D0782171

Queen
Elizabeth's
Wardrobe
Unlock'd

Queen Elizabeth's Wardrobe Unlock'd

The Inventories of the Wardrobe of Robes prepared in July 1600
edited from Stowe MS 557 in the British Library, MS LR 2/121
in the Public Record Office, London, and MS V.b.72 in the
Folger Shakespeare Library, Washington DC

*Edited and
with a Commentary by*
Janet Arnold

MANEY

© 1988 JANET ARNOLD

ISBN 0 901286 20 6

*All rights reserved. No part of this publication may
be reproduced, stored in a retrieval system, or
transmitted, in any form or by any means,
electronic, mechanical, photocopying, recording, or
otherwise, without the prior permission of the
author and publishers.*

PRINTED AND PUBLISHED IN GREAT BRITAIN BY
W. S. MANEY & SON LTD, HUDSON ROAD, LEEDS

Contents

Acknowledgements

Research for this book started over eighteen years ago and has been carried on continuously while working on other projects. My thanks are first due to the Trustees of the British Library, the Folger Shakespeare Library, Washington, DC, and the Public Record Office, London, for their permission to publish the manuscripts in their care. I would like to acknowledge the help given by a Winston Churchill Travelling Fellowship for three months in 1973 which enabled me to visit many museums and art galleries in France, Germany, Italy, Spain, and Sweden. I am also grateful for a Jubilee Research Fellowship in the Department of Drama and Theatre Studies at Royal Holloway College, University of London, for three years from 1978. Research on sixteenth-century terminology (for Chapter VI) and on the artificers of the Wardrobe of Robes and their work (for Chapter VIII) was a continuation of that undertaken for my book *Patterns of Fashion: the cut and construction of clothes for men and women c. 1560–1620*, and it would not have been possible to carry out this work, nor to prepare the indexes, without the very generous aid of a Fellowship awarded by the Leverhulme Trust Fund at the same college in 1980–85.

I would like to thank the Directors, Curators, and Assistants of the museums, art galleries, and costume collections which I have visited over the last eighteen years, for all their kindness and help while compiling the material for this book. I am also very grateful to members of the staffs of the British Library, the Public Record Office, the National Art Library at the Victoria and Albert Museum, and the Westminster and Bristol Central Reference Libraries for their assistance.

I have received encouragement and help from many people. This has included driving me to (and wrapping me with rugs in) cold country churches while studying details of dress on monumental effigies; carrying cups of tea up numerous flights of stairs; holding my notebooks and steadying my position while perched on chairs and stepladders taking photographs of inaccessible paintings and tombs; spending time to personally discuss or to write long letters on various aspects of sixteenth-century manuscripts, clothing, textiles, and portraits. Several friends have been particularly helpful with proof-reading and advice on preparing the indexes. I take full responsibility for all the final decisions and any mistakes. The latter are probably inevitable with a book of this size, but I hope there will be very few. There is not enough space to mention everyone, but I would particularly like to thank Mrs Alison Adburgham, Miss Jane Apple, the late Lord Astor, Professor George Brandt, the late Professor Julian Brown, Miss Anne Buck OBE, Dr Mary Westerman Bulgarella, Miss Christine Bullick, the late Dr Lionel Butler, Mrs Kathleen Chambers, Mrs Margie Christian, Miss Pamela Clabburn, Dr Christopher Coleman, Miss Elizabeth Ann Coleman, the late Mr T. Cottrell Dormer, Miss Gudrun Ekstrand, Sir Geoffrey Elton, the late Dr John Fletcher, Miss Norah Fuidge, Mr Robin Gibson, Mrs Caroline Goldthorpe, Dr Rainald Grosshans, Mr Robin Harcourt Williams, Miss Avril Hart, Miss Wendy Hefford, Miss Patricia Higgins, Mrs Millie Jaffé, Dr Mary de Jong, Mrs Joan Kendall, Mr John Kerslake FSA, Miss Mildred Lanier, Miss Ella McLeod, Sir Oliver Millar KCVO, Dr Roy Miller, Mr and Mrs Michael Morgan, Mrs Anne Wood Murray, Mr Revel Oddy, the Earl and Countess of Oxford and Asquith, Mr Stephen Parks, Miss Joyce Plesters, Mrs Esmé M. Plumbly, Miss Judith Prendergast, Mrs Susan Ranson, Dr Malcolm Rogers, Miss Natalie Rothstein, Mr Sidney Sabin, Dr Ann Saunders FSA, Miss Jennifer Scarce, Dr Karl Schütz, Miss Anna Southall, Miss Anneliese Streiter, Dr Frank Stubbings, Miss June Swann MBE, the Marquess of Tavistock, the Hon. Mrs Phyllis Thorold OBE, the Lord Tollemache, Miss Erika Weiland, Mr William Wells, Miss Norma Whittard, Dr Leonie von Wilckens, Miss Lorraine Williams, Miss Sarah Wimbush, Professor Katharine Worth and Mrs Laetitia Yeandle. My thanks are also due to Mrs Winifred Underwood for preparing numerous clean typescripts from my handwritten drafts over the years, no easy task. I owe a particular debt of gratitude to Miss Santina M. Levey, who read the manuscript at various stages, has given endless help in identifying and dating laces, produced photographs of various pieces of embroidery and designs at a moment's notice, and joined in the task of proof-reading and checking the indexes. Finally I would like to thank Miss Ann Campbell, Mr Derek Brown, and Mr Graham Maney for their kindness and inexhaustible patience while this book was going through the press.

Photographic Acknowledgements

Many of the photographs in this book were taken by the author, with the unstinting help of private owners and members of the staffs of art galleries, museums, and costume collections. Every effort has been made to trace owners of paintings, but some pictures have changed hands several times over the years and records have been lost. It has sometimes proved impossible to trace copyright holders of photographs: in some cases the prints are over twenty years old, and the firms of photographers have closed down. Even since this book went to press one picture has changed ownership; the portrait of an unknown lady in Figure 391 has been purchased by the Ferens Art Gallery, Kingston upon Hull. Each source is acknowledged beside the photograph. Figures 4, 8, 8a, 18, 23, 38, 76, 234, 236, 243, 338, and 339 are reproduced by Gracious Permission of Her Majesty the Queen.

The following are reproduced by kind permission of their owners and from their own or museum photographs:

College of Arms, London, 351
Society of Antiquaries of London, 89
Ashmolean Museum, Oxford, 306, 309, 310
The Marquess of Bath, Longleat House, 162, 196
Beaverbrook Art Gallery, Fredericton, 246
Bodleian Library, Oxford, 49, 159, 167, 283
British Library, 88, 94, 104, 108, 226–28, 252, 259, 336, 337, 409, 416, 439
British Museum, 27, 78, 92, 99, 100, 105, 114, 172, 307
The Duke of Buccleuch and Queensberry, KT (photo Tom Scott) 65, 138, 164–66, 231
Christ Church, Oxford, 59
Christies, 272
Colonial Williamsburg Foundation, 186
Courtauld Institute of Art, 102, 106, 150, 161, 240, 324, 410
Viscount De L'Isle, Penhurst Place, 34
Department of the Environment (Crown Copyright) 22, 72
Mr Simon Wingfield Digby, 75
Elizabethan Club of Yale University, 32, 145
Fitzwilliam Museum, 176
Folger Shakespeare Library, 260, 395
Guildhall Library, London, 250, 251
Jesus College, Oxford (photo B. J. Harris, City Centre Studio) 66, 67, 70
Kunsthistorisches Museum, Vienna, 169, 194, 205
Livrustkammaren, Stockholm, 248, 248a, 267, 267a
Madresfield Court Collection (photo Tom Bader) 37
Manchester City Art Gallery, 14
Metropolitan Museum of Art, New York, 238, 300, 302, 303, 327, 328, 356

Lt. Col. Meyrick, 128
Monasterio de Pederalbes, Barcelona, 322, 354
Museo del Prado, Madrid, 190, 192, 193, 197, 203, 340, 353, 355
National Gallery, London, 220, 262
National Gallery of Ireland, 214, 239
National Galleries of Scotland (photo Tom Scott) 5
National Maritime Museum, Greenwich, 43
National Portrait Gallery, London, 3, 21, 24, 26, 34, 40, 54, 71, 71a, 79, 86, 113, 120, 140, 140a, 142, 162, 183, 191, 201, 212, 215, 217, 221, 237, 242, 275, 369, 418, 430, 438
National Trust, Hardwick Hall, 129, 131, 423
Newbery Smith Associates, English Life Publications, 44
Norton Simon Foundation (photo A. Dolinski Photographic) 152, 152a
Parham Park, 148–148b, 404, 413
Pinacoteca di Siena, 28, 29, 341
Reading Borough Council (photo Walton Adams) 20, 20a, 436
Rijksmuseum, 211, 390
The Govenors of St Olave's Grammar School, 45
The Marquess of Salisbury, Hatfield, 140, 140a, 183, 217
J. B. Speed Art Museum, Louisiana, 7
Staatliche Kunstsammlungen, Kassel, 6
Staatliche Museen, Preussischer Kulturbesitz, Gemäldegalerie, Berlin-Dahlem, 224
Sudeley Castle, 56
The Governors of Queen Elizabeth's Hospital, Bristol (photo Cedric Barker) 101
Tate Gallery, 93, 174, 287, 364, 365
Marquess of Tavistock and the Trustees of the Bedford Settled Estates, 52, 149, 160
The Lord Tollemache, 240, 324, 422, 431
Toledo Museum of Art, Ohio, 64, 419, 441
Mr William Tyrwhitt-Drake, 55
Victoria and Albert Museum (Crown Copyright) 69, 81, 85, 116, 125, 126, 130, 131, 155, 156, 230, 274, 313, 377, 452, 453
Walker Art Galleries, Liverpool (photo John Mills Photography Ltd) 25, 25a, 311, 451, 463
Warburg Institute, 216
Westminster Abbey (photo Malcolm Crowthers) 109
Yale Center for British Art, Paul Mellon Collection, 57, 95, 229, 411
York City Art Gallery, 198

Abbreviations of Principal Works Cited

The following abbreviated forms have been used for references to manuscripts, books, and articles cited more than once. Many other works have been cited once only, and are fully described in the notes which follow each chapter. In some cases different editions of early works have been used, and the dates of publication are given in the notes. The place of publication of all books is London, unless otherwise stated. This list takes the place of a bibliography, and readers are also advised to consult Conyers Read (ed.), *Bibliography of British History: Tudor Period 1485–1603* (Oxford, 1959, 2nd edition) and the *Annual Bibliography of British and Irish History* (Royal Historical Society 1975–).

Alcega   Juan de Alcega, *Libro de Geometria, Pratica y Traça*, translated and edited by Jean Pain and Cecelia Bainton as *Tailor's Pattern Book 1589*, introduction and notes by J. L. Nevinson (facsimile edition, Carlton, Bedford, 1979).

Alciati   Andreas Alciati, *Clarissimi viri D. Andreae Alciati Emblematum Libellus* (Paris, 1542).

Anderson   Ruth M. Anderson, *Hispanic Costume 1480–1530* (Hispanic Society, New York, 1979).

Arnold, 'Cassock'   Janet Arnold, 'An Early Seventeenth Century Woman's Riding Doublet or Cassock', in *Waffen-und Kostümkunde* (Munich, 1980), part 2, pp. 113–28.

—— *'Coronation Portrait'*   Janet Arnold, 'The "Coronation" portrait of Queen Elizabeth I', in *The Burlington Magazine*, CXX (November 1978), pp. 727–41.

—— *'Doublet'*   Janet Arnold, 'A Woman's Doublet of about 1585', in *Waffen-und Kostümkunde* (Munich, 1981), part 2, pp. 132–42.

—— *'Lost from HMB'*   Janet Arnold, *'Lost from Her Majesties Back'*, Costume Society, Extra Series no. 7 (Wisbech, Cambridgeshire, 1980).

—— *'Mantle'*   Janet Arnold, 'Jane Lambarde's Mantle', in *Costume*, 14 (1980), pp. 56–72.

—— *'Neckwear'*   Janet Arnold, 'Three examples of late sixteenth and early seventeenth century neckwear', in *Waffen-und Kostümkunde* (Munich, 1973), part 2, pp. 109–24.

—— *'Nils Sture's Suit'*   Janet Arnold, 'Nils Sture's Suit', in *Costume*, 12 (1978), pp. 13–26.

—— *Patterns*   Janet Arnold, *Patterns of Fashion: the cut and construction of clothes for men and women c. 1560–1620* (1985).

—— *Patterns 1660–1860*   Janet Arnold, *Patterns of Fashion: Englishwomen's Dresses and their construction, c. 1660–1860* (1964; revised edition, 1977).

—— *'Smocks and Shirts'*   Janet Arnold, 'Elizabethan and Jacobean Smocks and Shirts', in *Waffen-und Kostkümkunde* (Munich, 1977), part 2, pp. 89–110.

—— *'Sweet England's Jewels'*   Janet Arnold, 'Sweet England's Jewels', in *Princely Magnificence: Court Jewels of the Renaissance 1500–1630*, edited by Anna Somers Cocks (Victoria and Albert Museum catalogue, 1980), pp. 31–40.

Ashmole   Elias Ashmole, *The Institution, Laws and Ceremonies of the Most Noble Order of the Garter* (1672; facsimile edition, 1971).

Auerbach, Tudor Artists   Erna Auerbach, *Tudor Artists* (1954).

—— *Hilliard*   Erna Auerbach, *Nicholas Hilliard* (1961).

Boissard   Jean Jacques Boissard, *Emblematum Liber* (Metz, 1584).

Boynton   Lindsay Boynton (ed.), *The Hardwick Hall Inventories of 1601* (The Furniture Society, 1971).

Bradford, Helena   Charles Angell Bradford, *Helena Marchioness of Northampton* (1936).

BL   British Library, London.

—— Add.   Additional manuscripts, especially 4712, collection of sixteenth-century manuscripts, formerly owned by Sir Robert Cotton; 5751A, collection of warrants and other documents; 5751B, larger documents from the previous volume, now bound separately; 46,348, 1550 inventory; 35,324, containing pictures of Queen Elizabeth's funeral procession.

—— Cotton   Manuscripts in the Cottonian Library deposited in the British Library, especially Caligula CI, Otho CX, Vespasian F III, and Vitellius F V, groups of sixteenth century letters and other documents.

—— Egerton   Egerton manuscripts, especially 2806, formerly Phillipps MS 8853, *A boke of Warrantes to the great Guarderobe Tempore Regine Ylizabethae towchyng her majesties Roobes and Apparell in the chardge of John Roynon and Rauf Hoope yeoman of the Guarderobe of Roobes*, 20 March 1568 to 19 February 1589.

—— Harl.   Manuscripts from the Harleian Library.

—— Lansdowne   Manuscripts in the Lansdowne collection.

—— Royal   Manuscripts in the old Royal and King's Collections, especially App. 68, *A booke of soche Jewells and other parcel[les] as are delivered to the charge and custodie of Mrs Mary Radclyffe one of the gentlewom[en] of the Quenes Majesties privie chamber. [All which] were parcell of soche Jewells as were in [the] charge of Mrs Blanche Parrye. Mense Julij 1587*.

—— Stowe   Stowe manuscripts collected by George Temple Nugent-Greville, Marquis of Buckingham, and kept at Stowe, his country seat, especially 557, transcript printed in full on pp. 251–334.

—— *Briquet*   C. M. Briquet, *Les Filagranes: Dictionnaire Historique des Marques du Papier dès leur apparition vers 1282 jusqu'en 1600*, 4 vols (Paris, 1907).

Byrne, Erondell   Muriel St Clare Byrne (ed.), *The Elizabethan Home Discovered in Two Dialogues by Claudius Hollyband and Peter Erondell* (revised edition, 1949).

Cal. Pat. Rolls   *Calendar of the Patent Rolls Preserved in the Public Record Office: Elizabeth I*.

CSP, Dom.   *Calendar of State Papers of the Reigns of Elizabeth and James I, Domestic Series, Preserved in Her Majesty's Public Record Office*.

CSP, Foreign   *Calendar of State Papers, Foreign Series of the Reign of Queen Elizabeth preserved in the Public Record Office*.

CSP, Spanish   *Calendar of State Papers, Relating to English Affairs of the Reign of Elizabeth preserved principally in the Archives of Simancas*.

CSP, Venetian   *Calendar of State Papers and Manuscripts relating to English Affairs existing in the Archives and collections of Venice and in other libraries of Northern Italy*.

Carter, 'Mary Tudor's Wardrobe'   Alison Carter, 'Mary Tudor's Wardrobe', in *Costume*, 18 (1984), pp. 9–28.

Cennini   Cennino d'Andrea Cennini, *The Craftsman's Handbook: 'Il Libro dell'Arte'*, translated by Daniel V. Thompson Jr. (New York, Dover edition, 1960).

Chambers   Edmund Kerchever Chambers, *The Elizabethan Stage* (Oxford, 1923), vol. I.

Christensen Sigrid F. Christensen, *De Danske Kongers Kronologiske samling paa Rosenborg. Kongedragterne fra 17. og 18. Aarhundrede* (Copenhagen, 1940).

Clode, Memorials Charles Mathew Clode, *Memorials of the Guild of Merchant Taylors of the Fraternity of St John the Baptist, in the City of London* (1875).

—— *Merchant Taylors* Charles Mathew Clode, *The Early History of the Guild of Merchant Taylors of the Fraternity of St John the Baptist, London*, 2 parts (1888).

Collins Arthur Jefferies Collins, *Jewels and Plate of Queen Elizabeth I: the inventory of 1574* (1955).

Colthorpe, Bateman Marion Colthorpe and Linley H. Bateman, *Queen Elizabeth I and Harlow* (Harlow, 1977).

Cotgrave, Dictionarie Randle Cotgrave, *A Dictionarie of the French and English tongues, London, 1611* (facsimile edition, Amsterdam and New York, 1971).

Cunningham, Revels Accounts Peter Cunningham (ed.), *Extracts from the Accounts of the Revels at Court, in the Reigns of Queen Elizabeth and King James I* (1842).

Cunnington, Handbook Cecil W. and Phillis Cunnington, *A Handbook of English Costume in the Sixteenth Century* (1954; revised edition, 1962).

Dawson, Kennedy-Skipton Giles E. Dawson and Laetitia Kennedy-Skipton, *Elizabethan Handwriting 1500–1650: A Guide to the Reading of Documents and Manuscripts* (1968).

Dekker Thomas Dekker, *The Shoemaker's Holiday*, written in 1598–99. Revels edition, edited by R. L. Smallwood and Stanley Wells (Manchester, 1979).

—— *Old Fortunatus* Thomas Dekker, *The Pleasant Comedie of Old Fortunatus. As it was plaied before the Queenes Majestie this Christmas . . .* (1600).

De Maisse André Hurault, Sieur de Maisse, *A journal of all that was accomplished by Monsieur de Maisse, Ambassador in England from King Henri IV to Queen Elizabeth, Anno Domini 1597*, translated, edited, and with introduction by G. B. Harrison and R. A. Jones (1931).

Denholm-Young, Handwriting Noël Denholm-Young, *Handwriting in England and Wales* (Cardiff, 1954).

D'Ewes Sir Simonds D'Ewes, *The Journals of all the Parliaments during the Reign of Queen Elizabeth both of the House of Lords and House of Commons Collected by Sir Simonds D'Ewes of Stow-Hall in the County of Suffolk . . . Revised and published by Paul Bowes* (1682).

Digby, Eliz. Embroidery George Wingfield Digby, *Elizabethan Embroidery* (1963).

DNB Leslie Stephen and Sidney Lee (eds), *The Dictionary of National Biography* (1885–1900, and supplements).

Edmond, Hilliard Mary Edmond, *Hilliard and Oliver* (1983).

Egerton Papers J. Payne Collier, *Egerton Papers* (Camden Society, 1840).

Ellis, Letters Henry Ellis (ed.), *Original Letters Illustrative of English History*, first series, 4 vols (1824).

Fanshawe Sir Thomas Fanshawe, *The Practice of the Exchequer Court with its severall offices and officers* (1658). (By Peter Osborne.)

Feuillerat Albert Fueillerat (ed.), *Documents relating to the Office of the Revels in the Time of Queen Elizabeth* (1908).

Foedera Thomas Rymer (ed.), *Foedera, conventiones, literae et . . . acta publica etc.* (photographic reprint of edition published at The Hague 1739–45, Farnborough, Hants, 1967).

Folger Manuscripts in the Folger Shakespeare Library, Washington, D.C. 20003, especially V.b.72 (see below); X.d.265, receipt for petticoats delivered to Mrs Elizabeth Marbery, or ε of the Chamberers to the Queen, by Ralph Hope, Yeoman of the Robes, 24 June, 1565; X.d.428(16), (120), (127), (128), (130), letters relating to gifts for Queen Elizabeth (presented by the Countess of Shrewsbury) from various writers; Z.d. 12–17, New Year's Gift Rolls, 1564, 1565 (incomplete), 1575, 1579, 1585, 1599.

—— inventory MS V.b.72, inventory of 1600, transcript printed in full on pp. 335–50.

Fragmenta Regalia, Paul Hentzner, *Paul Hentzner's Travels in England during the Reign of Queen Elizabeth translated by Horace Walpole late Earl of Orford to which is now added Sir Robert Naunton's Fragmenta Regalia* (1797).

Gerard John Gerard, *The Herball or Generall Historie of Plantes* (1597; photographic reprint, Amsterdam, 1974).

Giles, Ascham Revd Dr J. A. Giles, *The whole works of Roger Ascham now first collected and revised, with a life of the author*, 3 vols (1864–65).

Guiseppi M. S. Guiseppi, *A Guide to the Manuscripts in the Public Record Office*, 2 vols (1963 edition).

Harrison Frederick J. Furnivall (ed.) *Harrison's Description of England in Shakespeare's Youth. Being the second and third books of his Description of Britaine and England edited from the first two editions of Holinshed's Chronicle AD 1577, 1587, 1877–1908*; issued in 3 parts, with a supplement.

Hartshorne Albert Hartshorne, 'Notes on Collars of SS', in *The Archaeological Journal* XXXIV (1882), pp. 376–77.

Haydn, Dignities Joseph Haydn and Horace Ockerby, *The Book of Dignities* (1894 edition).

Haynes, State Papers Samuel Haynes, *A collection of State Papers relating to affairs in the reigns of Henry VIII, Edward VI, Mary and Elizabeth, from 1542 to 1570. Transcribed from original Letters and other authentic memorials left by W. Cecill, Lord Burghley, and now remaining at Hatfield House* (1740).

Heath J. B. Heath, *An Account of material furnished for the use of Queen Anne Boleyn and the Princess Elizabeth by William Loke, the Kings Mercer, between 20 January 1535/6 and 27 April 1536* (1863).

Hind Arthur M. Hind, *Engraving in England in the Sixteenth and Seventeenth Centuries*, vol. I, *The Tudor Period* (Cambridge, 1952), vol. II, *The Reign of James I*, (Cambridge, 1955).

HMC, Hatfield, Salisbury MSS Historical Manuscripts Commission. *Calendar of the Manuscripts of the Most Honourable the Marquess of Salisbury preserved at Hatfield House, Hertfordshire* (1888–).

HMC, Pepys Historical Manuscripts Commission. *Report on the Pepys Manuscripts preserved at Magdalene College, Cambridge* (1911).

Holme, Academy Randle Holme, *Academy of Armory, or, a Storehouse of Armory and Blazon* (Chester, 1688; facsimile edition, Menston, 1972).

Jenkins, Eliz. Great Elizabeth Jenkins, *Elizabeth the Great* (1972 edition).

—— *Eliz. and Leicester* Elizabeth Jenkins, *Elizabeth and Leicester* (1972 edition).

Johnson Paul Johnson, *Elizabeth I* (1976 edition).

Klarwill Victor von Klarwill (translated by T. H. Nash), *Queen Elizabeth and some Foreigners*, 1928. Description of Travels by Lupold von Wedel starting on 14 August 1585, part II, pp. 303–43. Herr Johann Jacob Breuning von Buchenbach chosen by Duke Frederick of Württemberg to be Leader of Embassy to Queen Elizabeth starting in March 1595, part III, pp. 347–423.

Levey Santina M. Levey, An Elizabethan Embroidered Cover' in *Victoria and Albert Museum Year Book*, no. 3 (1972), pp. 76–86.

—— *Lace* Santina M. Levey, *Lace: A History* (1983).

Linthicum M. C. Linthicum, *Costume in the Drama of Shakespeare and his Contemporaries* (Oxford, 1936).

MacCaffrey, 'Place and Patronage' Wallace T. MacCaffrey, 'Place and Patronage in Elizabethan Politics', in *Elizabethan Government and Society: Essays presented to Sir John Neale* (1961).

Madden Frederic Madden, *Privy Purse Expenses of the Princess Mary, daughter of King Henry the Eighth, afterwards Queen Mary, December 1536 to December 1544* (1831).

Melville Sir James Melville, *Memoirs of His Own Life 1549–93*, edited by F. A. Stewart (1929).

Merrifield, Treatises Mary P. Merrifield, *Original Treatises on the Art of Painting* (1848; New York, Dover edition, 1967).

Middleton, Dekker Thomas Middleton and Thomas Dekker, *The Roaring Girl*, 1611, probably written around 1608. New Mermaid edition, edited by Andrew Gomme (1976).

Millar, Inventories Oliver Millar (ed.), *The Inventories and Valuations of the King's Goods 1649–1651*, Walpole Society, vol. 43 (1972).

—— *Tudor Pictures* Oliver Millar, *The Tudor, Stuart and Georgian Pictures in the Collection of Her Majesty the Queen* (1963).

Minsheu John Minsheu, *The Guide into Tongues* (1617). (Unless otherwise stated, all references are from the first edition of 1617).

—— *Dialogues* John Minsheu, *Pleasant and Delightfull Dialogues in Spanish and English, profitable to the learner, and not unpleasant to any other Reader*, 1599.

Morse H. K. Morse, *Elizabethan Pageantry* (New York, 1934).

Moryson, Itinerary   Fynes Moryson, *An Itinerary written by Fynes Moryson, Gent* (1617; facsimile edition, New York, 1971).

Nichols, Ordinances   John Nichols, *A Collection of Ordinances and Regulations for the Government of the Royal Household made in divers reigns from King Edward III to King William and Queen Mary, also divers receipts in Ancient Cookery* (1790).

—— *Illustrations*   John Nichols, *Illustrations of the Manners and Expences of Antient Times in England* (1797).

Nichols, Literary Remains   John Gough Nichols, *The Literary Remains of King Edward the Sixth* (Roxburghe Club, 1857).

Norgate, Miniatura   Edward Norgate, *Miniatura, or the Art of Limning 1650*, edited by Martin Hardie (Oxford, 1919).

Nugae Antiquae   Henry Harington (ed.), *Nugae Antiquae, being a miscellaneous collection of original papers by Sir John Harington* (1779).

O'Donoghue   F. M. O'Donoghue, *A Descriptive and Classified Catalogue of Portraits of Queen Elizabeth* (1894).

OED   *The Oxford English Dictionary*, edited by James A. H. Murray, Henry Bradley, W. A. Craigie, and C. T. Onions, 12 vols (Oxford, 1933).

Paradin   Claude Paradin, *The Heroicall Devises of M. Claudius Paradin* (Anvers, 1563 edition (in French); 1563 edition (in English); 1591 edition (in English)).

Post, Royal Portraits   Margaret Post, *Royal Portraits from the Plea Rolls* (1974).

Praz, Imagery   Mario Praz, *Studies in 17th Century Imagery* (1964, 2nd revised edition).

Princely Magnificence   Anna Somers-Cocks (ed.), *Princely Magnificence: Court Jewels of the Renaissance 1500–1630* (Victoria and Albert Museum catalogue, 1980).

Progr. Eliz.   John Nichols, *The Progresses and Public Processions of Queen Elizabeth* (1788–1821), 3 vols and vol. 4, part. 1, (reprint of 1823 edition, 3 vols, New York, 1977). (Unless otherwise stated, all references are from the 2nd edition, 1823.)

Progr. James I   John Nichols, *The Progresses, Processions, and Magnificent Festivities of King James the First, His Royal Consort, Family and Court*, 4 vols (1828; reprint of 1828 edition, New York, 1977).

PRO   Public Record Office, London

—— *AO*   Exchequer and Audit Department, especially 1/2339–2344, Declared Accounts of the Great Wardrobe, 1558–1603 (paper rolls in very fragile condition); 3/907–910, Various Accounts of the Revels, of Keeper of the Great Wardrobe, etc., 1571–1623; 3/1106–1121, Various Accounts, 1559–1632.

—— *Baschet*   Transcripts by Armand Baschet and others, from documents in the National Archives at Paris, relating to the affairs of Great Britain and Ireland, 31/3 (203 bundles), 1504–1714.

—— *C*   Chancery, especially 47/3/38, 39, 40, and 41, New Year's Gift Rolls, 1563, 1577, 1598, and 1603; 115/L2/6697, day book of the Wardrobe of Robes, from the Duchess of Norfolk Deeds, printed in full in *Arnold, 'Lost from HMB'*.

—— *E*   Exchequer, especially 101/429/4, account of silks used for Queen Elizabeth's coronation; 101/429/5, bundle of 50 warrants for Queen Elizabeth's coronation; 101/403/2, 420–29, payment books for the Privy Purse, 1571–93.

—— *inventory*   LR 2/121, duplicate copy of Stowe 557, the Stowe inventory.

—— *LC*   Lord Chamberlain's Department, especially 5/32–37, 49, 54, 84, 182, books of copies of warrants and other documents; 9/52–93, Accounts of the Great Wardrobe, 1558–1603.

—— *LR*   Land Revenue, especially 2/121, duplicate copy of the Stowe inventory.

—— *SP*   State Paper Office, especially 12/221 and 78/7.

Putnam   Clare Putnam, *Flowers and Trees of Tudor England*, 1972. Selection of colour plates from MS Ashmole 1504 which dates from 1520–30, in the Bodleian Library.

Puttenham   George Puttenham, *The Art of Poesie* (1589).

Remembrancia   W. H. Overall and H. C. Overall, *Analytical Index to the Series of Records known as the Remembrancia preserved among the Archives of the City of London, 1579–1664* (1878).

Robertson, Inventaires   Joseph Robertson, *Inventaires de la Reyne Decosse Douairiere de France: Catalogues of the Jewels, Dresses, Furniture, Books and Paintings of Mary Queen of Scots 1556–1569* (Bannatyne Club, Edinburgh, 1863).

Rye   William Brenchley Rye, *England as seen by Foreigners in the Days of Elizabeth and James the First* (1865).

Shakespeare   The Arden edition of the works of William Shakespeare.

Smythe, Household Expenses   P. C. S. Smythe, *Household Expenses of the Princess Elizabeth during her residence at Hatfield, 1 October 1551–30 September 1552* (Camden Miscellany, 1853).

Soc. Antiquaries MS   Manuscript in the library of the Society of Antiquaries of London.

Stow   Charles Lethbridge Kingsford, *A Survey of London by John Stow reprinted from the text of 1603*, 2 vols (Oxford, 1908).

Stow, Annales   John Stow, *The Annales, or Generall Chronicle of England, begun first by maister John Stow, and after him continued . . . unto the end of this present yeere 1614* (1615).

Stowe inventory   Stowe manuscript 557, in the British Library, printed in full on pp. 251–334.

Strickland   Agnes Strickland, *Lives of the Queens of England: Elizabeth*, vol. VI (1843), vol. VII (1844), vol. IV (revised edition, 1851) reprinted as *Life of Queen Elizabeth* (1906 edition, unless otherwise stated).

Strong, Icon   Roy Strong, *The English Icon: Elizabethan and Jacobean Portraiture* (1969).

—— *Portraits*   Roy Strong, *Portraits of Queen Elizabeth I* (Oxford, 1963). NOTE the publication of *Gloriana*, in 1987 with further information on the portraits.

—— *'Three Jewels'*   Roy Strong, 'Three Royal Jewels: the Three Brothers, the Mirror of Great Britaine and the Feather', in *The Burlington Magazine*, CVIII (July 1966), pp. 350–52.

—— *Tudor Portraits*   Roy Strong, *Tudor and Jacobean Portraits*, 2 vols (1969).

Strype   John Strype, *A Survey of the Cities of London and Westminster . . . written at first in the year* MDXCVIII *by John Stow . . . enlarged by John Strype* (1720), 6 books in 2 vols.

Stubbes   Phillip Stubbes, *The Anatomie of Abuses* (1583, and other editions of 1585, 1595; facsimile edition Amsterdam and New York, 1972, collated from three copies of the 1583 edition in the Bodleian Library, Oxford). NOTE the spelling varies considerably in all these editions, and even in different copies of the same edition.

Suffolk Collection   John Jacob, *The Suffolk Collection, Ranger's House, Blackheath: Catalogue of Paintings* (1975).

Sydney Papers   Arthur Collins (ed.), *Letters and Memorials of State in the reigns of Queen Mary, Queen Elizabeth, King James, King Charles the First, Part of the reign of King Charles the Second and Oliver's Usurpation, written and collected by Sir Henry Sydney*, 2 vols (1746; facsimile edition, Ann Arbor, Michigan, USA, 1978).

The Ancestor   *The Ancester*, no. II (July 1902).

Thomson, Inventories   T. Thomson, *A Collection of Inventories and other records of the Royal Wardrobe and Jewelhouse; and of the Artillery and Munition in some of the Royal Castles 1488–1606* (Edinburgh, 1815).

Tout   T. F. Tout, *Chapters in the Administrative History of Mediaeval England, The Wardrobe, the Chamber and the Small Seals*, 6 vols (1920–33).

Tudor Court   Roy Strong, with contributions from V. J. Murrell, *Artists of the Tudor Court: the portrait miniature rediscovered 1520–1620* (Victoria and Albert Museum catalogue, 1983).

Veale   E. M. Veale, *The English Fur Trade in the Later Middle Ages* (1966).

Vecellio   Cesare Vecellio, *Habiti antichi, et moderni di tutto il Mondo* (Venice, 1598), reprinted in English edition as *Vecellio's Renaissance Costume Book* (New York, 1977).

Waugh, Corsets   Norah Waugh, *Corsets and Crinolines* (1954).

Whitney   Geffrey Whitney, *A Choice of Emblemes and other Devises* (1586).

Williams, Platter   Clare Williams, *Thomas Platter's Travels in England, 1599* (1937).

Yates, Astraea   Frances A. Yates, *Astraea: the imperial theme in the sixteenth century* (1975).

—— *Valois Tapestries*   Frances A. Yates, *The Valois Tapestries* (1975).

In loving memory of my mother
Adeline Arnold
who gave me constant encouragement

Introduction

If any excuse is needed for writing a book of such length on the subject of one woman's wardrobe, then my excuse must be that the careful and abundant records kept for Queen Elizabeth I give a unique source for the study of dress during the second half of the sixteenth century. The wealth of material which came so readily to hand made my task fairly straightforward, although I did not realize some eighteen years ago that it would be so time-consuming. The wardrobe in the title of this book refers not only to the Queen's clothes, but also to the Wardrobe of Robes, a sub-department of the Great Wardrobe. The yeomen and clerks who worked there kept records of all materials used, and work carried out, by a small band of skilled craftsmen making clothes and accessories for the Queen throughout her reign. They were also responsible for storing them safely in the Tower of London, the Wardrobe of Robes store near Blackfriars, and in other stores in various palaces, wherever the Court stayed.

The Stowe inventory, *The Booke of all suche Robes Apparell Silkes Jewells and other stuffe in the chardge of Sir Thomas Gorg knight gentleman of her majesties wardrobe of Robes*, which has provided the foundation of this book (pp. 251–334), was an accidental discovery. A short extract from it, which caught my interest in my student days in the early 1950s, was printed in *The Progresses and Public Processions of Queen Elizabeth* by John Nichols. This was first published in 1788, at which time the manuscript now known as the Stowe inventory, from which the extract was taken, belonged to Mr Craven Ord. In 1969, during a chance conversation about the correct names for different parts of dress in paintings at *The Elizabethan Image* exhibition at the Tate Gallery, Santina M. Levey told me that she had noticed an entry for an inventory naming loose gowns, French gowns and kirtles in the catalogue of Stowe MSS in the British Library, which might be helpful. Some months later, passing the shelves of catalogues of manuscripts just before closing time at the British Library, the two volumes of the Stowe catalogue caught my eye. With only a few minutes to indulge in serendipity, I put out my hand at random and the book fell open at the page listing Stowe MS 557. On the following morning I looked at the manuscript, and beneath the inscription on the title-page — 'This book belonged to Sir Simeon Stewart' — was a note — 'afterwards to Mr Craven Ord who placed it in 1790 in my M.S. Library' — written by antiquarian and palaeographer, Thomas Astle.

My first intention was to use extracts from the Stowe inventory as background material for my book *Patterns of Fashion: the cut and construction of clothes for men and women c. 1560–1620* (1985). However, after making a transcript, I felt that it should be published in full as A. J. Collins had done with the 1574 inventory in his *Jewels and Plate of Queen Elizabeth I* (1955). The clothes, with names of fabrics, of a wide variety of colours, and descriptions of embroidery, offered material to extend our knowledge of the terminology of sixteenth-century dress, while the scribbled marginal notes provided evidence of systematic checking which had been carried out between 1600 and 1604, casting light on the organization of the Wardrobe of Robes. I traced the duplicate copy of the inventory mentioned in the Stowe MS to the Public Record Office, London, in the Records of the Land Revenue Auditors (LR2/121). Mrs Laetitia Yeandle of the Folger Shakespeare Library, Washington DC, very kindly called my attention to what we thought might be a third copy of the inventory. This proved to be the list of other items remaining in store at the Great Wardrobe site near Blackfriars, and is printed here on pp. 335–50.

I wondered how long the large number of garments noted in the two inventories had been in the various stores of the Wardrobe of Robes. Obviously the Coronation robes were there from 1559, but what about the rest? The New Year's Gift Rolls, lists prepared each year to record gifts made to, and by, Queen Elizabeth on New Year's day, were already familiar to me. Many items of clothing were among those presented to her. One of the first I recognized, which also appeared in the Stowe inventory, was a purple taffeta forepart decorated with roses of white cypress presented by the Lady Mary Vere in 1578. Once this connection had been made I went through all the surviving rolls, preparing transcripts of several of them, for which there is not enough space in the present volume: these are being printed separately. A number of the descriptions differed slightly, apart from minor variations in spelling. For example, some French gowns in the New Year's Gift Rolls appeared as round gowns in the Stowe and Folger inventories, suggesting that the garments had been altered. Later research proved this to be the case. Searching the British Library catalogues for evidence of the tailors' work, I found Egerton MS 2806, *A boke of Warrantes to the great Guarderobe* (formerly in the library of Sir Thomas Phillipps) which recorded all the work carried out by tailors, embroiderers, and other craftsmen for the Wardrobe of Robes between 1568 and 1588. I decided to transcribe it completely, to make easier work of linking the pieces of clothing described in it with those in the Stowe and Folger inventories. Some had been in store for forty years, others were recent acquisitions, and many had been altered one or more times. In order to trace other garments before 1568 and after 1588, I returned to the Public Record Office, and found an almost complete run of copies of warrants from 1560 to 1603 among the Records of the Lord Chamberlain's Department (LC5/33–37), duplicating those contained in Egerton MS 2806. Here again I made a full transcript and continued to link the items. I have listed the dates and places where warrants for the Wardrobe of Robes were signed by the Queen on pp. 244–46, as they give the names of some of the palaces and country houses to which the Court travelled each year. Although there were delays in signing, and obviously other places were visited between the dates given, the warrants do give some idea of the number of removes undertaken by the Wardrobe staff. Although garments were frequently altered and re-used, some being given to the Queen's women, it soon became apparent that many more had been given to, and made for, Elizabeth than were finally listed in the inventories in 1600. I wondered what had happened to them and decided to look for a day book for the Wardrobe of Robes which recorded items of clothing and jewels lost or given away by the Queen between 1561 and 1585. This is mentioned in Agnes Strickland's account of the life of Queen Elizabeth, printed in 1843, at which time it was in the library of Sir Thomas Phillipps. Miss Norah Fuidge had come upon it some years before in the Public Record Office and very kindly traced the accession number (the Duchess of Norfolk Deeds, MS C/115/L2/6697) among her notes for me. Over one hundred and fifty lengths of material and items of clothing which had belonged to Elizabeth were recorded as gifts. Already in 1980 it was clear that there would not be enough space to print my transcript in the present volume and I published it with a commentary in 'Lost from Her Majesties Back'.

A number of jewels were listed in the Stowe inventory, and I had hoped to include in the present book my transcript of the inventory of the Queen's jewels which were in the charge of Blanche Parry and transferred to the care of Mary Ratcliffe in 1587 (BL, Royal App. 68). Again, there was insufficient space, and it is being published separately with a more detailed commentary on the jewels than would have been feasible here. I have linked individual jewels with donors, tracing some back to earlier inventories.

Research on the coronation robes listed in the Stowe inventory, together with the 'Coronation' portrait and miniature, led to the discovery of a manuscript titled *Materials for the apparel of her majesty and the persons engaged about her Coronation* in the Public Record Office, among the Various Accounts of the King's Remembrancer at the Exchequer (E101/429/3). I prepared a transcript and linked the entries with relevant extracts from the account of Sir Edward Waldegrave, Master of the Great Wardrobe, of all 'Clothes of Tishewe clothes of golde Sylver and Tyncell Velvet Satten Damask and other kindes of Sylkes' used for the coronation (E101/429/4). This unfortunately is again too long to include in the present book, but it was published as an appendix to my article 'The "Coronation" Portrait of Queen Elizabeth I' in *The Burlington Magazine* in November 1978.

The profusion of documentary evidence soon made it apparent that the scope of this book would have to be limited in some way. Some of the material directly relating to it has been, and will be, published separately, as I have explained. By the time I had transcribed and indexed the copies of warrants for forty years I began to realize that it would be impossible to write a book about the Stowe and Folger inventories without bringing in the clerks, yeomen and artificers of the Wardrobe of Robes. Although it would have been best if the complete run

of warrants could have been printed together with the inventories, the volume of material was too great. However, numerous extracts have been used to cast light upon many entries in the inventories. When the whole run is published, possibly on microfiche, I intend to incorporate the prices of all materials and work done taken from the Accounts of the Great Wardrobe, where the entries appear in clerks' Latin, using a personal computer to make the task easier and quicker. It will then be possible to carry out more research on the type of materials used and the silkwoman's supplies, to note variations in prices, the exact number of new gowns, remodelled items, alterations, and cost of workmanship, and to make a comparative study of the annual expenditure of the Wardrobe of Robes during Elizabeth's reign. It would appear that in some years, when many gifts of clothing were made to the Queen, she would spend less on herself and present a number of gowns made in the Wardrobe of Robes to her women, often to the young Maids-of-Honour. Clothes of her own which Elizabeth gave to her ladies-in-waiting were frequently first remodelled or lined with new taffeta.

It may seem strange for the Queen to give cast-off gowns to women of rank, such as Lady Warwick, but it must be remembered that the materials from which they were made, such as elaborately patterned velvets, cloths of gold and silver, richly embroidered silks and satins, sometimes cut and pinked, were of high quality and extremely expensive. In passing, I am indebted to Miss Jane Apple for a fascinating insight into the way in which one lady at Court obtained a quantity of rich material. Edward Stafford wrote from Paris to Sir Francis Walsingham on 10 July 1588 reporting that an unknown gentleman 'telleth me he sawe a pasport which he shewed him from you, and he knoweth your hand and he thinketh ytt to be cownterfetted, butt he telleth thatt ytt cost him seventie yeards of velvet to a ladie of the court to gett ytt him' (BL, Harl. 288, f. 218). Perhaps some of the velvet was eventually presented to the Queen — but by whom? Clothes were frequently left as bequests in wills during the period under study, as the value of the material was so much greater than the cost of making up the garment — hence the number of alterations. The elaborately embroidered gowns from the later part of the reign listed in the inventories may have been considered unsuitable to be given away. Many had been presented as gifts, and the embroidered motifs were often rich with symbolism, as well as heavy with gold thread. They were probably considered to be state treasure by the Queen. Certainly great care was taken of them in the Wardrobe stores.

The realization that all that had been written about Queen Elizabeth's dress might not be entirely accurate came early in my research. Gifts of clothes to the Ladies and Gentlewomen of the Bedchamber and Privy Chamber, and lengths of black satin, velvet, and taffeta suitable for two mourning gowns presented to Mary, Queen of Scots, make it clear that the claims of numerous writers that Elizabeth never gave anything away are untrue. I had originally intended to use eye-witness descriptions of the Queen's appearance on a number of public occasions, and to link them with entries in the Stowe and Folger inventories. By chance, within the space of a week, I read ten accounts of her visit to Tilbury in August 1588, to review the troops at the time of the threatened invasion by the Spanish Armada. These were all by authors writing from the seventeenth century onwards. Elizabeth was described variously as wearing a silver breastplate, a white velvet gown, great white plumes in her hair, a white satin gown, and a masque

PLATE IA *(Right) Queen Elizabeth I. Panel painting by an unknown artist, c.1590–92. The sleeves and stomacher are embroidered with lilies, strawberries, eglantine (sweet-briar) and other flowers in coloured silks. The interlocking linear pattern is in gold thread set with pearls. Toledo Museum of Art, Ohio*

PLATE IB *(Below) Detail of stomacher in Plate IA*

PLATE IC, D and E *(Bottom) Details from a bodice worn by Queen Amalia Sophia around 1640, pieced together from white silk camlet embroidered around 1590. The motifs include clasped hands denoting friendship, a blazing heart pierced by arrows, which signifies love, and pansies for thoughts. The linear pattern is in couched gold thread. Rosenborg Castle, Copenhagen*

Comitatu Serbio. Et
filium predicti Thomas Cokin

PLATE IIA (*Above left*) *Detail from a portrait of Queen Elizabeth I, by an unknown artist. The sleeves date from around 1570 and the hairstyle from around 1585. She fingers a jewel which appears in a later portrait, incorporated into a fan handle (Figs 143 and 143a). Elizabethan Club of Yale University*

PLATE IIB (*Above centre*) *Detail from the illumination of Queen Elizabeth I on the Ashburne Charter, by Nicholas Hilliard, 15 July 1585. Queen Elizabeth's Grammar School, Ashbourne, Derbyshire*

PLATE IIC, D, E, F, and G *A figure representing Astrology, a lion, an armillary sphere, a flagon with dolphin grotesques, a bird with strawberries, and a thunderbolt, details from an embroidered white satin panel, probably from a petticoat, c.1600. Victoria and Albert Museum, London (T.138–1981)*

PLATE III (*Opposite*) *Queen Elizabeth I. Panel painting by an unknown artist, 1590. Jesus College, Oxford*

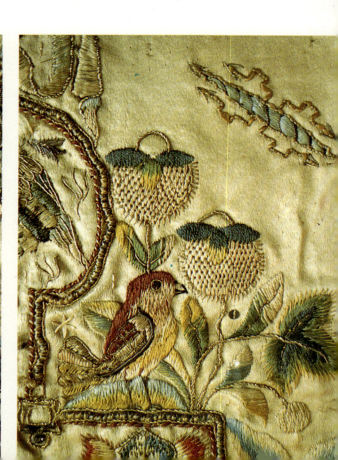

AÑO 1590:

PLATE IVA (Above) 'Armada' portrait of
Queen Elizabeth I. Panel painting by an
unknown artist, c. 1588–89. W. Tyrwhitt-
Drake, Bereleigh, Petersfield

PLATE IVB (Far left) The 'Welbeck' or
'Wanstead' portrait of Queen Elizabeth I,
attributed to Marcus Gheeraerts the
Elder, c. 1580–85. Private collection

PLATE IVC (Left) Detail of a river, a
cloud with raindrops, and a rainbow,
from an embroidered white linen smock,
c. 1600. Whitworth Art Gallery,
Manchester

costume. The longest account, apparently based on an engraving, from which some of these images were partly drawn, came from Agnes Strickland, published in 1844: 'She wore a polished steel corslet on her breast and below this ... a fardingale of such monstrous amplitude that it is wonderful how her mettled war-horse submitted to carry a lady encumbered with a gaberdine of so strange a fashion.' Intrigued to find so many discrepancies, I turned to the panel painting in the Church of St Faith, Gaywood, Norfolk, which shows the Queen mounted on a white horse and wearing a gown with a wide farthingale, her ruff opening to a wide square neckline, dating from around 1605 or a little later. It is not known if this was painted by someone who was eye-witness to the event, up-dating the clothes worn by the Queen, or from other people's memories of the occasion. The picture was heavily restored in 1905.

Miller Christy, in his article 'Queen Elizabeth's visit to Tilbury in 1588' (*English Historical Review*, CXXXIII, 1919), points out that there are at least two contemporary accounts of the occasion, one by James Aske, who seems to have been present, and another by Thomas Deloney, who may have had it at second hand. Both are in verse and neither of them gives detailed descriptions of the Queen's clothes. Aske describes her as 'like to Mars, the God of fearefull Warre ... Bellona-like renowned' reviewing her troops on foot, 'She thence some way still marching King-like on'. Later she was 'Most bravely mounted on a stately steede / With trunchion in her hand (not used thereto)', and was 'In nought unlike the Amazonian Queene'. Her coach was apparently studded with emeralds, diamonds, and rubies, 'set checker-wise by strange invention', and embroidered with gold knots. Deloney's ballad was set to the tune of 'Wilson's wild'. In his words she '... from fair St James's took her way, / With many Lords of high degree, / in princely robes and rich array; / And to barge upon the water / (being King Henry's royal daughter!) / She did go with trumpets sounding, / and with dubbing drums apace, / Along the Thames, that famous river, / for to view the Camp a space'. She viewed her 'armèd soldiers bright'on foot, 'Whereat her royal heart so leaped, / on her feet upright she stepped. / Tossing up her plume of feathers / to them all as they did stand, / Cheerfully her body bending / waving of her royal hand'. The description of the Queen on horseback is for the following day when 'The morrow after her abiding, / on a princely palfrey riding; / To the Camp she came to dinner / with her Lords and Ladies all. / Then came the Queen, on prancing steed, / attired like an angel bright'. We certainly have the image of a regal presence, but in neither account is the colour of Elizabeth's clothes mentioned. Space does not permit a full discussion of the Queen's appearance at Tilbury here, but my article 'The "Armada" portraits of Queen Elizabeth I', appearing in *Apollo* early in 1989, explores the subject more fully.

The problems of finding a detailed and reliable report of the Queen's appearance at one of the most important events of her reign are repeated on lesser occasions. In the end only a few personal accounts have been used and these are mainly by foreigners who wrote in greater detail than English observers. I have concentrated more on the portraits of Elizabeth, although it has not been possible to link conclusively items in the inventories with any of them, with the exception of the Coronation and Parliament robes. However, the magnificent clothes in paintings and miniatures, with their lavish embroidery, jewels, veils, and other accessories, offer visual evidence of fashions described in the inventories. I hope that the publi-

cation of this book will lead to some fragments of the Queen's embroidered clothes being traced. Even as it was being printed I saw a portrait, from a private collection, of Princess Magdalena Sibylla of Saxony who married Christian, the Prince Elect of Denmark, in 1634 (*Christian IV and Europe*, Exhibition Catalogue, Denmark, 1988, no. 119). Her gown was made from embroidered ivory silk dating from around 1600, which could well have belonged to Elizabeth, sent to Denmark by James I's consort, Queen Anne. A bodice dating from around 1640 worn by Queen Sophia Amalia, preserved at Rosenborg Castle in Copenhagen (*Christensen*, II, Plates LIV, LV), pieced together from silk dating from around 1590, seems likely to have had a similar history. The material is a white silver camlet, exquisitely embroidered with an interlacing design in gold thread, with motifs including clasped hands, hearts with crossed arrows and flames, daffodils, gillyflowers, and dolphin grotesques (Plates IC, ID, IE). In the same collection I found the kirtle, or surcoat, which was worn with the Garter mantle sent to Denmark for Christian IV in 1606 (*Christensen*, II, Plate IL). It was described in the Rosenborg inventory in 1718 as 'Een Carmesin Røed fløyels Polsk Kiortel', and was thought to have been part of the Polish dress worn by Frederick III around 1640–50. These discoveries encourage further research.

The transcripts complete, I worked on the first seven chapters of the book, concentrating on aspects of the Queen's appearance from contemporary accounts, her portraits, ceremonial robes, designs for jewellery and embroidery, their sources and symbolism, gifts of clothing and jewels to and from Elizabeth, fashions worn by her, and the work of clerks and yeomen in the organization of the Wardrobe of Robes. Most women will acknowledge the feeling of confidence and well-being which comes from wearing beautiful clothes in the latest fashion with complementary hairstyle and accessories. Elizabeth was a fascinating woman: she had a powerful charisma, and this was reinforced by clothes and jewels which reflected not only her own taste, but, in many cases, that of her loyal subjects who had presented them to her throughout her reign. Good organization was essential to ensure that the right clothes and accessories were ready when required. The posts of Gentleman, Yeoman and Groom of the Robes, Ladies and Gentlewomen of the Bedchamber and Privy Chamber, and Maids of Honour were no sinecure. Each had the safe keeping of portions of the Queen's apparel and jewels. A large number of persons shared the responsibility of making certain that Elizabeth would create the right impression at her audiences, on her Progresses, and on all occasions when she was in the public eye.

While working on *Patterns of Fashion: the cut and construction of clothes for men and women c. 1560–1620* I gathered a great deal of material on the work carried out by the artificers of the Wardrobe of Robes. In the end there was insufficient space to use it, and I decided therefore to publish this research in Chapter VIII, although it has made the book rather long. However, the contents of the Stowe and Folger inventories are far more interesting when seen in relation to the practical work carried out by tailors, embroiderers, skinners, silkwomen, shoemakers, and other craftsmen, together with the way in which the clothes were ordered and cared for. Unfortunately there was insufficient time for a full genealogical search to be carried out for every individual working for the Wardrobe of Robes, nor space to print the results, but some time spent with the Indexes and Printed Lists in the Society of Genealogists

Library, London, may discover many examples of family ties among the craftsmen. It seemed more useful to undertake the even more time-consuming task of providing an index of paintings, persons, places, and events, with a separate index, partly a glossary, for clothing, textiles, jewels, woven and embroidered motifs, symbolism, fashion terminology, and other related topics. I hope this will make the inventories more readily accessible and of use to the general reader, because terms for dress and textiles can be very confusing. There may be several words for the same item, as in our own time, for example, sweater, jumper or woollie, with cardigan for the same garment when buttoned down the front. What is a gown, what is a dress, what is a suit? We may have an evening gown or evening dress, wedding gown or wedding dress, but a bathing dress, bathing suit or swim suit, as well as a tailored suit to be worn with a blouse. These same difficulties were encountered by the International Committee for the Museums and Collections of Costume of ICOM when attempting to rationalize the terms for cataloguing costume in 1971–76. The same problems faced me when choosing terms for the different parts of dress in the sixteenth century, particularly as I had much new material which would be unfamiliar to the reader. Decisions have not been reached easily but I hope the reasons for them will be apparent in each case.

The reader is advised to study the list of abbreviations on pp. ix–xi and the key to signs and abbreviations in the transcripts on p. 243, as these are used in the text of the book as well as in the Stowe and Folger inventories. Those unfamiliar with Roman numerals, Imperial weights and measures, and Elizabethan currency will find some explanation on p. 242. It became apparent as I was writing this book that many younger readers have difficulty in reading Roman numerals because they are used so infrequently today, so in many places I have given Arabic figures in square brackets to help them.

On several occasions I have been asked if the preparation of the Stowe and Folger inventories in 1600 was not an example of the Queen's vanity and love of display. There is nothing unusual in the preparation of such inventories. Bearing in mind that Elizabeth probably considered the gowns enriched with gold thread as state treasure, it would seem she wished to leave everything in order and carefully recorded before her death. The Stowe inventory was kept by the officers of the Wardrobe of Robes as a record and was used to check the contents again when James I came to the throne in 1603. From this study we find the glittering lists prove, paradoxically, not that Elizabeth was extravagant, but that in the words of the Master of the Great Wardrobe, Sir John Fortescue, in 1593: 'As for her apparel, it is royal and princely beseeming her calling, but not sumptuous nor excessive.'

I

In the Eye of the Beholder

There is probably no other monarch whose appearance is so familiar to every school child. Horace Walpole remarked 'A pale Roman nose, a head of hair loaded with crowns and powdered with diamonds, a vast ruff, a vaster farthingale, and a bushel of pearls, are the features by which everybody knows at once the portraits of Queen Elizabeth' (Fig. 1).[1]

F. M. O'Donoghue gives the view which has been generally accepted about Elizabeth's elaborate gowns in the later years of her reign, following the lead given by Francis Bacon:

Though in her girlhood, when her position was one of great uncertainty and some danger, she discreetly affected an extreme simplicity of dress, and a dislike for outward show, after her accession to the throne her natural vanity and love of admiration led her to adopt every expedient calculated to enhance her charms, and in her later years, 'imagining' as Francis Bacon observes 'that the people who are much influenced by externals, would be diverted by the glitter of her jewels from noticing the decay of her personal attractions' she indulged in an absolutely barbaric display of rich fabrics and jewellery.[2]

What is the truth of this statement? Was it just vanity and love of admiration or can the change in the Queen's taste be attributed to other factors? The quantities of clothes recorded in the Inventories taken in 1600 would seem, at a cursory glance, to suggest sheer vanity: after relating them to the surviving New Year's Gift Rolls and the warrants for the Wardrobe of Robes for forty years a different picture begins to emerge. It is one of careful organization and economy. As the Chancellor of the Exchequer, Sir John Fortescue, told the House of Commons in February 1593: 'As for her apparel, it is royal and princely, beseeming her calling, but not sumptuous nor excessive'.[3]

Lack of space prevents a detailed comparison between Elizabeth's expenditure on her clothes and that of other princesses and queens during the sixteenth century. However, even a cursory glance at the wardrobe expenses of Katherine of Aragon in 1520,[4] the list of materials used for Anne Boleyn's clothes in 1536,[5] the clothes worn by Mary Tudor in 1553–54, the inventory of the wardrobe of Mary, Queen of Scots, at Holyrood in 1562[6] and the list of clothes for Christina di Lorena when she married Ferdinando I de'Medici in 1589[7] shows that these words were quite true. Elizabeth's wardrobe expenses each year during the last four years of her reign were £9,535, while those for James I during the first five years of his reign, were £36,377, annually.[8]

Contemporary accounts record Elizabeth's elegant appearance as a princess and during the first years of her reign. Her preference for black and white — 'These are my colours' as she told Don Diego Guzman da Silva, the Spanish Ambassador, at a masque in July 1564[9] — gave dramatic emphasis to the rich jewels which she wore. Black velvet and satin were a perfect foil for the pearls, gold embroidery, and pieces of gold and enamelled jewellery depicted in the 'Phoenix' portrait, one of the paintings which show Elizabeth at her most elegant (Fig. 26). The fashions of the first half of her reign were more flattering to the figure than later styles; and the small waist, constricted body, widening sleeves and cone-shaped Spanish farthingale would have made Elizabeth appear even slimmer and taller than she was. The elaborate clothes worn during the later years of the reign created an impression of wealth and majesty. Although less flattering, as it tended to cut the figure in half and thus make it appear shorter, the wide drum-shaped farthingale, fashionable from the early 1590s onwards, was certainly impressive and offered a larger area of skirt for ornamentation.

Signor Francesco Gradenigo reported back to Venice in November 1596 that 'Her Majesty is about sixty-four years of age, short and ruddy in complexion; very strongly built'.[10] The ruddy complexion is borne out by the portrait at Jesus College painted in 1590 (Fig. 66) and Elizabeth had certainly put on a little weight over the years. In 1581, when she was forty-eight, William Whittell, one of her tailors, had the job of 'alteringe enlarginge newe making & lyninge of thirtye peire of bodies & slevis with Jagges parte cloth of golde cloth of silver vellat satten taphata & netteworke perfourmed with like stuff and lyned with taphata'.[11]

William Jones, the Queen's tailor, carried out several large groups of alterations between 1585 and 1588.[12] In 1585 he was engaged in 'alteringe enlarginge pecinge longer and wider in the bodies slevis & skyrtes of fower score and eight peire of bodies for Gownes Dublettes and Jacquettes parte cloth of golde tyssue, cloth of golde, cloth of silver, vellat, satten striped, taphata, netteworke curle, and tufte taphata perfourmed with like stuff the lyninges perfourmed with sarceonett & taphata'.[13] In the same year Arthur Middleton, an

1   *Queen Elizabeth I encircled by the Tudor rose on the left and eglantine on the right. Woodcut from 'The Light of Britaine' by Henry Lyte, 1588. Private collection*

2   *Design, or drawing from an inventory, of a brooch, possibly for the Princess Elizabeth. Pen and ink drawing by Hans Holbein the Younger c. 1536. British Museum, London (5308–ECM 86/G347)*

alterations hand, was employed in 'alteringe & enlarginge of fower Gownes fower Dublettes six payer of bodies & one Jaquett parte of cloth of golde cloth of silver vellat tufte taphata satten & netteworke florished with golde silver & silke perfourmed with like stuff the lyninges perfourmed with sarceonett taphata canvas bayes hookes & eyes'.[14] Between September 1587 and April 1588 Jones altered, enlarged, and lengthened the bodices and sleeves of forty gowns and doublets.[15] By September 1588 he had carried out similar work on another thirty[16] and by April 1589 on thirty-two more.[17] During the summer of the same year Jones was then engaged in 'alteringe pecinge Longer enlarginge in the bodies and slevis of xxxiiij gownes saffegardes and Petycoates the bodies lykewyse of them enlardged and of dublettes and Jacquettes parte Cloth of Gold, clothe of Silver, velvet Satten and Taffeta perfourmed with lyke stuff and plushe Networke florished with gold, with Taffata to border and lyne the said garmentes, and Canvas bayes hookes and eyes to perfourme them of our great warderob'.[18] These may have been further alterations to garments first altered a year or more before. However, safeguards and petticoats were now on the list, so it seems likely that these were yet more clothes, which may not have been worn for some time, made ready in case the Queen wished to wear them.

The slow change in fashion from Spanish cone-shaped farthingale to wider drum-shaped variety accounts for all the alterations to the length of cloaks, gowns, petticoats, and safeguards which first appear in 1578,[19] but these references to 'pecinge longer and wider in the bodies' indicate a change in the Queen's size as well as in the fashions at this time. This, in addition to fashionably padded sleeves, must have given the impression of a strongly built figure, while the wide farthingale made Elizabeth appear short to Signor Gradenigo.

The wide-skirted fashions enhanced the regal presence while the slow and stately movements described by George Puttenham in 1589 would have made an impressive display of rich fabrics:

And in a prince it is decent to go slowly and to march with leisure, and with a certain grandity rather than gravity; as our sovereign lady and mistress, the very image of majesty and magnificence, is accustomed to do generally; unless it be when she walketh apace for her pleasure, or to catch her a heat in the cold mornings.[20]

Dignity might be sacrificed on occasion; Elizabeth could walk quickly to get warm and she probably looked very graceful when 'dancing high' in the Italian manner.[21]

The New Year's Gift Rolls show that an increasing number of items of clothing were given to Elizabeth as the years went by. It is hardly surprising that both embroidery and fabrics became more and more elaborate, since the donors were not only striving to please the Queen and show their loyalty, but also to keep abreast of each other. During the closing years of her reign, Elizabeth became not only a glittering symbol of church and state but also a cult figure — Pandora, Gloriana, Cynthia, Belphoebe, Astraea, Queen of the Sea[22] — and the mixture of Queen and Divine Goddess was well served by the image which she presented. The often complex symbolism expressed in the rich embroideries was in many cases carefully chosen by close friends and loyal subjects as well as those trying to climb the ladder of preferment. While the effect must often have been spectacular, it might not necessarily have been elegant. Although the ladies-in-waiting could advise donors on colours and fashions, and gifts were often altered by the Queen's tailor, to a certain extent Elizabeth's clothes in the closing years of her reign reflected her subjects' attitude towards her and their taste.[23]

Elizabeth's apparent need for compliments and admiration of her appearance has also been put down to sheer vanity, but was it just that? On occasion Elizabeth made it quite obvious that a compliment was expected from ambassadors and courtiers, but in some of these cases it may simply have been a feminine manoeuvre for gaining time. The oft-quoted conversation with Sir James Melville may have been as much to test him and gain information about the Queen of Scots as to obtain compliments for herself.[24] Sir Richard Baker described her as short sighted;[25] the compliments would have given her time to get a clear view of the speaker.

As Queen of England, Elizabeth played an intricate game of matrimonial alliances with suitors from all over Europe for

3   *Detail from Figure 191, 'Lady Jane Dudley', commonly called 'Lady Jane Grey'. Panel painting attributed to Master John, c. 1550. She wears a chain of antique cameos with a miniature watch above the deep crimson silk tassel. The deep red forepart, probably velvet, is decorated with interlaced lines of gold cord and braid forming a trellis-work, with stylized gold leaves and flowers enriched with pearls, and knots of pearls. Most of the gold leaf has worn away, or been removed with cleaning, revealing the ochre-coloured bole beneath. National Portrait Gallery, London*

years.[26] The game's success depended a great deal on her appearance and the illusion of eternal youth. She dressed carefully for the part, but the story of Elizabeth's vast wardrobe turns out to be one of careful budgeting and good organization, not wild extravagance and vanity. She certainly loved beautiful clothes and always dressed in the latest fashion but the impression gained is that she regarded the rich silks and velvets, gold embroidery, and spangles as state treasure; they were looked after most carefully. Some items dating from the 1560s were still there, unaltered, in 1600.

Some of the more familiar descriptions of Elizabeth are repeated here, with others not so well known, to build up the whole picture of the Queen and her choice of dress. These accounts from her tutor, close friends, onlookers in the crowds and ambassadors, some written shortly after seeing Elizabeth, others from memory years afterwards, give another slant on the subject before considering the portraits.

As a small child she was dressed most attractively. William Loke, the King's mercer, supplied some materials to Queen Anne Boleyn for Elizabeth in the spring of 1536, when 'my lady princess' was two and a half years old.[27] A yard of white sarsenet was bought to line a gown of orange velvet and the Tudor pale red gold hair and white skin would have been enhanced by a kirtle of russet velvet, newly edged with matching velvet. A kirtle of yellow satin was edged with yellow velvet and one of green satin with green velvet while two yards of 'white capha damaske' were used to make a kirtle edged with white velvet (white was one of Elizabeth's favourite colours in later years.) There were two pieces measuring a quarter of a yard each of black velvet and satin to make partlets, both lined with black taffeta sarsenet and a quarter of a yard of purple sarsenet to line a sleeve of purple embroidered satin.

After Anne Boleyn's execution Elizabeth's status changed, as in June 1536 Parliament passed an Act declaring her illegitimate. The child's household was reduced and her governess, Lady Margaret Bryan, a widowed cousin of Anne, wrote a worried letter to Thomas Cromwell, Lord Privy Seal:

Now et es so my {Lady Eliza}bethe es pot from that degree she was afor what d{egree she is at n}ow, I know not bot be heryng say therfor I know not how {to order her, n}or my self, nor non of hars that I have the rowl of {that is her} women and har gromes besychyng yow to be good lord {to my lady and to} al{l} hars, and that she may have som raymant for {She hath neither} gown, nor kertel nor petecot nor no maner of t{hinges as linen} for smokes, nor cerchefs, nor sleves, nor rayles, nor {body stitchets, nor hand}cerchers, nor mofelers nor begens. al{l} thys hir grac{e must have. I have} dreven of as long as I can, that be my trothe {i can drive i}t no longer. besychyng you my lord that ye wel{l see that her Grace m}ay have that es nedful for her, as my trust is ye wel{l do.}.[28]

The theory that Elizabeth's early memories of not having enough clothes to wear suitable for a child of her rank might have made her compensate for it in later life may be true. However she was only about three and a half years old when this letter was written and is unlikely to have understood Lady Bryan's worries. It may have been a case of 'out of sight, out of mind' as Lady Bryan also had difficulty in dressing the baby Prince Edward suitably for his rank for the visit by the Lords of Council in September 1538.[29] She wrote that she would

acompleche et to the best of my power with syche thynges as her es to do et with al, wyche es but very bare for syche a time. The best cot [coat] my Lord Prinses grace hath es tensel, and that he shal have on at that teym; he hathe never a good jewel to set on his cape [cap]; howbet I shal order al things for my lordes honer the best I can.[30]

Elizabeth may not have had a great many clothes as princess but she does not seem to have been unsuitably clad after this early episode. She certainly had some pretty jewels, although perhaps none of great value. In 1540 Katherine Howard gave her a 'Brooche of Golde wherin is set an Antique hedd of Agathe vj verey small Rubyes and vj verey small Emeradds. Litle thing worthe'.[31] A trifle, but no doubt the cameo would

Pink Garment

4 'Elizabeth I when Princess'. Panel painting attributed to
William Scrots, c. 1547. Royal Collection. Reproduced by
Gracious Permission of Her Majesty the Queen

have fascinated a seven year old child. The Queen also gave
some beads 'to the Lady Elysabethe, the kynges dowghter';
they were 'of golde that is to say x Longe stones enamuled with
white and garneshed with peerle & redstones every of them
havyng peerlles and x other stones ennamuled with blewe like
cuppes havyng also a pillar garnesshed with peerll and
redstones and a buttone of golde with divers small cheynes of
golde with black knoppes'.[32] Designs by Holbein for two little
brooches, with the words 'My Ladi Prinsis' (Fig. 2) may have
been commissioned by Henry VIII for his two daughters,
perhaps when Jane Seymour was Queen.

Princess Mary gave her sister more valuable jewels, among
them 'a grene Tablet garnished with golde havying the Picture
of the trinite in it' and a 'pomander of golde with a Diall in yt'
(perhaps similar to the watch in Fig. 3). Both were 'geven to my
Lady Elizabeth grace'. On 21 September 1553, when Mary
was Queen of England, she gave Elizabeth 'a Broche of thistory
of piramys & tysbie [Pyramus and Thisbe] with a fayr table
Diamond garneshed with iiij Rubies' and a 'payr of Bedes of
Corall . . . white trymmed with gold'.[33]

The portrait at Windsor Castle, probably painted in 1547,
shows Elizabeth as a serious young girl of thirteen with fair
skin, red-gold hair and long, slim-fingered hands (Fig. 4). Her
love of simplicity in dress, described by Ascham and Aylmer, is
not borne out by the richly patterned fabrics used for the
undersleeves and gown. Perhaps her most elaborate clothes
were chosen for the portrait, as befitting a princess, both
daughter and sister of a king.[34] The deep pink gown is

fashionably cut and the material is described in the records of
Edward VI's collection of pictures '. . . the ladye Elizabeth her
grace with a booke in her hande her gowne like crymsen clothe
of golde with workes'.[35]

Elizabeth dressed simply in her teens according to her tutor
Roger Ascham. She had just passed her sixteenth birthday
when he wrote in a letter to John Sturm:

It is difficult to say whether the gifts of nature or of fortune are most
to be admired in that illustrious lady. The praise which Aristotle gives
wholly centres in her — beauty, stature, prudence and industry. She
has just passed her sixteenth birthday and shows such dignity and
gentleness as are wonderful at her age and in her rank . . . . In
adornment she is elegant rather than showy, and by her contempt of
gold and head-dresses, she reminds one of Hippolyte rather than
Phaedra . . .[36]

Perhaps it was a method of self-defence, as O'Donoghue
suggests in *A Descriptive and Classified Catalogue of Portraits
of Queen Elizabeth*. Or it may have been simply a lack of any
great interest while her mind was occupied with the fascina-
tions of Greek and Latin. She must also have realized that she
looked very attractive in the plain styles which accentuated the
pallor of her skin and set off the red gold hair.

John Aylmer, Lady Jane Grey's tutor, who was made Bishop
of London in 1576, must have found it difficult to reconcile his
praise of Elizabeth's love of simplicity with some of her richly
embroidered gowns after she came to the throne. In *An
Harborowe for Faithful and Trewe Subjectes*, printed in 1559,
he wrote that in seven years after her father's death Elizabeth
had only once looked at the jewels he left her and continued:

I am sure that her maidenly apparel, which she used in Kyng
Edwardes tyme, made the noblemens daughters and wyves to be
ashamed to be drest and paynted lyke pecockes, being more moved
with hir most vertuous example: than with all that ever Paule and
Peter wrote touchyng that matter. Yea this I know that a great mans
daughter, receavinge from Ladye Marye before she was Quene,
goodly apparel of tynsyll, cloth of golde, and velvet, layd on with
parchement lace of gold: when she sawe it, sayde, what shal I doo
with it? Marry saide a gentlewoman weare it. Nay quoth she, that
were a shame to followe my lady Mary against Gods woorde and
leave my Lady Elyzabeth, whiche foloweth Gods woorde.

Aylmer recounted another interesting story which may be
true, although it is told from a staunch Protestant viewpoint.
When the Scottish Queen Regent, Mary of Guise, broke her
journey at the English Court on her way back to Scotland from
France in October 1551, both she and her retinue were
wearing the newest fashions and hairstyles which captivated
all the English ladies, with the exception of one — Elizabeth —
according to Aylmer: 'And this all men knowe, than when all
the ladies hent up thattire of the Scottish skyttes at the
commyng in of the Scottishe Quene, to go unbrydled, and with
their heares frounsed and curled and double curled she altered
nothing, but to the shame of them all kepte hir olde maydenly
shamefastness'. This was, perhaps, not the best way to be
unobtrusive at Court. Elizabeth must have stood out with
dramatic emphasis against the other ladies, if the story is true,
but it seems that neither Elizabeth nor her sister Mary
appeared at Court during this visit.

Aylmer apparently made one attempt to reform Elizabeth's
love of fashions in the early 1590s. He died in 1594 at the age
of seventy-three and Sir John Harington's story, although
undated, appears to refer to 1593:

One Sunday (April last) my Lorde of London, preachede to the
Queens Majestie, and seemede to touche on the vanitie of deckinge

the bodie too finely — Her Majestie tolde the Ladies, that if the Bishope helde more discorse on suche matters shee wolde fitte him for Heaven, but he shoulde walke thither withoute a staffe and leave his mantle behind him; perchance the Bishope hathe never soughte her Highnesse wardrobe, or he woulde have chosen another texte.[37]

Another tactless sermon was preached to the Court at Richmond in 1596 by Anthony Rudd, Bishop of St David's, on the infirmities of old age. Elizabeth was, not unnaturally, displeased at his observation that time had 'furrowed her face and besprinkled her hair with meal'.[38]

A brief glimpse is given of the young Princess in the procession from the Tower to the Palace of Westminster for the coronation of Queen Mary on the last day of September 1553: 'Next came a triumphal chariot covered with silver, in which was the Lady Elizabeth, sister of her Majesty, and Madam Anne of Cleves, wife of King Henry the Eighth and afterwards divorced by him, attired in cloth of silver.' Another eye-witness account in a manuscript used by Planché gives crimson velvet instead of cloth of silver, but the account here agrees with that of the French Ambassador.[39]

Giovanni Michiel, the Venetian Ambassador in England during the reign of Queen Mary, described Elizabeth shortly before she came to the throne in his *Relazione d'Inghilterra* presented to the Senate on his return in 1557:

My Lady Elizabeth was born in September 1533 so she is now twenty-three years old. She is a young woman whose mind is considered no less excellent [bello] than her person although her face is comely [gratiosa] rather than handsome but she is tall and well formed with a good skin although swarthy [anorchè olivastra]; she has fine eyes and above all a beautiful hand of which she makes a display [della quale ne fa professione].[40]

Paul Johnson points out that 'swarthy' or olive-skinned may reflect the fact that Elizabeth was apparently suffering from jaundice.[41]

There are a few other references to the Princess during 1557 and 1558, at which time she was in the charge of Sir Thomas Pope. She must have been beautifully dressed at the Shrovetide Pageant of 1557 in the great hall at Hatfield with forty-six or more gentlemen and ladies dressed in crimson satin embroidered with wreaths of gold and garnished with pearls.[42] This apparently incurred the displeasure of Queen Mary, but in spite of this Elizabeth was allowed to make visits to Court. On 25 February 1558 she rode from Hatfield to Somerset Place beyond Strand bridge and was received by the Queen on 28 February at Whitehall. On 4 March Elizabeth rode to her Palace at Sheen with a large company and in April she was escorted to Enfield Chase from Hatfield by a retinue of twelve ladies clothed in white satin and twenty yeomen in green, all on horseback, so that she might hunt the hart. In the summer of the same year she paid a visit to the Queen at Richmond, travelling by water from Somerset Place in the Queen's barge which was hung with garlands of artificial flowers and covered with a canopy of green sarsenet wrought with branches of eglantine in embroidery and powdered with blossoms of gold, accompanied by Sir Thomas Pope and four ladies of her chamber. Six boats attended this procession filled with her highness's retinue, richly dressed in russet damask and blue embroidered satin, tasselled and spangled with silver, with bonnets of cloth of silver plumed with green feathers. During the time of the Princess's residence at Hatfield she also spent Christmas at Hampton Court with the Queen and King Philip, but retired before the revels, maskings and disguisings began. On St Stephen's day she heard matins in the Queen's closet

adjoining the chapel, dressed in a robe of white satin strung all over with pearls.[43]

On her accession to the throne many more accounts might be expected but, although there are a large number of surviving portraits, there are remarkably few really detailed descriptions of Elizabeth's appearance until late in her reign. The best are written by foreigners, particularly the Venetians; the description of the coronation robes in 1559 is most illuminating when related to both portrait and miniature which show Elizabeth wearing them.[44] Unfortunately no authorized diplomatic functionary was accredited by the Signory of Venice to the English Court from 5 July 1557, when Giovanni Michiel left England with King Philip, until 1602;[45] the letter describing the coronation of Queen Elizabeth was written by Il Schifanoya, a Venetian in London, to the Castellan of Mantua.[46] The greater part of the Venetian despatches relating to Elizabeth were written from the Court of France, where Venice was represented by a succession of Ambassadors in Ordinary. One of the last audiences which Elizabeth gave in 1603 was described by another Venetian, with the same attention to detail shown by Michiel and Il Schifanoya. If only diplomatic relations had been maintained throughout the reign we might have had a series of similar eye-witness records of the Queen's appearance on many important occasions.

The English accounts frequently refer to Elizabeth's splendid presence. The dominant personality, Gloriana, Astraea, Belphoebe, must have impressed observers more than the clothes, as rarely is there more than a mention of colour and material, or a note that the Queen was richly dressed with many jewels. Perhaps letters were written by ladies at Court to relations in the country, describing the Queen's latest gowns and the lavish embroidery, but none seems to have survived. In one way the lack of description of her clothes may be a subtle compliment to Elizabeth's tailors for creating gowns in which she must have felt supremely confident and assured and which did not dominate her personality. However, it may simply be that the English were less observant of the detail which fascinated Venetian eyes.

Most of the accounts give no more than tantalizing glimpses of Elizabeth. For example we know that she was 'apparelled in purple velvet, with a Scarf about her neck' when she rode on horseback to take possession of the Tower after her accession to the throne on 28 November, 1558, but no further detail is given.[47] At the end of May 1559 the Queen received an Embassy from France at Whitehall for supper when she was 'dressed entirely in purple velvet, with so much gold and so many pearls and jewels, it added much to her beauty'.[48] On the occasion of her visit to Cambridge in 1564, again on horseback, she was described as wearing a gown of pinked black velvet with her hair in a caul set with pearls and precious stones and a hat over it, spangled with gold, with a bush of feathers.[49] Although the colour, fabric, and decoration are given, the gowns cannot be definitely identified with similar items in the inventories or portraits with any certainty, as there is insufficient detail. However, these brief descriptions do give an idea of the Queen's appearance on particular occasions. Only the Coronation, Parliament, and Garter robes are easily recognizable (Figs 86, 87, 99–102, 104–07, 109 and 114).

Her appearance, but not her dress, was carefully recorded by the Scottish Ambassador, Sir James Melville, after an interview with her in 1564. He wrote that her hair was more reddish than yellow and 'curled in appearance naturally. She desired to know of me what colour of hair was reputed best; and whether my Queen's hair or hers was best; and which of the two was fairest. I answered, the fairness of them both was not their worst faults . . . She inquired which of them was of highest stature? I said, My Queen. Then saith she, she is too high; for I myself am neither too high nor too low'.[50]

Lupold von Wedel who started his travels in England in August, 1585, was fascinated by the Queen and described her, with her retinue, at Hampton Court:

It being Sunday she attended Divine Service in the church or chapel which is in the castle . . . Before the Queen marched her bodyguard. They are all tall, strong, picked men. There are said to be two hundred of them, but this day they were not all present. They bore gilt halberds and wore red coats trimmed with black velvet. On their coats in front and behind are the Queen's arms in beaten gilt silver. Then came the most distinguished lords and councillors. Two of them bore a royal sceptre each. Then came one bearing the royal sword in a red velvet scabbard embroidered with gold and studded with precious stones and pearls. Him followed the Queen in black, because she is in mourning for the Prince of Orange and the Duke of Alençon. On either side of her crisp hair hung a great pearl about as large as a hazel-nut. The common people, who formed two rows on either side her path, fell upon their knees. The Queen's demeanour, however, was gracious and gentle and so was her speech, and from rich and poor she took petitions in a modest manner. Behind her walked a countess bearing her train. Then followed twenty-two maids of honour, mostly the children of Earls and other Lords. These were followed by twenty-four noblemen who bore small gilt pikes tipped with iron and adorned with long plumes. Although she has a hundred of these, they are not all on duty at the same time but discharge their office in turns. The Queen's path up to the chapel was guarded on both sides by the aforesaid bodyguard.[51]

Her 'crisp hair' would be described today as 'curled' or 'waved'. Shakespeare gives 'crispèd, snaky golden locks' for hair 'often known to be the dowry of a second head'[52] and the style was probably that seen in Figures 39 and 217. Pearls were often used to decorate Elizabeth's coiffure and are to be seen in many portraits.

Von Wedel also described the Queen arriving in London on 12 November in the same year to take up residence at St. James's for the Accession Day Tilts:

Before the Queen in her progress had reached the City, the Burgomaster or Mayor rode out to meet her with a cavalcade of some hundred horse. Amongst them were all the Aldermen and other burghers and craftsmen. Amongst these were very many goldsmiths, all dressed in black velvet coats, with fine trimmings. Each of them wore a gold chain over his coat. With them, but on foot, was a large crowd of the populace, not only men, but also women and girls. The Queen's train then came up. Riding ahead were her servants, then followed two of her guards, then came her equerries, and behind these her chamberlains, of whom there were about twenty. Then came the Privy Councillors. In front of the Councillors rode three bishops, amongst them the Bishop of Canterberg [Canterbury] who is the Primate of all England. On this occasion he had with him fifty of his horsemen. Behind the Bishops rode some councillors, but immediately before the Queen the Treasurer, who has been created a baron or knight, and a Secretary named Walsinger [Walsingham]. They were followed by the Queen in a gold coach, open all round, but having above it a canopy embroidered with gold and pearls. On the front and on the back of the coach were three plumes of various colours. The coach was drawn by four bays in royal trappings. The coachman was clad in red velvet, and on his coat both before and behind was the Queen's coat-of-arms and a rose of chaste silver-gilt. The Queen sat alone in the carriage. She was dressed in white and cried to the people: 'God save my people', to which the crowd responded with 'God save Your Grace.' This they repeated many

5 *Travelling carriage studded with gilt nails, similar to that described by Lupold Von Wedel. Water-colour drawing c. 1610. Scottish National Portrait Gallery, Edinburgh*

times, falling upon their knees. The Queen sitting all alone in her splendid coach appeared like a goddess such as painters are wont to depict. Behind the Queen's coach rode my Lord Lester, who is an Earl of princely blood. He had long been Master of the Horse. Beside him rode yet another of the Queen's Privy Councillors. Then followed the Queen's Maids of Honour, twenty-four in number. All were on horseback and beautifully attired. Behind them came the Queen's guards who on this day were fifty strong. They were all armed with bows and dirks. Then came a gilt coach embroidered with gold and silver, which however did not rival that of the Queen, and behind it yet another coach studded all over with nails of gold [Fig. 5]. In neither of these coaches was anyone seated. Behind this followed those who, as already related, had ridden out to meet the Queen. They accompanied her up to the house. On her entry all the bells pealed.[53]

Von Wedel certainly conjures up a splendid scene. The expenses of most of this and other similiar occasions can be pieced together from the almost complete run of yearly Accounts for the Great Wardrobe from 1558 to 1603 preserved in the Public Record Office, discussed further in Chapter VII.

Von Wedel's most detailed description of the Queen's appearance was for 27 December, when he went five miles down the Thames to Greenwich, where she was in residence:

Arrived at the palace, I first went into the chapel which is hung with gold. The pulpit is covered with red gold-embroidered velvet. In one-half of the church stands a large, high, gilded altar and there, divided off from the rest, is a recess entirely of gold cloth out of which the Queen comes when she is about to receive the Sacrament. Then I went into a large room before the Queen's chamber hung with tapestry wrought in silver and gold. Here I waited until she went to church. As at Hampenkort, as I have already related, she was accompanied to church by her gentlemen and ladies-in-waiting, who, however, on this occasion, it being Christmas-tide, were more gorgeously dressed. But the Queen being in mourning for the Duc d'Alençon and the Prince of Orange, was dressed in black velvet sumptuously embroidered with silver and pearls. Over her robe she had a silver shawl, that was full of meshes and diaphanous like a piece of gossamer tissue. But this shawl gleamed as though it were bespangled with tinsel, which, however, was not the case, and it hung down over her robe as low as the hem of her skirt.[54]

Shawl would be better translated as 'veil' or 'mantle'. Here again, although the detail is insufficient to connect these clothes with items in the Inventories, one gains an impression

6 'Queen Elizabeth receiving the Dutch Ambassadors in the Presence Chamber'. Water-colour drawing by an unknown artist, c. 1570–75. Staatliche Kunstsammlungen, Kassel (GS 10430)

of the Queen's appearance when in mourning which can be linked to the description of the whole Court wearing black when the news of the Massacre of St Bartholomew's Day was brought to Kenilworth in 1572.[55]

André Hurault, Sieur de Maisse, Ambassador Extraordinary from Henri IV to Queen Elizabeth, gives some of the best eye-witness accounts of the Queen's gowns in 1597. Several of his familiar descriptions are quoted here, as they also give the setting in which the Queen appeared and the way in which she spoke of herself and her attire. Unfortunately the original manuscript has apparently disappeared but six seventeenth-century transcripts survive. The translation by G. B. Harrison and R. A. Jones was based on a modern copy of one of these transcripts.[56] I have included some of the French terms of clothing from this copy, enclosing them in square brackets. De Maisse uses the New Style of reckoning throughout. His dates are therefore ten days in advance of current English reckoning. The English dates are given in square brackets. He wrote:

On the 8th of December [28 November] . . . about one hour after noon there came a gentleman from the Queen who . . . brought me in a coach to take me down to the river where one of the barges awaited me, and we went thence to the gate of the Queen's palace. At our landing there came to seek me a gentleman who spoke very good Italian, called Monsieur Wotton . . . He led me across a chamber of moderate size wherein were the guards of the Queen, and thence into the Presence Chamber, as they call it, in which all present, even

though the Queen be absent, remain uncovered. He then conducted me to a place on one side, where there was a cushion made ready for me [Fig. 6]. I waited there some time, and the Lord Chamberlain, who has the charge of the Queen's household (not as *maître d'hôtel*, but to arrange audiences and to escort those who demand them and especially ambassadors), came to seek me where I was seated. He led me along a passage somewhat dark, into a chamber that they call the Privy Chamber, at the head of which was the Queen seated in a low chair, by herself, and withdrawn from all the Lords and Ladies that were present, they being in one place and she in another. After I had made her my reverence at the entry of the chamber, she rose and came five or six paces towards me, almost into the middle of the chamber. I kissed the fringe of her robe [le bas de sa robe] and she embraced me with both hands. She looked at me kindly, and began to excuse herself that she had not sooner given me audience, saying that the day before she had been very ill with a gathering on the right side of her face, which I should never have thought seeing her eyes and face: but she did not remember ever to have been so ill before. She excused herself because I found her attired in her night-gown [sa robe de nuit], and began to rebuke those of her Council who were present, saying, 'What will these gentlemen say' — speaking of those who accompanied me — 'to see me so attired? I am much disturbed that they should see me in this state'.[57]

This reference to a 'nightgown' does not imply that the Queen was wearing the equivalent of a modern dressing-gown. The term is nearer in meaning to the eighteenth-century 'dress' and 'undress' and the modern 'formal' and 'informal'. 'Fringe' might be better translated as 'hem'. The rest of the description gives details of the gown:

She stood up while I was speaking, but then she returned to her chair when she saw that I was only speaking of general matters. I drew nearer to her chair and began to deal with her in that wherewithal I had been charged; and because I was uncovered, from time to time she signed to me with her hand to be covered, which I did. Soon after she caused a stool to be brought, whereon I sat and began to talk to her.

She was strangely attired in a dress [robbe] of silver cloth, white and crimson [toile d'argent blanche et incarnate], or silver 'gauze' [gaze d'argent], as they call it. This dress [robbe] had slashed sleeves [manches ouvertes] lined with red taffeta, and was girt about with other little sleeves that hung down to the ground [et estoit ceincte d'autres petites manches qui pendoient jusques à terre], which she was for ever twisting and untwisting.[58]

'Ouverte' is translated as 'gaping wide' by Cotgrave in his *Dictionarie of the French and English Tongues* printed in 1611; the sleeves may have been Spanish sleeves (Fig. 196), open at the front for the arm to pass through, rather than heavily slashed, or similar to those in Figure 7, where the opening can be fastened with gold buttons. Incarnate according to Cotgrave is 'carnation & more particularly, light or pale carnation: flesh coloured, or of the colour of our damaske Rose'.

It is interesting that Elizabeth should have fidgeted with her sleeves in this way, sometimes considered a sign of nervousness. Each period, however, has its own idiosyncratic mannerisms connected with dress or hairstyle; the twisting and untwisting of sleeves may be equated with the gesture familiar in the late 1960s and 1970s, of pushing long hair back and allowing it almost immediately to fall back on the face. De Maisse continues:

She kept the front of her dress [robbe] open, and one could see the whole of her bosom, and passing low [tout sa gorge et assez bas], and often she would open the front of this robe [manteau] with her hands as if she was too hot. The collar of the [said] robe [manteau] was very high, and the lining of the inner part all adorned with little pendants of rubies and pearls, very many, but quite small. She had also a chain [carcan] of rubies and pearls about her neck. On her head she wore a garland of the same material [estoffe] and beneath it a great reddish-coloured wig, with a great number of spangles [papillottes] of gold and silver, and hanging down over her forehead some pearls, but of no great worth. On either side of her ears hung two great curls of hair, almost down to her shoulders and within the collar of her robe, spangled as the top of her head. Her bosom [la gorge] is somewhat wrinkled as well as [one can see for] the collar that she wears round her neck, but lower down her flesh is exceeding white and delicate, so far as one could see.[59]

Cotgrave translates 'robbe' as 'a robe, gowne, mantle, coat; any long upper garment' and 'manteau' as 'a cloke'. De Maisse's description seems to be of a very elaborate style, but from the Queen's remarks her crimson cloth of silver night-gown with high collar, Spanish sleeves and narrow hanging sleeves behind may have been the type of dress she would have worn among her women, less formal than an ensemble considered suitable for an audience. This nightgown might also have been described as a loose gown.[60] It would have been worn over a kirtle or jacket and petticoat, but de Maisse does not appear to have seen enough to be able to describe them. 'Carcan' is translated by Cotgrave as 'a carkanet, or collar of gold, etc; worne about the necke' and the garland on the Queen's head was made of rubies and pearls to match it.

7 *'Portrait of an unknown lady', by an unknown artist, c. 1585. J. B. Speed Art Museum, Louisiana, Kentucky*

De Maisse continues:

As for her face, it is and appears to be very aged. It is long and thin, and her teeth are very yellow and unequal, compared with what they were formerly, so they say, and on the left side less than on the right. Many of them are missing so that one cannot understand her easily when she speaks quickly. Her figure is fair and tall and graceful in whatever she does; so far as may be she keeps her dignity, yet humbly and graciously withal.[61]

This description of the face is very close to the portrait of Elizabeth painted in 1590 when she was fifty-seven years of age, which is at Jesus College, Oxford (Fig. 66).

Elizabeth was dressed differently on the next occasion when de Maisse saw her, and again he gives a good description:

15th [5th] December. I thought that I should have appeared before the Queen. She was on point of giving me audience, having already sent her coaches to fetch me, but taking a look into her mirror said that she appeared too ill and that she was unwilling for anyone to see her in that state; and so countermanded me.

To-day she sent her coaches and one of her own gentlemen servants to conduct me. When I alighted from my coach Monsieur de Mildmay, formerly ambassador in France, came up to me and led me to the Presence Chamber, where the Lord Chamberlain came to seek me as before and conducted me to the Privy Chamber where the Queen was standing by a window. She looked in better health than before. She was clad in a dress [robbe] of black taffeta, bound [bandée] with [broad] gold lace [de passement d'or fort large], and like a robe in the Italian fashion with open sleeves and lined with

8 Detail from 'Queen Elizabeth I and the Three Goddesses' by an artist who uses the monogram HE, 1569. Royal Collection. Reproduced by Gracious Permission of Her Majesty the Queen

8a Detail of glove from Figure 8

would have been easy for any man, particularly a foreigner, to confuse the terms for different parts of an Englishwoman's dress. In this portrait, for example, the lace-edged neckline of the smock just shows above the jewelled stomacher. The ruff is attached to what appears to be another smock but the sitter might have described it as a lining or a facing.

Even the names for the parts of the body may be misleading. Cotgrave gives 'The Stomacke; the gorge; also . . . the breast (being the seat of the stomacke)' as translations of 'estomach' and the use of the word 'nombril' may be de Maisse's exaggerated way of indicating the waist level. Cotgrave further defines 'gorge' as 'in a woman, the outward, and upper part of the breast, betweene the necke and pappes', so that the area seen by de Maisse may, in fact, have been rather higher than the description suggests. The word 'bandée' is given by Cotgrave as 'garded, or welted' and 'entrouvre' as 'halfe to open, to make way through'. The gown was therefore guarded with broad gold lace as a decorative feature rather than bound with it, and when the Queen put her hands on each side it would have parted slightly, half opening to reveal the garments beneath.

De Maisse also mentions Elizabeth's height:

When anyone speaks of her beauty she says that she was never beautiful, although she had that reputation thirty years ago. Nevertheless she speaks of her beauty as often as she can. As for her natural form and proportion, she is very beautiful; and by chance approaching a door and wishing to raise the tapestry that hung before it, she said to me laughing that she was as big as a door, meaning that she was tall.[66]

De Maisse gives a third account of the Queen's appearance:

The same day (24th [14th] December) I went to see the Queen, and she sent me her coaches. I found her very well and kindly disposed. She was having the spinet played to her in her chamber, seeming very attentive to it . . . She was clad in a white robe of cloth of silver [robe de toile d'argent blanche], cut very low [eschancrée fort bas] and her bosom uncovered [le sein descouvert]. She had the same customary head attire, but diversified by several kinds of precious stones, yet not of any great value. She had a little gown of cloth of silver of peach colour, covered and hidden, which was fair.[67]

Cotgrave's translation of 'eschancrée' is 'cut or made hollow and into a halfe-round' and a neckline of this style would certainly have left the bosom uncovered (Figs 140 and 153).

The Queen's beautiful hands also attracted de Maisse's attention on his visit in 1597:

Having told her at some point that she was well advertised of everything that happened in the world, she replied that her hands were very long by nature and might, an nescis longas Regibus esse manus; whereupon she drew off her glove and showed me her hand, which is very long and more than mine by more than three broad fingers. It was formerly very beautiful, but it now very thin, although the skin is still most fair.[68]

crimson taffeta. She had a petticoat [une robbe desoulz] of white damask, girdled, and open in front, as was also her chemise [chemise], in such a manner that she often opened this dress and one could see all her belly [l'estomach], and even to her navel [nombril]. Her head tire was the same as before. She had bracelets of pearl on her hands, six or seven rows of them. On her head tire [coiffure] she wore a coronet of pearls, of which five or six were marvellously fair. When she raises her head, she has a trick of putting both hands on her gown [robe] and opening it [l'entrouvre] insomuch that all her belly [l'estomach] can be seen.[62]

This curious description may be a confusion of terms made in transcription and translation. It is unlikely that the Queen's women would have been so careless as to allow her to appear in public without fastening her clothes properly; this has since been described as a 'shameless occasion'.[63] The word 'chemise' may originally have been written as 'chemisette' or 'petite chemise', translated as 'waistcoat' by Minsheu in The Guide into Tongues (1617). Short embroidered jackets are seen in many portraits by the 1600s. A number of linen, flannel and silk waistcoats are listed in the warrants for the Queen's tailor. One, made in 1570, was 'of camerick enbrodered allover with silver'.[64] Another, altered in 1577, was of 'lynen cloth, quilted with blak silke'.[65]

Alternatively if the word was 'chemise', for which Cotgrave gives the translation 'a shirt or smocke', and it really was worn open as described, perhaps Elizabeth was wearing a style similar to that worn by an unknown lady in c. 1585 (Fig. 7). It

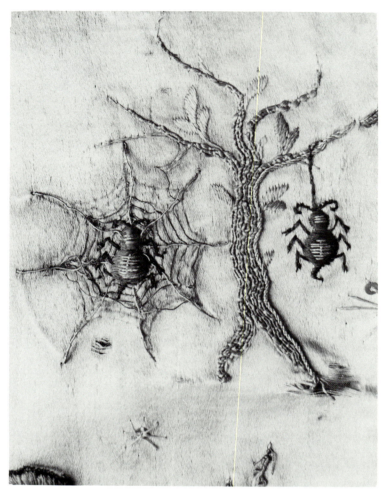

9 *Detail of spiders and a cobweb from a panel of embroidered satin c. 1600. Victoria and Albert Museum, London (T.138–1981)*

Here Elizabeth was wearing gloves while listening to music in the Palace. This may have been a matter of etiquette but would also have been a way of keeping the hands warm in a cold room in December. The other descriptions of Elizabeth wearing gloves are all on public occasions. Fifteen portraits, among over seventy I have examined, show her holding a glove or a pair of gloves in one hand and she is described as holding gloves in her hand in the Recognition Procession on 14 January 1559.[69] One picture shows her wearing gloves, *Queen Elizabeth and Three Goddesses* painted in 1569, where she is regally clad in a magnificent gown, as she must often have appeared before the people (Fig. 8). The gloves have narrow cuffs and are decorated with rows of fine silver cord, giving a striped effect. The beautiful gloves with very deep embroidered cuffs preserved in museums are not in evidence in portraits until after *c.* 1600. Those in the paintings of Elizabeth have richly decorated cuffs, but they are not usually more than about two inches deep.

De Maisse continues in his report of 1597:

. . . save for her face, which looks old, and her teeth, it is not possible to see a woman of so fine and vigorous disposition both in mind and in body . . . This day she was habited, as is her custom, in silver tissue [toile d'argent], or 'gauze' [gaze], as we call it in French; her robe was white and the overvest of gold and silk of violet colour [sa promelle de soye d'or et de couleur violette]. She wore innumerable jewels on her person, not only on her head, but also within her collar [qu'au dedans de son collet], about her arms and on her hands, with a very great quantity of pearls, round her neck and on her bracelets. She had two

bands [carcans], one on each arm, which were worth a great price. She preserves a great gravity amidst her own people. Having entered this time into the Chamber, she walked in a manner marvellous haughty, having Secretary Cecil near her; and I believe she did so expressly that I might see her while she pretended not to see me.[70]

Cotgrave translates 'gaze' as 'also (the sleight stuffe) Tiffanie'. 'Promelle' does not appear in Cotgrave's *Dictionarie* but is probably better translated as 'mantle'.[71] The description calls to mind the Ditchley portrait (Fig. 71).

Duke Frederick of Württemberg chose Herr Johann Jacob Breuning von Buchenbach to lead an embassy to Elizabeth in March 1595 on a quest for the Order of the Garter. Von Buchenbach reported back to the Duke:

I cannot pass over in silence the fact that at the last audience, as already reported, Her Majesty came forward a few paces to meet me and that she did not sit down. She stood for longer than a full hour by the clock conversing with me; which is astonishing for a Queen of such eminence and of such great age, for on the coming Michaelmas Day she attains the sixty-fourth year of her life. I have not heard that Her Majesty is wont often to do this.

Her Majesty was this time dressed in a red robe interwoven with gold thread, and on her head was the usual royal crown of pearls. She wore a collar that looked almost exactly like that worn by the Knights of the Order on St George's Day. Everything was studded with very large diamonds and other precious stones. Over her breast, which was bare, she wore a long filigree lace shawl, on which sat a hideous large black spider that looked as if it were natural and alive. Many might have been deceived by it.[72]

The 'long filigree lace shawl' was probably a network scarf like the eight which were lined with taffeta sarsenet and edged with gold and silver lace and fringe by Roger Mountague for the Queen in 1587.[73] The black spider may have been a jewel or, if the network was designed to look like a cobweb, it might have been a piece of applied raised embroidery (Fig. 9).

Paul Hentzner's description of the Queen at Greenwich written in 1598 also conjures up an image very similar to that of the Ditchley portrait, painted around 1592–94 (Fig. 71):

We arrived next at the royal palace of Greenwich, reported to have been originally built by Humphrey Duke of Gloucester, and to have received very magnificent additions from Henry VII. It was here Elizabeth, the present queen, was born, and here she generally resides; particularly in summer, for the delightfulness of its situation. We were admitted by an order Mr Rogers had procured from the Lord Chamberlain, into the Presence-chamber, hung with rich tapestry, and the floor after the English fashion, strewed with hay, through which the Queen commonly passes in her way to chapel: At the door stood a Gentleman dressed in velvet, with a gold chain, whose office was to introduce to the Queen any Person of Distinction, that came to wait on her: It was Sunday, when there is usually the greatest attendance of Nobility. In the same hall were the Archbishop of Canterbury, the Bishop of London, a great number of Counsellors of State, Officers of the Crown, and Gentlemen, who waited the Queen's coming out; which she did from her own apartment, when it was time to go to Prayers, attended in the following manner:

First, went Gentlemen, Barons, Earls, Knights of the Garter, all richly dressed and bare-headed; next came the Lord High Chancellor of England, bearing the Seals in a red silk Purse, between Two; one of which carried the Royal Scepter, the other the Sword of State, in a red scabbard, studded with golden Fleurs de Lis, the point upwards: Next came the Queen, in the Sixty-fifth year of her Age, as we were told, very majestic; her Face oblong, fair, but wrinkled; her Eyes small, yet black and pleasant; her Nose a little hooked; her Lips narrow, and her Teeth black; (a defect the English seem subject to, from their too great use of sugar) she had in her Ears two pearls, with very rich drops; she wore false Hair, and that red (crinem fulvum sed

10 'An unknown lady wearing a scarf'. Panel painting by an unknown artist, 1606. Present whereabouts unknown

Thomas Platter records seeing her at the Palace of Nonsuch in 1599 and although he mistakes her age — she was only sixty-six — the rest of his description is very similar to those of de Maisse and Hentzner:

We were led very soon into the presence chamber where we were placed well to the fore, so as better to behold the queen. This apartment like the others leading into this one was hung with fine tapestries, and the floor was strewn with straw or hay; only where the queen was to come out and up to her seat were carpets laid down worked in Turkish knot.

After we had waited awhile there, somewhere between twelve and one, some men with white staffs entered from an inner chamber, and after them a number of lords of high standing followed by the queen, alone without escort, very straight and erect still, who sat down in the presence chamber upon a seat covered with red damask and cushions embroidered in gold thread, and so low was the chair that the cushions almost lay on the ground, and there was a canopy above, fixed very ornately to the ceiling.

She was most lavishly attired in a gown of pure white satin, gold-embroidered, with a whole bird of paradise for panache, set forward on her head studded with costly jewels, wore a string of huge round pearls about her neck and elegant gloves over which were drawn costly rings. In short she was most gorgeously apparelled, and although she was already seventy-four, was very youthful still in appearance, seeming no more than twenty years of age. She had a dignified and regal bearing.[75]

One interesting discrepancy between these last accounts is the description of the hands. Hentzner writes that when Elizabeth drew off her right glove her hand was sparkling with rings and jewels, while Platter describes 'elegant gloves over which were drawn costly rings'. In Hentzner's description she was on her way to chapel and the glove was presumably fairly loose-fitting to permit it to be drawn off easily when a courtier was allowed to kiss her hand, a mark of favour. Platter saw her in the Presence Chamber at Court and the gloves must have fitted her hands very smoothly, with rings worn on top.

Giovanni Michiel wrote of Elizabeth's beautiful hands 'of which she makes a display' in 1557. She certainly drew attention to them, sometimes with words and sometimes by drawing her gloves on and off. Louis Aubery, Seigneur du Maurier, wrote in his memoirs: '& sur ce sujet, j'ay oüy dire à mon Pere, qu'ayant été dépêché vers elle, dans chaque Audience qu'il eut, elle se déganta plus de cent fois pour luy faire voir ses mains qui étoient tres-belles & tres–blanches'.[76] Even allowing for exaggeration, taking her gloves on and off so many times during an audience seems more like a nervous habit, but it certainly attracted attention to the beautiful white hands.

Sir Robert Sidney writing to Sir John Harington in 1600 gives an account of the Queen's appearance and the entertainments when she visited his house in 1600.

I do see the Queen often, she doth wax weak since the late troubles and Burleigh's death doth often draw tears from her goodly cheeks ... Her Highnes hath done honour to my poor house by visiting me and seemed much pleased at what we did to please her. My son made her a fair speech, to which she did give most gracious reply. The women did dance before her, whilst the cornets did salute from the gallery; and she did vouchsafe to eat two morsels of rich comfit cake, and drank a small cordial from a gold cup. She had a marvellous suit of velvet borne by four of her first women attendants in rich apparel; two ushers did go before, and at going up stairs she called for a staff, and was much wearied in walking about the house, and said she wished to come another day. Six drums and six trumpets waited in the court, and sounded at her approach and departure. My

factitium); upon her Head she had a small Crown, reported to be made of some of the gold of the celebrated Lunebourg table. Her Bosom was uncovered, as all the English ladies have it, till they marry; and she had on a Necklace of exceeding fine jewels; her Hands were slender, her Fingers rather long, and her Stature neither tall nor low; her air was stately, her manner of speaking mild and obliging. That day she was dressed in white Silk, bordered with pearls the size of beans, and over it a Mantle of black silk, shot with silver threads; her Train was very long, and the end of it born by a Marchioness; instead of a Chain she had an oblong Collar of gold and jewels. As she went along in all this state and magnificence, she spoke very graciously, first to one, then to another, whether foreign Ministers, or those who attended for different reasons, in English, French, and Italian; for besides being well skilled in Greek, Latin, and the Languages I have mentioned, she is mistress of Spanish, Scotch, and Dutch: Whoever speaks to her, it is kneeling; now and then she raises some with her Hand. While we were there, William Slawata, a Bohemian Baron, had letters to present to her; and she, after pulling off her glove, gave him her right Hand to kiss, sparkling with rings and jewels, a mark of particular Favour: Wherever she turned her Face, as she was going along, every body fell down on their knees. The Ladies of the Court followed next to her, very handsome and well-shaped, and for the most part dressed in white; she was guarded on each side by the Gentlemen Pensioners, fifty in number, with gilt halberds; in the antechapel next the Hall where we were, Petitions were presented to her, and she received them most graciously, which occasioned the acclamation of GOD SAVE THE QUEEN.[74]

wife did bear herself in wondrous good liking and was attired in a purple kyrtle fringed with gold; and myself in a rich band and collar of needlework, and did wear goodly stuff of the bravest cut and fashion, with an under body of silver and loops. The Queen was much in commendation of our appearances, and smiled at the ladies, who in their dances often came up to the stepp on which the seat was fixed to make their obeysance, and so fell back into their order again'.[77]

Sir John Harington wrote to Sir Hugh Portman in the troubled time of Essex's rebellion and described the Queen as 'quite disfavour'd and unattir'd' and that 'so disordered is all order, that her Highnes hathe worne but one change of raiment for many days . . .'.[78] In spite of her advancing years Elizabeth recovered her spirits sufficiently to be described as walking like an eighteen-year old in 1602. Her interest in clothes revived and she wore spectacular jewels and gown for an audience with the Venetian Secretary in England in February 1603.

Another foreign visitor, Frederic Gerschow, saw the Queen closely on the occasion of the Duke of Stettin's visit to Oatlands on 26 September, 1602. The Queen had given orders that they should walk in the garden close to the palace 'and her Royal Majesty passed us several times, walking as freely as if she had been only eighteen years old, always taking off her mascara [mascaram] and bowing deeply to his princely Grace, who, however, not willing to make himself known, stood almost behind'.[79] 'Mascara' is better translated as 'mask' (Fig. 289). The fashion for wearing masks seems to have started in the early 1570s; Harrison records that 'Women's Maskes, Buskes, Mufs, Fanns, Perewigs, and Bodkins, were first devised and used in Italy by Curtezans, and from thence brought into France and there received of the best sort for gallant ornaments, & from thence they came into England about the time of the Massacar in Paris [St Bartholomew's Day, 24 August 1572]'.[80] Emmanuel Van Meteren, a merchant of Antwerp who settled in London, lived there throughout Elizabeth's reign and was Dutch consul in England from 1583 to 1612, noted in about 1575 that 'ladies of distinction have lately learned to cover their faces with silken masks or vizards and feathers'.[81] Apparently the Queen's masks might be lined with perfumed leather: 'Item to Raffe Abnett . . . for one dozin of sweet skynnes to lyne maskes'.[82]

Elizabeth certainly wore a mask when hunting on a Progress at Basing Park in September 1601,[83] probably to protect her face from the elements, rather than as a disguise. The mask she wore at Oatlands, which Gerschow observed, may have been made from the two and a half yards of satin delivered by Baptist Hickes 'for Maskes and byllements' recorded in the warrants in April 1602.[84] Gerschow continues:

Her Majesty also gave him to understand that she would like to see his princely Grace, according to the English fashion, kiss her hands, which however, his Grace, for various weighty reasons, politely declined to do. At last the Queen, to show her royal rank, ordered some of the noble lords and counsellors to approach, and they, in their stately dress, were obliged to remain on their knees all the time

the Queen addressed them. Meanwhile, the Queen uncovered herself down to the breasts, showing her snow white skin [Inmittelst entblöste sich die koniger. bis an die Brüste und liess ihre schneeweisse Haut sehen]. To judge from portraits showing her Majesty in her thirtieth year there cannot have lived many finer women at the time; even in her old age she did not look ugly, when seen from a distance.

The description of Elizabeth uncovering herself down to the breasts probably means that she removed a light gauzy scarf from around her neck. Elizabeth had many exquisitely decorated scarves. One, made in 1590, was of 'white Syvework Lawne' edged with 'one ounce di of gold & silver Lace to perfourme the same.[85] Another, in 1591, was of white silk cypress, embroidered with scaling ladders, armed men and other devices in the borders at each end.[86] Stubbes described them as extravagant accessories in 1583:

Then must they have their silke scarffes cast about their faces, and fluttering in the wind with great tassells at every ende, eyther of gold, silver or silke. But I know wherefore, they will say, they weare these scarffes, namely, to keep them from Sunne burnyng.[87]

A scarf, apparently made of fine, semi-transparent silk, is tucked into the neckline in the portrait of an unknown lady painted in 1606 (Fig. 10).

One of the last audiences which Elizabeth gave was attended by Giovanni Carlo Scaramelli, Venetian Secretary in England, at Richmond on 16 February, 1603. He wrote to the Doge and Senate that he had been taken to the Presence Chamber and immediately after that into the room where her Majesty was:

The Queen was clad in taffety of silver and white trimmed with gold; her dress was somewhat open in front and showed her throat encircled with pearls and rubies down to her breast. Her skirts were much fuller and began lower down than is the fashion in France. Her hair was of a light colour never made by nature, and she wore great pearls like pears round the forehead; she had a coif arched round her head and an Imperial crown, and displayed a vast quantity of gems and pearls upon her person; even under her stomacher she was covered with golden jewelled girdles and single gems, carbuncles, balas-rubies, diamonds; round her wrists in place of bracelets she wore double rows of pearls of more than medium size. Her Majesty was seated on a chair placed on a small square platform with two steps, and round about on the floor and uncovered were the Archbishop of Canterbury Metropolitan of England, the Lord Chancellor, the Lord Treasurer, the Lord High Admiral, the Secretary of State and all the Privy Council; the remainder of the Chamber was all full of ladies and gentlemen and the musicians who had been playing dance music up to that moment.

At my entry the Queen rose and I advanced with reverences made in due order, and reaching her was in act to kneel down upon the first step and to kiss her robe, but her Majesty would not allow it, and with both hands almost raised me up and extended her right hand, which I kissed with effusion, and at the same moment she said 'Welcome to England, Mr Secretary'.[88]

Scaramelli's description is not that of an old lady; he leaves us with the image of the Ditchley portrait, the magnificent, regal figure of Gloriana.

Notes

1 Horace Walpole, *Anecdotes of Painting in England* (1862), I, p. 150. Quoted in *O'Donoghue*, p. vii.

2 *O'Donoghue*, p. vii.

3 *D'Ewes*, p. 473; quoted in *Johnson*, p. 209.

4 John Rylands Library, MS 239. Transcribed in preparation for publication.

5 *Heath*, pp. 10–13.

6 *Carter*, 'Mary Tudor's Wardrobe', pp. 23–28, and *Robertson, Inventaires*, pp. 60–74.

7 Martha McCrory and Anna Maria Testaverde Matteini, 'Fashion in Florence around 1589: The marriage of Ferdinando I de'Medici and Christina de Lorena', a paper prepared for the CIETA conference in Prato, September 1981.

8 Menna Prestwich, *Cranfield: Politics and Profits under the Stuarts* (Oxford, 1966), p. 12.

9 *CSP Spanish*, 1558–67, I, p. 368. Letter dated 10 July 1564.

10 *CSP Venetian*, 1592–1603, IX, p. 239. Letter dated 2 Nov. 1596.

11 BL, Egerton 2806, f. 166, warrant dated 6 April 1581.

12 For example ibid., f. 208ᵛ, warrant dated 27 Sept. 1585; f. 213ᵛ, warrant dated 27 Sept. 1586; f. 223, warrant dated 26 Sept. 1587.

13 Ibid., f. 204, warrant dated 16 April 1585.

14 Ibid., f. 208ᵛ, warrant dated 27 Sept. 1585.

15 Ibid., f. 227ᵛ, warrant dated 3 April, 1588.

16 Ibid., f. 232, warrant dated 27 Sept. 1588.

17 PRO, LC5/36, f. 100, warrant dated 3 April 1589.

18 PRO, LC5/36, ff. 119, 120, warrant dated 27 Sept. 1589.

19 BL, Egerton 2806, ff. 124, 124ᵛ, warrant dated 12 April 1578.

20 George Puttenham, *The Art of Poesie* (1589), quoted in *O'Donoghue*, p. xviii.

21 *De Maisse*, p. 95.

22 Thomas Dekker, *The Pleasant Comedy of Old Fortunatus as it was plaied before the Queenes Majestie this Christmas...* (1600). The symbolism is discussed in *Yates, Astraea.*

23 See Chapter V.

24 *Melville, Memoirs*, pp. 95–97.

25 Quoted in *Progr. Eliz.*, I, p. xiii.

26 Discussed in Martin Hume, *The Courtships of Queen Elizabeth* (1904, rev. edn.).

27 *Heath*, pp. 10–13.

28 BL, Cotton MS Otho CX, f. 230 (new no. 234). Quoted in *Strickland*, pp. 7, 8. The MS is badly damaged and the parts given in brackets in my transcript are either illegible or missing.

29 *Nichols, Literary Remains*, p. xxxvi.

30 Ibid., p. xxxvii. This letter is undated but seems to refer to the visit of the Lords of Council.

31 BL, Stowe 559, f. 58.

32 Ibid., f. 64.

33 *Madden*, pp. 178, 194, 197. The story of Pyramus and Thisbe is used in William Shakespeare, *A Midsummer Night's Dream.*

34 See Chapter II for further details.

35 *Millar, Tudor Pictures*, cat. no. 46, p. 65.

36 *Giles, Works of Ascham*, I, p. lxiii.

37 *Nugae Antiquae*, II, p. 215.

38 *Progr. Eliz.*, 1788–1805 edn., III, p. 8.

39 Antonio de Guaras, *The Accession of Queen Mary*, ed. Richard Garnett (1892), pp. 119, 139.

40 *CSP Venetian*, 1556–57, VI, pt. 2, p. 1058, report dated 13 May 1557.

41 *Johnson*, p. 13.

42 Thomas Warton, *Life of Sir Thomas Pope* (1780), pp. 86–87.

43 For these events see ibid. pp. 86–91, John Strype *Historical Memorials of Events under the Reign of Queen Mary I* (1721), pp. 108, 444–45 and BL, MS Cotton Vitellius F V. This MS, on which all the accounts in Warton and Strype are based, has been badly damaged and some folios removed. References to the pages in Strype are given on each folio.

44 *Arnold*, 'Coronation Portrait', pp. 729, 732.

45 *CSP Venetian*, 1558–80, VII, p. vii–viii.

46 Ibid., pp. 11–19, letter dated 23 January 1559. Il Schifanoya appears to be the true name of the writer, not an assumed one, ibid., pp. viii–ix.

47 *Progr. Eliz.*, I, p. 32.

48 *CSP Venetian*, 1558–80, VII, p. 92, letter dated 30 May 1559.

49 *Progr. Eliz.*, I, p. 160.

50 *Melville, Memoirs*, pp. 95–96.

51 *Klarwill*, pp. 322–23.

52 Shakespeare, *Merchant of Venice*, III, sc. 2.

53 *Klarwill*, pp. 328–29. For further details about the Accession Day Tilts see Roy Strong 'The Popular Celebrations of the Accession Day of Queen Elizabeth I', *Journal of the Warburg and Courtauld Institutes*, XXI (London, 1958) and Frances A. Yates, 'Elizabethan Chivalry: the Romance of the Accession Day Tilts' ibid., XX (1957). A superb coach was presented by Queen Elizabeth to Czar Boris Godunov in 1603, but not delivered until 1625, 20 years after his death. It was remodelled in 1678 and is now in the Kremlin. I am indebted to Miss Santina Levey for this information. Illustrated in Valeri S. Turchin, *Moscow* (1981), Fig. 142; B. A. Rybakov, *Treasures in the Kremlin* (1962), Figs 77–79. I am grateful to Miss Lorraine Williams for tracing these illustrations.

54 *Klarwill*, pp. 335–36.

55 *Jenkins, Eliz. and Leicester*, p. 222.

56 *De Maisse*, p. xvi. The copy of Paris Bibliothèque Nationale, fonds français 15974 is among the Baschet transcripts of French archives, PRO, 31/3/29.

57 Ibid., pp. 23–24. PRO, 31/3/29, ff. 204–04ᵛ.

58 Ibid., pp. 24–25. PRO, 31/3/29, ff. 204ᵛ–05.

59 Ibid., p. 25. PRO, 31/3/29, f. 205.

60 For futher details about nightgowns and loose gowns see Chapter VI.

61 *De Maisse*, p. 256. PRO, 31/3/29, f. 205.

62 Ibid., pp. 36–37. PRO, 31/3/29, ff. 210–10ᵛ.

63 A. L. Rowse, *The English Spirit* (1945), p. 121.

64 BL, Egerton 2806, f. 22, warrant dated 12 April 1570.

65 Ibid., f. 118ᵛ, warrant dated 27 Sept. 1577.

66 *De Maisse*, pp. 38–39, PRO, 31/3/29, f. 211.

67 Ibid., pp. 55–56. PRO, 31/3/29, f. 218ᵛ.

68 Ibid., p. 59. PRO, 31/3/29, ff. 220–21ᵛ.

69 *CSP Venetian*, 1558–80, VII, p. 12, letter dated 23 Jan. 1559.

70 *De Maisse*, pp. 82–83. PRO, 31/3/29, f. 230ᵛ.

71 For full discussion of mantles see Chapter VI.

72 *Klarwill*, p. 394.

73 BL, Egerton 2806, f. 224ᵛ, warrant dated 26 Sept. 1587.

74 *Rye*, p. 104.

75 *Williams, Platter*, p. 192.

76 Louis Aubery, Seigneur du Maurier, *Memoires pour Servir à l'Histoire de Hollande* (1680), p. 256.

77 *Nugae Antiquae*, II, pp. 255–56.

78 Ibid., pp. 64, 66.

79 Dr Gottfried von Bulow (ed.), 'Diary of the Duke of Stettin's Journey September 10–October 3, 1602' in *Transactions of the Royal Historical Society*, new series, VI (1892), pp. 1–67. The original MS is lost. This is a translation of a transcript dated 1757.

80 *Harrison*, pt. 1, p. 34.

81 *Rye*, p. 73.

82 PRO, LC5/37, f. 72, warrant dated 28 Sept. 1595.

83 *Progr. Eliz.*, III, pp. 566–67.

84 PRO, LC5/37, f. 258, warrant dated 19 April 1602.

85 PRO, LC5/36, f. 147, warrant dated 28 Sept. 1590.

86 See Chapter VIII, note 168, for full details.

87 *Stubbes*, p. 42ᵛ (1585 edn.).

88 *CSP Venetian*, 1592–1603, IX, pp. 531–32, despatch dated 19 Feb. 1603.

II

Portraits of the Queen

Fashions, face patterns and variations in the Queen's portraits

The clothes in many portraits of Queen Elizabeth are painted in great detail. Identifying them with entries in the inventories of 1600, the warrants for the Wardrobe of Robes,[1] the New Year's Gift Rolls[2] and the day book recording items leaving the Wardrobe of Robes between 1561 and 1585[3] would seem to be a simple matter. However, after indexing the warrants and linking these other manuscript sources with them, it gradually became clear that the numerous alterations carried out to Elizabeth's clothes had made them very difficult to trace with any certainty. The gowns depicted in some of the paintings may well have been painted exactly as Elizabeth wore them, but they could easily have been altered out of all recognition by the time they were entered in the Stowe and Folger inventories in 1600. Gowns opening at the back were sometimes altered to open at the front[4] and embroidery was often taken from one gown and mounted on another, perhaps of a different fabric and colour, thus completely changing its appearance.[5] Each costume depicted in the paintings was composed of a large number of detachable pieces: ruff, partlet, sleeves, forepart, petticoat, stomacher, gown, and veil were all separate items, and interchangeable. In addition to this each painter had his own style and the same item of clothing may thus appear in different portraits with subtle variations as, for example, the embroidered forepart in the three 'Armada' portraits of Elizabeth and other related pictures, discussed later in this chapter.

We know that some of the Queen's gowns were passed on to the Yeomen, Grooms and Pages of the Robes as gifts and fees.[6] Part of a purple velvet gown which had belonged to Mary Tudor was lost when some of her clothes were borrowed for a play presented before Elizabeth at Oxford in 1566.[7] When Thomas Platter visited the London playhouses in 1597 he noted that:

The actors are most expensively and elaborately costumed; for it is the English usage for eminent lords or Knights at their decease to bequeath and leave almost the best of their clothes to their serving men, which it is unseemly for the latter to wear, so that they offer them then for sale for a small sum to the actors.[8]

Although there seems to be no surviving evidence, the staff of the Wardrobe of Robes may have sold or hired some of Elizabeth's discarded gowns, given them as fees, to the players and also to some of the unknown artists who painted the Queen's portrait, for use as studio properties. This might account for the fact that the same forepart appears more than once, observed by several painters, in the three 'Armada' portraits and other pictures of the Queen.

Sir Roy Strong has discussed the different types of portraits of Elizabeth in his book *Portraits of Queen Elizabeth I*. He shows that the early ones were not good likenesses and provides documentary evidence that she was painted by, and probably sat personally for, at least these five artists during her reign — Levina Teerlinc in 1551, Nicholas Hilliard sometime about 1572, Federigo Zuccaro in 1575, an unknown French Master in 1581 and Cornelius Ketel. He also suggests another three who were likely to have had sittings — George Gower, John de Critz I, and the elder Marcus Gheeraerts.[9] Isaac Oliver would also have had a sitting around 1590–92 for his unfinished miniature (Fig. 81) and Elizabeth must surely have posed for the painter of the life-like Jesus College portrait in 1590 (Fig. 66). Although there is no evidence that it was ever put into effect, a proclamation drafted by Sir William Cecil in 1563 was designed to keep some control over production of the royal likeness. It prohibited painters, printers, and engravers from drawing the Queen's picture until 'some speciall conning paynter might be permitted access to hir Majesty to take ye natural representation of hir Majestie wherof she hath bene allweise of her owne riall[?] disposition very unwillyng'. After this 'hir Majestie will be content that all other paynters, or gravors . . . shall and maye at ther plesures follow the sayd patron or first portraictur'.[10] The face patterns were copied both officially and unofficially but we do not know exactly how the clothes and jewels in Elizabeth's portraits were arranged for the painters to work from. Some of the most beautiful pictures of the Queen, among them the 'Pelican', (Fig. 25), the 'Phoenix' (Fig. 26), the 'Cobham' or 'Darnley' (Fig. 215), the 'Ermine' (Fig. 217), the 'Welbeck' or 'Wanstead' (Fig. 218), the portrait at Jesus College, Oxford (Fig. 66) and the Ditchley (Fig. 71), show properly mounted gowns, the jewels and perfectly set ruffs arranged with loving care. This would have taken expert hands some time to do. In *Lingua or the Combat of the Tongues* Thomas Tomkis complains that . . . 'a ship is sooner rigged by far than a gentlewoman made ready'.[11]

Freeman O'Donoghue classified the Queen's portraits according to ruff styles.[12] Early in the reign the ruff was set in small figure-of-eight pleats, often with two layers, packed closely together beneath the chin. From the 1570s to about 1586 the ruff grew slowly wider and deeper, the sets radiating out from the neck. From about 1587 to 1589 a wide, shallow ruff was also fashionable, and towards 1590 was sometimes worn open a little at the front. In the 1590s the deeper style of ruff was worn wide open, framing the sides of the square neckline and standing high at the back of the neck. Each of the Queen's face patterns continued in use for several years, but the ruff, together with sleeve width, shape of farthingale and hairstyle, can date a portrait fairly closely, no matter which face pattern was used.

Although the original portraits are obviously preferable for costume study, copies made at a later date can also be useful. Many were made only a few weeks or months after the first picture. In a few cases meticulously painted Victorian water-colours are a record of miniatures which have since faded and paintings which were later heavily cleaned, thus removing much of the detail;[13] occasionally the original picture cannot now be traced and may have been destroyed. Each painting must be evaluated carefully before accepting the visual evidence.

According to the draft proclamation the Queen apparently did not like having her portrait painted, probably because of the time involved. Edward Norgate describes the number of hours and sequence of work for painting a miniature in *Miniatura or the Art of Limning*.[14] The first sitting usually took up to two hours and sometimes longer 'to dead colour the face only, not troubling your selfe . . . with ground, apparrell etc . . .' The second sitting

> ordinarily takes up three or fower howres, or more . . . The third and last sitting is commonly of two howres or three according to the patience of the Sitter or skill of the Lymner . . .

Norgate does not mention using a model or lay figure for the clothes, but he might have used one, on occasion, to get the correct folds in the material:

> for the apparrell, Linnen, Jewells, pearle and such like, you are to lay them before you in the same posture as your designe is, and when you are alone, you may take your owne time to finish them with as much neatnes and perfection as you please, or can.

Although the official face patterns of the Queen were used many times and some of the surviving portraits of Elizabeth are uninspired copies, others are the work of painters who used a face pattern but observed the details of clothing most carefully. In some cases the gowns and ruffs have been unskilfully mounted and the heads do not fit the bodies properly (Fig. 57). The portraits already listed, which show gowns, jewels and ruffs arranged convincingly, were probably completed when a lady-in-waiting was standing in for the Queen. This point is discussed later in this chapter. Other portraits appear to have been painted partly from a face pattern and partly from clothes propped up in the studio, possibly bought or borrowed from the staff of the Wardrobe of Robes. Jewels were probably copied from drawings and other paintings when they were not available in the studio. Variations in hairstyles and ruffs, sometimes of a later date than the

11 *'Queen Elizabeth I'. Engraving by Remigius Hogenberg, c. 1570. Private collection*

particular style of gown used in several pictures, may indicate the painters' efforts to record the latest fashions,[15] but the changes are sometimes the result of cleaning and restoration.

Subtle differences may be detected between a portrait and the engraving apparently made from it. One example, an engraving of Elizabeth made around 1570 by Remigius Hogenberg, shows a gathered partlet with very fine dotted lines running out from the neck, probably representing lines of decorative stitching (Fig. 11). It may have been taken from the portrait in the collection at Syon House,[16] but, if so, the painting has been altered slightly at a later date, possibly during cleaning. The fine dotted lines are not shown in the painting and the partlet has been incorrectly depicted on Elizabeth's left shoulder, where it covers the gown. On the right shoulder it is arranged correctly, beneath the gown. Pearls round the neckline and the ring on a cord at the neck appear in both pictures.

The Hogenberg engraving is from a portrait, but probably not the one at Syon House. A comparison of these two images and a portrait at Anglesey Abbey using the same face image (Fig. 12) gives rise to the theory that the engraving was taken from another picture which may no longer exist. The 'Anglesey' portrait has a slightly deeper ruff, an intricately embroidered partlet, deep embroidered guards and a heavy jewelled chain round the shoulder. The square neckline is bordered with pearls, as in the other two pictures, but it is far more carefully observed. The partlet extends right to the edge

12   'Queen Elizabeth I'. Panel painting by an unknown artist, c. 1570–72. The Queen wears a fine whitework partlet with the embroidered smock showing at the front. National Trust, Anglesey Abbey

13   'Frances Croker'. Panel painting attributed to workshop of George Gower, c. 1585–87. Victoria and Albert Museum, London

of the wide neckline, and it is easy to see how this may have been misinterpreted in the Syon portrait. The edge of a lace-trimmed exquisitely embroidered smock, 'embroidered round the square',[17] shows at the centre front, beneath the partlet.

Paintings showing identical pieces of clothing

The same pieces of clothing appear in several portraits of the Queen. The paintings of *Frances Croker* (Fig. 13) and *Mary Cornwallis* (Fig. 14) offer an example of a duplicate item of dress worn by two different women in about 1585–87. Both of them are wearing sleeves with the same embroidery. Those worn by Frances Croker miss one or two curly sprigs, but otherwise the pattern is identical; she has a wrist ruffle to match her ruff and the embroidered frill of the sleeve shows beneath it. Mary Cornwallis has an almost transparent covering for her sleeve and the embroidered sleeve frill can be seen more clearly. Did the two women use the same draughts-man to draw out the embroidery design? Did one of them admire the other's sleeves and ask if she might copy them? Or did George Gower (or one of of his assistants) use the detailed designs of the embroidery from the portrait of Mary Corn-wallis, the more skilfully painted picture of the two, for that of Frances Croker? No documentary evidence survives to answer these questions. All the other details are completely different

— aglets, jewels, foreparts and fans. A miniature of *Frances Croker*[18] shows different jewels again, but the likeness is sufficiently close to the painting in Figure 13 to prove that both pictures are not of Mary Cornwallis.

Another pair of portraits show identical costumes of about the same date; *Elizabeth Stafford, Lady Drury*, attributed to Segar (Fig. 15) and an *Unknown lady said to be Queen Elizabeth I*, at Trerice House, which has had the face over-painted, probably in the late eighteenth or early nineteenth century (Fig. 16). Was the portrait at Trerice House originally a second version of Lady Drury or was it a portrait of Queen Elizabeth, or of another lady? The ruffs, jewels and other details of the costume have been very carefully observed. If the pictures are of the Queen and Lady Drury, then there is ample evidence that the Queen gave presents of her clothes to ladies-in-waiting and others in the Court circle,[19] and it would have been possible for the recipient of the gown and ruff to order a duplicate portrait of herself wearing them. If the pictures are of two different women then we have a similar problem to that presented by the portraits of Frances Croker and Mary Cornwallis.

Portraits of two sisters in identical costumes may be seen in the Suffolk collection at the Ranger's House, Blackheath; *Diana Cecil, Countess of Oxford* and *Anne Cecil, Countess of Stamford*, both painted in c. 1615 and attributed to Larkin, wear white satin gowns heavily slashed to show the yellow silk

14 *'Mary Cornwallis', formerly at Hengrave Hall. Panel painting attributed to George Gower, c. 1585–87. Manchester City Art Galleries*

15 *'Elizabeth Stafford, Lady Drury'. Panel painting attributed to Sir William Segar, c. 1585. Present whereabouts unknown*

lining. The lace ruffs and cuffs are of a different design, but apart from that, although Anne Cecil is smaller than Diana, every crease, slash and spangle is virtually identical. Apparently the same gown has been used for both portraits.[20] In two other paintings of c. 1620, both attributed to Daniel Mytens, the dress is similar but the ruffs and cuffs are identical, with scalloped borders, alternate scallops caught down, exquisitely embroidered with black silk in a design resembling ermine tails; the portrait of Elizabeth Howard, Countess of Banbury, is also at the Ranger's House[21] and that of her sister Frances, Countess of Somerset, is in the collection at Woburn Abbey.

At the moment there is no conclusive evidence to answer the questions presented by these examples of pairs of paintings showing identical costume detail. However they do offer a note of warning that we should not accept the evidence of all the portraits of Queen Elizabeth at their face value. A few costumes depicted in early seventeenth-century paintings still survive today and can be compared with the artists' representations, among them *Sir Richard (?) Cotton* and his slashed satin suit,[22] *Margaret Laton* and her embroidered jacket[23] and *Jane Lambarde* and her crimson velvet mantle.[24] These three examples give us an insight into the type of detail to expect of a portrait where the painter has been able to make a careful study of the clothes.

16 *'Unknown lady said to be Elizabeth I'. Panel painting attributed to Sir William Segar, c. 1585. National Trust, Trerice House, Cornwall*

17   *(Above left) Fragment of rich crimson woven silk. Victoria and Albert Museum, London (563.1884)*

18   *Detail from Figure 4 of 'crymsen cloth of gold with workes' used for the gown worn by Princess Elizabeth. Panel painting attributed to William Scrots, c. 1547. Royal Collection. Reproduced by Gracious Permission of Her Majesty the Queen*

19   *Detail from Figure 90, a fragment of 'cloth of silver tissued with gold', woven with a design of looped gold thread in two sizes on a yellow silk ground with an additional weft of silver wire. Much of the metal thread has disappeared. A similar material with looped metal pile and satin ground is used for the undersleeves and forepart in Figure 18. Probably Italian, c. 1550. Victoria and Albert Museum, London (641.1883)*

The portrait of Elizabeth when princess

One early portrait of Elizabeth, in the Royal Collection, was painted when she was a girl of thirteen (Fig. 4). It is described in the inventory prepared for Edward VI in 1547 as 'A table with the picture of the ladye Elizabeth her grace with a booke in her hande her gowne like crymsen clothe of golde with workes'.[25] The fabrics are painted in minute detail; the artist has put flecks of yellow to give the effect of gold thread on the sleeves, bodice front and sides of the skirt. The 'workes', in a bold linear design, may have been cut velvet, but it is more likely that the material was of a similar weave to a surviving fragment of silk in the Victoria and Albert Museum (Fig. 17). The undersleeves and matching forepart are in very rich material with a white satin ground and raised looped pile of gold thread (Figs 18 and 19). Faint traces can still be seen of the red silk embroidery on the wrist ruffles and 'pullings out' of the white linen smock showing beneath the undersleeves. A band of white embroidery with fleurs-de-lis linked by a curvilinear design worked around the top of the smock emerges beneath the square neckline of the gown.

The portrait is a companion piece to that of her brother (Fig. 339); Sir Oliver Millar points out that both are by the same hand.[26] Sir Roy Strong suggests that the pictures are by the court painter, William Scrots, who served both Henry VIII and Edward VI.[27] The picture may have been commissioned by Henry VIII in 1546, but alternatively it might be one that Elizabeth sent to her brother at his request, with a letter in which she wrote '. . . the face, I graunt, I might wel blusche to offer, but the mynde I shal never be asshamed to present'.[28] The letter ends 'from Hatfield this 15th day of May': the year was probably 1547. It is unlikely that Edward would have asked for another picture if such a recent portrait had already been in the Royal Collection. The inscription 'Elizabetha/ [?Filia] Rex/Angliae' may originally have read 'Soror'.

Not very much is known about the exact length of periods of mourning in Royal households in the sixteenth century and customs varied in different countries. James V of Scotland and Mary of Guise spent weeks in mourning for their two sons who died in August 1541 and for Margaret Tudor who died later in the same year. However, when Mary visited the French Court in 1550 Diane de Poitiers advised her against wearing full

20 *'Queen Elizabeth I'. Panel painting by an unknown artist, c. 1571–75. By courtesy of Reading Borough Council*

The first portrait, at the Guildhall, Reading (Fig. 20) shows clothes carefully arranged and observed in great detail. The bodice is high-necked and fits closely. The term 'strait' is defined as narrow and tight-fitting in the sixteenth century and this style may resemble the French gown 'with a straite Bodie' made in 1562.[30] The term continues in use and may later be interchangeable with 'high bodies'.[31] There is an entry 'for alteringe and newe lyninge of a strayte bodyed Gowne of white Satten lyned with white bayes the bodyes being enlarged with white Satten' in April 1571,[32] about the time this picture was painted, but no further detail is given in the warrant. Perhaps the style might have been described as Spanish, as it is high necked, although made without hanging sleeves. Walter Fyshe is entered in the September warrant for 1572 'for making of a Spanyshe Gowne of white Satten with whole bodies and hangyng slevis with an enbrauderid garde of golde and silver and gowne lyned with blak sarceonett the bodies with canvas and buckeram and cotton in the ruffes'.[33] Here the 'whole bodies' probably means high-necked, but 'Spanyshe gown' implies that it might also have had hanging round sleeves open at the front, the 'manga redonda' familiar from the Spanish tailors' pattern books.[34] However the tabbed skirts at the waist of the bodice in Figure 20, copying men's fashions, make it seem likely that this is a doublet. Doublets for women appear to have been something of a novelty in 1574 and the term first appears in the warrants in 1575,[35] but this garment may have been an earlier gift.

From the late 1560s onwards the pleats at the waist were interlined and the skirt was worn over padded cotton rolls which gradually increased in size, giving a dome shape. The waistline rose slightly over the padding in the mid-1570s (Figs 203 and 205) still keeping the point at the front. The Reading picture was cleaned in 1977[36] and it was then discovered that there were two layers of paint on the left side of the skirt, the top one almost transparent: they are clearly visible in Figure 20. The second layer had been added a couple of years after the picture was first painted, when the panels had moved slightly. The gap was filled, probably by the original artist, and he updated the skirt to the newly fashionable line, worn over wider hip-pads.

The white satin bodice or doublet fastens down the front, left over right, with gold buttons like roses and worked buttonholes. On either side of the centre front, bordering the row of buttons, are bands of curving vines with bunches of grapes embroidered in gold thread. This design is repeated down both sides of the skirt opening at the front and on the forepart beneath. The forepart is slashed to match the doublet.

Each of the long regular slashes is bound with gold 'binding lace', which would be termed braid today. Decorative gold buttons, set alternately with diamonds and rubies, are placed between them. The armhole is bordered with a wing made of doubled strips of satin embroidered to match the front. Each strip is made up separately. The tabbed skirts are embroidered and assembled in the same way. Beneath the wing is a border cut in scallops which may be compared with one where scallop shapes have been cut away (Fig. 174). A long strip of fine white silk or cobweb lawn is caught down with jewels round the armhole, just above the wing.

The long, full sleeves are made of either very fine lawn or cypress, embroidered with daisies and roses in silver and gold thread. A gold armlet set with jewels catches the right sleeve to the arm, just below the wing, forming loose folds in the fine material. Two rather pronounced folds near the wrist on each

mourning, although her father had died recently; a Queen might only wear mourning for her husband without damaging her dignity. Diane added, however, that Mary might wear black clothes at Court, without any explicit evidence of mourning.[29]

Elizabeth would have worn mourning black for a few weeks after her father's death at the end of January, but Edward VI's coronation was on 20 February 1547 and after that she would, no doubt, have been ready to wear her best gown for a portrait to please her brother. Unfortunately Elizabeth did not describe the clothes in which she sat for the picture in her letter, but until another portrait or perhaps a miniature of her painted at this time is discovered, it may be conjectured that this is the picture she sent to Edward. It is a good example of the type of work carried out by a painter who had all the clothes and jewels in front of him, properly mounted, to complete the work.

Three portraits of the Queen in a white gown embroidered with gold thread

Three portraits painted in the early 1570s show the Queen in what appear to be the same clothes. Comparison between them suggests that the bands of embroidery from neck to waist have been altered, although it is possible that the differences are due to artists' interpretations or restoration work.

20a   *Detail of ruff and collar of smock in Figure 20*

21   *'Queen Elizabeth I'. Panel painting by an unknown artist, c. 1575. National Portrait Gallery, London*

sleeve may be standing 'in ruffes'. A French gown of ash-coloured cypress made in 1575, had 'sleeves made very long to stand in ruffes along the arm'.[37] The word 'ruffes' refers to gathered material. For permanent 'ruffes' or gathers, rows of evenly spaced stitches would be put in, pulled up and stroked to form any size from small folds to what would be termed 'cartridge pleats' today, depending on the length of stitch. A ruff, the name for the familiar figure-of-eight piece of linen neckwear, is abbreviated from 'ruff-band': 'They be full of wringles and crumples' in Minsheu's words. The word 'band' means 'neck-band' according to Minsheu and a 'ruff-band' is simply a gathered neck-band. The figure-of-eight shapes were achieved by starching and careful setting with heated sticks, first of wood and later of steel.[38]

The ruff in the portrait is embroidered with little white flowers (Fig. 20a). Beneath it, also embroidered, is a flat band or collar. It seems as if the ruff may be tacked to a plain linen smock and that the flat band is part of an upper smock of cypress, with the embroidered sleeves showing below the satin of the gown. Beneath this filmy material covering the arm is an area of white. This is probably the sleeve of a plain, fine linen smock. The carcanet, a close collar of jewels round the neck, is set with groups of four pearls placed between quatrefoil shaped rubies which alternate with diamonds: beneath each jewel hangs a pendent pearl. Two gold chains with alternate pairs of pearls and single jewels are looped across the chest and a larger chain of gold enamelled armillary spheres (celestial spheres with the band of the Zodiac around them), daisies with petals of pearls, gold enamelled Tudor roses, and gold lozenges set with diamonds, hangs over the shoulders. The girdle

matches the carcanet of pearls and jewels in the hair, with a long pendent end at the front.

Two other portraits almost reaching the waist, both facing right, have a greenish blue ribbon holding the Badge of the Garter, the Lesser George, round the neck instead of jewelled chains. That in the National Portrait Gallery shows the same bodice or doublet as the Reading portrait, except that the two bands of embroidery are placed side by side, without buttons (Fig. 21). The carcanet of jewels beneath the ruff differs slightly from the Reading version; there are sets of five pearls instead of four. The embroidery may have been remounted on a new bodice or doublet now fastening edge to edge with hooks and eyes. There are many examples of this type of remodelling and re-use of embroidery: 'To William Jones our Taylor . . . for making of a doublet of white satten cut and embroidered . . . the bodies stiffened with canvas and bucke-ram . . . the embroidery taken from another doublet of our store of the charge of Sir Thomas Gorges'.[39]

The sleeves in Figure 21 are different from those in the Reading portrait, being in satin, decorated with jewels and slashed to match the doublet, with horizontal bands of the gold 'curving vine' embroidery. Over these satin sleeves are coverings of almost transparent white silk with horizontal bands of embroidery in gold thread, spaced far apart. White flowers which appear to be embroidered on this covering are apparently showing through from a layer beneath the satin sleeve. The paint has become less opaque with age. The painter presumably started the picture with a pair of embroidered sleeves similar to those in the Reading portrait. These were later overpainted with the satin pair, probably by the original

22 'Queen Elizabeth I'. Panel painting by an unknown artist,
c.1575. Department of the Environment

23 'Queen Elizabeth I'. Panel painting by an unknown artist,
c.1575. Royal Collection. Reproduced by Gracious
Permission of Her Majesty the Queen

painter. Perhaps the Reading portrait in its first state had narrow satin sleeves, which were then covered with the embroidered ones. The satin sleeves in Figure 21 may have been altered from them: 'for alteringe and enlarginge the slevis of a straight bodied Gown of white Satten and new pasting the ruffes and lyninge them with white taphata'.[40] 'New pastinge the ruffes' may mean that the gathers over the sleevehead were stiffened with paste of flour and water or some kind of gum brushed over the wrong side of the satin. Alternatively the term refers to 'pasteboard', a type of cardboard made from layers of unsized paper of varying thickness, worked between the layers of material. This is seen in surviving examples of women's bodices dating from the seventeenth century.

Overpainting has occurred elsewhere. During cleaning in 1980 a serpent symbolizing wisdom was discovered held in the Queen's right hand and twisting round it. This was later covered over with a rose and another layer of paint on the back of the hand, perhaps not long after the picture was painted. X-ray examination showed that this whole portrait was painted on an old panel, over the portrait of a lady dating from the late 1550s.[41]

The third portrait has the same collar of jewels beneath the ruff and wings with scalloped borders as those in the Reading version and the embroidery uses the curving vine motif (Fig. 22). The sleeves are different again, with diagonal slashes in the satin. The same carcanet or biliment appears in all three

portraits: this band of jewels in the hair is of gold set with oval rubies alternating with single pearls and sets of four pearls alternating with square, pointed diamonds. The veil is pinched into pleats in the same way as that in the 'Phoenix' portrait (Fig. 26) but only the Reading portrait also has the tiny silk tufts to mark the depth of each pleat (Fig. 20a). The other two portraits show small pearls in their place and instead of a plain white veil have a black one, decorated with a trellis-work of puffed silk caught with pearls in gold settings at the intersections.

It is fairly certain that the Reading portrait, with a plain veil, was painted first in a properly set pose, probably during the summer months, at some time between 1571 and 1573, with the lightweight sleeves. The National Portrait Gallery version shows careful observation and may have been painted from the same clothes after alterations had been made by the Wardrobe staff perhaps a year or so later. The matching satin sleeves would have been tied in with ribbon points laced through eyelet holes worked in strips stitched into the armholes under the wings.[42] The wings in this portrait have been padded to form rolls over the shoulders. The third picture may have been painted just after this with a different set of sleeves. It is possible that by this time the gown was owned by the Yeoman of the Robes and used by the painters unofficially. Another portrait, in the Royal Collection, may have been copied from the third portrait, the painter varying the embroidery design to one of fleurs-de-lis and other flowers.[43]

24   'Queen Elizabeth I'. Miniature by Nicholas Hilliard, 1572.
National Portrait Gallery, London

25   The 'Pelican' portrait of Queen Elizabeth I. Panel
painting by Nicholas Hilliard, c. 1574–75. Walker Art
Gallery, Liverpool

The chest is shaped rather oddly in this picture, but this may be the artist's attempt to show a three-quarter view (Fig. 23).

As we have already seen, no evidence to show where or how the Queen's clothes were arranged for the painters has materialized so far, and the facts must still be a matter for conjecture. One of the duties of Ralph Hope, the Yeoman of the Robes, may have been to make gowns and jewels available for official portraits.

The 'Pelican' and 'Phoenix' portraits

As Sir Roy Strong has pointed out, the face mask of the 'Pelican' portrait facing right (Fig. 25) was reversed for the 'Phoenix' portrait (Fig. 26).[44] The clothes and jewels, which are beautifully observed in both pictures, would probably have been worn by a lady-in-waiting for Hilliard to finish the work, or a lay figure may have been used.

The 'Pelican' portrait takes its name from the pelican jewel worn by the Queen. From the evidence of bodice length, sleeve rolls and size of ruff the picture was painted around 1574–75. Hilliard's miniature of Elizabeth dated 1572 (Fig. 24) shows sleeve rolls 'drawn out' with fine striped silk: 'for drawinge out the slevis and downe before of a frenche gowne of plain blak vellat with a garde embroidered like Cheines drawne out with Sipers'.[45] These rolls seem to have been stiffened with bents: 'And for eightene yerds of great Bente occupied in the slevis of our Gownes'.[46] In the 'Pelican' portrait these rolls are even larger and more heavily padded showing the evolution of the fashion. The sleeves in the 'Phoenix' portrait painted around 1575–76 (Fig. 26) are formed over similar rolls to give a high

sleevehead: ' Frenche gowne of wrought vellat the grounde satten . . . with rolles of bent in the slevis coverid with fustian and sarceonett'.[47] These two portraits provide a useful example of the natural development of the tailors' work, one style growing out of another.

The 'Pelican' portrait shows a complete understanding of the qualities of different fabrics, their weight and the way in which they hang when folded, gathered and pleated. On her right arm Elizabeth wears a wide jewelled armlet over the delicate covering of the sleeve; caught round the left arm is a narrow red velvet hanging sleeve, no more than a decorative strip. This calls to mind de Maisse's description in 1597 of Elizabeth's gown 'girt about with other little sleeves that hung down to the ground, which she was for ever twisting and untwisting'.[48] The brown leather glove in her hand has a short yellow leather cuff decorated with three rows of little beads and a jewel mounted on a green and white ribbon bow.

Elizabeth had many pairs of sleeves, smocks, and partlets embroidered in blackwork on fine white lawn, sometimes with gold thread as well. This portrait shows matching sleeves and partlet embroidered with black silk in a design with curving tendrils joining the flowers, but the gold threads are not worked in the linen. A complete covering of cypress, which is almost transparent, is laid on top of the embroidered lawn; narrow gold lace is mounted in horizontal stripes on the sleeves and in lines radiating out from the neck. These coverings were originally plain, probably intended to protect the embroidery beneath, but gradually they became more and more ornate themselves. In this example the covering gives an added sparkle of gold. The partlet is open at the front neck, the edges bordered with black needle lace. The edges of the

25a *Detail from Figure 25 of partlet and lace with the edge of the smock showing at the front of the square neckline. The loop of pearls is caught under the pelican jewel*

26 *The 'Phoenix' portrait of Queen Elizabeth I. Panel painting by Nicholas Hilliard, c. 1575–76. National Portrait Gallery, London*

covering are bordered with gold bobbin lace (Fig. 25a). The top of the smock, embroidered in black silk and edged with gold lace, shows above the square neckline of the light crimson velvet gown. Similar gold lace, though wider, may be seen in Figure 322.

The bodice opens at the centre front with hooks and eyes beneath the pelican jewel. Comparison may be made with a similar gown worn by an unknown lady painted in 1569 (Fig. 174) where the top of the gown has been left unfastened, revealing a gold chain hanging above the smock, beneath the embroidered partlet. These bodices are cut in one piece, all the shaping being done at the opening on the centre front line. This style of cutting, first seen in the 1560s, was probably of French origin.[49]

Although the face is a copy of the 'Pelican' pattern in reverse, the detailed observation shows that gown and jewels in the 'Phoenix' portrait were arranged most carefully for the painter around 1575–76. The carcanet at the Queen's neck is similar to that in the 'Pelican' portrait, with gold enamelled links set with diamonds and pearls. Over her shoulders lies a heavy collar of jewels of the type seen in portraits of Henry VIII[50] and apparently worn only by the monarch. Those worn by noblemen were the collars of SS, the Garter and other orders. Another example of one of the monarch's collars of jewels may be seen in the 'Ermine' portrait (Fig. 217). The 'Phoenix' collar has large gold and white enamelled roses set with single diamonds. The other links are of gold enamelled red and black set with pearls, diamonds, and rubies.

The partlet is made of fine linen with blackwork embroidery, covered with network and edged with black needle lace. The smock beneath is bordered with black needle lace of a different design and the blackwork embroidery is of a more delicate pattern. This can be seen just above the edge of the bodice, at the front. The wrist frill of the smock, also embroidered with blackwork, may just be seen beneath the wrist ruff. Behind these ruffs are turn-back cuffs in what appears to be black, semi-transparent silk or cypress, edged with a band of black velvet. The bodice opens at the centre front beneath the phoenix jewel and is cut in the same way as that in the 'Pelican' portrait. The long sleeves widen at the top of the arm, with the fullness rising up at the shoulder in a similar way to those in Zuccaro's drawing of the Queen dated 1575 (Fig. 27), the watercolour sketch of her receiving the Dutch ambassadors (Fig. 6), and an engraving of a Parisian woman by de Bruyn (Fig. 175). Jewels are pinned to hold the puffs of fine silk in position over the sleevehead. The white veil is pinched into small pleats and tiny tassels of silk on the edge stand up above each one, over the top of the head.

In the 'Siena Sieve' portrait (Figs 28, 29, and 341) tufts of black silk may be seen on top of each pleat, with large, round black spangles or beads between them. The white veil is pinned round a wire frame curving over the shoulders; a few spangles or beads are just visible among the folds, between the silk tufts. Only half the number of tufts are allowed on the length over the head, so that they stand on top of the pleats, but not below. The even spacing of these silk tufts enabled the pleats to be

27   'Queen Elizabeth I'. Red and black chalk drawing by Federigo Zuccaro, May 1575. British Museum, London (G91–47, 402131 R3)

28   Detail from Figure 341 of wired veil from the 'Siena Sieve' portrait of Queen Elizabeth I, attributed to Cornelius Ketel, c. 1580. Pinacoteca di Siena

29   Detail of veil pinched into pleats over the head and extremely fine cutwork ruff with white pasteboard supportasse from the 'Siena Sieve' portrait of Queen Elizabeth I, attributed to Cornelius Ketel, c. 1580. Pinacoteca di Siena

made exactly the same size and pinned into position quickly and easily. The veil in the 'Ermine' portrait is pinned on a folded edge, without silk tufts, and the pleats are a little uneven (Fig. 217).

A third portrait, also by Hilliard (Fig. 30) uses the face mask of the 'Phoenix' and 'Pelican' portraits, dating from the mid-1570s, but the size of sleeve and ruff shows that it was painted around 1583–84. The black gown provides an admirable background for the wealth of jewellery. Beneath the ruff Elizabeth wears a carcanet of the type which can be seen more clearly in the 'Pelican' portrait (Fig. 25) where the ruff is much smaller. From this carcanet are suspended a number of pendent pearls and a large gold and enamelled jewel of a pelican in her piety. This is of a different design from that in the 'Pelican' portrait and Elizabeth had several others. Lady Mary Sidney gave her one at the New Year in 1573, which the Queen presented to the young Countess of Huntingdon: 'Item one juell of golde, whearin is a pellycane garnished with smale rubyes and diamondes, hanginge by a small cheyne and one pearle pendaunte'.[51] Another was the gift of Lady Stafford on

30 'Queen Elizabeth I'. Panel painting by Nicholas Hilliard, c. 1583–84. Private collection

31 'Queen Elizabeth I', by an unknown artist, c. 1570–75. Sir Nicholas Bacon, Raveningham Hall, Norfolk

New Year's day, 1580: 'Item a juell of golde being a pelicane of mother-of-pearle garnished with smale sparcks of rubyes and dyamondes'.[52] An even richer jewel is recorded in the inventory of the Queen's jewels made in 1587: 'Item on[e] Pellican of golde with a table diamond in her hed a rock Rubie in her brest and with five small rubies and one little Emerod with a cluster of pearles pendaunt thereat'.[53] Another is listed in the Stowe inventory of 1600: 'Item one Jewell of golde like a Pellican garnished with diamondes of sondrie sorts and bignes under her feete thre Rubies and a triangle diamonde with three small shorte cheines and a knobbe garnished with sparks of diamondes and Rubies'.[54]

Beneath the pelican in Figure 30 there are enamelled daisies and roses on either side of a large pointed diamond, with a fleur-de-lis in smaller diamonds below it, all set in gold, and three large pendent pearls. A matching set of round gold buttons, each made with a single large pointed diamond set in the centre with four smaller stones at the edge and four white enamelled daisies, are used for decoration. They are placed in a row over the roll of hair at the back of the head, alternating with jewels set with large pearls. On the padded sleeve rolls they are arranged between flowers made of fringed silk encircling a single large pearl and there are another three at the centre front bodice, beneath the pelican jewel. The fan handle is decorated with similar jewels, with a few more white enamelled daisies. Two chains hanging round Elizabeth's neck are designed *en suite* with the short girdle at the waist. The links are gold jewels with table-cut stones and treble loops of

graduated pearls. More of these loops are used to decorate the sleeve rolls. These pearls are probably 'lased upon thredds', as described in the inventory of Elizabeth's jewels in 1587.[55] The white silk sleeve is slashed and caught together with bands studded with enamelled flowers and pearls. Over the shoulders the curved wire of the veil is bordered with gold lace, small pearls, and black silk tassels. These pearls were probably of the same type as the five hundred and twenty purchased for the Queen at some time between July 1566 and April 1569, at one penny each, apparently for trimming partlets and ruffs.[56]

Hairstyles, embroidery, ruffs, and jewels in a group of portraits of Elizabeth

There are examples of hairstyles and ruffs of a later date than the gowns in several portraits of Elizabeth. The Yale picture (Fig. 32) shows fairly close-fitting embroidered sleeves, worn beneath light silk coverings, which were fashionable, according to dated portraits,[57] between 1567 and 1570. The wide hairstyle, elaborate pearl-trimmed head-dress and similar ruff appear in the 'Ermine' portrait, painted in 1585 (Fig. 217). The blackwork sleeves, decorated with jewels, and shape of the gown are similar to those in the Stansted Park portrait (Fig. 33). This shows the arched curve of the neckline seen in the 'Pelican' and 'Phoenix' portraits (Figs 25 and 26) but has a slightly wider ruff. It was probably painted around 1576–77. The veil is pinched into pleats over the head as in the

32 *'Queen Elizabeth I', by an unknown artist. The sleeves date from about 1570 and the hairstyle from about 1585. Elizabethan Club of Yale University*

33 *'Queen Elizabeth I', by an unknown artist, c. 1576–77. Ex. coll. Earls of Bessborough, Stansted Park. Present whereabouts unknown*

'Phoenix' portrait, the depth of each one marked with a pearl rather than a silk tuft. Black veils decorated in a similar way, with a similar pose are seen in Figures 21 and 22: these are almost transparent, but the Stansted Park veil appears to be lined with patterned silk. This may be seen more clearly in the Penshurst portrait (Fig. 34), which shows the same pose in reverse, with an alternative pair of embroidered sleeves. The Yale portrait is even closer to another version (Fig. 31) where the embroidered sleeves, partlet, gown, jewel, and fan are identical in design.[58]

The head and network ruff in the Yale portrait appear slightly disjointed and it seems likely that the picture was updated around 1585 by adding ruff and hairstyle of the latest fashion. The veil is decorated with vertical stripes of narrow spangled gold braid. Bands of gold embroidery in a geometric design border the veil, with gold spangles standing away from the outer edges. It falls over the shoulders, attached to the back of the head-dress. The same veil is used in three other portraits (Figs 40, 42, and 44) where it is held out by a wire frame, a fashion also seen in the 'Ermine' portrait. A gold jewel with two enamelled figures of men with tridents holding dolphins and Venus rising from the sea, standing on a sphere, is attached to the bodice below the yellow silk scarf. It is set with three table-cut diamonds and a ruby, with a pendent pearl below. A double rope of pearls is pinned to the scarf to hang in a loop round the jewel. We shall see this jewel again, in a version of the 'Rainbow' portrait, incorporated into the fan handle (Figs 143 and 143a).

A number of paintings of Elizabeth wearing gowns of a similar style, dating from the mid-1570s to the late 1580s, reveal subtle differences of fashion in hairstyles, ruffs, wrist ruffs, embroidered sleeves, accessories, and skirt shapes (Figs 35, 37, 38, 40, 42, 43, 44, and 46). The earliest of the group (Fig. 35) shows a black velvet gown of the high-necked style which also appears in the later portraits. The width of ruff and shape of hair indicate a date of about 1575–76. The veil has a row of decorative silk tufts and what appear to be spangles or beads placed alternately on the edge, which, like those in the 'Phoenix', 'Siena Sieve', and other portraits, enable it to be pleated evenly and pinned into position on top of the head to the back of a jewelled band, or carcanet.[59] The hair is frizzed in a similar way to the 'Darnley' portrait (Fig. 215). Beneath the cutwork ruff is a gold collar, or carcanet, set alternately with square table-cut rubies and cinques of pearls with a diamond at the front and pendent pearls. The front of the gown and shoulder wings are decorated with what may be an early and rare example of straw embroidery (Fig. 36) although it is more likely to be the painter's technique for depicting gold and silver couched thread. The white network coverings have darned embroidery of flowers with four petals and fleurs-de-lis. Blackwork embroidered sleeves may be seen just beneath them.

The second portrait, at Madresfield Court, is attributed by Sir Roy Strong to John Bettes the Younger (Fig. 37). It gives a three-quarter length view of a gown with a similar style of bodice, with bands of decoration on either side of the centre

34 'Queen Elizabeth I', by an unknown artist, c. 1577–78. Viscount De L'Isle, v.c., Penshurst Place, Kent

35 'Queen Elizabeth I'. Panel painting by an unknown artist, c. 1575. Present whereabouts unknown

36 Straw embroidery on crimson velvet. Early seventeenth century. Museo Parmigianino, Reggio Emilia

front opening. These guards are embroidered with fine gold thread couched in a flowing pattern; two kinds of heavier gold thread are used to border this design on either side, with spangles standing away from the edge. The embroidery is enriched with a few jewels with square table-cut stones, probably diamonds, placed at regular intervals down the front. The hair and semi-transparent striped veil are arranged in a similar way to those in Figure 35, but there is apparently a separate strip of linen pinched into pleats over the top of the head, behind the carcanet, edged with pearls. The pleats are not part of the veil, as in the 'Phoenix' and other portraits. The blackwork sleeves and ruff are much larger than those in Figure 35, and comparison with dated portraits shows that this picture was painted in about 1585. In her right hand Elizabeth carries a sieve, a symbol of chastity, and in her left, a pair of gloves with embroidered cuffs. The Queen's ear is apparently pierced for a pendent pearl earring; the 'Siena Sieve' portrait is one of the earliest which seems to show pierced ears (Fig. 29). A New Year's gift in 1597, however, does not make it entirely clear if Elizabeth wore earrings with hooks or if they were tied on: 'Item two Eringes of gold sett with Sparkes of Dyomondes and Rubies and fowre rynges of small pearles to hang them by'.[60] The Ditchley portrait shows an earring made like an armillary sphere, which seems to be tied on with red ribbon (Fig. 79).

37 *'Queen Elizabeth I'. Panel painting attributed to John Bettes the Younger, c. 1585. Madresfield Court collection*

38 *'Queen Elizabeth I'. Panel painting by an unknown artist, c. 1585. Royal Collection. Reproduced by Gracious Permission of Her Majesty the Queen*

The third portrait, in the Royal Collection (Fig. 38) shows the Queen wearing what seems to be the same gown, but its appearance is altered by a number of pearls mounted on the embroidered guards. The centre front fastens edge to edge, probably with hooks and eyes and there are gold jewels set with square table-cut gems on top of this opening. These are solely for decoration. The semi-transparent veil is arranged in a similar way to that in Figure 37, but it is embroidered with wide bands of an intricate design in gold thread. On top of these bands, as part of the pattern, are gold jewels set with square table-cut diamonds and pearls. The wings are decorated with jewels to match the front, instead of the double row of puffs, or 'pullings out'[61] of fine silk in the Madresfield Court portrait. The differences between the embroidery on the linen sleeves in these two pictures may be due partly to artistic licence but similar motifs on both would suggest that the same sleeves had been rearranged. The bunch of grapes and large rose on the Queen's right sleeve, beside the fan, may also be seen in the Madresfield portrait (Fig. 37).

The hair in the Royal Collection portrait is now arranged in tight curls and waves, and this is probably the fashion described by Lupold von Wedel when he saw the Queen in 1585.[62] The hair is waved and curled in a similar way in the Yale, National Maritime Museum, Arbury Hall and 'Ermine', portraits (Figs 32, 43, 44, and 217), although the outline shape changes slowly over five years. The Tatton Park portrait (Fig. 39) shows an extreme version. These elaborately dressed styles are wigs, to conceal the Queen's hair, now turning grey.

Wigs were fashionable accessories: it is well known that Mary, Queen of Scots, wore a red wig on the day of her execution in 1587, as it fell off when the executioner lifted the head.[63] Mary wore a wig much earlier than this, and it must have been very well made, according to a letter written to Cecil on '28 June 1568 at Mydnight' by Sir Francis Knollys, soon after Mary's arrival in Carlisle:

Mystres Marye Ceaton, who is praysed by this Q. to be the fynest busker, that is to say, the fynest dresser of a Woman's heade and heare that is to be seen in any Countrye, whereof we have seen divers experiences since her comyng hether, And among other pretie devyces yesterday & this Day, She did sett sotche a curled Heare upon the Queen that was said to be a Perewycke that shoed very delycately.[64]

Whether Mary wanted to conceal grey hair, or whether wigs were simply a matter of convenience, is uncertain. Ten years later the Countess of Essex made a gift to Elizabeth of 'ruffs of lawnde white worke, edged with sede perle, and a yelo here, and another like black'.[65] These yellow and black 'hairs' were probably wigs, although they may have been 'heads of hair' which were used for making cauls, lace (Fig. 329), and other decorative items. We do not know if Elizabeth ever wore a black wig; all the portraits show her hair as reddish gold and often dark red or deep golden brown in later years. The Queen did not wear wigs to conceal baldness, as some writers have suggested.[66] They were simply a fashionable accessory and covered greying locks. Elizabeth was certainly wearing a variety of wigs in the 1590s. Roger Mountague, her silkman,

39 'Queen Elizabeth I'. Panel painting by an unknown artist, c. 1585. Tatton Park, Cheshire

delivered 'vij heads of haire to make attiers, flowers, and other devices for Attiers, Two periwigs of haire' in 1592[67] and in 1595 he supplied 'iiij lardge fayre heddes of heaire iiij perewigges of heaire'.[68]

A similar way of dressing the hair, but less tightly curled and waved, worn with a slightly wider ruff may be seen in a fourth portrait, at the National Portrait Gallery (Fig. 40). This was probably painted around 1585–86, and Sir Roy Strong attributes it to John Bettes the Younger. The black velvet gown is also decorated with two wide decorative guards at the centre front. 'Fives'[69] or cinques of pearls and gold buttons, set alternately with square table-cut diamonds and rubies, are placed in spaces formed by what appear to be rows of stitches in gold thread, bordered by a line of small pearls on each side of the band. The girdle is made of double strips of five pearls linking jewels matching those on the gown. Three rows of pearls, one large pearl alternating with two small ones, hang round the neck and the bottom row is caught up above the jewel with a heart-shaped ruby[70] surrounded by two rows of small diamonds and pendent pearl below. The heavy black-work embroidery on the sleeves is similar to a surviving example (Fig. 41). The same veil as that in Figures 31, 32, 42, and 44 is pinched into pleats over the top of the head and then wired to stand out over the shoulders. The top of the fan handle is set with a large table-cut ruby and four pearls and there is a square table-cut diamond at the other end of the shaft.

The fifth portrait, at Hever Castle (Fig. 42) is very close to Figure 40, but there are a number of variations in both jewels and embroidery. The gown, ruff, cuffs, wrist ruffs, and veil are

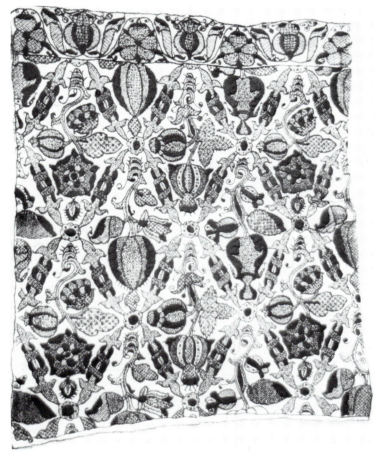

40 'Queen Elizabeth I'. Panel painting attributed to John Bettes the Younger, c. 1585–86. National Portrait Gallery, London

41 Panel of white linen with blackwork embroidery, c. 1585. Present whereabouts unknown

42 *'Queen Elizabeth I'. Panel painting attributed to John Bettes the Younger, c. 1585. Lord Astor, Hever Castle, Kent*

43 *'Queen Elizabeth I'. Panel painting attributed to John Bettes the Younger, c. 1586–87. National Maritime Museum, Greenwich*

apparently the same; minor differences can be put down to artistic licence. The sleeves in both portraits are covered with fine silk or cobweb lawn coverings, caught down with gold jewels set alternately with rubies and diamonds. However, the embroidered motifs of acorns, leaves, honeysuckle, roses, and daisies are in different positions on the sleeve of the linen smock beneath. The sleeve would appear to have been moved round on the arm. Instead of the heart-shaped jewel, the Queen wears a round gold one, set with a large table-cut diamond, two rubies, and four small diamonds. Her waist girdle is composed of gold links set alternately with diamonds and rubies, a large pearl between each one. The fan handle is of the same design as that in Fig. 40, but a large pointed diamond has replaced the table-cut ruby in the centre. There are rubies on each side of it instead of diamonds, with diamonds instead of rubies below, while at the other end of the shaft there is a large rock ruby. This counterchange effect suggests that the fan handle was reversible, and this was an intentional part of the design, not an example of a jeweller resetting the gems.

The sixth picture, at the National Maritime Museum, Greenwich (Fig. 43) was painted around 1586–87. It shows the same black velvet gown as that in Figures 40 and 42, but larger blackwork sleeves are worn with it. Hanging sleeves attached to the black velvet gown may be seen behind them. The decoration made of long strips of fine cobweb lawn or silk, caught down in puffs with gold jewels, may be attached to the

openings of these hanging sleeves, rather than mounted on the embroidered ones. Elizabeth wears a large jewel on her left sleeve, in a similar way to that in Figure 46. The wide lace-trimmed ruff is still closed all round.

The seventh picture, at Arbury Hall (Fig. 44) shows a wide shallow ruff which Santina Levey describes as cutwork with insets of needle lace bordered with a strip of drawn and pulled thread work, with points of detached needle lace round the edge. This is the style seen in the 'Armada' portraits of 1588–89 (Figs 52, 54, and 55) although here they are closed at the front. A ruff of this type worn slightly open at the front appears in the portrait of an unknown girl by John Bettes dated 1587, at St Olave's Grammar School (Fig. 45). From this evidence, the Arbury Hall picture was painted between 1587 and 1589. The embroidered guards at the front of the crimson velvet gown are carried out in gold thread in a stylized, flowing design. Gold jewels set with table-cut rubies and diamonds are mounted on top of the embroidery. The waist girdle is similar to that worn in Figure 40; the Queen holds the pendent end in her left hand showing the jewel set with pearls and a large pointed diamond attached to it. Three ropes of pearls are worn round the shoulders, one hanging low almost to the waist, the other two just showing at the opening of the ruff. Beneath the second rope is a gold chain, the links set with pointed diamonds and pearls. These pearl links are apparently those used for the waist girdle in the Hever Castle portrait (Fig. 42).

44 'Queen Elizabeth I'. Panel painting attributed to John Bettes the Younger, c. 1588–89. The Viscount Daventry, Arbury Hall, Nuneaton, Warwickshire

45 'Portrait of an unknown lady aged twenty'. Panel painting by John Bettes the Younger, 1587. The Governors of St Olave's Grammar School, Orpington, Kent

From this chain hangs a large gold jewel with an antique head at the top and two reclining white enamelled figures, one on each side of a large table-cut diamond.

The cutwork cuffs in the Arbury Hall portrait (Fig. 44) match the ruff; as in the National Maritime Museum portrait (Fig. 43) wrist ruffs are not worn with them. In the mid-1550s ruffles from smock sleeves are seen at the wrists in portraits. These increase in size and by the end of the 1550s were made separately from smocks, so that they could be more easily laundered and set in figure-of-eight shapes. Small wrist frills from smock sleeves may sometimes be seen beneath the ruffs (Fig. 26) but smocks were more usually finished with plain wrist-bands, to which the ruffs were tacked. By the early 1570s longer cuffs were sewn to wrist-bands and these may often be seen in portraits, turned back over the ends of gown sleeves, behind the wrist ruffs. By the end of the 1580s the fashion for wearing turn-back cuffs without wrist-ruffs was established and continued into the seventeenth century. The blackwork embroidered sleeves in the Arbury Hall portrait (Fig. 44) are decorated with gold jewels and covered with fine white silk or cobweb lawn, probably to protect the embroidery and help to keep it clean.

Strawberries and gillyflowers are scattered among the acorns, roses, eglantine, borage, and honeysuckle used for the blackwork embroidery motifs on the linen sleeves and stomacher in the portrait of Elizabeth at Pollok House, Glasgow[71] (Fig. 46). The clothes show similar lines to those in Figure 66,

46 'Queen Elizabeth I'. Panel painting by an unknown artist, c. 1590. Pollok House, Glasgow

47 'Queen Elizabeth I'. Detail from the illumination on the Mildmay Charter, by Nicholas Hilliard, 1584. Emmanuel College, Cambridge

48 'Queen Elizabeth I'. Detail from the illumination on the Ashburne Charter, by Nicholas Hilliard, 1585. Queen Elizabeth's Grammar School, Ashbourne, Derbyshire

and the Pollok House portrait was probably also painted in 1590. The gown is open at the front to show a blackwork embroidered panel to match the sleeves, covered quite closely with cobweb lawn or very fine silk cypress. The covering is slightly looser on the sleeves; earlier these transparent coverings on sleeves were considerably larger than the embroidered areas and hung in loose folds as in Figures 25 and 40. Another very close covering may be seen on the sleeves in the portrait of *A lady called Elizabeth, Queen of Bohemia*, painted in 1612 probably by Marcus Gheeraerts the Younger.[72] Gold jewels, or buttons, are stitched to the embroidered sleeves and front panel for extra decoration in the Pollok House portrait. Sometimes these jewels were lost while the Queen was wearing them and recorded in a day book: 'Lost from her Majesty's back, the 14th of May, Anno 21, one small acorn and one oaken leaf of gold at Westminster'.[73] If many of the jewels were pinned, like the one on her left sleeve, it is no wonder that they were lost. It would be very easy indeed for a pin to work loose. The scalloped outline apparently belonging to the embroidered sleeves is somewhat misleading. The painter observed the gown from the front and the scallops are, in fact, the edges of the black velvet gown sleeves, which can be seen more clearly on her right arm. These gown sleeves are lined with white silk and bordered with pearls. The farthingale is now quite wide and a tuck forming a flounce is arranged round the skirt, pinned to the edge of the frame or hip pads. The waist girdle is made of groups of three strings of pearls with gold jewels, set alternately with square table-cut rubies and diamonds; the end is looped up to the waist to display a gold tablet,[74] or jewel, set with a large table-cut ruby, a smaller diamond and a pendent pearl. The Queen holds a fan made of

four rows of feathers; three rows are white and one is red. In her left hand she carries a pair of brown leather gloves with narrow white cuffs.

The pearls apparently floating in the air above Elizabeth's head in the Pollok House picture are, in fact, attached to a very fine hair net (Fig. 296). This is made of hair, 'a heare cawle', threaded with pearls. The faint outline can be seen just above the hair. It is similar to one recorded in the inventory of the Queen's jewels made in 1587: 'Item one Cawle of heare sett with pearle of sundrie sorte and bignes with sede pearle betwene them chevernewise Ciiij^xx xj [191]'.[75] Another very decorative caul was a new Year's gift presented by Lord Russell in 1579, 'a cawle of here, garneshed with buttons of golde, within enamuled, and set with ragged perle'.[76] The detail in this caul shows that this portrait is another where the painter had the opportunity to work at his own speed from a costume which he could study closely, probably arranged by staff from the Wardrobe of Robes, even though he used the 'Darnley' face mask, familiar from other portraits.

The illuminations from the Mildmay and Ashburne Charters

Some portrait initial illuminations on charters and other official documents have received detailed discussion and analysis in Erna Auerbach's *Tudor Artists*.[77] Those of the Queen on the Mildmay and Ashburne[78] Charters of 1584 and 1585 respectively are of extremely high quality and seem almost certain to have been painted by Nicholas Hilliard. The two little pictures appear to be identical at first sight, but there are a number of variations between the costumes and regalia

49 'Queen Elizabeth I'. Frontispiece to a poem by Georges de la Motthe, a Huguenot refugee, presented to the Queen, 1586. Bodleian Library, Oxford (MS Fr. e.1.)

50 Queen Elizabeth I, or a lady-in-waiting, wearing a gown similar to that in the 'Armada' portraits for the artist to draw. Drawing by Nicholas Hilliard, c. 1588. Victoria and Albert Museum, London (P9–1943)

depicted in them which cannot be dismissed simply as artistic licence. The quality of the work bears evidence of the careful observation described by Norgate.[79]

The ruff and lace cuffs in the Ashburne Charter (Fig. 48) are much wider than those in the Mildmay Charter (Fig. 47) painted a few months earlier. In 1579 Elizabeth had framed sumptuary legislation[80] in an attempt to curb the fashion for increasingly large ruffs; it was entirely unsuccessful. Ruffs slowly grew wider and by the 1590s were open at the front, framing the neckline. The ruff in the 1584 Charter is quite large and that of 1585 reaches almost to the shoulders, showing the development of the fashion. In an illumination dating from 1586 the ruff is even wider, and slightly shallower, foreshadowing the style seen in the 'Armada' portraits of 1588–89. This is the frontispiece to a poem by Georges de la Motthe, a refugee asking for assistance, and it shows the Queen in a similar pose to that in the two Charters (Fig. 49). The detail here is sufficiently fine to see tiny gold daisies probably buttons, set in the three wide bands of the skirt, between the guards.

The gown in the Ashburne Charter has only one guard across the top of the bodice and it is elaborately embroidered, unlike the two on the Mildmay Charter. The skirt is turned back to reveal the lining right up to the waist, while in the Mildmay Charter the guards on either side of the front may be seen. In both pictures the black skirt is lined with orange/gold silk, with a woven pattern in dark tan, and the forepart beneath is of blue silk with a silver metal thread stripe. This is covered with strips of pale blue fine silk, caught down with jewels giving a trellis-work effect. There is a wide embroidered guard at the hem. Different jewels are placed on the centre front of the bodice in the two illuminations. The sceptre in the Ashburne Charter is longer and of a different design from that in the Mildmay Charter, as are the crosses on the orbs. The flatter shape of the crown in the Ashburne Charter may simply be the result of the artist's attempt to make it fit on top of the fashionable hairstyle more attractively.

These differences between the two illuminations suggest that the Wardrobe staff set up the gown twice for the same artist. On the second occasion the bodice had been altered and new ruff and cuffs arranged with it. There are descriptions of one orb and two sceptres in the 1574 inventory of items in the charge of John Astley.[81] There may have been others kept in the Secret Jewel-Houses at the Tower and Whitehall;[82] not all the inventories have survived, so this can only be conjecture.

The 'Armada' portraits and others showing similar clothing

When the Queen gave one of her infrequent sittings for a painter it is unlikely that it would have been for more than the face and the outline of the pose (Fig. 27). A lay figure may have been used or perhaps a lady-in-waiting posed in the Queen's clothes so that the artist could record all the details of embroidery, lace and jewels.

The line of the clothes in the three 'Armada' portraits shows a marked resemblance to those in the illuminations in the Mildmay and Ashburne Charters of 1584 and 1585, (Figs 47 and 48), the miniature by Hilliard in the Mauritshuis (Fig. 51) and a drawing sometimes said to be of Queen Elizabeth,

51 *'Queen Elizabeth I'. Miniature by Nicholas Hilliard, c. 1588. The Mauritshuis, The Hague*

although the face is not at all like her, attributed to Hilliard (Fig. 50). The drawing is remarkably similar to the Mauritshius miniature in the arrangement of bows on the shoulders and the fine lawn sleeves. Bearing in mind the number of alterations made to Elizabeth's clothes, it is quite possible that the black velvet gown in the miniature is the same one seen in the 'Armada' portraits, but with different sleeves.

Although the likeness is not of Elizabeth, the collar of jewels with pendent pearls depicted in the drawing certainly belonged to the Queen. A similar one may be seen in the 'Phoenix' portrait (Fig. 26). Many ladies in Elizabethan paintings have masses of chains, strings of pearls and other jewellery, but none wears these large collars except Elizabeth. The ruff in all three 'Armada' portraits almost conceals the collar of jewels, but the edge is just visible. In 1595 von Buchenbach wrote that the Queen's collar resembled that of the Knights of the Garter.[83] Hentzner also describes her wearing one of these collars in 1598 at Greenwich.[84] It is possible therefore, that, even if not of Elizabeth, the drawing is of a lady-in-waiting wearing Elizabeth's clothes, jewellery and collar of state for the sitting.

There are slight differences between the three versions of the 'Armada' portrait, which are considered separately here. Alternate bows of ribbon in the Woburn Abbey painting are faintly textured with blue (Fig. 52). It looks as if this was not an attempt to show shot silk or shadow, but that the ribbons may have been patterned with a tie-dye technique called ikat, which was certainly known at that date in the Middle East.[85] There may have been a short length which could not be matched to account for alternate bows of ribbon being plain pink. The Tasburgh family group,[86] painted in c. 1605 (Fig. 53) shows

two small boys before they had been breeched. They are wearing doublets and petticoats in cream silk with a brown, red and yellow streaked pattern which also appears to be an ikat fabric. As there was both diplomatic and commercial contact between Elizabethan England and Persia, it is possible that the 'Armada' portrait ribbons and the silk worn by the Tasburgh children came from a Persian source.

Returning to the Woburn 'Armada' portrait, the embroidery design of suns-in-splendour (a heraldic motif) with square pointed diamonds set in their centres and stylized flowers with pearl centres is outlined more intricately on the sleeve than on the skirt. An additional line of gold cord has been put in on the sleeve. The 'Armada' picture at the National Portrait Gallery (Fig. 54) is a very close copy of the Woburn version, but for one detail. The ribbons do not have the ikat pattern on them, but as a great deal had happened to this painting before it was acquired by the Gallery — including being cut down in size[87] — it is impossible to tell if these ribbons were originally like the others. If at one time full-length, the portrait may have shown a gown with bows round the hem like those in the drawing (Fig. 50). The costume in the Tyrwhitt-Drake 'Armada' portrait (Fig. 55) differs from the other versions in five ways. First the ribbon bows are alternately pink and blue without the ikat pattern; secondly, the lace cuffs are of a different design; thirdly, the wrist ruffles seem to be plain white, while the others are delicately embroidered in black silk and edged with black lace; fourthly, the suns-in-splendour on the embroidery have only four sharp points, while those in the other portraits have five; fifthly, the jewels holding down the bows of ribbon are of a different design, having curled gold wires standing out at the ends. Perhaps the first set of lace cuffs was being laundered and another set had to be used for the second portrait. The difference between the wrist ruffles may be due to cleaning of the picture many years ago. Variations between the numbers of points for the suns-in-splendour are seen in several paintings. One can only surmise that some painters found difficulty in drawing the more complicated five-point shape. In this case it does not appear to have been a new piece of embroidery. The jewels in the Tyrwhitt-Drake 'Armada' portrait are similar to those used in the Trinity College portrait of Elizabeth (Fig. 62).

The 'Armada' sleeves and forepart appear in a version, formerly attributed to Lucas de Heere (Fig. 57) of the well-known picture at Sudeley Castle, *The Family of Henry VIII accompanied by Peace, Plenty and Mars* (Fig. 56). De Heere died in 1584 and the 'Armada' portraits date from 1588–89. The costume detail shows that the picture is by another artist: the ruff is arranged with the open neckline at the front, and there is a wired veil behind similar to that seen in the Ditchley portrait, painted in c. 1592–94. The skirt is worn over big hip pads and this, together with the details of neckwear and hairstyle, point to a date of c. 1590–92. The engraving of *The Family of Henry VIII* by Will Rogers (Fig. 58) shows a completely different gown, with a drum-shaped farthingale. Rogers may have worked from another version of the painting dating from c. 1592–95.

The portrait of Elizabeth at Christ Church, Oxford (Fig. 59), has been cleaned and restored, but the same forepart as that used in the Woburn 'Armada' painting (Fig. 52) can still be seen. Some of the suns-in-splendour have five points, others have four. The fans in the two pictures are not of the same design. The gown is in a warm brown velvet, or possibly a dull surfaced satin. The line of the costume is similar to that in the

52 'Armada' portrait of Queen Elizabeth I. Panel painting attributed to George Gower, c. 1588–89. By kind permission of the Marquess of Tavistock and the Trustees of the Bedford Estates, Woburn Abbey

53 Detail of one of the young boys wearing what appears to be ikat-dyed silk, from 'The Tasburgh Family'. Panel painting by an unknown artist, c. 1605. Present whereabouts unknown

54 'Armada' portrait of Queen Elizabeth I. Panel painting by an unknown artist, c. 1588–89. National Portrait Gallery, London

55 'Armada' portrait of Queen Elizabeth I. Panel painting by an unknown artist, c. 1588–89. W. Tyrwhitt-Drake, Bereleigh, Petersfield

56   *Detail of Queen Elizabeth from 'The Family of Henry VIII accompanied by Peace, Plenty and Mars'. Panel painting attributed to Lucas de Heere, c. 1570–75. Sudeley Castle, Winchcombe, Gloucestershire.*

57   *Detail of Queen Elizabeth from 'The Family of Henry VIII accompanied by Peace, Plenty and Mars', by an unknown artist, c. 1590–92. Yale Center for British Art, Paul Mellon Collection*

'Armada' portraits and it too was probably painted in late 1588 or 1589, but this is probably an example of a costume set up in a studio, without a proper sitting, as the skirt and sleeves look as if they had been propped up. The whole portrait has a slightly disjointed effect which is not, I think, the result of copying from another portrait.

The Christ Church ruff is similar to the ruff in the 'Armada' portraits, with circular motifs at the ends of the sets, or pleats. There are 'esses' worked as part of the design of the lace, first facing the right way, then reversed, in alternate sets. Each set between them is decorated with a single row of pearls. 'Esses' are frequently found in the Stowe inventory of 1600, used as embroidery motifs, for example '. . . one peticoate of Murrey satten allover embroidered with Esses of venice silver and golde . . . lyned with yellow taphata'.[88] The use of an 'S' shape as an embroidery and lace motif may be linked with the collars of SS worn, as Ashmole describes, by the Lord Mayor of London, the Lords Chief Justices, Kings-and Heralds-of-Arms and some other servants of the monarch. According to Ashmole the SS stands for 'Saint Simplicius',[89] but 'Seneschallus', 'Sanctus' and other suggestions have also been made.[90] There is another theory that as some of the SS in the collars resemble stylized swans, they might derive from this bird, to which deeds of arms were sworn by knights at a banquet celebrating the knighting of the Prince of Wales and the marriage of King Edward's grandchild, Jeanne de Bar, to John de Warenne in 1306.[91] It is unlikely that the truth will ever be

known but the subsequent employment of SS as the livery of the Lancastrian party during the reigns of Henry IV, Henry V, and Henry VI is illustrated in almost endless variety by effigies and brasses of this period, with both men and women wearing the collars.[92] After the reigns of the Yorkist Kings, when the collar of SS was out of favour, Henry VII restored its use, with the addition of the Tudor badges of a pair of portcullises for fastening and a pendent rose.[93] The SS or 'esses', used for some of the Queen's jewels, as well as lace and embroidery motifs on her gowns, suggest that Purey-Cust's theory that S in the Collars of SS stands for 'Soverayne' may well be correct.[94]

To return to the Christ Church portrait, the gown fronts are edged with what is probably 'binding lace of venice gold', as described in the warrants and inventories, which would be termed 'braid' today. The borders are decorated with cinques of pearls, jewels, and red roses, which are probably silkwoman's work, made of some fabric such as ribbon or cypress. Two items in the warrants for 1588 give an idea of the numbers involved: 'for making of iiij^{xx}xiiij [94] flowers and devices made of pearle of our store and for garneshing them with oringe colour sleeve silk . . . ' and 'for making of devices of towers ribbon in graine like double roses to set iiij^{xx} [80] Jewels in of mother o'pearle . . .'[95] The latter 'devices' may be those on the gown in this portrait; the colour is correct.

The brown velvet sleeves are cut in open shapes and mounted upon white silk with a glint of silver in the weave, possibly 'silver chamblet'. A design of flowers, probably

58   *Detail of Queen Elizabeth from 'The Family of Henry VIII accompanied by Peace, Plenty and Mars'. Engraving by Will Rogers, c. 1592–95. Private collection*

59   *'Queen Elizabeth I'. Panel painting by an unknown artist, c. 1588–89. By courtesy of the Governing Body, Christ Church, Oxford*

60   *'Queen Elizabeth I'. Panel painting by an unknown artist, c. 1590. National Trust, Charlecote Park, Warwickshire*

embroidered ones, although they may be painted, shows through the cut shapes. Some of the cuts are bordered with gold lace; others have been left plain. The reason that they have not frayed is that, first, the material is firmly woven, and secondly, it has probably been sized with gum. In 1562 'William Myddleton our Enbrauderer' was paid 'for Sisynge and Cuttinge of a kirtle of black velvet with a Trayne And the Bodies cut allover with a small Cutt for workemanship therof xxx s'.[96]

This method of treating material for pinking is fully described in books on dressmaking in the mid-nineteenth century, when pinking was a popular way of trimming frills on dresses.[97] An alternative method of treating the edges of velvet, from the evidence of the suit worn by Nils Sture, preserved in Uppsala Cathedral since 1567, was to seal the edges with wax to prevent the tufts of silk falling out.[98]

A portrait of the Queen at Charlecote (Fig. 60) shows the same pose and some pieces of the costume. It is interesting to see the different ways in which the painters have interpreted the details of lace, jewellery, and sleeve embroidery. Unlike the Christ Church portrait, all the 'esses' on the ruff face the right way, and the pattern is more delicately painted. Santina Levey points out that the main part is cutwork and that the small band near the neck is drawn thread work. The gap at the neck of the ruff is filled in with a carcanet of pearls and small jewels. Both ropes of pearls are arranged in twisted rows, but are pulled more widely apart in the Charlecote version; the collar of jewels, partly concealed by the ruff, is larger and heavier than that in the Christ Church picture, and the clasps fastening the centre front bodice are of a different design. The forepart is embroidered with the same motifs and the skirt of the gown is

61 *'Queen Elizabeth I', by an unknown artist, c. 1590 with later additions. Jesus College, Oxford*

62 *'Queen Elizabeth I', by an unknown artist, c. 1590–93. By courtesy of the Master and Fellows of Trinity College, Cambridge*

propped up in a similar way. Although the sleeves appear to be different at a cursory glance, closer examination reveals that this is partly the Charlecote painter's interpretation of the same shapes of embroidery, lace, and cinques of pearls, and partly restoration work. Both painters must have had the costume in front of them; it is difficult to say which portrait is the more accurate representation, particularly as both pictures have been restored. Certainly the painter of the Charlecote portrait observed the details carefully. In her right hand Elizabeth holds a jewel which is attached to the bodice front with a red ribbon. It is probably a miniature gold sieve; the inscription on the side can be seen quite clearly. On the outer side of the ring are the letters 'ATERA IL BEN IL MA' and on the inside 'DIMORA IN SELLA'. The sieve was the symbol of the Vestal Virgin Tuccia and an emblem of chastity much favoured by the Queen. The legend 'A terra il ben mal dimora in sella' [the good falls to the ground while the bad remains in the saddle] is written on the sieve in the 'Plimpton' portrait of the Queen and in the 'Siena Sieve' portrait (Fig. 341); Sir Roy Strong suggests that this makes the sieve also fulfil its customary role as an emblem of the discernment of good from evil.[99] A New Year's gift of 'A ⟨Juell⟩ roundelett of golde Lyke

a Syve, garnished on thone syde with sparckes of Dyamonds having A Rocke Rubye pendant without foyle'[100] was made to Elizabeth in 1590, and might be the one shown in this portrait (Fig. 435), although the ruby has been replaced by a pearl, and the inventory does not mention an inscription.

A full length portrait of Elizabeth at Jesus College, Oxford, shows what appears to be the same gown, but it is in rich peacock green (Fig. 61). The large number of apparently deep folds towards the hem of the forepart makes the material look as if it were cut on the bias grain of the fabric, which it cannot be, from the placing of the embroidered motifs. Another puzzling feature is the shadow cast on the right side of each roundel. The embroidery on the other foreparts of this design is painted as a flat decorative surface. A possible explanation is that the embroidery had been remounted and the painter observed the shadows cast by the raised portions of the design. John Parr, the Queen's embroiderer certainly carried out work of this sort. One example in 1591 was for

alteringe and enlarginge of thenbrauderie of a gowne of whit Satten richelie wrought alover with flowers of gold, Tawney silke and gold Spangles, the whole work Cut out of the old grounde, and

62a *Detail of embroidery in Figure 62 showing the stitches and petals bordered with seed pearls*

62b *Detail of green silk point, or lacing ribbon, at the waist, and printed, or stamped, satin sleeve lining in Figure 62*

63 *Dark green velvet printed, or stamped, with hot irons to make the pattern, c. 1600. Museo de Valencia de Don Juan, Madrid*

afterwardes enbraudered upon a new ground of whit Satten and perfourmed with new enbrauderie in the slevis and skirtes.[101]

However, this shadow treatment is unusual in the sixteenth century and, together with the deep folds, may be the result of restoration at a later date. The sleeves and ropes of pearls are similar in interpretation to those in the Christ Church portrait (Fig. 59) and may have been copied from it, but the collar of jewels beneath the ruff is closer to that in the Charlecote painting (Fig. 60). Sir Roy Strong suggests that the angels are probably a late seventeenth-century addition.[102] The whole pose has a curiously disjointed look. X-ray photographs are needed to trace the stages of work on the picture.

A beautiful full-length portrait dating from the early 1590s at Trinity College, Cambridge, shows what seems to be the same forepart again (Fig. 62). Here the folds fall from the gathers at the waist, as they should, but the shape is much wider and a drum-shaped farthingale is worn beneath it. As Scaramelli, the Venetian Secretary, noted in 1603: 'Her skirts were much fuller and began lower down than is the fashion in France'.[103]

When compared with the earlier versions, there are a number of differences between the foreparts. In the Trinity College portrait there are no pearls in the intersections of the linear design; the roundels are larger and painted in far more detail than the other pictures. Each one is a stylized flower with the petals bordered with seed pearls. The suns-in-splendour have four sharp points, not five, seed pearls are sewn on top of them, and a gold button set with a diamond is placed in the centre of each. This may be a new piece of embroidery, a repeat, with variations, but it may be another painter's way of looking at the same object (Fig. 62a).

At the bottom of the bodice front is tied a pink silk ribbon. This is threaded through a ring at the top of a gold jewel set with a large ruby and pendent pearl, and caught to the side of the skirt. A little green silk point, or lacing ribbon, tied in a bow, holds the two sides of the gown together at the front (Fig. 62b). It may also pass through eyelet holes at the top of the petticoat. Attached in this way, the various parts of the dress would be prevented from swivelling in different directions. Eyelet holes through which points would have been

passed to attach a hip roll, or French farthingale, may be seen in a surviving corset of 1598.[104]

The gown is in brown velvet, or perhaps satin, and the hanging sleeve linings are in ivory printed satin, which would today be described as stamped. Elizabeth had several gowns of printed satin in the 1580s and 1590s. The technique was carried out with hot irons, which stamped the pattern into the material. Some pieces of satin and velvet where the pattern has been made in this way are still preserved in museums today.[105] The design shows more clearly in velvet than satin because the pile is crushed and looks a different colour (Fig. 63). The sleeves in the portrait are of creamy white satin embroidered with an intricate interlocking pattern in two shades of gold thread, studded with seed pearls. A rich collar of gold set with rubies, with large pendent pearls, is worn beneath the open ruff.

The half-length portrait of Elizabeth dating from about 1590 at Toledo Museum, Ohio, shows a similar collar of gold, and what appears to be the same gown, forepart and ruff (Fig. 64). The designs for the embroidery of the sleeves in the two portraits have one basic similarity. The interlocking linear patterns of both are studded with seed pearls. The ground here seems to be 'gold chamblet' and coloured silks have been used for the flowers, with pearls in their centres, among them eglantine (sweet-briar), strawberries, gillyflowers (pinks), and lilies. The stomacher is embroidered to match. A row of pearls borders the edge of the gown and hanging sleeve in both paintings.

One more version of what may be the 'Armada' forepart with a deep tuck arranged round it, as seen in the 1590s, appears in a half-length portrait at Boughton House. There are

64 'Queen Elizabeth I'. Panel painting by an unknown artist, c. 1590–92. Toledo Museum of Art, Ohio

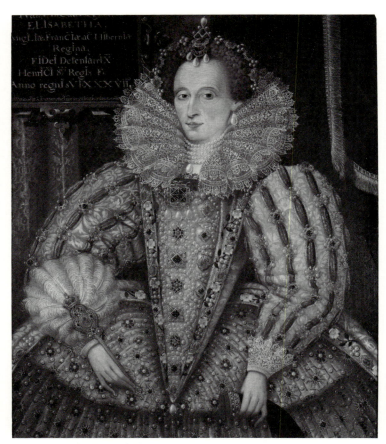

65 'Queen Elizabeth I', by an unknown artist, 1594–95. The Duke of Buccleuch and Queensberry, KT, Boughton House, Kettering, Northants

more pearls and the suns-in-splendour have six sharp points (Fig. 65). The gown has turn-back fronts forming lapels, embroidered with eglantine. They are bordered with binding lace, or braid, and set with jewels and groups of four pearls. This same decoration is continued down both edges of the skirt of the gown. The sleeves are of the same damask as the gown, the long slashes caught at regular intervals with jewels. It looks as though the various parts of the costume had been arranged separately for the painter as, although they are closely observed, the pose is stiff and rather disjointed. There is another version of this picture at the Deanery House, Westminster, where the face has been overpainted in the eighteenth century.[106]

These sixteenth-century pictures with similar pieces of clothing demonstrate the variations which can still be seen today in any life class in an art college. A group of fifteen people may draw or paint the same model in a set pose and at the end of the sitting there will be fifteen completely individual statements. The quality will vary according to the skill and interest of the draughtsman or painter. In the studio each version is recognizable from the model, but when the pictures are viewed beside each other, away from the model, it is sometimes difficult to appreciate that the same pieces of clothing have been portrayed. One hand will exaggerate the surface texture, another will emphasize jewellery or buttons, while a third will concentrate on folds of material. Differences do occur, but not to such a marked degree, between copies of paintings and the originals. With Elizabethan paintings these are sometimes the result of work by restorers, but they may also be attempts to update the fashions in the sixteenth century.

The portrait at Jesus College, Oxford

A comparison between the group of paintings discussed above and a portrait at Jesus College, Oxford, dated 1590 (Fig. 66) shows the difference between pictures where a face mask was used with various pieces of costume, probably arranged by the staff of the Wardrobe of Robes, and one where the painter was surely given a sitting. The unknown artist who painted this natural, life-like representation shows the features familiar from the later Ditchley portrait of c. 1592–94 (Fig. 71). But the Queen is no remote goddess here: she is a very shrewd old lady. The face is thin, as de Maisse described, and the cheeks slightly sunken from missing teeth,[107] more on the left side than the right. The complexion is rosy, and this too is confirmed by Gradenigo's report in 1596 where he describes Elizabeth as 'ruddy in complexion'.[108] The portrait is touching in its understanding of the sitter: it is truthful, kind but not flattering, and full of delightful details. There is a fern in the hair, a pansy on the ruff, a strawberry pinned to the stomacher; Elizabeth wears cherries as an earring and holds a thistle in her left hand. A determined lady, but also one who might have a nervous habit of fidgeting with her sleeves and gloves. It is also the Elizabeth who, after a season with a large number of alterations to her clothes, sent 'to Arthur Middleton for his pains taken in mending and altering our apparel, 40 shillings'.[109]

The painter has indicated a woven check in the white material beneath the black silk embroidery for the material of sleeves and stomacher (Fig. 67). This is probably linen, with either a damask weave or alternating groups of closely set threads and finer threads set further apart in both warp and

66 *'Queen Elizabeth I'. Panel painting by an unknown artist, 1590. Jesus College, Oxford*

67 *Detail of embroidered linen and aglets in Figure 66*

weft. The stomacher, undersleeves, facings of the gown and lining of the gown sleeves are all decorated with matching blackwork embroidery; similar embroidery but with the addition of gold thread may be seen in Figure 68. On the inside of the ruff, by the neck, is a smooth collar with blackwork embroidery, which is probably attached to a smock beneath.[110] It would have protected the ruff and been more easily laundered. The Hilliard miniature of Elizabeth painted around 1595–1600, formerly in the collection of the Earl of Radnor and now at the Victoria and Albert Museum, also shows a second collar in addition to the large ruff (Fig. 69). Here it is a 'chynne ruff', a small ruff encircling the neck beneath the chin, attached to a smock or partlet. The two curls hanging down recall de Maisse's description of 1597 'on either side of her ears hung two great curls of hair, almost down to her shoulders'. The small ruff would have concealed a sagging chin line, while the partlet or smock would have prevented the large ruff from being soiled, as well as concealing wrinkled skin over the chest.

Returning to the Jesus College portrait, aglets are tied all the way down the openings of the gown over-sleeves and at the top of the stomacher for decoration. They are of gold, enamelled red in a spiral design, with dark red ribbons. Aglets were originally the metal tags of laces, or points, intended primarily to make them easier to thread through eyelet holes. Gradually they grew larger until they were purely decorative features. Here the ribbons are very short and the aglets stand on end. A gold ring, enamelled black and set with a pointed diamond, is attached to a string of beads with a tiny red ribbon. Another black enamelled ring is tied in the hair. The custom of wearing rings on chains or tied on in this way is seen clearly in the Hilliard miniature of Elizabeth dated 1572 (Fig. 24) and in the

Hogenberg engraving of *c.* 1570 (Fig. 11). There are several portraits of other people wearing rings after this fashion. Good examples are those of Sir Henry Lee, painted around 1565,[111] wearing rings on cords round his neck, round his left arm and left wrist, over his shirt embroidered with armillary spheres, and *An Unknown Lady in Persian Dress* painted around 1592–95.[112] She wears two rings tied to a cord round her neck. Sir Martin Frobisher, painted in 1577,[113] has a single ring on a cord round his neck, as do Robert Cecil, 1st Earl of Salisbury,[114] painted in 1602, and Katherine Somerset, Lady Petre,[115] painted in 1599.

In the Jesus College portrait, Elizabeth wears a long string of beads which is twisted twice round her neck and then falls to below the waist (Fig. 67). The beads may be made of glass, like those in the collection at Schloss Ambras, near Innsbruck in the Tyrol;[116] the spotted variety have gold mounts. An intricately designed gold jewel enamelled in white, red, and black, set with a large diamond and pendent pearl, is attached to the beads at the neck with a little red ribbon. Another six strings of beads hang from the shoulders. There are five sorts of beads — tiny black ones which may be jet, larger reddish brown and pearly ones, which may be glass, with both round and long spiral beads of gold, enamelled black. The girdle is made of dark brown material, probably velvet, decorated with knots and circles of pearls. Several similar ones are listed in the inventory of the Queen's jewels made in 1587, for example: 'a waste girdle of blacke silke breaded [braided] sett with xvij caters of pearle sett in golde'.[117] The girdle stands out against the gown of black silk damask, or possibly cut velvet on a satin ground.

The folding fan has carved ivory sticks and is attached to the waist girdle with a red ribbon (Fig. 70). The leaf is made of pale

68   *Panel of white linen embroidered with black silk and gold,*
c. 1585–90. Royal Museum of Scotland, Edinburgh (1929.152)

69   *'Queen Elizabeth I'. Miniature by Nicholas Hilliard,*
c. 1595–1600. Victoria and Albert Museum, London (P1–1974)

cream parchment, or possibly silk, decorated with fine gold
braid and a linear design of red flowers, perhaps embroidered
rather than painted. This may be one of 'three Fannes with
braunches of Iverye one perfumed lether enbraudered'
repaired by Roger Mountague in 1588.[118] He may have
repaired it again in 1595: 'For mending of two Fannes of
perfumed lether with foure new branches of Ivorie bone, with
revettes and skales of silver'.[119] Silver rivets and scales may just
be seen where the ribbon passes through the hole at the end of
the fan. Feather fans, seen in many other portraits, continued
in use at the same time as these folding fans. In 1596
Mountague was employed in 'mending of iij fannes parte of
perfumed lether & of lawne stained in colours, one of fethers
stained with like colours & for seaven new braunches of Iverie
bone; & one of the fannes perfourmed with pearles all with
new revets & skales of silver'.[120] The fan 'perfourmed with
pearles' may be that in the Ditchley portrait (Figs 71 and 424).

The clothes in the Ditchley portrait and other pictures

One of the most familiar full length portraits of Elizabeth by
Gheeraerts the Younger was traditionally painted after her

70 *Detail of the folding fan with carved ivory sticks in Figure 66*

71 *'The Ditchley portrait of Queen Elizabeth I', by Marcus Gheeraerts the Younger, c. 1592–94. National Portrait Gallery, London*

71a *Detail of gown in Figure 71*

visit to Sir Henry Lee's house at Ditchley in 1592, but may be a year or two later (Fig. 71). Three other paintings were probably commissioned by Lee from Gheeraerts and that of Captain Thomas Lee is dated 1594.[121] In the Ditchley portrait the Queen wears a gown with hanging sleeves made from white silk with a secondary weft of silver metal threads, patterned with a large design in a raised looped pile of gold thread similar to that in Figures 19, 90, and 91. This can just be seen at the back of the wide French farthingale (Fig. 71a). The edge of this gown is bound with silver binding lace. The forepart (or petticoat), matching stomacher, sleeves, and lining for the hanging sleeves of the gown are in white silk apparently with a secondary weft of fine silver metal threads, probably 'silver chamblet'. This is decorated all over with a trellis-work of strips of puffed cypress caught down at the intersections with jewels mounted on rosettes of the same material.

These jewels, or buttons, are of three designs. Two are lozenge shaped, the gold mounts enamelled and elaborately chased, with fleur-de-lis at the points, set with either an oval ruby, or a square table-cut diamond; the claws may be seen on the rubies. The third is oval, the gold mount enamelled and set with four pearls. The three designs of jewels are arranged in diagonal lines, in alternating vertical and horizontal positions, at the intersections of the fine silk cypress trellis-work. At least forty-five buttons of each design were required for this decoration and over three hundred and seventy pearls to outline the edge of each hanging sleeve. The buttons are similar to those 'of golde ennameled with diverse colours eache with a diamonde xxiiij^tie', and 'of golde ennamelled with diverse colors eache with a Rubie xxiiij^tie' in the Queen's 1587 inventory of jewels.[122] These buttons are included in the Stowe inventory of 1600 with other lots, varying in the size of stone, making up 127 diamond and 50 ruby buttons. The pearl buttons seem to be the group of 147 listed in the same inventory 'called Trueloves each set with fower pearle, viz of the firste sorte lxxviij, of the seconde sorte xj, of the thirde sorte xxx and of the fourthe sorte xxviij';[123] they are probably the same as these entered in the 1550 inventory of Henry VIII's possessions as 'Cxxx trueloves of golde everie of them having iiij pearles taken from garmentes of the kinge that dead' and

later, in the 1587 inventory, as 'buttons with trueloves of pearle, one lacking one pearle Clij [152]'.[124] Twenty-two had been added before 1587 and five apparently 'lost from her Majesties back' by 1600. The girdle is probably that listed in the 1587 inventory as 'a shorte girdle with xiiij Rubies and xiij diamondes sett in gold like buttons with xxvij Scinques of pearle sett betwene them wantinge a pearle. The pearles lased upon a thredd'.[125] The carcanet and band of jewels bordering the neckline are made *en suite* with the girdle. There are over one hundred pearls in each of three ropes caught up on either side of the neckline, beneath the ruff. The earring of an armillary sphere (a celestial sphere with the band of the Zodiac round it) is tied on with a red ribbon. The crown is set with diamonds, rubies and a large red stone which may be the painter's representation of the Black Prince's Ruby. This great balas ruby, irregular in shape, may be seen today, set in the Imperial State Crown.[126] The wired veil is caught to her

72 'Queen Elizabeth I', by an unknown artist, c. 1592–1600.
Formerly at Blair Castle, the Department of the Environment

shoulders and stands in two hoops at the back. It is decorated round the edge with pearls and small hanging jewels. The material is apparently cobweb lawn or cypress.

The Queen holds a folding fan in her left hand. It has very dark brown wooden sticks which originally may have been black. The leaf is of some light brown material, either leather or silk, patterned with silver. On the fan's guardsticks are five pearls, each set on a tuft of red silk. This may be a fan mended by Roger Mountague in 1588 'with braunches of blacke wodde'.[127] He was also entered in a warrant of 1590 for 'mending of an Indyan Fanne with ij faire new braunches of Iverie' and 'new Tuftinge of a Fanne of perfumed Lether, the Tufts Canacion Silke ingrayne, and for new glewinge and revetinge the same'.[128] Mountague apparently mended the latter fan again in 1596 with five others 'of perfumed Lether and sondry other fations with braunches of Iverie bone'. He was employed in 'tufting parte of them with carnation ingrayne silke, for glewinge & revetting them, parte with revettes of gold, and parte of silver, with one ounce quarter di [1⅜ oz] of pearle to perfourme the edginge'.[129]

One half-length version of the Ditchley portrait, formerly at Blair Castle, (Fig. 72) shows the same forepart or petticoat, but without the tuck and the sleeves are slightly wider. The wired veil has a pronounced check of heavier threads in the weave and is bordered with a different arrangement of pearls, while a smaller crown and other jewels are worn in the hair. The ruff is a more elaborate one, with two bands of cutwork. The lace at the top of the stomacher, probably attached to the smock

beneath, has almost disappeared with cleaning and the first knot of three in the rope of pearls is arranged on top of it; the single knot is lower down in the Ditchley portrait. The carcanet, with a jewel hanging from it at the neck, and girdle are the same as those in the Ditchley portrait, but there are two jewels to match those in the hair together with a large jewel incorporating some kind of star-shape arranged across the top of the stomacher. The same sets of buttons hold down the intersections of fine silk cypress trellis-work, but they are in different positions. This trellis-work appears on the hanging sleeve linings, but is not shown in the Ditchley portrait, where the linings are only trimmed with rosettes and buttons. This may be artistic licence, as the bands of cypress do not seem to have been removed with cleaning. Gheeraerts may have felt that this extra decoration would be too fussy in the Ditchley portrait. Alternatively the trellis-work may not have been in position when he was working on the picture. The Queen fingers her pearls and does not carry fan or gloves. She stands beside what is probably the Chair of Estate, although not much of it can be seen.

Another half-length version of the Ditchley portrait of Queen Elizabeth at Blickling Hall (Fig. 73) differs from it in several details, but again gives the impression that the artist may have worked directly from the gown and jewels rather than copying from another painting. Beneath the chin is a small ruff of the type seen in the 'Rainbow' portrait at Hatfield House (Fig. 140) and the Hilliard miniature in Figure 69. The veil has extra pearls on wires standing away from the edge which would probably have trembled when moved. The folding fan is held at a different angle, in the left hand instead of the right. This is the same fan, decorated on both sides with five pearls, each mounted on a fringe of red silk. It is attached to the same jewelled waist girdle, with a red ribbon. The tuck at the edge of the farthingale is at the sides only, while that in the Ditchley portrait is arranged right across the front. The same crown as that in the Ditchley portrait, set with diamonds and rubies, is worn with similar, but not identical, jewels to those pinned to the edge of the wired veil in the Ditchley portrait. These decorate the wig in this picture. The painter has observed the same buttons attached to the sleeves, forepart, stomacher and lining of the gown sleeves as those in the Ditchley portrait, but interpreted them in a different way. The Queen stands beside the Chair of Estate, as in the Blair Castle portrait.

A third version (Fig. 74) in the Pitti Palace, Florence, also differs in detail from the Ditchley portrait. Elizabeth again stands by the Chair of Estate; more can be seen of it here than in the two previous portraits and may be compared with the chair upon which she sits in her Parliament robes, in the Helmingham Hall portrait (Fig. 102). Here, as in the Blickling Hall version, the fan is held in the left hand, attached to the waist girdle with a red ribbon. This is a different fan; there are at least eight pearls on each side, without silk tufts beneath. This may show Roger Mountague's handiwork, or may be the result of cleaning and restoration work on the painting. The ruff is decorated with rows of pearls radiating out from the neck instead of the rose in the Ditchley and Blickling Hall portraits. The same wired veil as that in the Blickling Hall portrait is worn, with additional jewels set with rubies and diamonds hung on the outer edge. The same crown as that in the Ditchley and Blickling Hall portraits appears again, but with a different arrangement of jewels in the wig, including many more pearls. There is no tuck in the forepart or petticoat

73 'Queen Elizabeth I', by an unknown artist, c. 1592–1600. The picture has been cleaned but the little ruff under the chin is still visible in some lights. The National Trust, Blickling Hall, Norfolk

74 'Queen Elizabeth I', by an unknown artist, c. 1592–1600. Detail of fan in Figure 425. Pitti Palace, Florence

as in the Blair Castle portrait, and the buttons are placed in the same arrangement on the fine silk rosettes.

The Queen wears what seems to be the same gown as that shown in all these portraits in a painting where she is carried in procession under a canopy (Fig. 75). The bodice here has short tabbed skirts bordered with pearls, but adding skirts would have been a minor alteration for Elizabeth's tailor. The hanging sleeve is trimmed inside with a trellis-work of silk cypress in the same way as the version in Figure 72.

A drawing of the Queen by Isaac Oliver (Fig. 76), with the reversal of orb and sceptre made for the engraving from it by Crispin van der Passe the Elder (Fig. 77) shows a gown remarkably like that in the Ditchley portrait. Sir Roy Strong notes the similarity of the Will Rogers engraving (Fig. 78) to the Ditchley portrait and has suggested that the drawing is a posthumous one deriving from the former.[130] However, this is unlikely as the clothes are more carefully observed than in Rogers' engraving: the Queen was still alive when this was printed, as there are verses beneath hailing her as a living monarch.

There are a number of small differences between the details of the clothing in the two engravings and the drawing. The wired veil in the Ditchley portrait is bordered with an arrangement of pearls and other jewels and the back of it is concealed by the hanging sleeves. That in Rogers' engraving is bordered with lace and the back length hangs down over the

sitter's left side, trailing on the ground. The Oliver drawing and de Passe engraving show what is probably the same lace, but depicted in a completely different way; it is unlikely that the veil in either drawing or de Passe's engraving was copied from Rogers' engraving. The number of jewels down the centre of the petticoat in Rogers' engraving is the same as that on the Ditchley petticoat — five — but the puffs of fine silk are arranged in a different way, being caught down at the intersections with pearls, not jewels mounted on silk rosettes, and there are no pearls in the lozenge shapes. The Oliver drawing shows seven jewels at the centre front skirt, the trellis-work of puffed silk is set much closer together and caught at the intersections with jewels; single pearls are set in the lozenge shapes, as in the Ditchley portrait.

The Ditchley portrait hemline is bordered with pearls, that in the Rogers' engraving has a deep fringe, while the hem in the Oliver drawing has a narrow binding and reveals the bottom of the farthingale beneath, as does de Passe's engraving. The tuck in the skirt is higher in the Oliver drawing and de Passe engraving than in the Ditchley portrait, and has a much more pronounced edge to it. The three long ropes of pearls hanging to the waist are shown in the same way in both engravings but the shorter ropes in the centre are differently arranged and the jewels at the neck are not the same. Two different materials have been used for the linings of the hanging sleeves of the gown. That in the Ditchley portrait has already been

75   Detail from 'Queen Elizabeth I carried in procession', by an unknown artist, c. 1600. By courtesy of Mr Simon Wingfield Digby, Sherborne Castle, Dorset

76   'Queen Elizabeth I'. Drawing by Isaac Oliver, c. 1592–95. Royal Collection. Reproduced by Gracious Permission of Her Majesty the Queen

77   'Queen Elizabeth I'. Engraving by Crispin van de Passe after Isaac Oliver, probably around 1592–95, with the later inscription 'Isaac Oliver effigiebat. Crispin van de Passe incidebat. procurante Joanne Waldnelio' in its third state, after the Queen's death in 1603. Victoria and Albert Museum, London (E3288–1960)

described. The Oliver drawing and both engravings seem to have used the same fabric, although there are a few minor variations. However, these may be accounted for by the different media in which the artists were working. The Queen's right foot in the Will Rogers engraving is turned to her right, showing a wedge heel; the shoes are heavily decorated. Those in the drawing are plain and without a wedge, although they are in the same position as those in the engraving. In the painting both feet point forwards. Will Rogers' engraving shows the Queen facing the same way as in the Ditchley portrait. The reversed image from which this was worked was probably a drawing which included the Chair of Estate, perhaps by the painter of the Pitti Palace version of the Ditchley portrait (Fig. 74). This drawing would have faced right, probably with the position of orb and sceptre reversed,

78 'Queen Elizabeth I'. Engraving by Will Rogers, c. 1593–95.
Detail of wedge-heeled shoe in Figure 307. British Museum,
London (1901–4–17–35)

79 Detail from 'The Ditchley portrait of Queen Elizabeth', by
Marcus Gheeraerts the Younger, c. 1592–94. National Portrait
Gallery, London

(as in Oliver's drawing) for Will Rogers' engraving, facing left,
to have been made from it.

After analysing all these differences in detail, it may be
conjectured that the clothes were set up, with fresh roses on the
ruff, for Gheeraerts to draw and paint. Elizabeth may have
worn the gown again and then, with the addition of a fresh
ruff, wired veil and jewels, it could have been remounted for
Isaac Oliver's drawing, with reversed orb and sceptre for the
engraver. The trellis-work of puffed silk and the tuck in the
skirt were arranged a little differently for this sitting. When
one considers the time taken in rearranging a simple drapery
on a model in a life class, after a rest, it is easy to understand the
differences between the three versions if the costume had been
moved; there is also the additional evidence of frequent
alterations to Elizabeth's gowns. Oliver's drawing is neither
signed nor dated, but it was probably made not long after the
Ditchley portrait sitting, using the same gown refurbished. De
Passe's engraving need not necessarily be posthumous. He
could have added the inscription referring to the Queen's
demise in 1603 to an engraving which he had already
completed. John Woutneel, the book and print seller who
obtained Oliver's drawing for de Passe to engrave, may have
had the work in hand before Elizabeth died. An alternative
suggestion given by Sir Roy Strong is that on the Queen's death
there must have been a ready market for prints of her and John
Woutneel took the old drawing because of the need for
haste.[131]

'Virtutis Amore'

Until recently Hilliard's miniature of the unknown woman in
Figure 80 has been described as Mary Queen of Scots since it
was listed by Vertue as 'Qn. Scots in White'.[132] At one time it
was thought to show her after the birth of James in 1566 and
later that it was a memorial portrait painted after her
execution in 1587. Sir Roy Strong has noted that it bears little
resemblance to Mary's portraits and dates it around 1615.[133]
Mary Edmond places it a little earlier and makes a convincing
suggestion that the sitter could be Elizabeth Cooke who died in
1609: her first husband was Sir Thomas Hoby and second,
Lord John Russell.[134] As Miss Edmond points out, identifying
portraits is a notoriously subjective affair. After looking for
some time at the miniature I wondered if it might be one last
portrait of Queen Elizabeth painted from life at some time
between 1600 and 1603. She had already seen her ageing
features depicted by Isaac Oliver around 1592 (Fig. 81). This
face pattern was used for some engravings and portraits but
the Queen returned to Hilliard for kinder interpretations of the
unmistakeable marks of advancing years.[135] The miniature
may have been painted at some time after 25 February 1601,
when the Earl of Essex was beheaded. Elizabeth suffered from
insomnia and was troubled with rheumatism at the end of
1602.[136] She may well have stayed in bed to keep warm. It was
very cold and wet when she travelled to Richmond in January
1603; perhaps she was resting after this journey or recovering

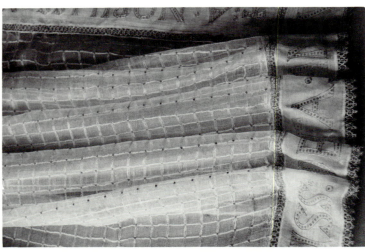

82   *Detail of ivory gauze veil, by tradition worn by Mary, Queen of Scots, at her trial. The added border is made of a more closely woven ivory gauze and bears an inscription embroidered in gold thread, which states that it is more recent than the veil, c. 1587. The Earl of Oxford and Asquith*

80   *'An unknown Lady, possibly Queen Elizabeth I'. Miniature by Nicholas Hilliard, c. 1601–03. Private collection*

81   *'Queen Elizabeth I'. Unfinished miniature by Isaac Oliver, c. 1590–92. Victoria and Albert Museum, London (P8–1940)*

from a cold and decided to give Hilliard a sitting in an informal pose.

The miniature shows the features familiar from the Ditchley portrait (Fig. 79). The veil is of some white, semi-transparent material, perhaps cobweb lawn, gauze or cypress, apparently woven with stripes of threads set closely together alternating with stripes of finer threads set further apart. A surviving example of a veil made from two layers of fine gauze, which is said to have been worn by Mary Queen of Scots at her trial (Fig. 82) shows the open texture of the silk (Fig. 82a). The top layer has a woven check, formed in the warp by three loosely spun, open-spaced silk threads, just under 3 mm (⅛″) wide and in the weft by three more closely packed threads 1.5 mm (1/16″) wide. The two layers of gauze are caught together at the intersections of the check with tiny gilt spangles 1.5 mm (1/16″) in diameter. Each layer of the veil is made of two pieces of gauze 43.8 cm (17¼″) wide and about two metres (2¼ yards) long, joined together. White lace decorates the edge of the veil in Figure 80 and a single pearl is attached to each of the points. It seems unlikely that a veil decorated in this way would have been worn by a widow as Sir Roy Strong suggests:[137] From the evidence of tombs and brasses from the late 1580s to the 1630s[138] it would seem that only plain linen veils were used for mourning. Elizabeth Kytson (Figs 84 and 84a) shows a stiffened veil standing away from the face, a double row of tucks gathered up to form a ruche like a ruff over the back of the head. This feature is seen in Figure 80, trimmed with pearls. A veil with a more pronounced stripe is seen in Oliver's miniature dating from around 1600 of an unknown lady formerly called Frances Howard, Countess of Somerset (Fig. 85). This curves down over the forehead more sharply than that in Figure 80 and a linen coif embroidered with gold and black silk can be seen higher up, under the veil, echoing the line over the forehead.

Beneath the veil at the front in Figure 80 is the edge of the coif, or possibly the triangular forehead cloth, dipping into a point over the forehead. This is bordered with narrow lace and tiny pearls. The use of the forehead cloth is uncertain. Elizabeth was presented with many coifs and forehead cloths

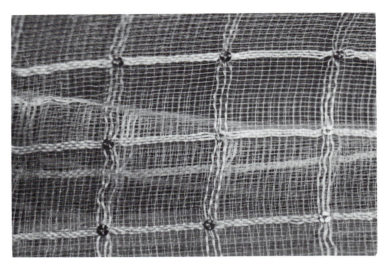

82a *Detail of veil in Figure 82 showing the open texture of the silk and the tiny silver-gilt spangles at the intersections of the check holding the two layers together. The inside measurement of each check is 14 mm (9/16″) by 15 mm (5/8″)*

as New Year's gifts.[139] They were certainly worn during illness as Fynes Moryson wrote in 1617: 'Many weare such crosse-clothes or forehead clothes as our women use when they are sicke'[140] (Fig. 83).

The white silk cape has a fine silver linear pattern on it, which appears to be woven rather than embroidered: the detail is so faint that it is difficult to be certain. Narrow gold bobbin lace radiates out from the neck and borders the edge of the cape above the ermine. It is apparently made from thread of gold strip wrapped round a silk core couched with red silk, as the gold is picked out with tiny touches of vermilion. The cape is open at the front and both sides are turned back showing ermine lining and collar. Beneath it the sitter wears a fine white linen smock with sleeves gathered in at the wrist, softly set wrist ruffs and a ruff of moderate size at the neck, a little larger than the 'chynne ruff' seen in Figure 69. Presumably this is a night smock, as turn-back cuffs are more usual for fashionable wear after the late 1580s. The sleeves are still quite full, as seen in the 1580s (Figs. 40, 42, 43, and 44). Although no sixteenth-century smocks known to have been used for nightwear appear to have survived, a plain style with wide sleeves such as this would have been comfortable to wear in bed.

The veil is carefully arranged behind the sitter, over a large pillow which seems to be finely embroidered, perhaps with drawn thread work, the blue/grey paint indicating shadows. The curtain at the right side of the state bed is bluish/grey and silver. In her hands the sitter holds a small book covered in pale cream leather with a gold design on it and gold edges to the tops of the pages. A prayer book about this size which belonged to Queen Elizabeth, in which she wrote six prayers in English, French, Italian, Latin, and Greek on sixty-five vellum pages, was decorated by Hilliard with portraits of herself and Alençon, probably in 1581. Its whereabouts are no longer known but there is a black and white facsimile in the British Library printed in 1893[141] which records the original as being 'bound in shagreen with gold enamelled clasps; in the centre of each is a ruby'. If the pale cream leather had become shabby or discoloured, the prayer book might well have been rebound by one of its later owners: James II, the Duke of Berwick, Horace

83 *White linen coif and forehead cloth embroidered with fleur-de-lis in black silk. The wide strip of bobbin lace was probably added a few years after the set was made, c. 1600. Lord Middleton Collection, Museum of Costume and Textiles, Nottingham*

84 *Detail from tomb of Elizabeth Kytson, showing her veil from the side, 1608. Hengrave Hall, Suffolk*

84a *Back of veil in Figure 84 showing ruching over top of head*

Walpole, the Duchess of Portland, Queen Charlotte or the Dowager Duchess of Leeds. The last known owner was Mr J. W. Whitehead, in 1902.

Sir Roy Strong feels that stylistically the miniature in Figure 80 must date from around 1610–15. A similar jewelled border may be seen in the portrait of Prince Charles dated 1614.[142] There is, however, no reason why Hilliard should not have painted a copy of his own earlier miniature.

85   *Unknown lady, formerly called Frances Howard, Countess of Somerset. Miniature by Isaac Oliver, c. 1600. Victoria and Albert Museum, London (P12–1971)*

Notes

1 Transcripts of the warrants for the Wardrobe of Robes, covering over forty years, are in preparation for publication.

2 List given in *Collins*, pp. 249–52.

3 Printed in full in *Arnold, 'Lost from HMB'*, pp. 22–83.

4 For example PRO, LC5/34, f. 22, warrant dated 30 Sept. 1567 and BL, Egerton 2806, f. 8ᵛ, warrant dated 16 Oct. 1568. See Chapter VI, notes 57 and 58.

5 For example BL, Egerton 2806, f. 12ᵛ, warrant dated 26 April 1569 and PRO, LC5/37, ff. 190–91, warrant dated 8 April 1600. See also the work of embroiderers in Chapter VIII.

6 *Arnold, 'Lost from HMB'*, p. 69, no. 298 and Folger inventory, ff. 17ᵛ–18ᵛ.

7 Ibid., p. 33, no. 61. This was apparently used for the play *Palamon and Arcite* by Richard Edwards, performed at Oxford in Sept. 1566. See *Strickland*, pp. 224–25.

8 *Williams, Platter*, p. 167.

9 *Strong, Portraits*, pp. 7, 25.

10 *Auerbach, Tudor Artists*, pp. 102–11. See also *Strong, Portraits*, pp. 8–10.

11 See Chapter VI, p. 110.

12 *O'Donoghue*, pp. xiv, xix.

13 Examples may be seen in many country houses and museums in England. Miniatures of John Croker and his wife Frances, at the Victoria and Albert Museum, are now thought to be copies of Hilliard's work.

14 *Norgate, Miniatura*, pp. 26–27.

15 For further details see pp. 19, 26 below.

16 *Strong, Portraits*, p. 58 suggests that the Syon portrait is a copy of the Hogenberg engraving.

17 *Arnold, 'Smocks and Shirts'*, p. 95.

18 This miniature in the Victoria and Albert Museum is now thought to be a later copy of an original by Hilliard.

19 Lady Drury was presented with some most attractive clothes, see *Arnold 'Lost from HMB'*, pp. 13–14. Also see Chapter V.

20 *Suffolk Collection*, cat. no. 10.

21 Ibid., cat. no. 16.

22 Janet Arnold, 'Sir Richard Cotton's suit' in *The Burlington Magazine*, CXV, May 1973, pp. 326–29 and *Arnold, Patterns*, pp. 28–29, 88–89.

23 *Arnold, Patterns*, pp. 51, 121.

24 *Arnold, 'Mantle'*, pp. 55–60.

25 *Millar, Tudor Pictures*, cat. no. 46, p. 65.

26 Ibid., pp. 64–65.

27 *Strong, Icon*, p. 74.

28 BL, Cotton MS Vespasian F III, no. 46. Quoted in *Progr. Eliz*, I, p. *28. See Janet Arnold, 'The 'Pictur' of Elizabeth I when Princess' in *The Burlington Magazine*, CXXIII, May 1981, pp. 303–04.

29 Rosalind K. Marshall, '"Hir Rob Ryall": The Costume of Mary of Guise' in *Costume*, 12, 1978, pp. 5–6. For details of royal mourning in Spain see *Anderson*, pp. 14, 251.

30 PRO, LC5/33, f. 4, warrant dated 20 Oct. 1562.

31 See Chapter VI.

32 BL, Egerton 2806, f. 30, warrant dated 4 April 1571.

33 Ibid., f. 44ᵛ, warrant dated 28 Sept. 1572.

34 See Chapter VI and *Arnold, Patterns*, p. 7.

35 See Chapter VI.

36 I would like to thank Miss Anna Southall for her kindness at the Area Museums Service for South Eastern England, Kenwood, London, while she was working on the picture in 1977.

37 BL, Egerton 2806, f. 80. Linked with Stowe inventory, f. 22ᵛ/68.

38 *Arnold, 'Neckwear'*, pp. 109, 112–15.

39 PRO, LC5/37, f. 190, warrant dated 8 April 1600.

40 BL, Egerton 2806, f. 34, warrant dated 24 Sept. 1571.

41 I would like to thank Mr Robin Gibson, of the National Portrait Gallery, and Miss Christine Bullick, who cleaned the picture, for their kindness in showing me the picture and X-ray photographs, and for interesting and helpful discussions.

42 For tying in sleeves see *Arnold, Patterns*, pp. 43–44, 107, 109.

43 *Millar, Tudor Pictures*, cat. 48, p. 66.

44 *Strong, Portraits*, p. 60.

45 BL, Egerton 2806, f. 71, warrant dated 14 Oct. 1574.

46 Ibid., f. 37ᵛ, warrant dated 24 Sept. 1571.

47 Ibid., f. 78, warrant dated 13 April 1575.

48 See Chapter I, note 58.

49 This style is discussed further in Chapter VI and in *Arnold, Patterns*, p. 9.

50 *Princely Magnificence*, pp. 32, 34, 100.

51 *Progr. Eliz.*, I, p. 324.

52 *Progr. Eliz.*, II, p. 289.

53 BL, Royal App. 68, f. 4.

54 The Stowe inventory, f. 100ᵛ.

55 BL, Royal App. 68, f. 19.

56 *Progr. Eliz.*, I, p. 270. Account of money paid by John Tamworth, deceased, between 8 July 1566 and 23 April 1569. The sum of £8.3s.4d. was paid to 'Mrs Launder for 520 pearles for the Quenes use at 1d apece, with 6 l for her half yeres wages for translating the Quenes pertlets'.

57 For dated portraits with fairly close fitting sleeves see *Mary Hill, Mrs Mackwilliam* (1567), Fig. 240, *Unknown Lady* (1569), Fig. 174. See also *Strong, Icon: Katherine de Vere* (1567), no. 55; *Edward, 3ʳᵈ Lord Windsor and his family* (1568), no. 60.

58 See *Strong, Portraits*, pp. 63–64 for provenance of these portraits.

59 For futher details about carcanets see *Arnold, 'Sweet England's Jewels'*, p. 35.
60 BL, Add. 5751A, f. 243ᵛ.
61 For other examples of 'pullings out' see Figs 24, 25, 26 and 35.
62 Chapter I, note 50.
63 *Progr. Eliz.*, II, pp. 503, 506.
64 BL, Stowe 560, f. 24ᵛ, quoted from BL, Cotton MS Caligula CI.
65 New Year's Gift Roll 1578 in *Progr. Eliz.*, II, p. 68.
66 Elizabeth Jenkins deals with this point in *Elizabeth the Great* (1972 edn.) pp. 7–8.
67 PRO, LC5/36, ff. 212–13, warrant dated 6 June 1592.
68 PRO, LC5/37, f. 90, warrant dated 29 April 1595.
69 For this term used in 1587, see *Progr. Eliz.*, II, pp. 498–99.
70 This may be a foiled crystal. See *Princely Magnificence*, cat. nos. 105, 106.
71 Elizabethan Exhibition, London, 1933, cat. no. 43. 'Mr Antrobus of Hatfield whose wife is descended from the Madingley Cottons, suggests that this portrait may have been given to the Hyndes of Madingley, one of whom was Maid of Honour to Queen Elizabeth'. I am indebted to Mr Brian Blench for this information.
72 Illustrated in *Strong, Icon.*, p. 293.
73 *Arnold, 'Lost from HMB'*, p. 64.
74 For other tablets see *Princely Magnificence*, p. 36.
75 BL, Royal App. 68, f. 36ᵛ.
76 *Progr. Eliz.*, II, p. 253.
77 *Auerbach, Tudor Artists*, pp. 119–32. Descriptions of the colours are given but no difference noted between Coronation and Parliament robes in the monochrome plates.
78 I would like to thank Mrs E. M. Plumbly, Chairman of the Governors of Queen Elizabeth's Grammar School at Ashbourne, for all her help when I took photographs of the Ashburne Charter. (Note: the school retains the original spelling of Ashbourne in its title).
79 *Norgate, Miniatura*, pp. 26–27.
80 *Nichols, Illustrations*, p. 11. Also see Chapter VI, notes 357, 359.
81 *Collins*, pp. 266–68.
82 A. J. Taylor, *The Jewel Tower, Westminster* (1965 edn.), pp. 13, 17.
83 See Chapter III, note 81.
84 See Chapter I, note 74.
85 There are surviving examples of brown, blue and white ikat cottons woven in the Yemen in the ninth and tenth centuries (Nancy P. Britton, *A Study of some early Islamic textiles in the Museum of Fine Arts, Boston* (1938), pp. 72–75). Blue and white linen ikat fabrics with tapestry woven bands are known from Egypt in the twelfth century (Nancy Reath and Eleanor Sachs, *Persian Textiles* (Yale, 1937), p. 71, pl. 10) and an example of striped blue silk ikat woven in Persia in the early seventeeth century is preserved in the Textile Museum, Washington (Alfred Buhler, *Ikat Batik Plangi*, Band I–III (Basle, 1972). I am very grateful to Miss Jennifer Scarce for these references.
86 Roy Strong, *The Elizabethan Image*, Tate Gallery Exhibition catalogue, 1969, no. 123.
87 *Strong, Tudor Portraits*, I, p. 103.
88 The Stowe inventory, f. 58/30.
89 *Ashmole*, p. 224.
90 *Hartshorne*, pp. 376–77.
91 C. K. Jenkins, 'The Collars of SS: A Quest' in *Apollo*, March 1949, XLIX, p. 60.
92 *Hartshorne*, p. 378.
93 Illustrated in *Princely Magnificence*, nos. 18 and P3.
94 A. Purey-Cust, *The Collar of SS* (1910), p. 55.
95 BL, Egerton 2806, f. 230, warrant dated 3 April, 1588.
96 PRO, LC5/33, f. 19, warrant dated 20 Oct. 1562.

97 *Arnold, Patterns 1660–1860*, p. 17.
98 *Arnold, 'Nils Sture's Suit'*, p. 19 and *Arnold, Patterns*, p. 100. For similar use of wax in ordinance of 1546 see *Anderson*, p. 253, note 128.
99 *Strong, Portraits*, p. 66. The portrait owned by Francis T. P. Plimpton is illustrated on p. 67.
100 BL, Add. 5751A, f. 223.
101 PRO, LC5/36, f. 189, warrant dated 27 Sept. 1591.
102 *Strong, Portraits*, p. 72.
103 *CSP Venetian*, IX, p. 531, no. 1135. Letter dated 16 April 1603.
104 *Arnold, Patterns*, pp. 46, 112–13.
105 There are also complete suits in printed, or stamped, satin dating from the 1630s and 1640s in the Victoria and Albert Museum, London.
106 Listed in *Strong, Portraits*, p. 78, no. P80.
107 See Chapter I, note 62.
108 See Chapter I, note 10.
109 See Chapter VIII, note 34. BL, Egerton 2806, f. 80ᵛ, warrant dated 13 April, 1575.
110 *Arnold, 'Smocks and Shirts'*, pp. 89–110.
111 Illustrated in Graham Reynolds, *Elizabethan and Jacobean 1558–1625* (1951), plate 4.
112 Illustrated in *Arnold, 'Smocks and Shirts'*, p. 98, with further details about the clothes on pp. 100–04.
113 Illustrated in *Strong, Icon.*, p. 154.
114 Ibid., p. 260.
115 Ibid., p. 278.
116 Illustrated in *Princely Magnificence*, p. 66, cat. no. 57.
117 BL, Royal App. 68, f. 20.
118 BL, Egerton 2806, f. 234, warrant dated 27 Sept. 1588.
119 PRO, LC5/37, f. 74, warrant dated 28 Sept. 1595.
120 PRO, LC5/37, f. 104, warrant dated 28 Sept.1596.
121 See *Arnold 'Smocks and Shirts'*, p. 104.
122 BL, Royal App. 68, f. 25ᵛ.
123 The Stowe inventory, f. 102/[3].
124 BL, Add. 46,348, f. 149ᵛ (1550 inventory) and BL, Royal App. 68, f. 25 (1587 inventory)
125 BL, Royal App. 68, f. 20.
126 Thomas Butler, *The Crown Jewels and Coronation Ritual* (1976) pp. 7, 12.
127 BL, Egerton 2806, f. 234, warrant dated 27 Sept. 1588.
128 PRO, LC5/36, f. 147, warrant dated 28 Sept. 1596.
129 PRO, LC5/37, f. 91, warrant dated 29 April 1596.
130 *Strong, Portraits*, p. 152. Here Strong suggests that the drawing is also by Crispin van de Passe I and not Isaac Oliver. In *Tudor Court*, p. 125, he suggests that the drawing was 'worked up at a later date over a tracing from the engraving'. This seems unlikely.
131 *Tudor Court*, p. 126.
132 *Vertue, Notebooks*, IV, p. 41.
133 John Murdoch (with Jim Murrell, Patrick J. Noon and Roy Strong), *The English Miniature* (New Haven and London, 1981), p. 59. *Tudor Court*, p. 91.
134 *Edmond, Hilliard*, p. 156.
135 *Tudor Court*, p. 124.
136 *Johnson*, pp. 435–36.
137 *Tudor Court*, p. 91.
138 They are described as 'arched hoods' in *Cunnington, Handbook*, pp. 177–78.
139 For examples see New Year's Gift Rolls 1562 (*Progr. Eliz.*, I, p. 116); 1578 (*Progr. Eliz.*, II, p. 77); 1579 (*Progr. Eliz.*, II, p. 259); 1589 (*Progr. Eliz.*, III, p. 12).
140 Quoted in *Cunnington, Handbook*, p. 177.
141 BL, MS Facsimile 218.
142 *Tudor Court*, p. 91.

III

Robes of Ceremony

Although numerous alterations to Elizabeth's clothes have made it difficult to link items of clothing in the Stowe and Folger inventories to particular portraits with certainty, the ceremonial robes for the Coronation, Parliament, and the Order of the Garter can be recognized immediately. A description of the Mourning robes is given in the Stowe inventory, but it seems that no pictures of the Queen wearing them have survived. Apparently Elizabeth did not wear any special robes for the Maundy, although she is said to have given away her 'best gown' at the ceremony.

The Coronation robes

The coronation robes, comprising an ermine trimmed mantle and kirtle, were also known as the 'Robes of Estate' and are described in this way in a list prepared for Mary Tudor's coronation in 1553.[1] In the Stowe inventory they are entered for Elizabeth as the 'Coronation Robes'.[2] Mantle and kirtle appear in the 'Coronation' portrait of Queen Elizabeth, formerly at Warwick Castle and now in the collection at the National Portrait Gallery (Fig. 86) and in the 'Coronation' miniature by Nicholas Hilliard (Fig. 87). These pictures have already been examined in considerable detail and the robes and regalia related to the lists of materials ordered for the coronation,[3] so that the subject requires no more than a brief notice here.

The panel painting has generally been described as an original of 1559 but some have believed it to be of later date. It has now been established through tree-ring dating by John Fletcher that the boards which made up the panel were used about 1600.[4] The 'Coronation' miniature by Nicholas Hilliard has usually been described as a copy of this unknown artist's painting.[5] We now know from the tree-ring dating that this was not so and it might be suggested that the painting was based on the miniature. However, there are considerable differences between the details of the costume depicted by Hilliard and those in the large portrait. Some are caused by different techniques and media, some by cleaning and restoration to the painting, while others seem to be the result of another sitting, or at least a second arrangement of robes and regalia. Pigments and techniques were closely examined by Jim Murrell for the exhibition *Artists of the Tudor Court* at the

Victoria and Albert Museum in 1983, and Hilliard's miniature is now considered to date from around 1590–1600 on technical grounds.[6] Documentary and visual evidence suggest that the robes in both portraits were probably copied from two earlier pictures painted on separate occasions, one in 1559 and the other around 1571.

The mantle and kirtle of 'Clothe of golde and silver tissue' depicted in both portrait and miniature had been kept from Queen Mary's coronation in 1553.[7] Although the various entries for the robes do not give detailed descriptions of the design of the fabric, on close examination the panel painting of Elizabeth shows that fabrics of the same type, but of different design, were used for the bodice of the kirtle and the mantle; the folds in the skirt break up the pattern too much for detailed comparison to be possible. This observation by the painter is correct. Before her coronation Elizabeth had a new bodice and pair of sleeves made for the kirtle which had previously been worn by Mary. This kirtle may originally have followed the lines of the loose kirtles belted at the waist worn by Henry VIII and Edward VI which appear in several Plea Rolls.[8] Mary Tudor is shown wearing one in a Plea Roll illumination of 1553[9] and although the illuminator may simply have been copying an old design, Mary's kirtle may well have looked very much like this. Elizabeth is shown in a similar kirtle on the obverse of the first Great Seal of 1559 (Fig. 88) but here again the artist may have been repeating an earlier design with the Queen's head. The kirtle worn by Elizabeth in a Plea Roll of 1572 has a fitted bodice.[10] If Mary's kirtle did follow the loose style Elizabeth would certainly have found the shape and heavy folds unflattering. Mary wears a gown made from similar material in Eworth's portrait of 1554 (Fig. 89) and the fitted bodice is rather clumsy simply because it was difficult to cut and stitch through the large areas of pattern formed with looped metal thread.

Four yards of 'Clothe of Tishewe the grounde golde and Tyshewe Sylver',[11] which cost £4 a yard, were delivered for the alterations to the kirtle. This was £2 a yard cheaper than the original material and probably had less metal thread in it. It would therefore have been lighter in weight, and more pliable. Four yards of material, approximately eighteen inches wide, would have been enough to make the new close-fitting bodice with its high neck and long sleeves. Although the Hilliard

86 'The 'Coronation' portrait of Queen Elizabeth I. Copy of an earlier portrait of c. 1559, now missing. Panel painting by an unknown artist, c. 1600. National Portrait Gallery, London

87 The 'Coronation' miniature of Queen Elizabeth I. Miniature by Nicholas Hilliard, copy of an earlier miniature of c. 1571, c. 1600. Private collection

miniature is very small, the same differences between the continuous curving design on the kirtle and isolated motifs of sprays of roses, rosebuds, and fleurs-de-lis on the mantle may be seen. The folds of the mantle are caught up a little higher in the painting, so that the fleurs-de-lis are in a different position from those in the miniature. Hilliard's detailed work shows that the woven design was carried out in silver metal thread with a raised looped pile on a golden yellow silk ground with a secondary weft of fine gold threads, a similar fabric to those shown in Figures 90 and 91. In the panel painting this detail has been obscured by cleaning and restoration.

An eye-witness account of the Queen in the recognition procession through London on the day before the coronation gives further detail about the robes. Il Schifanoya, an Italian, wrote to the Castellan of Mantua that Elizabeth was 'dressed in a royal robe of very rich cloth of gold with a double-raised stiff pile, and on her head over a coif of cloth of gold beneath which was her hair, a plain gold crown without lace, as a princess, but covered with jewels and nothing in her hands but gloves'.[12] On Sunday, 15 January, he saw her again, after the coronation:

The mass and all the ceremonies being concluded and the Queen having twice changed her apparel, they returned into Westminster Hall . . . her Majesty carrying in her hands the sceptre and orb and wearing the ample royal robe of cloth of gold. She returned very

cheerfully with a most smiling countenance for every one, giving them all a thousand greetings, so that in my opinion she exceeded the bounds of gravity and decorum.[13]

The differences between the arrangements of the powderings of black fur on the cape and lining of the mantle shown in portrait and miniature are possibly due to alterations by the skinner carried out in 1570–71. However, it must be remembered that the panel has been heavily restored, obscuring much of the evidence. The ermine cape on the mantle in the painting has a plain border, while that in the miniature shows small white tails hanging round the edge. The powderings of real ermine tails or little pieces of black fur from the legs of black lambs[14] are arranged with the pointed ends uppermost in the painting, the hairs separating below. In the miniature the black hairs are stroked downwards into points, the widest parts of the shapes being at the top.

Adam Bland, the Queen's skinner, was paid 'for mendinge the furre of our Coronation Mantle and kyrtle of Tishue with v tymber of Armions [i.e., ermines] and iij thowsand powderinges' in 1571.[15] A timber was a bale containing forty skins. This work, which could account for the different appearance of the fur, was carried out at some time between October 1570 and April 1571. The old fur, although regularly brushed and aired, might have been attacked by moths. It would probably have started to shed hairs near the joins in the skins, and would almost certainly have started to discolour with age.

88 *Queen Elizabeth I wearing the Robes of Estate used at her coronation. Obverse of the first Great Seal, 1559. British Library, London (Add. Ch.5706)*

89 *'Mary Tudor'. Panel painting by Hans Eworth, 1554. The Society of Antiquaries of London*

90 *Fragment of 'cloth of silver tissued with gold'. Probably Italian, mid-sixteenth century. This is a brocaded satin woven with a looped pile in two sizes of gold thread wrapped round a yellow and white silk core, a 'double-raised stiff pile' shown in detail in Figure 19. The ground is 'cloth of silver', consisting of a yellow silk warp and cream silk weft, satin weave, with an extra weft of silver wire, for which there is a separate twill binding warp. Most of this metal wire has disintegrated, as well as large areas of the looped pile. Victoria and Albert Museum, London (641–1883)*

91 *Fragment of 'cloth of gold yellow tissue', the wrapped metal thread forming a looped pile of two sizes on a twill weave yellow silk ground. Probably Italian, mid-sixteenth century. This is the type of material which covered the Chair of Estate at the coronation of Queen Elizabeth, which is shown in Figure 102. Museo Valencia de Don Juan, Madrid*

92 *Two earrings from the Cheapside Hoard, c. 1600. A large number of pearls are missing. British Museum, London*

93 *'Unknown Lady aged twenty-nine'. Panel painting by Hans Eworth, 1557. Tate Gallery, London*

It seems likely that in 1570, or early in 1571, the young Hilliard painted a miniature of the Queen in the splendid golden robes, newly furred, and that the 'Coronation' miniature is a later copy of it. Hilliard may have painted others, which, like the original, are now missing. The Queen's face is young and her long hair is arranged loosely over her shoulders as she wore it in the recognition procession on Saturday, 14 January, 1559. In 1570–71, when Hilliard probably painted his original miniature, she was thirty-seven, so he must have copied her features from an earlier image, perhaps that of the original 'Coronation' portrait. Although this can only be conjecture, it seems very likely that Elizabeth would have had a portrait painted to commemorate the event in 1559. The robes of 'Clothe of golde and silver tissue', which she had watched her sister wear in 1553, must have seemed like a triumphant and tangible symbol of safety and freedom.

Sir Roy Strong suggests that the Hilliard miniature 'ought to derive from one by Levina Teerlinc, recording the Queen in her coronation regalia, the basis for the official image on her Great Seal and state documents'.[16] It is possible that Hilliard copied the face from Teerlinc's image, but he must have observed the robes and regalia from life for his original miniature, as the looped metal pile and jewels are depicted in such minute detail. Perhaps the work of replacing the fur in 1570–71 created the opportunity for young Hilliard to test his skill. The material of the Robes of Estate would have been a challenge to any miniaturist, with its rich surface texture. In the version of 1600, as Mary Edmond points out, the jewels are so convincing that at first glance the tiny real diamond set in the centre of the cross on the orb cannot be distinguished from the surrounding counterfeits.[17] The pearls have the characteristic

dark spot (originally silver) in the centre seen in the 1572 miniature of the Queen (Fig. 24) and in many others (not only of Elizabeth) which Hilliard painted throughout his life — his own technique for giving pearls a lustrous appearance. Two small openwork gold pendants, probably earrings, from the Cheapside Hoard are set with what appear to be small pearls which show these dark spots[18] but are, in fact, white enamel with black enamel centres. These are arranged alternately with rows of real pearls (Fig. 92). This effect may have been inspired by the use of silver to highlight pearls in miniatures.

Although some areas of the panel painting have been extensively restored, the proportions of the figure are correct and the line of clothes of about 1559 can still be seen. The kirtle sleeves follow the shape of embroidered sleeves which fitted the arm closely. These were worn beneath gowns with short puffed sleeves in the late 1550s and throughout the 1560s (Fig. 93). Sleeves increased in size from about 1570 and were often bombasted or supported with whalebone from the 1580s to the 1600s, so the artist in 1600 copied the original line quite carefully. Wide sleeves turned back to reveal rich silk or ermine linings with detachable undersleeves (Figs 89, 94, and 95) might have been expected. This is the style worn by Mary Tudor which Giacomo Soranzo described in 1554: 'a gown and bodice with wide hanging sleeves in the French fashion, which she wears on state occasions'.[19] Elizabeth wears it on horseback on the reverse of the first Great Seal (Fig. 94). However, the weight of the coronation mantle would have made it impractical to wear the kirtle with anything other than very plain sleeves.

The kirtle bodice from the natural waist level to the point at the front, outlined by the jewelled girdle, is slightly longer in

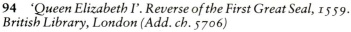

94 'Queen Elizabeth I'. Reverse of the First Great Seal, 1559. British Library, London (Add. ch. 5706)

95 'Mary Fitzalan, Duchess of Norfolk (?)'. Panel painting by Hans Eworth, 1565. Yale Center for British Art, Paul Mellon Fund

the panel painting than in the miniature. It is close in length to several shown in portraits of the late 1550s. This line was repeated in even more exaggerated form from the late 1580s to the early 1600s, when the panel was painted. The Queen is seated more convincingly in the miniature than the panel painting and it might be conjectured that Hilliard shortened the bodice deliberately to give this effect. However, by the early 1570s, slightly shorter waists are seen in portraits. Sir Roy Strong has suggested that the bodice in the miniature relates more closely to fashions after c. 1590,[20] but comparison with a few portraits of the 1570s shows a similar waist-line created partly by the rounded shape of the skirt, sometimes accentuated by little tabbed skirts at the waist (Figs 20 and 205).

The kirtle skirt is fully gathered and springs away from the waist in big loose folds in both pictures. The shape is seen, supported by a cone-shaped Spanish farthingale with small padded rolls, in the portrait of Mary Fitzalan, Duchess of Norfolk (Fig. 95). The pleats lie more smoothly in her plain velvet gown but the metal thread in the 'Clothe of golde and silver tissue' worn by Elizabeth would have been too springy to press into flat pleats. There is some question as to the date of this portrait and the identity of the sitter.[21] The red velvet gown and turned-back sleeves in cloth-of-gold revealing the richly embroidered undersleeves suggest that the ensemble may have been worn to the coronation in 1559. The painting is inscribed on the right A°/AETA.SV./16 and on the bottom right 1565/HE. If the painting is not a copy of an original painted in 1559 showing the Duchess of Norfolk (and at that date it would have been Margaret Audley, not Mary Fitzalan)

96 'Eleanor Benlowes aged twenty'. Panel painting attributed to Steven van der Meulen, 1565. St John's College, Cambridge

it may be a young relative of hers, or one of the other forty-two ladies who attended the coronation ceremony. They were each given sixteen yards of crimson velvet and two-and-a-half yards of cloth-of-gold for 'turning up the sleeves'.[22] The painting shows a gown of rich red velvet. There was one delivery of red velvet among all the lengths of crimson velvet,[23] so this may have been used for the gown, or the colour in the painting may have changed from crimson with cleaning.[24] The wide turned-back sleeve facings are in what might well be 'Clothe of golde greene with woorkes'.[25] Although the sleeves are becoming a little old-fashioned by 1565, the rich gown, possibly a gift from the Queen for the coronation, was still suitable for a visit to Court, a wedding or other festive occasions. It would have been passed on to another wearer if the original owner had put on weight.

The kirtle for the Queen's Parliament robes followed the same lines as the coronation robes and the skirts widened to follow the fashions throughout the reign; the edge of the drum-shaped farthingale with the skirt pinned to it may be seen quite clearly in a drawing by Hilliard of the Queen wearing her Parliament robes, probably made for a design for the Great Seal of Ireland in c. 1590–95 (Fig. 105).[26] However, there is no sign of a drum-shaped farthingale beneath the kirtle of 'Clothe of golde and silver tissue' in the panel painting, which might be expected if the coronation robes had been mounted for the painter around 1600.

Similarly, the double ruff, rising high at the back of the neck (Fig. 96) appears in many dated portraits between 1557 and 1569.[27] Ruffs slowly widened during the 1570s and the 1580s and retained their exaggerated size during the 1590s and early 1600s. If the coronation robes had been arranged for a portrait during these years it is unlikely that a ruff as old-fashioned as this would have been mounted with it. By 1600 a wider one, open at the front, would have been used.

It is not clear how often Elizabeth wore the Robes of Estate after her coronation. They may have been used at some time during the annual Accession Day celebrations and on other similar state occasions, although this can only be conjecture. The Queen may not have worn the kirtle or even the mantle of Estate again after the early 1580s. The fashionably padded sleeves, cumbersome hip rolls, ever increasing in size, and wide skirt in such stiff material would have been very awkward to manage beneath the heavy fur-lined mantle. It must have been quite difficult to move in the velvet Parliament robes, and cloth of gold would have been even heavier. During the later part of the reign, the mantle may simply have been carried in procession. A list of participants drawn up for the procession to Parliament, from the Palace of Whitehall to Westminster, in 1596[28] includes 'The Queene's Majestie's cloake and hatt, borne by a knight, or an Esquire'. Later in the procession the Queen, on horseback or in her chariot (presumably if it rained) would wear 'her roabes of estate, her trayne borne by a Dutches, or Marchioness'. Eyewitness accounts of the Queen at other openings of Parliament show that she wore the Parliament robes in the procession. Perhaps the 'cloake' was the mantle of Estate, and the Queen did wear her Parliament robes, not the 'roabes of estate' on this occasion.

Other differences between portrait and miniature also give weight to the theory that there were two separate sittings for the robes and regalia.[29] The bodice of the kirtle opens at the centre front, revealing a line of ermine in both pictures; that in the miniature shows very clearly in an almost unbroken line, while the fur in the painting is partly concealed by the mantle

97   *Silk mantle lace and tassels from the grave clothes of Cosimo de' Medici, 1574. Pitti Palace, Florence*

lace 'of silk and gold with buttons and tassels to the same' (Fig. 97).[30] This lace, or cord, is not arranged in the same way in both pictures. In the miniature it is arranged over the top of the large jewelled collar, while in the panel painting it lies underneath it.

The small jewelled collar fitting closely round the neck is designed *en suite* with the large collar in the panel painting. In the miniature there is a Tudor rose with red and white enamelled petals set in gold at the centre front of the small collar, while the centre piece of the large collar is a big sapphire, surrounded with smaller sapphires. The large collar in the miniature is of a different design from that in the panel painting; there are no hanging pearls and there are sets of only four pearls surrounding the jewels instead of six.

The evidence of the costume in both pictures related to the contemporary documents together with the tree-ring dating points to the panel painting being a copy of a portrait painted in 1559 or shortly afterwards, now missing. This theory might have been proved conclusively if restorers at various times had documented the condition of the painting before they started work. Unfortunately, as is so often the case, detailed records were not kept of cleaning and restoration in the past.

98 *Detail from the tomb of Richard Alington, showing his daughters with their sleeves untied, 1561. Rolls Chapel, London*
98a *Detail of sleeve from Figure 98*

The Mourning robes

A kirtle, surcoat, and mantle of purple velvet furred with powdered ermine are listed as 'the mourning Robes' in the Stowe inventory.[31] These were presumably State mourning robes which the Queen would have worn for obsequies for foreign royalty, but also seem to have been worn at the coronation. The description of what appears to be the same kirtle, surcoat, and mantle is given in a list entitled 'Materials for the apparel of her Majesty and the persons engaged about her Coronation'.[32]

Elizabeth's coronation does not seem to have differed materially from that of her sister Mary, but in neither case is it quite clear when these purple robes were worn as there are some discrepancies between various accounts of the ceremonies. Both Elizabeth and Mary went to the Abbey Church at Westminster in their Parliament robes of crimson velvet[33] and previous to the anointing, retired to the traverse to the left of the high altar and changed into kirtle, mantle, and surcoat of crimson velvet.[34] For the anointing Mary wore the Colobium Sindonis of white taffeta with a purple mantle.[35] Elizabeth had 'White Sarcennett for a tabarde to be putt on the Queens gowne when she is anoynted',[36] but it is not clear whether she wore a crimson or purple gown beneath the white Colobium Sindonis. The French Ambassador, Antoine Seigneur de Noailles, records a different sequence of changing robes from that of the Form and Order of Queen Mary's coronation.[37] At the end of the service the Order directs the Queen to lay aside 'all her regalies' and to wear the usual robes of purple velvet with her crown on her head. Elizabeth apparently wore the golden coronation robes, according to the Italian observer: 'The mass and all the ceremonies being concluded and the Queen having twice changed her apparel, they returned into Westminster Hall . . . Her Majesty carrying in her hands the sceptre and orb and wearing the ample royal robe of cloth of gold . . . In the meanwhile the Lord Marshall, Duke of Norfolk and the Lord Steward, Earl of Arundel . . . proceeded to arrange the banquet . . . the Queen during this interval having divested herself of her heavy robe'.[38] Perhaps Elizabeth wore these purple velvet robes for the banquet.

Not very much is known about the length of periods of mourning in Royal households in the sixteenth century, nor the exact details of dress.[39] We know that Elizabeth was joined by the entire Court in wearing mourning black when the French Ambassador was summoned to an audience[40] after the massacre of the Huguenots, which took place on St Bartholomew's Day, 24 August 1572. Lupold von Wedel described Elizabeth wearing black in mourning for the Prince of Orange and the Duke of Alençon in 1585.[41] The purple velvet robes may perhaps have been worn on state occasions at these times.

The furs were mended in 1571 with four timber of ermine skins and two thousand powderings,[42] but far more work was carried out in 1580. There is an entry among the warrants for 'Adam Blande our Skynner for mendinge the furre of our Robe kyrtell and Circoate of purple vellat with tenne Tymber of armyons fower thowsande powderinges and fower thowsande Pynkes of our great warderobe'.[43] The mourning robes were not worn very often, apparently, as there are few direct references to them among the warrants. They would, however, have been regularly aired and brushed with all the other garments, to keep them in good condition.

The Parliament robes

The Queen is depicted wearing her Parliament robes in several paintings, illuminations, engravings, and seals. The crimson velvet kirtle and mantle are entered in the Stowe inventory of the Wardrobe of Robes prepared in 1600.[44] There is a second kirtle listed in the Folger inventory, which may have been out of fashion.[45] Like the coronation robes, Mary Tudor's Parliament robes were apparently refurbished for Elizabeth to wear in the procession to the Abbey Church at Westminster at her coronation.[46] They were probably of very good quality velvet and little worn. A new kirtle was made in 1563 by Walter Fyshe 'a parliamente robe of crimsen velvet lined in the bodies and sleves with whit sarscenet all of our great warderobe'.[47]

99 'Queen Elizabeth I enthroned as the Patroness of Geography and Astronomy'. Detail from the engraving in its first state, attributed to Remegius Hogenberg, 1579. Frontispiece to 'Atlas of England and Wales' by Christopher Saxton. British Museum, London

100 'Queen Elizabeth I enthroned as the Patroness of Geography and Astronomy'. Detail from the engraving in its second state, attributed to Remegius Hogenberg, 1579. Frontispiece to 'Atlas of England and Wales' by Christopher Saxton. British Museum, London

During Elizabeth's long reign of forty-four years she held only ten parliaments (with a total of thirteen sessions) of an average of ten weeks.[48] The Parliament robes were brushed, aired and fur was replaced at intervals to keep them in good condition, throughout the reign,[49] and the kirtle was altered and remodelled to keep it in fashion. Walter Fyshe is listed in 1571 'for making of a gatherid foreparte with new bodyes and slevis of crymsen vellat for our parliament kyrtle lyned with white taphata and Canvas in the bodies, of our greate guarderobe'.[50] Later in the same year the kirtle was altered again and this time Fyshe was entered 'for alteringe and enlarginge the hinder parte of a kyrtle of crymsen vellat for the parliament and for perfourmynge the sarceonett of our greate guarderobe'.[51] Next year the kirtle needed more work and Fyshe was listed in the warrant: 'for alteringe of a kyrtle of crymsen vellat for the parliament and enlarginge it the lyninge perfourmed with white taphata and borderid aboute with like taphata of our great guarderobe'.[52] By 1576 the kirtle was out of fashion and Fyshe worked on it again, apparently trimming it with gold lace as well: 'altering the bodies and making newe slevis and Jagges for our parliament kyrtle lased with a passamayne lase of venice golde & lyned with white sarceonett of our great guarderobe'.[53] There were now 'jagges', or tabbed sleeve wings, set in the armholes. Apparently the alteration was not enough, as in the autumn of the same year Arthur Middleton, an alteration hand, is entered 'for making of newe bodies slevis & Jagges of crymsen vellat for our parliament Robe lyned with white sarceonett layed with passamaine lase of venice golde'.[54] In 1581 Fyshe carried out another alteration, either to replace a worn area, or, more probably, to make the skirt fashionably wider: 'for alteringe of our Parliament kyrtle of crymsen vellat & settinge in two panes half the bredth

of vellat the lyninge perfourmed with white sarceonett of our great guarderobe'.[55] A similar alteration was carried out for the Garter kirtle in 1580. It is not entirely clear, but up to 1585 the kirtle seems to have been made with the bodice high to the neck, the style still seen in the Helmingham portrait (Fig. 102). In the spring of 1585 William Jones made a new bodice with a low square neckline: 'for making of a peire of square bodies with Jagges and enlarginge the slevis of a kyrtle of crymsen vellat for our parliament Robe edged with golde lase lyned with white sarceonett with like stuff & canvas to perfourme them of our great guarderobe'.[56] This neckline is seen in Figures 106 and 107.

The ermine lining the mantle seems to have been too hot and heavy for the Queen. In 1571 Walter Fyshe had the job of 'alteringe and takinge out the furre in the shoulders of our parliament Mantell and perfourmynge it with white taphata'.[57] This was apparently renewed in the following year: 'for lyninge of our parliament Robe from the waste upwarde with white taphata of our great guarderobe'.[58] The weight of the fur attached to the taffeta may have torn it in places.

The ermine was kept in good repair. Each year there were entries of this type: 'for mending the furre of our parliament Robes and sweetinge them with a perfourmance of powderid armyons of our great guarderobe'.[59] Sometimes big repairs were needed: 'to Adam Blande our Skynner for mending the furre of our parliament Robe kyrtell Circoate whoode & Cap of Maintenance perfourmed with vj tymber of armyons thre thowsande one hundreth & fyvetie pynkes & powderinges'.[60]

Parliament was always opened in state, with a service at Westminster Abbey. The same Italian who had described the Coronation robes, wrote about the Queen's robes for the opening of Parliament on 25 January 1559 to Octaviano

101 'Queen Elizabeth I in her Parliament robes'. Detail from the illumination on the Charter for Queen Elizabeth's Hospital, Bristol, 1590. The Governors of Queen Elizabeth's Hospital, Bristol

102 'Queen Elizabeth in her Parliament robes'. Panel painting attributed to Marcus Gheeraerts the Younger, c. 1585–90. She wears a cutwork ruff edged with needle lace. Lord Tollemache, Helmingham Hall, Stowmarket

Vivaldino, Mantuan Ambassador with King Phillip at Brussels:

Her Majesty came to the Abbey . . . in her ordinary litter, wearing a royal crimson robe lined with ermine, but not with the hood as generally worn by former [sovereigns]. The robe fitted close to the body and was high up to the throat, with a lace trimming at the top, and a round cape of ermine like the one worn by the Doge of Venice and a cap of beaten gold covered with fine oriental pearls on her head and a necklace from which was suspended a most marvellous pendant.[61]

The lace mentioned here is the silk cord which fastened the mantle at the front.

The two versions of the frontispiece of Christopher Saxton's *Atlas of England and Wales* printed in 1579 show Queen Elizabeth, enthroned as the Patroness of Geography and Astronomy, wearing the Parliament robes. An interesting set of variations emerges when the two plates are compared. The first state (Fig. 99) shows the ermine cape worn low at the neck, in a similar way to the drawing of c. 1590–95 by Hilliard (Fig. 105). The kirtle beneath has sleeves fastening on the outside, which are left open with the ribbons untied. The style may be seen more clearly in three dimensional form on Richard Alington's tomb of 1561. His three daughters show the side view of this sleeve (Fig. 98). Some of the ribbons are left hanging loosely, allowing the undersleeve to show. The sleeves are still fairly close to the arm in 1561; those in Saxton's *Atlas* are much wider. The second state of the engraving (Fig. 100) shows plain sleeves without ribbons and

the ermine cape is higher at the neck. The faint marks where the original neck edge was beaten out of the plate are still visible to the naked eye. The decorative jewelled band down the front of the kirtle has been removed completely and that round the hemline replaced with a border of ermine. A. M. Hind lists three copies of the Atlas with the plate in its first state,[62] there are many others with the plate in its second state. It is particularly puzzling since the first state of the engraving shows the Parliament robe low in the neck, as it appears later in the reign (Fig. 105) and the kirtle in the second state has been simplified, not made more fashionable. One explanation may be that Elizabeth herself ordered the alteration. The kirtle for the Parliament robe as described in the Stowe inventory of 1600 is certainly plain crimson velvet trimmed with ermine and this is how it is shown in the Helmingham portrait (Fig. 102).

Many of the illuminations of Elizabeth in the Parliamentary robes on official documents[63] show her wearing a pink mantle, not crimson as described in the inventory, with an ordinary gown, sometimes a little out-of-date, beneath it (Fig. 101). In some cases the paint has faded, but in others it is likely that more consideration was given to the decorative colour scheme for these delightful little pictures and the appearance of the page than accurate costume detail. The change from fashionable gown to ermine-trimmed kirtle in the two stages of the engraving for Saxton's *Atlas* would seem to indicate that the crimson velvet Parliament kirtle would normally have been worn beneath the Parliament mantle.

103 *'Portrait of an unknown lady'. Panel painting attributed to Marcus Gheeraerts the Younger, dated 1592 in what may be a later inscription. She wears a ruff with similar cutwork motifs to that in Figure 102. The Trustee of the Will of the Earl of Berkeley, Berkeley Castle*

104 *Queen Elizabeth I in her Parliament robes. Obverse of the Second Great Seal, pattern drawn in 1584 and in use from 1586 to 1603. British Library, London. (Seal XXXVI:19)*

Both versions of this engraving show the Parliament mantle fully lined with ermine. Von Wedel described it in 1585 as being lined only as far as the waist, although, as the Queen was sitting in a litter, this may have been all he could catch sight of in the crowd. His whole account is of interest, as it paints a detailed picture of the opening of Parliament:

Then came the Queen in a semi-covered litter that looked like a half-canopied bed. The litter was entirely of wood upholstered all over with gold and silver cloth. The cushions, too, on which the Queen reclined were of gold and silver material. The long red velvet parliamentary cloak she wore was trimmed to the waist with a lining which was white with black dots. On her head she wore a crown. The litter was borne by two white steeds with yellow manes and tails. On the horses' heads and tails were plumes of yellow and white, their saddles and cloths being of gold material. Behind the Queen was another led horse. It had a red velvet saddle-cloth garnished with gold borders and gold lace. Following this horse came four-and-twenty women and maidens who rode in single file, each of them outvying the others in raiment, adornment and horse-trappings. Behind the women followed two coaches. The one was upholstered in red, gold-embroidered velvet, the other in black velvet with gold embroidery; but in them was no one. On either side of the Queen was her bodyguard, not however in their usual uniform, for their tabards were wholly of red cloth trimmed with beaten gold. In such state did the Queen progress to Westminster Abbey, where all the Kings lie buried. Then she went into the church, where prayers were said and psalms sung, and from there into the House of Parliament which is hard by. Here she was led into a chamber where upon a dais a canopy was erected. This was most splendidly made of gold coverlets and velvet embroidered with gold, silver and pearls. Under the canopy stood her chair which was likewise fitted out in regal splendour.[64]

The Parliamentary robes described here would have looked like those in the portrait of the Queen at Helmingham Hall, dating from around 1585–90 (Fig. 102). The colour is red, but

may have changed from crimson with cleaning. The ermine lining of the mantle is turned outwards at the front, the wide cape being concealed beneath the ruff. Elizabeth sits in an informal pose, a fan in her left hand, her right arm resting on the arm of what appears to be the Chair of Estate which is covered in 'Clothe of golde yellow tissue'.[65] She wears a crown and a small jewelled anchor is pinned in her hair. The collar of jewels is similar to that in the 'Ermine' portrait (Fig. 217). The wide sleeves are padded with cotton bombast or held out with whalebones. The wrist ruffs of the smock are carefully set below the ermine cuffs. The velvet of the skirt is gathered at the waist and supported by a large French farthingale, a roll padded with cotton, tied round the waist. The kirtle opens at the centre front and the edges are bordered with ermine. The ruff is remarkably similar to one depicted in the portrait of an unknown lady, dated 1592 in what is probably a later inscription (Fig. 103). The cutwork flowers on both have raised petals. This effect has been produced by the stiffly starched, fine linen easing back after the ruff was set with hot irons. The ruff worn by the unknown lady might have been a gift from the Queen after she had worn it a few times, with a new border, or perhaps Gheeraerts simply used the detail of the cutwork from the same ruff in both pictures.

The Parliamentary mantle in the Second Great Seal, which was in use from 1586 to 1603 (Fig. 104), is the same as that depicted in the Helmingham portrait. It shows a closed ruff with the mantle high at the neck, held away at the sides by hands emerging from clouds. On 8 July 1584 Nicholas Hilliard and Dericke Anthony, graver at the Mint, were ordered 'to embosse... patterns for a new Great Seal according to the last pattern made upon parchment by you Our Servant Nicholas Hilliard'.[66] The drawing for another Great Seal, Sir Roy Strong suggests for Ireland, also by

105 *'Queen Elizabeth I in her Parliament robes'. Possibly a design for a Great Seal of Ireland. Pen and ink and wash drawing over pencil by Nicholas Hilliard, c. 1590–95. British Museum, London (1912–7–17–1)*

106 *(Left) 'Queen Elizabeth I in her Parliament robes', by an unknown artist, c. 1595. T. Cottrell Dormer, Rousham House*

107 *(Above) 'Queen Elizabeth I in her Parliament robes'. Panel painting by an unknown artist, 1598. Corporation of Dover*

Hilliard, shows an open ruff dating from the early 1590s and the mantle is low in the neck (Fig. 105). It is of particular interest as it shows the Queen seated, and the line of the farthingale supporting the kirtle may be seen above the knees. The material is caught up and pinned to the edge of it.

The portrait of Elizabeth wearing her Parliament robes at Rousham House (Fig. 106) may have been worked from the same sitting as this Hilliard drawing, or perhaps from the drawing itself. It was cleaned and restored in 1804. A letter from the restorer, William Delamotte to Sir Clement Cottrell-Dormer, the owner, survives but does not give very much detail about the work carried out: 'I have never had any pictures so bad to do. The Queen Elizabeth has turned out well and looks as fresh as ever'.[67] Comparison with the Hilliard drawing shows that during restoration the folds of velvet over the edge of the farthingale were probably altered a little; the arrangement with pins is no longer visible. The knees appear to protrude rather suddenly; originally the highlights on the velvet were probably less pronounced. The kirtle is bordered with ermine at the hem and appears to have opened at the centre front, as there is a narrow line of ermine, part of which has been removed with cleaning. Hilliard's drawing does not show this opening, but there is a band of fur bordering the

108 *Detail from the Funeral Procession of Queen Elizabeth I. One of a series of water colour paintings, 1603. British Library, London (Add. MS 35,324 Rothschild Bequest vol. XV f.376)*

109 *Queen Elizabeth I in her Parliament robes. Marble effigy carved by Maximilian Colte. Orb, sceptre and collar of jewels are modern replacements. 1605. Westminster Abbey, London*

hem. Both pictures show the ermine cuffs at the ends of the sleeves with wrist ruffs beneath.

The mantle in the drawing has a deep ermine cape with tails round the edge, over which a heavy jewelled collar is worn in the same way as that in the Saxton's *Atlas* engraving (Figs 99 and 100). It can just be seen beneath the open ruff. There is a second jewelled collar beneath the mantle which shows at the front. The cape in the portrait has a scalloped edge, perhaps the result of restoration; originally it may have had tails. There is no jewelled collar.

The pair of mantle laces in the drawing pass through holes in the ermine cape at the neck, are knotted together at chest level, then fall loosely into the lap and the tassels reach the hem. In the painting the laces are knotted correctly but are tied in a bow in the lap, which seems to be the work of the restorer. The tassels are correctly observed.

Another portrait of the Queen in her Parliament robes purchased in 1598 'to be sett up in the halle' in the Maison Dieu, Dover, shows a kirtle with tabbed skirts to the bodice (Fig. 107). The ruff is open and there is no wide ermine cape to the crimson velvet mantle, although the ermine lining can be seen. The artist may not have been able to observe the mantle at first hand, or he may have found difficulty in painting the white ruff over the white fur and therefore left the crimson velvet background beneath it, concealing the Queen's left shoulder with a dark green velvet curtain and turning back the mantle on her right shoulder. The kirtle is in rich crimson velvet, the bodice decorated at the front and round the square neckline with pearls and jewels. The tabbed skirts are outlined with pearls. The edge of the farthingale can be seen beneath the carefully arranged flounce. In her right hand the Queen holds a rope of large pearls which is attached to a jewelled girdle.

The Parliament robes were used for the last time in Elizabeth's funeral procession from Whitehall to the Abbey Church at Westminster on 28 April 1603.

The Lively Picture of her Majesties whole body, in her parliament robes, with a crowne on her head, and a scepter in her hand, lying on

110   *Detail of ruff and smock collar from the effigy in Figure 109*

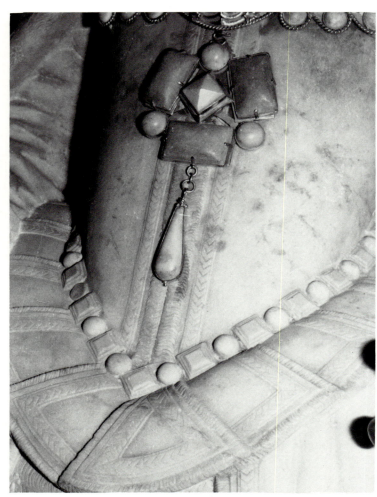

111   *Detail of tabbed skirts bordered with ermine and two rows of braid from the effigy in Figure 109. The 'Three Brothers' jewel is a modern replacement*

the corpse inshrined in leade, and balmed; covered with purple velvet; borne in a charriot, drawne by foure horses, trapt in blacke velvet.[68]

One of a series of water colour paintings[69] of this procession shows that the 'lively picture' was a life-size effigy (Fig. 108) 'carved in wood and coloured so faithfully that she seems alive' as Scaramelli, the Venetian Secretary in England, wrote to the Doge and Senate.[70] However, the 'Clothe of golde and silver tissue' kirtle of the Robes of Estate, with long folds caught in at the waist in the old style, rather than the Parliament kirtle is depicted in this picture. The Parliament mantle lined with ermine lies beneath the effigy. It is not certain which version is correct, but the Parliament kirtle and mantle seem more likely to have been used, as they appear in the monument in Westminster Abbey. The superb marble effigy of the Queen by Maximilian Colte[71] shows the Parliament robes in great detail (Fig. 109). The wide ruff is open at the front as in the Ditchley portrait (Fig. 71). and the lace-bordered collar of the smock is arranged over it (Fig. 110). The kirtle bodice has small tabbed skirts similar to those in the Dover portrait (Fig. 107) and opens at the centre front. Both fronts and tabbed skirts are bordered with ermine and two rows of braid, or 'passamayne lace of venice golde' (Fig. 111). A wider braid is used on either side of the skirt, which is open to reveal an ermine forepart (Fig. 112). This use of more ermine than before, with an ermine forepart as well as the customary cuffs, kirtle hem, and

mantle lining, is reflected in the portrait of Lucy Russell, Countess of Bedford, daughter of Lord John Harington, and patroness of poets (Fig. 113). She wears an ermine lined mantle, deep ermine cuffs, an ermine stomacher elongated to lie over the front of the farthingale, and a deep band of ermine at the hem, curving up at the front. The rich red velvet may originally have been crimson.[72] This painting probably shows the Countess in her robes and coronet for the coronation of James I and Anne of Denmark in 1603. A portrait of the same sitter, wearing similar robes painted around 1615 shows an even deeper band of ermine at the hem and ermine linings to hanging sleeves.[73] The ermine forepart may have been added to Elizabeth's Parliament robes for the funeral procession in 1603, and this appears in Maximilian Colte's sculpture.

The Garter robes

An early record of the Queen in her Garter robes was presented to her as a New Year's gift in 1568 'By Mrs Levina Terling a paper paynted with the Quenis Majestie and the Knightes of thorder'.[74] It was delivered to Blanche Parry but unfortunately does not seem to have been preserved. The Queen wears the Garter robes in Gheeraerts' etching of the procession at Windsor in 1576 (Fig. 114). The crimson velvet kirtle and purple velvet mantle are listed in the Stowe inventory.

112 *Detail of ermine forepart from the effigy in Figure 109*

113 *'Lucy Russell, Countess of Bedford', by a follower of Robert Peake, c. 1603. She wears robes of red velvet trimmed with ermine. National Portrait Gallery, London*

A selection of extracts from the warrants for the Wardrobe of Robes shows that, like the Parliament kirtle, the Garter kirtle was altered throughout the reign. Walter Fyshe is entered in 1564 'for makinge of a paire of Bodies of crimsen velvet for a kirtle of Thorder of the garter Lyned with white sarcenet of oure greate warderobe'.[75] Although a ceremonial habit, the lines of current fashion are to be detected in the kirtle. Walter Fyshe worked on the kirtle again in 1571 'making of a gatherid foreparte of crymsen vellat and alteringe the bodies and making newe nether slevis for a kyrtle of crymsen vellat of our order of the Garter of our greate guarderobe'.[76] In 1575 he is entered again 'for alteringe of a Robe of crymsen vellat for thorder of the garter & making of newe bodies and slevis of like vellat lyned with white sarceonett of our greate guarderobe'.[77] Two years later he made the sleeves even larger 'alteringe the bodies and slevis of a kyrtle of crymsen vellat for thorder of the garter the ruffes being enlarged of our great guarderobe'.[78] The term 'ruffes' refers to the gathered areas over the sleeveheads. They may have been stiffened in the way described when Fyshe altered and enlarged the sleeves of a white satin gown in 1571, 'newe pasting the ruffes and lyninge them with white taffeta'.[79] In 1578 Fyshe worked on the kirtle again 'alteringe the bodies and slevis and enlarginge the ruffes of our Robe of thorder of the garter of crymsen vellat layed with passamaine of venice golde the ruffes drawen oute with lawne the lyninge performed with white sarceonett of our greate guarderobe'.[80] Many portraits show strips of fine cobweb lawn or silk pulled out of the gathers at the tops of sleeves or arranged round the armholes (Figs 12 and 26).

Fyshe enlarged the skirt of the Garter kirtle to keep it in fashion in 1580: 'for alteringe the skyrtes of a frenche kyrtle of crymsen vellat of our order of the Garter and settinge in of two panes of the bredth of vellat the lyninge perfourmed with white sarceonett of our greate warderobe'.[81] In the following year Arthur Middleton, the alterations hand, was given the job of making a new bodice for the kirtle. This now had 'jagges', or tabbed sleeve wings, set in the armholes: 'for making a peire of bodies & Jagges of crymsen vellat for our order of the garter the lyninge perfourmed with sarceonett'.[82]

In 1583 William Jones, now the Queen's tailor in place of Walter Fyshe who had retired, first of all altered the kirtle 'with like vellat and taphata'[83] and then, presumably because it still looked unfashionable, was employed in 'making of a payer of square bodyes of crymsen vellat for a kyrtell of our order of the garter bounde aboute with a lase of venice golde lyned with canvas styffened with buckeram the Jagges Drawen oute with

114   *Queen Elizabeth I in her Garter robes in procession with the Knights of the Most Noble Order of the Garter at Windsor. Details from an etching by Marcus Gheeraerts the Elder, dated 1576, altered to 1578 by a contemporary hand. British Museum, London*

lawne of our great guarderobe'.[84] This style of bodice had a square neckline. In 1587 Jones made a new bodice. The old velvet may have been shabby but it was at this time that the Queen put on weight:[85] 'for making of a peire of bodies of crymsen vellat for our Robe of thorder of the garter layed on with golde lase stiffenid with canvas and buckeram and for enlarginge the slevis with like vellat of our great guarderobe'.[86] The entry for a new bodice which Jones made in 1595 gives details about the way in which it was fastened: he was employed in 'alteringe and makinge new bodies to a Robe of our Order of the Garter, of Crimsin velvet with gold lace aboute and drawne out with Copwebbe Lawne the bodies stiffened with Canvas and buckeram hookes and eyes of our great warderobe'.[87]

The purple velvet mantle was kept in good order by Walter Fyshe; in 1570 he was entered 'for lynyng a Mantle of our order of the Garter with whyte taphata'.[88] Two years later he carried out more work 'making of a coller for a Robe of our order of the garter of purple vellat of our greate guarderobe'.[89] William Jones carried out unspecified alterations to the mantle in 1583[90] and in the same warrant he is entered 'for makinge of a Mantell of purple vellat for our order of the garter lyned with white taphata serceonett the coller styffenid with canvas, with Robes lases of our great Guarderobe'.[91] This may have been a replacement for the old mantle, but Ashmole records that both Sovereign and Knights-Companions of the Order each left a spare mantle in the vestry of St George's Chapel, Windsor, for times when they were required unexpectedly. The second mantle was used for all other occasions elsewhere.[92]

The purple velvet mantle fastened with 'a mantle lace of purple silke and golde'. The word 'lace' may at first be misleading; today we would call it a cord. Elias Ashmole described the lace fully in 1672:

For further Ornament, the Mantle had fixed to its Collar, a pair of long strings, anciently woven of Blue Silk only; (called Cordans, Robe-strings, or Laces) but of later times twisted round, and made of Venice Gold, and Silk of the Colour of the Robe; at each end of which, hung a great Knob or Button wrought over and raised with a rich Caul of Gold; and Tassels thereunto of like Silk and Gold.[93]

We would describe both 'button' and 'tassell' together as the tassel today.

Herr Johann Jacob Breuning von Buchenbach, who headed an Embassy from the Duke of Württemberg, described the procession of the Order at Windsor in 1595:

The Knights of the Garter wore the following garb. The usual articles of attire, the breeches and doublet, were for the most part of silver cloth and other material. Over this they wore a red velvet gown which hung down to their calves. This gown was girded with a broad gilt belt, from the front of which tassels of gold and silk depended. Over this gown they wore another long cloak of fig-brown velvet, which trailed somewhat upon the ground. Both cloak and gown were lined with white taffeta or silk. Over the fig-brown cloaks they wore slung across the shoulders a special tippet in old Franconian style, of the same stuff and colour. On one side of this tippet was a round hole, lined with white. Round this hole in embroidered letters was the motto, 'Hony soit qui mal y pense'. These tippets were similar to those worn by the Venetian nobility, or by the town-councillors of Siena, or by the rectors of the university of Padua. There they are styled Liripipium. Over the very long fig-brown cloaks they wore a rather broad gold enamelled, bejewelled collar resting upon their shoulders and having large rings like those of the Golden Fleece. Suspended from the collar is a medallion of St. George of fair size, and round this in enamelled letters, 'Hony soit qui mal y pense'. On their heads they wore little black bonnets and atop of these a white plume. On the left thigh they wore the Garter like a girdle, on which were embroidered in pearls and precious stones the words quoted above. Each of them bore a gold dirk or rapier. Some bore white rods in their hands. There were also three others present wearing almost similar garments, which were, however, of red satin. Two of them carried black staffs and they were the Chancellor and the Secretary of the Order. The third carried a large book bound in red velvet with silver-gilt clasps, wherein the statutes of the Order are written. When formed up for the procession to the chapel, he with the book marched at the head, then followed the two with the black rods and then the knights two by two.[94]

For most of the Order's history the mantle has been blue, except between 1564 and 1637 when, as Ashmole describes:

But in Queen Elizabeth's reign (upon what ground is no where mentioned) the Colour of Forreign Princes Mantles, was changed from Blue to Purple: for of that Colour were the Mantles sent to the French Kings Charles the Ninth, anno 6 Eliz. and Henry the Third, an. 27 of the same Queen: So also to the Emperor Maximilian, an. 9 Eliz. to Frederick the Second King of Denmark, an. 24 Eliz. to John Casimire, Count Palatine of the Rhyne, an. 21 Eliz. and to Christierne the Fourth King of Denmark, an. Jac. R.4. but that sent to Frederick Duke of Wirtemberg in the same year, was of a mixt Colour, to wit, Purple with Violet. Thus the purple Colour came in and continued till about the 12. year of king Charles the First.[95]

The warrants show that each Knight was given eighteen yards of crimson velvet for gown or kirtle, hood and tippet and ten yards of white sarsenet for lining them.[96] Foreign princes invested with the Order were presented with these garments made up and also a mantle containing twenty yards of purple velvet lined with sixteen yards of white taffeta.[97] English Knights apparently provided their own mantles at this time, as material for them does not appear in the warrants. Von Buchenbach describes the colour of the mantles as fig-brown. One which survives today, presented to Christian IV, King of Denmark and Norway, when he was installed as Knight by proxy in 1606,[98] is in very dark purple velvet, which might almost be described as aubergine under some lights, when the rich colour is then similar to that of a ripe fig.

This, presumably, was the colour of Elizabeth's Garter mantle listed in the Stowe inventory of 1600 together with the crimson velvet kirtle. Ashmole explains that there were several solemn days and occasions when the Sovereign and Knights were enjoined to wear the whole habit of the Order. Less solemn occasions required them to wear the mantle, or collar of the Order only.[99] Von Buchenbach describes Elizabeth wearing cloth of silver in the Garter procession at Windsor in 1595:

After the Knights walked two Mylords in long black gowns, each carrying a golden sceptre. Then came another who, bearing a sword in a red velvet scabbard with gilt ornamentations, preceded Her Majesty. Then Her Majesty stepped out of the Privy Chamber, arrayed in silver cloth. On her robe were embroidered two obelisks crossed, which in lieu of a button had at the top a beautiful oriental pearl. The robe was further adorned with rare costly gems and jewels. On her head she wore a very costly royal crown. Her Majesty was escorted on either side by Knights and Earls. Her train was borne by a maid-of-honour. On stepping out of the chamber Her Majesty greeted all present. Then there followed in great numbers all the countesses and other noble ladies who had awaited her in the Presence Chamber.[100]

On this occasion the Queen would have put on the mantle of the Order at St George's Chapel, unless this is the train to which von Buchenbach refers, incorrectly described. As the Knights were dressed in the whole habit in the procession, the Queen was apparently departing from tradition in wearing a cloth of silver gown.

The Robes of the Order of St Michael

The Order of St Michael was a similar institution in France to the Most Noble Order of the Garter in England.[101] It was a military order and women were not admitted, but Charles IX conferred the Order on the Earl of Leicester and the Duke of Norfolk in January, 1566, as a compliment to the Queen.[102] The Robes of the Order of St Michael which remained in the Wardrobe of Robes in 1600 had belonged to Edward VI.[103] In 1575 Walter Fyshe, the Queen's tailor, was paid 'for lyninge of a Roabe of cloth of silver for thorder of St Mychaell of the chardge of Rauf Hope yeoman of our Guarderobe of Robes lyned with white Satten of our great guarderobe'.[104] Presumably the white satin had discoloured with age. In 1577 a 'Case

115 'Queen Elizabeth I at the Maundy ceremony'. Miniature by Levina Teerlinc, c. 1560–62. Madresfield Court Collection

of Jeane fustian'[105] was made to protect the robes, but I have found no evidence yet that they were ever used for any purpose during Elizabeth's reign.

The Maundy ceremony

No special gown is listed for the Maundy. A miniature (Fig. 115) shows Elizabeth in about 1560 ready to perform the ceremonial feet washing of the poor women, one for each year of her age. It may have been painted for the Queen as a New Year's gift by the miniaturist Levina Teerlinc. At New Year in 1562 she presented Elizabeth with 'the Queen's personne and other personages in a box fynely painted';[106] the group of people may well have been these participants in the Maundy ceremony.

In the miniature Elizabeth wears a fine cambric apron, The warrants for the ninth year of her reign, dated 28 March 1567, include an item: 'to William Dane lynnen Draper . . . for iiij elles of fyne Camerick to make an apron and a Towell to were at our Maundy'.[107] Among the warrants there are at least eleven repeat orders for 'one round Kirtle of white damask bound with gold lace', and one is listed in the Stowe inventory.[108] According to Strype 'she gave unto twenty women so many gowns and one woman had her best gown'.[109] It is possible that this white damask kirtle was her 'best gown', made specially for the Maundy when she did not have one that she wished to give away. In 1573 Lambarde mentions that Elizabeth gave each poor woman 'certain yards of broad cloth to make a gown' and twenty shillings in a red leather purse to

IV

Designs for Jewellery and Embroidery: their Sources and Symbolism

Jewellery designs

Portraits of the Queen conjure up the poet's words: 'when she came in like starlight, thick with jewels',[1] and suggest the wildest extravagance. However, this impression is quite unjustified. As the Chancellor of the Exchequer told the Commons in 1593: 'As for her apparel, it is royal and princely, beseeming her calling, but not sumptuous nor excessive'.[2] Many of the jewels were from her father's coffers and had been worn both by him and his six wives and, in turn, by her brother and sister.[3] In addition to this, the New Year's Gift Rolls record a large number of jewels presented to Elizabeth by members of the nobility, courtiers and their wives; many were of most imaginative design, often symbolic, and would have given her far more pleasure than purses of gold.

Several of the Queen's jewels show the use of initial letters, often E, and sometimes those of the donor. These jewels made attractive gifts. Henry VIII presented one to Katherine Howard in 1540: 'Item oone other hache of golde wherein is vj feir diamondes wherof iiij be table diamondes and two be poynted & a feir Emeralde in the myddes therof with also thre feir peerlls hanging at the same'.[4] This is apparently the same jewel listed in the 1587 inventory, the single emerald being replaced by a diamond: 'Item an H with seaven diamondes wherof two pointed and five tabled with three pearles pendaunte'.[5] Elizabeth may well have worn this jewel in remembrance of her father. Anne of Denmark wears the crowned S for her mother, Sophia of Mecklenberg, and the crowned C encircling a 4, which alludes to her brother, Christian IV of Denmark, in her portrait painted in about 1617 (Fig. 120). A chain 'of golde havinge twelve peeces & in every peece two diamondes lackinge one and eleven with two Rubies in eache with letters of H & R betwene them lackinge two diamondes'[6] also appears in the 1587 inventory. The letters

HR are for 'Henricus Rex' as those of ER are for 'Elizabetha Regina'. A pair of gold bracelets worn by Lady Speke, in her portrait painted in 1592, display the letters ER.[7] These may have been a gift to the Queen which she then presented to Lady Speke. Gifts might be passed on almost immediately.[8] Another jewel of gold, the front set with rubies, emeralds and diamonds was a New Year's gift in 1574 from the Earl of Ormond. It had Elizabeth's name in full: 'The backeside is a blewe christall, under it certayne verses, every of them beginning with the letters E.L.I.Z.A.B.E.T.H.'.[9]

The letter S was also used by goldsmiths for royal jewellery. Strings of beads and buttons decorated with 'esses' were worn by Henry's Queens.[10] Examples of 'esses' worked in the lace and embroidery used on Elizabeth's ruffs and gowns have already been discussed, with the suggestion that S probably stood for 'Soverayne'.[11] The motif was also used for her jewels, for example, two attractive gifts at the New Year in 1601 were 'Twelve Buttonnes of golde enamelled grene lyke bay leavis havinge in eche fyve small dyamonds like lettre S' and 'One paier of Bracelettes of golde conteyning viij peeces lyke Esses and viij peeces like Mullettes garnished with opalles and sparkes of rubyes and opalles'.[12]

Some of the jewels with designs of biblical inspiration which belonged to Elizabeth had been among Henry VIII's treasure.[13] 'A brouche of the force of Sampson set over with diamont' listed in the 1550 inventory[14] had originally been purchased by Anne of Cleves[15] and was delivered by Elizabeth to Mrs Katharine Howard's charge in February 1572,[16] so presumably it was in use at this time.

The Queen kept, and no doubt wore, jewels like the Sampson brooch and the 'Jhus of golde ennamuled conteignyng one Rubye xxiij diamondes and thre small Emeraldes with thre feir pearles hanging at the same',[17] which appears in the 1540 inventory of jewels given to Katherine Howard by

116 *Queen Elizabeth I, wearing a jewel shaped like a crescent moon in her hair and arrowhead jewels on her ruff. Miniature by Nicholas Hilliard, c. 1595–1600. Victoria and Albert Museum, London (Jones Collection, 622–1882)*

Henry VIII at the time of their marriage. However, jewels presented by courtiers during the last quarter of the sixteenth century reflect the classical aspects of the cults of Elizabeth — as Astraea and as Vestal Virgin — rather than biblical inspiration. Among the mythological subjects used for jewellery designs were the story of Prometheus, Ixion being broken on the wheel and Diana, moon goddess and chaste huntress.[18]

The Queen frequently appears as Diana or Cynthia in Elizabethan literature,[19] and among her jewels are several which use the crescent moon, symbol of the goddess (Fig. 116). A fan given to her by Sir Francis Drake in 1587, was 'of fethers, white and redd, the handle of golde inamuled, with a halfe moone of mother-of-perles, within that a halfe moone garnished with sparkes of dyamondes, and a fewe seede perles on thone side, having her Majesties picture within it, and on the backside a device with a crowe over it'.[20] Here the crescent moon is linked with Elizabeth's portrait, a flattering gift.

Other subjects, of secular inspiration, were chosen specially to please the recipient. In 1571, De Spes, the Spanish Ambassador, told Zayas, the Duke of Alva's Secretary, that Leicester had given the Queen a jewel in which she was represented as seated on a throne with the Queen of Scots in chains at her feet and France and Spain submerged by waves 'with Neptune and the rest of them bowing to this Queen'.[21]

The number of jewels presented as New Year's gifts to the Queen fluctuated from year to year, with a grand total of eighty on 1 January 1587, the twenty-ninth year of her reign. At this time one danger was past: Mary, Queen of Scots, had been executed on 8 February 1586. However, there were now threats of a Spanish invasion and the New Year's gifts in 1587 symbolize the loyalty of Elizabeth's subjects, often holding hidden messages. Some of these were taken from emblem books, which provided a useful source of inspiration for both jewellers and embroiderers. Mario Praz has described these books in great detail[22] so it is only necessary to say here that among the best known in England were Claude Paradin's *Devises Heroïques*, which first appeared in 1551 and was translated into English in 1591 as *The Heroicall Devises of M. Claudius Paradin*, and Geffrey Whitney's *A Choice of Emblemes and other Devises*, the first English emblem book, of

117   *Emblem of hands holding a trowel and a sword dedicated to John Payton Esquire, from 'A Choice of Emblemes' by Geffrey Whitney, 1586. Victoria and Albert Museum, London*

118   *Emblem of a crab and a butterfly dedicated to Francis Windham and Edward Flowerdewe 'most upright judges', from 'A Choice of Emblemes' by Geffrey Whitney, 1586. Victoria and Albert Museum, London*

1586. The latter drew heavily on later editions of *Viri Clarissimi D. Andreae Alciati . . . Emblematum Liber*, first published in 1531.

One jewel presented in 1587, for example, was a 'Jewell of golde having twoe handes, thone holding a sworde thother a Trowell both garnished with sparkes of diamondes and betweene the handes a garnishment of Opalles'.[23] This device, dedicated to John Payton, appears in Geffrey Whitney's *A Choice of Emblemes* (Fig. 117). It may have been Payton who gave the jewel to Elizabeth, conveying the message 'That to defend our country dear from harm/ For war or work we either hand should arm'.[24] The devices were copied from book to book, sometimes with slight changes in the meanings to suit the author's intentions. The device of the sword and trowel appears earlier in Paradin's book with the motto 'Ready to both' and this text: 'The Israelites after their returne from the captivitie of Babilon, taking in the one hand a trowell, in the other a sword (such were the continuall troubles of their enemies) built up the walls of Jerusalem. Which thing in a misterie did represent the ministers of the church of Christ who are bound to instruct the ignorant, and to bring againe those that do erre in the faith (which are very ruines in deed) & to fight manfully with the sword of God's word against the enemies thereof, which are vices and sinne'.[25]

The device of a crab and a butterfly appears in both Paradin's *Heroicall Devises* and Whitney's *A Choice of Emblemes* (Fig. 118). In Paradin's book the picture is accompanied by the motto 'Festina lente. Make hast[e] but slowly' and the following story: 'Augustus Caesar . . . commanded a butterflie cleaving to a sea crabbe to be ingraven in gold, insinuating by the slownesse of one, a kind of temperancie and slow deliberation: and by the fast flying of the other a certaine rashnesse or headlong fury. By both which joined together he signified that a certaine meane or temperature in all things is verie needfull for a prince'.[26] A jewel of this design was entered in the New Year's Gift Rolls of 1578: 'a juell, being a lylly of

golde, with a butterflye in the same, and a sea crabbe, garneshed with small ophalls, rubys, and diamunds with rooses of mother-of-perle and sparks of rubyes; brought into the said chamber by Mrs Skydmore, without report made by whom it was given'.[27] Perhaps this was intended as a piece of anonymous advice or as a tactful plea to Elizabeth in some suit: the motto 'Make haste slowly' also appears with the device in Whitney's book, where it is dedicated to 'the very honourable Francis Windham and Edward Flowerdewe most upright judges' (Fig. 118).[28] One of these men may well have sent the jewel to the Queen.

The design of another of Elizabeth's jewels listed in the Stowe inventory of 1600, a 'Jewel of gold like a Crossbow garnished with diamonds',[29] may also have been inspired by an emblem in Whitney's book (Fig. 119). His illustration is accompanied by the motto 'Ingenium superat vires' and the verse:

Man's wisdome great, doth farre surpasse his strengthe,
For proofe, behoulde, no man could bende the bowe:
But yet, his witte devised at the lengthe,
To winde the stringe so farre as it shoulde goe:
  Then wisedome chiefe, and strengthe, must come behinde,
  But bothe be good, and giftes from God assignde.[30]

Beside the entry in the inventory is a margin note: 'Taken by the Kings Majestie, the 19 of May, 1603'. This jewel may have been one of the first gifts which James I presented to Anne of Denmark on his accession. In her portrait, painted by an unknown artist in about 1617 (Fig. 120) Anne wears a diamond crossbow in her hair which fits the description in the Stowe inventory.

A miniature by Nicholas Hilliard in the Jones Collection at the Victoria and Albert Museum shows four little arrow-heads among the jewels pinned to the Queen's ruff (Fig. 116). These are similar to the set of six pinned in her hair in a miniature in the Madresfield Court collection (Fig. 121). An Irish dart, a light throwing spear, was used in the design of a gold jewel set

119 *Emblem of a crossbow from 'A Choice of Emblemes' by Geffrey Whitney, 1586. Victoria and Albert Museum, London*

with diamonds delivered by an Irish lackey as a gift from one of Sir Henry Norris's sons who was in Ireland when Elizabeth visited Rycote, in 1592.[31] With it was a letter 'I desire this Dart to be delivered, an Irish weapon', with the motto in Irish, 'I flye only for my Soveraigne'.

Other jewels were given to the Queen on this visit by absent members of the Norris family, designed to remind Elizabeth of the donors and their good wishes. Another son, in Flanders, sent a golden key set with diamonds, with the motto in Dutch 'I onlie open to you', a letter explaining that this was the key of Ostend, and Ostend the key of Flanders: 'The wards are made of true hearts; Treachery cannot counterfeit the Key, nor Treason herselfe picke the locke'. A third son, in France, sent a gold sword set with diamonds and rubies with the motto in French 'Drawen onlie in your defence'. His letter proclaimed that in the Queen's service 'I will spende the blood of my heart . . . what my words cannot effect my sword shall'.

The fourth son sent a truncheon, a symbol of office, with the motto in Spanish 'I do not commaunde but under you'. A letter accompanying it explained that, as he had to be obedient to the winds in his ship and could not visit Cheapside, he had nothing to offer but his truncheon. It was, however, a little jewel set with diamonds. Finally Sir Henry's daughter sent a daisy of gold set with rubies from Jersey, where her husband, Sir Anthony Paulet, was Governor. The messenger delivered it to the Queen with a speech to say that 'it hath no sweetnes, yet manie vertues; her heart no tongue, but infinite affections: in you, she saieth, are all vertues, and towards you all her affections'.

Although jewels dating from 1583, similar in design to the Norris gifts, have been described as stupid and ugly and it has been said that by 1586 Elizabethan emblems were lapsing into petty and purposeless naturalism,[32] these and other examples show that this was not so. Another jewel 'of golde, being an arrow thorowe a snake, garnished with smale diamonds and rubyes and three ragged perles pendant', given to Elizabeth by

120 *'Anne of Denmark', by an unknown artist, c. 1617. The Queen wears a jewel shaped like a crossbow in her hair, which may have belonged to Queen Elizabeth. A pendent ruby and pearl are worn beneath a large table diamond which may be the 'Mirror of France'. 'A small pendant rubie, to be worne on the forehedd' is listed among Elizabeth's jewels in 1587. National Portrait Gallery, London*

121 *Queen Elizabeth I, wearing jewels shaped like arrowheads in her hair. Miniature by Nicholas Hilliard, c. 1588. Madresfield Court collection*

124 *Emblem of a withered elm with a fruitful vine symbolizing eternal friendship, from 'A Choice of Emblemes' by Geffrey Whitney, 1586. Victoria and Albert Museum, London*

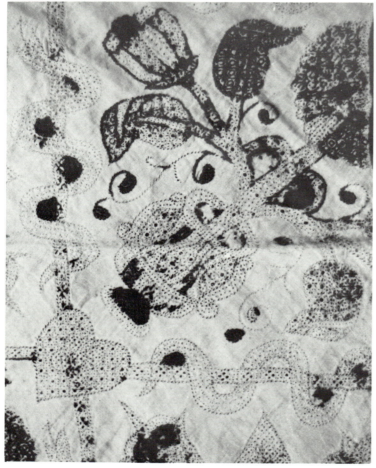

122 *Emblem of a serpent entwined around an arrow, from 'A Choice of Emblemes' by Geffrey Whitney, 1586. Victoria and Albert Museum, London*

123 *Fragment of embroidered linen which by tradition belonged to Queen Elizabeth I. It is worked in black silk with flowers in a pot, hearts and snakes. The black silk has almost disintegrated, but on the left holes of stitching show the shape of the snake. Royal Museum of Scotland, Edinburgh. (1929.152)*

the Countess of Oxford as a New Year's gift in 1583,[33] was also inspired by an emblem book (Fig. 122). In Alciati's book,[34] the emblem is accompanied by the motto 'Maturandum'. Whitney adds a verse in his book:

Aboute the arrowe swifte, ECHENIS slowe doth folde:
Which biddes us in our actions haste, no more than reason woulde.[35]

Snakes twisting round what seem to be the shafts of arrows transfixing hearts, arranged in a trellis design, appear in a surviving fragment of embroidery (Fig. 123).

In another gift of 'a juell of golde being a ded tre with mysaltow, set at the rote with sparks of diamonds and rubys',[36] the mistletoe was probably intended to be bunches of grapes. The gift may have been incorrectly described by a scribe who did not know the emblem of fruitful vine growing over a withered elm (Fig. 124). It appears in Alciati's book with the motto 'Amicitia etiam post mortem durant', symbolizing eternal friendship.[37] The picture may also be seen in Whitney with the same motto,[38] and in Boissard's *Emblematum Liber* with the motto 'Perfect is friendship which lives after death'.[39]

Among her jewels Elizabeth had many made in the shape of birds. There are swans,[40] cranes,[41] peacocks,[42] and owls[43] as well as a parrot[44] (Fig. 125), but the pelican (Fig. 126) and the phoenix were the most popular choice. The pelican jewels have already been mentioned (page 24). Whitney gives a picture of a pelican in *A Choice of Emblemes* (Fig. 127) with the motto 'Quod in te est, prome. Ad eundum' and these verses:

The Pellican, for to revive her younge,
Doth peirce her brest, and geve them of her blood:
Then searche your breste, and as you have with tonge,
With penne procede to doe our countrie good:
    Your zeale is great, your learning is profounde
    Then help our wantes, with that you doe abounde.[45]

The phoenix appears in Paradin's *Heroicall Devises* with the motto 'But always one Phoenix in the world at once'.[46] It was one of the Queen's favourite emblems, often appearing in

125   *Pendant of gold enamelled in white, blue, green, yellow, red, and ochre in the form of a parrot, set with a table-cut foiled crystal in the chest. c. 1600. Victoria and Albert Museum, London (337–1870)*

126   *Pendant of gold enamelled in white, black, blue, yellow, red, and green in the form of a pelican, set with red foiled glass in the chest. c. 1550–75. Victoria and Albert Museum, London (335–1870)*

jewels presented at the New Year. One in 1586 was the gift of Lord Howard, the Lord Admiral: 'a juell of golde, being an armlett, containing 11 letters, being SEMPER EADEM, garnished with sparks of rubyes; and 12 peses, with three ragged perles in a peece, and in the middest a fenix of golde, garnished with opalls and smale sparks of rubyes on the one side'.[47] Another beautiful phoenix jewel worn by Elizabeth may be seen in Figure 26. The Drake jewel, dating from 1588, contains a Hilliard miniature of the Queen facing a painting of a phoenix on the inside of the lid[48] (Fig. 128). This is of the same type as that appearing on the Phoenix medal, one example of which is in the British Museum, dated 1574.

Elizabeth gave many of her courtiers and suitors nicknames and references to them are sometimes made in the design of the jewels presented as gifts. Walter Raleigh was 'Water'; Hatton, jealous of him, sent the Queen a gold bodkin and a gold charm made like a little bucket, with a letter saying that he knew she would need the latter as 'Water' was sure to be near her.[49] This may be the jewel entered in the 1587 list: 'Item a watche of golde sett with small Rubies small diamondes and small Emerodes with a pearle in the topp called a Bucket wanting two Rubies';[50] another was given to her at the New Year in 1596 'one small Juell of gould like a Buckett garnished with sparkes of ⟨dyomondes⟩ rubies and two small pearles pendant'.[51]

Elizabeth's nickname for her suitor François, Duke of Alençon, was 'frog'. Many enchanting little jewels with gold and enamelled frogs were given to her during the time of his

127   *Emblem of a pelican from 'A Choice of Emblemes' by Geffrey Whitney, 1586. Victoria and Albert Museum, London*

128   *The Drake jewel of enamelled gold set with a sardonyx cameo containing a miniature of Queen Elizabeth I, the inside of the lid covered with parchment painted with a phoenix. 1588. Lt Col Sir George Meyrick Bart, M.C.*

129 *'Queen Elizabeth I', by an unknown artist. Possibly 1599, as a portrait brought to Hardwick from London at this date is mentioned in the accounts. The embroidery may have been worked by the Countess of Shrewsbury as a gift for the Queen. National Trust, Hardwick Hall, Derbyshire*

130 *Fragment of white satin with applied sage green velvet. The bird is 'stained' or painted with pink and green dyes and outlined in black, probably with pen and ink. c. 1570. From the back of embroidery worked by Mary, Queen of Scots, at Oxburgh Hall. Victoria and Albert Museum, London (T33LL–1955)*

courtship, for example 'a leafe of golde ennameled grene with a frogge of golde thereon, garnished with sparckes of dia-mondes'[52] and 'One greene frogg, the back of emeraldes, smale and greate and a pendaunte emeralde, with a smale cheyne of golde to hang by'[53] which was presented by the Countess of Huntingdon. Another was obviously a gift from François himself, containing his picture. A pair of bracelets bore his name as the donor. Both gifts are listed in the 1587 inventory of jewels: 'Item one little flower of golde with a frogge thereon and therein Mounsier his phisnamye and a litle pearle pendaunt'[54] and 'Item one paire of Bracelettes of golde ennameled sett with lettres of sparckes of diamondes with this name Francos de Valos contayninge viij peces'.[55]

At the New Year in 1582, to express his eternal devotion to her, François presented the Queen with 'a shackyll of golde with these words graven SERVIET ETERNUM DULCIS QUEM TORQUET ELIZA. And a paddlock of golde hanging by a little cheyne of golde'.[56] At the same time he gave her

'more, a juell being a shipp of golde garnished with six fayre dyamondes, and other smale dyamondes and rubyes, the sayles spredd abrode, with a word enamuled on them'. A ship in sail was a favourite sixteenth-century design for jewels (one is worn by Frances Cobham in Fig. 162) and Elizabeth had several others. One of them 'A Shippe of golde garnished fullye with diamondes lacking two and sett with one Rubie and one pearle pendaunte',[57] may be that listed among Katherine Howard's jewels in 1540: 'A Ship of golde saylyng conteig-nyng one feir rubye in two Fysshes mowthes and xxix diamondes greate and small in the same ship with a Few peerle hanging at the same'.[58] Another entered in the 1587 inventory of jewels was 'a shipp of mother of pearl garnished with golde and sparckes of Rubies and diamondes':[59] these designs may have been inspired by the emblem books. Alciati gives a ship in his book, with the motto 'SPES PROXIMA'. A picture in Whitney's book is accompanied by the motto 'Constantia comes victoriae' and two verses ending:

> Though master reste, thoughe Pilotte take his ease
> Yet night, and day, the ship her course dothe keepe:
> So, whilst that man dothe saile theise worldlie seas
> His voyage shortes: althoughe he wake or sleepe.
>   And if he keepe his course directe, he winnes
>   That wished porte, where lasting joye beginnes.[60]

Boissard's *Emblematum Liber* also gives a ship, with the motto 'A Ship in troubled waters is like the days of Man'.[61]

Some of the jewels presented to the Queen incorporated the badges of their donors. The Earl of Leicester, for example, often used the bear and ragged staff, sometimes just the latter, in the design of his gifts. On New Year's Day in 1580 he gave Elizabeth, among other presents, a black velvet cap with 'a bande abowte it with 14 buttons of golde garnished with dyamonds, being raged staves and true-love knotts, garnished with rubyes and dyamondes and 36 smale buttons, being true love knotts and raged staves'.[62] An earlier gift, at New Year in 1574, used only the bear: 'a fanne of white fethers, sett in a handle of golde . . . on each syde a white beare and twoe perles hanging, a lyon ramping with a white moseled beare at his foote'. The muzzled bear with the lion rampant was probably intended to show Leicester's allegiance and devotion to the Queen. Her nickname for Leicester was 'Eyes' and it is tempting to suppose that he also gave her 'a ringe of golde with an Agatt made like two eyes with sparckes aboute it of Rubies'.[63] However, this can only be conjectured, as the Earl of Hertford gave her 'a paire of braceletts of golde, conteining

131 *One of nine panels of velvet with painted decoration, c. 1570. The ground is of dull green velvet, faded in places, with strapwork pattern in darker green, oulined with fine silk cord. The couching stitches are worked through both velvet and canvas lining. The roundels of ivory velvet are painted or 'stained' with watery dyes of brown, pale green, and yellow-beige, which have probably faded. The outlines of birds, slips of flowers, and other motifs are worked in black silk in back or running stitch. National Trust, Hardwick Hall, Derbyshire*

132 *Heron catching an eel. Detail of a polychrome embroidered white satin panel, probably from a skirt, c. 1600. Victoria and Albert Museum, London (T.138–1981)*

seven peeces, three of the saide peeces having eies' at New Year in 1583,[64] and there are several other gifts with eyes in the design which were not presented by Leicester.

Embroidery designs in the Hardwick portrait

The full length painting at Hardwick Hall, Derbyshire, (Fig. 129) shows Elizabeth wearing one of the most elaborate gowns seen in any of her portraits. A. F. Kendrick commented 'It must be confessed that the pattern of the Queen's dress is at times so fanciful that one hesitates to regard it as a faithful representation of what the painter saw with his own eies'[65] and it has been suggested that the portrait was pieced together from a woodcut extended to a full length.[66] Some of the descriptions of fantastic and elaborate pieces of embroidery in the Stowe inventory make it clear that this is not the case. The painter observed carefully a richly decorated gown. The main problem of interpretation lies in deciding whether the white silk forepart, or petticoat, is 'stained' or embroidered (Figs 130, 131, 132, 133, and 134). Unfortunately no stitches are visible, as they are in some pictures, to provide definite proof (Figs 62 and 62a).

Methods of staining, or painting with dyes and pigments, for banners and hangings are described in Cennino d'Andrea Cennini's treatise *Il Libro dell'Arte*[67] and a manuscript compiled by Jehan Le Begue.[68] The former was copied out in 1437, in Florence. Cennini describes stretching linen or silk taut on a frame with nails and tacks, painting the material first with a coat of size, then a very thin layer of gesso and finally drawing with charcoal. After this he explains how to lay diadems or grounds in gold so that the cloth may be rolled up and folded without damage. The colours were to be applied in the same way as for panel painting, tempering them with yolk of egg.[69] Cennini also describes working on velvet. The design

is drawn with a pen and either ink or tempered white lead. The area to be gilded or painted is coated with size, and an equal amount of white of egg and a little white lead; this is then pressed flat on the pile.[70]

Jehan le Begue compiled his manuscript in Paris in 1431 from a collection of works on painting made by Jehan Alcherius. The latter visited Bologna in February 1410 when he was given recipes for preparing and using 'coloured waters' by one Theodore, a Flemish embroiderer, who had had them from Gian Galeazzo Visconti, his employer in Pavia. The latter had obtained the recipes in London.[71] One recipe is apparently for a discharge technique, to leave a white pattern on a coloured ground.[72] Theodore also gives recipes for several 'coloured waters'. Red, for example, is 'an ounce of Brazil in powder and a sixth part of alun de glace, and make it boil well in a vessel of clear water until it is reduced to one half, and then use it'.[73] He describes the way in which

. . . in England painters work with these waters upon closely woven cloths, wetted with gum-water made with gum-arabic, and then dried, and afterwards stretched out on the floor of the soler [solario, upper storey of a house], upon thick woollen and frieze cloths; and the painters, walking with their clean feet over the said cloths, work

133 *Sprig of columbine, probably embroidered professionally, with fish and caterpillars apparently added a little later by an amateur. Detail from a large panel of white ribbed silk with an additional weft of silver threads, embroidered with polychrome silks, said to have belonged to Blanche Parry. It was used as an altar cloth. c. 1590–1600. The Church of St Faith, Bacton*

134 *Detail of a fragment of embroidered white satin, with padded raised work for the strawberries and acorns. The acorn cups and mossy bank on which the unicorn sits are made of tiny pieces of coiled wire twisted over with shades of dark green silk. Early seventeenth century. Burrell Collection, Glasgow*

and paint upon them figures, stories and other things. And because these cloths lie stretched out on a flat surface, the coloured waters do not flow or spread in painting upon them, but remain where they are placed, and the watery moisture sinks into the woollen cloth [below], which absorbs it; and even the touches of the paintbrush made with these waters do not spread, because the gum with which, as already mentioned, the cloth is wetted, prevents their spreading. And when the cloths are thus painted, their texture is not thickened or darkened any more than if they had not been painted because the aforesaid watery colours have not sufficient body to thicken the cloth.[74]

This description would seem to be for large items such as hangings and banners, but the technique could have been applied to materials intended for clothing. Ten recipes for 'coloured waters' or dyes are given. Japanese kimonos are still hand-painted with delicate designs today, following traditional techniques. The English work may have been similar, although few examples are recorded. The Queen had a black velvet French gown with white sarsenet 'stained like clouds' and a cloak lined with straw coloured 'stained' velvet, but the design is not described.[75] Experiments made by Roger Thorpe in 1977 at the West Surrey College of Art and Design, Farnham, showed that, with care, dyes might be painted on the

reverse side of velvet without bleeding: the dye ran down into the pile of the velvet, giving a clear design on the right side. The velvet in Figure 131 was probably 'stained' in this way.

The delightful variety of motifs in the Hardwick portrait include pansies, roses, iris, sea monsters, a crab, snakes, butterflies, fish, a sea horse, a kingfisher, and a swan, among other birds, executed in a wide range of colours. These are scattered over the white silk in a random arrangement. All this suggests that the design is probably embroidery rather than staining. The petticoat may have been a New Year's gift worked by the donor. The motifs might be drawn out professionally, but their choice and arrangement are those of an imaginative and enthusiastic domestic embroiderer, rather than the carefully planned, usually geometrically arranged design of a professional (Figs 26 and 135). The latter would give consideration to repeats and the all-over finished effect. Geometric designs, often resembling strapwork in Tudor panelling, were taken from books like Gormont's *Le Livre de Moresques, tres utile et necessaire à tous orfevres, tailleurs, graveurs peintres, tapissiers, brodeurs, lingeres et femmes quis besongent de l'aiguille*, printed in Paris in 1546. The birds in Figure 131 appear to have been adapted from woodcuts in

135 *'Queen Elizabeth I'. Panel painting by an unknown artist, c. 1583. The Queen wears a black gown with gold embroidery and white silk doublet slashed chevronwise on the sleeves. Mr and Mrs Salway, Overton, Herefordshire*

136 *Sea monsters and animals of the North Atlantic and northern lands. Detail from woodcut by Sebastian Munster, c. 1580. British Library, London*

Pierre Belon's *L'Histoire de la Nature des Oyseaux, avec leurs descriptions, & naïfs portraicts*, printed in Paris in 1555.

Inspiration for monsters in the Hardwick portrait come from a variety of sources, one of them probably Sebastian Munster's *Cosmographia*. This first appeared in 1544 and then in more profusely illustrated volumes — there were thirty-three editions before 1600. By the 1590s there would have been copies in many English libraries. There were other map-makers at work as well, who put these decorative sea monsters in their oceans. Dr John Dee wrote in 1570 'Some, to beautify their Halls, Parlors, Chambers, Galeries, Studies or Libraries . . . liketh, loveth, getteth and useth, Maps, Charts, and Geographicall Globes',[76] so the Elizabethan embroiderer would have been able to copy from them quite easily. A whale spouting at the bottom of a navigation chart, or an animal similar to it (Fig. 136) must have been the inspiration for the creature in the middle of the Queen's petticoat, in the Hardwick portrait (Fig. 129). Conrad Gesner's *Historia Animalium* appeared in 1551. It is difficult to know if he copied his sea beasts from Munster, or the other way round, without comparing complete runs of the editions of both books.

Many slips of flowers are worked on the Queen's petticoat in the Hardwick portrait. Embroiderers made designs from books illustrated with engravings of plants, of which John Gerard's *Herball*, printed in 1597, is probably one of the best known,[77] and in addition to this there were all the real flowers in Elizabethan gardens to provide a living copy for embroidery

designs. As well as interesting shapes and colours, the symbolism of flowers was, no doubt, borne in mind. The meanings, among them the white lily for purity and 'rosemary, that's for remembrance: pray, love, remember; and there is pansies, that's for thoughts',[78] were familiar to sixteenth-century embroiderers. More obvious symbols than these, the Tudor rose and the French fleur-de-lis, or flower-de-luce, are embroidered on the Queen's sleeves in the Williamsburg portrait (Fig. 186).

Slips of flowers were often embroidered separately, then cut out and mounted on a larger piece of material, as well as being embroidered directly as part of a carefully arranged design (Figs 133 and 137). In this example it appears that a domestic embroideress later added small items, including caterpillars, butterflies, fish, dogs, stags, frogs, squirrels, dragonflies, and rowing boats with their occupants, between the original slips of flowers which were probably worked by a professional embroiderer. The original effect must have resembled the petticoat worn by Elizabeth Vernon (Fig. 138). The embroidery, on finely ribbed white silk with a secondary weft of silver metal strip, termed 'silver chamblet' in the sixteenth century, is from Bacton Parish Church, Hereford.[79] At one time it was cut up for a communion table cover and parts are pieced together from small scraps. It dates from the last decade of the sixteenth or the early years of the seventeenth century.

The material may originally have been a petticoat or forepart, but no crease marks can be detected, as the silk is very fragile, close to disintegration, and kept in a frame behind glass

Nil penna, sed usus.

To. Pr.   Dr.

137   *One section of a panel of white ribbed silk with an additional weft of silver threads, embroidered with polychrome silks, said to have belonged to Blanche Parry. It was used as an altar cloth. c. 1590–1600. The Church of St Faith, Bacton*

138   *'Elizabeth Vernon, Countess of Southampton'. Detail from Figure 164, panel painting by an unknown artist, c. 1600. The Duke of Buccleuch and Queensberry, KT, Boughton House, Kettering, Northamptonshire*

139   *Emblem of an ostrich, from 'A Choice of Emblemes' by Geffrey Whitney. 1586. Victoria and Albert Museum, London*

for protection. The slips of flowers are worked so that they lie in rows with heads towards one selvedge. If viewed in this way, as if they were growing, there would be a selvedge join running round the body when made up or the petticoat would not be long enough. However, without all the pieces, it is impossible to conjecture the original shape of the garment. The embroidery is said to have belonged to Blanche Parry, who died on 12 February 1590 and is buried at Bacton. Perhaps it was one of Elizabeth's petticoats given for use in the church after Blanche's death, possibly after the death of the Queen, although there is no documentary evidence to support this suggestion. However, there are examples of ecclesiastical vestments and furnishings made from fashionable clothes worn by royalty and nobility still preserved today in cathedrals, churches, and museums.

Some of the other motifs on the petticoat in the Hardwick portrait have been taken from emblem books, although they are not quite such straight copies as the examples on the embroidered panel 'The Shepherd's Buss' at the Victoria and Albert Museum.[80] On the left side of the skirt, below the tassel

hanging from the cushion, is an ostrich. This appears in Whitney's book with its head turned to the right (Fig. 139), accompanied by the motto 'Nil penna, sed usus' and the verses:

> The Hippocrites, that make so great a showe,
> Of sanctitie, and of Religion sounde,
> Are shaddowes meere, and with out substance goe,
> And beinge tri'de, are but dissemblers found.
>   Theise are compar'de unto the Ostriche faire,
>   Whoe spreades her winges, yet sealdome tries the aire.[81]

Whether this was intended as a symbolic message to the Queen or if, as seems more likely in this particular case, it was simply a matter of using an interesting picture as a source for an embroidery motif, is uncertain.

This portrait is probably one of three of Elizabeth recorded at Hardwick Hall in 1601.[82] It is possible that the elaborate embroidery was carried out by the Countess of Shrewsbury, Bess of Hardwick, who was a notable needlewoman. It may have been a New Year's gift to Elizabeth, perhaps made up by William Jones, the Queen's tailor. The Hardwick accounts show a payment of £50 to him in 1601.[83] It may not be too fanciful to suppose that Bess wanted to keep a record of her work for posterity, and commissioned the portrait for this reason. The jewel attached to the girdle with a red ribbon in this portrait is of a similar design to the 'Jewell of golde lyke a Pyramides sett with Saphyers one Rubye one small diamonde triangled and three small pearles' presented to the Queen in 1595, which was later given to Mr Killigrew's daughter.[84] There are several jewels of this design recorded, presumably inspired by Whitney's *A Choice of Emblemes* (Fig. 151).

140 The 'Rainbow' portrait of Queen Elizabeth I, by an unknown artist, c. 1603. By courtesy of the Marquess of Salisbury, Hatfield House

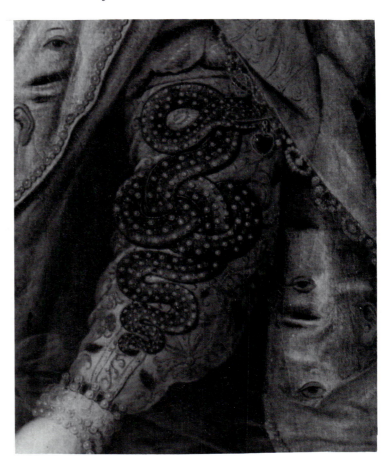

140a Detail of jewel in Figure 140

Embroidery and jewels in the 'Rainbow' and other portraits

It has been suggested that the clothes and jewels in the 'Rainbow' portrait (Fig. 140) painted around 1603, have little concern with plain fact.[85] However, a detailed study of the picture shows that the painter observed each item very carefully. The Queen wears a fairly long-waisted jacket embroidered with flowers and what may be an Irish mantle,[86] loosely draped round her waist on the right side, falling over her left shoulder. One side of the mantle is made of some type of light silk woven with a fine silver stripe and the other an orange-gold silk, probably satin, upon which numerous eyes and ears appear to be stained (i.e., painted) rather than embroidered. On her left sleeve are three pieces of jewellers' work linked together; a twisted serpent, with a red, heart-shaped jewel hanging from its mouth, and an armillary sphere above the head. This celestial sphere represents the heavens, with the band of the Zodiac encircling it; Elizabeth wears armillary spheres as earrings in the Ditchley portrait (Fig. 79). The serpent may be the 'Jewell of golde like a Snake wound togeather garnished with small Opalls and Rubies' listed in the Stowe inventory in 1600.[87] The Queen's hair is arranged with long curls hanging down to her shoulders as described by de Maisse in 1597.[88] It is shown arranged in this fashion by Hilliard in a miniature dating from about 1595–1600 (Fig. 69), where she also wears a small ruff beneath the chin similar to that in the 'Rainbow' portrait. One of 'three paire of Chynne ruffs of Lawne' given to the Queen at the New Year in

1599 by Abraham Speckard, a silkman,[89] may have been used in the latter picture. In her right hand Elizabeth holds the rainbow which gives the portrait its name.

The symbolism of the 'Rainbow' portrait has been interpreted in different ways by René Graziani and Frances Yates. Graziani sees professions of religious faith in the rainbow, the serpent and the eyes and ears on the mantle.[90] Dr Yates finds rather more likely links with Cesare Ripa's *Iconologia*,[91] the eyes, ears, and mouths on the Queen's mantle symbolizing her 'Fame', although as the creases in the satin give a misleading appearance of mouths, there are, in fact, only eyes and ears. They may still signify 'Fame', but another possible symbol for Elizabeth, also depicted in *Iconologia*, is 'Ragione di Stato', 'Reason or Interest of State', or perhaps 'The Art of Government':[92] 'She is represented in a garment of turquoise woven with eyes and ears to symbolise her jealous hold over her dominion, and her desire to have the eyes and ears of spies, the better to judge her own plans and foil those of others' (Fig. 141). This seems apt for Elizabeth. Dr Yates relates other symbols to *Iconologia* and Pierio Valeriano's *Hieroglyphica*; the combination of the serpent and the armillary sphere on the left sleeve represents 'Intelligenza', reflecting the Queen's wisdom in both heavenly and earthly matters, with the heart of 'Consiglio', 'Counsel', which comes from the heart and is necessary for making a wise choice.[93]

Both the jeweller who made the serpent and the painter who decorated the mantle may have been directed to use the symbols in *Iconologia* for their designs. Although it would have been easier to work from the illustrated edition which was printed in Rome in 1603, and the portrait may date from

141   *The figure of 'Ragione di Stato' from 'Iconologia' by Cesare Ripa, 1603. British Library, London*

142   *'An unknown lady called Arabella Stuart', by an unknown artist. She wears the serpent jewel with a heart hanging from its mouth shown on Elizabeth's sleeve in the 'Rainbow' portrait. c. 1605–10. Present whereabouts unknown*

that year, possibly being completed after the Queen's death, there are full descriptions in the first edition, which appeared in 1593. The twisted serpent jewel was apparently given away after it was checked in the Stowe inventory in 1604, as it appears on the left sleeve of an unknown lady who was painted at about that time (Fig. 142). The artist has varied the shape slightly, but the jewel is the same size in relation to the arm in both pictures. The minor differences seem to be due to the artist's interpretation.

The fantastic head-dress, copied from the 'Sponsa Thessaloniciensis' in Boissard's *Habitus variarum orbis gentium* has a jewelled crown with a crescent moon fitted into it. Frances Yates suggests that this indicates Elizabeth's role as Diana, the moon-goddess, the Virgin Queen, and that the picture records Elizabeth's presence on some occasion when allegories in her honour were presented by various personages and were later summed up in a composite portrait of herself.[94] The Queen may, however, have worn parts of the ensemble, if not the whole of it, herself. If we take the component pieces separately — large open ruff, small closed ruff, wired veil, embroidered jacket — each item could be worn as part of her ordinary dress. Although the eyes and ears on the mantle may seem somewhat

theatrical, as if the garment had been specially designed for a masque, the Queen did have other clothes embroidered and stained with similar motifs. The mantle might have been a gift bearing a symbolical message from a loyal subject. Eyes appear as motifs worked on an embroidered New Year's gift in 1581: 'By the Barroness Shandowes Dowager a paire of Slippers of carnacion vellat enbraudered withe a border of perle and handes and Eyes enbraydered'.[95]

One interesting feature of the dress in the 'Rainbow' portrait is the absence of a farthingale to support the petticoat concealed beneath the mantle. It may be conjectured that this is because the costume was specially designed for a masque or, possibly, that not all the parts of the ensemble were arranged for the portrait painter. The hairstyle, wired veil and other details of the dress make it unlikely that the portrait would have been painted after the farthingale had gone out of fashion, and there is no sign of any later alteration to the mantle at waist level.

Another version of the 'Rainbow' portrait, known only from a photograph (Fig. 143) might at first appear to be simply an unskilful copy, leaving out the fantastic head-dress, rainbow and serpent. The picture has also apparently been cleaned

143 'Queen Elizabeth I'. Panel painting by an unknown artist, c. 1603. The Queen is in the same pose as the 'Rainbow' portrait, but wears a jacket of woven patterned silk with guards embroidered with eyes and stylized flowers. Present whereabouts unknown

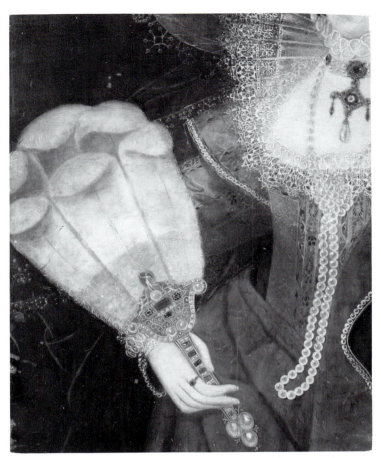

143a Detail of fan and guards embroidered with eyes and stylized flowers beneath the rope of pearls in Figure 143

and restored. However, there are several interesting details which show that this painter too probably had access to some items in the Wardrobe of Robes. The Queen seems to be wearing a very small French farthingale, or hip roll, although this cannot be seen. The mantle is apparently of velvet, lined with silk upon which there are faint traces of a woven linear pattern. The jacket is made of silk with a woven lozenge design; embroidered guards, or bands of decoration, one wide bordered by two narrow, are mounted at the centre front and on the sleeves over the front seams. The wide band is embroidered with stylized flowers; the narrow bands are embroidered with eyes linked by a continuous curving line. Although this might seem an unlikely motif for embroidery, we have already seen that it was used on a pair of slippers. A surviving bias strip of aubergine satin 5.7 cm (2¼″) wide in the Victoria and Albert Museum (Fig. 144) shows what the band on this jacket might have looked like. It is embroidered with weeping eyes, arrows through hearts, leaves, flowers, and caterpillars. French knots are worked all over the design and along the folded edges of the band. These borders are clipped, or 'snipped at thedges', as it was described in contemporary accounts. The gloves, with cuffs embroidered with cornucopia and flowers, have been carefully observed, but perhaps the fan deserves even more attention. The lower part of the handle is the same as that depicted in the Yale portrait (Fig. 32) but incorporated into the top of the handle, immediately below the feathers, is the jewel the Queen holds in her fingers in that picture (Figs 143a and 145). Perhaps the painter copied the

details from the Yale portrait, but there is plenty of evidence that jewels were altered and gems recut and reset; the square, table-cut diamonds, one on each side of the ruby in the jewel, have been recut with facets before being mounted on the fan. Cutting gems with facets is an early seventeenth-century development, the first signs of which are seen towards the end of the 1580s.[96]

If the 'Rainbow' portrait is a record of the Queen's appearance at a masque, it may have taken place when she visited Sir Thomas Egerton, the Lord Keeper, at Harefield Place in July 1602. She was offered a poem, 'the humble petition of a guiltless Lady, delivered upon Munday morninge when the [robe] of rainebowes was presented to the Queen by the Lady Walsingham'.[97] In it, St Swithin apologized for the wet weather and explained that it was the fault of Iris:

> From her her rayneie robes he tooke
> Which heere he doth present to you
> It is fitt it should with you remaine
> For you know better how to raine
> Yet if it raine still as before
> St Swythin praies that you would guesse,
> That Iris doth more roabes possesse.
> And that you should blame him no more.

The motto 'Non sine sole Iris', 'No rainbow without the sun', with Elizabeth holding a rainbow, does suggest that the picture may have been painted shortly after this visit to Harefield, possibly commissioned by Sir Thomas Egerton to commemorate the occasion. The head-dress and mantle may have been

144   *Detail of aubergine satin guards embroidered with weeping eyes, leaves, flowers, and caterpillars in satin stitch, couched cord, and French knots in polychrome silks, c. 1600. Victoria and Albert Museum, London (T.378A–1976)*

145   *Detail of jewel worn by Queen Elizabeth I in Figure 32, c. 1570–85. The Elizabethan Club of Yale University*

worn in a masque which took place then, and Sir Thomas may also have given Elizabeth the jewelled serpent, although no record of the gift seems to have been preserved.

The rainbow appears in Paradin's *Heroicall Devises* with the motto 'The raine bow doth bring faire weather', and this text: 'The most faire and bountifull queene of France Katherine used the signe of the rainebow for her armes, which is an infallible signe of peaceable calmenes and tranquillitie'.[98] The rainbow is used as an embroidery motif on many of Elizabeth's gowns and may be seen on one surviving fragment of a smock (Fig. 146) which is of high quality and may well have belonged to the Queen. Here the rainbow appears with clouds, apparently with raindrops below. This, however, may show the partial use of an emblem from Paradin's book, where manna is shown falling from the clouds to outstretched hands beneath, with the motto 'Not those things which are upon the earth'.[99]

The Queen wears a jewelled gauntlet pinned to her ruff in Figure 140 which Frances Yates suggests may possibly relate the 'Rainbow' portrait to some ceremonial tilt in which Queen Elizabeth's knights showed their prowess in honour of 'the most royall queene or empresse'.[100] This may be so, or the jewel may be that given to Elizabeth at the New Year in 1582 by Sir Thomas Perrot: 'Item, one gauntlet of golde, garnished with smale seede perles, and sparcks of diamounds'.[101] Another jewel which she might have chosen to wear for her portrait, as an alternative to the gauntlet, was a 'Jewell of golde like a Rainebow and the sunne over yt garnished with sparkes of Dyomondes', given to her at the New Year in 1597.[102]

Symbolism in embroidery designs in other late sixteenth- and early seventeenth-century portraits

The use of symbolism in embroidery during the sixteenth century was not, of course, confined solely to Elizabeth's gowns. Hidden meanings in designs, some taken from emblem books, for embroidery on furnishings worked by Mary, Queen of Scots, are fully discussed by Margaret Swain in *The Needlework of Mary Queen of Scots*. The cloth of estate,

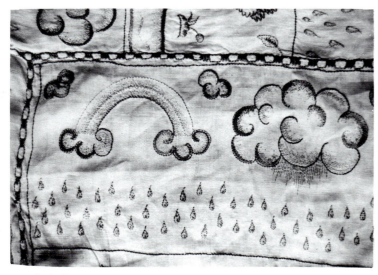

146 *Detail from a white linen smock embroidered with polychrome silks in a design incorporating rainbows and flowers. c. 1585–1600. Whitworth Art Gallery, Manchester*

147 *Detail of embroidery incorporating the ragged staff, the Earl of Leicester's badge, seen in Figure 196, the portrait of Lettice Knollys, Countess of Leicester. Painting attributed to George Gower, c. 1585. Reproduced by kind permission of the Marquess of Bath, Longleat House, Warminster, Wiltshire*

148 *A lady said to be Eleanor Verney, Mrs William Palmer, the Queen's god-daughter. Panel painting attributed to Sir William Segar, c. 1590. The Collection at Parham Park*

under which Mary sat to receive Nicholas White in 1569, bore the embroidered motto 'En Ma Fin Gît Ma Commencement' from Marie de Guise's impresa of the phoenix rising from the flames — also used by Elizabeth. However, Mary does not appear to have worked on — or worn — gowns with emblems incorporated in the design of the embroidery. This fashion seems to have developed in the 1580s. Lettice Knollys for example has ragged staves, the Earl of Leicester's badge, embroidered all over her black gown (Fig. 147) in her portrait painted around 1585, but there are a few portraits of ladies wearing clothes embroidered with motifs which seem more appropriate for Elizabeth, dating from the 1580s onwards. We may be looking at items of the Queen's clothing in portraits other than her own without realizing it. A surviving day book records numerous gowns given to ladies-in-waiting and others between 1561 and 1585.[103] The warrants for the Wardrobe of Robes list many others from 1585 until the end of the reign. Several of the items in the Stowe inventory were given away after 1600, and the names noted in the margin. Unfortunately the records are incomplete and the gifts cannot be linked conclusively with the portraits. However, it may be conjectured that any lady who received a piece of beautifully embroidered clothing once worn by the Queen might well decide to have a portrait painted to display the gift.

A lady said to be Eleanor Verney, Mrs William Palmer, the Queen's god-daughter, painted around 1585–90[104] (Fig. 148) wears a black velvet gown with sleeves embroidered all over with pillars of seed pearl surrounded with cinques of pearls, similar to descriptions of those embroidered for Elizabeth, although none can be positively identified as not enough details are given. The motif was taken from the emblem of the pillars of Hercules in Paradin's book, where it appears with the motto 'Hee conceiveth hope to proceed further'.[105] Mrs

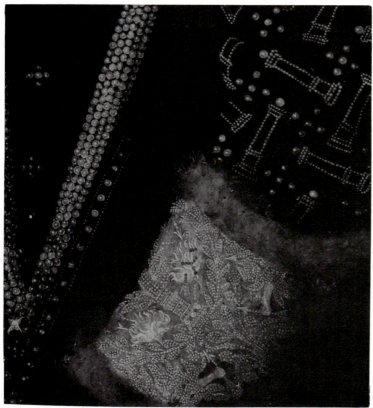

148a   *Detail of ruff from Figure 148*

148b   *Detail of muff and embroidered pillars from Figure 148*

149   *'Frances Clinton, Lady Chandos', by Hieronimo Custodis, 1589. Her doublet and forepart are embroidered with pearls in a design of butterflies and altars. By kind permission of the Marquess of Tavistock, and the Trustees of the Bedford Estates, Woburn Abbey*

Palmer's ruff is embroidered in black and white silk with ragged staves and spotted serpents. This and the muff may also have been gifts originally presented to the Queen. The muff is lined with russet coloured fur and heavily embroidered with seed pearls in a design of wreaths of leaves and a pillar with leaves growing from it, possibly adapted from Whitney's *A Choice of Emblemes* (Fig. 151). Flames of fire are carried out in red and yellow silk, with two crossed arrows on top, worked in seed pearl. A hand holding an arrow is worked on each side below. A hand with a sword in Paradin's book is accompanied by the motto 'Without all falsehood or deceipt'.[106]

Frances Clinton, Lady Chandos, painted in 1589 by Custodis (Fig. 149), wears a gown embroidered with seed pearls in a design of butterflies and altars. This again is similar to gowns embroidered for the Queen listed in the Stowe and Folger inventories. The motifs were probably embroidered separately and mounted in the same way as some pillars and 'esses' from one of Elizabeth's gowns: John Parr was employed in 'stichinge downe the pillers and esses of gold upon the traine and bodies of a gowne of clothe of silver' early in 1593 and in 'rippinge of[f] Certaine Pillers from a peire of Slevis for a gowne of cloth of silver and new setting them on Againe' later in the same year.[107] These pillars, like those on Mrs William Palmer's gown, were probably taken from the emblem of the pillars of Hercules.

The portrait of an unknown lady at Cowdray Park (Fig. 150) shows a petticoat which may have been a New Year's gift embroidered by the donor; the design seems to be domestic rather than professional work. It is similar to one listed in the Stowe inventory: 'Item one Peticoate of white Satten embroidered allover like peramydes and flowers of venice golde and silke'.[108] New Year's gifts from the last three years of the reign were not entered in the Stowe and Folger

inventories and only the final Roll survives.[109] In this Roll there are fifty-one items of richly embroidered clothing, many of which have similar motifs used for the embroidery. Once again Whitney's *A Choice of Emblemes* provided the source of inspiration for the design (Fig. 151). The spire or 'pyramid', as it was also described, was the emblem of the Cardinal of Lorraine — and Paradin shows it in his book, where the ivy and the 'four-squared pillar' represents the bishop clinging to his faith. Whitney has changed the meaning of the Cardinal of Lorraine's emblem, as may be seen by the poem beneath:

A mighty spyre, whose toppe doth pierce the skie,
An ivie greene imbraceth rounde about,
And while it stands, the same doth bloome on high
But when it shrinkes, the ivie standes in dowt:
The Piller great, our gracious Prince is:
The braunche, the Churche: whoe speakes unto hir this

I that of late with stormes was almost spent,
And brused sore with Tirants bluddie bloes,
Whome fire and sworde, with persecution rent
Am nowe sett free, and overlooke my foes,
And whiles thou raignst, oh most renowned Queene
By thie supporte my blossome shall bee greene.

After Anne of Denmark's death in 1619, James 'caused to be perticulerly inventoried . . . with Intent to have the same soulde for our best Advantage', among other things, 'Remnantes of Stuffes of sondry kindes, olde Robes and Garmentes of former Queenes of this Realme with divers other thinges belonging unto our sade late Deere Consort'. These were of

150   *Unknown lady wearing a gown embroidered with an emblem seen in Figure 151, painting by an unknown artist. c. 1603. The Viscount Cowdray, Cowdray Park*

150a   *Detail of embroidery from Figure 150*

151   *An emblem, variously described as a spire, pillar, obelisk, and pyramid, from 'A Choice of Emblemes' by Geffrey Whitney. 1586. Victoria and Albert Museum, London*

152 *'Portrait of an unknown lady', attributed to Marcus Gheeraerts the Younger, c. 1605–10. She wears a white silk doublet with red ribbon points at the waist and a red velvet petticoat with a covering of what is possibly 'mezza mandolina', a type of netting, in a design of cobwebs. The flounce is arranged with red ribbon points at the edge, probably hiding pins below. Norton Simon Foundation, Pasadena, California*

152a *Detail from Figure 152*

153 *'Lady Julius Caesar', by an unknown artist, c. 1610. She wears a richly embroidered petticoat beneath her gown. Present whereabouts unknown*

small value 'and not fytt to be by Us preserved.' Any of the 'Appearall Robbes and other furniture of our late Deere Consort, as weare by her used and worne in her Lyfe tyme, and are not nowe meete to be by Us kepte and preserved', were to be disposed of among the 'Ladies and others as served or attended upon our said late Consort'.[110]

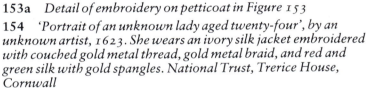

153a   *Detail of embroidery on petticoat in Figure 153*

154   *'Portrait of an unknown lady aged twenty-four', by an
unknown artist, 1623. She wears an ivory silk jacket embroidered
with couched gold metal thread, gold metal braid, and red and
green silk with gold spangles. National Trust, Trerice House,
Cornwall*

155   *White satin panel, probably from a petticoat, embroidered
in polychrome silks with a lion, trees, birds, an armillary sphere,
cherubs, a castle, spiders, flies, and other insects. c. 1600. Victoria
and Albert Museum, London (T.138–1981)*

It is also clear that any of Elizabeth's gowns which had
passed into Anne of Denmark's wardrobe may have been given
to ladies-in-waiting at any time from 1603 to 1619. An
unknown lady painted in about 1610 (Fig. 152) wears a
covering over her red velvet petticoat which is not unlike a
description in the Stowe inventory of 1600: 'Item, one mantle
of white network diamondwise wrought like small cobwebb
roundell work laid with silver plate'. A mantle could easily
have been adapted to cover a skirt.

Lady Julius Caesar[111] (Fig. 153) wears a richly decorated
gown very similar in line to that in the portrait of a *Lady called
Elizabeth of Bohemia*, which is dated 1612.[112] Beneath it can
be seen a tantalizing glimpse of an elaborately embroidered
petticoat which may once have belonged to Queen Elizabeth.
A white satin petticoat in the Stowe inventory of 1600,
'embroidered allover with Rockes, fishes and such like with a
broade border like cloudes Seas fishes and Rockes',[113] is
similar in design, but Lady Caesar's petticoat also includes
castles and the sun.

One last portrait, not of Elizabeth, but of an unknown
lady aged 29, painted in 1623, shows a rather strangely

embroidered jacket (Fig. 154). The design was obviously not drawn out to fit the pattern shapes. It may not be too fanciful to suppose that this could be one of Elizabeth's petticoats translated. A surviving white satin panel, probably for a skirt, shows how the ovals on the front bodice might originally have been placed (Fig. 155). The Stowe and Folger inventories, the warrants for the Wardrobe of Robes, and the New Year's Gift Rolls have provided much information but more is needed in the form of correspondence and diaries, with personal reminiscences about the Queen's embroidered gowns. It is perhaps surprising that so much material about the Wardrobe of Robes and the contents should have survived and there may well be more to be discovered.

Colour symbolism

Colour symbolism in Elizabethan England has been discussed extensively by M. C. Linthicum in *Costume in the Drama of Shakespeare and his Contemporaries*[114] and only a brief account drawn from the same sources is given here. Certain meanings had already been associated with colours from earliest times: white with purity; black with darkness, constancy, woe and death; red with blood, denoting power; yellow with the sun, thence warmth and fruitfulness; green with spring, denoting youth and hopefulness; brown with the dying year and despair; grey with winter and barrenness. These associations were adapted early in the Christian era to symbolize Christian beliefs. Thus, for example, white came to represent purity of the soul, while red was for the blood of Christ, thence justice and mercy.

By the sixteenth century heraldry had done a great deal to consolidate the association of various colours with virtues and vices. Early treatises on blazonry were limited to the colours borne in arms, but widening interest in the subject gradually increased the range until all colours were included to symbolize abstract concepts such as envy, fame, honour, and prudence. Morality plays, masques, and pageants all helped to make colour symbolism familiar to ordinary people.[115]

The most widely-read early book on colour-symbolism, written under the name of Sicile, Herald of Alphonso V, King of Aragon, dates from the early sixteenth century.[116] A copy of the first edition has not yet been traced, but one of the eight known French editions is dated 1528 in what seems to be the sixth edition, titled *Le Blason des couleurs en Armes Livrees et devises*. There were Italian translations published in 1565, 1593 and 1595. An English translation by R(ichard) R(obinson), *A Rare True and Proper Blazon of Colours and Ensignes Military with theyre Peculiar Signification . . . translated oute of a little French Booke printed at Paris 1546*, was published in 1583.

As Linthicum points out, the influence of Sicile's book must have been widespread. His work was mainly drawn from traditional meanings of colour symbolism, but Rabelais accused him of attributing some meanings on his own authority.[117] Fulvio Pellegrino Morato's *Del significato de'colori* was published in 1535. This book does not cover the blazoning of arms and is based on references from the Bible, Homer, Virgil, Plautus, Ovid, Petrarch, and the author's own Italian contemporaries. It was reprinted in 1545 and then, after Morato's death in 1547, in 1551, 1559, 1564, 1584, 1586, 1593, and 1599. Morato's colour symbolism agrees fairly closely with that of Sicile with the exception of green, ash, incarnate, and turquoise. Briefly, in Sicile's treatise, white

showed faith, chastity, and humility; black, grief and constancy; obscure grey, patience; bright grey, despair; ash, trouble and sadness; silver, purity; yellow, hope, joy, magnanimity; russet, prudence; yellow-red, deception; green, love, joy; blue, amity; turquoise, jealousy; perse (bluish grey) knowledge; red, prowess; vermilion, courage. Morato's green is obscure or willow green, denoting grief and misery, and he explains that throughout the ages turquoise had symbolized contemplation and elevated thought before its association with jealousy.[118] Sicile also gives various colour combinations, for example, white and black denote grief; white and blue courtesy; white and green, virtuous youth; white and grey, hope of coming to perfection; white and tawny, patience in adversity; blue and violet, loyalty in love.[119]

Coronato Occolti's *Trattato di Colori* published in 1557, followed by a second edition in 1568, gave some similar meanings to Sicile and Morato but there were several differences: for example obscure grey denoted lack of firmness, deceit and death of good instead of patience; vermilion denoted scorn and wrath instead of courage. Occolti also gave meanings for various colour combinations.[120] Ludovico Dolce's *Dialogo nel quale si ragiona delle qualita diversita e proprieta dei colori*, published in 1565, gives much the same material as Morato, with some extra colours. His work was known and copied in England. Giovanni Rinaldi's *Il Mostrovissimo Mostro*, drawing largely on the earlier writers, was printed in Ferrara and Venice in 1584 and 1592, 1593, 1599, and 1626.

There were no books solely on colour symbolism produced in England, but the works of Italian writers must have been familiar to many. Gerard Legh's *Accedens of Armory* published in 1562 covers the blazoning of arms and discusses the symbolism of the seven colours used in blazonry both separately and in combination with others.[121] Sir John Ferne's *Blazon of Gentrie*, published in 1586, follows Legh's symbolism, but also attributes colours to the seven ages of man: white to infancy, azure to juveniles of 7–14 years, yellow to adolescents of 14–20 years, green to 'lusty green youth' of 20–30 years, vermilion to virility of 30–40 years, purple to 'grey hairs' of 40–70 years and black to old age.

Elizabeth and her courtiers would have been familiar with this language of colours. At a masque in July 1564 she told Don Diego Guzman da Silva, the Spanish Ambassador, of her preference for black and white, saying 'These are my colours'.[122] As they represented eternal virginity (white for chastity and black for constancy, according to Sicile, although he also gave the meaning of grief to a combination of black and white) it would seem that in spite of anxiety about the succession at this time, the Queen was already determined to remain single. The symbolism was presumably understood by the Spanish Ambassador.

It would, however, be a mistake to think of Elizabeth as always in black and white. Many other colours are listed in the Stowe and Folger inventories. An analysis of the loose gowns in the Stowe inventory, for example, shows that, although there were twenty-three white and twenty-two black gowns, there were also nine tawny, eight ash colour and one of ash or dove colour, seven of carnation in varying shades, four each of orange and peach, three of russet, two each of crimson, hair colour and purple, and one each of bee colour, clay, drake's colour, horse-flesh, lady's blush, maiden's blush, murrey, partridge, and straw. The French gowns in the Stowe inventory also show a considerable range of colours, with black predominating: there are thirty-nine black gowns, about twenty of cloth of gold, cloth of silver, or gold and silver camlets (in shades varying from black, white, and ash to carnation, orange, peach, pink, purple, and tawny), twelve white, eight hair colour, five tawny, two each of ash, carnation, orange, and russet and one each of horseflesh, Isabella, murrey, and peach. In the Folger inventory there are another eleven black French gowns, three of cloth of gold or silver, three of ash and two each of white, hair colour, paul, russet, and tawny.

Much could be conveyed by the wearing of a particular colour, often confined to favours or knots of ribbons, providing that the wearer's meaning was interpreted correctly. Shirley satirized the use of 'such variety of Ribbands every day' in *Captain Underwit*:

DEVICE: Your colours to an understanding Lover carry the interpretation of the heart as plainly as we express our meaning one to another in characters. Shall I decipher my colours to you now? Here is Azure and Peach. Azure is constant and Peach is love; which signifies my constant affection.

SISTER: This is very pretty.

DEVICE: Oh, it saves the trouble of writing, where the Mistress and Servant are learned in this amorous blazon. Yesterday I wore Folimort, Grisdelin, and Isabella. Folimort is withered, Grisdelin is absent, and Isabella is beauty, which put together, express I did wither and languish for your absent beautie.

SISTER: But is there any reason for these distinctions?

DEVICE: Yes, Lady: for example, your Folimort is a withered leafe, which doth moralize a decay; your yellow is joy, because—

SISTER: Why, yellow, Sir, is Jealous.

DEVICE: No, your Lemon colour, a pale kind of yellow is Jealous. Your yellow is perfect joy. Your white is Death; your milk white, innocence; your black, mourning; your orange, spiteful; your flesh colour, lascivious; your maide's blush, envied; your red is defiance; your gold is avaritious; your straw, plenty; your green, hope; your sea-greene, inconstant; your violet, religion; your willow, forsaken.[123]

As we see here, some different interpretations are given from those in Sicile and Morato's books where red, for example, symbolized prowess. White obviously did not symbolize death

for Elizabeth and it seems unlikely, if orange signified spite to all the world, that Sir Francis Walsingham would have presented her with an orange-tawny satin French gown in 1584.[124] Elizabeth herself chose orange for a satin round gown in 1590[125] and there are many other orange French gowns, round gowns, foreparts, and petticoats recorded in the Stowe and Folger inventories. Presumably the accepted meaning of orange and orange-tawny at the English Court at this time was 'a certainty of nobleness of mind or high courage', the attribution found in Occolti's book.[126] Sea-green symbolized a changeable nature and inconstancy: perhaps neither the widowed Countess of Lincoln nor Mr Wolley, one of the Queen's secretaries, was aware of the meaning, as they each presented gifts of beautifully embroidered sea-water green satin petticoats at the New Year in 1588.[127] There may, however, have been a sudden fashion for the colour at this time, and the meaning was disregarded.

Although some of the clothes in the Stowe and Folger inventories would have had colour significance, particularly when they were gifts from friends and courtiers seeking to convey good wishes or climb the ladder of preferment, other colours were doubtless chosen because they were fashionable or because the Queen's women suggested them. Lady Sussex, for example, advised the Countess of Shrewsbury to present Elizabeth with a watchet satin cloak and safeguard as a New Year's gift because she had no garments of that colour already and 'she hathe sondery garmentes off as[h] coullore all Rede and begenes to be wery off the coullore'.[128] Ash colour was certainly popular with the Queen, and the Countess of Shrewsbury was anxious to please: neither Elizabeth nor the Countess appears to have worried about Morato's meaning of 'a disposition to deceive' for ash colour.[129] Lady Sussex was presumably not thinking of 'fayned stedfastenesse'[130] when she suggested watchet satin be used for the cloak and safeguard. She was concerned only to suggest an attractive alternative colour which the Queen would like, and the gift was certainly very well received.[131]

It is possible that the clothes worn by the Queen for masques, for appearances on Progresses, at ceremonies such as the Accession Day Tilts and on other public occasions would have been chosen with colour significance in mind. At other times any symbolism was probably confined to the embroidery motifs on her clothes and jewels worn with them.

Notes

1 Quoted in *Jenkins, Eliz. Great*, p. 317.
2 *D'Ewes*, p. 473.
3 *Arnold, 'Sweet England's Jewels'*, pp. 31–40.
4 BL, Stowe 559, f. 21.
5 BL. Royal App. 68, f. 6.
6 *Ibid.*, f. 11.
7 Noted by Anna Somers Cocks in *Princely Magnificence*, p. 106.
8 Several examples are given in *Progr. Eliz.*, I, p. 324 (list of jewels given at the New Year 1573), p. 381 (list of jewels given at the New Year 1574).
9 *Ibid.*, p. 380.
10 *Arnold, 'Sweet England's Jewels'*, p. 39.
11 See Chapter II, notes 88–94.
12 BL, Add. 5751A, ff. 256–57.
13 For a description of this treasure see *Arnold, 'Sweet England's Jewels'*, pp. 31–36, 39.
14 BL, Add. 46,348, f. 154.

15 Neville Williams, *Henry VIII and His Court* (1973 edn.), p. 178.
16 *Progr. Eliz.*, I, p. 295.
17 BL, Stowe 559, f. 59ᵛ.
18 *Arnold, 'Sweet England's Jewels'*, pp. 39, 40.
19 *Yates, Astraea*, p. 29.
20 *Progr. Eliz.*, II, p. 499. 'Crowe' may possibly be 'crowne'.
21 Quoted in *Jenkins, Eliz. and Leicester*, p. 200.
22 Mario Praz, *Studies in 17th Century Imagery* (1964, 2nd rev. edn.).
23 BL, Add. 5751A, f. 213ᵛ, New Year's list January 1587 and also the Stowe inventory f. 102ᵛ/11.
24 *Whitney*, p. 66.
25 *Paradin* (1563, French edn.), p. 69; (1591, English edn.), p. 145.
26 *Ibid.*, (1563, French edn.), p. 153; (1563, English edn.), p. 162ᵛ; (1591, English edn.), p. 324.
27 *Progr. Eliz.*, II, p. 79. A similar jewel is listed in the Stowe inventory, f. 100/4.

28 *Whitney*, p. 121.

29 Stowe inventory, f. 97/[36].

30 *Whitney*, p. 168. This emblem also appears in *Paradin* (1563 edn.) p. 176, with the motto 'Wit or pollicie excelleth strength'.

31 *Progr. Eliz.*, III, pp. 169–72. Listed in the Stowe inventory, f. 98/61.

32 Joan Evans, *A History of Jewellery 1100–1870* (2nd edn. 1970) p. 117.

33 *Progr. Eliz.*, II, p. 397.

34 *Alciati*, p. 120.

35 *Whitney*, p. 188.

36 New Year's Gift Roll 1579, *Progr. Eliz.*, II, p. 253.

37 *Alciati*, p. 40.

38 *Whitney*, p. 62.

39 *Boissard, Emblematum*, p. 65.

40 For example, New Year's Gift, 1586, *Progr. Eliz.*, II, p. 451.

41 For example, New Year's Gift 1585, ibid., p. 426.

42 For example, BL, Royal App. 68, f. 4ᵛ.

43 Ibid., f. 30ᵛ. and New Year's Gift Roll 1585, Folger, Z. d.16, gift of the Earl of Cumberland.

44 New Year's Gift Roll 1579, *Progr. Eliz.*, II, p. 255.

45 *Whitney*, p. 87.

46 *Paradin*, (1563, French edn.), p. 85ᵛ; (1591, English edn.), p. 110.

47 *Progr. Eliz.*, II, p. 451.

48 *Princely Magnificence*, cat. no. 40, illus. p. 61.

49 Quoted in *Jenkins, Eliz. Great*, p. 315.

50 BL, Royal App. 68, f. 9.

51 BL, Add. 5751A, f. 242.

52 BL, Royal App. 68, f. 33.

53 New Year's Gift Roll 1582, *Progr. Eliz.*, II, p. 389.

54 BL, Royal App. 68, f. 35ᵛ.

55 Ibid., f. 15ᵛ.

56 New Year's Gift Roll 1582, *Progr. Eliz.*, II, p. 387.

57 BL, Royal App. 68, f. 6.

58 BL, Stowe 559, f. 59ᵛ.

59 BL, Royal App. 68, f. 33ᵛ.

60 *Whitney*, p. 137.

61 *Boissard, Emblematum*, p. 25

62 *Progr. Eliz.*, II, p. 289.

63 BL, Royal App. 68, f. 23.

64 *Progr. Eliz.*, II, p. 396.

65 A. F. Kendrick, *English Needlework* (1933), p. 76.

66 *Strong, Portraits*, p. 83.

67 *Cennini*, pp. 103–08.

68 *Merrifield, Treatises*, I, pp. 1–321.

69 *Cennini*, pp. 103–04.

70 Ibid., p. 107.

71 *Merrifield, Treatises*, pp. 1–7.

72 Ibid., pp. 7, 85–86.

73 Ibid., p. 86.

74 Ibid., pp. 88, 90.

75 Stowe inventory f. 19ᵛ/27 and f. 65ᵛ/11.

76 Quoted in R. A. Skelton, *Decorative printed maps of the 15th to the 18th centuries* (1952), p. 1.

77 For further details and illustrations from various herbals see Geoffrey Grigson, *The Englishman's Flora* (1958, 1975); Ann Leighton, *Early English Gardens in New England* (1970), and Clare Putnam, *Flowers and Trees of Tudor England* (1972).

78 Shakespeare, *Hamlet*, Act IV, sc. 5.

79 *Proceedings of the Society of Antiquaries* (1883–84), second series, Vol. 10, no. 1, p. 329.

80 J. L. Nevinson, 'English Domestic Embroidery Patterns of the Sixteenth and Seventeenth Centuries', in *Walpole Society Journal*, XXVIII, 1939–40, p. 1 and *Digby, Eliz. Embroidery*, pp. 46, 105–06, pl. 50.

81 *Whitney*, p. 51.

82 *Strong, Portraits*, pp. 83–84.

83 I am indebted to Mr David Durant for sending me this reference.

84 BL, Add. 5751A, f. 238ᵛ.

85 F. M. Kelly, 'Queen Elizabeth and her Dresses', in *The Connoisseur* CXIII, 1944, p. 71.

86 For Irish mantles see *Arnold, Mantle*, pp. 56–72.

87 Stowe inventory, f. 104/[29].

88 See Chapter I, note 59.

89 New Year's Gift Roll 1599, Folger, Z.d.17.

90 René Graziani, 'The 'Rainbow Portrait' of Queen Elizabeth I and its Religious Symbolism' in *Journal of the Warburg and Courtauld Institutes*, XXXV, 1972, pp. 247–59.

91 *Yates, Astraea*, pp. 216–17.

92 Cesare Ripa, *Iconologia* (1603 edn.), p. 426. I am very grateful to Mr Michael Morgan for translating this passage and suggesting the possible alternative of 'Art of Government' to 'Reason or Interest of State'.

93 *Yates, Astraea*, p. 217.

94 Ibid., pp. 217–19 and *Allegorical Portraits of Queen Elizabeth I at Hatfield House*, Hatfield House Booklet, no. 1, 1952.

95 New Year's Gift Roll 1581, Eton College, BLA 18/192.

96 *Arnold, 'Sweet England's Jewels'*, p. 35.

97 *Progr. Eliz.*, III, pp. 591–93. For payment for rainbow robe see Chapter V, note 10.

98 *Paradin* (1591, English edn.), p. 76.

99 Ibid., p. 65.

100 *Yates, Astraea*, p. 219.

101 *Progr. Eliz.*, II, p. 389, here given as 'Sir Thomas Parrat'.

102 BL. Add. 5751A, f. 243.

103 Printed in *Arnold, 'Lost from HMB'*.

104 Strong, Icon, p. 223. I am indebted to the Collection at Parham Park for the following information from James Wentworth Fitzwilliam, *Parham in Sussex* (1948), pp. 46–48. The painting has two inscriptions on the back (i) '. . . Said to be Eleanor Palmer, daughter of the first Lord Paget of Beaudesert . . . and wife of William Palmer of Parham' and (ii) '. . . Oct. 24, 1836. Lady which appears to be Eleanor Palmer by the inscription on the back of the picture . . .'. William Palmer's wife was in fact Elizabeth Verney and not Eleanor Paget as stated (p. 47). Elizabeth was born at Chislehurst on 2 September 1556 and was named after the Princess who was her godmother (p. 48).

105 *Paradin* (1563, French edn.), p. 18ᵛ; (1591, English edn.), p. 32.

106 *Paradin* (1563, French edn.), p. 56; (1591, English edn.), p. 111.

107 PRO, LC5/36, f. 256, warrant dated 10 May 1593 and f. 261, warrant dated 28 Sept. 1593.

108 Stowe inventory, f. 60/58.

109 PRO, C47/3/41, in preparation for publication.

110 *Foedera*, 7, pt. 3, pp. 112–13 and 117–18. See also *Chambers*, I, p. 210 for Elizabeth's gowns used for masque costumes, and *Anderson*, p. 259, note 404 for sale of royal clothes.

111 I am grateful to Mr Sidney Sabin for drawing my attention to this painting.

112 Illustrated in *Strong, Icon*, p. 293.

113 Stowe inventory, f. 61/79.

114 *Linthicum*, pp. 13–23, for colour symbolism. Ibid., pp. 24–52 for costume colours in the drama.

115 For example see ibid., p. 16 and texts and articles in *Medieval English Theatre* (Lancaster University, 1979–).

116 *Linthicum*, p. 17.

117 Ibid., p. 18.

118 Ibid., p. 19.

119 Ibid., pp. 17–18 for further examples.

120 Ibid., p. 20.

121 Ibid., p. 22.

122 See Chapter I, note 9.

123 Quoted in *Linthicum*, pp. 25–26. The play was given before 1641.

124 Stowe inventory, f. 21ᵛ/54.

125 Folger inventory f. 4ᵛ/[13].

126 *Linthicum*, p. 20.

127 Stowe inventory, f. 58ᵛ/36 and 38.

128 See Chapter V, note 19.

129 *Linthicum*, p. 35.

130 Ibid., p. 16.

131 See Chapter V, note 20.

V

Gifts of Clothing and Jewels

Gifts of clothing and jewels to the Queen

The custom of presenting gifts to the monarch at the New Year had been established in a formal pattern well before Elizabeth's reign. A. J. Collins lists a number of Rolls of New Year's gifts[1] which have survived from the reigns of other Tudor monarchs, Henry VIII, then Edward VI, and Mary, as well as Elizabeth. Members of the nobility, clergy, and senior officials presented the Queen with purses of gold according to their rank and wealth, and she made carefully graded gifts of quantities of silver-gilt plate in return. In 1562,[2] for example, the Archbishop of Canterbury gave £40 and the Bishop of London £20, in half sovereigns, while the Bishop of Exeter presented £10 in angels. The Duke of Norfolk gave £20 'in sundry coynes of golde' and the Earl of Northumberland presented £10 in angels. The ladies gave much less. Lady Butler, for instance, gave £6 in French crowns. All these gifts of money were sent in little purses of coloured silk, velvet, and satin, or of knitted silk and metal thread.

The Earl of Huntingdon recorded the procedure of presenting a New Year's gift to James I very soon after the King had come to the throne. This was, presumably, the way the system had worked throughout Elizabeth's reign:

You must buy a new purse of about v s price, and put thereinto xx peeces of new gold of xx s a piece, and go to the Presence-Chamber, where the Court is, upon New-Yere's day, in the morninge about 8 o'clocke, and deliver the purse and the gold unto my Lord Chamberlin, then you must go down to the Jewell-house for a ticket to receive xviii s vi d as a gift to your paines, and give vi d there to the box for your ticket; then go to Sir William Veall's office, and shew your ticket, and receive your xviii s vi d. Then go to the Jewell-house again, and take a peece of plate of xxx ounces weight and marke it, and then in the afternoone you may go and fetch it away, and then give the Gentleman who delivers it you xl s in gold, and give to the box ii s and to the porter vi d.[3]

Early in Elizabeth's reign there are only a few gifts of jewels and clothing among the purses of gold, mainly from the Queen's close women friends, who would have known her taste. By the 1580s an increasing number of elaborate jewels and exquisitely embroidered clothes, some of which must have been very expensive, are listed in the New Year's Gift Rolls. These were presented by courtiers, the Earl of Leicester and Sir

Christopher Hatton among them. This number continues to rise during the 1590s, presumably because the Queen showed greater signs of appreciation to the donors on receiving these personal gifts, preferring them to purses of gold.

Smaller and less expensive presents were made by courtiers of lower rank and their wives, and also by some of the Queen's servants and tradesmen. At the New Year in 1563, for example, Robert Robotham, Yeoman of the Wardrobe of Robes, presented 'two peire of black silke hose knytt' and Mrs Elizabeth Shelton gave 'fowre peire of Sockes wrought with blak silke'.[4] In 1565 Mrs Dane, wife of William Dane the Queen's linen draper,[5] gave 'clx flowers for pullinges owte of cameryke wrought with venice golde and silver with a partelet and a Coller wrought with like golde & silver',[6] small accessories which would have looked charming worn with a black velvet gown and also shown the quality of the donor's wares. Robert Robotham gave only one pair of knitted black silk stockings in 1568, so perhaps they were far more elaborate than his earlier gifts although no details are given. At the same time Adams, 'Scolemaster to the henchmen', the Queen's pages, presented 'two patrons for slevis drawen upon Cameryke'[7] (Fig. 156). This would have been within the schoolmaster's means, and he may have drawn out the design himself. Perhaps the cost of embroidery was more than he could comfortably afford. The sleeves were probably later embroidered by one of the women attending on the Queen, perhaps Lady Cobham. Small gifts of this type were presented throughout the reign.

Gowns and jewels were given to Elizabeth on many other occasions than at the New Year. The custom of presenting such gifts on her Progresses was often made part of a small ceremony. In September 1592 at Rycote Sir Henry Norris made a speech and presented the Queen with a gown on the first day of her visit. On the Sunday he met Elizabeth in the garden 'with sweete musicke of sundry sorts' and introduced gifts from his sons, each with an accompanying letter expressing their loyalty, as has already been described in Chapter IV. On the last day, as the Queen was leaving, a daisy of gold set with rubies was presented by a messenger from Jersey, with a letter from Norris's daughter, making a charming farewell present.[8]

On 13 December 1595 Rowland Whyte described a series of gifts presented to the Queen by the Lord Keeper at his house at

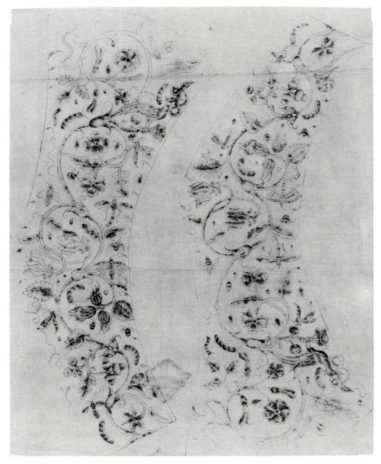

156 *One of a pair of sleeves drawn out on a piece of white linen, embroidered in black silk which is now disintegrating. c. 1605–10. Victoria and Albert Museum, London*

Kew: 'At her first Lighting, she had a fine Fanne, with a Handle garnisht with Diamonds . . . In her Bed Chamber, presented her with a fine Gown and a Juppin, which Things were pleasing to her Highnes'.[9] The rainbow robe, presented to her when she visited Harefield Place on a Progress in 1602, was the gift of Sir Thomas Egerton. Care had been taken to make sure that it would be the right size by employing William Jones, the Queen's tailor, to make it. Sir Arthur Mainwaring received £553. 6s. to pay for the expenses of the Queen's visit and on 10 August he 'Payde to the mercers, the imbroderer, the silkeman, and Queenes taylor lxxv li xvs [£75. 15s]'[10] for the rainbow robe. Part of the poem apologizing for the wet weather, read out when the robe was given to the Queen by Lady Walsingham, has already been quoted.[11]

These beautifully embroidered clothes, many still in the Wardrobe of Robes in 1600, must have taken much time and thought to prepare. They usually cost large sums of money, although in some cases embroidery was carried out by donors who were skilful needlewomen, such as Bess of Hardwick, Countess of Shrewsbury. Margaret Swain has noted that the Queen of Scots, who was held captive at Hardwick, embroidered a petticoat for Elizabeth. Mary wrote to the French ambassador in London in 1574 for satin and silk:

I must give you the trouble of acting for me in smaller matters, viz. to send me as soon as you can eight ells of crimson satin of the colour of the sample of silk which I send you, the best that can be found in London, but I should like to have it in fifteen days, and one pound of the thinner and double silver thread.[12]

Mary completed the gift, a skirt of crimson satin lined with matching taffeta, in May and asked the French ambassador to present it to the Queen on her behalf 'as evidence of the honour I bear her, and the desire I have to employ myself in anything agreable to her'. At the same time Shrewsbury, who held Mary in his custody, wrote to Walsingham that: 'Some in my house are infected with the measles, and it may be dangerous for the Queen to receive anything hence before it has been well aired. God preserve her. She is a precious jewel to all men'. The petticoat was no doubt aired thoroughly, as it was later in May when the French ambassador described its reception in a letter to his King.

The Queen of Scots, your sister-in-law, is very well, and yesterday I presented on her behalf a skirt of crimson satin, worked with silver, very fine and all worked by her own hand, to the Queen of England, to whom the present was very agreable, for she found it very nice and has prized it much; and she seemed to me that I found her much softened towards her.[13]

It is easy to understand why petticoats, foreparts, loose gowns, ruffs, and smocks were popular gifts. They required very simple sets of measurements, and were easier to make than close-fitting garments like doublets, where the measurements would have to be exact; the wrong size or a poor fit would make the gift unacceptable. The 'Vestal Maydens' played safe with the gifts of 'a vaile of white, exceeding rich and curiously wrought; a cloke and safegard set with buttons of gold, and on them were graven emprezes of excellent devise; in the loope of every button was a Nobleman's badge, fixed to a pillar richly embroidered'. These they presented at the Tiltyard at Westminster on 17 November 1590, during the Accession Day Tilts.[14] All three garments were loose fitting. Some clothes were not made up when given to the Queen, and so allowed her tailor to make adjustments without unpicking. One 'foreparte of purple Taphata set with Roses of whit Cipers and Cheines betweene of venice golde with a brode passa-maine of venice golde unlyned and unmade', the gift of the Lady Mary Vere in 1578, was still unlined and unmade when it was entered in the Stowe inventory in 1600, so presumably the Queen had not liked it enough to have it made up. This was a risk the donors had to take with gifts of jewels and clothes; however carefully chosen, the Queen might not find the design, materials or colour to her taste.

Sir William More had better luck than Lady Mary Vere with his gift; Lady Wolley wrote to her father 'Since my coming to the Court, I have had many gratious words of her Majesty . . . yesterday she wore the gown you gave her'.[15] This letter was probably written after the Queen's visit to Loseley in 1591. When the Queen visited Mitcham, in September 1598, Sir Julius Caesar presented her with 'a gown of cloth of silver richly embroidered; a black networke mantle with pure gold; a taffeta hat, white with several flowers and a jewel of gold set therein with rubies and diamonds',[16] but there is no mention of her wearing the gown, or of her reaction to the gifts.

Advice about the gifts to present was given by members of the Royal Household. In August 1597 one of Burghley's secretaries, Henry Maynard, wrote from London to Michael Hicks who was anticipating a visit from the Queen to Ruckholt in Essex. He had told the Lord Chamberlain that Hicks was troubled at the insufficient accommodation he could provide for the royal train and wrote 'His awnsweare was that you weare unwise to be at anie such charge: but onelie to leave the howse to the Quene: and wished that theare might be presented to hir Majestie from your wief sum fine wastcoate or fine ruffe, or like thinge, which he said would be acceptablie taken as if it weare of great price'.[17]

A series of letters records the trouble which Ladies of the Privy Chamber and Bedchamber took to make sure that the gifts of the formidable Bess of Hardwick, Countess of Shrewsbury (Fig. 157), would be acceptable to the Queen. The wrong choice of colour or embroidery motifs could spoil a gift, so friends at Court did their best to help. Anthony Wingfield wrote a letter to his wife on 13 October, 1575, telling her that he had consulted Lady Cobham and Lady Sussex about the Countess of Shrewsbury's gift. Lady Cobham had suggested money or a gold cup, while Lady Sussex thought that an embroidered cloak and safeguard would be more acceptable and suggested that Walter Fyshe, the Queen's tailor should make them. Wingfield's letter shows his concern:

I have Dylte with my lade off sysex and my lade cobame Fore my ladys gyfte onto the quene, and my lady off sousex opynneone was that my lade should have gevene the fayere bede that my lady makes to hur hangynges and my lady co(bame) would in nowyes that ytt should be so, but would have my lade geve forte pound in monne, or a coupe off gould aboute that walleur but in onne wyes my lady off sysex would have my lade geve a safegard and a clouke off sume wacheche sattyne or peche coullore, and inbroyderyd with sume perete flowares and leves with sondery coullares made with gould sponggulles and sylke. thes fantaskecalle thynges wyll be more exsyptyd thane coupe or Juell and my lady off susex would have waltare fyeses to have the Dowynge off ytt.[18]

The pretty flowers and leaves for the embroidery motifs were later defined as pansies (Fig. 158), the Queen's favourite flower, according to Lady Sussex. Anthony Wingfield wrote again to his wife on 13 December:

I could not speke with my lade off susex tyll yestardaye att nyte for that she was not well and yestaredaye whan I had Deleveryd the lyttares thane I Dylte with hur for her Jugmente for the neueresgefte. and thys ys hur mynde that she would have the coullere to be off a lyete wacheyte sattene and gardyd with small garges off carnasyon vellvete. and apone the garde imbroyderyd with pansys off all fasyenes so that in them be all mannar off coulloures and to be trymed with gleysterynge gould and sylver to the byste shoue. and not with grete pourell but to the best shoue off small purell. the garde to be a good ennche broude and not above for in a naroue garde the panse floware wyll shoue best becaues that small flower and lefe wyll shoue best in a small garde. thys ys my lady off s[usex] opynneone and as she sayes ye quene lekes byst off that floware and to have the satten a lyte wacheytt becaues she hathe no garmente off that collore all Rede and she hathe sondery garmentes off as[h] coullore all Rede and begenes to be wery off the coullore.[19]

Presumably Walter Fyshe was given the order to make the cloak and safeguard just after this letter was written. It must have been a rush job with only about two and half weeks for the embroidery as well. The guards, a good inch broad, of carnation velvet embroidered with pansies and trimmed with small pearls, each one sewn on by hand, would have taken hours of work. The tailor would have mounted the guards as they came from the embroiderers, one at a time, on the light watchet satin. Apparently this shade of blue was most acceptable, as Elizabeth Wingfield wrote to Bess of Hardwick on 2 January, to tell her how Elizabeth received the gift. Her words at the beginning of the letter probably refer to her work in finding embroiderers:

my humbil duty remembred, yow honour shall know that after my c[osin] wilame and my carefull toyll, by reason of the shurt tyme, we

157 'Elizabeth, Countess of Shrewsbury', known as 'Bess of Hardwick'. c. 1580. National Trust, Hardwick Hall, Derbyshire

158 Detail of a pansy from the Hardwick portrait of Queen Elizabeth I in Figure 129. c. 1599. National Trust, Hardwick Hall, Derbyshire

have reped such recompence as could not dissire better. furst her majestie never liked any thinge you gave her so well. the color and strange triminge of the garments with the redie and grat[e] cost bestowed upon yt hath caused her to geve out such good speches of my lord and your ladyship as I never hard of better. she toulde my lord of Lester and my lord chamberlen that you had geven her such garments thys yere as she never had any so well lyked her and sayd that good nobell copell the[y] show in all things what love the[y] bere me and surely my lord I wyll not be found unthankefull if my lord and yow ladyship had geven v hundrd pound. in my opennon yt would not have bene so well taken.[20]

159 *Queen Elizabeth I, wearing a short silvery-white cloak, or possibly a shoulder rail, over a black gown with a black muff, embroidered with gold thread, hanging on a ribbon. Illumination in the margin of a poem written by Georges de la Motthe, a Huguenot refugee, presented to the Queen, 1586. Bodleian Library Oxford (MS Fr. e.1, f.13v)*

Although the year is not given in the dates of the last two letters it seems as if they must refer to the cloak and safeguard, particularly in view of 'the short time' which Elizabeth Wingfield mentions. The two months from 13 October, when the gift was first planned, to 13 December when Anthony Wingfield wrote again about it to his wife, was probably just long enough for several letters to travel between the Court and Derbyshire, asking questions and then confirming the choice of gift. Bess was probably relieved that she did not have to send the embroidered bed hangings.

Lady Frances Cobham had helped her on an earlier occasion when the Countess of Shrewsbury was still Lady St Loe. She had tacked up a pair of sleeves embroidered by Bess to the width which she knew that the Queen would prefer, while resting at Cobham in October during her pregnancy, waiting for the week before St Andrew's Day. This must have been between 1561, when Bess spent seven months in the Tower under suspicion of being involved in Catherine Grey's secret marriage, and 1568 when she married the Earl of Shrewsbury. Lady Cobham also sent Bess the measurements for a 'caylle' for the Queen, to be embroidered to match the sleeves. Derbyshire was obviously rather out of the way for the latest fashions and she suggested that it should be returned unmade. The ten yards for 'the roufes of the neke and hands' to which she refers was a length of joined strips of fine linen to be gathered up for a set of neck and wrist ruffs, probably six yards for the neck and two yards for each wrist ruff, not the total quantity of material required:

i have resevyd your letter mi good ladi to me very wellcom as Frome her i love dearely and most desyr to see. i wolde yow had as good caus to com to ley in thes partes as i colde wyshe and thene yow shulde be as grete a stranger in darbi shere as now yow ar[e] in London. i am now at cobhan wher[e] i intende god wyllyinge to be browght a bed. i loke a weke before sente anderous day. i pray praye for me. i know i shall spede much the better for a good womianes prayer. I have bassted the scleve of that wydenes that wyll best contente the quyne. the len[g]th all wrott wyll be shourte innoufthe i know the[y] wyll be well leked. the[y] ar[e] fyne and strange. i have heyr sent yow inclosen the brede and len[g]th of a caylle for the quyne of the same worke for to shute wyth the scleves. yow may send yt up unmade for that the fasshuyne ys much altared senes yow were heyr. x yarde ys innoufe for the roufes of the neke and hands.[21]

It is not entirely clear what a caylle was. Cotgrave gives cale, a kind of little cap, in the 1650 edition of *A Dictionarie of the French and English Tongues*. However, the description of this item being made to match the sleeves sounds more like a partlet as they were so often made in sets. Perhaps the word should have been raylle, not caylle. Minsheu defines raile as neckerchief and the word appears in this sense as early as 1482. It may have been used as an alternative word for partlet. Apparently a rail could also be made in heavier materials than linen. Walter Fyshe was entered for 'making of a shoulder Raile of bayes gatherid thicke of our great guarderobe' in the warrant of 12 April 1577. Perhaps a caylle or raylle was a shoulder cape gathered into the neck, similar to the little cape in Figure 159.

Sometimes there were short delays in obtaining the silks to carry out the embroidery. Gilbert Talbot wrote to the Countess of Shrewsbury on Friday 13 October 1575 from Sheffield:

It apereth by a note yt came with the stuffe yt there is suche things comme as Nicholas Steward wrytt for, as thredd & silke or such like; but it is lapped amonge so many other roulles of the lyke, and nothing wrytten on the backsyde, yt we can not tell which is for your Ladyship from other folkes. If therefore my cosen Jane will wryte what your Ladyship sente for, we shall send them: they appeare to be but small thinges.[22]

No doubt the Countess kept a large stock of silks in hand, but the wait, particularly when a gift for the Queen was involved, would have been irksome.

Francis Walsingham always gave the most beautiful presents and devoted considerable time and thought to them. In the New Year's Gift Roll of 1577 he is listed among the knights as 'Francis Walsingham also Secretary'.[23] A gap had been left; presumably a knighthood had been expected. However, Elizabeth had obviously decided not. 'Mr' is written into the gap, in a different shade of black ink. Walsingham received his knighthood on 1 December 1577 at Windsor. He obviously wanted to make Elizabeth an acceptable New Year's gift and a few days later Amyas Paulet wrote to him from Paris:

I will despatch Dannett in convenient time to be with you three or four days before New Year's day . . . This bearer had put a piece of silk to working for you, as the only thing that seemed to your purpose and was promised assuredly that it should be ready before the 18th [8th]; whereof being disappointed, after the French manner, I was forced to seek another merchant.[24]

He went to some trouble for Walsingham and wrote again on 25 [15] December:

Please receive by this bearer, Mr Dannett, a piece of silk containing 20 yards, being sorry I can provide no better stuff. The plague in Italy and the disorder of the money here are thought to be the true causes that nothing comes out of those parts. The Queen and ladies here, for want of better stuff, make all their new garments of coloured satin garnished with gold and silver. If by ignorance I shall send anything to her Majesty that seems unfit for her, please to take order that it may not be delivered; and I shall pray you to extend their favour towards a trifle which I send by this bearer, referring the delivery of the same to your friendly consideration. I wish to send something to her Majesty; and, therefore, have resolved upon this because I can find no silk of any new fashion.[25]

This twenty yards of silk was presumably made up in about five days, as it is listed in the New Year's Gift Roll of 1578, 'By Sir Fraunces Walsingham knight, principall Secretary; a Gowne of blewe Satten, with rewes of golde and two small pasmane laces of venice golde, Faced with powdred Armyons. Delivered to Rauf hoope'.[26] Walsingham wrote to Paulet that the parcels had arrived safely: 'I am much beholding to you for the piece of satin you sent me, which liked her Majesty so well that I have never had greater thanks of her for any present I have made her', but 'the good acceptance of Paulet's gift' had to be seen in Secretary Wilson's report as 'he had the delivery of it, I being absent'.[27]

Amyas Paulet was also instructed to get Elizabeth a muff 'or countenance (so they call it here)' in Paris in 1579. He sent one, 'the best I can find at this time thinking it better to send this as it is when there is some cold stirring, than to wait for a better till the cold be clean gone. I have caused this countenance to be furred as well as it can be done in this town, but have not perfumed it because I do not know what perfume will be most agreeable to her Majesty'.[28] The Queen carries a muff in Figure 159.

A rich jewel or beautiful gown was far more likely to please the Queen than a purse of sovereigns. Mrs Wingfield wrote to the Countess of Shrewsbury advising her on a gift rather than sending money:

presently after I re[ceved] yow ladyships leter I went to my lady cobham and we longe confarde of the matter. I se[e] by her she was muche against yow honour giveinge money. mr W and I founde her so muche agannst the same that we ment if we coulde have founde any fine reare thinge to have bestowed thurty or fortye pounde of some suche thinge, but how she woulde like the best coulde be hade beinge not her owne doinge we muche douted. now we have concluded she shall provide the same whiche she sayth she wyl do to her magisty likinge. truly if yow honour had geven money I feare yt woulde have bene ell liked.[29]

This would have been for a New Year's Gift as the letter was written on 4 December but the year is not given. As we have seen already the same thought is expressed in another of her letters '. . . if my lord and yow ladyship had geven v hundred pound. in my opennon yt would not have bene so well taken'.[30]

When Sir John Harington, the Queen's godson, was involved in a lawsuit to recover some lands, probably Harington Park, which had been forfeited by Sir James Harington for supporting Richard III, he decided to try and further his suit by sending the Queen a gift, although obviously aware that there were dangers in doing so. He wrote to a friend, probably Sir Robert Sidney:

Yet I will adventure to give her Majestie five hundred pounds in money, and some pretty jewel or garment as you shall advyse, onlie praying to her Majestie to further my suite with some of her lernede Counsel; which I pray you to find some proper tyme to move in; this some hold as a dangerous adventure, but five and twentie manors do well warrant my trying it.[31]

Elizabeth, Dowager Lady Russell, mother of Elizabeth Russell, one of the Maids of Honour, had given much more than Sir John. She wrote to her nephew, Sir Robert Cecil, on 5 March 1600:

Good Mr Secretary, move her Majesty to grant my lease, promised to your father in his days, to me now for Bess Russell's good. It cost me truly, twelve years since, a gown and petticoat of such tissue as should have been for the Queen of Scots' wedding garment; but I got them for my Queen, full dearly bought, I well wot. Beside, I gave her Majesty a canopy of tissue with curtains of crimson taffety, belited gold. I gave also two hats with two jewels, though I say it, fine hats; the one white beaver, the jewel of the one above a hundred pounds price, beside the pendent pearl, which cost me then 30 l more. And then it pleased her Majesty to acknowledge the jewel to be so fair as that she commanded it should be delivered to me again, but it was not; and after, by my Lady Cobham, your mother-in-law, when she presented my new year's gift of 30 l in fair gold, I received answer that her Majesty would grant my lease of Dunnington. Sir, I will be sworn that, in the space of 18 weeks, gifts to her Majesty cost me above 500 l, in hope to have the Dunnington lease; which if now you will get performed for Bess's almost six years' service, she, I am sure, will be most ready to acquit any service to yourself.[32]

Perhaps the tissue gown and petticoat were eventually altered for Anne of Denmark, the Queen of Scots as she was then, after Elizabeth's death.

Sometimes even gifts of clothing were granted a mixed reception, as a series of letters from Rowland Whyte to Sir Robert Sydney show. He wrote on 5 January 1599:

Her Majestie is in very good Health and comes much abroad these Holidayes; for almost every Night she is in the Presence, to see the Ladies dawnce the old and new cowntry Dawnces, with the Taber and Pipe. Here was an exceeding rich new Yeares Gift presented, which came, as it were in a Clowde no Man knows how; which is nether receved nor rejected; and it is in the Hands of Mr Controller. Yt comes from the poor Earle, the Downfall of Fortune (it is thought).[33]

The Earl of Essex seems to have been unsuccessful with his gift as Rowland Whyte reported that the Queen was still very angry with him on 12 January but 'the Lady Lester sent the Queen a rich New Year's Gift which was very well taken'.[34] This good reception probably made her decide to venture another gift to help Essex. On 25 February Whyte wrote again: 'My Lady Lester hath now in Hand a Gown she will send to the Queen which will cost her 100 l at lest'.[35] However, Elizabeth was obviously very angry still and on 3 March Sydney received another letter with the latest gossip from Whyte:

Yesterday the Cowntess of Leicester sent the Queen a curious fine Gown, which was presented by my Lady Scudmore. Her Majestie liked yt well, but did not accept it, nor refuse yt, only answered that Things standing as they did, yt was not fitt for her to desire what she did, which was to come to her Majesties Presence to kiss her Hands, upon her going now to her poor home.[36]

It is difficult to tell how much the good words put in by the person who presented the gift for the donor influenced the Queen's decisions. In this case Lady Scudamore may have softened the Queen's reply, as although Elizabeth did not accept the gift, she did not refuse it.

As we have seen, much depended on the advice given by the Queen's women for the choice of colours and motifs for the embroidery or the style of a gown. They must have been consulted all the year round by many people who wished to make sure that their gifts would please the Queen and help their suits. The timing of the presentation of a gift would also have needed careful consideration. Any gown, however richly embroidered, would have paled into insignificance beside the gifts from the Czar, Ivan the Terrible. These were presented by Sir Jerome Horsey who recorded his audience with the Queen in 1587:

I delivered to her highness — she touching every parcel with her hand — first 4 pieces of Persian cloth of gold and two whole pieces of cloth of silver of curious work: a large rich cloth of estate of white arras — a representation of the sun shining in his full splendancy gold and silver beams interwrought with most orient colours, silks, silver and gold, the thread 'sliked' flat to illustrate the beauty thereof; a fair large Turkey carpet; four black very rich 'timbers' [bales each containing 40 skins] of sables; six white well grown spotted 'luzerance' [lynx]; two 'shubs' or gowns of white ermines. The Queen did even sweat by taking pains to handle the canopy of cloth of gold and especially the rich sables and furs; commanded Mrs Mary Skidmore and Mrs Mary Radcliff, both of Her Majesty's bed-chamber, and Mr John Stanhope [Vice-Chamberlain] to help to lay them into Her Majesty's closet.[37]

Some of the gifts presented to the Queen were made the occasion for a small ceremony, as at Rycote in 1592. Others were accompanied by letters expressing loyalty and devotion from their donors. One of these was sent by Francis Bacon. It probably accompanied the gift of an embroidered satin petticoat as a New Year's gift in 1600, which is listed in the Stowe inventory.

Most excellent Sovereign Mistress, the only New Year's Gift which I can give your Majesty, is that which God hath given to me: which is, a mind in all humbleness to wait upon your commandments and business: wherein I would to God that I were hooded, that I saw less; or that I could perform more: for now I am like a hawk, that bates, when I see occasion of service, but cannot fly because I am tied to another's fist. But, meanwhile, I continue my presumption of making to your Majesty my poor oblation of a garment, as unworthy the wearing, as his service that sends it: but the approach of your excellent person may give worth to both: which is all the happiness I aspire to.[38]

Gifts of clothing from the Queen

John Chamberlain wrote in 1603 that Elizabeth 'made no will nor gave anything away so that they which come after shall find . . . a rich wardrobe of more than 2,000 gowns'. However, the evidence is quite clear that Elizabeth made gifts of clothing and lengths of material to her women, her servants, and many people of high rank, throughout her long reign. One of the earliest was noted at the end of May, 1559, when the Queen gave presents to an Embassy from France. There were gifts of gold, silver, horses, and dogs valued at 10,000 crowns for M. de Montmorency[39] and 'to the brother of M. de Montmorency: most valuable clothes which had belonged to King Edward her brother, and suitable to his person, he being of the same age [as that King was]'.[40] She made many other gifts of clothing to children. One in 1599, to Sir Robert Cecil's son — 'a gallant faire Boy' — of a coat, girdle, dagger, and hat with feather and jewel to wear in it, must have given a great deal of pleasure.[41] Sometimes lengths of material were set aside for them. In 1574, Lady Buckhurst was given some purple satin for a coat for one of her children and Lady Sheffield had velvet for a gown for her daughter.[42]

Pieces of clothing, some new but many previously worn, were perfectly acceptable as gifts from the Queen in sixteenth-century England, even though the recipients might be of high rank. Elizabeth had clothes remodelled to wear

again herself and there was no reason for others to find fault with the gifts. Materials like velvet, cloth of gold and satin were extremely expensive and the clothes worn by the Queen were superbly embroidered. They were sometimes presented without alteration, like the black satin round kirtle given to Mary Scudamore in 1577,[43] but many were relined and altered at considerable expense. One round gown which had been given to Elizabeth at the New Year in 1578 by the Earl of Warwick is listed in the Stowe inventory.[44] It was given to the Countess of Kildare on 16 December 1602 at Whitehall and she put her signature in the inventory as a form of receipt. William Jones had been given the work of altering and new making up again a high bodied gown of black uncut velvet given to the Countess of Kildare while John Parr enlarged the embroidery and added three new guards,[45] so that it could be given as a present.

Mary, Queen of Scots, wrote to Elizabeth after her escape from Lochleven to Carlisle in 1567 and told her that she had no clothes but the gown she stood up in. She asked for some of the Queen's gowns but none were sent, although so many were given to other ladies. Elizabeth Jenkins suggests that there was something more in this than the reluctance of a vain, greedy woman to part with her possessions, that the demand's symbolic meaning was out of all proportion to the practical one; it was as if Mary had come to take the throne. For Elizabeth to send a present of clothes and jewels to the Queen of Scots would have required an effort of which she was incapable.[46] This may well be true but perhaps there is another explanation. The Spanish Ambassador reported that he had heard that the parcel delivered by Sir Francis Knollys contained two worn out chemises, a length of black velvet and a pair of shoes, while Mary's own version to France was that the Queen of England had sent her a little linen. An item among the warrants for the Wardrobe of Robes lists 'Sixtene yerdes of blak vellat: Sixtene yerdes of blak Satten: and tenne yerdes of blak taphata Delyvered by our Commaundement to our trustie and right welbeloved Counsailor Sir Fraunces Knolles knight vice chamberlen of our Chamber, for the Quene of Scottes, of our great guarderobe',[47] This seems very likely to have been the 'length of black velvet', so often quoted, but the satin and taffeta are never mentioned. If these three pieces of black material were in the parcel sent to Carlisle it would seem that the gift was a subtle message to the Queen of Scots rather than an example of the Queen of England's clutchfisted ways, the usual interpretation of the story. It was a quiet hint that Mary should go into suitable mourning. Elizabeth might as easily have sent some plain black gowns of her own, but she would have known from Melville[48] that the Queen of Scots was taller than herself and probably larger in the waist since the birth of James. Lengths of rich black velvet, satin and taffeta were, therefore, quite appropriate for the message which Elizabeth wished to convey to Mary, who had remarried so hastily after the violent death of Lord Henry Darnley, with all the attendant rumours.

Elizabeth made gifts of Garter Robes to foreign royalty when they were admitted to the Order. In 1572 the Duke of Montmorency was presented with robes made from:

xviij yerdes of crymsen vellat: xx yerdes of purple vellat xxiij yerdes iij quarters of white taphata and two yerdes & a half of yellowe cloth of golde with one riche Robe lace of purple silk and golde garnesshed with thre great buttons of purple silke and golde and a great tassell with a cawle of venice golde and two ounces and a half of crymsen and white spanyshe silke all whiche percelles were employed upon a

Mantle of our order of the garter a kyrtle a whodde with a Typpett and a Mantle for a helmett by us given to Duke Memorance all of our greate guarderobe.[49]

Duke Casimir, son of the Elector Palatine, was made a Knight of the Order in 1579. Thomas Ludwell, the livery tailor, made his hood, kirtle and purple velvet mantle 'with a Garter enbroderid with venice golde seede pearle sett on the shoulder'.[50]

More details are given of the robes presented to Frederick II, King of Denmark, entered in a warrant of 1582. He was elected to the Order in 1578. Thomas Ludwell was employed in:

makinge of a Robe of our order of the garter of purple vellat by us sent to ⟨the⟩ our deare brother the Kinge of Denmarke borderid with buckeram and lyned with white taphata sarceonett: for makinge of a kyrtell & a whodde of crymsen vellat (for him) borderid with buckeram and lyned with white taphata sarceonett: One Cusshion of purple vellat backed with satten with a tyke fylled with fethers: And asmuche crymsen vellat as will serve to cover a Booke of our greate guarderobe.[51]

The buckram interfacing would have kept the edges of the mantle and kirtle firm, without puckering. From Roger Mountague there was 'one Robe stringe of venice golde and silke made on the fingers with two cawles & buttons with tasselles of like golde & silke employed upon the said Robe all of our great guarderobe'.[52] An order went 'to James Hewishe for thirteene elles of hollande cloth to make One peire of Sheetes to carye the said Robes in of our great guarderobe'.[53] This would have protected the velvet and helped to prevent creasing during the journey to Denmark.

David Smith, the Queen's Embroiderer, was entered in the warrant 'for enbrauderinge of a Scutchion for the said Robe with venice golde silver pearle and damaske purle ammountinge to the summe of Fower poundes of our great guarderobe'.[54] This escutcheon was the Garter set on the shoulder, as described for Duke Casimir's mantle, and is included in the total cost of the embroidery for the robes in the warrant for April 1583:

to Davide Smyth our Embrauderer for sundrye percelles of stuffe and workmanshipe by hym employed uppon our garmentes before written And for embrauderinge of a Banner cloth for our Deare Brother the Kynge of Denmarke, ammounting to the Somme of Thre score one poundes seven shillinges and fower pence, of our great Guarderob.[55]

Roger Mountague, the Queen's silkman, supplied:

two lardge tasselles of crymsen spanyshe silke garnisshed with fayer cawles of venice golde and silver wrought with knotted panes and under cawled with like golde and silver, employed upon a banner a helmett and a Sworde, for thenstawlinge of our sayde Brother the Kinge of Denmarke are to be payed for at our great guarderobe.[56]

No details of the prices are given here. A delivery of materials, apparently from James Hewish, includes the material for the King's banner:

Item eleven yerdes of cloth of golde: sixe yerdes of cloth of silver: twelve yerdes di quarter of crymsen vellat: and fyve yerdes of blewe vellat employed in enbraudering of a Banner cloth for our deare brother the Kinge of Denmarke at his enstawlinge at Wyndesor of our greate guarderobe.[57]

The garter was not apparently listed as a separate piece of work but it survives in the Danish Royal Collections.[58]

The robes were carried to Denmark in two trunks. There was also a velvet-covered case containing the Collar of the Order.[59] King Frederick's collar has not been preserved, but that of Christian IV, King of Denmark and Norway, dating from 1606 may be seen today at Rosenberg Castle in Copenhagen, together with the purple velvet mantle.[60]

Gifts of clothing to the Queen's women

It seems as if gifts of the Queen's clothing were one of the perquisites of the Ladies and Gentlewomen of the Privy Chamber and Bedchamber, the Maids of Honour and some servants. A gift of an orange velvet safeguard and a pair of sleeves was made to an Irish gentlewoman in 1583. It was entered in what, as far as I know, is the only surviving day book of the Wardrobe of Robes, noting that these things were given by the consent of the gentlewomen of the Privy Chamber, Mrs Scudamore, Mrs Blanche Parry, Mrs Hawkes, Mrs Chaworth, and others.[61] When it was decided that a gown was due to be discarded, the Queen and her ladies may have discussed among themselves who would be the most suitable recipient for the gift, perhaps according to rank or length of service. The pieces of clothing seem to have been allocated rather unevenly; from the evidence of the day book, some ladies apparently received more gifts than others. However this one manuscript does not give the whole picture. The total number of gifts has to be pieced together from other sources, and some of the evidence is missing. Many gifts of clothing which had been altered or specially made were entered in the warrants for the Wardrobe of Robes and some of them have duplicate entries in the day book. Gifts of clothing would have been recorded in other day books kept in each department of the Wardrobe of Robes, but these books have not yet been traced. The uneven allocation of gifts may also have been due to absence from Court from time to time, as, for example, Lady Cobham when she was pregnant and stayed at Cobham. The gifts would also have depended to a large extent on the Queen's humour. As Sir John Harington wrote: 'When she smiled, it was pure sun-shine that every one did chuse to bake in, if they could; but anon came a storm from a sudden gathering of clouds and the thunder fell in wondrous manner on all alike'.[62]

It is not certain exactly how many Maids of Honour and Ladies and Gentlewomen of the Privy Chamber and Bedchamber attended on the Queen at any one time throughout the reign, nor to what extent the gifts of clothing were intended to show royal favour, or were given in part payment for their services. The number of attendants seems to fluctuate. According to E. K. Chambers there were six Maids of Honour, not salaried, but girls of good birth who attended on the Queen to hold her train and perform other similar tasks.[63] Lupold Von Wedel records that there were twenty-two Maids of Honour in a procession which he saw in August 1585 and twenty-four in November of the same year.[64] It is likely that the Ladies and Gentlewomen of the Privy Chamber and Bedchamber were included in these numbers, as no mention is made of any other female attendants on either occasion.

Gifts of clothing show that there were certainly six Maids of Honour in 1565, as they were presented with yellow satin gowns by the Queen to wear at the marriage of Lady Anne Russell, the Earl of Bedford's daughter, to Ambrose, Earl of Warwick on 11 November:[65]

160 *'Lady Anne Russell, Countess of Warwick'. Panel painting by an unknown artist, c. 1569. By kind permission of the Marquess of Tavistock, and the Trustees of the Bedford Estates, Woburn Abbey*

First to Walter Fyshe our Taylour . . . Item for makinge of vj gownes for our six maides of honour viz Mris Mary Howarde Anne Windesoure, Katherine Bridges Katherin Knevit Mary Ratlyf and Dorothye Broke of yellow Satten garded with grene vellat cutt cheverne wise and laid with silver lace the slevis drawne out withe Grene Tincell Sarcenet lined in the nether partes with Buckeram and cotton in the plaites and in the bodies and straite sleves lyned with fustian and in the ruffes with Frize all of oure great warderobe.[66]

Lady Anne (Fig. 160) had been a Maid of Honour before her marriage and, like the other young girls, had been in the charge of 'the Mother of the Maids' at Court. This term was used in Henry VIII's reign and may well be older than this. In 1598 the post was held by Elizabeth Wingfield: her gift is entered in the New Year's Gift Roll, 'By Mrs Wyngfeilde mother of the Maides one night rayle of Lawne wrought with black silke'.[67] It can have been no easy task to supervise these lively young creatures at Court, surrounded as they were by Elizabeth's courtiers.

The number of Maids of Honour was definitely limited and the coveted places were difficult to get. Rowland Whyte wrote to Sir Robert Sydney on 5 January 1599: 'The young faire Mrs Southwell, shall this Day be sworn Mayde of Honor. My Lady Newton sought yt for her Daughter. It is thought that your Cousen Gifford of Hampshire, shall marry Mrs Onslow, the Mayde of Honor'.[68] It was even better to be one of the Privy Chamber, as the ladies had more influence, and salaries were attached to these posts. 'Learn before your access her

Majesty's disposition by some of the privy chamber, with whom you must keep credit, for that will stand you in much stead' wrote Robert Beale,[69] and a letter from Rowland Whyte makes it clear which post was preferred, if there were a vacancy: 'Mrs Lettice Garrett shalbe a Maid of Honour, and if my Lord Borough cannot bring his Daughter to the Privy Chamber, tis thought she shalbe another of the Maides'.[70] On some occasions sisters were at Court together. The positions depended as much on the vacancies caused by marriage as on the influence exerted by parents and friends. 'Lady Mary Talbott is to be of the Privy Chamber; and the Lady Elizabeth, her Sister, Maid of Honor', wrote Rowland Whyte in another gossipy letter on 28 June 1600.[71]

Many of the girls received gifts of gowns and kirtles from the Queen, some of which had belonged to her, like the purple velvet loose gown presented to 'Mrs Mary Howarde one of the Maydes of honour' in 1566.[72] Others were made specially at the Queen's command, by her own tailor. Walter Fyshe, for example, made 'a frenche Gowne of blak vellat (for Fraunces Vaughan one of our Maydens of honour) layed with one brode and two narrowe lases of venice silver with spangelles lyned with sarceonett the bodies and slevis lyned with fustian and a Rolle of cotten and buckeram in the pleites the lase silke & other garnishement receyved of our said Silkewoman' in 1578.[73]

Some of the groups of gowns may have been a form of livery, as they were identical. They were in the latest fashion and all gifts of the Queen. One group of eleven in 1572 must have looked enchanting. Walter Fyshe used a large quantity of material and trimmings for them:

Clx yerdes of crymsen vellat: lxvj yerdes of blewe taphata: xvij yerdes of murrey satten; with fourtye two poundes iiij oz quarter di of brode compas lase made like Esses of watchett silke and silver cheine frenge lase: xxiij oz quarter of watchett white and crymsen spanyshe silke to sett on the said lase and xiij dozen & a half of watchett white and crymsen towers Rebande all the said percelles employed upon eleven Gownes by us geven to the Lady Susan Bowser: Mary Ratclyff: El[ea]ner Bridges: Elizabeth Garrett: Katheryn Howarde: Ysbell Holcrofte: Fraunces Howarde: Elizabeth Knolles: Anne Weste: Elizabeth Stafforde: and Mary Shelton of our great guarderobe.[74]

Six of the eleven were Maids of Honour and five held positions in the Privy Chamber and Bedchamber. Mary Shelton, for example, is listed as a chamberer in a warrant for livery in 1571.[75]

Groups of gowns continued to be ordered specially for gifts throughout the Queen's reign. In 1596 William Jones made

three highe bodied gownes of velvet, thone for the Ladie Elizabeth Somerset and thothers for the Ladie Katherine Somerset and the Ladie Elizabeth Clinton the bodies and slevis lyned and the gownes bordered withe sarcenet, the slevis & stomachers of white Satten cut and Raysed uppon silver Chamblet, with thre payre of verthingale slevis of our great warderobe.[76]

John Parr was entered in the same warrant:

For enbraudering of thre gownes of drake coloure velvet (for the sayd thre Ladies) on the slevis & bodies richlie wrought alover with spangles, and two brode borders downe the foreventtes and a welte round aboute the skyrttes of every gowne of the same worke, & pullinge out the sayd thre gownes with Copwebb lawne and tufted with carnacion silke: For raysinge up thre payre of slevis and thre stomachers of whit Satten raysed uppon silver chamblet and sett betwene every raysinge a tuft of venice stuff with hanging spangles and a garland of silver purle aboute them, for workmanship hanginge spangles, pinchte plate and spangles: And for Canvas thred and other necessaries to sett the same workes in frames of our great warderobe.[77]

These were richer and more expensive gowns than those given as livery. Mary Shelton's livery warrant in 1571, addressed to John Fortescue, Master of the Great Wardrobe, gives details of the materials allowed:

We woll and Commaund you fourthwith upon the Sight hereof to deliver or cause to be delivered unto our welbeloved woman Mary Shelton one of our Chamberers for her lyvery against the Feast of Christmas last past These parcells folowinge That is to say Fyrst xiiij yardes of Satten for a gowne Item iij yardes of velvet for gardinge of the same gowne And also Six yardes of Sarcenet for Lyninge the same Gowne. And that ye yearly from hensfourth at the Feast of St Andrewe the Apposte delyver unto her for her lyvery against the Feast of Christmas the lyke parcells duringe our plesure And these our Lettres shalbe your suffycyent warraunt dormaunt and dischardge for the yearly delyvery of the premisses in fourme aforesaid. geven under our signet at the pallace of Westminster the xiiij day of February in the xiijth yere of our Raigne.[78]

Mary Shelton was second cousin and Gentlewoman of the Privy Chamber to Elizabeth. She married John Scudamore, a Gentleman Usher to the Queen, without the royal consent, a breach of etiquette, particularly since she was a distant relation. Eleanor Bridges, a Lady of the Privy Chamber, wrote to the young Earl of Rutland 'The Queen hath used Mary Shelton very ill for her marriage: She hath telt liberall bothe with bloes and yevell wordes, and hath not yet graunted her consent'.[79] The secret wedding apparently took place in January 1574. The Queen had probably got used to the idea of the marriage by October, as there is a gift of a forepart to Mrs Mary Skydmore at that time,[80] but John Scudamore was not knighted until 1596. Mary seems to have had charge of the day book recording gifts of clothing from the Queen and jewels lost by her,[81] which is preserved in the Public Record Office.

It is not clear what differences there were between the position and duties of the women variously described as Ladies and Gentlewomen of the Privy Chamber and Bedchamber, and Chamberers. E. K. Chambers suggests that Chamberers were below the others in rank,[82] but it seems that Ladies and Gentlewomen of the Privy Chamber and Bedchamber and Chamberers may have had alternate periods of duty, although this can only be conjectured. Dorothy Broadbelt, who married John Abington (or Habington), is referred to variously as 'a Gentlewoman of the Chamber' in 1568,[83] 'a Gentlewoman of the Privy Chamber' in 1570[84] and 'one of our Chamberers' in 1575.[85]

Elizabeth Marbery, who had attended on Elizabeth when Princess, is described as 'one of the Chamberers' in 1570[86] and as 'a Gentlewoman of the Bedchamber' in 1580.[87] She was granted a pension of £20 yearly during her lifetime and, like Mary Shelton, each year on St Andrews Day received the material for a livery gown of satin guarded with velvet, 'agaynste the feaste of Christmas'.[88] In 1574 she and her husband, Thomas, made a petition for a re-grant of certain lands and tenements in the Manors of Warden and Southill, County Bedfordshire, together with certain tenements and a warren of conies of the yearly rent of £9. 10s. 4d.[89] In consideration of this, Mrs Marbery was willing to resign the pension of £20 granted to her at the beginning of the reign, as also the £60 of arrearages of the same due at Christmas 1573. An endorsement signed by Thomas Sackford states that at Hampton Court on 1 February, 1573, the Queen was pleased to grant the petition.

There were about 350 people receiving annuities in 1573, a large proportion of them serving courtiers already on the Crown pay-roll.[90] These annuities were negotiable, the market value depending on the life expectancy of the holder, and might be sold or used against a debt. They might also, as in the case of Elizabeth Marbery's pension, be exchanged for a lease of crown land. She continued in her place at Court and was presented with many attractive gifts of clothing after this time. One gown recorded in the day book in 1580, when it left the Wardrobe of Robes at Court, was also entered in the warrants for the same year:

for alteringe and newe makinge of a lose gowne of wrought vellat (for Elizabeth Marberye) layed with blak silke lase lyned with London dye Cotten and in the bodies & slevis with fustian with a steye of like fustian the forequarters & coller lyned with vellat the gowne being of our store of the chardge of the said Rauf Hope savinge one yerde of vellat to enlarge the slevis make newe Jagges & collar.[91]

An extract from a copy of a warrant giving a detailed list of wages with the names and titles of posts is given below.[92] It dates from 22 May 1589 according to a note made in a later hand. It is certainly after 1586, as Sir Thomas Gorges has been knighted and is entered for a fee of £20 as a Groom of the Privy Chamber. It cannot be much later than 1589, as Blanche Parry died on 12 February 1590. Margin notes indicate the date when the warrant for each post was made out. Lady Cobham, Lady Carew, Blanche Parry, and Lady Stafford, for example, were with the Queen from the first year of her reign.

per Warrant

The Wages of the Privey Chamber and others, for one whole yeare

The Bed Chamber

The Lady Cobhame	— xx *li* [£20]
The Lady Carewe	— xxxiij *li* vjs viijd [£33. 6s. 8d.]
Mrs Blanch a Parry	— xxxiij *li* vjs viijd [£33. 6s. 8d.]

RMN per warr' dat' tertio Januarij anno primo Reg' Elizabethe
— lxxxvj *li* xiijs iiijd [£86. 13s. 4d.]

Gentlewomen of ye Privey Chamber

The Lady Haward	— xxxiij *li* vjs viijd [£33. 6s. 8d.]

RMN — per warr' dat' tertio Jan' anno primo Reg' Elizabethe

The Lady Stafford	— xxxiij *li* vjs viijd [£33. 6s. 8d.]

RMN — per warr' dat' 13° Aug' anno primo Reg' Elizabethe

The Lady Layghton	— xxxiij *li* vjs viijd [£33. 6s. 8d.]

RMN — per warr' dat' v^to Junij anno Octavo Reg' Elizabethe

The Lady Hartforde	— xxxiij *li* vjs viijd [£33. 6s. 8d.]

RMN — per warr' dat' 28° Novemb' anno xij^mo Reg' Elizabethe

Dorrathy Edmundes	— xxxiij *li* vjs viijd [£33. 6s. 8d.]

RMN — per warr' dat' 5to Novemb' anno xij^mo Reg' Elizabethe
Clxvj *li* xiiijs iiijd [£166. 13s. 4d.]

Chamberers

The Lady Drewrye	— xx *li* [£20]

RMN per Warr' dat' 28° Novemb' anno xj^mo Reg' Elizabethe

Mary Skudamore	— xx *li* [£20]

RMN per Warr' dat 2° Januarij anno xiij° Reg' Elizabethe

Katherin Newton	— xx *li* [£20]
Jane Bruxsiles	— xx *li* [£20]

RMN per Warr' dat' xvij^mo Julij anno xix^no Reg' Elizabethe
lxxx *li* [£80]

Elizabeth Marbery, as we have seen, resigned her pension for a grant of land and Mary Ratcliffe may have done the same.

161 *'Lady Drury and one of her children', by an unknown artist, c. 1578. Lady Drury's doublet and petticoat are of white silk with rows of grey and gold braid, stitched in white. Her black gown is decorated with red, white, and black twisted cord with gold buttons on the shoulder wings. The child wears brown patterned with darker chestnut, trimmed with gold braid, and sleeves to match Lady Drury's doublet. Private collection*

Mary started as a Maid of Honour in 1561, being presented at Court on New Year's Day by her father, the younger son of the first Earl of Sussex. She never married and remained in the Queen's service until the end, outliving her. Her name appears in the Stowe inventory, still in charge of the personal jewels, in 1603. Neither of these two women is listed here, although Mary Ratcliffe was certainly a Gentlewoman of the Privy Chamber.[93]

Blanche Parry, as a Gentlewoman of the Privy Chamber, apparently received board and lodging for herself and servants, horses and stabling with carriage accommodation when the Court moved and various allowances in kind, in addition to the salary of £33. 6s. 8d.,[94] and presumably this applied to all the Queen's women. Elizabeth might also give an occasional present of money to a favourite. Mary Scudamore, for example, had £400 in 1591 and £300 in 1594.[95]

It is interesting to follow the sequences of gifts of clothing to a few of the Queen's women. Dorothy Broadbelt, described as a Gentlewoman of the Chamber,[96] is entered for her livery in the same warrant as Elizabeth Marbery. She was given a gown and kirtle when she married John Abington, a Clerk of the Kitchen, in 1567:

Item to the said Walter Fyshe for makinge of a flaunders Gowne of blacke velvet with Satten Grounde for the mariage of Dorothy

Bradbelte to Mr abington welted with blacke velvet layed with silver Lace faced with blacke velvate and Lyned with bayes and with a border of Sarcenete aboute the skyrtes with fryse to the ruffes and Buckeram to lyne the Coller frynged aboute with silke and silver and for makinge of a frenche kyrtelle for her of murrey velvete with bodies to it welted with murrey velvete layed with silver lace lyned with Crymsen Sarcenette lett Downe with crymsen Taffata and lyned in the plites with Red Cotton all of our Great warderobe.[97]

By 1572 Abington had risen to the position of Chief Clerk of the Kitchen of the Household and the couple were leased some lands and properties in Northampton for forty-one years in consideration of the surrender of a patent dated 29 June 1560 which leased some of the properties to Dorothy at a rent of £18. 12s. for forty-one years from Michaelmas 1569. They were also leased the Rectory of Utterby, in Lincolnshire in 1570, with a yearly rent of £5. 6s. 8d. and in the lease she is described as a Gentlewoman of the Privy Chamber.[98] In 1575 the Queen gave Dorothy one French kirtle of russett wrought velvet with a satin ground and another of black velvet cut all over.[99] Her name does not appear again in the day book after this date, and these may be the last gifts.

Elizabeth Stafford's warrant dormant for livery in 1569 gives details of materials. Apparently, like the other women, she had to pay the tailor for his work, as the entry for making the gown has been deleted:

We Will and commaunde you fourthewith upon the Sighte hereof to deliver unto Elizabeth Stafforde one of our Chamberers for her lyverye xiiij yardes of Russet Satten for a gowne iij yardes of velvet for gardinge and vj yardes of Sarcenet for lyninge ⟨together with the makinge of⟩ the same in lyke maner as other our Chamberers usually have heretofore had and so yearly at the Feaste of St Andrew the Appostle in lyke maner duringe our pleasure.[100]

She was given twenty yards of black velvet with a white satin ground on 6 November 1573 before her marriage to Mr Drury, possibly for her wedding day.[101] This was made up for her in the Wardrobe of Robes into a French gown with a long train. In the warrant she is described as 'Elizabeth Drury one of our chamberers'.[102]

On 28 November Elizabeth Drury (Fig. 161) was presented with one of the Queen's petticoats of crimson wrought velvet with an embroidered border, probably as a wedding gift.[103] On 20 January 1575 she was given one of the Queen's French kirtles in cloth of gold[104] and Walter Fyshe made her a crimson wrought velvet bearing cloth trimmed with gold and silver lace at the Queen's command; in the warrant, she is again described as a chamberer.[105] She may have worn the kirtle when the bearing robe was used at her daughter's christening, probably in January 1575. Her husband was knighted and on 20 November 1578 Elizabeth, Lady Drury, received one of the Queen's round kirtles of cloth of silver.[106] Other gifts followed, some for her little girl. In 1578–79 Walter Fyshe made

a gowne of carnacion satten (for the Ladye Drurye her Doughter) layed with silver lase edgid with white satten borderid with white sarceonett the bodies lyned with buckeram and fustian and pockettes of fustian: & for making of a payer of slevis of white satten cutt (for her) lased over with golde lase lyned with carnacion sarceonett all of our greate warderobe.[107]

On 20 December 1579 a gift was made of one of the Queen's petticoats in green wrought velvet to make another gown for the child. Again Walter Fyshe made the material up for her, probably for her fourth birthday, into

a streighte bodied gowne of grene vellat (for Fraunces Drurye) layed with lase of venice silver & carnacion silke the bodies & slevis lyned with fustian with a rolle of cotten & buckeram in the pleites the gowne bordered with like fustian the Jagges drawen oute with white lawne the vellat to make the gowne of our store being thouteside of a Petycoate of the chardge of the said Rauf Hope, threst of our greate warderobe.[108]

Lady Drury received a French kirtle of cloth of silver striped with purple silk on 20 January 1580.[109] Perhaps this was to wear on the little girl's birthday, when the child wore her green velvet gown. Lady Drury had more daughters and in 1592 William Jones is entered

for makinge of two highe bodied gownes with Traines facings, and stomagers of watchett velvett by us geven to two of the ladie drurie her daughters, with a silver lace about them, the bodies, sleves, facinges and stomagers laced alover with silver lace, cutt & drawne out with copweb lawne, lined with silver Tincill and white Fustian, the bodies stiffened with canvas and buckeram, with buckeram to laye about them the traines lined, and the gownes bordered with sarcenett, with two paires of vertingale sleves of white Fustian to them all of our great warderobe.[110]

The warrant does not specify if one of them was for Frances.

Among the group of women who stayed with the Queen for life, with Blanche Parry, who died unmarried in 1590, and Mary Ratcliffe, also unmarried, who outlived Elizabeth, was Lady Dorothy Stafford, wife of Sir William Stafford. She was the daughter of Henry, Lord Stafford, only son of Edward, last Duke of Buckingham. A widow from the age of twenty-seven, Lady Dorothy died in September 1604 aged seventy-eight, after forty years in the service of the Queen.[111] Only one gift of clothing from Elizabeth is recorded for her, a black taffeta Flanders gown, and that is early in the reign,[112] but there may have been other gifts entered in books not yet traced. However Lady Dorothy may have been larger than Elizabeth and the clothes would not have fitted her in this case.

Lady Anne Russell, a gentle person with a sweet disposition, was highly favoured by Elizabeth when serving as a Maid of Honour. The Queen and Leicester made the arrangements for her marriage to the Earl of Warwick in 1565,[113] and at that time she was presented with a superb gown and kirtle. Both had previously been worn by the Queen and Walter Fyshe was given the work of

new makinge of a french gowne for the Countesse of warwick of purple Cloth of Tishue garded with purple velvet lyned with purple Taffata the slevis Lyned with frise the said gowne of our store receyved out of the charge of the said Rauf Hope out of our Towre of London all the rest of our great warderobe. Item for alteringe and new makinge of a round kyrtle for the said Countesse of purple velvet the forepart alover enbradered with gold and Lyned with purple taffata the said kyrtle of our store and receyved as afore the velvet to pece the forepart of our great warderobe.[114]

The Countess of Warwick remained one of Elizabeth's closest friends throughout the reign. After the Queen's death at Richmond, she was one of the three women who stayed with the body and was in charge of the arrangements there.[115]

A post in the Privy Chamber or Bedchamber was no sinecure. The Queen's women gave her loyal and devoted service. Each had her own particular tasks to perform, and was in charge of certain valuables. It would appear from the evidence of New Year's Gift Rolls and the day book that Blanche Parry acted as librarian. Jane Brussels looked after the Queen's ruffs, a task also undertaken at various times by Bridget Carr and Mary Scudamore. Mary Ratcliffe and Katherine Carey, Countess of Nottingham, were each responsible for certain personal jewels,[116] and Lady Carewe

162 Detail of Lady Cobham from the family group of William Brooke, Lord Cobham, Frances his wife, and their six children. Panel painting attributed to the Master of The Countess of Warwick, 1567. Reproduced by permission of the Marquess of Bath, Longleat House, Warminster, Wiltshire

apparently coped with French hoods. Mary Scudamore seems to have had charge of the day book recording gifts of clothing from the Queen and lost jewels.[117]

There was apparently no hierarchy. Lady Cobham (Fig. 162) appears to be first Lady of the Bedchamber in the list of wages of the Privy Chamber, but she was only paid £20, the same as the Chamberers, while others in the Bedchamber and Privy Chamber were paid £33. 6s. 8d. Gifts of the Queen's clothing do not give any clues as to precedence. Although Elizabeth gave some very beautiful gowns to those who had been with her many years, she seems to have given even more to the young Maids of Honour when they first came to Court. Elizabeth and Ann Knollys, for example, were presented with complete outfits of French gowns, kirtles, farthingales, hats, hose, and shoes. Frances Johnson, Katherine Howard, Mary Sidney, Frances Vaughan, the Countess of Essex's two daughters, Frances and Elizabeth Howard, Lord Hunsdon's daughters, Margaret, Philadelphia, and Katherine Carey, and many others, received equally generous gifts.[118] Gifts from the Queen must have been treasured possessions. A scarf of Elizabeth's which George Tenecre had been given by Mrs Bridget Chaworth, one of the Queen's women, was recorded in his will in 1591: 'Item 1 skarfe of Ash cullor cypers with ij edges of gould & Sylver yt was ye Queenes yt Mrs ⟨E⟩ Chaworthe gave me'.[119]

Although the title 'Mistress of the Robes' is given to Frances, Lady Cobham (Fig. 162) by Don Diego Guzman da Silva, the

Spanish ambassador, in a dispatch dated 17 September 1565, there seem to be no other contemporary references to the post. Neither transcript nor translation of the original document, which is probably in the Archives of Simancas, could be traced at the Public Record Office. However, it seems likely that the term was simply one used by the translator in the 1890s. An occasional use of the title, if it existed in the sixteenth century, might be expected among the warrants, together with the 'Mother of the Maids'.

Sir Thomas Gorges held the post of Gentleman of the Robes from 1586 until the end of the reign. There is a warrant dated 26 July 1603 signed by Queen Anne, appointing Lady Audrey Walsingham, one of the Ladies of the Privy Chamber, as 'guardian and keeper of the robes'.[120] Lady Walsingham was given a yearly fee of 40 marks with authority to buy 'all stuffs of gold, silver, tinsel silk etc. needful and to convert the same into apparel according to Her Majesty's direction'. She was also to choose tailors, embroiderers, haberdashers, and others necessary; none was to be employed or have access to the Queen but at her choice.

Haydn, in *The Book of Dignities*, mentions that Mary, Duchess of Ancaster and Kesteven, held the appoinment of Mistress of the Robes in the Household of Queen Charlotte, Consort of George III. He gives a list of Mistresses of the Robes from 1837 onwards and states that 'This lady performs for the Queen, whether regnant or consort, duties analagous to those performed by the groom of the stole for the king; but mistress of the robes to a queen regnant is an office of more political importance than that of mistress of the robes to a queen consort'.[121] Apparently after the reign of William and Mary, the office of groom of the stole, though somewhat incongruous in name, was continued between 1702 and 1714, when Queen Anne was on the throne, and combined the duties of mistress of the robes.[122] The appointment of Lady Audrey Walsingham to be 'guardian and keeper of the robes' in 1603, after Sir Thomas Gorges had held the post of Gentleman of the Robes for Queen Elizabeth, makes it seem likely that the title of 'Mistress of the Robes' evolved at some time during the seventeenth century for another Queen Consort.

Whatever her title, Lady Cobham seems to have attended on the Queen at regular intervals from 1558 until her death in 1592, and may well have been responsible for supervising the choice of clothes and making certain that everything required for several days ahead was in the correct place at Court: many items were stored at the Tower and in the office of the Wardrobe of Robes while a few garments would usually have been in the tailor's hands for alterations and renovations.

The Maids of Honour had less responsible tasks to perform, carrying the Queen's train and running errands for her. In later years it must have been difficult for these young girls to be at the beck and call of an imperious old lady with an uncertain temper. The older women, such as the Countess of Warwick, Lady Dorothy Stafford, Lady Mary Scudamore, and Mrs Mary Ratcliffe, who had been with the Queen so long, understood how many cares of state Elizabeth carried on her shoulders, and weathered the storms with her. A letter from William Fenton to Sir John Harington in 1597 casts light on the ageing Queen's treatment of her women when under stress. The letter concerns Lady Mary Howard, who had been extremely troublesome:

I have not seene her Highnesse save twice, since Easter last, bothe of which times she spake vehementlye and with great wrathe of her servante, the Ladie Marie Howarde, forasmuche as she had refused to bear her mantle at the hour her Highnesse is wontede to air in the garden, and on small rebuke did vent suche unseemlie answer as did breede much choler in her mistresse. Again, on other occasion, she was not ready to carry the cup of grace during the dinner in the privie-chamber, nor was she attending at the hour of her Majesties going to prayer. All whiche dothe now so disquiet her Highnesse, that she swore she would no more shew her any countenance, but out with all such ungracious, flouting wenches; because forsoothe, she hathe much favour and marks of love from the younge Earl, which is not so pleasing to the Queene, who dothe still muche exhort all her women to remaine in virgin state as muche as may be. I adventured to say, as far as discretion did go, in defence of our friende, and did urge muche in behalfe of youthe and enticinge love, which did often abate of righte measures in faire ladies; and moreover related whatever might appease the Queene, touching the confession of her great kindness to her sister Jane before her marriage; all which did nothinge soothe her Highnesse anger, saying, 'I have made her my servante, and she will now make herself my mistresse; but in good faith, William, she shall not, and so tell her' . . . It might not be amisse to talke to this poor younge Ladie to be more dutiful, and not absent at meals or prayers, to bear her Highnesse mantle and other furniture, even more than all the reste of the servantes, to make ample amends by future diligence; and always to go first in the morninge to her Highnesse chamber, forasmuche as suche kindnesse will muche prevail to turne awaie all former displeasure. She must not entertaine my Lorde the Earl in any conversation but shunne his companye; and moreover be less carefull in attiringe her own person, for this seemethe as done more to win the Earl, than her mistresse good will . . . If we consider the favours shewed her familie, there is ground for ill humour in the Queen, who dothe not now beare with such composed spirit as she was wont, but, since the Irish affairs, seemethe more froward than commonlie she used to bear herself toward her women, nor dothe she holde them in discourse with such familiar manner, but often chides them for small neglects, in such wise as to make these fair maids often cry and bewail in piteous sort as I am tolde by my sister Elizabeth.[123]

This would seem to be the same 'Ladie M. Howard' in the story told about the Queen by Sir John Harington in a letter to Mr Robert Markam in 1606:

I wyll tell a storie that fell oute when I was a boye; She did love rich cloathynge, but often chid these that bought more finery than became their state. It happenede that Ladie M. Howarde was possesede of a rich border powdered wyth golde and pearle, and a velvet suite belonginge thereto, which moved manie to envye; nor did it please the Queene, who thoughte it exceeded her owne. One daye the Queene did sende privately, and got the Ladies rich vesture, which she put on herself, and came forthe the chamber amonge the Ladies; the kirtle and border was far too shorte for her Majesties height; and she askede every one, How they likede her new-fancied suit? At lengthe she asked the owner herself, If it was not made too short and ill-becoming? — Which the poor Ladie did presentlie consente to. 'Why then if it become not me, as being too short, I am minded it shall never become thee, as being too fine; so it fitteth neither well'. This sharp rebuke abashed the Ladie, and she never adorned her herewith any more. I believe the vestment was laid up till after the Queenes death.[124]

If this story is true, it was probably because Lady Mary had been flirting with the Earl of Essex. Elizabeth might certainly be angry if a Maid of Honour wore very rich clothes, unsuitable for her age and station; they represented wealth and therefore power. But there is plenty of evidence, as we have seen, that many ladies did wear clothes as elaborately embroidered as the Queen's own, since they were those Elizabeth had worn herself and which she had given to them. On this occasion her anger was directed at a young woman who was not only a rival, youth against age, but had also behaved badly to her.

Gifts from the Queen to her fool, dwarf and other servants

Elizabeth made many gifts of clothing to her servants, in most cases to women, but there are some entries for clothing, as well as lengths of cloth, presented to men. Occasionally Ralph Hope, the Yeoman of the Robes, accepted them as part of his fees, although he also received a few gifts.[125] Apparently clothes were sometimes given as payment for services to the state. A rather mysterious present of three and a half yards of russet satin to make a doublet for the Steward of the Cardinal of Chatillon's house[126] may be explained as a payment for spying on his master. In April 1569 Killigrew wrote to Sir William Cecil that 'Sir H. Norreys had a packet intercepted in which there were letters to the Cardinal of Chatillon, since which time he is straightly looked unto'.[127]

A particularly fine suit was made for Arthur Middleton, a servant of Elizabeth Knollys. He first worked for the Queen in an unofficial capacity, carrying out a large number of alterations to her clothes in 1574. By 1576 he was numbered among the Queen's artificers. She must have been very pleased with his work. A warrant to Thomas Ludwell, the head livery tailor, allowed

for making of a Cloake of blak cloth (for Arther Middleton) lyned with silke saye fased with tufte taphata edged with taphata lyned with cotton & canvas in ye coller: for making of a Dublett of carnacion satten (for him) cutt and lyned with grene sarceonett fustian and canvas bumbasted & fased with taphata: for making of a peire of gasken hose of tufte taphata (for him) lyned with lynen cloth, cotten, canvas, bumbasted with cotten woll: one peire of garnesey knytt stockinges: one vellat Cap: A Gyrdle & a peire of Garters of taphata and two Shirtes of holland cloth all of our great guarderobe.[128]

These clothes, particularly the gaskin hose, or breeches, would have roused Phillip Stubbes' anger: 'yea every one, Servyng man, and other inferiour to them in every condition will not stick to flaunt it out in these kinde of Hosen, with all other their apparell sutable thereunto'.[129] The knitted stockings would not have pleased him either: 'Then have they nether-stockes to these gaie hosen, not of cloth (though never so fine) for that is thought to[o] base, but of Jarnsey, Worsted, Crewell, Silke, Thred, and suche like, or els[e] at the least of the finest Yearne that can bee got, and so curiously knitte with open seame downe the legge, with quirks and clocks about the ancles and sometyme (haply) interlaced with golde or silver thredds, as is wonderful to beholde . . . every one (almost) though otherwise very poore, havyng scarce fortie shillynges of wages by the yere will not sticke to have two or three paire of these Silke nether stockes, or els[e] of the finest Yearne that may bee got'.[130] Stubbes published his *The Anatomie of Abuses* in 1583, so Arthur Middleton would have been typical of the serving men he berates for extravagance in dress.

Lengths of carnation and russet satin for doublets were given to Leckener, one of the Queen's footmen,[131] Anthony Crane, servant to the Earl of Hertford,[132] Michael Stanhope,[133] and Oliver Twiste, the son of Anne Twiste the Queen's laundress.[134] Walter Trimmell was presented with a cloth cloak, a doublet bombasted with cotton wool, kersey hose bombasted with cotton wool and trimmed with silk lace with sarcenet canions, all made by Thomas Ludwell, and a pair of knitted stockings with girdle and garters.[135] Robert Hayles received a similar gift of a watchet kersey cloak, jerkin, doublet, and round hose, with knitted stockings, garters, and girdle.[136] One servant, George the Sweeper, had a red cloth

coat trimmed with silk lace and buttons[137] and a felt hat with a cypress hat band.[138] No doubt all these gifts were for work over which servants had taken particular trouble, as Arthur Middleton had done with the alterations.

Elizabeth gave many presents of clothing to the people who entertained her. William Shenton, the fool, received three complete outfits in 1574 and 1575, all made by Thomas Ludwell. None seem to be recorded after this date, so he may have left the Queen's service. His first suit included a gaskin coat of grey cloth striped with silk lace, with a pair of matching gaskins, or breeches, trimmed with lace of several colours and ribbon points. The doublet was of striped sackcloth trimmed with silk lace, and he also had a taffeta girdle, nether stocks, garters, and grey cloth hat. The last was lined with buckram and taffeta and decorated with silk lace devices and a feather covered with gold spangles.[139]

The second suit was much more elaborate and at the same time Shenton was given other gifts, including bedding. Thomas Ludwell was entered in the warrant

for making of a Coate of wrought vellat and tufte taphata (for William Shenton foole) paned red grene and yellowe striped with lase buttons & loupes sowed on with silke fased with taphata lyned with bayes and buckeram: for making of a Cassocke (for him) of chaungeable mockeado striped with billement lase, sowed on with silke with buttons of silke fased with taphata and lyned with bayes and buckeram: for making of a Dublett (for him) of striped sackeloth trymmed with lase sowed on with silke with silke buttons fased with taphata bumbasted lyned with canvas and fustian: for two yerdes of leven taphata for a gyrdell for him: for makinge of two Cases for his Instrumentes thone chaungeable mockeado striped with billement lase thother, tufte taphata paned and striped and lyned with buckeram: One fetherbedde a bolster: A Coveringe: a peire of Blankettes: two peire of Sheetes: six Shirtes: two quilted nighte Cappes and six peire of Showes for the said fole all of our greate guarderobe.[140]

The description of the paned red, green, and yellow coat sounds much more like a court jester's costume than the grey cloth suit.

Shenton was also given two pairs of gaskins, or galligaskins, so called because the Gascons first wore them, according to Minsheu. Apparently these were large wide breeches reaching to the knee,[141] but sometimes they were padded and worn with canions, tubular extensions fitting closely to the leg above the knee, as in these two pairs made for Shenton:

Item for making of a peire of gascons (for the said foole) with six yerdes of chaungeable mockeado trymmed with billement lace with canyons with lyninges of lynen, wollen, cotten, heare, canvas, with pockettes, poyntes, silke garters: & a peire of nether stockes to them: for making of a peire of gascons (for him) with two yerdes of wrought vellat and foure yerdes of tufte taphata layed on with billement lase sowed on with silke with canyons & lyninges of lynen, wollen, and buckeram, pockettes of fustian with canvas & heare, one peire of nether stockes of garnesey yarne: a dossen of Poyntes & a peire of Garters trymmed with lase of colours all of our great guarderobe.[142]

At the same time Raphael Hammond, the Queen's capper, made Shenton a hat from a yard of tuft taffeta, decorated with lace of several colours and a coloured feather trimmed with gold spangles. He also made 'a red felte (for him) trymmed with taphata & lase & a bande wrought with colours and a fether of colours with gold spangelles to the same hatt'.[143]

There are no details of the colours used for the third and last suit given to Shenton. Ludwell made him a frieze coat with decorative cuts and lined with mockado, and gaskins of mockado trimmed with 'billement lace'. The latter were lined with linen and wool, stuffed with canvas and hair, and had fustian pockets. The doublet was of striped sackcloth, perhaps of the same design as the first one he was given. He also had two pairs of knitted stockings, two knitted caps, garters, and girdle of taffeta, two shirts and four pairs of shoes.[144]

Monarcho, an Italian jester, was sufficiently well known for Shakespeare to write about him in *Love's Labour's Lost*: 'A phantasime, a Monarcho and one that makes sport to the Prince'. He apparently first appeared at Court in 1568, when Thomas Ludwell made him

a Gowne of Red grograine chamblett (for an Italian named Monarko) garded with thre gardes of blewe vellat layed on with copper golde lase sowid on with silke and buttons and loupes of like copper golde and pockettes of fustian: for making of a foure quarterid Jerken for him of like grograine striped downe with blewe vellat layed on with copper golde lace sowid with silke and copper golde buttons: And for making of a Dublett for him of striped sackecloth welted with the same fased with red taphata lyned with fustian and canvas bumbasted with cotten wolle with buttons of silke and button holes made of silke all of our greate guarderobe.[145]

Adam Bland, the Queen's skinner, furred this gown and jerkin with twelve fox skins and 151 lamb skins,[146] for winter wear.

Henry Herne made Monarcho two pairs of hose, probably trunk hose from the description:

of red Stamell garded with blewe vellat layed with copper golde lace sett on with silke with lyninges of kersey Cotten and lynen and with pampillion in them and pockettes of fustian all of our greate Guarderobe.[147]

Monarcho wore a hat, made by Raphael Hammond, with these clothes

of blewe taphata (for the said Monarke) striped with golde lace and enbrauderid with Egles of golde and silke with a Felte in it all of our greate Guarderobe. Item to David Smyth for enbrauderinge of the said Hatt with devices of copper golde and silke on it for stuff & workemanship thereof xxvs of our greate guarderobe.[148]

The felt foundation would have held the shape of the hat, beneath the taffeta.

A separate entry in the warrant describes the copper gold lace used for gown, jerkin and hose, as braid. In the sixteenth century the term 'lace' is often used for 'braid', so it is interesting to find an example where both words are used for the same material. The jerkin buttons may have been of Scottish origin, or the term may have described a particular type of design:

Item Delyverid to the said Thomas Ludwell by him employed upon a Gowne and a Jerken for the said Monarke xxvij oz of fine copper golde brayde doble gilte: thre dossen of longe buttons & loupes wrought on the fyngers of fine copper golde doble gilt: and two dossen and a half of skottyshe buttons of copper golde for his Jerken all of our greate guarderobe. Item Delyverid to Henry Herne by him employed upon the said Monarke his hoose xij oz quarter of fine copper golde brayde being doble gilt of our greate guarderobe.[149]

Thomas Ludwell made another gown for Monarcho in the summer of 1569,[150] in 'blue unwaterid Chamblett with a garde of crymsen vellat'. Accompanying it were a doublet of 'striped golde Canvas' bombasted with cotton wool; and a jerkin of tawny Spanish leather, with a decorative pattern cut in it, both with copper gold buttons. Henry Herne made the slops, or breeches, to match the gown and provided kersey nether

stocks while Garrett Johnson made him two pairs of Spanish leather shoes. Monarcho also received a velvet cap, a girdle, a pair of garters, a pair of gloves, and six shirts.

A third gown, which Thomas Ludwell made for Monarcho in 1574, was of blue damask 'garded with foure gardes of grene vellat endentid layed on with silver lase sowed on with silke'. A jerkin was made to match and the doublet was of striped canvas trimmed with silk lace.[151] Monarcho was also given two shirts, a pair of Spanish leather shoes, a pair of leather pantobles, and two yards of narrow green taffeta for a girdle.[152] Adam Bland furred the gown with twelve white fox and forty-six hare skins, powdered with sixty black genets tails. Henry Herne is entered for 'canvas blewe buckeram heare Cotten kersey for stockes for the said Monark lynen lyninges pockettes of fustian Two dossen of Poyntes and making of his garters and Hose all of our great guarderobe'.[153]

The fourth gown, and apparently the last for Monarcho, which Ludwell made in the summer of 1575, was of 'olde Tyncell'.[154] This was probably some material from a gown of Elizabeth's or perhaps old stock in the Wardrobe. It does not seem to be a scribe's error for gold tinsel, as it is entered in the same way in another copy of the warrant.[155] This gown was guarded with yellow velvet and faced with changeable or shot mockado. Jerkin and gaskin hose, or breeches, were made in matching mockado, striped all over with 'billement lace', or braid. Monarcho's doublet of striped sackcloth was trimmed with lace and his nether stocks, or stockings, were of stammell kersey, with girdle and garters of taffeta. The jerkin was furred with forty-four black coney skins and ten white lamb skins. This seems a lot of fur for a jerkin, and it was probably used for the gown as well.

A small Negro page boy attended on the Queen in 1574. He was given 'a gasken Coate for a litell blak a More of white taphata cutt lyned under with tyncell striped downe with golde and silver lyned with buckeram and bayes poynted with poyntinge Rebande and fased with taphata'.[156] The bombasted doublet was made to match, with silver buttons. Henry Herne made 'a peire of gaskens for the said little blak a More with canvas cotten heare pockettes of fustian and lyninges of fustian in the canons'. The boy also had a pair of knitted stockings, a pair of white shoes and a pair of white pantobles, a dozen points to truss his hose and a pair of garters.[157]

The little blackamoor received one more gift of clothes in 1575. No others seem to have been recorded after this date. Thomas Ludwell made him 'a Cassocke of carnacion stammell trymmed with silver lase and on either side a purle lase of grene silke sowed on with silke with buttons of silke and silver fased with taphata lyned with bayes and buckeram'.[158] The hose, or breeches, were made of silver and silk lace-trimmed stammel to match, with taffeta trimmed with silver lace pulled out between the panes. They were lined with linen, stuffed with hair and canvas to make them stand out, and had fustian pockets. The green taffeta doublet was decoratively cut, pulled out with sarsenet and trimmed with lace to match the cassock. These garments were worn with a pair of knitted stockings, taffeta girdle and garters, and a carnation velvet cap. There was also a tuft mockado gown faced with thirty-seven black coney skins, a gaskin coat of changeable mockado and a matching doublet and another taffeta girdle, with six pairs of shoes.

Elizabeth Smithson and Anne Twiste,[159] the Queen's laundresses, were among the women servants who received gifts of clothing from Elizabeth. Anne's were for her daughter

Winifred. Some women were given livery, as in the case of Ippolyta the Tartarian, who was in the Queen's service by 1561. She seems to have been a child, perhaps a midget, although described as 'our woman' in the warrants, as Alice Mountague the silkwoman, 'delivered to Katherin Asteley for the said Ipolitaine one Baby of pewter' in 1562.[160] This doll may have been similar to that illustrated in Figure 163. There is a warrant dormant for her livery in June 1564:

A warrant for Ipolita the Tartarian. We woll and comaunde you that ye deliver or cause to be delivered to oure deare and welbeloved woman Ipolita the Tartarian, by hir to be taken of our guifte by vertue of this our warraunte dormaunte yearely duringe our pleasure at the Feast of St Michell tharcangell theise parcelles of stuff folowinge viz First oone Gowne & kirtle of damaske gardid withe velvett drawne oute with sarceonett with poyntynge Ribande lined with cotton fustian and linnin Item one other Gowne and kirtle of grograyne chamlett garded with velvett poyntynge Ribande Item one other gowne of clothe And a kirtle of grograyne drawne out with sarceonett lyned as afore Item one peticote of red clothe or grograyne And one varthingale of mockeado Item vj smockes, vj kercheves, vj partelettes with Ruffes & iiij payre of lynen sleves Item half a pound of Threde to make hir said smockes & kercheves vj oz of silke to worke the said partelettes and Sleves, fyve oz of venice golde & silver to make other workes one cloute of spanyshe nedles, one skarfe of sarceonett One hatt & ij cawles of golde silver & silke And theise our lettres signed with oure owne hande shalbe your sufficiente warraunt & dischardge in this behalf geven under our Signett at our manoure of Richemounte the xvj[th] of June the sixte yere of our Reigne.[161]

Details of prices of some of these items are given in a later note:

Theise parcelles conteyned in the Tertarians warraunte
Item ix elles of whited canvas for vj smockes at ijs the ell — xviij s
Item ij elles of hollande for sleves for the same vj smockes price the elle iij s — vj s
Item v elles of fyne hollande For vj partelettes with bandes and ruffes for the same at vj s viij d thell — xxxiij s iiij d
Item vj elles of hollannde to make vj kercheves price the elle vj s viij d — xls
Item ij ells hollande for iiij payre sleves at vj s viij d — xiij s iiij d.
Item di lb of systers thred at xx s lb. — x s
Item vj oz of granado silke at ij s viij d oz — xvj s
Item v oz of venice golde & silver at vj s viij d oz — xxxiij s iiij d
Item j clout spanishe nedles — xls.
Item one skarf of Sarceonett — xxv s vj d
Item one velvett hatt — xxxiij s iiij d
Item ij caules of gold silver & silke at xl s pece — iiij li.[162]

Ippolyta was still in the Queen's service in 1569, as Adam Bland furred a short damask cloak for her in that year with five dozen black coney skins.[163] This was an extra gift from the Queen, as furs were not included in the livery warrant. There seem to be no other entries for her after this date, but as she received this generous livery allowance, she may simply not have been given any extra clothes.

An unnamed woman dwarf appears among the warrants in 1577,[164] perhaps taking Ippolyta's place. She received two gowns and in the following year another three, of white damask, blue camlet and 'changeable red and white Damaske', with three petticoats of mockado, red kersey and red and green dornex.[165] More gifts followed in 1579, three gowns with close fitting bodices of white bayes, white damask, and orange damask, white satin sleeves, a petticoat, three network part-lets, two little gilt rings, eight yards of 'fyne white Thred bonelace', six pairs of Spanish gloves, and a looking glass.[166] Later in the same year 'Thomasen a woman dwarf'[167] was given two more 'streighte bodied' gowns, of unwatered camlet

163 *A pewter doll, or 'baby', height 80 mm (3 ⅛ inches) found in the River Thames in London. The caul, pleated skirt and what appears to be a decorative apron are similar to German and Swiss fashions of c. 1550. The doll may have been imported.*
A. G. Pilson collection

and watchet taffeta, the latter with hanging sleeves 'layed with lase of counterfett silver and silke'. There was also a pair of carnation taffeta sleeves, and three petticoats of 'red mockeado striped with copper golde', 'stammell colour cloth' and 'fryzeado stammell colour' each with 'bodies lined with fustian'. The 'bodies' for the two latter were of crimson taffeta. The material used for the first is not specified, but was presumably made to match the petticoat. At the same time Thomasina's sister, Prudence de Paris, was given a violet cloth gown.[168]

Thomasina was probably the dwarf first listed in 1577. Her name is usually given in the warrants after 1579, as 'Tomasen the woman dwarf' or 'Tomasin de Paris'. There does not seem to be a livery warrant for her, but she was regularly presented with most attractive gowns throughout the reign. The last, in 1603, was a loose gown of tuft taffeta, trimmed with silk and silver lace, with sleeves and stomacher of white satin and a damask petticoat.[169] Thomasina apparently did not stay at Court after James I came to the throne, as her name no longer appears among the warrants.

Some of Thomasina's clothes were quite as fine as those worn by the Queen, indeed some of them were made from her old gowns. One in 1584 was

a frenche Gowne of white and blak tufte taphata (for the said Dwarf) layed with lase borderid with buckeram the bodies lyned with canvas & buckeram the slevis drawne oute with lawne sett with bugelles allover, the outeside being a kyrtell of our store of the chardge of the said Rauf Hope threst of our great guarderobe.[170]

In 1587 Thomasina was given a petticoat of orange and black 'figured satten frengid upperbodied with taphata lyned with fustian the skirtes lyned with bayes the outeside made of an olde Gowne of our store'.[171] With this she had two gowns of new material, one of gold-striped white satin, the other of murrey and black tuft taffeta both trimmed with gold and silver lace. Both gowns had bodices stiffened with buckram and fustian pockets. At the same time William Jones made Thomasina two pairs of white satin sleeves, altered another gown of black and white tuft taffeta, binding the skirts with black and white silk lace, and made a bodice and paned sleeves for a gown of orange, gold and black tuft taffeta.

These are typical entries for the dwarf throughout the reign. She was also given three pairs of holland cloth sheets, 'one dozen of diaper Napkyns',[172] two dozen table napkins and a dozen towels,[173] which would have lasted her a lifetime: linen is a hard-wearing fabric. There are often lengths of holland cloth for her,[174] probably to make smocks and ruffs, and pretty gifts including silver and gold cauls,[175] two taffeta

aprons,[176] a green taffeta scarf [177] and several ivory combs[178] and looking glasses.[179] The latter items may have been intended for Thomasina to dress the Queen's hair. She was obviously able to write, as 'one penner and Inkehorne' were delivered to her by Roger Mountague in 1581.[180] Thomasina was frequently given 'a payer of knyves in a sheathe with Sheares in thende':[181] The knives may have been for table use, although Peter Erondell refers to 'the knife to close Letters' in his book of French/English dialogues reflecting life in a noble household, *The French Garden*, published in 1603.[182] The shears, or scissors, may have been for embroidery work.

Thomasina was always dressed in the latest fashion, although she was so small, receiving, for example, two pairs of 'verthingale sleeves of whales bone covered with fustian' to hold out her satin sleeves in 1588.[183] This would suggest that she was a midget, proportioned like a child. She was probably like an elegant doll and, as she remained at Court until the end of Elizabeth's reign, was doubtless an entertaining companion.

Notes

1 *Collins*, pp. 248–53

2 New Year's Gift Roll 1562, *Progr. Eliz.*, I, pp. 108–28.

3 *Progr. James I*, I, p. 471.

4 New Year's Gift Roll 1563, PRO, C47/3/38.

5 See Chapter III, note 107.

6 New Year's Gift Roll 1565, Folger, Z. d. 13.

7 New Year's Gift Roll 1568, Society of Antiquaries of London MS 538. I am indebted to Miss Santina M. Levey for the suggestion that the schoolmaster may have drawn out the embroidery design, as other examples are known.

8 See Chapter IV, note 31.

9 *Sydney Papers*, I, p. 376.

10 *Egerton Papers*, p. 343.

11 See Chapter IV, note 97.

12 *Swain, Needlework*, p. 82.

13 Ibid., p. 83.

14 *Progr. Eliz.*, III, p. 49.

15 Ibid., pp. 82–83.

16 Ibid., p. 429.

17 *Ellis, Letters*, first series (1824), II, pp. 274–76.

18 Folger, X. d. 428 (127).

19 Letter dated 13 December, no year given but probably 1575. Folger, X. d. 428 (128).

20 Letter dated 2 January, no year given but probably 1576. Folger, X. d. 428 (130).

21 Letter dated 21 October, no year given but between 1561 and 1568. Folger, X. d. 428 (16). For 'shoulder raile' see BL, Egerton 2806, f.109ᵛ, warrant dated 12 April 1577.

22 Joseph Hunter, *Hallamshire* (1819) p. 86.

23 PRO, C47/3/39.

24 *CSP Foreign*, 1577–78, p. 388, letter dated 18[8] December 1577. New Style dates are apparently used for these letters from France and are therefore ten days in advance of current English reckoning. English dates are given in square brackets.

25 *CSP Foreign*, 1577–78, p. 403, letter dated 25[15] December 1577. See note 24 above.

26 Society of Antiquaries of London, MS 537, printed in *Progr. Eliz.*, II, p. 74.

27 *CSP Foreign*, 1577–78, p. 457, letter dated 14[4] January 1578.

28 *CSP Foreign*, 1578–79, p. 409, letter dated 6 February [27 January] 1579.

29 Letter dated 4 December, no year given but possibly 1585. Folger, X. d. 428 (131).

30 Letter dated 2 January, no year given but possibly 1576. Folger, X. d. 428 (130).

31 *Nugae Antiquae*, II, p. 253.

32 *HMC Hatfield, Salisbury MSS* (1904) X, p. 51. Letter dated 5 March 1600.

33 *Sydney Papers*, II, p. 155.

34 Ibid., pp. 158–59.

35 Ibid., p. 172.

36 Ibid., p. 174.

37 E. A. Bond (ed.), *Travels*, p. 234, quoted in Bradford, *Helena*. p. 101. Other rich gifts were sent by the Sultana Mother of Turkey in 1599. They are recorded in a letter written to Elizabeth by Esperanza Malchi, a Jewess: . . . 'Besides your Majesty having sent a distinguished Ambassador into this Kingdom, with a present for this most serene Queen my mistress, in as much as she has been willing to make use of my services, she has found me ready. And now at the departure of

the noble Ambassador alluded to, the most serene Queen wishing to prove to your Majesty the love she bears you, sends to your Majesty by the illustrious Ambassador a robe and a girdle, and two kerchiefs wrought in gold, and three wrought in silk, after the fashion of this kingdom, and a necklace of pearls and rubies; the whole the most serene Queen sends to the illustrious Ambassador by the hand of the Sieur Bostanggi Basi; and by my own hand I have delivered to the illustrious Ambassador a wreath of diamonds from the jewels of her Highness, which she says, your Majesty will be pleased to wear for the love of her, and give information of the receipt. And your Majesty being a Lady full of condescension, I venture to prefer the following request; namely that, since there are to be met with in your Kingdom distilled waters of every description for the face, and odiferous oils for the hands, your Majesty would favor me by transmitting some by my hand for this most serene Queen; by my hand, as, being articles for ladies, she does not wish them to pass through other hands. Likewise if there are to be had in your Kingdom cloths of silk or wool, articles of fancy suited for so high a Queen as my Mistress, your Majesty may be pleased to send them, as she will be more gratified by such objects than by any valuable your Majesty could send her. I have nothing further to add, but to pray the Lord God that he may give your Majesty the victory over your enemies: and that your Majesty may ever be prosperous and happy. Amen. From Constantinople the 16th November 1599. Your Majesties most humble Esperanza Malchi' (*Ellis, Letters*, first series (1824), III, p. 53).

38 Quoted in *Progr. Eliz.*, III, p. 468. See Stowe inventory f.61/77.

39 *CSP Venetian*, 1558–80, VII, p. 97. Letter dated 11 June 1559 from Paolo Tiepolo, the Venetian Ambassador with King Philip, to the Doge and Senate.

40 Ibid., p. 94. Letter dated 30 May 1559 from Il Schifanoya to the Castellan of Mantua.

41 *Sydney Papers*, II, p. 156. Letter from Rowland Whyte to Sir Robert Sydney, dated 5 January 1599.

42 BL, Add. 5751A, f.87. Signet warrant for deliveries dated 19 May 1574.

43 Arnold, 'Lost from HMB', no. 220.

44 Stowe inventory, f.26/15.

45 PRO, LC5/37, ff.283, 284.

46 *Jenkins, Eliz. Great*, p. 147.

47 BL, Egerton 2806, f.11, warrant dated 16 Oct. 1568.

48 Chapter I, note 50.

49 BL, Egerton 2806, ff.49, 49ᵛ, warrant dated 28 Sept. 1572.

50 Ibid., f.140ᵛ, warrant dated 10 April 1579.

51 Ibid., ff.181, 181ᵛ, warrant dated 28 Sept. 1582.

52 Ibid., f.181ᵛ.

53 Ibid.

54 Ibid.

55 Ibid., f.186, warrant dated 20 April 1583.

56 Ibid., f.187.

57 Ibid., f.196ᵛ, warrant dated 26 April 1584.

58 *Christensen*, p. 30. pl. IV.

59 Arnold, 'Lost from HMB', no. 355.

60 *Christensen*, pp. 21–28, pls I and II.

61 Arnold, 'Lost from HMB', no. 362.

62 *Nugae Antiquae*, II, p. 141.

63 *Chambers*, I, p. 45. However, see *Progr. Eliz*, I, p. 269 where 'Mary Radclyffe, one of the Madens of Honoure' was paid 'for her stipend of £40 per annum for two years and a half, ended at the Annunciation of oure Lady, 1569 £100.0s.0d'.

64 See Chapter I, notes 51 and 53. There is one reference to 'The 15 ladies of

honnour hath fee £750.0.0' in a list titled 'The officers & servanntes in the householde and what their fees and allowance is' apparently dating from 1586. BL, Harl. 6839, f.317ᵛ. I am indebted to Miss Jane Apple for this reference.

65 *Jenkins, Eliz. and Leicester*, pp. 147–48 for description of wedding.

66 PRO, LC5/33, f.167, warrant dated 25 March 1566.

67 A letter from Elynor, Countess of Rutland, to Lady Lisle mentions Mother Lowe: '. . . And where ye be verey desirous to have youre daughter maistres basset to be oon of the Quenes graces maides, and that ye wold I shuld move hir grace in that behalf. This shalbe to doo yow Ladishipe {to wit} that I p{erceve} right well the kingis highnes pleasure to be suche that no more maides shalbe taken in, untill suche tyme as some of them that nowe be with the quenes grac[e] be preferred. Albeit if ye will make some meanes unto mother Lowe who can doo as moche good in this matier as any {. . .} woman here that she maye make some meanes to get yow said doughter with the quenes said grace' (BL, Cotton Vespasian F xiii, article 121, f.172). The letter is dated 17 February; no year is given but it is likely to have been 1537. Elynor assisted the chief mourner at Queen Jane Seymour's funeral in November of that year. Lady Lisle died in March 1539. (G.E.C., *The Complete Peerage*, rev. ed., Geoffrey White.) See New Year's Gift Roll 1598 (Folger, Z. d. 17) for Mrs Wingfield, Mother of the Maids. There is one reference to 'The Mother of the ladies of honnour hath fee 66li. 3s. 4d.', BL, Harl. 6839, f.317ᵛ, see note 64.

68 *Sydney Papers*, II, p. 156.

69 *Treatise of the office of a councillor and Secretary to Her Majesty* (1592) quoted in G. R. Elton, *The Tudor Constitution* (Cambridge, 1965), p. 126.

70 *Sydney Papers*, II, p. 16.

71 Ibid., I, p. 204.

72 Arnold, 'Lost from HMB', no. 47.

73 BL, Egerton 2806, f.135, warrant dated 26 Sept. 1578.

74 Ibid., f.49, warrant dated 28 Sept. 1572.

75 PRO, LC5/49, f.174, warrant dated 14 Feb. 1571.

76 PRO, LC5/37, f.88, warrant dated Lady Day 1596.

77 Ibid., f.89.

78 PRO, LC5/49, f.174, warrant dated 14 Feb. 1571.

79 HMC Rutland, I, p. 107, quoted in *Jenkins, Eliz. Great*, p. 225.

80 Arnold, 'Lost from HMB', no. 179.

81 PRO, The Duchess of Norfolk deeds, MS C/115/L2/6697 printed in full in Arnold, 'Lost from HMB'.

82 Chambers, p. 44.

83 *Cal. Pat. Rolls, Eliz.*, IV, 1566–69, no. 1418, lease dated 16 April 1568.

84 *Cal. Pat. Rolls, Eliz.*, V, 1569–72, no. 302, lease dated 27 June 1570.

85 BL, Egerton 2806, f.82, warrant dated 13 April 1575.

86 Arnold, 'Lost from HMB', no. 117. She is entered as 'Mistres Morberye' in 1552, *Smythe, Household Expenses*, p. 36.

87 Arnold, 'Lost from HMB', no. 280.

88 PRO, LC5/49, f.126, warrant dated 28 Nov. 1559.

89 HMC Hatfield, Salisbury MSS, pt II, (1888) p. 69, no. 184, dated 1 Feb. 1574.

90 MacCaffrey, 'Place and Patronage', pp. 114–15.

91 BL, Egerton 2806, f.152, warrant dated 12 April 1580.

92 BL, Lansdowne 59, f.43.

93 She is described thus in a draft commission dated 6 Oct. 1600, CSP Dom. 1598–1601, CCLXXV, p. 476.

94 C. A. Bradford, *Blanche Parry* (1935), p. 6.

95 MacCaffrey, 'Place and Patronage', p. 116.

96 PRO, LC5/49, f.126, warrant dated 28 Nov. 1559.

97 PRO, LC5/34, f.26, warrant dated last day of Sept. 1567.

98 *Cal. Pat. Rolls, Eliz.*, V, 1569–72, no. 2574, 20 August 1572 and no. 302, 27 July 1570.

99 Arnold, 'Lost from HMB', no. 198.

100 PRO, LC5/49, f.170, warrant dated 20 Nov. 1569.

101 Arnold, 'Lost from HMB', no. 159.

102 BL, Egerton 2806, f.68ᵛ, warrant dated 16 April 1574.

103 Arnold, 'Lost from HMB', no. 163.

104 Ibid., no. 186.

105 BL, Egerton 2806, f.82ᵛ, warrant dated 13 April 1575.

106 Arnold, 'Lost from HMB', no. 256.

107 BL, Egerton 2806, f.137ᵛ, warrant dated 10 April 1579.

108 Arnold, 'Lost from HMB', no. 278 for the gift and BL, Egerton 2806, f.152, warrant dated 12 April 1580 for the tailor's work.

109 Arnold, 'Lost from HMB', no. 279.

110 PRO, LC5/36, f.210, warrant dated 6 June 1592.

111 Joseph Hunter, *Hallamshire* (1819), p. 92. See also her tomb in St Margaret's Church, Westminster.

112 Arnold, 'Lost from HMB', no. 70.

113 *Jenkins, Eliz. and Leicester*, pp. 147–48.

114 PRO, LC5/33, f.166, warrant dated 25 March 1566.

115 *Johnson*, p. 438.

116 The Stowe inventory, ff.100, 104.

117 Arnold, 'Lost from HMB', p. 11.

118 These are recorded among warrants throughout the reign and in Arnold, 'Lost from HMB'. An article with further information on this subject is in preparation.

119 Will of George Tenecre, 20 April 1591, PCC 58 Harrington. I am very grateful to Miss Jane Apple for this reference.

120 CSP Dom. Add. vol. XXV, 1603–10, p. 427. Mr David McKeen writing a

book on William Brooke, Lord Cobham of Kent, has found no references to the title 'Mistress of the Robes' in his MS sources for Lady Frances.

121 *Haydn, Dignities*, p. 304.

122 Ibid., p. 303.

123 *Nugae Antiquae*, II, p. 232–35, letter dated 23 May 1597.

124 Ibid., pp. 139–40.

125 Arnold, 'Lost from HMB', nos 56, 101, 115, 151, 242, 292, 381.

126 Ibid., no. 130.

127 HMC Hatfield, Salisbury MSS, pt I (1883) p. 403, no. 1287, letter from H. Killigrew to Sir William Cecil, dated 2 April 1569.

128 BL, Egerton 2806, f.107ᵛ, warrant dated 26 Sept. 1576.

129 *Stubbes*, 1583 edn, p. 26; 1585 edn, p. 24; 1595 edn, p. 30.

130 Ibid., 1583 edn, pp. 26, 26ᵛ; 1585 edn, pp. 24, 24ᵛ; 1595 edn, p. 31.

131 BL, Egerton 2806, f.107ᵛ, warrant dated 26 Sept. 1576.

132 Ibid.

133 Ibid., f.133, warrant dated 26 Sept. 1578.

134 Ibid., f.167ᵛ, warrant dated 6 April 1581.

135 Ibid., f.114, warrant dated 12 April 1577.

136 Ibid., f.91ᵛ, warrant dated 28 Sept. 1575.

137 Ibid., f.75, warrant dated 14 Oct. 1574.

138 Ibid., f.84ᵛ, warrant dated 13 April 1575.

139 Ibid., f.75, 75ᵛ, warrant dated 14 Oct. 1574. Shenton is described here as 'a Foole', not by name.

140 Ibid., f.84, warrant dated 13 April 1575.

141 *Stubbes*, 1583 edn, p. 25ᵛ; 1585 edn, p. 23ᵛ; 1595 edn, p. 30. Stubbes gives them as 'Gally hosen'.

142 BL, Egerton 2806, f.84ᵛ, warrant dated 13 April 1575.

143 Ibid.

144 Ibid., f.92, warrant dated 28 April 1575.

145 Ibid., f.6ᵛ, warrant dated 14 April 1568.

146 Ibid.

147 Ibid., f.7.

148 Ibid.

149 Ibid., f.7ᵛ.

150 Ibid., f.20, 20ᵛ, warrant dated 6 Oct. 1569.

151 Ibid., f.69ᵛ, warrant dated 14 April 1574.

152 Ibid., f.70.

153 Ibid.

154 Ibid., f.91ᵛ, warrant dated 28 Sept. 1575.

155 PRO, LC5/34, f.310, warrant dated 28 Sept. 1575.

156 BL, Egerton 2806, f.70, warrant dated 14 April 1574.

157 Ibid.

158 Ibid., f.83ᵛ, warrant dated 13 April 1575.

159 Ibid., f.126ᵛ, warrant dated 12 April 1578 for Smithson, f.185, warrant of 20 April 1583 for Twiste and Arnold, 'Lost from HMB', nos 17, 46, 122, 250.

160 Ippolyta appears as 'a Tartarian woman' in a gift list for 1561 printed in *The Gentleman's Magazine and Historical Chronicle* (1754) XXIV, pp. 162–63, reprinted in *The Needle and Bobbin Club* (New York, 1925) IX, no. 2, pp. 15–17. Both are dated to 16 May, 'the thirde yeare of our reigne, 1560', which should be 1561. I am indebted to Miss Santina M. Levey for these references. For the pewter baby see PRO, LC5/33, ff.10, 11, warrant dated 20 Oct. 1562.

161 PRO, LC5/49, f.149.

162 Ibid., f.339.

163 BL, Egerton 2806, f.20, warrant dated 6 Oct. 1569.

164 Ibid., f.112, warrant dated 12 April 1577.

165 Ibid., f.123ᵛ, warrant dated 12 April 1578; f.131, dated 26 Sept. 1578.

166 Ibid., ff.138, 142, warrant dated 10 April 1579.

167 Ibid., f.145ᵛ, 146, warrant dated 12 Oct. 1579.

168 Ibid., f.149ᵛ.

169 PRO, LC5/37, ff.283, 284, warrant dated 21 May 1603.

170 BL, Egerton 2806, f.195ᵛ, warrant dated 12 April 1584.

171 Ibid., f.221ᵛ, warrant dated 12 April 1587.

172 Ibid., f.159ᵛ, warrant dated 28 Sept. 1580, for one pair of sheets made of eight ells of holland cloth from James Hewish; f.167ᵛ, warrant dated 6 April 1581, for two pairs of sheets 'contayning two bredthes and two elles longe the pece' and the diaper napkins.

173 Ibid., f.181ᵛ, warrant dated 28 Sept. 1582.

174 For example, ibid., f.133ᵛ, warrant dated 26 Sept. 1578 and f.148, warrant dated 12 Oct. 1579.

175 For example, ibid., f.156, warrant dated 12 April 1580 and f.173ᵛ, warrant dated 15 Sept. 1581.

176 Ibid., f.158ᵛ, warrant dated 28 Sept. 1580.

177 Ibid., f.193, warrant dated 26 Sept. 1583.

178 For example, ibid., f.181, warrant dated 28 Sept. 1582; f.193, warrant dated 26 Sept. 1583; f.217ᵛ, warrant dated 27 Sept. 1586.

179 For example, ibid., f.142, warrant dated 10 April 1579; f.193, warrant dated 26 Sept. 1583; f.198ᵛ, warrant dated 12 April 1584; f.211ᵛ, warrant dated 27 Sept. 1585; f.217ᵛ, warrant dated 27 Sept. 1586.

180 Ibid., f.172ᵛ, warrant dated 15 Sept. 1581.

181 For example, ibid., f.181, warrant dated 28 Sept. 1582; f.193, warrant dated 26 Sept. 1583; f.198ᵛ, warrant dated 12 April 1584; f.211ᵛ, warrant dated 27 Sept. 1585; f.217ᵛ, warrant dated 27 Sept. 1586.

182 *Byrne, Erondell*, p. 40.

183 Ibid., f.232, warrant dated 27 Sept. 1588.

VI

The Pursuit of Fashion

'A gentlewoman made ready'

The fashionable woman in sixteenth-century England took some time in dressing, with the assistance of one or more maid-servants. The following description in *Lingua, or the Combat of the Tongues* by Thomas Tomkis, printed in 1607, gives an idea of the number of component parts needed at the turn of the century and conjures up a picture of the Ditchley portrait of the Queen (Fig. 71). Although five hours is a little exaggerated, it would have taken at least an hour to set a starched ruff and pin the flounce round the edge of a drum-shaped farthingale in position.

Five hours ago I set a dozen maids to attire a boy like a nice gentlewoman; but there is such doing with their looking glasses, pinning, unpinning, setting, unsetting, formings and conformings, painting blew veins and cheeks; such stir with sticks and combs, cascanets, dressings, purls, falls, squares, busks, bodies, scarfs, necklaces, carcanets, rebatoes, borders, tires, fans, palisadoes, puffs, ruffs, cuffs, muffs, pusles, fusles, partlets, frislets, bandlets, fillets, crosslets, pendulets, amulets, annulets, bracelets, and so many lets [hindrances] that yet she is scarce dressed to the girdle; and now there's such a calling for fardingales, kirtles, busk-points, shoe ties, etc., that seven peddler's shops — nay all Stourbridge Fair — will scarce furnish her: a ship is sooner rigged by far, than a gentlewoman made ready.

The sequence of events is described by Peter Erondell in his vivid account of the Lady Ri-Mellaine getting dressed in the morning, assisted by Prudence, the chamber-maid, and Jolye, the waiting gentlewoman: his book of French/English dialogues reflecting life in a noble household, *The French Garden*, was published in 1605.[1] Muriel St Clare Byrne suggests that Lady Ri-Mellaine's character may be based on Lady Elizabeth Berkeley, the only child of George Carey, Baron Hunsdon, and godchild of the Queen.[2] Her husband, Sir Thomas Berkeley, whom Erondell had instructed in the French language, was very extravagant. Lady Elizabeth apparently paid off his debts and restored financial order by firm retrenchment fourteen years after their marriage, which was in 1596. Sir Thomas's mother, Lady Katherine, was an equally masterful character — 'of stomache great and haughty' — and Erondell may have met her as she did not die until 1596.[3] His dialogues certainly conjure up the daily conversations dominant personalities such as Lady Elizabeth and her mother-in-law — or the Queen

— would have had with their women: 'Hoe! who is in the inner Chamber? how now, Maidens, heere you not? are you deafe? . . . O God! how long you make me tarrye! Kindle the fire quickly, warme my smocke and give it me'. Linen feels cold to the touch and taking the chill off the smock in front of the fire would also have ensured that it was properly aired.

Her smock on, the Lady next calls for her 'pettycoate bodyes: I meane my damask quilt bodies with whalebones, what lace doe you give me heere? this lace is too shorte, the tagges are broken, I cannot lace myself with it, take it away, I will have that of greene silke'. This garment would have resembled that in Figures 164 and 232. The room must have been draughty, in spite of the fire, and once the 'damask quilt bodies' stiffened with whalebone was laced up over the smock, she asks 'when shall I have my under-coate? Give me my peticoate of wroughte Crimson velvet with silver fringe: why doe you not give me my night-gowne? For I take colde: Where be my stockens? Give me some cleane sockes, I will have no woorsted hosen, showe me my Carnation silk stockins: where laid you last night my garters?' The socks were presumably of very fine linen and worn beneath the knitted silk stockings to prevent damage from perspiration. The stockings and garters would have been similar to those worn by Eleanora of Toledo (Fig. 301). Lady Ri-Mellaine then cries 'Take away these slippers, give me my velvet pantofles; send for the shoomaker that he may have again these turn-over shooes, for they be too high. Put on my white pumpes; set them up I will have none of them: Give me rather my Spanish leather shooes for I will walke today . . . Tye the strings with a strong double knot, for feare they untye themselves'.

At this stage a combing cloth was placed over Lady Ri-Mellaine's shoulders[4] while her hair was rubbed with a warm cloth to remove grease and dandruff, then combed with ivory and boxwood combs. Her protests of 'O God! you combe too harde, you scratch me, you pull out my hayres' calls to mind the inscription 'menez moi doucement' on the comb in the portrait of Elizabeth Vernon (Fig. 165). In the Queen's case from the late 1570s a wig would have been ready dressed to put on over her hair.[5] Jolye asks her mistress 'Will it please you to weare your haires onely, or els to have your French Whood?' and the reply comes 'Give me my whood, for me thinketh it is somewhat colde, and I have a rewme which is falne on the left side of my head'. Jolye points out that it is a

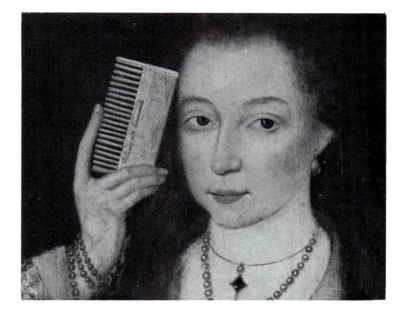

164 *'Elizabeth Vernon, Countess of Southampton, at her toilet'. Panel painting by an unknown artist, c. 1600. She wears a pink silk 'pair of bodies' or corset with rows of stitching to hold whalebones or bents for stiffening. It laces at the centre front. The Duke of Buccleuch and Queensberry, KT, Boughton House, Northamptonshire*

165 *Detail of comb in Figure 164*

166 *Detail of pincushion and jewels in Figure 164*

fine day and Lady Ri-Mellaine drily comments 'I perceive that you would have me take an other attyre . . . Set up then my French whood and my Border of Rubies, give me an other head attyre'. The long box where she keeps the jewels for her hair is produced from the closet and the hair dressing finished to an accompaniment of 'what is become of my wyer? Where is the haire-cap? Have you any ribbons to make knots? Where be the laces for to bind my heares?' Next, the Lady Ri-Mellaine washes herself, while Jolye is sorting out the jewels. By this time only her face and hands are left uncovered, so this activity must have been somewhat restricted, perhaps because of the cold weather. The page brings water: paste of almonds is preferred to a musk ball, as it 'scoureth better'. Lady Ri-Mellaine asks for 'my piece of Scarlet to wipe my face', which seems to have served as a flannel, and then 'Give me that napkin' — a linen cloth to dry herself. A carcanet of precious

stones is put on after this, either round her neck or, more probably, in her hair. No mention is made of cleaning her teeth, but Queen Elizabeth had numerous 'tooth clothes'[6] and obviously tried to remove plaque, although as she was so fond of sweetmeats her teeth were badly decayed.[7]

Lady Ri-Mellaine seems to have decided to wear a new gown — or perhaps one that had been altered — as she directs her attendants to 'call my Taylor to bring my gowne, not the close one, but my open gowne of white Sattin layd on with buttons of Pearl. . . Shall I have no Vardingale? . . . Do you not see that I want my buske? what is become of the buske-poynt?' The space for a busk and the eyelet holes for a busk point to secure it may been seen at the front of the 'pair of bodies' in Figure 232.

The final touches are given by neckwear, purse, clean handkerchief, gloves (it is too warm for a muff), mask, fan, 'Chayne of pearls', and girdle with these items in a case hanging from it: scissors, pincers, pen-knife, a knife to close letters, bodkin, ear-picker, and seal. Jolye asks 'What dooth it please you to have Madame, a ruffe band or a Rebato?' Lady Ri-Mellaine examines the ruff first of all but 'How is it that the supporter is so soyled? I know not for what you are fit, that you cannot so much as keep my clothes cleane . . . take it away give me my Rebato of cutworke edged'. This did not meet with

167 '*Queen Elizabeth I dressed in a crimson gown*', possibly the Parliament kirtle, looking at her reflection in a glass. Illumination in the margin of a poem written by Georges de la Motthe, a Huguenot refugee, presented to the Queen, 1586. Bodleian Library, Oxford (MS Fr.e.1, f.14)

168 '*Isaac Oliver's wife, Sarah Gheeraerts*'. Miniature by Isaac Oliver, c. 1602. She wears a white linen jacket with polychrome silk embroidery, similar to others in many English portraits. The coif and hairstyle resemble those in Dutch portraits after 1600. The smock is worn with the flat turndown collar open at the neck, in an informal pose. Private collection

approval either: 'is not the wyer after the same sort as the other? It is a great wonder if it be any thing better'. Small pins from the pincushion were used to fasten the cuffs, probably of brass or steel such as those in Figure 166, although a black pin is also mentioned. The Queen's clothes would have been pinned in the same way (Fig. 167).

Fashions for Elizabeth

It is quite a complex task to trace the origins of any particular style of dress in a given period, to tell how widespread it was and to judge the duration of its popularity. The evolution of fashion is a gradual process, dependent on many factors. In sixteenth-century England fashions were set at Court, partly by the personal dictates of courtiers and the skill of their tailors, working within limits imposed by the weight, texture, and width of the materials available. They were also partly adapted from styles described by travellers returning home from abroad or brought to the country by foreign visitors.

At this date, designs for clothes apparently were not made, although costumes worn by participants in the ceremonies for the Accession Day Tilts would probably have been sketched for tailors by a number of painters or draughtsmen, and the over-all effect of the spectacle master-minded by Sir Henry Lee.[8] Similar results would have been achieved for costumes worn in masques and other entertainments performed for the Queen on her Progresses, the forerunners of those designed by Inigo Jones for Court masques in the early seventeenth century.[9] However, as we have already seen, the Queen's everyday appearance was the result of her women assembling the component parts of gown, kirtle, sleeves, forepart, ruff, jewels, and so on to her choice.[10] The tailors were artist/craftsmen, producing *toiles* in buckram with samples of arrangements of braid and decorative pinking so that Elizabeth could select those she preferred.[11] The Queen's embroiderers may have drawn out some of their own designs as well as employing draughtsmen, or 'pattern drawers' to do this work. Again, samples were presented to Elizabeth, from which she could make her choice.[12]

Foreign styles exercised a considerable fascination: the Scottish Ambassador, Sir James Melville, recorded a discussion of the fashions which he had had when he met Queen Elizabeth in 1564. He wrote that 'The Queen my Mistress', [Mary, Queen of Scots]

had instructed me to leave matters of gravity sometimes, and cast in merry purposes, lest otherwise I should be wearied, she being well informed of that Queen's natural temper. Therefore in declaring my observations of the customs of Dutchland, Poland, and Italy, the Buskins of the Women was not forgot, and what Countrey Weed I thought best becoming Gentlewomen. The Queen said she had Cloth[e]s of every sort, which every day thereafter, so long as I was there, she changed. One day she had the English Weed, another the French, and another the Italian and so forth. She asked me which of them became her best? I answered, in my judgement the Italian dress, which answer I found pleased her well, for she delighted to shew her golden coloured hair, wearing a Caul and Bonnet as they do in Italy.[13]

What is the evidence for named styles from abroad in the inventories and warrants for the Queen's Wardrobe of Robes? There are not many such entries in over forty years and almost all of them belong to the 1560s and 1570s. Elizabeth had a black taffeta Flanders gown in 1562,[14] another of black 'barred velvet' in 1563[15] and a few others were made and altered between 1563 and 1571.[16] After this there seem to be only alterations to those she already had. Walter Fyshe, her tailor, remodelled a Dutch gown of black velvet, with a Spanish sleeve in 1567,[17] and there is a reference to 'alteringe and making longer' of a black velvet Polish gown in 1568,[18] so these two gowns may have been in the Wardrobe for some time. Walter Fyshe also made a Venetian gown of crimson velvet, which was given to Elizabeth Knollys in 1565,[19] two 'traine gownes of the French fation' and five gowns of the Italian fashion in 1568 and 1569.[20] Four Spanish gowns were made between 1571 and 1577[21] and Fyshe was also engaged in 'alteringe and enlarginge of the slevis of a gowne of orange colour satten of the Irishe facion' in 1576.[22] Apart from these references and a few others, garments are usually described as loose gowns, French gowns, round gowns, kirtles, petticoats, and doublets. The Italian fashion mentioned by Melville obviously included the hairstyle with 'caul and bonnet'. Elizabeth already had a Flanders gown, made in 1562, when Melville met her. Perhaps the Polish gown remodelled in 1568 was hurriedly made during his visit in 1564.

It seems as if foreign fashions were adopted and modified so quickly that their names were soon dropped from the warrant entries. The difference between each style of dress, as worn by an Englishwoman, may not have been quite so pronounced as Melville's description implies. Our eyes have become familiar with a certain range of portraits known to be of English-women. Although we differentiate between Spanish and French farthingales, and recognize the different fashions depicted in paintings of foreigners, all the subtle variations in sleeves, fastenings, necklines, and bodice lengths in English portraits tend to be accepted as English dress without querying if the fashions were of Spanish, French, Dutch, Italian or Polish inspiration, and if they were known as such by their wearers.

It is no straightforward matter to make comparisons with portraits of foreigners, as an Italian woman may well be wearing a French fashion, a French woman an Italian fashion, or a Bohemian woman a Spanish fashion. Just to add to the confusion, some pictures are of Englishwomen living abroad (Fig. 203), some of foreigners living in England[23] (Fig. 168) and others of Englishwomen painted by foreigners. No matter what the sitter is wearing, a painter sometimes will give a faint hint of the fashions of his own country to a portrait, quite unconsciously. Not only this, but the slight variations in past fashions which would have been noticed immediately at the time, for example the raising or lowering of the waistline by an inch, can often only be detected with difficulty at a later date. The main features of Spanish, French, Italian, and other styles as they appeared in the countries of origin throughout the reign must first be established. The details may then be traced in portraits where they are seen subtly transmuted into English fashions.

French gowns and a French tailor

In 1520 Katherine of Aragon's tailor received instructions 'for translating of iij gownes after the devysing of Sir Thomas Bullen When he came owte of france'[24] and was paid thirteen shillings and four pence for his labours. How much these gowns looked like the original French fashion after an English tailor had altered them to an Englishman's description, it is difficult to say. Perhaps these three gowns marked the beginning of a particular style of sleeve or neckline which, to our eyes, is an English fashion. Giacomo Soranzo, the Venetian Ambassador, described Mary Tudor's clothes in a despatch in 1554:

Her garments are of two sorts; the one, a gown such as men wear, but fitting very close, with an underpetticoat which has a very long train; and this is her ordinary costume being also that of the gentlewomen of England. The other garment is a gown and bodice, with wide hanging sleeves in the French fashion, which she wears on state occasions.[25]

169 'Elizabeth of Valois, Philip II of Spain's Queen', by Alonso Sanchez Coëllo, 1564. She wears a silk gown, embroidered with silver metal thread. The forepart is of white silk with a raised looped pile in silver metal thread. The white silk sleeves are slashed diagonally and caught together with aglets for decoration. Gemäldegalerie, Kunsthistorisches Museum, Vienna

The portrait of Elizabeth when Princess, probably painted early in 1547 (Fig. 4) shows the latter style, described as 'the French fashion' by an Italian. Perhaps the instructions received by Katherine of Aragon's tailor in 1520 resulted in a gown similar to this. Elizabeth of Valois, Philip II of Spain's queen, wears a gown with similar square neckline, slightly more arched and filled in with a partlet, in her portrait some seventeen years later (Fig. 169): the sleeves are of a later style.

The Stowe and Folger inventories prepared in 1600 include many items from earlier years. These descriptions may be compared with dated warrants for the Wardrobe of Robes and entries in New Year's Gift Rolls. We can see that the same name was used for certain types of gown for over forty years, although portraits show considerable changes in cut and shape. A 'French gown', from the numerous entries, seems to

9

170   'Aulica Franca: French lady at court' wearing what is probably a round gown. From Omnium Poene Gentium Imagines by Abraham de Bruyn, 1577. British Library, London

171   Louise de Lorraine and her sister from the Valois tapestries, ordered by Catherine de 'Medici as a gift to her native city of Florence, c.1575. Galleria degli Uffizi, Florence

be the name for one of the basic styles of dress, not 'a gown of the French fashion' — although the name obviously came originally from a style of dress imported from France. Walter Fyshe, the Queen's tailor, made 'a french Gowne of blak vellat with doble bodies of the Italion fation' in 1568,[26] altered and new-made 'a frenche Gowne of blak satten with a spanishe garde' in 1573[27] and made 'a frenche Gowne with a longe traine of purple cloth of golde the bodie made with a highe Coller and great pendaunte slevis of the spanishe facion' in 1576.[28] These entries show that the basic French gown might incorporate fashion features from other countries.

Descriptions of French gowns in the Stowe and Folger inventories are very close to those of round gowns and sometimes gowns were altered from the former style to the latter. For example in 1575 Fyshe altered and new-made

a frenche Gowne with a traine of blak vellat wrought with a very brode garde of blak silke like cheines the same Gowne made into a rounde Gowne ye traine made into slevis and two newe panes in the skyrtes.[29]

The essential difference between the styles in this instance seems to be that a French gown had a skirt which trailed on the ground at the back, while the hem of a round gown was level all the way round, just touching the floor. The skirt of this French gown after its alteration to a round gown would probably have resembled those worn by a French lady at court in Figure 170 and by Louise de Lorraine and her sister in Figure 171.

The term 'traine gowne'[30] found in the Stowe inventory may simply be an abbreviation for 'a french gown with a train'. There is, however, one reference to a French gown 'with a traine to take of and on'[31] and another to a round kirtle with a similar detachable train in 1563,[32] so it is possible that a separate train was a feature of 'a traine gowne'. Certainly trains were made separately. Walter Fyshe made 'a Trayne of crymsen tyssue lett downe with crymsen Satten lyned with purple sarconett welted with blewe vellat' in 1569.[33] This may have been worn with several different gowns.

The length of trains probably varied considerably. The example given above of the black velvet train being used to make sleeves and 'two newe panes' for the skirt of a round gown suggests that this too was made separately. Paintings, drawings,[34] woodcuts, and engravings show that trained skirts might rest on the ground for two or three yards and more behind the wearer (Figs 172 and 184), but this material would probably have been too soiled and shabby with wear to re-use for sleeves. The purple cloth of gold French gown made in 1576, cited above, is one of several which had a train sufficiently long to be noted as a feature. The skirt at the back of an ordinary French gown may only have been a yard or so longer than the rest of the hem. There are entries for 'a Gowne of blak vellat with a trayne of the frenche fation' and 'a traine Gowne of the frenche fation of black unshorne vellat'[35] among the warrants in 1569. This is an unusual way of phrasing the description and, as it is just after the Queen had tried to get a French tailor, the term may refer to a certain style of cutting.

Although Elizabeth employed only two tailors to make her own clothes during her reign, Walter Fyshe from 1558 to 1582 and William Jones from 1582 onwards, an attempt to get another tailor was made in 1567. Sir William Cecil wrote early in that year to Sir Henry Norris, appointed Ambassador at Paris in 1566:

The Queen's Majesty would fain have a tailor that had skill to make her apparel both after the Italian and French manner, and she thinketh that you might use some means to obtain some one that serveth the French queen, without mentioning any manner of request in our queen's majesty's name. First cause your lady to get such a one.[36]

Sir Henry Norris wrote back on 1 March, 'As for a tailor for the Queen, my wife and I will do what we may'.[37] There seem to be no further letters on the subject, so apparently this was beyond the Ambassador's ingenuity to contrive. Perhaps Lady Norris, Elizabeth's 'own Crow', could not arrange satisfactory terms, as no French tailor's name appears in the warrants for the Wardrobe of Robes. The secret of Italian and French cut was conveyed to England in another way.

There are entries among the warrants in 1572 for Walter Fyshe 'alteringe and newmaking of a straight bodied Gowne of striped silke (brought out of Fraunce) the bodies and slevis striped thicke with golde lase cutt and turned in lyned with buckeram ye slevis lyned with white Satten the bodies with white sarceonett and a pockett of blak taphata',[38] then 'alteringe of the said Gowne of striped silke and lyninge it with purple flanell',[39] presumably for winter warmth. Fyshe worked on it again later in the same year

making of a payer of upper slevis for a Gowne of striped silke that was brought out of fraunce cutt & turned in layed with golde lace lyned with white Satten cotten buckeram and white taphata drawen out with lawne and the gowne borderid with blak taphata of our great guarderobe'.[40]

This was apparently the same gown which Fyshe worked on again in April 1574, 'alteringe and newe lyninge the bodies and slevis of a Gowne sent oute of Fraunce lyned with white taphata'[41] and 'borderinge of a Gowne sente oute of Fraunce

171a *Detail of embroidered guard at hem of round gown in Figure 171*

172 *Huntsman reporting the evidence of a hart to the Queen, whose trained skirt is held up by a Maid of Honour. Woodcut from 'The Noble Art of Venerie or Hunting' by George Turbervile. 1575. British Library, London*

with blak taphata' in October of the same year.[42] This 'bordering' was repeated in 1575.[43] It is probably the same gown which appears in the warrants in 1576, now described as a round gown, and again sent to Walter Fyshe for bordering with black taffeta.[44]

173 *'Nobilis Virgo Francica: Unmarried French noblewoman'*
wearing a French gown with hanging round, or Spanish, sleeves,
holding a folding fan. From Omnium Poene Gentium Habitus *by*
Abraham de Bruyn, 1581. British Library, London

174 *'Portrait of an Unknown Lady aged twenty-one'. Panel*
painting by an unknown artist, 1569. She wears an embroidered
linen partlet with matching sleeves, or possibly a smock, filling in
the square neckline. Beneath it at the front may be seen the square
neckline of the smock worn beneath. Tate Gallery, London

These entries are all for alterations, so the gown must have
arrived in the Wardrobe before 1572, perhaps sent by Lady
Norris in 1567. It would have been easier for Walter Fyshe
simply to take a pattern from a gown made in France and
adapt it for the Queen, rather than import a French tailor and
risk malicious comments about the deficiences of English
tailoring from the French Court.[45] Lady Norris probably told
the tailor that the gown was a present for one of her relatives in
England. In 1576 Walter Fyshe was called into service again
for

alteringe and newe making of a gowne of cloth of silver sent oute of
Fraunce the bodies and slevis new lased & all ye gowne newe lyned
with white sarceonett with a Rolle of white bayes in the pleites ye
bodies lyned with canvas the slevis made larger and a peire of slevis of
venice golde carnacion and watchett silke nettworke payed for at our
prevye purse threste of our great guarderobe.[46]

By 1577 the problem of ordering gowns from France without a
chance of fitting them seems to have been solved. Fyshe made
buckram gowns, or *toiles* as we would describe them today, to
send across the Channel.[47] The French tailor would have been
able to find a woman who fitted them exactly, and then make
the gown to her size. Elizabeth could have worn her new
gowns immediately they arrived at Court, without any alterations.

It seems likely that the superbly cut gown in the 'Phoenix'
portrait (Fig. 26) resulted from the influence of this unknown
French tailor's work. All the bodice shaping is done at the
centre front, with the centre back on the straight grain of the
material. The centre front neckline is thus forced upwards into
a curve. There are no side or side front seams. The front
pattern shape is similar to that of a 1780s bodice,[48] giving a
most elegant line. This may be a 'gown of the French fashion'
following the lines of that listed in 1569 which was probably
copied from one sent from France by Lady Norris. A gown
with bodice of similar cut and round hanging sleeves of the
Spanish style, worn by a young French noblewoman carrying a
folding fan, may be seen in Figure 173. In Figure 174 the front
opening of the same style of bodice is clearly visible, as it has
been left unfastened at the top. The distinctive sleeves in the
'Phoenix' portrait are a French fashion and may be seen worn
by a Parisian woman in Figure 175. The style presumably
evolved from arranging material over padded sleeve rolls
(Figs 24, 25, and 174) thus making firm supports for the full
sleeveheads.

The evidence of portraits suggests that the French gown of
the early 1560s continued on the lines of those of the 1550s,
with turn-back sleeves and close-fitting bodice with low square
neckline and pointed waist at the front, following the line of
the girdle. The bodice seems to have been joined to the skirt
which was smooth at the front and pleated at the sides, rather
than being made separately as were the later doublet and
petticoat. However, the purple cloth of gold French gown

175 'Femina Parisiensis ornatus: A Parisian woman', from
Omnium Poene Gentium Habitus by Abraham de Bruyn, 1581.
British Library, London

176 'Unknown Lady, formerly called Queen Mary I when
Princess', attributed to Hans Eworth, c. 1557–60. She wears a
black satin gown with partlet and turn-back sleeve linings in black
velvet. Undersleeves and forepart are in crimson satin.
Fitzwilliam Museum, Cambridge

made with a high collar in 1576, cited above, shows that the
square neckline may not necessarily have remained a distinguishing feature of the style. Earlier the square was
frequently covered with a partlet in matching material, and the
low neckline was not always particularly obvious (Fig. 176).
When cut with a high collar, the French gown might be
described as 'a Frenche gowne with high bodies'[49] or 'a highe
bodied gowne'.[50] This is probably the type of gown which the
Queen wears in Figure 177. Presumably the cut remained the
same, with the shaping at the centre front, the style evolving
simply from cutting the partlet in one with the square-necked
bodice. A small dart, or fish, would probably have been made
horizontally across the bust line, in a similar way to those in
eighteenth-century riding habits.[51]

There are a few references to French gowns 'with a straite
Bodie'[52] and 'straighte bodied' gowns[53] throughout the reign.
One, as we have seen, was sent from France in 1572,[54] and
another, also from France, was altered in 1577 'drawne oute
before with white lawne, with two newe panes sett into the
nether partes the bodies lyned with blak sarceonett and
pockettes of sarceonett'.[55] The word 'strait' is defined as
narrow or tight-fitting in the sixteenth century. As all French
gowns appear to have fairly tight bodices, it is not quite clear
what the difference was, unless it describes the cut of the gown
in the 'Phoenix' portrait (Fig. 26). 'Strait' may also mean
close-fitting up to the neck. Alternatively, the word may
indicate extra stiffening with bents (the fore-runner of whalebone), the use of a rigid busk, or fastening with lacing rather
than hooks and eyes. Lacing enables a gown to be pulled in to
fit very tightly.[56]

A French gown could apparently open at back or front.
Walter Fyshe altered one French gown of purple velvet[57] and
another of black velvet,[58] making them 'open before' in 1567
and 1568. The portrait of Princess Elizabeth (Fig. 4) shows a
bodice closed at the centre front, probably fastening at the
centre back[59] with lacing through eyelet holes (Figs 178 and
179). An unknown lady painted in 1569 wears a bodice with a
centre front opening, fastening edge to edge with hooks and
eyes; it is undone for a few inches at the top (Fig. 174).

The miniature of Elizabeth painted by Nicholas Hilliard in
1572 (Fig. 24) shows the same style, but the hooks and eyes are
fastened at the top of the bodice. The 'Pelican' portrait painted
about three or four years later, shows larger rolls over the
shoulders, but it is the same type of gown, fastening at the
centre front (Fig. 25). The high-bodied gown in Figure 30
probably fastens in the same way, with hooks and eyes, but the
opening cannot be seen, as the gown is black and three large
jewels are placed on the centre front line, below the pelican
jewel. There are even larger rolls over the tops of the sleeves.
Padded shoulder rolls were fashionable in many European
countries during the middle years of the sixteenth century. A
woman's embroidered velvet doublet of c. 1585 preserved in
the Germanisches Nationalmuseum, Nürnberg,[60] has large

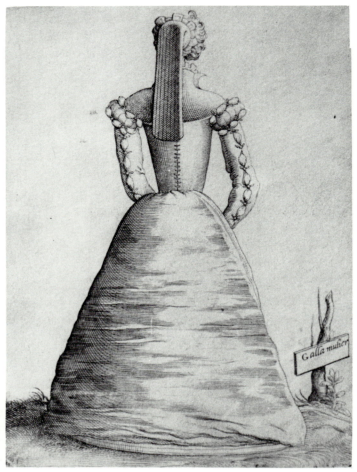

177 'Queen Elizabeth I', by an unknown artist, c. 1580–84. She wears what is probably a 'French gown with high bodies' with contrasting sleeves and forepart of white semi-transparent linen or silk embroidered in white silk, with very fine cutwork and needle lace ruff, and cuffs. Present whereabouts unknown

178   Back view of a French woman showing the lacing in the bodice and the bottom hoop of the farthingale beneath the hem of the skirt. The sleeves are open at the seam, with puffs of smock pulled through. From 'Habitus Nostrae Aetatis' by Enea Vico, c. 1556. Victoria and Albert Museum, London

sleeve rolls padded with linen, or hemp, folded in and pleated to shape (Fig. 180). Pieces of felt cut into small shapes and joined together with butted edges are placed on top. Shaped pieces of velvet are mounted over this smooth surface.

A French gown might be recut from another gown. For example in 1572 Walter Fyshe altered

a Gowne of blak vellat with a garde of crymsen Satten enbrodered with pearle the garde taken of[f] and the Gowne made into a frenche Gowne with newe bodies with a highe collar and slevis cutt very thicke and edged with blak Satten bordered with buckeram and lyned with sarceonett the rolles in the slevis coverid with fustian of our greate guarderobe.[61]

There would have been plenty of material in a loose gown to make a French gown with a short trained skirt.

It is apparent that among the French gowns in the Stowe inventory of 1600 there are examples of bodices, sleeves, and skirts of the latest 'French fashion' of different dates throughout Elizabeth's reign. Among the French gowns of the early type are a few which had belonged to Queen Mary.[62] As we have seen, these had a tight bodice with square neckline, often worn with a matching or contrasting partlet, and wide sleeves with rich linings turned back to be caught behind the upper arm revealing undersleeves in contrasting material (Figs 4, 176, and 191): there may still have been a few of these gowns

dating from the 1560s among Elizabeth's French gowns in 1600. This style evolved into the tight bodice with arched square neckline revealing an embroidered smock or partlet (Figs 24, 25, and 174) and later the alternative high-necked bodice with standing collar (Figs 1 and 177). Both styles had short sleeves or padded sleeve rolls over the shoulders, with 'pullings out' of lawn or silk and embroidered sleeves, often in fine linen, showing beneath. The high-necked bodice might also be made with hanging sleeves (Figs 52, 54, and 55). Another style of French gown had a tight bodice with arched square neckline and long sleeves with full sleeve-heads supported by padded rolls (Figs 6, 26, and 175). During the 1580s the French gown bodice lengthened and grew narrower at the front, following the lines seen at the French Court (Figs 185 and 187) and might be high to the neck (Figs 181 right and 182 left) or open in a square (Figs 181 left and 182 centre and right). The trained skirts were worn over Spanish farthingales which gradually increased in size, with extra padded rolls over the hips. By the mid-1580s the distinctive rounded skirt shape seen in paintings of the Valois Court in the early 1580s (Fig. 187) was established in England, the forerunner of the drum-shaped farthingale. Another style seen in these pictures, the bodice opening at the front and folded back to show facings which often match the stomacher (Figs 181 centre and 185) was established in England by about 1590 (Fig. 66).

179   *Front view of the French woman in Figure 178*

180   *Woman's doublet in embroidered black velvet with padded rolls over the shoulders, c. 1585. Germanisches Nationalmuseum, Nürnberg (T 832)*

181   *'Nobilis Femina Francica, Virgo Francica, Virgo Francica' from 'Habitus Variarum Orbis Gentium' by Jean Jacques Boissard, 1581. Three styles of dress worn by French women. Private collection*

185   *Detail from a painting of a ball at the court of Henri III called 'The Ball for the wedding of the Duc de Joyeuse'. School of Clouet, c. 1581–82. Louvre, Paris*

186   *'Queen Elizabeth I'. Panel painting by an unknown artist, c. 1585–88. She wears a black French gown with 'high bodies', round or Spanish sleeves and immense wired veil. Gift of Mr and Mrs Preston Davie. Colonial Williamsburg Foundation, Virginia*

4 March 1577 Amyas Paulet wrote from St Die 'to send a gown by this bearer. It may not seem strange that the silver is counterfeit, which is commonly used here by the French Queen and the Queen of Navarre. This sad time of Lent must excuse the baseness of the gown'.[74] He prays Walsingham to advise him when to send another gown 'which shall be of better quality'. On 17 March Paulet wrote again when sending a farthingale 'such as is now used by the French Queen and the Queen of Navarre'.[75] No details are given, but this may have been one of the earliest examples of a cone-shaped Spanish farthingale extended with extra hoops at the hips, and probably padded hip rolls as well, to give the dome-shaped line to skirts familiar from paintings of the Valois Court in the 1580s (Fig. 185). Padded hip rolls were certainly worn in the 1580s, before the introduction of the drum-shaped farthingale. The gown and farthingale sent in March may have given some inspiration to Walter Fyshe, as during the summer he made 'a rounde gatherid kyrtle of the frenche facion of white Capha layed with thre laces of counterfett golde and carnacion silke lyned with white sarceonett of our great guarderobe'.[76]

The Queen sought eagerly after French jewellery as well as clothes. In May 1561 Sir William Cecil finished a letter to Sir Nicholas Throckmorton, Ambassador in France, with a plea for a goldsmith:

To end; the Queen's Majesty, I assure you, taketh your last writing in right good part, and willed me to require you that some goldsmith there might be induced indirectly to come hither with furniture of aglets, chains, bracelets etc: to be bought both by herself, and by the Ladies here, to be gay in this Court towards the progress. What is meant in it I know not; whether for that which many look for, or for the coming in of the Swede; but, as for me, I can see no certain disposition in her Majesty to any marriage, and any other likelihood doth not the principal here find, which causeth him to be perplexed.[77]

The quest for the newest foreign fashions may have been partly for diplomatic ends. The ladies at the Valois Court were pleased that Elizabeth favoured the French fashions in her portrait painted for Catherine de' Medici when the Anjou marriage negotiations were at their height. Henry Cobham wrote to Francis Walsingham on 22 January 1581:

The Quene moother this other daie shoed in Courte her Majesties picture made in full length and proportion by her owne frenche painter which was lately in England, of the which picture this Quene seemeth to make great estimation. The ladies did highly commend the Quene my Soveraines rare giftes and princely comliness with exceding prayses and admiracione Marvelinge very muche at the number of those great pearles wherewith her highnes gowne is set forth and beautified supposinge that all the other princes of Christendome had not the like quantite of pearles of ye sorte. The great princesses did note and weare very muche satisfied to see her Majestie apparaled and attyred all over alla francoyse.[78]

A full length portrait of Elizabeth (Fig. 186) now at Colonial Williamsburg[79] shows the line of the French farthingale (apparently widened slightly at the sides a couple of years after

187 *Detail from a ball at the court of Henri III called 'The Ball for the wedding of the Duc de Joyeuse'. School of Clouet, c. 1581–82. Louvre, Paris*

188 *'Nobilis femina Francica: French noblewoman'. From Omnium Poene Gentium Habitus by Abraham de Bruyn, 1581. She wears a pleated wired veil standing in two hoops behind the shoulders. British Library, London*

the picture was painted to bring it up to date) long narrow bodice and large ruff which developed in England following the fashions of the French Court (Fig. 187). These features are seen at their most exaggerated English form in the 'Armada' portraits of Queen Elizabeth (Figs 52, 54, and 55). Wired veils appear in de Bruyn's engravings of French fashions (Figs 188 and 247). The Williamsburg picture also shows masses of pearls decorating the black velvet gown and forepart. They are arranged in sets of one large and three small pearls all down the front. The white satin undersleeves beneath the Spanish hanging sleeves are heavily embroidered in gold thread with large fleur-de-lis and slightly smaller Tudor roses. The pointed bodice front and width of sleeves indicate a date of about 1585–88 in England, although the hairstyle looks a little earlier, around 1580. It may be conjectured that this picture is a copy made from the 1581 portrait sent to France, with the alterations in the line made to be in keeping with the latest fashion. The shape of the skirt in 1588–89 may be seen clearly in the 'Armada' portraits (Figs 52, 54, and 55). A slightly narrower line appears in an engraving of 1589, *Eliza Triumphans*, by Will Rogers (Fig. 189). The skirt and paned sleeves here have what seems to be an applied design of pomegranates. The ruff is slightly open at the front, the forerunner of the style seen in the Ditchley portrait (Fig. 71).

Spanish fashions

The power of the Habsburg dynasty reached across Europe. At the death of Emperor Charles V in 1558 Spain was more powerful than any of her neighbours on the Mediterranean shores and Spanish fashions soon challeged the earlier dominance of Flemish, French, German, and Italian styles. The change was the more rapid because the Austrian Habsburgs adopted Spanish fashions to a considerable extent, as well as wealthy people in Italian territories conquered or inherited by Spain. High-necked, stiff bodices topped with ruffs, round hanging sleeves, and cone-shaped farthingales appear in portraits of royalty and nobility all over Europe during the second half of the sixteenth century.

The influence of Spanish fashions was first felt early in the sixteenth century at the English court when Katherine of Aragon arrived to marry Prince Arthur in 1501, with a second impetus when Philip II married Mary Tudor in 1554. Katherine seems to have brought the first Spanish 'verdugado', (verdingale or farthingale) seen in England with her, but may have worn it very little, preferring to adopt English fashions. Certainly the style was novel enough for the English to observe on her arrival in 1501 that she and her ladies wore 'benethe ther wast certayn rounde hopys, beryng owte ther gowns from ther bodies after their countray maner'.[80] At this date the shape of the hooped skirt alone would have been 'the Spanish fashion' in England. Hall describes a masque at Greenwich on 7 March 1519,[81] in which eight masquers were dressed in

189 *'Eliza Triumphans'. Engraving by Will Rogers, 1589. The Queen wears a French gown with a square neckline. The forepart is embroidered with suns-in-splendour and knots of pearls. British Library, London*

190 *'Salome with the head of John the Baptist'. Panel painting by Juan Flamenco, c. 1470. She wears a 'verdugado' with double hoops in casings of patterned silk, Museo del Prado, Madrid*

black velvet gowns 'with hoopes from the wast douneward'. These would seem to have been farthingales. Perhaps some of the Queen's discarded clothes had been given to the masquers and the style was adopted as a novelty. A contemporary note to Latimer's sermon given before King Edward in 1552 says that 'vardingales are learned from players that decked giants after that manner'.[82] Apparently the word first appears in the Royal Wardrobe accounts in 1545 when 'vij virg. Satten de bruges crimson pro una verdingale' are entered for Princess Elizabeth.[83]

The 'verdugado', from the Spanish word 'verdugos' used to describe any smooth twigs put out by a tree that has been pruned (coppiced), was an underskirt originally held out with hoops of osiers from coppiced willows. It was cut in gored panels; hoops of ropes, bents, whalebone, and apparently tight rolls of material were also used for stiffening at various times. An account of a farthingale made in 1560 allows 5 yards of purple taffeta with 7¾ yards of purple velvet for the border and 7½ yards of kersey for the ropes.[84] Linthicum suggests that the kersey was for casings but the quantity is more than is needed for this purpose. It is more likely that the material was cut and joined to form long continuous strips about a foot wide, then rolled tightly to make 'ropes'.[85] After the 1580s

these methods of stiffening were generally replaced by whalebone.

The Spanish farthingale is first seen in a Catalan painting of about 1470, where Salome, dressed in fashionable contemporary clothes, bears John the Baptist's head to King Herod (Fig. 277). Salome and her attendants wear hoops on the outside of their skirts, encased in velvet bands as a form of decoration. A similar painting of about the same date by Juan Flamenco (Fig. 190) shows Salome with a gown over her hooped petticoat.

The fashion for this cone-shaped style of farthingale spread all over Europe with the Habsburg influence, the hoops concealed beneath the gown (Figs 178 and 191). A Spanish tailor's pattern book survives to show us the exact shape of both men's and women's clothes, including a farthingale, for the second half of the sixteenth century. This first printed book on tailoring, Juan de Alçega's *Libro de Geometria, Pratica y Traça* was published in Madrid in 1580.[86] Although it is a guide showing tailors the most economical layouts for various widths of cloth, and not a treatise on the technique of cutting patterns with scale diagrams, the roughly drawn pattern pieces may usefully be related to patterns taken of surviving garments.[87] Later books, *Geometria, y Traça Perteneciente al*

191 'Lady Jane Dudley, commonly called Lady Jane Grey'. Panel painting attributed to Master John, c. 1550. She wears a gown of ivory silk with a looped pile of silver metal thread. The sleeves are turned back to show the linings of lynx. The whole skirt is probably lined with fur. A line of white hairs may be seen under each side of the front opening, lying over the deep red forepart which is decorated with interlaced lines of gold cord, braid and pearls, matching the undersleeves. National Portrait Gallery, London

192 'Maria of Austria, wife of Emperor Maximilian II', by Antonio Mor, 1551. The round sleeves are decorated with ribbons and large aglets. Museo del Prado, Madrid

Oficio de Sastres by Francisco de la Rocha Burguen, published at Valencia in 1618 and Geometria, y Trazas Pertenecientes al Oficio de Sastres by Martin de Andúxar, published in Madrid in 1640,[88] show that there were few innovations to interrupt the gradual crystallization of Spanish styles.

Elizabeth had four Spanish gowns made for her between 1571 and 1577.[89] Earlier Spanish gowns made in the 1550s when Philip arrived at the English Court would probably have

been similar to that worn by Maria of Austria, wife of Emperor Maximilian II, in her portrait painted in 1551 by Antonio Mor (Fig. 192). It has a low arched square neckline, filled in with a partlet, Spanish round sleeves, and cone-shaped farthingale. The low square neckline was at this time just passing out of fashion in Spain, so Elizabeth's gowns in the late 1560s and 1570s would probably have had high necklines of the type seen in the portrait of Elizabeth of Valois, Queen of Spain, painted by Pantoja de la Cruz in about 1568 (Fig. 193). This sleeve style has a widely curved outer edge, open at the front to reveal the arm in a close-fitting undersleeve. The more moderate size in Figures 192 and 194 is described as a 'manga redonda' (round sleeve) in the Spanish tailors' books.[90] The same shape, deeply slashed at the back, is worn by Elizabeth of Valois in Figure 195. The large sleeve in Figure 193 may be the style entered as a 'great spanyshe sleve' made for a black velvet gown with a train for Elizabeth in 1569.[91] The flat pattern shape is rounded on both sides. Elizabeth wears round sleeves of the more moderate size in several portraits, but they are observed from the front (Figs 46 and 186). The clearest side view of the style worn by an Englishwoman is given in the portrait of Lettice Knollys painted in about 1585 (Fig. 196).

193 *'Elizabeth of Valois, Queen of Spain', by Pantoja de la Cruz, c. 1568. She wears large hanging sleeves, the curved outer edge caught together with jewelled clasps and knots of pearls to match the front. The sleeve linings are of white silk striped with silver. Museo del Prado, Madrid*

194 *'Anne of Austria, Queen of Spain', by Antonio Mor, 1570. The curved back seam of the round sleeve is caught together at intervals with ribbon points and aglets. Kunsthistorisches Museum, Vienna*

195 *'Elizabeth of Valois, Queen of Spain', by Antonio Mor, c. 1568. Her satin bodice, or doublet, is slashed down the front, a fashion worn by the noblewomen of Brescia, Verona and other cities in the province of Lombardy. The round Spanish sleeves are deeply slashed at the back and the satin lining is used to bind the cuts. This French princess, Queen of Spain, is thus wearing a mixture of Spanish and Italian styles. Present whereabouts unknown*

The black velvet is embroidered with silver ragged staves set among the curving lines of gold braid.[92] The ragged staff was the badge of Robert Dudley, Earl of Leicester, whom she married in 1578. Her white satin undersleeves are embroidered in gold thread. A pattern shape resembling the round sleeve, with more material allowed towards the top for the gathered sleevehead, gives the style seen in the 'Darnley' portrait (Fig. 215): this has a strip of gold and silver bobbin lace covering the seam, which runs down the outside of the sleeve, shaped in at the wrist.[93] The shape may have been

196 *'Lettice Knollys, Countess of Leicester', attributed to George Gower, c. 1585. Reproduced by permission of the Marquess of Bath, Longleat House, Warminster, Wiltshire*

197 *(Above) Infanta Isabella Clara Eugenia and her dwarf, Magdalena Ruiz, attributed to Felipe de Liano, c. 1584. Museo del Prado, Madrid*

198 *(Left) Mary Denton aged fifteen. Panel painting attributed to George Gower, 1573. York City Art Gallery*

adapted by Walter Fyshe from the 'spanyshe sleve', and gives an effect similar to the French sleeve in the 'Phoenix' portrait of the Queen (Fig. 26), where the seam is set towards the back.

Another good example of the large sleeve seen in Spanish paintings, which appears in modified form in England, is worn by Infanta Isabella Clara Eugenia in her portrait painted in about 1584 (Fig. 197). This long hanging sleeve, reaching to the ground, is caught at the front opening with aglets or jewels at wrist and shoulder. The English variety, cut straight and not caught at the wrist, appears in several portraits of Elizabeth (Figs 52, 54, 55, 62, and 71). This is probably the style variously described as pendant sleeves,[94] 'verie lardge pendaunte slevis',[95] hanging sleeves[96] or sleeves 'cut very longe to hange by the bodies'[97] in the inventories and warrants.

A pair of 'hangynge slevis to weare upon the arme with thre cuttes downeright the panes and cuttes lased thicke and with poyntinge rebande of venice silver and carnacion silke'[98] might at first be taken for a Spanish sleeve, but in the Spanish portraits the single cut is horizontal not 'downeright'. The

199 *Detail from the tomb of Lady Margaret, Countess of Lennox, 1578. Lady Margaret's daughters wear what may be 'Venetian gowns' with sleeves similar to those in Figure 198, the panes tied together at intervals with ribbons. Westminster Abbey, London*

199a *Back view of Lady Margaret's daughters in Figure 199*

three cuts, making a paned sleeve, may be seen in the portrait of Mary Denton painted in 1573 (Fig. 198). Similar sleeves, tied up with bows of ribbon, are worn by the Countess of Lennox's daughters (Figs 199 and 199a).

Walter Fyshe was engaged in 'upperbodying of a frenche Gowne of blak Satten enbrauderid with spanyshe garde lyned with fyne sackecloth and ashe colorid sarceonett'[99] in 1572. This was presumably a ready-made guard embroidered in Spain, purchased from a merchant. In the following year Fyshe altered and new-made the gown but no further detail is given about the Spanish guard.

In June 1577 when Dr Wilson, the English agent, was granted an audience with Don John of Austria, he took with him a miniature of Elizabeth borrowed from Fulke Greville. Wilson wrote to the Queen from Brussels:

And suerlie, Madame, Don Jhon was moche pleased with the sight of it, and perused it verie curiouselie a good longe tyme, and asked me yf Your Majestie wer not attired some tymes according to the spanyshe maner. I towlde hym Your Majestie used diverse attires, italian, spanyshe and frenshe, as occasion served and as yow pleased. He sayde the spanyshe attire was the most cummelie . . . He towlde me he is so enformed of Your Majestie, that if you wer in the cumpanie of your ladies, but in a blacke velvet frenshe gowne and a playne howde to the same, he myght discerne yow for the Queene, although he had never seen your picture before.[100]

Don John, perhaps not unnaturally as a Habsburg and half brother to King Philip of Spain, preferred the Spanish styles. Wilson continued, with a note of flattery:

I towlde hym indeede that God had doone moche for yow, not onelie to cawle you to the place of a queene and so represent hymselfe, but also to geave yow soche a shape fytte for any queene and there withal a mynde endewed with soche several and famowse vertues as therfore Your Majestie is had in admiration and a chief spectacle to the whole worlde.[101]

Italian fashions

Elizabeth was certainly interested in the fashions of Spain and Italy early in 1565. On 16 January the Earl of Leicester, in his official capacity as Master of the Horse, wrote with a request for white mares to Thomasso Baroncelli in Antwerp and added: 'The patterns of bodices which you have sent me for the Queen are beautiful, but not what she wants, having several of that make. She wants the kind used in Spain and Italy, worked with gold and silver'.[102] Baroncelli replied on 21 February 'I hope you will see everything together with the geldings and jerkins (colletti) which her Majesty wishes for. If she had sent me a pattern I should have tried to supply her before now'.[103] From the description, the 'patterns of bodices' were designs for embroidery rather than the tailor's pattern pieces. The rich, deep mulberry velvet jerkin illustrated in Figures 200 and 200a may have been the type sought by Elizabeth. It is elaborately embroidered with gold thread and pearls. She wears a similarly embroidered jerkin or doublet buttoning to the neck in Figure 201 with what may be one of the embroidered network veils listed in the Stowe inventory.

Five gowns of the Italian fashion were made for the Queen in 1568 and 1569. The descriptions help to explain what the style was. The first was a 'frenche Gowne of blak vellat with doble bodies of the Italion fation',[104] the second 'a Gowne of crymsen Satten of the Italion fation Raste allover with a garde of blewe vellat',[105] the third 'a Trayne Gowne of blak wrought

200 *'Portrait of an unknown Italian lady', by an unknown artist, c. 1570–80. Her deep mulberry jerkin is heavily embroidered with gold thread and pearls and lies open at the neck, revealing the striped silk beneath. Present whereabouts unknown*

200a *Detail of Figure 200*

201 *'Queen Elizabeth I'. Engraving by Jan Rutlinger, c. 1580–85. The Queen wears an elaborately embroidered jerkin or doublet similar to that in Figures 200–200a. Her veil hangs from a carcanet set with large pointed diamonds and she holds a jewel with the phoenix emblem. Private collection*

vellat of the Italion fation with doble bodies the upper bodies and slevis cutt very thicke with a chevern',[106] the fourth 'a Gowne of blak Satten with a Trayne of the Italion fation with two peire of bodies',[107] and fifth 'a straight bodied Gowne of blak taphata cutt allover with a lozenge cutt of the Italion fation with doble bodies layed with a lase of golde and carnation and blak silke lyned with crymsen cloth of golde with rolles of Cotten and Fustian in the slevis and a Pockett of carnation taphata'.[108] Four of these descriptions have 'double bodies', two bodices which were apparently worn at the same time. This style is seen in Italian portraits[109] and in the woodcuts of clothes worn by gentlewomen in Verona, Brescia, and other cities of Lombardy shown in Vecellio's *Di gli antichi et moderni di Diverse Parti del Mondo*, printed in 1590.

There are two slashes on either side of the centre front bodice of the gown worn by a noblewoman of Verona (Fig. 202).

202   *Dress worn by the noblewoman of Brescia, Verona, and other cities in the province of Lombardy. From 'De gli Habiti antichi et moderni di Diverse Parti del Mondo' by Cesare Vecellio, 1590*

203   *'Lady Jane Dormer, Countess of Feria', attributed to Antonio Mor, c. 1570. Museo del Prado, Madrid*

204   *'Queen Elizabeth I'. Panel painting by an unknown artist, c. 1568. The collar and sleeves are turned back to show the striped lining. The wings are 'jagged' and padded in rolls over the shoulders, with 'jagges' behind them. Present whereabouts unknown*

Lady Jane Dormer, Countess of Feria, one of Queen Mary's gentlewomen of the Bedchamber, was painted wearing the same style, with single slashes (Fig. 203). On 29 December 1558, she married the Count of Feria, who had come to England with King Philip of Spain. They left for Flanders in July 1559. Later they went to Spain, arriving in Toledo in August 1560. This portrait was painted in the late 1560s or early 1570s, when she was living in Spain. The design of the striped silk may be seen beneath the black velvet. The front is left open, in addition to the long slashes. All the edges are bordered with gold braid and trimmed with red ribbon bows and gold buttons, set with pearls.

Queen Elizabeth wears a gown with similar slashes in a portrait of about 1568 (Fig. 204). Another picture, painted in the mid-1570s, shows the slashes on a short waisted bodice with long sleeves (Fig. 205). This bodice is made with tabs at the waist, or 'little skirts' as they are described in the warrants. This is probably the Italian fashion in England at this date, a

205 'Queen Elizabeth I', by an unknown artist, c. 1575. Kunsthistorisches Museum, Vienna

206 (Left) 'Portrait of an unknown Venetian Lady' by Titian, 1560. Gemäldegalerie, Staatliche Kunstsammlungen, Dresden

207 (Above) 'Nobile Ornata Gentildonne a Feste Pubbliche: Venetian gentlewoman at a public festival'. From De gli Habiti antichi et moderni di Diverse Parti del Mondo by Cesare Vecellio, 1590

rather short-waisted bodice revealing another one beneath through deep slashes and sometimes an opening at the front.

In 1565 Walter Fyshe made 'a venecian gowne of crimsen velvet the ground satten for Elizabethe Knowles layed with iij silver laces the skyrtes lyned with buckeram and cotton with fustian in the bodies and frise in the ruffes the slevis drawne out with silver Sarceonet'.[110] This may have resembled the gown with a low square-necked bodice laced up at the centre front, with short puffed sleeves, seen in Titian's portrait of a young Venetian noblewoman painted in 1560 (Fig. 206). This style, but with a longer bodice and wider opening, is seen later in Vecellio's woodcut of 1590 (Fig. 207). Alternatively it may have resembled the gowns worn by Venetian noblewomen in Jost Amman's *Trachtenbvch* and Abraham de Bruyn's *Omnium Poene Gentium Imagines*, both published in 1577. These have the bodice closed at the front and a low square neckline filled in with a partlet left open at the front (Figs 208 and 208a). Gowns reminiscent of this style are seen in a few English tomb sculptures (Figs 199 and 199a) and portraits of the late 1560s and 1570s.[111]

Italian styles were seen at the English Court in 1595, according to a German visitor. Von Buchenbach, at the head of an embassy sent by Duke Frederick of Würtemburg, found the appearance of the courtiers most impressive:

208   'Fœmina ex praecipua nobilitate in urbe Veneta: Venetian noblewoman'. From 'Trachtenbuch' by Jost Amman, 1577. Germanisches Nationalmuseum, Nürnberg

208a   'Nobilis matrona Veneta, Virgo Veneta; Venetian noblewoman and young unmarried Venetian Lady' from 'Omnium Poene Gentium Imagines' by Abraham de Bruyn, 1577. Private collection

There were besides assembled many other earls, lords and knights. They all wore gold and silver dress and their raiment was embroidered with precious stones and pearls. At no other Court have I ever seen so much splendour and such fine clothes. This holds good both of the men and of the countesses and other noble ladies, who were of rare surpassing beauty and for the main part in Italian costume with breasts bared. In their hands they held large black plumes or other fans wherewith to cool themselves.[112]

As 'Italian fashions' in England seem to have referred to the 'double bodies' already described, von Buchenbach may have meant Venetian rather than Italian styles. He would have been looking at gowns similar to those in the Ditchley and Hardwick portraits of Elizabeth (Figs 71 and 129).

Giacomo Franco described Venetian costume in *Habiti delle Dame Venetiane* printed in 1610:

In Venice there are four classes of women who all dress nearly the same and are only to be distinguished by the greater or less profusion of jewels . . . The wives of the rich merchants of Venice dress and ornament themselves so brilliantly that they are hardly to be distinguished from the ladies of the nobles. Our picture presents one of them in summer costume and with the fan which it is their habit to use.[113]

The picture shows a gown with closed front and low square neckline (Fig. 209). The partlet beneath is left open, with a shallow standing ruff at the back of the neck. The skirt is gathered to the bodice waist. The gown as Franco describes is exactly like that of a bride of noble birth. Franco gives illustrations of the latter and of a married noblewoman (Fig. 210) as well as the merchant's wife. That of the married noblewoman has evolved from the style painted by Titian in 1560, except for the addition of the standing band or collar. The fashion is seen in England[114] developing from the standing ruff framing the square neckline in the 1590s to a shallower band standing at the back of the neck in the early 1600s (Fig. 120).

Flanders partlets, smocks, and gowns

Not only French, Spanish, and Italian fashions interested Elizabeth. In 1577 her attention was directed towards the Low Countries. On 30 August Wilson wrote from Oatlands to Davison, the English agent resident in Flanders, at the English Embassy in Antwerp:

I am further to desire you to confer with M. Fremin and to take him with you to the Marchioness of Havrech, and shew her that the Queen would gladly have a suit of her own linen partlets that she wear, and the same to be sent in a box, in such form and manner as she doth wear the same abyllements; for that the Queen, in seeing her picture, did marvellous delight in the manner of the wearing of her linen in such sort. Therefore, if it will please her ladyship to send me one of her own best linen suits for the Queen, I will send her whatsoever it shall please her to command that England yieldeth. This I pray you do with as great cunning as you can for the Queen's satisfaction, and commend me heartily to the Lord Marquis himself.[115]

The Marchioness of Havrech was the wife of Charles Phillipe de Croy, Ambassador from the Low Countries. It would be interesting to know how Davison phrased the request and if the Marchioness was flattered by it. The Queen was extremely anxious to obtain the partlets.

On 3 September Wilson wrote again, 'I pray you remember to deal with Mme de Havrech, to have one suit of her linen partlets as she wears them as her picture showed which I brought over. This is the Queen's desire'.[116] Davison replied to Walsingham on 9 September:

Yesternight I received yours of the 3rd by my man and last Wednesday another of the 24th ult., sent by Mr Beale. By the latter I perceive you had received but three packets from me, though this be the 7th I have dispatched since my coming. I learn from my man that the weather has stayed some of them at Dunkirk these seven or eight days.[117]

No further mention is made of the partlets but presumably, wind and weather permitting, Elizabeth eventually received them.

There must have been something very unusual about this neckwear; the linen may have been starched and pleated in some novel way which caught Elizabeth's eye. The portrait of the Marchioness has not yet been traced. It would be interesting to know if the style bore any resemblance to the Flanders partlet made in 1564 by Walter Fyshe:

Item for making of a flaunders partlet of Sipers for a frenche gowne of sipers doble lyned with taphata & buckeram of our great warderobe.[118]

The earlier partlet seems to have been a more solid arrangement as it was lined. It may have been similar to those in the picture of *Pierre de Moucheron and his wife Isabeau de*

209 'Venetian merchant's wife holding a fan' from 'Habiti delle donne Venetiane' by Giacomo Franco, 1610. Private collection

210 'A married Venetian noblewoman' from 'Habiti delle donne Venetiane' by Giacomo Franco, 1610. Private collection

211 Detail from 'Pierre de Moucheron and his wife, Isabeau de Berbier with their children in Antwerp'. Panel painting attributed to Cornelius de Zeeuw, 1563. Rijksmuseum, Amsterdam

212 *'Lady Anne Penruddocke aged twenty'. Panel painting attributed to Hans Eworth, 1557. She wears a black satin gown decorated with black velvet guards, which fastens at the front with hooks and eyes concealed by black satin ribbon bows. The velvet guards are bordered with rows of narrow black braid and cord. The red satin undersleeves are slashed vertically and held in with bands of what may be velvet of a deeper red than the satin, embroidered with lighter red silk, or possibly a woven braid, The ruff and wrist ruffs are edged with buttonhole stitch in red silk. The Lord Howard de Walden*

213 *Detail from the tomb of Richard Alington and his wife Joan, 1561. Joan wears a gown decorated with embroidered guards. Rolls Chapel, London*

Berbier with their children in Antwerp in 1563, attributed to Cornelius de Zeeuw (Fig. 211). There may have been some feature common to both the partlet made by Walter Fyshe and that worn by the Marchioness of Havrech.

Among the New Year's gifts presented to the Queen on 1 January 1559 are nine smocks: two, presented by Lady Throgmorton, are 'flandours Smockes wrought with white worke'.[119] It is possible that at this date these two Flanders smocks had high necks and the other seven were of the low-necked variety. However, the name might as easily have been derived from the source of the linen employed in making them, or may have referred to the use of rich white embroidery for which Flanders was famous. The other smocks were embroidered in coloured silks, with gold and silver thread.[120]

Even a contemporary definition can be misleading. As already noted, in 1554 Giacomo Soranzo, the Venetian Ambassador, described Mary Tudor's closely fitting gown worn over a trained petticoat as the ordinary costume of the gentlewomen of England. The style is seen in numerous portraits of the 1550s and 1560s, including a few of both Mary and Elizabeth.[121] Big puffed sleeves reaching to just below the elbow with decorative guards round armholes, down the front and on the high collars are frequently occurring features in many of these gowns (Fig. 212). It is possible that these are what were described as 'Flanders gowns' in England at that time. Analysis of the different styles of gown mentioned in the warrants for the Wardrobe of Robes and the Stowe and Folger inventories puts them in the broad category of 'loose gowns'.

Some of the 'loose gowns' in the Stowe and Folger inventories have been linked with references in warrants and Gift Rolls to show that they are also 'night gowns'. Others may well be Flanders gowns, but none of the descriptions is detailed enough to link them with named items among the warrants. However, Flemish paintings of the 1560s show several styles of gowns. One prominent feature is common to many of them — big, short puffed sleeves (Fig. 211). Gowns in these pictures are usually decorated with wide guards round the armholes and on the sleeves and collar, as well as the skirts. Ascham described 'French gowns' worn in Brussels, 'of black velvet guarded down right from the collar with broad guards, one nigh another'.[122] In England guards certainly seem to have been an important feature of Flanders gowns, judging from some of the entries in the warrants. One, in 1575, was 'for alteringe and newe makinge of a great flaunders Gown enlarged in the bodies and newe shoulder gardes and collar gardes, and newe slevis & winges made of tholde slevis'.[123]

These guards were long strips, often of contrasting material, made separately and tacked on. They could be changed from gown to gown, to give a completely new appearance. A new

Spanish gown made for Elizabeth in the mid 1570s was 'partelye garded with a garde taken from a Gowne of tawnie satten of our store'.[124] Those round the hem could be replaced when worn out. Guards were also called borders, and it would seem from some of the descriptions that very narrow strips were called 'welts': 'Item for making of a Gowne of blak vellat with a trayne of the frenche fation garded with crymsen vellat enbrauderid with pearle welted on each side the garde wrought with pearle . . . the same gardes taken from a frenche Gowne of crymsen Satten of our store in the chardge of Rauf Hope yeoman of our guardrobe of Roobes threst of our great Guarderobe'.[125]

Guards were used on the hems of all types of gown, so apparently those on a Flanders gown were simply a much more prominent feature. Lady Anne Penruddocke is probably wearing a Flanders gown in her portrait painted in 1557 (Fig. 212). Here black velvet guards are placed round the armholes on the sleeves and down the front on both sides. Guards might be plain, of contrasting material — velvet on satin for example — but they were more often decorated with cutting and pinking and/or embroidery. They provided a change of colour and surface texture from the rest of the gown.

Joan Alington is shown with embroidered guards on her effigy dating from 1561 (Fig. 213). Here they are arranged down the long sleeves from shoulder to wrist, round the sleeve ends, down both fronts and round the armholes. The high standing collar has guards running downwards. The gown is very full at the back and gathered up evenly. As this has long sleeves it may not be a Flanders gown, in spite of the prominent guards, but it would certainly have been described as a loose gown. However, Walter Fyshe made 'a paire of upper sleeves for a Flaunders gowne of Black Taffata' in 1562,[126] so it seems likely that there were lower parts there as well, and that a Flanders gown might therefore have long sleeves as an alternative to the short puffed ones. Further examination of the warrants for the Wardrobe of Robes shows that these long sleeves might have been described as 'French'. In 1570 Walter Fyshe was entered for 'newe making of A flaunders gowne of black Wrought Vellatt with A Frenche sleve garded with black Vellatt lyned with black sarcenett with A staye of Fustyan and canvas to lyne the coller, the slevis drawen out with Sypers the gown unmade and remayning in the charge of the sayd Raphe Hope with Vellatt to make the slevis of our great guarderobe'.[127] This French sleeve may have resembled those in Joan Alington's gown, an early version of the style with more fullness at the sleevehead worn by the Queen in the 'Phoenix' portrait (Fig. 26) and a Parisian woman in Figure 175. From the evidence of portraits and these contemporary accounts it may be conjectured that a Flanders gown had a high collar and was heavily decorated with guards. It is not clear if the body was always semi-fitted or if there might be fullness at the back. There were usually big puffed sleeves reaching to just above the elbows, sometimes with matching close-fitting extensions to the wrists, but an alternative sleeve style might also be used.

Dutch gowns, Dutch cloaks, and German fashions

Four Dutch gowns appear among the warrants, but the descriptions are not very detailed. Walter Fyshe was engaged in 'new lyning the bodies and bordering the skyrtes of a Dou[t]che Gowne of blak vellat with spanyshe slevis with

213a *Detail of back of effigy in Figure 213 showing the guards and fullness of material gathered into the shoulder seams and back of the collar*

213b *Detail of front of effigy in Figure 213 showing the embroidered guards*

214 'Alexander Farnese', by Alonso Sanchez Coello, c. 1560. Charles V's grandson, by Margaret of Parma, who followed Don John of Austria as Governor of the Netherlands. He wears a Dutch cloak with elaborately embroidered guards. National Gallery of Ireland, Dublin

215 The 'Darnley' or 'Cobham' portrait of Queen Elizabeth I, by an unknown artist, c. 1575. The gown is of ash grey silk with a woven design. The bodice, or doublet, fastens with buttons and loops with decorative 'froggings' after the Polish fashion. The latter are of gold and silver bobbin lace mounted on red silk, or possibly braid, with red silk and gold and silver metal thread tassels at the ends. The seam on the outside of the sleeve is covered with gold and silver bobbin lace. National Portrait Gallery, London

white taphata' in 1569,[128] 'borderinge of a Dou[t]che Gowne of blak wrought vellat with murrey sarceonett' in 1571,[129] 'alteringe of a Dou[t]che Gowne of blak vellat enbrauderid with bugell and making a peire of newe bodies with a square coller and litle skyrtes lyned with sarceonett and doble lyned with buckeram' in 1572[130] and 'lyninge of a Dou[t]che Gowne of tyncell of divers colours lyned with blak sarceonett' in 1574.[131] It is not entirely clear what features distinguished a Dutch gown in England, but not, apparently, the guards which were used so much on Flanders gowns.

Dutch cloaks were worn by both men and women. Elizabeth wore them on horseback, as they are listed together with safeguards in the Stowe inventory, and obviously then formed part of a riding habit. Many Dutch cloaks are listed among the warrants for the Wardrobes of Robes. A typical entry records Walter Fyshe 'alteryng newe makyng cuttyng and pynkyng of A Doutche cloak of black taphata enbrodered with bugle allover the Cloak newe lyned with Murrey Taphata the Cloak gyney us by the Ladye Sydney' in 1570.[132] It is not clear from this entry what features were characteristic of a Dutch cloak, but among those listed in the Stowe inventory are several which have undergone alterations at various times. These descriptions show that they had sleeves.[133]

Occasionally a cloak has sleeves but is not described as a Dutch cloak.[134] This may, however, be a scribe's omission. Short cloaks with sleeves may be seen in Dutch paintings but many of the clothes are black and it is difficult to see details in reproductions. However, a short cloak with sleeves, reaching to the waist, may be seen very clearly in the portrait of Alexander Farnese by Coello, painted in about 1560 (Fig. 214).[135] The feminine fashion in England probably resembled this, although there is no indication of length in the warrant entries.

German influence on fashions during the second half of the sixteenth century in England was seen more in men's than women's clothes. Indeed, no German styles are mentioned among the records of the Wardrobe of Robes, in spite of Rathgeb's comment in 1592, that 'All the English women are accustomed to wear hats upon their heads, and gowns cut after the old German fashion — for indeed their descent is from the Saxons'.[136] Perhaps this is because German styles were similar to those of Flanders and Englishwomen had already adopted them as such.

Polish fashions

Among the French, Spanish, Italian, and Flanders gowns, the Queen had one Polish gown. Walter Fyshe was employed in

216 *Polish and Hungarian gowns fastening with 'froggings'. From 'Omnium Poene Gentium Habitus' by Abraham de Bruyn, 1581. British Library, London*

217 *The 'Ermine' portrait of Queen Elizabeth I. Panel painting attributed to William Segar, 1585. By courtesy of the Marquess of Salisbury, Hatfield House*

'alteringe and making longer of a Gowne of blak vellat of the polony fation the vellat to alter the same of our greate Guarderobe' in 1568.[137] In the following year he worked on it again,[138] so the Queen must have worn it several times. However, there is neither a detailed account of its shape and design, nor any indication whether the feature which made it Polish was the fabric, the cut or perhaps the method of fastening.

The 'Darnley' or 'Cobham' portrait of Elizabeth (Fig. 215) shows her wearing a doublet of masculine style, as 'mannes apparell is, for all the worlde' complained Philip Stubbes:[139] the fashion was very popular. The portrait shows an interesting arrangement of braid stitched in lines across the chest beside each button, with loop buttonholes ending with little tufts of silk, a type of frogging, although the term was not used at this date. It may be conjectured that, whatever it was in 1568, this is the Polish fashion in about 1575. The national dress of Poland was of Eastern origin. De Bruyn shows this type of fastening on Polish and Hungarian gowns (Fig. 216) while Vecellio shows them on gowns worn by Poles, a Prussian merchant, a Lithunanian woman from Grodno and the Sultan of Turkey.[140] Surviving examples of sixteenth-century Turkish caftans,[141] have these fastenings with toggles instead of the buttons used on Elizabeth's doublet.

The same type of decorative fastenings are employed on the black gown in the 'Ermine' portrait of the Queen (Fig. 217) dated 1585. Here they are worked in gold thread and enriched with jewels. The tufts at the end of each one are made of gold thread, with gold spangles. Mention should be made of the superb jewel hanging from the rich carcanet which is one of several collars of state worn by the Queen in her portraits. The jewel is described in the 1587 inventory of Elizabeth's jewels delivered to Mary Ratcliffe as 'a faier flower with three great ballaces and in the middes a great pointed diamond and three great pearles sett with a faier great pendaunt pearle, Called the brethren'. It is known variously as 'The Three Brethren' or 'The Three Brothers' and is known to have been carried by Charles the Bold on his expedition against the Swiss and captured by the latter at Grandson on 1 March 1476. It later

218 *The 'Welbeck' or 'Wanstead' portrait of Queen Elizabeth I attributed to Marcus Gheeraerts the Elder, c. 1580–85. Private collection*

219 *Detail of gold cord or braid 'froggings' in Figure 218*

220 *'Christina of Denmark, Duchess of Milan'. Panel painting by Hans Holbein, c. 1538. National Gallery, London*

221 *'Katharine Parr'. Panel painting attributed to William Scrots, c. 1545. National Portrait Gallery, London*

came into the possession of Henry VIII and was worn successively by Tudor and Stuart sovereigns. Other legendary named jewels worn by them include the 'Mirror of Great Britain', the 'Feather', the 'Mirror of France', and the 'Portugal Diamond'.[142]

A gown fastened all the way down the front with heavy gold cord or braid 'froggings', finished with tufts of gold threads, and buttons of single rubies in gold settings appears in the 'Wanstead' portrait (Figs 218–19). This is also known as the 'Welbeck' portrait and was painted at about the same time as the 'Ermine' portrait. Probably the clearest example of a gown of Polish inspiration, the white silk is worked with flowers beloved of English embroiderers — pale pink roses, scarlet pimpernels, blue borage and flax, and pansies — alternating with stylized geometric motifs in gold thread, each with a ruby mounted in gold set in the centre. The collar of state appears to be the same as that in the 'Ermine' portrait, the minor variations caused by a different artist's interpretation. The Queen holds a pink feather fan with a gold handle set with rubies and pearls. Her light brown leather gloves have short, embroidered yellow silk cuffs. The black silk network mantle or veil falls from the shoulders in long graceful folds, the collar turned back behind the ruff, revealing the white silk lining. It is embroidered all over with what seem to be gold serpents, symbolizing wisdom, alternating with red flowers which may be stylized roses, although the leaves are not the right shape (Fig. 244). The mantle is bordered with two narrow bands of gold braid enclosing more embroidered serpents alternating with small geometric motifs.

222 'A lady aged thirty called Queen Elizabeth I', by an
unknown artist, 1563. She wears what appears to be a tan velvet
loose gown trimmed with brown fur. Gripsholm Slott

223 'An unknown lady aged thirty-four'. Panel painting by an
unknown artist, 1569. Emmanuel College, Cambridge

Night-gowns and loose gowns

Walter Fyshe and William Jones made a number of night-
gowns for the Queen. Others were presented to her as New
Year's gifts, among them one of tawny wrought velvet, lined
with carnation unshorn velvet, from the Earl of Leicester.[143]
The descriptions of work carried out on some of these night-
gowns at various times may be compared with final entries in
the Stowe and Folger inventories in 1600 where they are all
listed as 'loose gowns'.

'Loose gown' seems to be a generic term for over-gowns
worn with kirtles and probably included Flanders gowns, as
we have already seen. They might fall loosely from shoulders
to hem at both front and back, a style seen earlier in Holbein's
portrait of the Duchess of Milan, painted in about 1538
(Fig. 220). Katharine Parr wears a similar loose gown in rich
red silk with a woven design in her portrait some seven years
later (Fig. 221). It is decorated with deep crimson velvet guards
embroidered with gold thread, and gold aglets stand away
from the sleeves which reveal white linen smock frills embroidered with red silk at the wrists. The collar is lined with what
seems to be white embroidered linen, but may be a patterned
silk. A portrait of a woman said to be Elizabeth I, painted in
1563 (Fig. 222) shows a gown cut loosely at both front and
back, trimmed with brown fur. The pattern shapes for similar
gowns may be seen in *Libro de Geometria, Pratica y Traça* by
Juan de Alcega, printed in Madrid in 1580, with a second
edition in 1589.[144]

Alternatively the gown might be fitted at the waist on both
front and back side seams, with long or short sleeves
(Fig. 223). A loose gown might also be fitted at the front and
loose at the back as in Mor's portrait of Margaret of Parma
(Fig. 224). Here there are full, short upper sleeves and lower
sleeves which fit the arm quite closely. A long slash reveals the
carnation silk kirtle beneath. Pattern diagrams for both styles
with alternative sleeves may be seen in *Geometria, y Traça
Perteneciente al Oficio de Sastres* by Franciso de la Rocha
Burguen, published in Valencia in 1618.[145]

The term 'night gown' was probably first given to a loose,
comfortable gown worn in the bedchamber early in the
sixteenth century. At this time it was frequently made of
woollen or worsted fabrics, sometimes with a hood. After
Henry VIII came to the throne, night-gowns were made in
richer fabrics — satin, velvet, and taffeta trimmed with gold
and silver lace — and lined with shag, plush, and fur. While
doubtless still used in the bedchamber, night-gowns were later
worn during the day as well, probably as a kind of loose coat
for extra warmth. Count Egmont wore a red damask night
robe at his execution in 1568,[146] while Lady Anne Clifford
recorded in her diary on 28 December 1617: 'I went to Church
in my rich night gown'.[147] The Queen may have favoured
night-gowns for informal wear during the day among her
women; quite a number, entered as 'loose gowns' are listed in
the Stowe and Folger inventories.

Most of these night-gowns were still lined with soft, warm
materials although some were lined with sarsenet, probably

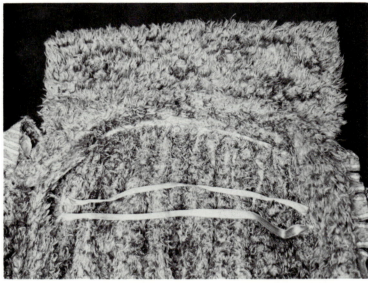

for summer wear. All were made in rich fabrics, often with buttons and loops to fasten sleeve and front openings. One made by Walter Fyshe in 1568, for example, was

a night Gowne of blak wrought vellat with a lace made of golde silver murrey and blak silke and eight dossen of buttons and loupes of like lace lyned with murrey sarceonett with fryse in the ruffes lyned in the skyrtes and coller with buckeram all of our greate guarderobe.[148]

Fyshe worked on it again shortly afterwards 'makinge newe slevis for a night Gowne of blak wrought vellat lyned with sarceonett the gowne new lyned with flanell'.[149] The flannel was probably for warmth in cold weather. The collar of this night-gown must have worn out at the edges and looked shabby, as Fyshe worked on it again in 1571 'alteringe and making a newe coller for a night Gowne of blak wrought vellat lyned with murrey sarceonett and faced with Sables the coller lyned with canvas and murrey sarceonett'.[150] This was probably a standing collar of the type seen in many portraits at this date. The canvas would have stiffened it. The lining was replaced again in 1572, when Fyshe altered the 'night Gowne of blak wrought vellat being lyned with murrey sarceonett and new lyned with flanell and for making of a newe staye of fustian covered with murrey sarceonett'.[151] Many of the Queen's loose gowns and night-gowns have stays as described here. The word probably originally meant 'support'[152] and this is borne out by Randle Holme in *The Academy of Armory and Blazon*, printed in 1688: 'In a Woman's Gown there are . . . the Stayes which is the body of the Gown before the Sleeves are put to or covered with the outward stuff'.[153] By this time the stays were a fully boned support, but in 1572 the word 'stay' probably referred to a strip of material stretching across the back inside, stitched to both armholes to hold the fullness of pleats or gathers in position. A loose gown preserved at Claydon House, Buckinghamshire, worn by Sir Francis Verney in the early seventeenth century,[154] still has two green silk stays across the grey shag lining (Fig. 225).

Another style of collar is noted in 1573, when Fyshe new-made a russet tuft taffeta night-gown with 'a newe fallinge coller lyned with canvas' for it.[155] This night-gown also had pockets and wings over the sleeveheads. When first made in 1572 it may have had a standing collar, but the description does not give this much detail:

for making of a night Gowne of russet tufte taphata layed with thre lases of silver and murrey silke the bodies lyned with blak taphata with pockettes and steye of like taphata the coller and winges lyned with buckeram of our great guarderobe.[156]

A night-gown which Fyshe new-made in 1574 gives a little more information about other features. The wings were now padded to make rolls over the shoulders (Fig. 204). 'Jagges', strips of doubled satin clipped at regular intervals giving a tabbed effect, or rows of separately made tabs with raw edges turned inwards, were stitched to the edge of the collar and into the armhole with the wings. His work is described as

newe making of a night Gowne of crymsen Satten with a brode garde wrought with a very busye worke of venice golde & silver lase the coller lyned with canvas the winges with buckeram with rolles in the winges coverid with fustian and Jagges made for the coller & winges of crymsen Satten of our great guarderobe.[157]

Another night-gown made in 1575 seems to have had a very deep collar described as 'a cape'. Perhaps this was a new development from the 'falling collar', unless this term refers to a separate short cape. Fyshe is entered

224   'Margaret of Parma', by Antonio Mor, c. 1562. She wears a semi-fitted black satin gown shaped on the side seams at the front. It is decorated with black velvet guards pinked and trimmed with diagonally-placed strips of braid. Gemäldegalerie, Staatliche Museen Preussischer Kulturbesitz, Berlin-Dahlem

225   Two green silk stays stitched to the armholes to hold the back pleats in position inside a loose gown of rich purple silk damask lined with grey silk shag, by tradition worn by Sir Francis Verney. c. 1605–15. Sir Ralph Verney, Claydon House (The National Trust) near Aylesbury

for makinge of a lardge night Gowne of wrought vellat ye grounde satten borderid aboute with brode silver lase the slevis layed thicke with like lase like Waves and in a space by thedge of the gowne lased byas very thicke like a garde the forequarters and cape lyned with russett unshorne vellat with a steye and pockettes and the gowne borderid beneth with russett taphata the Jagges lyned with like taphata and in the cape with canvas the vellat and brode silver lase of our store Receyved of the said George Brideman threst of our great guarderobe.[158]

All the Queen's night-gowns listed in the Stowe and Folger inventories would seem to have been very warm and comfortable to wear as they are mainly made of velvet and lined with fur or materials with a soft pile such as plush. Many were New Year's gifts and some very attractive ones were presented in the 1580s and 1590s.[159] One given by Sir John and Lady Scudamore in 1599 was of ash coloured velvet with a silver ground, with powdered ermine edgings and facings 'furred throughe with pure'.[160]

Riding gowns

The Queen spent a great deal of time on horseback as she enjoyed hunting. She also preferred this form of transport to travelling in a carriage and was, no doubt, seen to great advantage in this way, above the heads of the crowds. Always in the public eye, Elizabeth wore some beautiful gowns when mounted. Van Meteren wrote in 1575 that the English 'when they go abroad riding or travelling . . . don their best clothes, contrary to the practice of other nations'.[161] Perhaps this fashion was set by the Queen (Figs 94, 226, 227, and 228). Benedict Spinola presented her with an elegant riding crop, among other gifts 'all in a Case of Wodde coverid with grene vellat enbrauderid with Silver', at the New Year in 1559.[162] This was a thoughtful choice 'By Spynnolla a Straunger'. The 'Riding rodde garnisshed with Golde Silke and pearle' must have greatly pleased Elizabeth. It may not be entirely coincidence that there was a licence granted on 21 April 1559 for Benedict Spinola, a free denizen, to import and export certain kinds of cloth and merchandise, wines, and other items to a certain amount.

In 1562 David Smith was entered in a warrant 'for Enbraudringe of iiij rydinge hoodes ij of Blac velvet and ij of Blac Taffata for workemanship of them xxxvjs. Item for v oz of Spanyche Lace spent upon the same hoodes at ijs vjd thounce xijs vjd. Item for ij oz of Silke to worke the same hoodes iiijs'.[163] These hoods must have been very pretty and would have kept the Queen's hair from being wind-blown.

Walter Fyshe made one 'round ryding Kirtle of blac pynked velvet with bodies to the same with a gard and ij weltes of blac velvet lyned with blac Taffeta'[164] for Elizabeth in 1563. This would have been worn with a gown over it. There is, apparently, only one 'riding gown' entered in the warrants, which Fyshe altered and enlarged in 1568. It was of 'blak vellat striped with silver and garded with crymsen vellat' and was probably a gift, as it does not seem to be listed among the warrants before this entry.[165] At the same time Fyshe put in a crimson taffeta lining which was replaced in the following year. The riding gown probably had heavy wear. It was, presumably, like an ordinary French gown with a skirt made long enough to cover the feet when riding side-saddle. Fyshe was also employed in 'Takinge oute the Furre of a ridinge clok of Black wrought velvet and lynynge it with sarsenet of our great warderobe'[166] in 1563. This cloak was probably worn

226 *Queen Elizabeth I dismounted, after hunting the hart. Woodcut from* The Noble Art of Venerie *by George Turbervile, 1575. British Library, London*

227 *Queen Elizabeth I riding side saddle, hunting with falcons. Woodcut from* The Book of Faulconrie *by George Turbervile, 1575. British Library, London*

228 *Queen Elizabeth I riding side saddle. Reverse of the Great Seal, 1586. British Library, London (Seal XXXVI:19)*

with the black velvet riding kirtle and gown. These items, which appear to have formed an ensemble, are the only ones, apart from hoods, to be listed as 'riding' clothes. Subsequently the Queen wore safeguards with doublets, jupes, and cloaks.

Many of these cloaks are described as Dutch cloaks in the Stowe inventory and would therefore have had sleeves, much easier for riding. The safeguard was 'a kind of aray or attire reaching from the navill downe to the feete'.[167] Moll Cutpurse, the outspoken, fearless leading character in *The Roaring Girl* by Middleton and Dekker, often wears masculine clothes as an expression of her freedom and toughness. She appears in one scene 'in a frieze jerkin and black saveguard'[168] so presumably the safeguard was a complete skirt, rather than an apron-front. Randle Holme described it as part of the 'Riding suite for Women'; it was 'put about the middle, and so doth secure the Feet from cold and dirt'.[169] These descriptions show that the safeguard was a type of skirt, probably gathered at the waist, often, though not always, with pockets. One entry for alterations gives a little more detail:

for alteringe and gardinge downe ye sides with eight gardes on a Saufegarde of grene vellat the gardes welted with carnacion satten and a lase of venice golde silver & carnacion silke on every side the weltes the gardes borderid with grene taphata and pockettes of like taphata & stringes to it of our great guarderobe.[170]

The strings may have been tied round the foot or stirrup, to hold the skirt in position when mounted, a dangerous practice which was certainly followed in the 1880s, with a tab and an elastic stirrup; a safety foot strap was invented in 1886.[171]

From the late 1580s onwards 'juppes' seem to replace cloaks to a great extent. The term 'juppe', a name imported from France, was used in England in the late sixteenth century for a woman's upper garment usually accompanying a safeguard, apparently taking the place of the Dutch cloak. There are forty-three juppes with matching safeguards listed in the Stowe inventory.[172] These are in a wide range of colours and

materials including gold camlet, cloth of silver, velvet, satin, taffeta, lawn, grosgrain, and network, variously embroidered and decorated with gold and silver braids. It is to be hoped that the weather was usually kind to the Queen, particularly on her Progresses when watching entertainments put on in her honour. The entertainment devised for her by Thomas Churchyarde in 1578 received the full force of a heavy thunderstorm: 'We were all so dashed and washed, that it was the greater pastime to see us looke like drowned rattes than to have beheld the utterance of the shewes rehearsed. Thus, you see, a shew in the open fielde is always subject to the suddayne change of weather'.[173] The Queen would obviously have taken shelter in her carriage, but even a few drops of rain can spot velvet. Her hosts must have prayed for fine weather.

The French origin of the 'juppe' (from 'jupon') is doubly confirmed by an entry in the New Year's Gift Roll of 1589, where 'a safeguard with a Jhup or gaskyn Coate of haire Cullored satten like flames of fire of gold, and garnesshed with buttons, loupes and lace of venis silver' was given to the Queen by the Countess of Shrewsbury.[174] The latter term was already in use in 1578, as Lady Paget had given her 'a Gascone coate of black vellat, al over leyed with pasmane of silver and lyned white sarceonet' as a New Year's gift.[175] Gascons were natives of Gascony, a province of south-western France; many were soldiers of fortune and spent much time on horseback. The 'jhup or gaskyn coate' may therefore have copied some feature common to the riding coats worn by these men. It was probably a loose form of doublet, comfortable for riding, but fitting more closely than a Dutch cloak.[176] 'Juppe' may be an alternative name for a cassock, a garment which women had worn in England in the 1540s and 1550s, but this can only be conjecture. The term cassock is used for a masculine garment from the 1530s onwards but seems to be little used by women after the 1580s. The word 'juppe' appears in the 1570s.

Sixteenth- and early seventeenth-century costume terminology can be confusing. Minsheu gives English translations of the names of several Spanish garments and uses the word 'cassock' many times.[177] A 'sayuélo' for example, is 'a jerkin, a little cassocke such as women use in Spain'. Randle Cotgrave gives the French terms 'gippon' and 'jupon' while 'cassock' is translated as 'casaque, galleverdine, gippon, hoqueton, juppe'.[178] The word 'juppe' is then translated back into English as 'a shepheard's pelt, frocke or gaberdine; such a course long jacket as our Porters weare over the rest of their garments; (hence) also, a cassocke, long coate, loose jerkin'.

Masculine fashions: women's doublets, jackets, and jerkins

The introduction of masculine styles with the 'jhup or gaskyn coate', which women wore on horseback from the late 1570s onwards, has already been described. Whether other masculine fashions of doublet, jacket, and jerkin were originally adopted for riding and then became fashionable wear can only be a matter for conjecture.

The term 'doublet' first appears among the warrants in 1575, when Walter Fyshe made 'a dublett of yellowe Satten layed with silver lase lyned with yellowe sarceonett the same taken oute and lyned with white sarceonett and in the coller with canvas'.[179] Linthicum suggests that women wore doublets in the early sixteenth century, but this fashion would seem to have been a novelty in 1574, as Gascoigne in *Steele Glas*, asks 'What are they? Women? Masking in men's weedes? With Dutchkin dublets and with Jerkins jagged?'.[180]

There are numerous other references to women's doublets from this time until the end of Elizabeth's reign. Philip Stubbes complained in 1583 that

The women also there have dublettes and Jerkins, as men have here, buttoned up the breast, and made with winges, weltes and pinions on the shoulder pointes, as mannes apparell is, for all the worlde, and though this be a kind of attire appropriate onely to man, yet they blushe not to weare it.[181]

Stubbes may have disapproved, but he left us a very clear idea of the main features of a doublet which may be linked with portraits (Fig. 215) and warrant entries for tailors' work.

At first doublets followed masculine styles, buttoning up at the front with a high collar, although made without the exaggerated peascod belly at the centre front. The pointed waist reached its greatest length at the front towards the end of the 1580s and then slowly shortened again during the 1590s. A stiffened bodice, termed 'square bodies' came into fashion in the early 1580s. As we have seen, 'a peire of square bodies' was made for the Garter Kirtle in 1583 and for the Parliament Kirtle in 1585.[182] These 'square bodies' apparently followed the style of a doublet with tabbed skirts, but with a low square neckline (Fig. 109), and the opening cannot always be seen. The word 'doublet' seems to have been used for them by the 1590s, as eighty-five doublets are listed in the Stowe inventory but no pairs of 'square bodies' appear among them.

Many of these doublets with square necklines are seen in portraits, sometimes worn with matching petticoats (Fig. 10), but more often in contrasting colours and materials (Fig. 229). Petticoats and doublets together were presented to the Queen as New Year's gifts, usually in different fabrics. In one case, for example, a carnation taffeta petticoat accompanied a white satin doublet lined with carnation plush.[183] Here there is a link between the colour of the petticoat and the lining of the doublet but, although attractive together, they could also have been worn apart, with other doublets and petticoats.

Doublets were made in a wide variety of materials, including cloth of silver, cloth of gold, velvet, satin, taffeta, network, and lawn.[184] One entry among the warrants in 1576 records that William Whittell also used a fabric more often employed for linings in the Queen's gowns when

making of a Dublett of perfumed fustian of our store layed with lase of venice golde & grene silke lyned with grene taphata sarceonett canvas bumbaste hookes and eyes: for Making of a dublett of grene perfumed fustian layed with silver lase lyned with white taphata sarceonett with bumbaste canvas hookes & eyes: for making of xiij Cases of fustian for xiij dublettes: for making of a Case of yellowe Cotten for a Dou[t]che Cloake.[185]

No doubt this perfumed fustian was of extremely fine quality. Until the sixteenth century fustian had been imported into England and was consequently expensive, usually worn by royalty and the nobility.[186] In earlier times and during the sixteenth century 'Fustian-a-napes', or fustian of Naples, was apparently made of cotton, or flax mixed with wool, so silky-looking that it resembled velvet. Fustian had been made in England before 1554; in that year Norwich weavers who had been making 'fustian-a-napes' petitioned to be allowed to call their material 'Norwich fustian'. These fustians were fifteen yards long and half an ell wide in the loom. The spun cotton used for these fustians came from the Turkey Company and was the finest obtainable.[187]

229 'Lady Clopton of Kentwell Hall'. Panel painting by Marcus Gheeraerts the Younger, c. 1600. She wears a black velvet doublet, or 'square bodies', embroidered with triangles and curving drops in gold thread, with a covering of finest white cobweb lawn or silk. The petticoat is in white silk with what seems to be a woven pattern in black cut velvet. Yale Center for British Art, Paul Mellon Collection. New Haven, Connecticut

By the beginning of the seventeenth century the English manufacture of fustians had declined because they failed to keep up to standard, but they were still very popular at the end of the sixteenth century. The statute of 1597 concerning fustian manufacture states that 'the wearing of fustian has lately grown to greater use than ever it was before'.[188] The fustian with a soft, fleecy pile, linen warp and cotton weft, used for linings in surviving sixteenth- and early seventeenth-century doublets and suits[189] is of the cheapest variety; it is not at all like velvet.

Perhaps the perfumed fustian for the Queen's doublets was a gift from some Norwich weavers. Arthur Middleton made 'two peire of jeane fustian bodies' in 1576,[190] but this was imported Genoa fustian. The perfumed fustian doublets seem to have followed masculine styles more closely in 1576, as they were bombasted, unlike the first doublets made in 1575. The Queen may not have liked the results, as others made after this do not seem to have been padded. As we have seen, fustian was also used to make cases for doublets. These cases, or bags, were to protect clothes in store and when travelling.

Sometimes doublets were made from other garments. William Whittell altered a waistcoat to make a doublet in 1575, adding sleeves made by the Queen's silkwoman, Alice Mountague. The sleeves may have been detachable, but this is not specified in the warrant entry:

230   *Back of embroidered jacket without gussets, in white silk*
embroidered with polychrome silks and metal thread. It is lined
with pink silk shag. c.1590–1600. Victoria and Albert Museum,
London (173.1869)

for alteringe and newemakinge of a Dublett wrought with venice
golde silver & white silke the bodies being a wastecoate of our store
the slevis made by our Silkewoman the dublett lyned with white
satten and canvas with buttons hookes and eyes of our great
guarderobe.[191]

The canvas stiffening would seem to mark the difference
between waistcoat and doublet. As we shall see waistcoats are
usually lined with sarsenet, a light-weight silk, rather than
satin, and do not have canvas interlinings.[192]

Linthicum gives several references to jackets worn by men
and says that they were form-fitting, lined, waist-length
garments, with or without sleeves, worn for warmth.[193] The
fashion appears to have been adopted by women in the late
1570s; there are at least seven references to them among the
warrants for the Wardrobe of Robes between 1577 and 1580.
The descriptions are brief, so it is not clear if these jackets
copied masculine fashions very closely. William Whittell made
'a Jaquett of wrought vellat garded with vellat drawne with
satten layed with satten lase, with a peire of slevis of taphata
cutt lyned in the bodies with course canvas hookes and eyes'
for Elizabeth in 1577[194] and altered and made new wings for
four 'Jaquettes of vellat satten and taphata' later in the same
year.[195] He made a russet satin jacket 'layed with oringe colour
vellat and silver lase lyned thre severall tymes with sarceonett'
in 1578,[196] a velvet jacket 'bounde aboute with a passamaine
of venice silver sett allover with small buttons lyned with white
sarceonett' in 1579[197] and a 'Jaquett of blak satten cutt garded
with vellat the garde edgid with satten & wrought upon with
lase lyned with sarceonett & fustian' in the following year.[198]
William Jones was employed in 'makinge of a paire of
forebodies & Jagges for a Jacquett of Cloth of Silver with a
gold lace about yt lyned with Taffata' in 1595,[199] but only

three jackets appear in the Stowe inventory. They are entered
in the list of doublets, the first of cloth of gold, the second cloth
of silver, and the third embroidered with raised mosswork.[200]
It is not clear what differences there were between a jacket and
a doublet, from these descriptions, but it seems likely that the
word 'jacket' may have been used for the type of garment in
Figure 230, the forerunner of the jackets shaped at the waist
with gussets. The latter are seen in many portraits dating from
the early seventeenth century and several examples, mainly in
embroidered linen, are preserved in museums.[201] However,
the distinctions have been lost with the passage of time, and
this can only be conjecture.

Jerkins were another masculine fashion which women
copied, the Queen probably in the lead (Figs 200, 201).
William Whittell made her a black velvet jerkin lined with
straw coloured sarsenet in 1576[202] and lined one 'of leather
enbrodered' in 1577.[203] He made another of perfumed leather
'poynted with xij Aglettes' in 1577.[204] It is not clear if these
points, or laces, were to fasten the jerkin, or simply attached
for decoration. The aglets may have been small metal tags
enabling the laces to be threaded through eyelet holes, rather
than the large gold enamelled variety seen in portraits at this
date. The latter were purely for decoration.

Jerkins were often worn over doublets for extra warmth and
it is not easy to tell one garment from the other in portraits.
Even their wearers in the sixteenth century found difficulty in
doing so. Valentine mistakes Thurio's jerkin for a doublet in
The Two Gentlemen of Verona, and turns his error into a
punning joke.[205] William Whittell made 'a Dublett Jerkenwise
of russett satten cutt & drawne welted with white vellat lyned
with white sarceonett with canvas hookes & eyes bumbast and
buckeram' for Elizabeth in 1576.[206]

Linthicum states from the evidence of inventories that
jerkins were sometimes made with sleeves.[207] However,
stiffened wings at the armholes of both garments would make
it very difficult to pull on a sleeved jerkin over a doublet, even if
the latter was sleeveless. Inventories would list 'jerkins with
sleeves' if in matching material, even though made separately.
The sleeves would have been tied into the armholes of the
doublet beneath, or into the jerkin if worn alone. The same
kind of confusion often occurred with partlets and sleeves, as
Linthicum has explained.[208] Making a doublet 'jerkenwise'
probably meant that the sleeves were not sewn into the
armholes, and that the doublet was made without as much
stiffening as usual.

Jerkin making was a separate craft from tailoring.[209] A
tailor would make jerkins in addition to his other work, but a
jerkin maker probably specialized in this particular garment
because he was not skilful enough to master the most difficult
technique in the art of tailoring to satisfy fashion-conscious
customers, namely to set in a sleeve without any pulling under
the arm or wrinkling over the sleevehead. Separate sleeves,
easily tied into doublet or jerkin beneath the wings, presented
no problems.

A quotation from Rowlands' *Knave of Harts* would certainly seem to show that jerkins were normally sleeveless:

> Because we walk in jerkins, and in hose
> Without an upper garment, cloak or gown,
> We must be tapsters running up and down.[210]

Tapsters usually work with their shirt sleeves rolled up and
long sleeves in a jerkin would be uncomfortably warm.

Waistcoats

Waistcoats were worn by both men and women. The warrants for the Wardrobe of Robes list a large number made for the Queen. Linthicum states that a waistcoat was a waist-length undergarment, with or without sleeves, usually quilted or bombasted, and that, from the evidence of contemporary plays, a woman did not appear in public in a waistcoat unless she was a strumpet.[211] It would seem that these garments, although often very decorative, were seen only in the bed-chamber, worn over the smock and then covered with kirtle and gown. Norah Waugh suggests that the waistcoat is an early form of corset, taken from masculine fashions, later termed 'a pair of bodys'.[212] Examples of waistcoats worn by Elizabeth show that while they probably did give some support, with lines of decorative quilting and other embroidery, they were also worn for warmth: some are interlined with cotton wool, while others are made of flannel.

Elizabeth had several waistcoats made for her by Walter Fyshe in 1563.[213] One was of 'fyne hollande cloth lyned with lyke hollande'. Two others were of white satin, the first 'layed on with a lace of blacke sylke and sylver lyned with sarceonett and fyne hollande clothe' which was then altered with the addition of 'a lace of russet sylke and golde', and the second 'layed all over with a lace of black sylke and silver lyned with white sarceonet and fyne holland clothe'.

David Smith was entered in a warrant in 1565:

for enbrauderinge of a wastcote of white taphata sarceonet with a worke allover of black silke lyke a scallop Shell wrought upon fyne lynen clothe for workemanship therof xlvjs. Item for viij oz of granado silke to worke the same at iijs thoz xxiiijs. Item for bumbast spent upon the same wastcote ijs vjd.[214]

This bombast was probably a very thin layer of fine cotton wool, to avoid a bulky appearance, but give some warmth. Two years earlier, Smith had worked on a pair of waistcoat sleeves which were also padded:

Enbrauderinge of a paire of Sleves for a wastcoat of fyne lynnen Clothe wrought allover with a worke of white Cheyne silke lace powdered full of stitches for workemanshipp therof xls. Item for v oz of Cheyne lace and silke spente upon the same sleves at iijs iiijd thounce xvjs viijd. Item for an ell of fyne holland to worke the said sleves upon vjs. Item for half a pound of Cotton spent upon the same sleves xd.[215]

Some of the waistcoats appear to have been unpicked for laundering. Roger Mountague was entered in 1588 'for wasshinge starchinge mendinge & newe makinge up of two wastcoates wrought with blacke silke and golde nedleworke with fower elles and a halfe of camerike and thre quarters of an ounce of venice golde lase to them'.[216] This sounds as if both of them were given new linings of cambric and extra trimming of gold braid or lace.

Other attractive waistcoats in various materials worn by the Queen include one altered by Walter Fyshe in 1570, 'a wastecoate of Camerike enbrodered allover with silver' and another of white sarsenet which he made in 1573.[217] The latter was 'layed with lase of blak silk lyned with lynen cloth and fustian'. William Whittell made a 'Wastecoate of lynen cloth quilted with blak silke' in 1577[218] and William Jones altered and made wider one of 'sarceonett quilted with golde and silver' in 1584.[219] This quilting may simply have referred to lines of decorative stitching also giving stiffness, without a layer of cotton wool, but by the 1590s 'quilting' seems to have

described stitches holding padding in position. Jones, for example, made 'two Rowles of strawcolour taffata, quilted with bumbast', probably as sleeve supporters, in 1591.[220]

Although cotton quilted waistcoats would have been warm, Elizabeth also relied on wool to protect her against the damp English climate and draughty English houses and castles. She had, for example, two waistcoats of 'flanell bounde aboute with lase' in 1573,[221] which would have been very warm. In 1581 another two were described as 'of fyne flanell layed with silke lase'[222] and in 1586 she had 'two wastecoates thone flanell thother bayes bounde with reben'.[223]

Some of the waistcoats had sleeves, probably made separately. In 1577 Walter Fyshe made 'a wastecoate of white satten cutt & raveled allover striped with silver lase with doble Jagges and greate slevis bounde with passamaine lase of venice golde and silver lyned with strawe colour sarceonett'.[224] Other waistcoats seem to have been sleeveless but a pair of sleeves, perhaps of different material, could easily have been tied into the armholes if required. Fyshe made 'thre peire of wastecoate slevis of white sarceonett lyned with the same' and 'two peire of very fyne flanell slevis' in 1574.[225] William Jones made six pairs of flannel sleeves bound with ribbon in 1586,[226] at the same time as the two waistcoats of flannel and bayes. Flannel waistcoats would have been most welcome articles in any woman's wardrobe during the cold winter months in sixteenth-century England.

Bodies

'Bodies' are listed in the warrants for the Wardrobe of Robes right through Elizabeth's reign. The right and left sides of a bodice were collectively described as 'a pair of bodies', in the same way as a pair of sleeves or a pair of breeches. The meaning of the word 'body' usually has to be deduced from the context, as 'a pair of bodies' can be the foundation of the fashionable shape, an early form of corset, as well as the bodice of a kirtle or gown. The word 'corset' appears in Cotgrave's *Dictionarie of the French and English Tongues*, printed in 1611, as a French term for 'a little body, also a paire of bodies (for a woman)'. It is not used in England until the nineteenth century. During the seventeenth century the boned lining of a bodice was called 'the stays' and this term continued in use during the eighteenth century, when the garment was made as a separate item. The word probably originally meant 'support' and in the sixteenth century seems to have referred to a strip of material stretching across the back of a loose gown inside, to hold the fullness in position (Fig. 225).[227]

There are many examples of 'a pair of bodies' as part of a kirtle or gown. Walter Fyshe, for example, lined the 'bodies of a Dowche gowne of blak vellat embrauderid with bewgelles' in 1568[228] and made 'a payer of bodies and slevis for a Gowne of blak wrought vellat' in 1569,[229] while Arthur Middleton made 'a payer of bodies and slevis with Jagges of crymsen vellat for a kirtle with a passamaine lase of venice golde lyned with sarceonett canvas hookes and eyes' in 1579.[230] These were all bodices with skirts attached, like those in an entry for William Whittell 'alteringe & newe making of Eleven peire of bodies for gownes' in 1580[231] and those which William Jones worked on in 1584 'alteringe pecinge longer and enlarginge of Thirtye & seven peire of bodies and slevis for gownes'.[232]

Sometimes 'bodies' are described as 'upper bodies', a good example being 'a peire of upper bodies with large slevis and with doble skirtes and doble Jagges in the syse of white Satten

11

231 *'Elizabeth Vernon, Countess of Southampton'. Panel painting by an unknown artist, c. 1600. Detail from Figure 164 showing a pink silk 'pair of bodies' lacing at the front. c. 1600. The Duke of Buccleuch and Queensberry, KT. Boughton House, Northamptonshire*

layed thicke and cutt the cuttes edgid & the panes lyned with oringe colour taphata the bodies lyned with like taphata the coller lyned with canvas of our greate guarderobe', made by Walter Fyshe in 1574.[233] The double skirts were probably two rows of small tabs laid one over the other at the waist, unless the scribe had intended to put 'doble lyned', indicating extra stiffness. A single row of tabs may be seen in Figure 203. The 'doble Jagges in the syse' — scyes, or armholes — were two folded strips of material, clipped or 'jagged' for decoration, giving a tabbed effect. They might also be made from separate tabs with raw edges turned inwards. (Fig. 201). The term 'upper bodies' would seem to refer to an outer bodice worn over the kirtle bodice, as with the Italian fashion already described.

Many 'pairs of bodies' are listed as individual items, without any mention of kirtle or gown. Some of these are presumably the early form of corset, to be worn over a smock, beneath kirtles or close-fitting French gowns. This extra layer of stiffening compressed the bust and made a woman's figure more compact. It is much easier to fit a gown over a firm foundation (Fig. 231).

Walter Fyshe made 'a payer of bodyes of black cloth of Silver with litell skyrtes bound with gold lase lyned with black sarceonett' in 1571,[234] and this is typical of many others throughout the reign. In 1579 William Whittell altered 'a peire

of bodies of sweete lether',[235] which may well have been an early leather corset, similar to those made in the eighteenth century.[236] The Queen's early 'bodies' are lined with fustian, taffeta or sarsenet, but in 1583 William Jones made 'a payer of bodyes of blake vellat lyned with canvas styffenid with buckeram drawen oute with white sipers',[237] which may be the forerunner of the type of corset dating from 1598, worn by Pfalzgräfin Dorothea Sabina von Neuberg (Fig. 232). This is of ivory silk, still with rows of stitching forming casings for whalebones, although the latter, together with the linen lining, have disintegrated.[238]

Not all the 'pairs of bodies' listed among the warrants are necessarily separate garments. The scribe may simply have omitted to make a note of the gown or kirtle to which they were attached. For example, Walter Fyshe is entered for altering 'a payer of bodies of blak Satten garded chevernewise and making of a newe coller for the same' in 1569,[239] and 'for cutting out a paire of bodyes and slevis of the frenche fation of black vellat' in 1571.[240] Both these 'bodies', the former with a collar and the latter with sleeves, sound as if they would have been component parts of gowns, rather than corsets.

An entry for work carried out by William Jones for the Queen's dwarf in 1597 shows the use of the word 'bodies' to describe both the bodice of a gown and a corset, in conjunction with the term 'French' for the latter:

Item for making a highe bodied Gowne of drake colour velvet (for Tomasen our woman dwarfe) with two silver laces aboute the bodies and slevis wrought with silver lase with a paier of slevis and a stomacher of white satten cut and lined with serceonet the bodies lined and stiffened with canvas & buckeram the skirtes bordered with fustian with a rolle of cotton and paier of verthingale slevis of fustian. And for making of a petycoate of chaungable taphata and thre gold lases and a fring aboute the skirtes lyned with baies with a payer of french bodies of damaske lyned with sackecloth, with whales bone to them, of our great warderobe.[241]

Here the bodice of a high-necked gown was lined with canvas and buckram to stiffen it. There was also a stomacher lined with sarsenet to put over the front of the bodice. The sleeves were held out with a pair of hooped sleeve supports, hence the term 'verthingale slevis'. The fringed petticoat was lined with bayes, a cloth of worsted and woollen mixture with a nap. This was presumably for warmth, as well as to stiffen the garment. The 'rolle of cotton' was a hip pad to hold out the skirt: 'a role to weare under womens gowns, a French verdingale' as Minsheu described it,[242] or the 'French Vardingale; or (more properly) the kind of roll used by such women as weare no Vardingales' according to Cotgrave.[243] Thomasina's 'french bodies' of damask, lined with sackcloth and stiffened with strips of whalebone, would probably have been similar in appearance to the corset in Figure 232. Here there is a wide casing at the front to take a busk of wood or whalebone for extra stiffening. William Jones provided 'xij Buskes of Whalesbone and wyer coverid with sarceonet quilted' for Elizabeth in 1586.[244] Thomasina must already have had a suitable busk.

In 1597 the three children of a gentleman named Starkie living in Lancashire were possessed of the devil and made accusations of witchcraft. The eldest girl, aged fourteen, screamed and yelled to her possessing demon:

Come my lad. Come on and set my partlet on one side as I do on the other . . . Thus, my lad, I will have a fine Smocke of silke, it shall be finer than thine, I will have a Petticoat of silke, not redde but of the finest silk that is, it shall be guarded and a foote high: it shall be laid on with gold Lace: it shall have a French bodie, not of whalebone, for

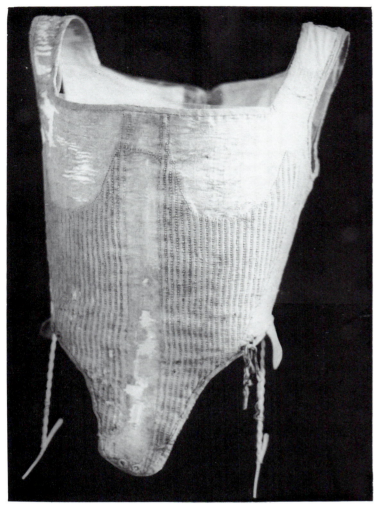

232 'Pair of bodies' in ivory silk worn by Pfalzgräfin Dorothea Sabina von Neuberg. The linen lining and whalebones have all disintegrated in the grave, but the lines of silk stitching remain. 1598. Bayerisches Nationalmuseum, Munich

233 Bents, the reedy stems of grasses grown on sand dunes, arranged in bunches of about twenty and held between two layers of linen by lines of stitching. Detail from the front of a linen 'pair of bodies' which has been cut off, perhaps to use as a stomacher. Early seventeenth-century or provincial eighteenth-century. Rocamora Collection, Barcelona

that is not stiff enough, but of horne for that will hold it out, it shall come, to keepe in my belly ... My lad I will have a Busk of Whalebone, it shall be tyed with two silke Points, and I will have a drawn wrought stomacher imbroidered with golde, finer than thine.[245]

The term 'French bodies' does not seem to have been used before the 1590s. In 1577 Jérôme Lippomano wrote that

French women have inconceivably narrow waists; they swell out their gowns from the waist downwards by whaleboned stuffs and vertugadins, which increases the elegance of their figures. Over the chemise they wear a corset or bodice, that they call a 'corps piqué' which makes their shape more delicate and slender. It is fastened behind which helps to show off the form of the bust.[246]

The 'French bodie' probably took its name from this early French fashion, a quilted, or stitched bodice. The idea of putting strips of whalebone between the rows of stitching may have originated in France. Mr Starkie's daughter wanted her 'French bodie' to be stiffened with horn, to produce an even more rigid effect than the strips of whalebone used for Thomasina's 'pair of french bodies', with a whalebone busk at the front.

Both 'bodies' and corsets were stiffened with bents, a type of stiff hollow-stemmed grass, before whalebone was introduced (Fig. 233). William Jones is entered in the warrants in 1582:

for alteringe of a peire of bodies and enlarginge the slevis with a partelett of prented cloth of golde coverid with a Shadowe of blak nettworke the slevis drawen oute with white nettworke the bodies lyned with sackecloth and buckeram aboute the skyrtes with bentes coverid with fustian with prented cloth of silver to perfourme it.[247]

This form of stiffening continued in use until the eighteenth century, as surviving garments show.[248]

There are a number of entries for 'square bodies' from 1583 onwards. William Jones made, for example, 'two payer of square bodyes of satten lyned with serceonett & canvas with satten and vellat to perfourme them' in that year.[249] The 'square bodies' made for the Parliament kirtle in 1585 followed the lines of a doublet, but with a low square neckline (Fig. 107). Another 'payer of square bodies' made by William Jones in 1586 were of 'carnacion satten striped with golde & silver lyned with sarceonett & fustian'.[250] By the 1590s the word 'doublet' seems to have been used for this style, although not always fastening with buttons at the front by this time, (Fig. 229) and clerks gradually drop the word 'square' from descriptions. They still refer to 'high bodies', as in 1595, when William Jones made

a highe bodied gowne of ashe colour tussued taffeta with a gold and silver bone lace aboute, with two payre of slevis, faces and Stomacher of silver Chamblet covered over with Copwebb Lawne, and upon

234 *'Queen Mary I'. Panel painting by an unknown artist,*
c. 1554. Royal Collection. Reproduced by Gracious Permission
of Her Majesty the Queen

them white lawne wroughte with gold and silver plate, the bodies
stiffened with canvas and buckeram hookes and eyes and duble lyned
with Sarceonet of our great warderobe.[251]

Stomachers

Stomachers are treated briefly here as, although not listed
separately in the Stowe and Folger inventories, these items are
capable of changing the appearance of a gown to a considerable degree. Many stomachers were made by the Queen's
tailors and they are also considered as part of the work of
embroiderers and silkwomen described in Chapter VIII.

The stomacher or placard was a small decorative piece of
material worn by both men and women over the chest and
abdomen to fill in the front opening of doublet or kirtle body.
It is first recorded being worn by men in 1450[252] and may be
seen later in many portraits during the first half of the sixteenth
century. Women apparently first adopted the stomacher in the
first decade of the sixteenth century[253] and it continued in use
long after Elizabeth's reign, until the end of the eighteenth
century. A woman's stomacher might also conceal obtrusive
fastenings, as well as filling in the front opening.

Some stomachers were stiffened: four made for the Queen in
1576 were of 'paste bourde coverid with taphata'.[254]
However, most of those listed among the tailors' work in the
warrants were not rigid. Typical examples include six stomachers 'of white Satten layed at the toppes with bone lase of
venice golde & silver', made by Walter Fyshe in 1575, which
were lined with white fustian,[255] eight made by William Jones

in 1586 'of white satten, layed on with golde lase lyned with
sarceonett' and another four 'of white satten with gold and
silver lace, and lyned with Sarcenet and fustian' in 1596.[256] No
stiffening of any kind is mentioned. It was presumably not
needed because the stiffened pair of 'bodies' worn beneath the
kirtle frequently had a wooden busk at the front. The 'French
bodie' stiffened with horn and the whalebone busk tied in with
silk ribbons, or points, which Mr Starkie's daughter called for
in 1597, had a stomacher embroidered with gold thread to go
on top.[257] A bodice and matching train made for the Queen by
William Jones in 1592 had a stomacher lined with silver
camlet, and again there is no mention of stiffening inside it:

a paire of bodies with hanginge slevis, and a traine of heare colour
tuft Taffata the ground Silver with a gold and silver Lace about yt sett
with buttons and tassells the hanginge slevis drawne out with Lawne
striped with gold and Silver, the hanginge slevis facinges and
stomacher lyned with Silver Chamblet and lawne don with silver
plate the bodies stiffened with canvas and buckeram hook and eyes
lyned with Sarcenet and the trayne lykewise Lyned with Sarcenet of
our great warderobe.[258]

William Jones made one 'stomacher of white lawne bound
with silver lace with hookes and eyes' in 1594.[259] The warrants
are not clear on the methods used for attaching other
stomachers. The lack of hooks and eyes in the descriptions
would suggest the use of pins.

White satin was the most popular material for the Queen's
stomachers, although other fabrics were also used. For
example, Walter Fyshe made her three of white velvet in
1575,[260] one of black velvet lined with black sarsenet in
1576[261], and two of 'strawe colour satten layed with golde lase
lyned with sarceonett' in 1587.[262] The first straw coloured
satin stomacher was apparently made in 1577,[263] and there are
many others of this colour after that date, as well as white
ones. Walter Fyshe also made Elizabeth 'fower Stomachers of
fyne skarlett layed with golde and silver lase at the toppes'
during the winter months of 1581.[264] These were presumably
for warmth, as scarlet was a very fine cloth of wool.

During the first twenty years of the reign Elizabeth's
stomachers were usually trimmed with gold or silver lace, or
braid. Later they became more ornate and were often made to
match sleeves and gown facings. William Jones made 'a peire
of slevis & a Stomacher of white satten cutt in risinge panes
lyned with silver chamblett & sarceonett' in 1587,[265] while
John Parr was employed in 'augmentinge of the embroidery of
a paire of sleves, coller, stomager and facinges of white lawne
richly wrought alover with gold & colored silkes' in 1591.[266]
The latter items sound very similar to the sleeves, sleeve
linings, collar lying over the ruff, stomacher and gown facings
seen in the Jesus College portrait of the Queen (Fig. 66).

John Parr worked on other elaborately decorated stomachers. In 1596 he was employed in

enbrauderinge on of pearle beinge raysed upon a payer of slevis &
stomacher of cloth of silver and blacke stiched cloth the pearle beinge
ripped of[f] & new thredded & twisted uppon silver wier with xj
ounces di of silver wier.[267]

These were probably small pearls, and the twisted silver wire
would have held them away from the cloth of silver stomacher
and sleeves in the same way as the spangles in Figure 460.

Jewels were used to decorate stomachers and may be seen in
many portraits (Fig. 71). John Parr was entered in a warrant of
1595 for 'enbrauderinge on of Jewells upon a plackett &
stomacher of silver sarcenet, wrought with arches of

pearle'.[268] The placket, according to Linthicum, is the short opening at the top of a woman's petticoat or kirtle skirt, usually in front, and not to be confused with the 'placard', or stomacher.[269] However, John Rider in his *Bibliotheca Scholastica: a double dictionarie*, printed in 1589, describes the placard as the 'fore part of a woman's peticote' and a 'Placarde or foreparte of a kirtle of purple cloth of gold', which had belonged to Queen Mary, is listed in the Folger inventory.[270] Walter Fyshe made one 'payer of kyrtle bodies the foreparte being of tyssue and the back of white Satten with a wreth of white Satten enbrodered with golde lyned with white sarceonett the tyssue being of a placarde received of the said Rauf Hope' and another 'peyre of kyrtle bodies the foreparte of crymsen tyssue the backe of crymsen Satten with two golde laces aboute lyned with crymsen sarceonett the tyssue being a placarde' in 1569.[271] The amount of material needed for the front of a kirtle bodice would presumably be more than could be cut from a stomacher, unless it was pieced with satin. However, Walter Fyshe worked on 'a foreparte and placarde of nedleworke' in 1573[272] and here the 'placard' appears to be a stomacher. The word seems therefore to have had both meanings and should always be considered in context.

There are several references with sexual innuendo to plackets in Shakespeare's plays.[273] These indicate that they were skirt openings at the front, as, for example, when Thersites calls for vengeance on the whole camp 'or rather the bone-ache! for that, methinks is the curse dependant on those that war for a placket'.[274] During the seventeenth century the word 'placket' acquires the meaning of 'pocket' as well as an opening, presumably because pocket bags were stitched there.[275]

Partlets and sleeves

Partlets and sleeves, although not listed separately in the Stowe and Folger inventories, are treated briefly here as they are fashion features which can completely change the appearance of a gown. Partlets were originally short jackets worn by men, but from the late fifteenth century the term was used for a garment which covered the upper part of the chest and neck.[276]

Women's partlets were made with standing collars in material to match the gown from the 1530s to the 1550s. They may be seen in portraits, covering low square necklines, in some cases fitting so closely that the edge is hardly visible, giving the appearance of a yoke seam (Figs 176 and 234). By the end of the 1550s a second variety of partlet, resembling the top of a smock, filled in these necklines (Fig. 174) following the lines of the masculine shirt. This style of partlet remained in fashion until about 1580, at first with a narrow frill at the top of the standing neckband. This frill slowly developed into the ever-widening ruff, which was made as a separate item for easier laundering by the 1560s.[277] These partlets were made of elaborately embroidered lightweight materials, including satin, lawn, cypress, and network (Fig. 235), and were frequently made with a pair of matching sleeves. As Linthicum points out, the descriptions of 'partlets with sleeves' in contemporary accounts have often confused lexicographers.[278] The sleeves were not attached to the partlet. The edge of a low square-necked smock may sometimes be visible beneath the partlet (Figs 12 and 25a), but usually it is virtually impossible to detect the difference between a partlet with matching sleeves and a high necked smock in portraits.[279] The smock in the painting of *Queen Elizabeth I and the Three*

235 *'Queen Elizabeth I', by an unknown artist, c. 1575–80. She wears a network partlet decorated with seed pearls. The ruff is embroidered with drawn thread work and bordered with needle lace. Cambridge University Old Schools*

Goddesses (Fig. 236) is embroidered all over, with ruffs at neck and wrists. When worn beneath a gown it would have had a similar appearance to the smock, or partlet with matching sleeves, in the portrait of a young lady in Figure 174: both paintings date from 1569.

Some of the Queen's partlets were presented to her as gifts, others were made by Walter Fyshe and embroidered by David Smith, while many more were supplied by Alice Mountague, her silkwoman. In 1565, for example, Alice was entered in the warrants

for working half way of a gathered partelet of lawne with drawne worke of crimsen silk for workinge of viij yardes of lawne Ruffes with spanishwork of crimsen silk edgid with viij yardes of bobin lace of gold and crimsen silke.[280]

The eight yards of 'lawne Ruffes' was the length of gathered frill stitched to the top of the neckband. It is not clear why Alice only worked half of the partlet: perhaps one of the Queen's women finished the embroidery, or possibly the back was left plain.

Another partlet made by Alice in the same year had lawn ruffs measuring twelve yards round the edge. This was probably arranged in two lengths of six yards, one above the other (Fig. 174):

a gathered partelet of laune beinge wrought alover with diverse <colours> workes of silk of sondry colours with xij yerdes of laune Ruffes beinge wrought with spanishe worke and edgid with turnid frindge of gold being whipped withe flat Damask Pirle.[281]

236   *Detail from 'Queen Elizabeth I and the Three Goddesses'. Panel painting signed HE, 1569. The Goddess Venus sits on a white linen smock embroidered in stripes with a geometric design. The ruffs at neck and wrists are still clearly joined to the smock, not detachable. Royal Collection. Reproduced by Gracious Permission of Her Majesty the Queen*

Portraits often show delicately made silk strings to tie the neck of the partlet (Fig. 237). Alice Mountague 'delivered to Dorothy bradbelt to our use vij Paire of partelett laces of venice gold and Silver with acrons [acorns] at thendes' for Elizabeth in 1564.[282] Other partlets have hooks and eyes[283] fastening the band at the front. These may also be seen in portraits (Fig. 238).

Some partlets were very richly decorated and one is thus described in the warrants for 1565:

Item to David Smith Enbrauderer . . . for enbrauderinge of a very rich partelet upon silver sarceonet with cheynes of gold and grea[t] pearles beinge wrought with straight stripes downe right with a twiste of venice gold on ether syde of the cheynes and p(ear)les for workmanshipp of the same partelet and new setting on of the Jewells in the band xls.[284]

Here the partlet had jewels set on the neckband beneath the ruff, as well as large pearls used for the embroidery.

Walter Fyshe made a very elaborate partlet in 1576:

a rufte partelett of the frenche facion of tawnye satten layed betwene the ruffes with lase of venice golde & silver with a small welte enbrodered with pirle lyned with white taphata & sarceonett the Jagge at the coller bounde aboute with a passamaine lase of venice golde & silver.[285]

The satin was ruched all over the partlet and decorated with gold and silver braid. The effect would probably have been similar to that of red silk embroidered with gold thread and pearls seen in the portrait of the Countess of Kildare (Fig. 239). However the exact appearance of a partlet 'of the French fashion' can only be conjectured, as with the 'Flanders partlet' discussed earlier.

Economies were practised by altering and re-using old trimmings on new partlets. David Smith, for example, in 1565 was entered 'for enbrodering on of sundry old flowres made of black silk and gold and set upon a new partelet of white launde gathered for workmanshipp therof Lvs'.[286]

There are many examples of matching partlets and sleeves. One set embroidered with gold and silver birds and flowers in 1565 gives details of the price of materials and workmanship:

Item to David Smith Enbrauderer . . . for enbrauderinge of a gathered partelet and a paire of wide slevis of lawne wrought allover with sondry sortes of byrdes and floures made of gold and silver of sondry colours for workmanshipp therof xiij*li* xiij*s* iiij*d*. Item for xiij ounces of gold and silver p(ur)les spent upon the same partelet and slevis at vj*s* viij*d* thounce iiij*li* vj*s* viij*d*.[287]

The wide sleeves would probably have looked like those worn beneath the Flanders gown in a portrait of an unknown lady painted by Hans Eworth in 1563.[288] The portrait of Mary Hill, Mrs Mackwilliam, painted in 1567 shows both wide sleeves and gathered partlet of embroidered lawn (Fig. 240). The description 'wide' is relative, as may be seen in Figure 14.

237 Detail from 'Mary, Queen of Scots', by an unknown artist, 1578. She wears her ruff open, with falling band strings. Beneath the ruff a black necklace of what may be jet is visible, with pendent M initials. National Portrait Gallery, London

238 Portrait of an unknown lady, by an unknown Flemish master, c. 1545–55. Metropolitan Museum of Art, New York

239 The Countess of Kildare, 'the Fair Geraldine', by an unknown artist, c. 1575. National Gallery of Ireland, Dublin

240 'Mary Hill, Mrs Mackwilliam aged thirty-four'. Panel painting attributed to the Master of the Countess of Warwick, 1567. The Lord Tollemache, Helmingham Hall, Stowmarket

241   *Blue silk knitted jacket with a diagonal striped pattern in self colour. The design of 'froggings' across the front is knitted in gold metal thread to match the imitation guards round armholes and waist and down the centre back, side seams and centre of each sleeve. The 'froggings' are inspired by the Polish style of fastenings seen in the 'Darnley' and other portraits and imitate intricate knots in narrow braid. The buttons are worked in gold metal thread over wooden bases. c. 1600. Germanisches Nationalmuseum, Nürnberg (T 3638)*

Not all the matching partlets and sleeves were embroidered. In 1565 Alice Mountague supplied 'a partelet and a peire of slevis of whit knit work with braunches of gold'.[289] Here the word 'branches' obviously means 'patterns' or 'designs'. Knitted silk jackets with patterns in gold and silver thread (Fig. 241) may be seen in several museums.[290] At the same time Alice supplied 'vj paire of garnesey knit slevis'.[291] The terms 'garnsey', and jersey or 'jarnsey' are apparently interchangeable. The latter is included among the threads described by Stubbes in 1583 for making fine knitted stockings: 'Jarnsey, Worsted, Crewell, Silke, Thred and such like or els[e] at the least of the finest Yearne that can bee got'.[292] Although Linthicum suggests that these were fine worsted stockings from Jersey,[293] Stubbes's use of the word 'Jarnsey' as well as worsted would seem to show that it was a type of thread. This is confirmed by a document written by Thomas Caesar probably in December 1596:

Spinninges of wooll are of three sortes, viz. either upon the greate wheele which is called woollen yarne, . . . or upon the small wheele, which is called Garnesey or Jarsey yarne, bicause that manner of spynning was first practised in the Isle of Garnsey or Jarnesey (sic) . . . or upon the rock, which is called worsted yarne . . . Jersey and Worsted yarnes be made of combed wooll . . . Jarsey yarne maketh warpe for the finest stuffes.[294]

J. de L. Mann suggests that the small wheel refers to what is sometimes known in England as the Saxony wheel, which appeared in Germany about 1480. It gradually spread over western Europe and might well have been introduced into the Channel Islands by Protestant refugees during Elizabeth's reign.[295] Randle Holme gives further information in *The Academy of Armory and Blazon*: 'Jersey is the finest Wool taken out of other sorts of Wool by Combing it with a Jersey-Comb'.[296] Perhaps this comb was a Channel Island invention and gave the wool its name rather than the method of spinning, because apparently there is no tradition of the Saxony wheel

there although the inhabitants certainly knitted and presumably spun their yarn from combed wool. The 'garnesey knit' sleeves for the Queen were probably of very fine wool, perhaps as fine as that used for delicate knitted Shetland shawls in the nineteenth century, both light and warm.

The items dealt with so far have all been from the 1560s and 1570s. Although partlets slowly went out of fashion after about 1580, pairs of sleeves made separately from gowns, and of contrasting materials, continued in use until the end of the reign. Many of the sleeves listed in the warrants were component parts of the Queen's gowns but others, as we have already seen, were made to match partlet, stomacher and facings of a gown. There were also a number of individual pairs of sleeves which could be worn with different gowns, tied into the armholes with points, or lacing ribbons. Some were gifts to Elizabeth, while others were made, embroidered, and often altered, in the Wardrobe of Robes.

Many different fabrics and methods of decoration were used. Walter Fyshe was employed in 'altering and making longer of a peire of slevis of blak vellat with longe byas cuttes edged with white Satten and lyned with white taphata' and making 'a payer of slevis of blak Satten lased at the handes & downe tharme with blak silke lase lyned with tawney sarceonett of our great guardrobe',[297] in 1573 and 1575 respectively. The latter pair might have resembled those in Figure 135. Fyshe was also entered for 'makinge up of a peire of slevis of fine lynen cloth enbrodered allover with silver lyned with sarceonett'[298] in 1575. These may have been a gift to the Queen, delivered unmade, so that they could be fitted properly. William Jones made a pair of sleeves of 'white fillasella wrought with gold & lined with Sarcenet' in 1596[299] but no details are given of their size. Presumably they were full and gathered, similar to those in Figure 177.

Three pairs of sleeves of the 'French fashion' are listed in the warrants in 1575, 1576, and 1579. A style worn by Parisian women (Fig. 175) is seen in a water-colour drawing of the Queen in about 1575 (Fig. 6) and the 'Phoenix' portrait (Fig. 26). The sleeves are cut with very high sleeveheads, padded inside for support, with a seam running down the back of the arm.[300] Perhaps this was the French style of sleeve which Walter Fyshe made in 1575, 'a peire of slevis of the frenche facion for a Dublett of oringe colour Satten cutt & pinked lased downe tharme thicke lyned with white sarceonett'.[301] The second pair, which he made in the following year, 'a peire of slevis of the frenche facion of white satten rufte allover verie thicke and the ruffes cutt verie thicke with small cuttes and lased betwene with white silke lase lyned with white taphata',[302] were heavily gathered, probably using a lot of material. This would have helped to hold out the sleeveheads. The third pair which Fyshe made, in 1579, 'a payer of slevis of the frenche facion with doble ruffes cut in panes of carnacion and white satten snipte lyned with white taphata'[303] were cut in panes which were probably shaped to give fullness at the top of the sleeve. They may have resembled the paned sleeves worn by the Countess of Lennox's daughters (Fig. 199).

In 1581 Fyshe made a fourth pair of sleeves which are very close to the description of those made in 1579: 'a peire of slevis of cloth of silver cutt in panes with a worke rufte up layed with golde lase lyned with tawnye satten striped with golde and lyned with white sarceonett'.[304] By this time the words 'of the French fashion' had been dropped.

Sleeves, like other garments in the Wardrobe of Robes, were sometimes made from material which had been used before. In

1580 Walter Fyshe, for example, made 'a peire of slevis of white satten enbrauderid allover the slevis lyned with yellowe sarceonett of our store being taken oute of another peire of slevis threst of our greate guarderobe'.[305]

The silkwoman, or silkman, undertook alterations to delicately embroidered sleeves. In 1589 Roger Mountague was entered in the Michaelmas warrant for 'alteringe and translatinge of a payre of wyde ruft slevis of white lawne, for rippinge of[f] the gold lace with devises of pearle and setting them on againe and makinge up the slevis'.[306] In the following year he also laundered two pairs of lawn sleeves, 'mendinge washinge and starchinge of ij paire of wyde Irishe slevis of white Lawne thone striped with golde Lace, thother with black Silk drawen worke'.[307] In 1592 Mountague worked on another 'paire of wide sleves of white lawne gathered in ruffes with vij yardes of fine white starched lawne to performe them, lyned with holland clothe and new striping them in diverse places with gold spangle lace, the lace of our store'.[308] The sleeves were indeed wide, as 3½ yards of lawn, probably at least 36 inches wide, was used for each one. The 'ruffes' are what we would call an even arrangement of gathers.

Most sleeves made for Elizabeth were lined with taffeta or sarsenet but many in museum collections are lined with fustian or linen. In 1572 Walter Fyshe made 'two peire of slevis of white Satten cutt and raste one peire lyned with flanell the other peire with lynen cloth'[309] for the Queen. The flannel lining was for warmth. We have already seen that some waistcoat sleeves were made of flannel. Other pairs of sleeves in this material include 'two peire of slevis of white flanell thone peire striped with silke lase'[310] made by Fyshe in 1581, possibly to be worn with two flannel waistcoats made at the same time, although this is not specified. Flannel waistcoat sleeves were also 'bounde with reben'. No details are given about the quantity of ribbon used.

A large number of sleeves 'of hollande clothe bounde with reben' were entered in the warrants. William Jones, for example, made fourteen pairs during the winter of 1584–85,[311] twenty-four pairs in the summer of 1585,[312] forty-eight pairs in 1586,[313] twenty-seven pairs during the winter of 1587–88,[314] and another fourteen pairs in the summer of 1588.[315] Some of these sleeves may have been given to the Queen's women, although this can only be conjecture. They were presumably worn as a support beneath wide sleeves of the latest fashion: more than one pair may have been worn at the same time.

As the fashionable sleeves slowly grew wider, the holland sleeves bound with ribbon were no longer stiff enough to hold out those of velvet and other heavy fabrics. Jones made 'two payer of slevis of fustian bented allover'[316] and 'fower payer of slevis of white fustian bented with whales bone'[317] in 1585 and in the following year 'Tenne peire of slevis bented allover with whales bone iiij peire of white fustian & vj peire of hollande cloth'.[318] In 1588 Jones made twenty-seven pairs of sleeves 'of hollande clothe bounde with reben with whales bone and bent' which would seem to combine the two forms of stiffening.[319] He is entered later in the same year 'for making of fowerteene payer of sleeves of hollande cloth bounde with reben and viij payre of verthingall sleeves of like hollande cloth bented allover with whales bone'.[320] The holland sleeves bound with ribbon continued in use at the same time as holland sleeves stiffened with whalebone, probably as an alternative for supporting fine lawn sleeves. They would have given a much softer effect (Fig. 242). Embroidered silks and velvets would

242   'Portrait of an unknown lady, formerly called Mary Queen of Scots', by an unknown artist, c. 1575–80. The sleeves and forepart are probably in white linen embroidered with a strapwork design in black silk, further enriched with what seem to be small strips of black braid or ribbon. National Portrait Gallery, London

have needed the firmer whalebone support. The stiff sleeve supports continued in use until the end of the reign. Jones made 'two paier of verthingale slevis of holland cloth bented about with whales bone and riben of our great guardrobe' in 1596.[321]

Foreparts and petticoats

The forepart was a detachable panel of material, usually richly decorated, worn beneath the gown, to fill in the triangular opening at the front of the skirt.[322] The word 'forepart' was also used occasionally to describe the front part of petticoats, sleeves, and bodices, as, for example in 'a foreparte for a Petycoate of white Satten'.[323] On its own, 'forepart' was usually the name for the front of the kirtle skirt, but it should always be considered in context for the correct definition.

The early forepart[324] was a smooth triangular piece of material (Fig. 191). As the skirt widened, so the forepart grew larger[325] (Fig. 50). Walter Fyshe was employed in 'newe making and enlarging of a foreparte of yellowe satten, and settinge in of two newe panes of the whole bredthe of satten enbroderid with venice silver and blak silke frengid with like silver and silke lyned with ashe colorid sarceonett'[326] in 1579. This would have been quite a large piece of material.

243 *Detail from 'Queen Elizabeth I and the Three Goddesses'. Panel painting signed HE, 1569. The Queen wears a black mantle with short sleeves and a standing collar, embroidered with a geometric design in couched gold thread and pearls. Royal Collection. Reproduced by Gracious Permission of Her Majesty the Queen*

There are 135 and 58 foreparts listed in the Stowe and Folger inventories respectively. Among them are a number of gathered foreparts. The fullness of material was presumably gathered in at the waist (Fig. 62). Clerks used the term 'gathered' to describe both the forepart and the kirtle with which it was worn. Walter Fyshe was entered in 1571 for both 'alteringe and newemaking of a gatherid foreparte for a frenche kyrtle of cloth of golde the guarding perfourmed with crymsen vellat and the lyning perfourmed with crymsen taphata'[327] and 'for alteringe and making of a newe foreparte of a gatherid kyrtle of white vellat'.[328] Some of these gathered foreparts were very decorative and would have completely changed the appearance of a kirtle. Walter Fyshe made 'a gatherid frenche foreparte of strawe colour satten cutt & raste allover layed with laces of venice golde and silver lyned with white sarceonett' in 1577.[329] This is probably a clerk's

shorthand for 'gatherid french kirtle foreparte' rather than a new French fashion, but this can only be conjecture.

Foreparts were made to match bodices, doublets, sleeves, and stomachers. Walter Fyshe was employed in 'alteringe making longer wider and making a peire of bodies with litell skyrtes for a foreparte of crymsen satten enbrodered with venice golde lyned with crymsen sarceonett and frenge of golde and crymsen silke' in 1571.[330] The 'litell skyrtes' were the tabs at the waistline of the bodice similar to those in Figure 243. In 1575 Fyshe made 'a gatherid Foreparte of lawne striped with golde wrought with purple silke with bodies layed with passamayne lase of venice golde & silver and two small laces layed by[as] lyned with white taphata'.[331] In these two examples the bodice and forepart together may have been worn instead of a kirtle, the forepart attached to the petticoat, beneath the gown. A 'foreparte and placarde of nedleworke of silkes of divers colours lyned with tyncell sarceonett and white sarceonett'[332] which Fyshe worked on in 1573 may have had a similar appearance to what appears to be a blackwork embroidered stomacher and forepart worn by Mrs Mack-william in 1567 (Fig. 240). Here the word 'placard' is used for stomacher and not 'forepart'.

In 1593 William Jones relined a forepart of orange coloured satin and made a pair of doublet sleeves to match.[333] At this date, the forepart would have been very wide, and possibly gathered. It is often impossible to tell the difference between a large forepart and a petticoat in portraits of the early 1590s. However, when the gown opened very widely at the front, it seems to have been more usual to wear a full petticoat, judging from the declining numbers of foreparts listed among the warrants in the last decade of Elizabeth's reign.

Petticoat, the name for a short coat worn by men in the mid-fifteenth century, was the term for a woman's underskirt by the mid-sixteenth century.[334] It was also used, apparently, for the skirt worn with a bodice or doublet, often in contrasting material, as seen in many portraits dating from the end of the sixteenth and the early seventeenth centuries (Fig. 229). In 1585 Kiechel described English women as 'somewhat awkward in their style of dress; for they dress in splendid stuffs and many a one wears three cloth gowns or petticoats, one over the other'.[335]

The Queen had a large number of beautifully embroidered petticoats presented to her as New Year's gifts. Among 125 and 27 rich silk and velvet petticoats listed in the Stowe and Folger inventories respectively, there is one which was probably an under petticoat, worn for warmth. It is a flannel petticoat of the Irish fashion, entered together with a smock.[336] Elizabeth had had many other flannel petticoats made throughout her reign. Walter Fyshe, for example, made two of red flannel 'bound aboute with crymsen lase' in 1568.[337]

Most of the warm petticoats made for the Queen in the Wardrobe of Robes were of flannel, bayes and kersey. These were cloths of wool, often dyed in bright colours. For example in 1569 Walter Fyshe made four of 'Flanell dyed Stamell colour'[338] and in 1571 two of 'grene bayes with a lase of grene silke and golde' and two more of 'purple bayes layed with lase of purple silke and silver'[339] with another two of 'crymsen Bayes layed with bone lase of venice golde and silver' in 1572.[340] A petticoat of crimson flannel made in 1573 was 'bounde aboute above and beneth with two penny brode rebande'.[341] These are typical of entries which appear among the warrants throughout the reign during both summer and winter months. No doubt a warm petticoat would have been a comfort in the cold, damp English climate, whatever the season. Five petticoats made in 1576 were 'of doble white bayes cottonid on thinside bounde above & benethe with lase of white silke'.[342] The term 'cottoned' refers to the nap raised on the material in its manufacture. Double bayes was woven with paired warp or weft threads, a very warm material.

Often rich silk petticoats, some presented as New Year's gifts, were given warm linings of flannel, bayes and kersey. For example in 1568 Walter Fyshe lined one of blue tufted yellow silk with blue kersey and another 'of cloth of silver with two brode borders enbrauderid with golde with bodies of crymsen Satten' with red flannel.[343] In 1569 he lined a petticoat of 'oringe tawny vellat with blewe bayes',[344] which would have been very warm. One white taffeta petticoat, made in 1576, was 'lyned with ye same taphata and doble lyned with verie fine white flanell with a bone lase of venice golde'.[345]

Petticoats lined with silk would have been worn in warmer weather. A few were made without linings, presumably for very hot summer days, as they are described as 'summer petticoats'; Walter Fyshe made one 'somer Petycoate of mockeado striped with grene with a bone lase of golde' in 1572[346] and 'two sommer Petycoates of taphata layed with bone lase of venice golde and silver borderid with like taphata' in 1579.[347] The clerks entering the tailors' work in the warrants do not give much information other than the colour, decoration and type of fabric for petticoats. However, in 1580 Arthur Middleton made one 'under Petycote of vellat lyned with sarceonett & flanell'.[348] Presumably many others of similar description among the warrants were also under petticoats. In 1576 Arthur Middleton made the Queen 'a shorte gatherid Petycoate of white taphata layed with bone lase of venice golde & silver lyned with white sarceonett'[349] which would presumably have been worn over a Spanish farthingale, beneath a gathered forepart or kirtle, giving fullness over the hips.

Occasionally clerks do not give full details of the material used for a petticoat. One made in 1573 was 'of paris gallante color with a lase aboute the same of venice golde and silver,[350] another, 'of opall with fowre gardes of crymsen vellat layed with bone lase of venice golde and silver',[351] was altered in 1576, 'the gardes removed and sett wider a sonder the lyninge perfourmed with flanell and crymsen taphata'. The word 'opall' would suggest an effect similar to that of changeable taffeta.

Many petticoats were made with 'a peire of bodies': Arthur Middleton made 'a newe backe of crymsen satten for a peire of bodies for a Petycoate of opall' described above.[352] These bodices were not stiffened. Walter Fyshe, for example, made 'a payer of bodies of oringe colorid taphata lyned with the same for a Petycoate of oringe colour vellat' in 1572,[353] and William Jones made 'Two payer of petycoate bodies of satten lyned with sarceonett' in 1585.[354] It seems that a 'petticoat bodies' was simply a support to take the weight of the petticoat on the shoulders and avoid too much bulk at the waist. Some petticoats are specified as 'without bodies' so presumably they fastened at the waist with ties, or perhaps with the 'flappes' and 'shoulder peces' which are mentioned in the warrants. Walter Fyshe, for example, is entered in 1576, 'for making of eighteene flappes and shoulder peces for Petycoates of sundrye kyndes of stuff & sundrye colours[355] and in 1580 'for making of Twentie flappes of satten & taphata for petycoates of sundry colours lyned with sarceonett'.[356] It can only be

244 *Detail from Figure 218, the 'Wanstead' portrait of Queen Elizabeth I, attributed to Marcus Gheeraerts the Elder, c. 1580–85. The black network mantle is embroidered with what appear to be golden serpents and red flowers. Private collection*

conjecture, but these flaps and shoulder pieces may have been some arrangement like a pair of braces.[357] The method used for supporting men's breeches, by points attached to eyelet holes worked in a strip sewn to the doublet waist inside, held the two garments together. A woman's petticoat would have to be held up equally securely to prevent a gap at the waist, as the doublets and bodices fitted so tightly. Surviving sixteenth- and early seventeenth-century women's doublets and jackets show no trace of lacing strips at the waist.[358]

Mantles and veils

The Stowe inventory groups together 94 mantles and veils, and there is one mantle listed in the Folger inventory. The mantles for the Coronation, Parliament, and Garter robes may be seen in portraits (Figs 87, 102, and 114). These were of 'cloth of gold tissued with gold and silver' and velvet, apparently semi-circular in shape, and lined with taffeta or ermine.

Another style of mantle may be seen in the picture of *Queen Elizabeth I and the Three Goddesses*, painted in 1569 (Fig. 243). Instead of falling loosely over the shoulders in long folds to the ground, it has short sleeves and a collar. Walter Fyshe was employed in 'making of a Mantle of blak taphata with a longe Traine welted with blak vellat wrought upon blak

248a *Back view of the doll in Figure 248*

249 *Lady Arabella Stuart, aged twenty three months, holding a doll which may have been made to convey fashion news and then handed down as a toy. Panel painting by an unknown artist, 1577. National Trust, Hardwick Hall*

In the summer of 1573 Elizabeth saw Lady Sidney in a most becoming new gown, which prompted the following urgent letter from Lady Sidney to Cockrame her steward:

Cockrame her Majestie lyeks so well of the velvet yt my Lord gave me last for a Gowen as she hath very earnestly willed me to send her so mouch of hit as will make her a loes gown. I understand my Lord had his at Coopers or Cookes I pray you fayle not to inquyre sertenly <for hit> of whom and what is left of hit. Yf thear be 12 yards it is inoughe. You may not slake the care hear of for she will tack it ill and it is now in the wourst tyem for my lord for divers consyderacions to dislyek her for souche a tryfle. Whearfore i ons againe ernestly requyre it.[373]

Did Cockrame manage to reach the mercer in time to purchase the last twelve yards, or had it already been sold? I have been unable to trace a length of velvet from Lady Sidney entering the Wardrobe of Robes at this time, so perhaps her hopeful attempt to keep Elizabeth happy at home while Sir Henry Sidney battled with the troubles in Ireland was unsuccessful.

Sumptuary legislation

The pursuit of fashion, in the sixteenth century as today, was an expensive business. As soon as a new fashion arrived at Court, wealthy merchants and their wives, and then their servants, would do their best to follow it. Van Meteren commented in 1575 that 'The English dress in elegant, light, and costly garments, but they are very inconstant and desirous of novelties, changing their fashions every year, both men and women'.[374] This situation was no different in the early seventeenth century, according to Moryson's account in 1617:

All manners of attire came first into the City and Countrey from the Court which being once received by the common people, and by very Stage-players themselves, the Courtiers justly cast off, and take new fashions, (though somewhat too curiously); and whosoever weares the old, men looke upon him as upon a picture in Arras hangings. For it is proverbially said, that we may eate according to our owne appetite, but in our apparell must follow the fashion of the multitude, with whom we live. But in the meane time it is no reproch to any, who of old did were those garments, when they were in fashion.[375]

This extravagance was strongly attacked by Philip Stubbes in his *The Anatomie of Abuses*.

Attempts had been made earlier to curb excesses in dress. The first recorded 'Act of Apparel' was passed early in the reign of Edward IV.[376] Tudor monarchs also tried to restrict extravagant displays on their courtiers' backs with sumptuary legislation. One act was passed in the twenty-fourth year of Henry VIII's reign and another after the accession of his daughter Mary.[377]

On 20 October 1559 a Proclamation against excess in apparel was signed by Elizabeth and was printed on the following day.[378] Articles were agreed upon by the Privy Council for reformation of their servants in abuses of apparel and they were bound to observe and enforce these regulations. Another Proclamation followed in 1574. Gilbert Talbot wrote to his mother, the Countess of Shrewsbury, on 28 June in that year from the Court at Greenwich:

Her majestie styrreth litell abrode, and since the stay of the navy to sea, here hathe bene all thinges very quieat; and almoste no other taulke but of this late proclamation for apparell which is thought shall be very severely executed both here at the cowrte, and at London.[379]

Another enforcement was passed in 1577, followed by a 'commandment' on 12 February 1580:

Her Majesties pleasure was, by advise of her saide Councell, that from the one and twentieth of this moneth, no person shall use or weare such excessive long clokes, being in common sight monstrous, as nowe of late are begonne to be used, and before two yeeres past hath not bene used in this Realme. Neither also shoulde any person use or weare such great and excessive ruffes, in or about the uppermost part of their neckes, as had not been used before two yeeres past; but that all persons shoulde in modest and comely sort leave off such fonde disguised and monstrous manner of attyring themselves, as both was unsupportable for charges and undecent to be worne.

And this her Majestie commanded to be observed upon paine of her high indignation, and the paines thereto due; and willed all officers to see to the reformation and redresse thereof, to the punishment of any offending in these cases, as persons wilfully disobeying or contemning her Majesties commandement.[380]

Sharp words, strong measures; but precisely how were these regulations enforced? Who had the job of walking up to some courtier wearing a long cloak and an immense ruff and telling him to take them off? And what was 'excessively long' — mid-calf, ankle-length or to the ground? Harrison wrote that apprentices in London might not wear gowns lower than their calves during Mary's reign and at the beginning of Elizabeth's reign, but 'the length of Cloakes being not limited, they made them Cloakes downe to their Shooes'.[381]

A letter from the Lord Mayor to the Lord Treasurer, dated 5 May 1580, goes some way to explaining why sumptuary legislation had so little effect. He wrote that 'in executing the commands of Her Majesty, for the reforming of Monstrous Ruffs, and other disorders, he had friendly admonished Mr Hewson, son-in-law of the Lord Chief Baron, for wearing excess of Ruffs, in the open street, after Easter, against Her Majesty's proclamation; that he replied in a very contemptuous speech, and for the credit of his office, he had been compelled to take further steps to enforce the Royal commands, whereby he had given great offence to the Lord Chief Baron, which he had expressed in his Letter enclosed, and by refusing to enter his house, and that, fearing his displeasure for the rest of his life, he prayed his Lordship's intercession in the matter'.[382] The proclamation may have curbed the fashion for wide ruffs for a few weeks, but probably not much longer than that. The Queen herself wears wider and wider ruffs in her portraits, culminating in the enormous shallow ruff seen in the 'Armada' portrait (Fig. 52). After this they were narrower, but much deeper, standing round the edge of the square neckline (Fig. 71). Another attempt was made to restrict the 'inordinate excess in apparell' in 1597.[383] One of the reasons given was 'the confusion allso of degrees in all places being great where the meanest are as richly apparelled as their betters, and the pride that such inferior persons take in their garments driving many, for their mayntenance, to robbing and stealing by the high waye'. Jacob Rathgeb certainly gave an account of fine clothes being worn every day in 1592:

The women have much more liberty than perhaps in any other place; they also know well how to make use of it, for they go dressed out in exceedingly fine clothes, and give all their attention to their ruffs and stuffs, to such a degree indeed, that, as I am informed, many a one does not hesitate to wear velvet in the streets, which is common with them, whilst at home perhaps they have not a piece of dry bread.[384]

In the words of the 1597 proclamation 'Her Majestie finding by experience that clemency, wherunto she is most inclinable as long as there is any hope of redresse, this increasing evil hath not been cured, hath thought fitt to seeke to remedy the same by correction'. A number of restrictions were laid down once again and, if they had been followed, it would have been possible to tell an Earl from a Baron and a Countess from a Viscountess, a Baroness, the wife of a Knight and also from the wife of a man with an income of £200 per annum. However, this piece of sumptuary legislation seems to have had as little effect as its predecessors.

Notes

1 Byrne, Erondell, pp. 36–40.
2 Ibid., p. xvi–xvii.
3 Ibid., pp. xvii–xviii.
4 See Leonie von Wilckens, 'Ein "Haarmantel" des 16. Jahrhunderts', Waffen-und Kostümkunde, 1980, pp. 39–44.
5 See Chapter II, note 65.
6 For example, 'By Mrs Twiste, six towthclothes wrought with blake silke, and edged with golde', New Year's Gift Roll 1579, printed in Progr. Eliz., II, p. 260.
7 Quoted in Jenkins, Eliz. Great, pp. 234–35.
8 See E. K. Chambers, Sir Henry Lee (Oxford, 1936).
9 For details of these entertainments see Progr. Eliz., 3 vols and Jean Wilson, Entertainments for Elizabeth I, (Woodbridge, 1980).
10 See also Chapter II.
11 See Chapter VIII, note 88.
12 See Chapter VIII, notes 152, 153, 154.
13 Melville, pp. 49–50.
14 PRO, LC5/33, f.4, warrant dated 20 Oct. 1562, for making a pair of upper sleeves for a Flanders gown.
15 Ibid., ff.39, 40, warrant dated 4 May 1563, for new lining.

16 PRO, LC5/33, ff.38, 39, 40, warrant dated 4 May 1563; BL, Egerton 2806, f.9ᵛ, warrant dated 16 Oct. 1568; ff.12ᵛ, 13, 13ᵛ, 14, warrant dated 26 April 1569; f.18, warrant dated 6 Oct. 1569; f.22, warrant dated 12 April 1570; ff.25ᵛ, 26, 26ᵛ, warrant dated 14 Oct. 1570; f.29, 30ᵛ, warrant dated 4 April 1571; ff.35, 35ᵛ, warrant dated 24 Sept. 1571.
17 PRO, LC5/34, f.22, warrant dated last day of Sept. 1567.
18 BL, Egerton 2806, f.2ᵛ, warrant dated 14 April 1568; for 'drawing out the sleeves of a gowne of the Polony fashion', f.12, warrant dated 26 April 1569.
19 PRO, LC5/33, f.145, warrant dated 20 Oct. 1565.
20 For 'traine gownes of the French fation' see BL, Egerton 2806, f.12ᵛ, warrant dated 26 April 1569 and f.16ᵛ, warrant dated 6 Oct. 1569. For gowns of the Italian fashion, f.3, warrant dated 14 April 1568; ff.12ᵛ, 13ᵛ, 14, warrant dated 26 April 1569; f.17ᵛ, warrant dated 6 Oct. 1569.
21 Four Spanish gownes made for the Queen, ibid., f.29, warrant dated 4 April 1571; f.44ᵛ, warrant dated 28 Sept. 1572; f.95, warrant dated 14 April 1576; f.111, warrant dated 12 April 1577. One Spanish gown made for Mary Ratcliffe, f.82ᵛ, warrant dated 13 April 1575. References to Spanish sleeves, f.2ᵛ, warrant dated 14 April 1568; ff.16ᵛ, 17, warrant dated 16 Oct. 1569; f.144, warrant dated 12 Oct. 1579. References to 'Spanish gardes', f.39ᵛ, warrant dated 9 April 1572; ff.52, 54, warrant dated 1 April 1573; f.72ᵛ, warrant dated 14 Oct. 1574.

22 Ibid., f.102ᵛ, warrant dated 26 Sept. 1576.
23 Edmond, Hilliard, p. 159.
24 Wardrobe Expenses of Queen Katherine of Aragon in 1520, John Rylands Library MS 239.
25 CSP Venetian, 1534–54, V, p. 533.
26 BL, Egerton 2806, f.3, warrant dated 14 April 1568.
27 Ibid., f.52, warrant dated 1 April 1573.
28 Ibid., f.93ᵛ, warrant dated 14 April 1576.
29 Ibid., f.79, warrant dated 13 April 1575.
30 Stowe inventory, f.18/7, 8, f.19ᵛ/21, 22.
31 Ibid., f.24ᵛ/102.
32 Arnold, 'Lost from HMB', no. 24.
33 BL, Egerton 2806, f.13, warrant dated 26 April 1569.
34 For examples see Strong, Icon, pp. 140–41 and drawings by Antoine Caron in Yates, Valois Tapestries, pl. xb.
35 BL, Egerton 2806, f.12ᵛ, warrant dated 26 April 1569 (see Chapter VIII, note 106 for full quotation) and f.16ᵛ, warrant dated 6 Oct. 1569.
36 Quoted in Strickland, p. 233.
37 HMC Pepys, p. 99. Letter dated 1 March 1566/7 from Sir Henry Norreys to Sir William Cecil.
38 BL, Egerton 2806, f.39ᵛ, warrant dated 9 April 1572.
39 Ibid.
40 Ibid., ff.45, 45ᵛ, warrant dated 28 Sept. 1572.
41 Ibid., f.64, warrant dated 14 April 1574.
42 Ibid., f.72ᵛ, warrant dated 14 Oct. 1574.
43 Ibid., f.85ᵛ, warrant dated 28 Sept. 1575.
44 Ibid., f.103ᵛ, warrant dated 26 Sept. 1576.
45 In 1574 Lord North, when he was English Ambassador at Paris, described Catherine de'Medici dressing up two dwarfs to mime what they supposed to be the manners of the Queen of England, although Fénélon discounted the story (quoted in Jenkins, Eliz. Great, p. 211). Relations were friendlier in 1581 when the Anjou marriage negotiations were at their height and ladies at the Valois Court were pleased that Elizabeth favoured French fashions 'attyred all over alla francoyse' (see note 78).
46 BL, Egerton 2806, f.93, warrant dated 14 April 1576.
47 See Chapter VIII and Arnold, Patterns, pp. 8–9.
48 Arnold, Patterns 1660–1860, pp. 36, 39 and Arnold, Patterns, p. 9, fig. 38.
49 Folger inventory, f.3/14.
50 Stowe inventory, f.19/18.
51 Arnold, Patterns 1660–1860, pp. 24, 25.
52 For example PRO, LC5/33, f.4, warrant dated 20 Oct. 1562.
53 For example BL, Egerton 2806, f.162ᵛ, warrant dated 6 April 1581 and the Stowe inventory, f.20ᵛ/39.
54 See note 38.
55 BL, Egerton 2806, f.111ᵛ, warrant dated 12 April 1577.
56 See Arnold, Patterns, pp. 43, 106, 108 for doublet lacing at front beneath buttons and buttonholes.
57 PRO, LC5/34, f.22, warrant dated last day of Sept. 1567.
58 BL, Egerton 2806, f.8v, warrant dated 16 Oct. 1568.
59 Two side back openings laced may be seen in Eleanora of Toledo's gown, 1562, Arnold, Patterns, pp. 103–04 and in the gown worn by Isabella Colonna in The Colonna Family painted by Scipio Pulzone in 1581, ibid., p. 41.
60 Arnold, 'Doublet', pp. 132–42 and Arnold, Patterns, pp. 43, 106–08.
61 BL, Egerton 2806, f.40ᵛ, warrant dated 9 April 1572.
62 Stowe inventory f.8. For further examples of Mary's gowns see Carter, 'Mary Tudor's Wardrobe' pp. 23–28.
63 C. Wriothesley, A Chronicle of England during the reigns of the Tudors, ed. W. D. Hamilton, Camden Society, New Series, XI (1875–77). p. 93.
64 See transcript in Carter, 'Mary Tudor's Wardrobe', pp. 23–27.
65 For examples see Stowe inventory f.46ᵛ/7 and 10.
66 BL, Egerton 2806, f.40ᵛ, warrant dated 9 April 1572.
67 Ibid.
68 Ibid., f.51, 51ᵛ, warrant dated 1 April 1573.
69 Arnold, Patterns, pp. 44, 109–10.
70 For a kirtle of this type worn by a plump woman see Catherine of Austria, Queen of Portugal, by Antonio Mor, 1552, ibid., p. 6, and worn by a slim woman see the portrait of a young girl by Clouet c. 1560, F. Boucher, History of Costume in the West, p. 225. Both wear these kirtles with girdles.
71 John Webster, The Duchess of Malfi, before 1614 (Revels edn 1964), II, 1, lines 7 and 148.
72 BL, Egerton 2806, f.72, warrant dated 14 Oct. 1574.
73 Ibid., f.93ᵛ, warrant dated 14 April 1576.
74 CSP Foreign 1575–77, no. 1317, p. 540, letter dated 4 March 1577.
75 Ibid., no. 1334, p. 546, letter dated 17 March 1577.
76 BL, Egerton 2806, f.116ᵛ, warrant dated 27 Sept. 1577.
77 Misc. State Papers from 1501–1726, vol. 1 (1778) p. 172.
78 PRO, SP 78/7, no. 12, Cobham to Walsingham 22 January 1581/2.
79 I am very grateful to Miss Mildred Lanier for slides, photographs and information about this picture.
80 Anderson, p.209.
81 Quoted in Linthicum, p. 179.
82 Ibid.
83 Ibid., p. 180.
84 PRO, LC9/52, quoted in Linthicum, p. 180.

85 This method was used most successfully in a home-made cotton petticoat in the late 1850s, now in the private collection of Mrs Helen Larson, Fig. 278.
86 There is a copy of the 1589 edition in the National Art Library at the Victoria and Albert Museum, London. Printed in a facsimile edition in 1979 as A Tailor's Book of 1589.
87 See Arnold, Patterns, pp. 4–10 and Arnold 'Cassock', pp. 126–27.
88 There are copies of both these rare volumes in the National Art Library, Victoria and Albert Museum, London.
89 See note 21.
90 For detailed discussion and comparison of pattern shapes see Arnold, 'Cassock', pp. 113–27.
91 BL, Egerton 2806, f.16ᵛ, warrant dated 6 Oct. 1569.
92 Noted in Strong, Icon, p. 180.
93 See Arnold, Patterns, p. 8, figs 33, 34, 35.
94 BL, Egerton 2806, f.8ᵛ, warrant dated 16 Oct. 1562.
95 Ibid., f.174ᵛ, warrant dated 6 April 1582.
96 Ibid., f.35, warrant dated 24 Sept. 1571.
97 Ibid., f.78ᵛ, warrant dated 13 April 1575.
98 Ibid., f.143ᵛ, warrant dated 12 Oct. 1579.
99 Ibid., f.39ᵛ, warrant dated 9 April 1572.
100 Kervyn de Lettenhove, Relations Politiques des Pays-Bas et de L'Angleterre (Brussels, 1890), ix, p. 336. Also recorded in CSP Foreign 1575–77, no. 1470, pp. 596–97, letter dated 11 June 1577.
101 Ibid.
102 HMC Pepys, p. 46, letter dated 16 January 1565 from Court.
103 Ibid., p. 51, letter dated 21 February 1565 from Antwerp.
104 BL, Egerton 2806, f.3, warrant dated 14 April 1568.
105 Ibid., ff.12ᵛ–13, warrant dated 26 April 1569.
106 Ibid., f.13ᵛ, warrant dated 26 April 1569.
107 Ibid., f.14, warrant dated 26 April 1569.
108 Ibid., f.17ᵛ, warrant dated 6 Oct. 1569.
109 For examples see Rosita Levi Pisetzky, Storia de Costume in Italia (Milan, 1966), fig. 51, pls 26, 27 and 55.
110 PRO, LC5/33, f.145, warrant dated 20 Oct. 1565.
111 For example Unknown girl attributed to Steven van der Meulen, 1567 illustrated in Strong, Icon, p. 129 and Elizabeth Cessil attributed to George Gower, c.1579, ibid., p. 179.
112 Klarwill, part III, pp. 376–77.
113 Giacomo Franco, Habiti delle Dame Venetiane (1610). Reprint of 100 copies, Venice, 1878.
114 Examples may be seen in Strong, Icon, pp. 249, 267, 283 and 293.
115 CSP Foreign 1577–78, no. 158, p. 120, letter dated 30 August 1577.
116 Ibid., no. 185, pp. 136–37, letter dated 3 Sept. 1577.
117 Ibid., no. 204, p. 149, letter dated 9 Sept. 1577.
118 PRO, LC5/33, f.108, warrant dated 27 Sept. 1564.
119 New Year's Gift Roll 1559. John Rylands Library, English MS 117.
120 Ibid., quoted in Arnold, 'Smocks and Shirts', p. 92.
121 Examples may be seen in Strong, Icon, pp. 89, 95, 105, 108.
122 Giles, Ascham, I, p. 246.
123 BL, Egerton 2806, f.78ᵛ, warrant dated 13 April 1575.
124 Ibid., f.95, warrant dated 14 April 1576.
125 Ibid., f.12ᵛ, warrant dated 26 April 1569.
126 PRO, LC5/33, f.4, warrant dated 20 Oct. 1562.
127 BL, Egerton 2806, f.25ᵛ, warrant dated 14 Oct. 1570.
128 Ibid., f.13ᵛ, warrant dated 26 April 1569.
129 Ibid., f.35, warrant dated 24 Sept. 1571.
130 Ibid., f.41, warrant dated 9 April 1572.
131 Ibid., f.71ᵛ, warrant dated 14 Oct. 1574.
132 Ibid., f.26, warrant dated 14 Oct. 1570.
133 Stowe inventory, f.67ᵛ/38, f.69/66, f.70ᵛ/84.
134 Ibid., f.68/50.
135 See also the portrait of Sir Jerome Bowes in Suffolk Collection, cat. no. 2.
136 Rye, p. 8.
137 BL, Egerton 2806, f.2ᵛ, warrant dated 14 April 1568.
138 Ibid., f.12, warrant dated 26 April 1569.
139 Stubbes, 1583 edn, 37ᵛ; 1585 edn, p. 38; 1594 edn, p. 44.
140 Vecellio, pp. 106, 107, 109, 110.
141 Examples may be seen in the Victoria and Albert Museum, London.
142 For further history of 'The Three Brethren' and other named jewels see Strong, 'Three Jewels', pp. 350–52 and Arnold, 'Sweet England's Jewels', pp. 32, 33, 107–08.
143 See Stowe inventory f.30ᵛ/9; the gift was made in 1585.
144 For examples see Arnold, Patterns, Fig. 41 and Alcega, Tailor's Book, p. 71.
145 For a gown shaped at the waist at both front and back side seams, see Arnold, Patterns, Fig. 50. For a gown fitted at the front and loose at the back, see ibid., Fig. 47.
146 Quoted in Linthicum, p. 185.
147 Ibid.
148 BL, Egerton 2806, f.9ᵛ, warrant dated 16 Oct. 1568.
149 Ibid.
150 Ibid., f.35ᵛ, warrant dated 24 Sept. 1571.
151 Ibid., f.43ᵛ, warrant dated 28 Sept. 1572.
152 OED
153 Holme, Academy, III, p. 94 quoted in Arnold, Patterns, 1660–1860, p. 3.

154 *Arnold, Patterns*, pp. 38, 98, 100.
155 BL, Egerton 2806, f.51, warrant dated 1 April 1573. See *Arnold, Patterns*, p. 98 for a loose gown with what may be a 'falling collar'.
156 BL, Egerton 2806, f.47, warrant dated 28 Sept. 1572.
157 Ibid., f.65, warrant dated 14 April 1574.
158 Ibid., f.80, warrant dated 13 April 1575.
159 For examples see Stowe inventory f.31/15, 16 and Folger inventory f.6/[21].
160 Folger inventory f.6/[26].
161 *Rye*, p. 71.
162 New Year's Gift Roll, 1559, John Rylands Library, Eng. MS 117. For Spinola's licence dated 21 April 1559, see *CSP Dom.* 1547–80, p. 128, no. 6.
163 PRO, LC5/33, f.17, warrant dated 20 Oct. 1562.
164 Ibid., f.39, warrant dated 4 May 1563.
165 BL, Egerton 2806, f.9, warrant dated 16 Oct. 1568 and for the replacement of the lining, f.14, warrant dated 26 April 1569.
166 PRO, LC5/33, f.64, warrant dated 2 Nov. 1563.
167 John Higgins, *The Nomenclator, or Remembrancer of Adrianus Junius, written in Latine, Greeke, French and other forrein tongues and now in English*, London 1585.
168 Thomas Middleton and Thomas Dekker, *The Roaring Girl*, written c. 1608, published 1611, II, sc.1 (New Mermaid edn, 1976, p. 33).
169 *Holme, Academy*, III, p. 95, quoted in *Arnold, Patterns, 1660–1860*, p. 4.
170 BL, Egerton 2806, f.86.
171 Irene Foster, 'The Development of Riding Costume c. 1880–1920', *Costume 3*, 1969, p. 56.
172 Stowe inventory, ff.76–79.
173 *Progr. Eliz.*, II, p. 201.
174 Stowe inventory f.78ᵛ/38.
175 New Year's Gift Roll, 1578. Society of Antiquaries of London MS 537, printed in *Progr. Eliz.*, II, p. 71.
176 *Arnold, 'Cassock'*, pp. 121–22.
177 *Minsheu*.
178 *Cotgrave, Dictionarie*.
179 BL, Egerton 2806, f.80ᵛ, warrant dated 13 April 1575.
180 Quoted in *Linthicum*, p. 200.
181 *Stubbes*, 1583 edn, p. 37ᵛ; 1585 edn, pp. 38, 38ᵛ; 1595 edn, p. 44.
182 See Chapter III, note 56 for the Parliament kirtle and note 84 for the Garter kirtle, and Chapter VI notes 249, 250, for other 'square bodies'.
183 New Year's Gift Roll 1588, see Stowe inventory f.61ᵛ/83.
184 For example BL, Egerton 2806, ff.184, 190 and Stowe inventory ff.80–85.
185 BL, Egerton 2806, f.96ᵛ, warrant dated 14 April 1576.
186 *Linthicum*, p. 106–07.
187 Ibid., p. 108.
188 Quoted, ibid., p. 106.
189 *Arnold, Patterns*, pp. 16–17, figs 89, 91, 100.
190 BL, Egerton 2806, f.104ᵛ, warrant dated 24 Sept. 1576.
191 Ibid., f.89, warrant dated 28 Sept. 1575.
192 See p. 145, notes 213 and 224.
193 *Linthicum*, p. 202.
194 BL, Egerton 2806, f.114, warrant 12 April 1577.
195 Ibid., f.118ᵛ, warrant dated 27 Sept. 1577.
196 Ibid., f.131ᵛ, warrant dated 26 Sept. 1578.
197 Ibid., f.139, warrant dated 10 April 1579.
198 Ibid., f.153, warrant dated 12 April 1580.
199 PRO, LC5/37, f.57, warrant dated 10 April 1595.
200 Stowe inventory f.80/1, 5 and f.85/84.
201 Examples in *Arnold, Patterns*, p. 51, figs 362–67.
202 BL, Egerton 2806, f.105, warrant dated 26 Sept. 1576.
203 Ibid., f.118ᵛ, warrant dated 27 Sept. 1577.
204 Ibid., f.114, warrant dated 12 April 1577.
205 Shakespeare, *Two Gentlemen of Verona*, II, iv, 20.
206 BL, Egerton 2806, f.105ᵛ, warrant dated 26 Sept. 1576. See also f.105 for another example in black taffeta.
207 *Linthicum*, p. 202.
208 Ibid., p. 162.
209 See examples Essex County Records Office lists.
210 Quoted in *Linthicum*, p. 193, note 3.
211 Ibid., p. 214.
212 *Waugh, Corsets*, pp. 17, 19. See also *Holme, Academy*, III, p. 95, for the term described in 1688 'Wastcoat, waistecoat; is the outside of a Gown without either stayes or bodies fastened to it; It is an Habit or Garment generally worn by the middle and lower sort of Women, having Goared skirts and some wear them with Stomachers'.
213 PRO, LC5/33, f.37, warrant dated 4 May 1563.
214 Ibid., f.131, warrant dated 16 April 1565.
215 Ibid., f.53, warrant dated 4 May 1563.
216 BL, Egerton 2806, f.233ᵛ, warrant dated 27 Sept. 1588.
217 Ibid., f.22, warrant dated 12 April 1570 and f.51, warrant dated 1 April 1573.
218 Ibid., f.118ᵛ, warrant dated 27 Sept. 1577.
219 Ibid., f.194, warrant dated 12 April 1584.
220 PRO, LC5/36, f.171, warrant dated 10 June 1591.
221 BL, Egerton 2806, f.54, warrant dated 1 April 1573.

222 Ibid., f.162, warrant dated 6 April 1581.
223 Ibid., f.213, warrant dated 27 Sept. 1586.
224 Ibid., f.117, warrant dated 27 Sept. 1577.
225 Ibid., f.65, warrant dated 14 April 1574.
226 Ibid., f.213, warrant dated 27 Sept. 1586.
227 See note 153.
228 BL, Egerton 2806, f.3ᵛ, warrant dated 14 April 1568.
229 Ibid., f.17, warrant dated 6 Oct. 1569.
230 Ibid., f.146ᵛ, warrant dated 12 Oct. 1579.
231 Ibid., f.152ᵛ, warrant dated 12 April 1580.
232 Ibid., f.200, warrant dated 27 Sept. 1584.
233 Ibid., f.71ᵛ, warrant dated 14 Oct. 1574.
234 Ibid., f.30, warrant dated 4 April 1571.
235 Ibid., f.139, warrant dated 10 April 1579.
236 P. and R. A. Mactaggart, 'Some aspects of the use of non-fashionable stays' in *Strata of Society*, The Costume Society, 1973, plates 7, 8 and 9.
237 BL, Egerton 2806, f.184, warrant dated 20 April 1583.
238 Karen Stolleis, *Die Gewänder der Lauinger Fürstengruft* (Munich, 1977), pp. 66–67, figs 26, 27. *Waugh, Corsets*, p. 18. *Arnold, Patterns*, pp. 112–13.
239 BL, Egerton 2806, f.17ᵛ, warrant dated 6 Oct. 1569.
240 Ibid., f.29ᵛ, warrant dated 4 April 1571.
241 PRO, LC5/37, ff.109–10, warrant dated 8 July 1597.
242 *Minsheu*.
243 *Cotgrave, Dictionarie*.
244 BL, Egerton 2806, f.213, warrant dated 27 Sept. 1586.
245 G. B. Harrison, *Elizabethan Journal*, quoted in E. Sitwell, *The Queens and the Hive* (1966 edn) p. 471.
246 Jérôme Lippomano, *Voyage de Jérôme Lippomano ambassadeur de Venise en France en 1577*, quoted in *Waugh, Corsets*, p. 27.
247 BL, Egerton 2806, f.175, warrant dated 6 April 1582.
248 There are examples in a few private collections in England.
249 BL, Egerton 2806, f.189ᵛ, warrant dated 26 Sept. 1583.
250 Ibid., f.213, warrant dated 27 Sept. 1586.
251 PRO, LC5/37, f.69, warrant dated 28 Sept. 1595.
252 *Linthicum*, p. 191.
253 Ibid.
254 BL, Egerton 2806, f.94ᵛ, warrant dated 14 April 1576.
255 Ibid., f.78, warrant dated 13 April 1575.
256 Ibid., f.213, warrant dated 27 Sept. 1586, and PRO, LC5/37, f.101, warrant dated 28 Sept. 1596.
257 See note 245 above.
258 PRO, LC5/36, f.219, warrant dated 28 Sept. 1592.
259 PRO, LC5/37, f.9, warrant dated 12 April 1594.
260 BL, Egerton 2806, f.89, warrant dated 17 Sept. 1575.
261 Ibid., f.95ᵛ, warrant dated 14 April 1576.
262 Ibid., f.124, warrant dated 12 April 1578.
263 Ibid., f.118, warrant dated 27 Sept. 1577.
264 Ibid., f.162, warrant dated 6 April 1581.
265 Ibid., f.223, warrant dated 26 Sept. 1587.
266 PRO, LC5/36, f.177, warrant dated 10 June 1591.
267 PRO, LC5/37, f.102, warrant dated 28 Sept. 1596.
268 Ibid., f.88, warrant dated 29 April 1595.
269 *Linthicum*, p. 192.
270 Folger inventory, f.1ᵛ/[4].
271 BL, Egerton 2806, f.13, warrant dated 26 April 1569.
272 Ibid., f.52ᵛ, warrant dated 1 April 1573.
273 For examples see Shakespeare, *King Lear*, III, iv, 98; *Love's Labour's Lost* III, i, 181; *Winter's Tale*, IV, iv, 245.
274 Shakespeare, *Troilus and Cressida*, II, iii, 21.
275 Lady Lambert's placket, 1663, cited in *OED*.
276 *Linthicum*, p. 162.
277 *Arnold, 'Smocks'*, p. 95.
278 *Linthicum*, p. 162.
279 *Arnold, 'Smocks'*, pp. 91, 92.
280 PRO, LC5/33, f.147, warrant dated 20 Oct. 1565.
281 Ibid., f.146.
282 Ibid., f.111, warrant dated 27 Sept. 1564.
283 There are a number of neckbands with hooks and eyes, as well as those tied with band strings, to be seen in portraits from the 1540s to the 1560s in both public and private collections.
284 PRO, LC5/33, f.153, warrant dated 20 Oct. 1565.
285 BL, Egerton 2806, f.95, warrant dated 14 April 1576.
286 PRO, LC5/33, f.153, warrant dated 20 Oct. 1565.
287 Ibid.
288 Illus. in *Strong, Icon*, p. 96.
289 PRO, LC5/33, f.147, warrant dated 20 Oct. 1565.
290 Examples in the Germanisches Nationalmuseum, Nürnberg, the Victoria and Albert Museum, London, and the Royal Museum of Scotland, Edinburgh.
291 PRO, LC5/33, f.147, warrant dated 20 Oct. 1565.
292 *Stubbes*, 1583 edn, p. 26; 1585 edn, p. 24; 1595 edn, p. 31.
293 *Linthicum*, p. 261.
294 PRO, SP15/33/71, transcript given in J. de L. Mann, 'A Document Regarding Jersey Spinning in the P.R.O.' in *Textile History*, 4, October 1973, pp. 140–41.

295 Ibid., p. 140.

296 *Holme, Academy*, III, Chapter VI, p. 287. According to Holme the combs were heated in a charcoal fire, putting 'a gentle heat into the teeth'. The wool was then combed and 'Drawing it out is to strike one Combs teeth into another, thereby to draw it fine. Cleaning the Comb is to take the course Wool remaining out of the Combs teeth. It is a stinking imploy, the workmen are fit Companions for Devils, for with them is heat, smoak, and stink enough to stiffle a body while seeing of them'.

297 BL, Egerton 2806, f.58ᵛ, warrant dated 20 Oct. 1573 and f.79ᵛ, warrant dated 13 April 1575.

298 Ibid., f.88ᵛ, warrant dated 28 Sept. 1575.

299 PRO, LC5/37, f.101, warrant dated 28 Sept. 1596.

300 For pattern see *Arnold, Patterns*, fig. 38.

301 BL, Egerton 2806, f.88, warrant dated 28 Sept. 1575.

302 Ibid., f.94ᵛ, warrant dated 14 April 1576.

303 Ibid., f.145, warrant dated 12 Oct. 1579.

304 Ibid., f.162, warrant dated 6 April 1581.

305 Ibid., f.151, warrant dated 12 April 1580.

306 PRO, LC5/36, f.122, warrant dated 27 Sept. 1589.

307 Ibid., f.147, warrant dated 28 Sept. 1590.

308 Ibid., f.213, warrant dated 6 June 1592.

309 BL, Egerton 2806, f.41, warrant dated 9 April 1572.

310 Ibid., f.162, warrant dated 6 April 1581.

311 Ibid., f.203ᵛ, warrant dated 16 April 1585.

312 Ibid., f.208, warrant dated 27 Sept. 1585.

313 Ibid., f.212ᵛ, warrant dated 27 Sept. 1586.

314 Ibid., f.227ᵛ, warrant dated 3 April 1588.

315 Ibid., f.231ᵛ, warrant dated 27 Sept. 1588.

316 Ibid., f.203ᵛ, warrant dated 16 April 1585.

317 Ibid., f.207ᵛ, 208, warrant dated 27 Sept. 1585.

318 Ibid., f.212ᵛ, warrant dated 27 Sept. 1586.

319 Ibid., f.227ᵛ, warrant dated 3 April 1588.

320 Ibid., f.231ᵛ, warrant dated 27 Sept. 1588.

321 PRO, LC5/37, f.101, warrant dated 28 Sept. 1596. Whalebone always seems to have been used to stiffen the Queen's sleeves, unlike Mr Starkie's daughter who called to her possessing spirit, 'I will have my Sleeves set out with wire, for stickes will breake and are not stiffe enough' (see note 245).

322 See Stowe inventory, ff.46–55.

323 BL, Egerton 2806, f.80, warrant dated 13 April 1575.

324 See *Arnold, Patterns*, p. 101 for pattern of triangular forepart.

325 Ibid., p. 115 for pattern of larger forepart.

326 BL, Egerton 2806, f.136, warrant dated 10 April 1579.

327 Ibid., f.34ᵛ, warrant dated 24 Sept. 1571.

328 Ibid., f.35.

329 Ibid., f.117ᵛ, warrant dated 27 Sept. 1577.

330 BL, Egerton 2806, f.36, warrant dated 24 Sept. 1571.

331 Ibid., f.85, warrant dated 28 Sept. 1575.

332 Ibid., f.52ᵛ, warrant dated 1 April 1573.

333 Stowe inventory, f.48/32 and PRO, LC5/36, f.252, warrant dated 10 May 1593.

334 Discussed in *Linthicum*, p. 187. 'Peticoat is the skirt of a Gown without its body; but that is generally termed a Peticoat, which is worn either under a Gown or without it' (*Holme, Academy*, III, p. 95).

335 *Rye*, pp. 89–90, quoted in *Harrison*, p. lxii.

336 Folger inventory, f.10/2.

337 BL, Egerton 2806, f.4ᵛ, warrant dated 14 April 1568. Mary, Queen of Scots, wore a red petticoat to lead the troops with Bothwell in June 1567: 'The Queen's apparel in the field was after the fashion of the women of Edinburgh in a red petticoat, sleeves tied with points, a partlyte, a velvet hat and a muffler', *CSP Foreign 1566–68*, no. 1313, pp. 253–54, letter dated 18 June 1567.

338 BL, Egerton 2806, f.14, warrant dated 26 April 1569.

339 Ibid., f.29, warrant dated 4 April 1571.

340 Ibid., f.39ᵛ, warrant dated 9 April 1572.

341 Ibid., f.51, warrant dated 1 April 1573.

342 Ibid., f.103, warrant dated 26 Sept. 1576. For 'cottoned' see *Linthicum*, p. 69.

343 Ibid., f.3ᵛ, warrant dated 14 April 1568.

344 Ibid., f.12ᵛ, warrant dated 26 April 1569.

345 Ibid., f.94ᵛ, warrant dated 14 April 1576. Cream camlet petticoat breeches worn by Karl X Gustavus of Sweden are interlined with fine wool for warmth in a similar way (Livrustkammaren, Stockholm, 3412b).

346 BL, Egerton 2806, f.50, warrant dated 28 Sept. 1572.

347 Ibid., f.144, warrant dated 12 Oct. 1579.

348 Ibid., f.153, warrant dated 22 April 1580.

349 Ibid., f.104, warrant dated 26 Sept. 1576.

350 Ibid., f.52ᵛ, warrant dated 1 April 1573.

351 Ibid., f.94, warrant dated 14 April 1576.

352 Ibid., f.104, warrant dated 26 Sept. 1576.

353 Ibid., f.40ᵛ, warrant dated 9 April 1572.

354 Ibid., f.208, warrant dated 27 Sept. 1585.

355 Ibid., f.103, warrant dated 26 Sept. 1576.

356 Ibid., f.151ᵛ, warrant dated 12 April 1580.

357 Strips of linen covered with silk were stitched to the shoulder seams inside a cassock to act as braces to support the breeches in a suit of Dutch camlet worn by Karl X Gustavus of Sweden (Livrustkammaren, Stockholm, 3415a).

358 For examples see *Arnold, Patterns*, pp. 51, 106, 107, 108, 120, 121.

359 BL, Egerton 2806, f.17ᵛ, warrant dated 6 Oct. 1569.

360 Ibid., f.190, warrant dated 26 Sept. 1583.

361 Ibid., f.25, warrant dated 12 April 1570.

362 Ibid., f.30ᵛ, warrant dated 4 April 1571, listed in Stowe inventory, f.11ᵛ/5.

363 Stowe inventory f.11ᵛ/5.

364 BL, Egerton 2806, f.53ᵛ, warrant dated 1 April 1573.

365 Stowe inventory, f.14/43.

366 PRO, LC5/37, f.157, warrant dated 19 April 1602. This may be the item listed in Stowe inventory f.14ᵛ/49.

367 BL, Egerton 2806, f.44, warrant dated 28 Sept. 1572.

368 Ibid., f.59ᵛ, warrant dated 20 Oct. 1573.

369 Ibid., f.52, warrant dated 1 April 1573.

370 Ibid., f.79ᵛ, warrant dated 13 April 1575.

371 Letter dated 2 April 1604 sent from Longford, *Bradford, Helena*, pp. 186–87.

372 A. M. Nylén, 'Dräktdocka från Karl IX's tid' in *Livrustkammaren*, XI, no. 1, 1967, pp. 1–22.

373 Kent County Archives Office. Document dated 22 July 1573.

374 *Rye*, p. 71.

375 *Moryson, Itinerary*, pt I, p. 199.

376 *Egerton Papers*, p. 247. See also Frances Elizabeth Baldwin, *Sumptuary Legislation and Personal Regulation in England* (Baltimore, 1926).

377 *Egerton Papers*, p. 247.

378 Ibid., document at the Society of Antiquaries of London.

379 Joseph Hunter, *Hallamshire* (1819), p. 84.

380 *Nicholas, Illustrations*, p. 11.

381 *Harrison*, pt 4, p. 37.

382 *Remembrancia*, p. 117, I, 13.

383 Printed in *Egerton Papers*, pp. 247–56.

384 *Rye*, p. 7. Rathgeb was private secretary to Frederick, Duke of Wirtemberg, Count Mümppelgart, and visited England with him in August 1592, keeping a record of his travels.

VII

The Wardrobe of Robes

The Great Wardrobe

Tout has fully described the organization and development of the Wardrobe as a government department in *Chapters in the Administrative History of Medieval England*. In the beginning the Great Wardrobe — 'great' meaning 'large' not 'important' —was a sub-department of the Wardrobe. The Great Wardrobe was originally a large store-house for bulk purchases and later carried out work such as making armour, tents, and liveries as well. In 1360 a permanent home was found for the Great Wardrobe on a site sold by the executors of Sir John Beauchamp to Edward III. It was in the Parish of St Andrews, north of Baynard's Castle and Puddle Wharf, close to the River Thames for convenient transport. Here Beauchamp had built a large town house with houses and shops beside it, giving onto a small square. On 1 October 1361, the Great Wardrobe moved to these premises.[1] The shape of the site is still there. Richard Newcourt's map of 1658 shows the buildings before the Great Fire, tucked behind the Church of St Andrews, not far from St Paul's (Fig. 250). *A large and Accurate Map of the City of London* made by John Ogilby and William Morgan printed in 1676 shows the size of the site, although all the buildings were destroyed in the Fire (Fig. 251). This historic site remains. The hidden courtyard of Wardrobe Place, is still surrounded by eighteenth-century, Victorian and Edwardian buildings, in spite of attempts to demolish two-and-a-half sides of it by Warnford Investments and British Telecom in 1981, as reported in letters to *The Times* on 12 June and 28 November of that year.

Long before the Tudor period the Armoury had broken away from the Great Wardrobe and was housed at the Tower of London. The Great Wardrobe remained at the Baynard's Castle site, a little world of its own, the property of the Sovereign and under the Sovereign's jurisdiction within the City of London. Before Elizabeth's reign there were letters to the Lord Mayor forbidding him 'to entre oure Wardrobe or anye of the Tennenteries of the same'.[2] On one occasion the Master of the Great Wardrobe asked him to stop 'diveres Malitious Persons' from electing

Richarde Stoughton Clarke within my Office of the quenes highnes great wardrobe in london to be Constable withein the parishe of Sainte Andrewe nexte Baynardes Castell not weyinge his daylye service and attendaunce uppon his sayde Office for deliverey in my absence of Suche her graces Stoore remayninge in my Saide Office of the greate warderobe as well for her majesties own use as others by her speciall Commaundmente nor yet consideringe the liberties and auntientte Costome of the saide great warderobe.[3]

The Wardrobe staff were to concentrate on their work for the Sovereign and not to be drawn into time-consuming, unpaid parish duties.

During Elizabeth's reign the Great Wardrobe dealt with supplies for the sub-departments of the Removing Wardrobe of Beds, the Stables and the Wardrobe of Robes. The Removing Wardrobe of Beds was concerned with furniture of all kinds, the cushions, carpets, and tapestries needed to furnish each residence as the Court moved every few weeks, visiting in turn Whitehall, Nonsuch, Woodstock, St James's, Somerset Place, Oatlands, Richmond, Greenwich, Hampton Court, and Windsor Castle, as well as going on Progresses. The Stables dealt with saddles, trappings, carriages, and litters both for the Sovereign's personal use and for the Court. The Wardrobe of Robes was concerned mainly with Queen Elizabeth's clothes, gifts of clothing for her ladies, robes for the Order of the Garter, materials needed for the Royal Maundy ceremony, and material for liveries for the artificers, among them the Queen's tailor, embroiderer, farthingale-maker, capper, hosier, shoemaker, skinner, locksmith, and cutler, as well as the Master Cook and the Clerk of the Wardrobe of Robes.

The Great Wardrobe also dealt with materials for State Funerals and obsequies for foreign royalty, some materials for the Office of Revels and liveries for the Lord High Treasurer of England, the Chancellor of the Exchequer, the Barons of the Exchequer, the Lord Chancellor or Keeper of the Great Seal of England,[4] the Lord Chamberlain,[5] and all those other people who were entitled to them — including over two hundred yeomen, grooms, and pages.[6]

The post of Master, or Keeper of the Great Wardrobe, formerly held by Sir Ralph Sadler and Sir Edward Waldegrave, was granted to John Fortescue for life in 1559, in consideration of his services to the Queen.[7] Fortescue was given his livery annually at Christmas. It consisted of 'Twentye and eighte yardes of fyne blacke Lukes [Lucca] velvett Twentye & foure yardes of fyne blacke Satten Twentye and foure yardes of

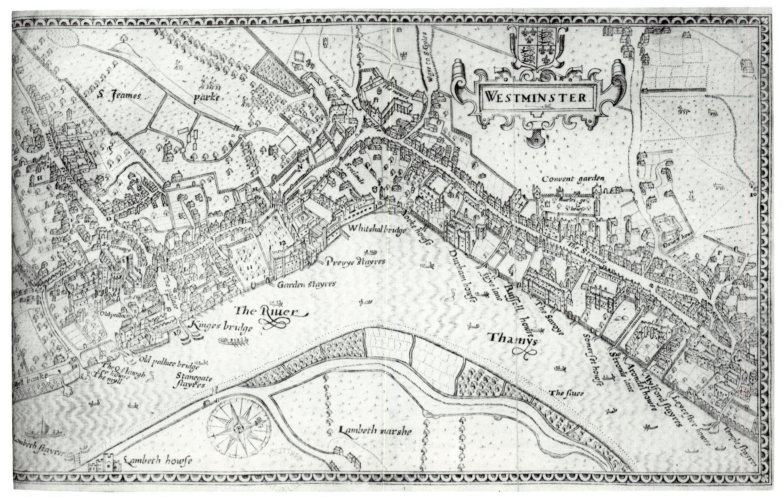

252 'Westminster' from 'Speculum Britanniae: Pars Middlesex' by John Norden, 1593.
The palace of Whitehall and the old palace of Westminster are on the left and Somerset
house on the right. British Library, London

by fire. In 1529, when Wolsey fell from power, Henry VIII confiscated his great house, York Place, legalizing the position with the next Archbishop of York.[19] In 1536 an Act of Parliament declared the limits of the King's Palace of Westminster.[20] York Place, later called Whitehall, was 'not moche distaunt from the same auncient Paleys', and Henry VIII 'uppon the grounde therunto adjoynyng, most sumptuously and curiously hath buylded and edified many and distincte beautifull, costely and pleasaunt lodgynges, buyldynges and mansions'.[21] By the authority of Parliament this mansion and the park surrounding it, together with the ancient Palace were to be named 'the Kynge's Palace at Westmynster for ever'. The limits were Charing Cross, the Sanctuary Gate at Westminster, the Thames on the East side and the wall of St James's Park on the west side. Within its precincts, at the old Great Hall of Westminster, Parliament assembled, courts of law sat and the Exchequer had its offices, while Whitehall Palace, which took its name from one of the rooms within it, the White Hall, was the chief seat of the sovereign.

The use of the name Westminster persisted for another fifty years overlapping with the name Whitehall and this has caused some confusion, but the Wardrobe of Robes at 'our Palace at Westminster' and at Whitehall during Elizabeth's reign are the same place. Thomas Platter visiting Whitehall in 1599 mentions the store there: 'This fine, but unfortified palace, contains the queen's wardrobe (Garde Robe) where she keeps her clothes and jewels which are worth an immense sum'.[22] He does not say if he was shown any of the contents.

George Brideman had been appointed Keeper of the Palace of Westminster by Mary Tudor.[23] He kept his post when Elizabeth came to the throne and continued in it until 1580. The last entry which mentions him is for 'eighte yerdes of like cloth of silver of our store Receyved of George Brideman deceassid sometyme keper of our Palloice at Westminster'.[24] His place was taken by Thomas Knyvett.[25] In c. 1578 Brideman's total fees as Keeper of the Palace of Westminster were recorded as £128. 13s. 4d. of which £18. 5s. 0d. was for keeping the house and garden with £15. 14s. 2d. for keeping the great wardrobe.[26] Variations in the fees may have been due to clerical errors. In 1593 Knyvett's fees totalled £131. 16s. 8d. of which only £8. 5s. 0d. is entered for keeping house and garden and £15. 4s. 2d. for the great wardrobe.[27] The £8. 5s. 0d. seems to be a mistake and it should again have been £18. 5s. 0d. Another account which appears to date from before 1588 gives the total fees as £127. 13s. 4d., of which £18. 5s. 0d. was for keeping the house and gardens and £15. 4s. 2d. for keeping the great wardrobe.[28]

In addition to these fees Brideman was also given summer and winter liveries as a Groom of the Privy Chamber. A warrant dated 16 October 1559 included liveries for three other Grooms of the Privy Chamber, as well as Brideman. They were allowed annually:

xiiij yeardes of good blacke velvett xiiij yeardes of good blacke
Damaske or satten to make them Gownes Cooates and doblettes
oon Furre of goode bodge [budge] for the saide gownes price eighte
poundes'
two yeardes di of fyne marble clothe to make them winter Cooates
two yeardes di of Russett velvett to garde the saide Cooates
two yeardes di of fyne grene clothe to make them Somer Cooates
two yeardes di of good grene velvett to garde the sayde cooates withe
makinge lynynge sylke bottones and all other necessarye thinges to
the saide gownes Cooates Doblettes Furres.[29]

The lining materials were not specified but might have been
linen or fustian with some parts in taffeta. The full details and
prices for each year during Elizabeth's reign may be examined
in the Accounts of the Great Wardrobe.[30]

Furs and lengths of material as well as clothes were stored at
the Palace of Westminster; in September 1559 Brideman
delivered skins and taffeta, among other items, to the Tower.[31]
The Robes of Estate and the Parliament robes were also
probably kept at Westminster from the beginning of the reign.
The warrants refer to Adam Bland, the Queen's skinner,
providing 'one grose of crimsen Satten swete Bagges and viij lb
of swete powder as well to make swete our Robes and apparell
remayning within our Wardrobe of robes as also remayning
within our Tower of London' in 1562.[32] This may be a
reference to the Wardrobe of Robes at the Palace of Whitehall,
Westminster, rather than at Baynard's Castle. Bland was
certainly at Westminster to beat the robes and furs in 1570.[33]

The Stowe inventory and the duplicate copy in the Public
Record Office taken in 1600, refer to 'the Guardrobe of Robes
as well within the Courte as at the Tower of London and
Whitehall'. The initial 'C' for Court in both refers to all the
clothes being used by the Queen at that time, wherever the
Court might be, on a Progress or in another of the royal
residences, in addition to those at Whitehall. The Folger
inventory lists the items remaining within the office of the
Wardrobe of Robes at the Baynard's Castle site.

The Wardrobe Tower at the Tower of London is shown in a
map printed in 1597 by Gulielmus Hayward and J. Gascoyne
(Fig. 253). Hentzner described his visit there in 1598:

Upon entering, we were obliged to leave our swords at the gate, and
deliver them to the guard. When we were introduced, we were shown
above a hundred pieces of arras belonging to the crown, made of
gold, silver and silk; several saddles covered with velvet of different
colours; an immense quantity of bed-furniture, such as canopies and
the like, some of them most richly ornamented with pearl; some royal
dresses so extremely magnificent, as to raise any one's admiration at
the sums they must have cost.[34]

The descriptions in the Stowe and Folger inventories make it
understandable that the gowns should have been displayed as
tourist attractions.

To judge from the increasing size of annual deliveries of
sweet powder for the clothes and fuel for fires to keep the
rooms aired, there must have been a large area in the
Wardrobe Tower to house the Wardrobe of Robes store,
which was in the charge of Ralph Hope for the first part of the
reign. The number of gowns and other items housed there by
the end of the reign can be calculated from the entries marked
'T' in the Stowe inventory. There was another store at
Somerset Place between 1568 and 1572, with records for
deliveries such as 'two poundes of Powder and two Loades of
Coales to ayer our Apparell in the chardge of John West at our
Manour at the Stronde'.[35] Whether this was a temporary store

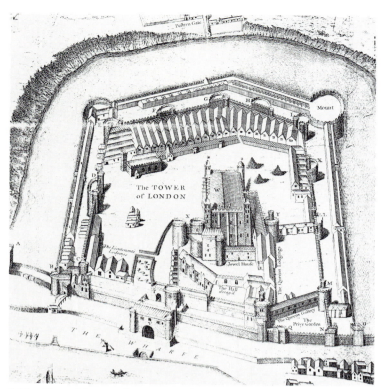

253 *Detail from 'The Tower of London' by Gulielmus Hayward and J. Gascoyne, 1597. Y marks the Wardrobe Tower, near the Queen's Lodgings. Private collection*

until more space could be allocated elsewhere, or if it
continued in use is difficult to tell, as later entries are often
simply for 'loades of coales to ayer our Apparell' not specifying
the location of the stores. It certainly sounds as if the number
of items had been reduced by 1570 as there was a delivery of
only 'one loade of Coales and one pound of powder to ayer our
Apparell remayning in chardge within our manor at the
Strande'.[36] In a later entry in 1572, where John West was
allocated his three yards of red cloth for a livery coat, there is a
delivery noted of 'one Loade of Coales and a pounde of
Powder to ayer our Apparrell in his chardge'[37] so perhaps this
store may already have been moved from Somerset Place.

Away from London, Thomas Platter visiting Windsor
Castle in 1599 wrote 'Then by way of the guard room we
entered the room where the queen's wardrobe is kept, thence
to the presence chamber where the queen appears in person.[38]
This area would probably have been simply for the Garter
robes and gowns needed by the Queen for the times when she
was in residence at Windsor, rather than permanent stores for
clothing, and probably included space for storing bed linen,
tapestries and other soft furnishings as well.

The removals of the Wardrobe of Robes

All these repositories and the continual moving of the Court
from place to place involved a considerable amount of
organization for the officers of the Wardrobe of Robes, as well
as the ladies-in-waiting who would have kept lists of all the
clothes needed by the Queen at each remove. Platter and
Rathgeb both mention the 300 carts needed for bag and
baggage on these occasions.[39] How many of these were needed
for the Wardrobe of Robes is not stated. There were many
difficulties to be surmounted, not only wet weather and bad
roads; the Queen might change her mind — again — about the

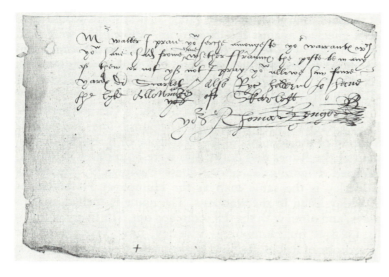

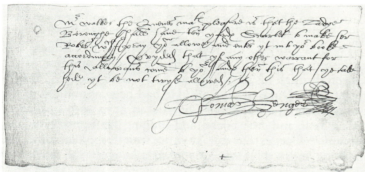

254 *Note from Thomas Benger to Mr Walker, searching for a lost warrant. Undated, between late November 1558 and early January 1559. Public Record Office, London*

255 *Warrant for material for the coronation, with a request that it should not be allowed twice, from Thomas Benger. Undated, between late November 1558 and early January 1559. Public Record Office, London*

the 'garments and stuffs' due to Hobbes, from those in his custody, as the usual fees which were given to the Yeoman and other officers of the Wardrobe of Robes. The items remaining were to be delivered to Ralph Hope, Yeoman of the Wardrobe of Robes. A similar commission was made to Mildmay after the death of Robert Robotham, another Yeoman of the Wardrobe of Robes, at the suit of Grace Robotham, his wife.[77]

Although many records for the Wardrobe of Robes survive, they are incomplete. Regulations governing the Office of the Wardrobe of Robes do not seem to have been preserved, if they existed at all, but the organization would probably have been similar to that described in the Regulations governing the Office of the Revels.[78] These Regulations are undated, but seem to have been devised in 1560, after Thomas Benger had been appointed Master of the Revels following his experience assisting in the preparations for the Coronation.[79] All items delivered to the Revels Office were entered in a book, after measuring lengths of cloth and weighing spangles and lace to make sure there were no short measures.[80] They were then locked up for safety in chests or presses. When removed from the chest the reason was given in the journal, or day book, and a note made of the quantity used. When a costume was finished, its description was written in a book and later entered in an inventory:

Anye suyte of garmentes newe made upon the fynyshinge of the same and anye other garment newe made woulde be entred into the Jornall bookes upon the fynyshinge of theym to thende they maye be afterwardes entred into the Indenture of Inuentorye This woulde be done before the tyme they be occupied in the Prince service to thende it maye be knowen what is lackinge if anye disorder happen in the tyme of service as many tymes it dothe.[81]

It seems likely that under the Pigeons' supervision, a similar routine was followed for the Wardrobe of Robes.

Both goods and workmanship were requisitioned by warrant. Every half year there were deliveries of 'necessaries' for the Wardrobe of Robes and among them were two reams of paper, two pay books, paper, parchment, a bottle of ink, and books 'occupied in making of warrants'.[82] Liveries provided by the Great Wardrobe for officials and servants in posts which continued unchanged were covered by warrants dormant. Clothes for the Queen, some of her ladies-in-waiting and the artificers, with other work carried out for the Wardrobe of Robes, were ordered by particular warrants, issued at Lady Day and Michaelmas for the preceding half year.

It seems likely that the price of each item and probably an estimate of the artificers' work in carrying out embroidery and making up the garments would have been agreed by the Clerk and Yeoman of the Robes. Other officials may have been involved as well; at the Office of the Revels it was the Master Clerk Comptroller.[83] The prices would then have been noted in a journal, or day book. When the work was delivered on completion, the bills were presented and the Clerk would enter them in a 'briefe booke' as at the Revels Office. Rough notes and a reorganized draft of one half-year's work carried out for the Wardrobe of Robes with prices still survives, but there is not enough space to print them here.[84] From this information the particular warrants were drafted and then details of workmanship and materials used by each artificer, without prices, were copied, not always very neatly, into books for reference at the Office of the Wardrobe of Robes. One survives for the years 1567 to 1585, inscribed on the title page *A book of Warrantes to the great Guarderobe Tempore Regine Ylizabethe towchyng her Majesties Roobes and Apparell in the charge of John Roynon and Rauf Hoope yeomen of the Guarderobe of Roobes.*[85]

Payment to artificers and suppliers by John Fortescue, Master of the Great Wardrobe, was authorized by Signet warrants for the Crown, written in a neat secretary hand. These Signet warrants would have been kept as a record, probably in the office which had obeyed their instructions since they formed the authority for the action taken, but were later dispersed. Examples may be seen in manuscript collections all over Europe and in America, the 'top copy' as it were, acquired by autograph hunters for the Queen's signature.

Copies of all warrants, both dormant and particular, were made in a series of books presumably as a record for the Lord Chamberlain's Office of materials and work carried out each year for the Stables, the Removing Wardrobe of Beds, the Wardrobe of Robes, and also for making liveries.[86] Very few entries include the price of materials and workmanship. Payment books for the Privy Purse between 1571 and 1593 have survived,[87] listing, for example, the details of the cost of embroidery for livery coats but there are very few items of personal clothing for the Queen.

The cost of materials and work for the Wardrobe of Robes is recorded in a series of books containing the annual Accounts of the Great Wardrobe from Michaelmas to Michaelmas[88] for almost every year throughout the reign. Among the entries in each book are the Master's receipts from the Exchequer, his standing allowances, income from rents and a contribution from the Court of Wards and Liveries of £2,000 annually. The materials in stock are listed with full details of length and price, and notes of 'novae empciones' (new purchases) made during that year. Following this are details of all the work carried out for the Great Wardrobe, complete with prices, copied from the warrants. These are fair copies, neatly arranged, but translated into clerk's Latin, sprinkled with a few English words.

Every item was checked most carefully when the copy of a warrant was made. One example for the Wardrobe of Beds notes three alterations: 'The originall of the next Warrant aforewritten was razed in three places. viz in the xxiij th Line these wordes were written upon a place razed viz Thomas Larkin. in the xxiiij th line Honor at hampton and in the last lyne (xxxvj th)'.[89] The copies of the warrants are signed with 'ex^r' or 'ex per', meaning 'examined by', and usually the name of the clerk responsible for the checking is given. Sometimes a double check was made. One warrant, for example, was 'perused and examyned this xv of Aprile 1577 per me Henry Sekeford';[90] Sackford was a Groom of the Privy Chamber and may have been checking for items to be paid from the Privy Purse, although none is specifically listed, and the usual mention of 'our great guarderobe' is made for every item. The signature of the Yeoman of the Robes 'R:Hope' is written under this note beside 'ex per N. Pigeon' to signify that it had also been checked by the Clerk of the Wardrobe of Robes. When second copies were made the original signature was faithfully copied too, for example 'signed thus. Ex. per N. Pigeon'.[91]

Almost all the warrants authorizing the purchase, transfer and use of materials seem to be neatly written Signet warrants, signed by the Queen herself, after the reorganization of the method of declaring accounts in 1560.[92] However, one small bundle of eighty warrants, roughly scribbled on small scraps of paper, survives from 1558–59.[93] All are addressed to Mr Walker, Clerk of the Great Wardrobe, and most of them are signed by Thomas Benger, one of the Queen's servants who was appointed Master of the Revels in 1560. They authorize allowances of scarlet cloth among other materials and cast some light on the frenzied activity of preparation for Elizabeth's coronation in the eight weeks following Mary's funeral. The size of the warrants varies from 8.9 cm (3½ in.) × 20.9 cm (8¼ in.) to 22.8 cm (9 in.) × 21.5 cm (8½ in.) and some are fairly neatly written in a set formula, for example:

Garrett Johnson — iiij [yards] di Redd clothe
Cuthbert Dyckynson — iiij [yards] di Redd clothe
Mr Walker I praie you allowe this men the proporcion above written in Redd clothe and enter it in your booke accordinglye

[Signature] Thomas Benger

Each warrant is marked with a small cross, presumably when it was entered in the book and the cloth handed out. In spite of all the care taken, warrants occasionally went astray in the rush, and the official formula changes to a worried personal note (Fig. 254):

Mr Walker I praie yow serche amongeste your warrantes which yow have had frome me, whether Fraunces the poste be in any of them or not yf not I pray yow allowe him foure yardes di Scarlet.

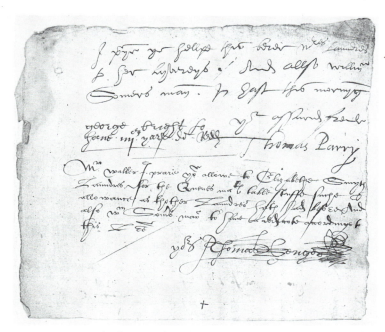

256 *Warrant for liveries for Elizabeth's coronation for one of the Queen's laundresses, Elizabeth Smith, and George Bright, William Somer's servant. Undated, between late November 1558 and early January 1559. Public Record Office, London*

Benger obviously suspected that some servant might try to get an extra ten yards of scarlet and wrote in another warrant (Fig. 255):

Mr Walker the Quenes majesties pleasure is that the Ladye Boroughe shall have ten yardes Scarlet to make her Robes which I pray yow allowe and enter yt into your booke accordingly {provyded} that yf any other warrant for this allowance come to your handes than this that ye take hede yt be not twyce allowed.

In some cases help was needed to obtain a warrant for livery. Thomas Parry, Elizabeth's cofferer when she was Princess, who had been appointed Treasurer of the Household at the end of 1558, scribbled a note to Thomas Benger at the top of one of these warrants: 'I praye you hellpe this berer Mrs Laundres to her lyvreys. And allso William Somers man. In hast this mornyng Your assured frend Thomas Parry' (Fig. 256). The warrant continues:

Mr Walker I praie yow allowe to Elizabethe Smyth Laundres for the Quenes majesties table stuffe suche allowance as thother Laundres hath had before And also William Somers man to have a red cote according to this Letter yours Thomas Benger.

The quantity of cloth for the servant of Will Somers, the Court Fool, 'george bright to have iiij yardes di Redd', is added in another hand.

The Signet warrant below was sent to George Brideman in February 1569.[94] It shows that these warrants were used for checking items. A note in another hand at the bottom explains that the number of skins and each length of material had been checked against a book of receipts.

Elizabeth R [signature]   By the Quene

We woll and commaunde you that upon the sight hereof ye delyver or cause to be delyverid unto Raffe hope yeoman of our Robes and Adam Blande our skynner thre score [[exper]] and six of the best of our sable skynnes being in your chardge at our pallaice of Westminster to furr as a night gowne of blak wrought vellat layd over with a passament lace of murry silke and golde. Also that ye delyver unto

Walter Fysshe our Taylor xvj [[exper]] yardes quarter of Murry sattyn to make a strayght bodied gowne for us. And one quarter of a yard [[exper]] of the same stuff to make paterns of gardinges. Tenne yardes [[exper]] of purple cloth of silver with workes to make us a frenche kyrtell. And six [[exper]] yardes & a half and half a quarter of Crymesyn cloth of gold tyssued with gold and silver to make the trayne of a Frenche kyrtell for us. And these our lettres signed with our hand shalbe your sufficient warraunt and dischardge for the delyverye of all the said percelles. geven under our signet at our said pallaice of Westminster the xxᵗʰ of February in theleventh yere of oure Raigne.

[[°exper the whole warr']]
To our trusty and welbelovyd servant George Bredyman keper of our forsaid Pallaice.

No 25°

[[This hath ben examined upon a booke of the receipt of the perticuler percelles above mencioned signid by the said Rafe hope and Walter fishe, testifyeng their receipt therof and used for her majestie

Exr per J. Somer]]

Although warrants were needed to authorize the transfer of materials for the use of the artificers, sometimes the rules were broken. In one case an acknowledgement was sent to George Brideman which he or Pigeon may have drafted, for his protection.[95]

Elizabeth R [signature]   By the Quene

Where as you have heretofore . . . delivered by our like commandement unto Raffe Hope yeoman of our robes & John Bate fardingale-maker aleven [[ex per]] yardes quarter of blewe satten to make us a fardingale for the which you have no warrant yet from us in writing: we have thought good for your indemputie herin by these presents to declare our good acceptacion of your delivery of the premisses and that these our lettres signed with our hande shalbe your sufficient warrant & discharge for the delivery therof. geven under our signet at our manour of Grenewich the xvjᵗʰ of May in the xjᵗʰ yere of our reign 1569.

No 26°

It was very important that careful records should be kept for the Wardrobe of Robes with its stores as far apart as the Tower and Whitehall. Each garment would have been entered in an inventory, as for the Office of Revels, with margin notes to indicate the new location when it was moved. On transfer from store to store the garments were accompanied by a list, and on delivery the recipient checked the items against it, copied them into a day book and returned the list duly signed. One of these lists sent with six petticoats to Mrs Elizabeth Marbery, one of the Gentlewomen of the Bedchamber, is printed below.[96] Each item is crossed off in the left margin except the first, where the petticoat was delivered to Dorothy Broadbelt:

xxiiij° Junii Anno Regine Eliz vijᵐᵒ [1565]
Petycoates delyverid to Mrs E Marbery one of the Chamberers to [the] Quenis majestie to her highnes [sent] by Rauf hope yeoman of the Robes
First one Petycoate of crymsen Satten razed [with] a brode border enbraudred with silver & frengid lyned with unshorne vellat
LMN 'and the sayd petycot delyvered to mrs dorothe'
Item one Petycoate of crymsen taphata allover layed with a Cawle of golde and silver
LMN 'X'
Item one Petycoate of crymsen cloth of golde reyzid with unshorne vellat frengid with golde and silke
LMN 'X'
Item one Petycoate of crymsen tuft taphata ⟨cutt upon⟩ with a border enbrauderid with silver
LMN 'X'

Item one Petycoate of crymsen vellat cutt upon golde sarceonet with a border enbrauderid with venice golde frengid and lyned with taphata
LMN 'X'
Item one Petycoate of crymsen Grograme with two brode borders of lase of crymsen silk and golde layed aboute the Skyrtes and bodyes
[Signature] 'Elyzabeth Marbry' LMN 'X'

There is a note in a surviving day book recording items leaving the Wardrobe of Robes which mentions a length of cloth of silver for Anne Knolles 'entered in a book for the Tower Chardge'.[97] The Yeoman and Grooms would have been able to find a gown quickly at any time when the Queen required it, using these books, and the inventories of 1600 would have been assembled from all this material. It is obvious from the change of wording, which differs in many cases from that first used in the warrants and New Year Gift Rolls, that each item was checked and scrutinized individually at that time.

How the original inventories were organized is not known; none has yet been traced. They may have been destroyed after the final inventories were made in 1600. Separate sections may have been kept for the different styles — loose gowns, French gowns, round gowns and so on. As new gowns were made or given to the Queen they would then have been entered in the appropriate category in sequence of their arrival in the Wardrobe of Robes. The classification by type of fabric was probably carried out in 1600.

Some of the Royal clothes became due to the Yeomen, Grooms and Pages as fees, and others were given to ladies-in-waiting. Examples are noted in the Folger inventory of 1600 and in a surviving day book,[98] which recorded all items leaving the Wardrobe of Robes, whether lost jewels, gifts or fees of clothing with signatures for proof of receipt. The ladies-in-waiting would probably have suggested which items might be disposed of, subject to the Queen's approval.

Each of the Queen's servants was accountable for the goods held for the Wardrobe of Robes until their discharge. Arthur Middleton, the alterations hand, accepted a delivery of silks from the mercer in 1578[99] and was responsible for their safe keeping until they were allowed for in the next warrant.

Silkes receyved by Arthure Middleton of Ambrose Smythe mercer and not allowed by warraunte for the wardrobe of the robes endinge at Michelmas Anno xx° Regne Elizabethe 1578 but to be answered by the said Arthure Midleton viz

Velvet blacke at xxviij s viij yardes iij quarters	xij li vs
Velvet Tawny at xxvj s viij d j yarde di quarter	xxxs
Velvet russet at xxvj s viij d di yarde	xiij s iiij d
Satten blacke at xiiij s iij yardes	xlij s
Satten yelowe at xiiij s vj yardes	iiij li iiij s
Satten Grene at xiiij s j yarde di	xxj s
Satten white at xvj s iiij yardes	lxiiij s
Satten Crimsin iij quarters yarde di	xiij s iiij d
Satten murry at xiiij s iiij yardes di	lxiij s
Satten ashecolour at xvj s iij yardes	xlviij s
Satten strawecolour at xvj s iij yardes	xlviij s
Taffata blacke at xvj s iiij yardes	lxiiij s
Sarcenet Blacke at ix s vj yardes	liiij s
Sarcenet White at ix s x yardes	iiij li x s

The whole list had been cancelled and a note in the margin, also cancelled, reads 'allowed in the next warrant for the warderob of the robes'.

The system seems to have been virtually foolproof. During Elizabeth's reign there appears to have been no spoiling of the wardrobe by 'evill disposed persons' with thefts of silk like that recorded in 1556 when John Banyarde 'Late yeoman Tailor of the said wardrobe and Thomas Fraunces of London Broker of divers Sortes of Silkes' stole damask, satin, taffeta and sarceonet amounting to some 864 yards.[100]

There are some examples of rough notes, first and second drafts, and final copy of memoranda with 'Pigeon' written at the top, of the charges of the warrants for the Wardrobe of Robes between 1584 and 1586.[101] They are of interest as they cover the period when Ralph Hope retired from his post as Yeoman of the Robes and Sir Thomas Gorges was appointed Gentleman of the Robes. Three examples of these drafts are included here. The first, for the year ending at Michaelmas 1584, gives the cost of all the work done by the Queen's artificers.

The totall chardges of the Warraunte for the Robes for one whole yeare endinge at the Feast of St Michell Tharkangell Anno Domini 1584

Wylliam Jones your majesties Tayloure — Clxvij *li* xvj *s* iiij *d* [£167..16s..4d.]

Roger Mountague for gold and silver lace, silke and silke riben and diverse other necessaries delivered into the warderobe of Robes amountinge unto — ix^c xxij *li* vj *s* [£922..6s.]

Adam Bland Skynner — xxxiiij *li* xviij *s* x *d* [£34..18s..10d.]

Roberte Sibthorpe verthingalemaker — xxxij *li* xvj *s* iiij *d* [£32..16s..4d.]

Henry Herne Hosyer — x *li* iiij *d* [£10..0s..4d.]

Garrett Johnson Shomaker — ⟨xliiij *li* xvj *s* x *d*⟩ xxv *li* ix *s* viij *d* [£25..9s..8d.]

Thomas Grene the Coffermaker — xliiij *li* xvj *s* x *d* [£44..16s..10d.]

James Hewishe Lynnen draper — lxxiij *li* ij *s* [£73..2s.]

John Parr Enbrauderer — Clx *li* x *s* x *d* [£160..10s..10d.]

Margaret Skettes whoodmaker — vij *li* vj *s* viiij *d* [£7..6s..8d.]

Gilbert Polson Locksmythe — ix *li* viij *s* vj *d* [£9..8s..6d.]

Diverse mercers for Sylkes — CCliiij *li* xij *s* [£254..12s.]

Silkes delivered of store of the greate warderobe Ciiij^xx xij *li* vj *s* [£192..6s.]

For Lyveries for xiij persons viz The Clarke of the Robes the Master Cooke the Taylour the Skynner shomaker hosier and vij other Artyficers in toto — iiij^xx ix *li* iiijs viij *d* [£89..4s..8d.]

M^t M^t xxiiij *li* xijs [£2,024..12s.]

The second draft gives the total charges of the warrants for three years, 1585, 1586, 1587. The total in 1587 is very close to that of 1584. Here a check was being made against Ralph Hope who was retiring as Yeoman of the Robes and Sir Thomas Gorges, in his new appointment as Gentleman of the Robes.

The Chardges of the Warraunte for the Warderobe of Robes for iij severall yeares viz

In the tyme of Raffe hope for ij severall yeares viz

The warraunte for the Warderobe of Robes for one whole yeare endinge at the Feaste of St Michell Tharkangell Anno xxvij° RRE [1585] — iiij^mt iij^c xxxvj *li* iiij *s* iiij *d* [£3,336..4s..4d.]

The warraunte for the warderobe of Robes for one whole yeare endinge at Michelmas Anno xxviij° Regine [nos]tre Eliz [1586] — m^t m^t vij^c iiij^xx xv *li* xxij *s* [£2,795..22s.]

Memorandum that Sir Thomas Gorges knight entered into the service for this xxviij yeare one quarter of yt wherby yt fell out to be the lesse.

Sir Thomas Gorges knight

The warraunte for the Robes for one whole yeare endinge at michelmas Anno xxix° Regine Eliz [1587] cometh to the some of M^t M^t xxiiij *li* xij *s* [£2,024..12s.] wherof

Imployed in presse sheetes and Curtains of hollande Cloth, Fustian for Cases and buckeram to lyne presses and other necessaries the some of Cxx *li* [£120]

257 *Muniment chest, with a few shreds of the original leather remaining on the wooden base. Sixteenth century. Private collection*

And so the Chardges of the xxix yeare ys not so muche as the xxviij yeare by the Some of — vij^c lxx *li* ix *s* x *d* [£770..9s..10d.]

difference M^t xij *li* [£1,012] Anno xxvij

Memorandum in pricinge thartifficers bill Anno xxviij — Cxij *li* [£112]

And abated in prysinge Anno xxix — lviij *li* xvj *s* [£58..16s.]

Item abated in the Pynners bill not mencyoned in this warraunte xxvj *li* xiijs iiijd [£26..13s..4d.] yearely

So ys abated in the whole prysinge CC *li* [£200] and upwardes

The third draft gives the details of the prices deducted from the Artificer's bills in 1586, mentioned above:

Prises deducted out of the Artyficers bills in a Warrant dated the xxvij of September 1586.

From Jones the Taylour his bill — xlvj *li* iiij *s* vj *d* [£46..4s..6d.]

From Blande the Skynner — xv *li* xv *s* [£15..15s.]

From Sipthorpe verthingale maker — xj *li* vij *s* iiij *d* [£11..7s..4d.]

From herne hosier — viij *s* iiij *d* [8s..4d.]

From Garret shomaker — liij *s* [53s.]

From Grene Coffermaker — v *li* iij *s* [£5..3s.]

From Polson locksmyth — ij *s* iiij *d* [2s..4d.]

From Ripon Cochmaker — vj *li* [£6]

From Mountague Silkman x *li* xij *s* [£10..12s.]

From Margaret Skettes whoodmaker — xvj *s* [16s.]

From Parr Enbrauderer — xij *li* [£12]

Summa Cx *li* xiij *s* vj *d* [£110..13s..6d.]

Not contayned in the Warraunt but paide for by Mr H. Sekeford for one quarter of a yeare

Lott Arnold Pynner — vj *li* ij *s* vj *d* [£6..2s..6d.]

William Cokesbury Capper — [no entry]

These prices deducted from the artificers bills seem likely to have been the amount for July to September when Sir Thomas Gorges took charge of the Wardrobe of Robes. As for nearly all other years of Elizabeth's reign, details of prices of materials and workmanship for this period may be studied in the Great Wardrobe Account books.[102]

Any collection of papers, whether kept as a record or being handled continually for reference, needs careful organization to prevent damage. In 1580 Nicholas Pigeon ordered 'one Cofer of wodde coverid with hide lether bounde with iron with lockes and keyes lyned with seare cloth and lynen to carye the Recordes of our Robes of our great warderobe'[103] from Thomas Grene, to keep the papers safe from damp and possible destruction by mice. It would probably have resembled the chest in Figure 257.

The dispersal of the contents of the Wardrobe of Robes

The extremely efficient organization of the Wardrobe of Robes kept Elizabeth perfectly dressed for all occasions throughout her long reign. It seems very likely that the Queen ordered the Stowe and Folger inventories to be prepared in 1600 because she thought of all these clothes and personal jewels as state treasure, which would have to be accounted for when James I came to the throne. Many of them were gifts or had been paid for at the charge of the Great Wardrobe. Some items were paid for by the Privy Purse but this was more usual in the early years of the reign. The gowns, as we may see in the inventories, were made of rich fabrics covered in gold thread and jewels. Although there were not the three thousand complete dresses mentioned in numerous costume books,[104] nor the six thousand gowns mentioned in 1603 by Scaramelli, the Venetian Secretary in England,[105] the total number of pieces of clothing, including doublets, foreparts, cloaks, petticoats, and gowns, with forty lengths of silk and numerous fans, groups of buttons and other jewels, amounted to over 1,900 items.[106] In a letter dated 30 March 1603, John Chamberlain wrote to Dudley Carleton on the death of the Queen, 'she made no will, nor gave anything away; so that they which come after, shall find a well-furnished jewel-house, and a rich wardrobe of more than 2,000 gowns, with all things else answerable.'[107] It is not certain if these were included among the 'treasures' referred to by Sir John Eliot in the House of Commons on 27 March 1626, 'Would that such a commission might be granted, if only that we then could search for the treasures and jewels that were left by that ever-blessed princess of never-dying memory, queen Elizabeth!'[108] They were certainly included by Scaramelli, writing to the Doge and Senate of Venice in 1603:

It is reckoned that what with the crown jewels, the dresses and private jewels of the late Queen the rich hangings of so many palaces, the silver and gold, including many sacred vessels — the heritage to which the king succeeds amounts to six millions in gold, not counting the two millions of revenue.[109]

The dispersal of the contents of the Wardrobe of Robes was started by Elizabeth herself. Throughout the reign gowns were remodelled and given away to ladies-in-waiting[110] and nine are noted as gifts to the 'Lady Marques' in the Stowe inventory between 1600 and 1603. The Queen's personal jewels were also bestowed as gifts in the same way. On 6 October, 1600, a draft of a commission[111] was made to 'Lord Treasurer Buckhurst, Lord Admiral Nottingham, Secretary Cecil and Sir John Fortescue' to check the number and condition of the Queen's personal jewels. Katherine, Countess of Nottingham, a Lady of the Privy Chamber, Mary Ratcliffe, a Gentlewoman of the Privy Chamber, and other lords, ladies and servants of the Queen who had any of her jewels in their care, were required to give an account of them, listing any defects. Jewels that were no longer suitable for Elizabeth's use, either from 'decay, imperfection or being out of fashion', were to be sold and 'converted into money', after inventories had been made. At the same time, the Commissioners were to sell any of the Queen's plate which was in poor condition, or out of fashion, reserving the gold and silver to be sent to the Mint for coinage. Reasonable sums were to be paid for the expenses of all those involved in the work of carrying out the survey and preparing the inventory. Some of the personal jewels remaining after this survey are listed at the end of the Stowe inventory, still in the

charge of the Countess of Nottingham and Mary Ratcliffe. The Commission made on 27 July, 1600, to list the whole contents of the Wardrobe of Robes, including the jewels, is noted at the front of this inventory (see p. 252).

What is the truth of the story that Anne of Denmark had Elizabeth's clothes cut up for her own use? Giovanni Carlo Scaramelli, Venetian Secretary in England, wrote to the Doge and Senate in July, 1603, that on leaving Edinburgh Queen Anne had generously distributed all her jewels, dresses and hangings in her rooms among the ladies who remained behind, and added:

In the late Queen's wardrobe she will find six thousand dresses, and though she declared that she would never wear cast clothes, still it was found that art could not devise anything more costly and gorgeous, and so the Court dressmakers are at work altering these old robes, for nothing new could surpass them.[112]

The number of six thousand was, as we have seen, an exaggeration and, as women's clothes continued to be made by tailors until the end of the seventeenth century, 'Court dressmaker' was simply a term used by the translator in the 1890s. He would have expected Queen Anne's clothes to be made by dressmakers, but only linen smocks, ruffs, and similar items were made by women at this time. These alterations to Elizabeth's gowns would have been carried out by tailors, and as Anne of Denmark seems to have been of a heavier build than Elizabeth, there would have been quite a lot of work. Detailed records apparently have not survived.

There are two other references to the dispersal of the contents of Queen Elizabeth's Wardrobe of Robes and her personal jewels. The first is found in a short note copied into the front of the Stowe inventory by Thomas Astle, an extract from a manuscript in Colchester Castle Library with the title *A Diarian Discourse or Ephemeridia Narration by Sir Symonds d'Ewes of Stowe Hall Com: Suffolk.* This is the story that James I gave away 'that inestimable Wardrobe for charitye preserved by all his Ancestors, to one onely Scott, namely Erle of Dunbar who breaking those venerable Robes of ancient Kings, and wickedlye transporting them into the Low Countrys, sold them for above One Hundred Thousand Pounds'.[113] D'Ewes wrote this on 21 January 1620, according to the note, but there seems to be no other supporting evidence for the truth of this account, nor can the original be checked. Apparently this was only a part of D'Ewes' diary, and A. G. Watson, in his book *The Library of Sir Simonds D'Ewes*, states that the manuscript of the diary for 1618–20 is now lost. D'Ewes died in 1640 and his private collection of books, including the original manuscript, was later sold for £450 to the Harleian Library. J. H. Marsden published anonymously in 1851 *College Life in the time of James I as illustrated by an unpublished diary of Sir Simonds D'Ewes*, and Watson quotes a letter from Marsden, written in 1885, in which he says that the D'Ewes diary 'was discovered by me many years ago in an old library in Colchester Castle. It is now missing having been taken out of the library by a member who never returned it and is now dead'.[114]

The second reference concerns the dispersal of Queen Anne of Denmark's personal effects in 1619. A Commission to prepare 'perfect Books inventories and Schedules' was set up in April of that year to record 'all such Jewells, precious Stones, Ornaments, Housholdstuffe, Implementes, and other Goods and Chattels, as did thentofore belong to our late Deare Consorte Queen Anne in her Lyfe tyme, with their Names,

Fashions, Qualities and Values'.[115] In July, after all this had been done, James decided to send the best jewels, 'precious Stones and Ornamentes' to the Secret Jewel House in the Tower of London 'for the Honor and Magnificence of our Crown and State'. Some were to be used for presents for Ambassadors thus thriftily saving 'the Expence of our Treasure', while others were to be put in the custody of Sir Henry Mildmay 'Mayster and Treasourer of our Jewells and Plate' or kept at Denmark House, either for ornaments there, or to be otherwise disposed of, at the King's pleasure.[116]

How many of Elizabeth's personal jewels listed in the Stowe inventory were among those being 'of smale Worth and Valewe' and therefore sold at this time may never be known, nor the number of her gowns which had been translated into furnishings or remodelled for Queen Anne to wear:

And furthermore, at touching such of the Apparell, Robbes and other Furniture of our late Deere Consort, as weare by her used and worne in her Lyfe tyme, and are not nowe meete to be by Us kepte and preserved, We are pleased, and by these Presents doe requier and geve Power and Authoritie unto you our said Commissioners, or anie three or more of you as aforesaid, to delyver distribute and dispose of the same to and amongst suche Ladies and others as served or attended upon our said late Consort, in such manner as you in your Wisdomes shall thinke meete; which said Sale Deliverie and Disposing of the said Jewelles, precious Stones, Ornaments, Robes and Apparell by you or anie three or more of you, to be had and made as aforesaid, Wee will and graunte shal be goode effectual and of Validitie to all Intentes and Purposes . . .[117]

On 10 August 1619 a further Commission gives another clue to the dispersal of Elizabeth's gowns, if, as seems likely, many of them were considered to be out of fashion after their first alterations and simply left in the Wardrobe store at the Tower of London.

Whereas divers Jewelles precious Stones, Plate and Ornamentes of our late deere Consort Queen Anne deceased, being of small Values and unfitt to be reserved, have bene by you lately soulde according to our Commission to you in that behalfe directed, and whereas there are yet remayning divers loose and ragged Pearles, some parcelles of Silver Plate, together with broken pieces and endes of Goulde and Silver, Lynnen which hath beene muche worne, Cabinetts, Rem-

nantes of Stoffes of sondry kindes, olde Roabes and Garmentes of former Queenes of this Realme, with divers other thinges belonging unto our sade late Deere Consort, all which beinge but of small Value, and not fytt to be by Us preserved, Wee have caused to be perticulerly inventoried and appraised, with Intent to have the same soulde for our best Advantage.[118]

'Olde Roabes and Garmentes of former Queens of this Realme' may be a description of some of the items in the Stowe and Folger inventories, written from the point of view of people too close to them to understand their future value. In 1619 they would have been nothing more than a lot of unfashionable clothes taking up storage space. Perhaps if they had been kept for another twenty or thirty years their value might have been apparent, although probably then they would have been dispersed with all the other effects of Charles I in 1649. It is interesting to see that in that inventory of 1649 there are listed 'Twoe Cypresse Chests' containing 'Queene Anns Parliament and Coronation Roabes'[119] which apparently escaped dispersal in 1619, as well as a number of robes, cloaks, and gowns belonging to Henry VIII, which are not listed in the Stowe or Folger inventories. It is possible that these garments really belonged to James I and not Henry VIII, unless some chests were discovered in the Tower which had been passed over accidentally in 1600, since several items belonging to Edward VI and Queen Mary were listed in the Stowe inventory.

Perhaps the truth lies somewhere among all these stories. Anne of Denmark probably took over some of the more fashionable items and gave others to her ladies-in-waiting, and relatives in Denmark. A number of richly embroidered gowns covered with gold thread, pearls, and spangles may have been given to the Earl of Dunbar to sell. Other pieces may have been given as fees to Yeomen, Grooms and Pages of the Robes, as in Queen Elizabeth's time. Some may have been cut up for masque costumes at Court[120] and given or sold to the players. After reading the inventories, the beauty of surviving fragments of Elizabethan domestic embroidery can only make us even more aware of the unsurpassed splendour of the Queen's gowns and regret that they have not survived intact.

Notes

1 *Stow*, II, p. 19. For medieval history of Great Wardrobe see *Tout* and for later history see L. B. Ellis, 'Wardrobe Place and the Great Wardrobe' in *Transactions of the London and Middlesex Archaeological Society*, New series IX, pt. III (1947), pp. 246–61.
2 PRO, LC5/49, f. 344.
3 Ibid., f. 370, dated 1 Dec. 1553.
4 These liveries are listed in PRO, LC5/182, 'A Generall Collection of all the offices in England with their Fees in her Majesties guift', 1593, and in PRO, LC9/52–96, the Accounts of the Great Wardrobe, 1558–1603, as well as in *Nichols, Ordinances*, p. 243. Further details will be given in an article now in preparation.
5 PRO, LC5/49, f. 236.
6 For example PRO, LC5/36, ff. 60–61, warrant for watching liveries for a total of 211 yeomen, grooms and pages, dated 20 March 1588: ff. 179–181, warrant for a total of 207 yeomen, grooms and pages, dated 16 July 1591.
7 *Cal. Pat. Rolls, Eliz.*, 1558–60, I, p. 90, 22 July 1559.
8 PRO, LC5/49, f. 126.
9 *Minsheu*.
10 *Stow*, II, p. 16.
11 *DNB*.
12 Ibid.
13 Henry Alfred Napier, *Historical Notices of the Parishes of Swyncombe and Ewelme in the County of Oxford* (Oxford, 1858), p. 401.
14 *CSP Dom., James I*, 1603–10, p. 13. Grant dated 1 June 1603. Commission to take up workmen etc., dated 1 June [?] 1603.

15 PRO, LC5/32, f. 363.
16 *Cal. Pat. Rolls, Eliz.*, 1558–60, I, p. 354, 7 Jan. 1560.
17 PRO, LC5/49, f. 330.
18 BL, Egerton, 2806, f. 6, warrant dated 14 April 1568. The *OED* gives 'lyor, lear: tape, binding for the edges of a fabric'. In the case of the round lyor with the curtain rings, the term may refer to a cord.
19 Neville Williams, *The Royal Residences of Great Britain* (1960), p. 101.
20 Ibid., p. 5.
21 Act of Parl. 21 Henry VIII, 1536, cap. 12.
22 *Williams, Platter*, p. 165.
23 BL, Lansdowne 156, f. 104v (old no. f. 96v) in a list of fees granted by Queen Mary, and *Feuillerat*, p. 447, note 112, where he gives Brideman's death as before 1594.
24 BL, Egerton 2806, f. 157v, warrant dated 28 Sept. 1580.
25 Ibid., f. 163v, warrant dated 6 April 1581.
26 *Nichols, Ordinances*, p. 255.
27 PRO, LC5/182, f. 34.
28 PRO, SP 12/221, unnumbered folio. This MS has a note 'Amias Powlites inheritance' on f. 33v, written in another hand. Paulet died in 1588. Separate fees are recorded on f. 18v for 'The Robes Yeoman Fee v *li* Groom Fee liijs iiijd page Fee xls'.
29 PRO, LC5/49, f. 45.
30 PRO, LC9/52–93.
31 BL, Add. 5751A, f. 57, warrant for deliveries dated 24 Sept. 1559.

32 PRO, LC5/33, f. 8, warrant dated Oct. 1562.
33 BL, Egerton 2806, f. 27, warrant dated 14 Oct. 1570.
34 *Fragmenta Regalia*, p. 26.
35 BL, Egerton 2806, f. 11, warrant dated 16 Oct. 1568.
36 Ibid., f. 28, warrant dated 14 Oct. 1570.
37 Ibid., f. 49v, warrant dated 28 Sept. 1572.
38 *Williams, Platter*, p. 211.
39 *Rye*, p. 13 and *Williams, Platter*, p. 199.
40 Letter quoted in Thomas Birch, *Memoirs of the Reign of Queen Elizabeth* (1754), I, p. 155. I am indebted to Miss Santina M. Levey for this reference.
41 *Colthorpe, Bateman*, p. 28.
42 Francis Osborne, *Historical Memoirs*, quoted in *Jenkins, Eliz. Great*, p. 225.
43 *Cal. Pat. Rolls, Eliz.*, 1569–72, V, p. 261, no. 2096, commission dated 3 April 1571.
44 Ibid., 1566–69, IV, p. 254, no. 1507. Grant dated 1 April 1568.
45 Ibid., 1569–72, V, p. 364, no. 2548. Grant dated 21 July 1572, surrendered by Nicholas Pigeon, the surviving grantee, 18 June 1582.
46 BL, Egerton 2806, f. 57v, warrant dated 1 April 1573. The word 'livery' is not mentioned in the entry: 'for making of a Gowne of chamblett (for Edmunde Pigeon Clerk of our Guarderobes) garded with vellat layed with lase stiched with silke & furred with bouge for making of a Jaquett (for him) of vellat garded with the same stiched with silke with buttons of silke lyned in the bodies with fustian & in the bases with cotten And for making of a Dublett (for him) of like vellat lyned with fustian & canvas and buttons of silke all of our greate guarderobe'.
47 Ibid., f. 62v, warrant dated 20 Oct. 1573: 'for enbrauderinge of a Jaquett of vellat for Edmunde Pigeon Clerc of our Guarderobes layed with lase for lase silke & workemanship thereof'. This probably refers to the jacket made earlier in the year, see note 46.
48 Ibid., f. 69v, warrant dated 14 April 1574. The entry is almost identical to that for his father in note 46.
49 PRO, LC5/32, f. 6, 24 Feb. 1556, and also LC5/49, f. 127, 28 Nov. 1559.
50 *Nichols, Ordinances*, p. 255.
51 PRO, LC5/49, f. 223, dated 17 March [?] 1590.
52 *Smythe, Household Expenses*, p. 31.
53 PRO, LC5/49, f. 116, dated 20 Dec. 1558.
54 *Nichols, Ordinances*, p. 251.
55 *Cal. Pat. Rolls, Eliz.*, 1560–63, II, p. 3. Lease dated 5 March 1561.
56 PRO, LC5/49, f. 116, dated 20 Dec. 1558.
57 A warrant dormant was an order for a delivery of specified items, such as livery, to be delivered at regular intervals, usually once, occasionally twice a year, during the Queen's pleasure. Particular warrants were made out for all the items delivered to various departments each half year, and these varied considerably.
58 Records of Merchant Taylors Company, Index of Freemen 1530–1929, Guildhall Library, London.
59 *Clode, Merchant Taylors*, I, p. 197.
60 William Herbert, *History of the Twelve Great Livery Companies of London* (1836), II, p. 395 (24 March 1578).
61 *Minutes of courts of Merchant Taylors*. Also see pp. 179–80.
62 He was Yeoman of the Wardrobe, *Smythe, Household Expenses*, p. 30.
63 PRO, LC5/49, f. 116, warrant for livery dated 20 Dec. 1558.
64 Ibid., f. 156, 10 Feb. 1565.
65 PRO, LC5/32, ff. 307–09.
66 PRO, LC5/35, f. 231, warrant for watching liveries dated 10 Nov. 1580.
67 PRO, LC5/36, ff. 2–4, warrant dated 15 Nov. 1585.
68 PRO, LC5/84, f. 121]. Thomas Gorges seems to have been knighted in 1586, probably on his appointment. The records are not clear, see W. A. Shaw and G. D. Burtchael, *The Knights of England* (2 vols), 1906.
69 PRO, LC5/49, f. 217, warrant dormant for livery dated 19 May 1588.
70 Ibid., f. 235, 'a certificate of alteration of thofficers of the Robes' dated 7 Nov. 1598. Richard Nightingale added this postscript: 'Mr Tias this is to certifie you that the hand above written is Mr Conwes hand, the Gentleman ussher that sware us your lovinge frend Richard Nightingale'. Thomas Conway addressed the certificate 'To my loving Frend Mr Robert Tias Clarke Controller of her Majesties Great Warderobe'.
71 *Bradford, Helena*, p. 60 also refers to BL, Lansdowne 59, f. 43, no. 22, where eighteen Gentlemen of the Privy Chamber have fees of £50 each, per annum. PRO, LC5/182, ff. 21–21v lists three Gentlemen Ushers of the Privy Chamber at fees of £30 each and grooms (not numbered) at £20 each, per annum.
72 *DNB* gives Helena as daughter of Wolfgang Suavenberg. *Bradford, Helena*, gives Helena Ulfsdotter Snakenborg, p. 25, and quotes a letter from her signed 'Elin Ulfsdotter', p. 48. P. W. Hasler (Ed.) *The History of Parliament: the House of Commons 1558–1603* (1981) Vol. II, under Sir Thomas Gorges, gives Helena as daughter of Ulf Henrikson von Snakenborg of East Gothland, Sweden.
73 *Bradford, Helena*, p. 65. See letter BL, Cotton MS Titus Bii, f. 346.

74 W. Shakespeare, *Twelfth Night* (Arden edn., 1975), II, sc. 5. See p. 64 where a note suggests that 'this example was invented'.
75 Leslie Hotson, *The First Night of Twelfth Night* (1954) pp. 181–82.
76 *Cal. Pat. Rolls, Eliz.*, 1560–63, II, p. 3. See also *Arnold, 'Lost from HMB'*, p. 24, no. 10.
77 *Cal. Pat. Rolls, Eliz.*, 1569–72, V, p. 261, no. 2096. Commission dated 3 April 1571.
78 *Feuillerat*, pp. 5–17.
79 *Chambers*, I, p. 75.
80 *Feuillerat*, pp. 12–13.
81 Ibid., p. 14.
82 For example, BL, Egerton 2806, f. 62v, warrant dated 20 Oct. 1573.
83 *Feuillerat*, p. 12.
84 PRO, LC5/32, ff. 100–106.
85 BL, Egerton 2806.
86 For holders of the post of Lord Chamberlain and the organisation of the Chamber, see *Chambers*, I, pp. 40–44. Copies of warrants, PRO, LC5/32–37. I am indebted to Sir Geoffrey Elton and Dr Christopher Coleman for information about Signet warrants.
87 PRO, E403/2, 420–29.
88 PRO, LC9/52–93. See also PRO, AO1, 2339–2344, but these paper rolls are very fragile and some are disintegrating.
89 PRO, LC5/37, f.6, dated 20 Feb. 1593.
90 PRO, LC5/35, f. 78, warrant dated 12 April 1577.
91 PRO, LC5/49, f. 214, copy of warrant dormant dated 7 Nov. 1581.
92 M. S. Guiseppi, *Guide to the Public Records* (1963 edn.), I, pp. 70–71. Examples of Signet Warrants for the Wardrobe of Robes signed 'Elizabeth R' in BL, Add. 5751B, f. 10, dated 28 March 1567; ff. 11–12, dated 28 Sept. 1593; ff. 13–14, dated 28 Sept. 1600; ff. 15–16, dated 19 April 1602.
93 PRO, E101, 429/5.
94 BL, Add. 5751A, f. 77, warrant dated 20 Feb. 1569. The signature may be 'Somer' or 'Sonner'.
95 Ibid., f. 79, warrant dated 16 May 1569.
96 Folger, X.d.265. I am indebted to Mrs Laetitia Yeandle, of the Folger Shakespeare Library, for this reference.
97 *Arnold, 'Lost from HMB'*, no. 104.
98 PRO, The Duchess of Norfolk deeds, MS C/115/L2/6697 printed in full in *Arnold, 'Lost from HMB'*.
99 PRO, LC5/34, f. 340.
100 PRO, LC5/49, f. 263, dated 21 Feb. 1556.
101 PRO/LC5/84, f. 118 (draft showing cost of work by artificers in 1584), f. 117 (draft giving total charges of warrants in 1585, 1586, 1587), f. 116 (draft showing prices deducted from artificers bill in 1586).
102 PRO, LC9/52–93.
103 BL, Egerton 2806, f. 159, warrant dated 28 Sept. 1580.
104 *Progr. Eliz.*, III, p. 504, note 2, quoting Sir George Hume seems to be the original source for this number, repeated in *Strickland*, p. 50, and in many other books.
105 *CSP Venetian*, 1603–07, X, p. 64, no. 91, dated 10 July 1603.
106 See Stowe and Folger inventories.
107 BL, Add. 4173, Birch Coll., f. 161v, quoted in *Progr. Eliz.*, (1st edn. 1785–1821), IV, pt. I, p. 36, letter dated 30 March 1603.
108 *Collins*, p. 3.
109 *CSP Venetian*, 1603–07, X, p. 23, no. 40, dated 15 May 1603.
110 For examples see *Arnold, 'Lost from HMB'*, and Chapter V.
111 *CSP Dom. Eliz.*, 1598–1601, CCLXVI, p. 476, no. 87. Commission dated 6 Oct. 1600.
112 *CSP Venetian*, 1603–07, X, p. 64, no. 105, dated 6 August 1603.
113 See Stowe inventory, f. 2v.
114 Andrew G. Watson, *The Library of Sir Simonds D'Ewes*, (1966), pp. 70 and 316. I am indebted to Sir Geoffrey Elton for pointing out that Marsden edited part of the D'Ewes diary in 1851 and that J. O. Halliwell edited 2 vols of the Autobiography in 1845 from BL, Harl. MS 646.
115 *Foedera*, VII, part 3, p. 112.
116 Ibid.
117 Ibid., p. 113.
118 Ibid., p. 118.
119 *Millar, Inventories*, p. 102.
120 'For the *Twelve Goddesses* warrants were issued to Lady Suffolk and Lady Walsingham to take Queen Elizabeth's robes from the wardrobe in the Tower', *Chambers*, I, p. 210. For details of the costumes in *The Vision of the Twelve Goddesses*, by Samuel Daniel, performed on 8 Jan. 1604 at Hampton Court, see T. J. B. Spencer and Stanley Wells (eds), *A Book of Masques*, (Cambridge, 1967, 1980 edn), pp. 26–28.

VIII

The Queen's Artificers

Today tradesmen and craftsmen are greatly honoured when they are allowed to show the royal coat of arms and the words 'By Appointment' to the sovereign. The Elizabethan equivalent of this honour was signified by the granting of livery and thereafter appearing as 'Our' artificer, or craftsman, in the warrants. Although there is insufficient space to deal fully with liveries here, it should be noted that certain colours, quality of cloth, and trimmings also clearly signified the rank and office of various members of the Royal Household.

The names and occupations of all the Queen's artificers working directly or indirectly for the Wardrobe of Robes are known throughout the reign, both from the letters patent for their fees and liveries and from the copies of warrants made during their time of service. There were, for example, thirteen men listed in the copy of a warrant dormant for liveries dated 7 November, 1587: 'Nicholas Pigeon, Clarke of our wardderobe of Robes and beddes ... John Smythson our Master Cooke, William Jones oure Tailor, Adam Bland oure Skynner, Henry Hern our hosyer, Garrett Johnson our Shomaker, Roberte Sibthorpe our verthingalemaker, John Parr our enbrauderer, Richard Mathewe our Cutler, Gilbert Polson our Locksmyth, William Cookesbury oure Capper, Richard Nightingale yeoman of our Male [mail, ie., post] and Arthure Myddleton' were to receive their liveries 'yearlie at the Feast of all Saintes duringe oure pleasure'.[1]

The colour of the livery made for Nicholas Pigeon, Clerk of the Wardrobe, is not stated, but it was probably black or russet. He had 'one Gowne of Chamblett garded with velvett Laied on with silke Lace and furred with budge. One Jaquett of velvett garded with the same and enbraudered with silke Lyned with fustian, with buttons of silke. and one Dublett of velvett Lyned with fustian and Canvas with lace silke & buttons to the same'. On the other hand the livery of John Smythson 'our Master Cooke' consisted of 'One Coate of grene cloth garded with velvett and Lyned with Cotton and one Coate of marble Cloth[2] Likewise garded with velvett and Lyned with cotton'. William Jones and all the other men received 'three yardes of read clothe to make everye of them a lyverie Coate, and two yardes of velvett a peece to gard the

same Coates with lynynge makinge and enbrauderinge of our Lettres for every of them'.

There were few changes of staff during the reign and these were due to death, retirement or promotion. There was apparently only one case of dismissal for inefficiency or some misdemeanour.[3] The work of these artificers provides the background to the clothes listed in the inventories and enables us to look at them not simply as examples of textiles and embroidery used in the second half of the sixteenth century, but to see them as the products of skilled craftsmen. The work of the Clerk of the Wardrobe of Robes has been dealt with in Chapter V and that of the Master Cook does not concern us here. The work of cutler and locksmith affected that of the wardrobe staff indirectly, although it may not at first seem relevant. The pinner and coachmaker were not listed in the 1587 livery warrant, but did receive livery, while the hood-makers apparently did not, although they made headwear for the Queen: the capper did receive livery. The work of all these craftsmen is discussed in this chapter, together with that of silkwoman and silkman, who did not receive livery. The linen drapers and mercers, such as William Dane, William Ferrars and Baptist Hicks,[4] who supplied all types of fabrics for the wardrobe, are outside the scope of this present book.

The tailors

Among the most important craftsmen, as far as Elizabeth's appearance was concerned, were the tailors (Fig. 258). Walter Fyshe, the Queen's first tailor, may have made her clothes when she was Princess. His name first appears in a warrant for surplusage in 1557[5] where he was owed £63.19s.4d. and he seems to have been appointed as Elizabeth's tailor as soon as she came to the throne, when it appears that a thorough reorganization of the Wardrobe of Robes took place. The records are incomplete for the early years, but he was entered as 'the quenes Tailor' in the accounts for the coronation, when he was paid 'for making her graces Roabes and others xiiij *li* xvij*s* iiij*d* [£14.17s.4d.]'.[6] He also appears as 'our Taylor' in a

258 *A tailor's workshop in Nürnberg. The tailor is cutting out with a large pair of shears, the small scraps left over being thrown into the box under the table. At the back of the room hang a pair of pluderhose, full baggy breeches of the type which the tailor wears, and a woman's gown with full pleated skirt. The pleats are being set permanently, held in position by horizontal bands with a weight beneath. These pleats are a peculiarly German/Swiss fashion. Woodcut from 'Eygentliche Beschreibung Aller Stände auff Erden' by Jost Amman and Hans Sachs, 1568. Private collection*

warrant dated 24 September 1559 to George Brideman to deliver fabrics.[7]

In 1560 there was a commission under the signet for John Fortescue, Master of the Great Wardrobe 'to take up workmen and to provide stuffs and carriage for the same for the great wardrobe at the queen's reasonable wages and prices'.[8] An unsigned, undated memorandum in a book of copies of warrants may have been prepared at this time by a clerk who wanted to know about earlier arrangements for fees and livery for the Sovereign's tailor when reorganising the Wardrobe of Robes:

Whereas ther was none allowance to any yoman taillore for wages or lyveries in the great warderobe all the tyme of king henry the vijth butt that George Lovekyne the kinges Tailloure made all kinge henry the vijth Apparell & the henxmen and all other to whome the kinge gave warraunte unto

Anno xxiij° H. Septimi Memorandum I fynde that Steven Jasper after the deathe of George Lovekyn made all the kinges Robes aswell kinge henrye the VIIth as kinge henry theighte and all other Particler warrauntes as henxmen & other & Trapers for horsses & other

Item I Fynde that Richarde Gibson came firste to be yeoman Tailloure in the firste yere of kinge henry the viijth

Item I can not fynde that Richarde Gibson ever wroughte or made any thinge for the kinge or made any other aparell for any warraunt the gardes cotes or eny other

Anno iij° R.H. viij[vi] Item I fynde that William Hilton was the kinges Tailoure after Stephen Jasper & made also all the kinges robes & all other warrauntes frome the kinge

Anno xij° R.H. viij[vi] Item I Fynde that John Parys was the kinges Tailoure and made all the kinges Roobes & other warrauntes as henxmen & others

Anno xl° R.H. viij[vi] Item I Fynde that John Malte was Tailloure to the kinge and made all the kinges Roobes & also all other warrauntes directed to the same warderobe. Memorandum that in all the yeares and accomptes aforesaide The lyninge of Arras & other thinges within the warderobe was done by the kinges Bedmaker or by whome the Master of the warderobe will appoynte[9]

In spite of the Queen's request to Sir Henry Norris in 1567 to try and get her a French tailor, Fyshe continued to make her gowns until 1582.[10] On 29 January 1574 he was promoted, on the death of John Arnold, to 'thoffice of yoman or keper of our vestures or apparell of all and singuler our Maskes Revelles and disguysinges and also of the apparell and trappers of all and singuler our horses ordeyned and appoynted and hereafter to be ordeyned and appoynted for our Iustes [Jousts] and Turneys'.[11] The post brought with it a fee of sixpence a day for life and 'one lyverye coate such as yeomen officers of our houshould have of vs to be yerely had and perceaved at our great warderobe by the handes of the keper or Clerke of the same for the tyme beinge'.[12]

Presumably Fyshe had several journeymen and apprentices working for him, to manage the work in both departments. William Jones is first listed as 'Our Tailor', as well as Walter Fyshe, in a warrant dated 6 April 1582.[13] In the next warrant Fyshe's name no longer appears, and he had presumably retired. His name is listed among those attending the Court of the Merchant Taylors Company during the 1580s, the last time being on 12 July 1585, and a reference to 'the said Walter Fyshe disceased' is made in a document dated 28 April, 1586.[14]

Walter Fyshe's skill as a cutter would have been most usefully employed in the Office of the Revels. There was 'A Platte of Orders to be observed for the better Management of the Office' drawn up, where his post is described:

The Yomane of thoffice whoe oughte to be of good Capacitie knowledge experience and acquaintaunce with thaffaires of the office aswell far understandinge of devise and settinge fourthe of the same, as for castinge and ymployeinge of the stuffe to the furdest stretche of sarvice and moste advauntaige / Shall doe or cawse to be cutte oute made and furnishedd all the garmentes and vestures with theire peeces utensilles and properties, Have take in chardge and sawfe keepe the same remaininge whole.[15]

This is also a fair description of the requirements for the Queen's tailor, with the addition of the virtues of discretion, tact and complete loyalty. A copy of a minute from Cecil around 1560 shows how much thought was given to the matter of security.

Certayn Cautions for the Queen's Apparell and Dyett. We think it very convenient that your Majestie's Apparell and specially all maner of Thyngs that shall touche any Part of your Majestie's Body bare, be circumspectly looked unto; and that no Person be permitted to come nere it, but such as have the Trust and Charge thereof.

Item, That no manner of perfume, ether in Apparell or Sleves, Gloves or such lyke, or otherwise that shall be appoynted for your

Majestie's Savor, be presented by any Stranger, or other Persone, but that the same be corrected by some other fume.

Item that no forrayn Meate or Dishes being dressed out of your Majestie's Court be brought to your Foode, without assured knowledge from whom the same cometh; and that no use be had hereof.

Item that it may please your Majesty to take the Advise of your Phisician for the Receaving wekely twise, some Preservatiff contra pestem & venena, as therbe many good Thyngs & Salutaria.

Item It may please your Majestie to gyve order who shall take the Chardge of the back Doores to your Chamberors Chambers, where Laundresses, Taylors, Wardrobers, and such, use to come; and that the same Doores may be duely attended uppon, as becommeth, and not to stand open but uppon Necessite.

Item that the privie Chamber may be better ordered with an attendance of an Usher and the Gentillmen and Groomes.[16]

In 1568 Walsingham had a report from Franchiotto, an Italian, about the danger of poison and to have great care for the Queen.[17] When Platter visited Nonsuch in 1599, he noted that 'but a short time before, an attempt had been made to poison the queen by smearing powder on the chair she was accustomed to sit and hold her hands on', and that she 'refused to allow anyone into her apartments without mylord Admiral's command'.[18]

It seems likely that the workrooms in which most of the Queen's clothes were made were at the Great Wardrobe, near the livery tailoring workrooms. Her hats and shoes may have been made in the craftsmen's own workshops, but security would have been much easier in a restricted area. No doubt it was Ralph Hope's job to examine all the work and gifts of clothing carefully to make sure nothing was poisoned.

The records for necessaries refer to shears and irons entering the Office of the Wardrobe of Robes, equipment for the Queen's tailors, unless they were intended for a small alterations workroom. Both the Queen's tailors made clothes for her ordered and paid for by private individuals; for example Walter Fyshe made a cloak and safeguard as a New Year's Gift from Bess of Hardwick in 1576[19] and William Jones made the Rainbow robe presented to Elizabeth when she visited Harefield on a Progress in 1602.[20] This might indicate that the tailors had their own workrooms but it is possible that they were able to carry out this private work in the Wardrobe of Robes as it was for the Queen; there is no mention of premises being used for a workroom in Walter Fyshe's will.[21]

The orders for the better management of the Office of the Revels, made long before Fyshe was appointed Yeoman, show that in the past tailors had probably taken too many perquisites in odd lengths of material and apparently some problems had been caused by temperamental cutters.

There woulde also be a speciall order that the yeoman shall cutte out noe garment but by the appoyntment of the Master or Clerke Comptroller and in the presence of theym or one of theym and the Clerke to thende it maye be entred into the Iornall bookes what cutt out and what remayninge yf the yeoman shall refuse so to doe, or be absent in tyme of necessitye of the Princes service Then that the officers maye have libertye to call some other workeman in his place to cutt out and make suche garments as shalbe requysite and needefull by reason of his absence or defaulte Otherwise shall the officers be subiecte to the wilfulnes of the yeoman in tyme of spede and the yeoman maye also committe that wast whiche the officers cannot helpe.[22]

Precautions were taken against petty thieving and probably similar rules applied in the Office of the Wardrobe of Robes.

For frynge lace and Buckerams &c. they maye remayne in presse or Chestes vnder the lockes and keys of the Clerke Comptroller and Clerke to be delyuered over in their presence by their servauntes to suche as shall neede it always entringe the same into the Iornall bookes the cause wherefore &c. and in like sorte other stuffe of diverse kindes.[23]

The Queen's tailor must have spent a considerable amount of time travelling from workroom to Court for fittings and alterations. Most of these fittings would probably have been arranged when the Queen was staying at Whitehall but they might occasionally have involved a journey to places as far away as Richmond and Greenwich. A list of expenses incurred by Walter Fyshe during 1577 and 1578, when he was Yeoman of the Revels, as well as the Queen's tailor, gives an insight into the transport situation. These expenses were all paid by the Office of the Revels.

Walter Fysshe for mony by him disbursed; viz For boate hier to Barmesey [Bermondsey] to speake with my Lord Chamberleyne;
iiijd.
For a Carre the next daie to carry ij Baskettes of stuffe to Barmesey to shewe my Lord Chamberleyne;   ijs.
For his owne boate hyer the same day;   iiijd.
Boat hier to Mr Brydemans to see what stuffe was there;   viijd.
For a Carre to fetch home the same stuffe; ijs.
For his boate hier when he wente to fetche awaie the same stuffe;   viijd.
For his boate hier to and from the courte when he wente to make the garmentes for the Amasons Musitions;   iiijs.
xs. iiijd.[24]

Ralph Hope, the Yeoman of the Robes, would have produced similar expenses sheets for his department in addition to those for travelling on Progresses[25]

Walter Fyshe was a puritan. His will,[26] proved in 1585 as a 'Citizen and Marchaunt taylour of London', made it quite clear that at his funeral there should be 'no blackes or suche like vayne pompe or ceremonye used, or in myne owne opinyon doe rather agree with poperie and paganisme, Than with the rule of the Ghospell of god'. He left his wife Elizabeth 'the use and occupacion of my dwellinge howse in the blacke Fryers in London, soe longe as she shall lyve, paieng the rent and performinge the covenntes to be paide and done by me and myne Assignes for the same', and 'all my lease interest and term of years . . . in the prebend of Shalford . . . in the countie of Essex'. His daughter Elizabeth was married to Charles Hales, gentleman, and Walter Fyshe had already provided for her. His sons Cornelius and Phillip were to receive a share of the goods and chattels; there is no indication that either of them had been apprenticed as tailors, following their father's trade. Among the friends to whom he left mourning rings 'of gould of fourtie shillings a peece' was 'Davye Smithe, Imbrauderer' with whom he had worked so closely for over twenty years on the Queen's clothes. In the summer of 1580 he made a charitable gift of a house and tenement in Cannon Street London (now number 60 Cannon Street and 16 Nicholas Lane) to the Merchant Taylors' Company for ever upon trust 'to employ the rent of the said premises between five poor studious scholars of St John's Oxford, which should be most like to bend their studies to divinity, to be yearly divided between them towards the amount of their victuals and battelings'.[27] He also endowed the almshouses next to the Church of St Martins Oteswich with an annual sum of £7 and an extra 20s. a year for each of the seven almsmen of the

259   *Scarlet parliament robes; robes of the Most Noble Order of the Garter, the mantle in pale brownish mauve, or fig brown, with crimson kirtle and tippet; and livery of a Halberdier in scarlet, guarded with black, and yellow paned trunkhose with pale crimson showing between the panes, worn with yellow hose. These are examples of clothing made by Thomas Ludwell. Pen*

and watercolour drawing from 'Corte Beschryvinghe van England, Scotland ende Irland' by Lucas de Heere, c. 1575. British Library, London (Add. MS 28330)

260   *A Spanish tailor's workshop, woodcut from 'Geometria y Traca' by Diego de Freyle, 1588. Folger Shakespeare Library, Washington, D.C.*

Merchant Taylors Company 'and their wives (if they had wives)'.[28]

William Jones, who took Fyshe's place as the Queen's Tailor in 1582, kept this position for the rest of the reign. He may have been related to Edward Jones, Queen Mary's tailor.[29] He was admitted to the Guild of Merchant Taylors on 29 August 1569 and was awarded livery on 18 May 1586.[30] Like Walter Fyshe, who was elected Master of the Company in 1576,[31] Jones was also an active member of the Guild and was elected third Warden in 1599 and first Warden in 1605.[32]

A third man, one Arthur Middleton, was employed as an alterations hand. He first worked for the Queen in an unofficial capacity, when he was the servant of Elizabeth Knollys in 1574, and was given by the Queen's commandment 'for his paynes taken in alteringe of our garmentes the summe of xxxs'.[33] In the Lady Day warrant for the Robes in 1575 there is an entry 'to Arther Middleton for his paynes taken in mendinge & alteringe of our Apparell fourtye shillinges of our great guarderobe';[34] and in the Lady Day warrant of 1576, he was given three yards of red cloth for a coat with the other artificers.[35] As well as the money, the Queen made him another gift; a warrant to Thomas Ludwell the head livery tailor, allowed for making Middleton a cloth cloak, satin doublet and tuft taffeta gaskin hose and supplying a pair of knitted stockings, a velvet cap, a girdle, a pair of garters and two linen shirts.[36]

Elizabeth must have been particularly pleased with Middleton's work. He continued to work in the Wardrobe of Robes mainly as an alterations hand but also making some doublets and other items for her. He was promoted to the post of Yeoman of the Male in the place of Richard Nightingale who was appointed Groom of the Robes,[37] but must have either proved incompetent or committed some misdemeanour, as there is a certificate dated 3 November 1594, 'for the admittance of Thomas Collins Yeoman of the Male in the rowme of Arthure Myddleton expelled from that place of service'.[38]

A fourth tailor, William Whittell, may originally have been employed as an alterations hand, like Middleton. He seems to have specialized in making and altering doublets, jackets and jerkins. He first appears by name in the warrant for 28 September 1575, employed in 'translatinge of a night Gowne of blak taphata lyned with white sarceonett', 'translating of fowre Gownes and sundrye Dublettes with a boxe to put a peire of bodies in' and 'alteringe and newemaking' a doublet and cloak as well as making doublets, sleeves and cloaks for the Queen.[39] He also made 'xiij Cases of fustian for xiij dublettes' and 'a Case of yellowe Cotten for a dou[t]che Cloake' in the winter of 1575–6:[40] this was part of a very large entry, almost all for altering and making doublets and sleeves. Whittell made jerkins and waistcoats later in the same year and he was also employed in 'alteringe translatinge and newe making of xxxiiij dublettes' at this time.[41] During the winter of 1576–7 he continued to work on doublets, including one which he made of 'satten the colour called soppes in wine'[42] and all the other types of garments previously listed with the addition of a forepart and several jackets. Whittell does not appear among the warrants after 1583.[43] He may have died, or perhaps did not get on well with William Jones, the Queen's new tailor, who had taken Walter Fyshe's place on his retirement in 1582.

Thomas Ludwell was the tailor in charge of livery making, specializing in men's clothes (Fig. 259). He did not make clothes for the Queen, but did supply some for her servants, such as those for Arthur Middleton already described. He also made items such as

a Robe of purple vellat of our order of the Garter (for our deare Cosen Duke John Cassimerus) borderid aboute with buckeram lyned with white taphata sarceonett sowid with silke with stringes buttons and tasselles of venice golde and purple silke with a Garter enbroderid with venice golde and seede pearle sett on the shoulder: for making of a kyrtle and a Whodde (for him) of crymsen vellat borderid with buckeram lyned with white taphata sarceonett sowed with silke.[44]

Tailors might be employed in espionage, as Kenelm Berney confessed to the Lords of the Council in 1572:

Among much Italian talk between Mather and Hearle they once brake out in English. Hearle said 'How might a letter come to the Duke's [Duke of Norfolk] hands?' 'Marry' said Mather 'the finest

261 *A needlemaker's workshop in Nürnberg. The needlemaker cuts the needles from iron wire, files them, makes eyes and sharpens the points, then strengthens them by heating. Woodcut from 'Eygentliche Beschreibung Aller Stände auff Erden' by Jost Amman and Hans Sachs, 1568. Private collection*

262 *'The tailor' by G. B. Moroni, c. 1570. The shears are held ready to cut the black cloth on the white lines marked with soap or chalk. National Gallery, London*

263 *A thimblemaker's workshop in Nürnberg. The thimble-maker manufactures his products from brass, which is heated, shaped and riddled with holes. Thimbles are used by cobblers, tailors, embroiderers and seamstresses. Woodcut from 'Eygentliche Beschreibung Aller Stände auff Erden' by Jost Amman and Hans Sachs, 1568. Private collection*

way is to write upon Holland cloth and to line his hose with the same and send it unto him by his Italian tailor, who not long since bare him a new pair, to which tailor he called to strike up his hose, saying 'It is said, I hear say, that I shall not live to wear these hose out, but I trust yeas or else I shall have worse luck than I look for'.[45]

There is no evidence that Walter Fyshe, William Jones or any of the other tailors working in the Wardrobe of Robes were employed in similar work.

The tailor's equipment

The tailor required little equipment; a clear working area, strips of parchment to take his measures, a yard stick, a table for cutting his cloth, a pair of shears, irons, pins, needles (Fig. 261) thread, chalk or soap for marking the cloth (Fig. 262) and a thimble (Fig. 263). Fynes Moryson in his *Itinerary* describes some Irish women sitting down by the fire 'with crossed legges like Taylors'[46] and this was the traditional position for work (Fig. 258) carried on into the twentieth century.

The deliveries of necessaries which entered the Office of the Wardrobe of Robes every six months included pieces of equipment used by tailor, embroiderer, groom and clerk. A typical example is given here, dated 14 October 1574:

Item Delyverid into thoffice of our Guarderobe of Robes to be employed upon sundry our necessaries theare thre dossen of Brusshes two dossen of rubbinge Brushes: two paper Bookes: two Reames of Paper: thre boultes of blak Thred: thre poundes of white Thred: thre poundes of Thred of colours: one pottell of Ynke: six yerdes of fryse: six yerdes of styff buckeram: two poundes of searing Candle: one

pounde of Hookes and Eyes: thre peces of fustian: thre peces of buckeram: one yerde of cloth to make rubbinge clothes: Two peire of Sheares: one pressinge Iron: six yerdes of white pennystone: CC [200] of Spanishe needles: & one cloute of Millen needles all of our great guarderobe.[47]

One item not listed is tailors' chalk, or soap, for marking out pattern shapes on the cloth. Moroni's portrait of an unknown tailor, standing with shears in his right hand, shows white marks on the piece of dark cloth on the table (Fig. 262). Tailors' chalk is mentioned by Cennini in *Il Libro dell'Arte* written in 1437. He describes drawing on black or blue cloth for hangings: 'You cannot draw with charcoal. Take tailors' chalk, and make little pieces of it neatly, just as you do with charcoal; and put them into a goosefeather quill, of whatever size is required'.[48] Alçega refers to the use of 'xabon'[49] in his *Libro de Geometria, Pratica, y Traça* printed in 1589, and white soap is still used by tailors, as well as chalk. On white silks the tailor might have used charcoal and on velvet 'a pen, with either ink or tempered white lead' as Cennini describes for embroidery designs.[50]

The brushes, rubbing brushes and yard of cloth to make rubbing cloths were for the groom and page of the Robes to clean the clothes and are discussed later. The two paper books and two reams of paper were used by the Clerk. Sometimes parchment was included in the order as well: 'for paper parchment ynke & Bookes occupied in making of warrauntes'.[51] Parchment was also used for tailors' measuring strips. Garsault describes a strip of paper which was notched on the edge for each separate body measurement of the individual client in *L'Art du Tailleur* printed in 1769:[52] tape measures do not seem to have been invented until the early

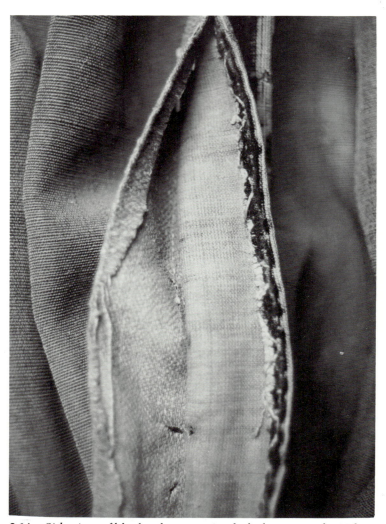

264 *Side view of black velvet pane in pluderhose worn by Nils Sture. The cut edges of the velvet are waxed to prevent fraying and are held down with catch stitch, c. 1567. Uppsala Cathedral*

nineteenth century. Thomas Clatterbrooke supplied 'parchement for Meazures ij *d*' for the Office of Revels [53] and this would have lasted much longer than paper. The Clerk of the Wardrobe of Robes would have supplied strips of parchment for the tailor when needed. There were many people to be measured for gowns presented as gifts by the Queen; the measurements were needed for alterations to existing gowns as well as making new ones. It is likely that Walter Fyshe would have taken one set of measurements for the Queen and continued to use this for his patterns, simply taking check measurements if she lost or put on weight.

At least three deliveries of measuring sticks are listed, 'thre brazell mett yerdes and thre brazell mett elles' in both 1578 and 1580[54] and 'sixe mett elles and yerdes of woode' in 1583.[55] There is a reference to the tailor having his 'mette yarde and his measure' written in 1553 and the term 'met yard' was still in use in the nineteenth century, defined in *A Glossary of words used in the neighbourhood of Whitby* as a measuring rod or draper's yardstick.[56] It is likely that some of the ell rods would have been used by the officer who measured off the lengths of cloth on arrival in the Wardrobe of Robes, to check that no short measures had been given. Two measuring sticks, probably dating from the sixteenth or seventeenth century, may be seen in the Gruuthusemuseum, Bruges. They are of

dark wood with lines roughly scratched on them. One is apparently an ell rod, marked in eight divisions, the other a yardstick marked in quarters and nails (2¼ inches). Both sticks are about an inch wide, and might have been narrower according to Thomas Dekker, writing in 1606: 'For as man is Gods ape, striving to make artificiall flowers, birdes, etc: like to the naturall: so for the same reason are women, Men's "she apes", for they will not be behind them the bredth of a Taylors yard (which is nothing to speake of) in anie new-fangled upstart fashion. If men get up French standing collers, women will have the French standing coller too'.[57]

Two pairs of an unspecified type of shears are entered in the Michaelmas warrant of 1574, given above, another two pairs each year in 1579, 1580 and 1583[58] and one pair in 1584.[59] 'One payer of taylers Sheares' are listed in 1584, 1587 and 1588,[60] with six pairs of unspecified shears in 1588.[61] Considerable skill and sharp shears would have been needed for 'newe dressinge rowinge and sheringe on both sides of eight yerdes di of Serge' and 'dressinge and sheringe on both sides of fyve yerdes of carnacion serge';[62] this work was apparently carried out by Walter Fyshe or one of his workmen. Shears would have been sharpened periodically but cutting silk makes them blunt very quickly and replacements would often have been needed.

A pressing iron is listed in the 1574 delivery of necessaries. Walter Fyshe would already have had several irons in the workroom; the new one was probably ordered because of the increasing amount of work in hand, or possibly as a replacement if one of the old ones had developed a rough surface. Gilbert Polson supplied a new pressing iron in 1580[63] and Thomas Larkin made another in 1594,[64] followed by one more in 1595: 'one pressing Iron beinge very well steled'.[65] This description presumably meant that the surface was made very smooth and hard, to avoid scratching. Larkin supplied one more iron at the end of the reign.[66]

Pins were made by Robert Careles the pinmaker and were entered separately in the warrants. Needles were usually imported and purchased from the silkwoman, although some of those listed in the deliveries of necessaries may have been made in England, probably those described as 'tronoye' needles. Harrison noted that 'The making of Spanish Needles, was first taught in Englande, by Elias Crowse a Germaine, about the Eight yeere of Queene Elizabeth; and in Queene Maries time, there was a Negro made fine Spanish needles in Cheapside, but would never teach his Art to any'.[67] Two hundred Spanish needles and a clout of Milan needles are listed in the Michaelmas 1574 delivery listed above and these were probably imported. There are several references in the warrants to Spanish and Milan needles, for example 24 'longe spanishe Needelles' in 1579, two clouts of Spanish needles in 1584 and 'CCL [250] myllen Nedelles of sundrie syzes' in 1587,[68] but there are many more entries of 'tronoye needells' in numbers ranging from one hundred and twenty five to five hundred at a time. The word 'tronoye' seems to be derived from 'tron' an obsolete word meaning steel.

Black, white and coloured thread were among the necessaries in the 1574 warrant and would have been made of linen: silk is listed separately. The tailor passed the thread through wax to prevent it fraying when it was pulled through several layers of cloth. This process is recorded in 1489 'Mawgys toke a threde of sylke and cered it well'.[69] It was no doubt used long before this, from very early times. Tailors traditionally used beeswax, and this is still used today. None is entered in the warrants, so either the tailor supplied his own or else used some of the searing candle listed. Two pounds of searing candle was a fairly regular order, and its use may be conjectured from surviving examples of costume and embroidery, although not described in the entries. Hot wax was dabbed along the cut edge of velvet to prevent it fraying and this finish may be seen in Nils Sture's breeches of 1567, preserved in Uppsala Cathedral (Fig. 264).[70] The process was also known in Spain. An ordinance of 1546 at Granada required, among other things, that seams of silk fabric hose and the edges of silk trimming should be waxed, which would prevent ravelling.[71] This technique was also used in France where the term 'bougier' was 'to ceare velvet or any silk cloth'.[72] Wax would also have been needed by the laundress to hold the sets of ruffs which were too narrow to pin. A ruff with the original wax on the sets still survives in the Bayerisches Nationalmuseum, Munich.[73] Wax was also used as an alternative to brushing with gum at the back of embroidery on open grounds to prevent the ends of the silks unravelling after removal from the frame.[74]

The tailor's patterns and choice of fabrics

'Two Bundelles of lardge browne paper' entered the Office of the Wardrobe of Robes in 1581.[75] Although it can only be conjectured, it is possible that this would have been for Walter Fyshe to cut patterns taken from the buckram and canvas *toiles* he made for the Queen and her ladies. Using the measurements on his parchment strip, the tailor would draw out the pattern shapes on a variety of cheap materials which might afterwards be used for interlinings. After cutting the pieces out and tacking them together, the *toile* would be fitted and any necessary adjustments made. There are numerous examples of these pattern *toiles*. A small selection is given here, to show the range of materials and variety of garments: 'First to Walter Fyshe our Tailor . . . for making of a patron of a Frenche gown with a straite Bodie, of Buckeram, the sleves drawn oute with white sarsenet' in 1562:[76] 'for making a payer of bodies of buckeram for pattron lyned with buckeram' and 'for making of a pattron for a trayne Gowne of buckeram' in 1571:[77] 'for making of thre pattrons for slevis of buckeram . . . for making of a pattron for a frenche Gowne of canvas . . .' and 'for making of a patron for a Vale of canvas . . .' in 1572:[78] 'for making of a payer of bodies of canvas for a pattron with litell skyrtes lyned with like canvas . . .' in 1573:[79] 'for makinge of a peire of upper bodies of white fustian for a pattron with greate slevis cutt and edgid with fustian & lyned with like fustian . . .' in 1574:[80] 'for making of two peire of bodies for a pattron of lockeram lyned with lockeram and for making of a payer of greate slevis of buckeram with greate ruffes and Jagges . . .' in 1575:[81] 'for making of a Pattron for a Dublett of striped Canvas lyned with white Fustian bumbasted with cotten woll the coller styffened with cotten and buckeram' and 'for cuttinge and makinge of a pattron of buckeram for a frenche gowne of tyssue' in 1579:[82] 'for making of a pattron of a night gowne of buckeram layed with lase & loupes of white thred the slevis lyned with white fustian' in 1580[83] and 'for cutting oute of a pattron for a Cloake of buckeram' in 1581.[84] The problem of sending the Queen ready-made gowns from France which would fit properly also seems to be solved here: 'for makinge of a pattron for a Gowne of buckeram being sent into Fraunce' in

1577,[85] and 'for making of Two pattrones of buckeram thone for a frenche gowne thother for a Petycoate sent into Fraunce . . .' in 1580.[86] It can only be conjecture, but these *toiles* may have been sent as a guide to size for the ambassadors and others who purchased gowns for the Queen; a parchment measurement strip may have been sent on previous occasions and not been entirely successful.

After the fitting the *toile* would have been unpicked, the pieces pressed and all the seam lines carefully marked out. The pieces of buckram, or brown paper patterns traced from them, were then laid on the silks and velvets, matching the grain lines and balancing any woven designs, while arranging the shapes to waste as little material as possible. This was not always an easy task, as silks came in varying lengths from the weavers and in slightly different widths from selvedge to selvedge. Sometimes another gown length would already have been cut from the piece by the mercer and the 'remnant' as it was described, although perhaps ten yards in length, would be impossible to match exactly. No two pieces, spun, dyed and woven by hand, would have been absolutely identical in colour; even minor variations in a new dye-bath would show when the silk was woven, in the same way that the difference between two batches of apparently identical knitting wool can be seen today when they are knitted up. The tailors had to cut their coats according to their cloth and often pieced gowns from two lengths, a time-consuming process. Walter Fyshe had to do this in 1579 for a new gown, the length for the sleeves arriving later: 'for cuttinge oute and pecinge of a frenche gowne of purple tyssue of our store with thre yerdes di quarter of like tyssue Retournid into our said office to make slevis'.[87]

The patterns described above should not be confused with patterns presenting sample arrangements of braid or lace such as this one: 'First to Walter Fyshe our Taylour . . . Item for makinge of two Pattrones of wrought vellat cutt billettwise thone layed with venice golde thother with silve lase'.[88] The Queen would have selected the one which she preferred for the gown.

When the flat pattern shapes had been marked out on satin, velvet or taffeta with tacking threads, or drawn out with tailor's chalk, a fine brush or pen, the uncut length of material was passed to the embroiderer to be stretched taut on a frame while the embroidery was carried out. On its return the shapes were cut out; one entry for Walter Fyshe in 1565 is for 'cuttinge oute of a streite bodied gowne of black satten remayninge at thenbroder unmade'.[89] The garment was then made up with interlinings and linings of suitable weight and stiffness. Among the fabrics used were 'xxiij yerdes of Flanell to lyne gownes petycoates and Cloakes' in 1576,[90] 'fourtye yerdes of Bayes of sundrye colours employed in lyninge of gownes and Cloakes and to styffen Dublettes Jerkens and gownes . . .' in 1578,[91] 'Thirteene elles of hollande cloth to lyne slevis: fower elles of lockeram to make under slevis' and one elle of Canvas to lyne slevis' in 1584[92] and 'xij elles of Canvas & vj elles of hollande cloth to be employed in stiffenynge the bodies of Gownes' in 1587.[93] This holland cloth might have been starched like that used for a gown in 1594, with 'bodies stiffened with Canvas and buckeram, lined with sarceonett the bodies downe before lined with starched holland cloth with hookes & eyes'.[94] Several different materials were used in each gown for the outer layer, linings and inter-linings; one simple French gown made by Walter Fyshe in 1568, 'of blak vellat with a garde enbrauderid with golde

265 *Detail from the effigy of Joan Alington in Figure 213 showing the hem with braid on the edge, 1561. Rolls Chapel, London*

and silver the Gowne lyned with crymsen sarceonett the pleytes lyned above with buckeram and the Ruffes with fryse with ventes of fustian in the Bodies & a Rolle of cotten',[95] used five fabrics with cotton wool padding as well.

The places where the lengths of silks and velvets were stored is usually given in the warrants and occasionally when they were paid for:

First to Walter Fyshe our Taylour . . . Item for making of a frenche Gowne of blak Satten with a verye brode garde of tyncell aboute the skyrtes enbrodered with blak Satten the bodies & slevis being all of tyncell enbrodered with blak Satten the gowne lyned with sarceonett with rolles of bent in the slevis coverid with fustian the Tyncell of our store of the chardge of Rauf Hope yeoman of our Guarderobe of Robes the Satten and sarceonett payed for in the last warraunte amonge necessaryes for our Robes threst of our great guarderobe.[96]

In a few cases the donor's name was listed in the warrants as well; one in 1570 records Walter Fyshe 'altering and newe making of a round kyrtle with Two payre of bodyes of cloth of silver welted with three weltes of black Vellatt the weltes overcast with gold and silver Lace the cloth of silver to make the kyrtle gyney by the Countyes of Bedforde threste of our great guarderobe.[97]

The various pieces of material for one gown might come from different stores, as in this example of 1580 where the skirt of a new French gown was made from a round kirtle in store, probably at the Tower, with an extra eight yards of cloth of silver collected from Whitehall. The taffeta lining, buckram interlining and other materials were from the Office of the Wardrobe of Robes.

First to Walter Fyshe our Taylour . . . Item for making of a frenche gowne with a shorte Traine of carnacion cloth of silver the gowne lyned with white sarceonett the bodies & slevis lyned with taphata and cloth of silver cutt chevernewise and bounde with lase of venice silver the cuttes drawen oute with <lase> lawne the ruffes lyned with buckeram and Rolles of bent coverid with fustian the skyrtes being a rounde kyrtle of our store of the chardge of Rauf Hope yeoman of our warderobe of Robes with eighte yerdes of like cloth of silver of our store Receyved of George Brideman deceassid sometyme keper of our Palloice at Westminster threst of our greate warderobe.[98]

The reference to the exchange of eighteen and a half yards of tawny satin for the same quantity of murrey satin in the

following entry in 1576 is a little confusing. One explanation is that the Queen changed her mind about the colour scheme and the mercer agreed to take murrey satin which had been in store in the Office of the Wardrobe of Robes and already paid for by the Great Wardrobe in return for the tawny satin required.

First to Walter Fyshe our Taylour . . . Item for making of a spanishe gowne of tawnye satten with a verye great pendaunte sleve with doble Jagges in the syse and small skyrtes to the bodies the gowne lyned with white sarceonett & edgid with white satten the slevis lyned with white satten cutt and raste allover & lyned undernethe with white sarceonett the small skyrtes edgid with white satten the gowne partelye garded with a garde taken from a Gowne of tawnye satten of our store Received of Blaunche Pary one of the gentilwomen of our prevye Chamber. xviij yerdes di of satten towardes the making of the same gowne exchaunged for so muche murrey satten of our store the satten to performe the same gowne of our great guardrobe.[99]

Skirt hems were protected with braid at the edge (Figs 265 and 266) which could be replaced when worn. Perspiration was absorbed by linen smocks worn next to the skin, but even so, a considerable amount of the work done by the Queen's tailor in any year was for freshening gowns with new linings. In some cases he completely changed their appearance as well, to keep them in fashion. These were not only for Elizabeth to wear but also for her ladies-in-waiting and others. Extracts from the warrants which have been linked with the Stowe and Folger inventories provide many useful examples where the whole style of a gown has been altered by recutting, adding new sleeves, changing the opening from front to back or changing the embroidered guards. In one example given below, a trained French gown was changed into a round gown by cutting off the train and using it for sleeves and two new panels in the skirt.[100]

The tailors' terms

Many of the terms which are frequently repeated in the warrants may need some explanation; in some cases their meaning can only be conjectured from visual evidence in portraits. The 'verye great pendaunte sleve' in the last entry quoted above was a hanging sleeve which might have reached the ground, possibly similar in style to those worn by the Queen in Figure 62. From the evidence of portraits the 'doble Jagges in the syse', in the same entry, were two strips of material, either cut in scalloped shapes or snipped to form tabs, set into the armhole above the sleevehead. Tailors still use the word 'scye' for the armhole. It seems to have been an abbreviation of 'armseye' or armhole. The 'small skyrtes to the bodies' was a narrow basque usually cut in tabs round the waist like those seen in several portraits of Elizabeth (Figs 25 and 111). The word 'skirt' should always be considered in context, as it also describes the lower part of a gown, from waist to ground. The term 'nether skirts' occurs occasionally, as in this entry for Walter Fyshe in 1579 'making the nether skyrtes of a frenche gowne of fine white lawne enbroderid allover with bugelles & sipers sett allover with Roses of sipers lyned with taphata the winges lyned with buckeram & cotten'.[101] Another, in 1581, refers to 'making of the nether partes of a frenche gowne of blak printed satten enbroderid with leaves of heare colour satten lyned with black sarceonett the satten of our store of the chardge of Rauf Hope yeoman of our guarderobe of Robes and the heare colour satten of our store of the chardge of Thomas Knevett keper of our Palloice of Westminster':[102] it is not clear if 'nether skirts' and 'nether parts' referred to a somewhat deeper area at the hem than that usually covered by a guard, or the whole skirt.

Guards were wide decorative bands bordering hemlines and other edges, sometimes round armholes and covering seams (Figs 212, 213, and 213a). They were usually made separately from the rest of the garment, often of a contrasting colour and material, and frequently embroidered and/or trimmed with braid. They could be transferred from gown to gown very easily, needing only two rows of tacking stitches to hold them in place, an easy way of renovating an old gown. In this example more work was carried out as well with new sleeves and shoulder wings made from the old sleeves, which may have been out of fashion:

First to Walter Fyshe our Taylour . . . Item for alteringe and newe makinge of a great flaunders Gowne enlarged in the bodies and newe shoulder gardes and coller garde and newe slevis & winges made of tholde slevis the gowne cutt allover and lyned with spanishe ashe colour taphata the coller newe lyned with canvas and the winges with cotten of our great guarderobe.[103]

It is interesting to note that the wings were lined with cotton. This may have been of the same quality as cotton cloth entered in a list of re-exports from the Levant in 1586, among the Earl of Leicester's accounts. This cotton cloth was 6d. a yard, while cotton yarn was 1s. 6d. a lb: 'Sipris cottons' were entered among other imported cloths at Dover in 1576–77.[104] The latter were possibly made in Cyprus, although the name may have been given simply because the goods were imported thence. Cotton was used on a few occasions for whole garments for the Queen. William Jones, for example, made 'a kirtle of whit Callacowe bounde with riben of our great Warderob' for her between Michaelmas 1594 and Lady Day 1595.[105] This calico, a term derived from Calicut in India, the original place of manufacture, would have been very fine cotton, of good quality and expensive.

Welts were narrow bands, often snipped on the edge, used at hems and placed beside guards as in this example:

First to Walter Fyshe our Taylour . . . Item for making of a Gowne of blak vellat with a trayne of the french fation garded with crymsen vellat enbrauderid with pearle welted on each side the garde wrought with pearle lyned with crymsen sarceonett and buckeram in the pleytes the ruffes lyned with <fustian> fryse with ventes of fustian in the bodies the slevis drawen oute with lawne the same gardes and weltes taken from a frenche Gowne of crymsen Satten of our store in the chardge of Rauf Hope yeoman of our guardrobe of Roobes threst of our greate Guarderobe.[106]

In this entry the pleats at the waist of the skirt were interlined with buckram to stiffen them. The 'ruffes' were tight gathers, or cartridge pleats as they are known today, a process still in use for theatrical costumes. The word 'ruff', used for the familiar piece of neckwear arranged in figures of eight at the outer edge (Fig. 268), is abbreviated from a 'ruff-band'. The word 'band' means a collar and a 'ruff-band' is simply a gathered collar.

The 'ruffes' in the entry above enabled the fullness of the skirt to be drawn up to fit the waist and a wide sleevehead to fit an armhole, although the material might be quite thick. They were interlined with frieze, a woollen fabric, to make them rounded in shape on the folded edge where they were attached to another piece of the garment. The sleeves 'drawen out with lawne' describes a long strip of fine white lawn being pulled out in puffs through holes made in seams, or in the material, for decoration (Fig. 240). Other fine materials such as cypress

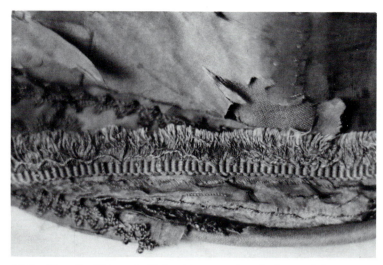

266   Detail of fringed silk braid protecting the hem of the petticoat in which Pfalzgräfin Dorothea Sabina von Neuberg was buried, 1598. Bayerisches Nationalmuseum, Munich

were also used. The strips of material are often termed 'pullings out' in the warrants.

'Rolles of cotten' were used in many gowns. These were pads of cotton wool bombast which would have given a little support beneath the pleats at the waist, so that they would fall in an attractive curve over the cone-shaped Spanish farthingale. They were also used beneath the shoulderheads of sleeves. The description in an entry for one gown in 1569 explains that the rolls of cotton were 'coverid with fustian'.[107] Another gown made in 1571 had rolls of fustian with bents to hold the shape inside the sleeves, which would have been more springy than a solidly packed cotton wool roll:

First to Walter Fyshe our Taylour . . . Item for making of a frenche Gowne of russett wrought vellat the grounde silver cutt asunder allover and sett together with a lase of golde silver and russett silke cheverne facion lyned with ashe colour sarceonett and buckeram in the pleites the bodies & slevis lyned with white Satten and purple tyncell sarceonett with rolles of fustian and bentes in the slevis the Stuff to make the Gowne and vj yerdes and a half of ashe colour sarceonett of our store Recevyed of the said Rauf Hope threste of our greate guarderobe.[108]

This was a very elaborate gown, involving a lot of work in cutting the velvet and arranging the braid in a chevron design.

Some of the tailors' terms are very descriptive. Walter Fyshe unpicked part of a French gown in 1581 and is described as 'alteringe rippinge and newe making of the nether partes' of it.[109] There are some references to tacking stitches among the warrants, as in the following example, but other stitches are individually named only among the entries for work carried out by hosiers and silkwomen: 'Fyrste to William Jones our Tayloure . . . Item for alteringe of a gowne of hare colour cloth of Silver printed and makinge of a paire of hanginge slevis to yt cut and tacte up, lyned with Silver Tincell and holland clothe covered over with lawne of our greate warderobe'.[110] The 'cloth of Silver printed' was stamped with hot irons to give a decorative pattern. This technique was used most successfully on velvet as the crushed pile gave variations in texture and a clear distinction between light and dark areas (Fig. 63). This work may have been carried out by the mercer or the tailor.

The terms 'cutt and raste' and 'razed and pinked' appear in the tailor's entries from about 1576 onwards.[111] Here 'rased'

267 *Razed pattern on a white satin cloak worn by Charles X Gustavus, 1654. Livrustkammaren, Stockholm (inv. no. 3389)*

267a *Detail from Figure 267 showing the razed surface of the satin*

268 *(Above) 'Queen Elizabeth I' by an unknown artist, 1589. She wears a doublet pinked with a variety of patterns, the larger slashes revealing striped silk beneath. Present whereabouts unknown*

or 'razed' describes a different process from 'raysed', used by the embroiderer when he padded or 'raised' certain areas of the embroidery with cotton wool, parchment, or other materials. The use of the word in the embroiderer's entries, usually in conjunction with 'uppe, 'uppon' or 'on', should be compared with its use in those for the tailor, for example:

Item to John Parr our enbrauderer . . . for raysinge up of a paire of slevis of white silke sipers upon Carnacion cloth of Silver richelie wrought with silver wormes spangles and purle upon the raysinges.[112]

To the tailor, 'razing' was a term applied to a particular method of cutting satin in a decorative pattern. The design was first outlined, probably using a simple template as a guide for the size, and then drawn freehand, scoring the surface of the satin. The shapes were then filled in with minute cuts measuring from 0.7 mm (1/32 in.) to 6 mm (1/4 in.) in length, with spaces of 0.7 mm (1/32 in.) to 4.7 mm (3/16 in.) between them. The cuts were made diagonally or straight across the grain of the satin and were only deep enough to sever the surface warp threads; the weft and main warps remained untouched. The surface was then gently razed with a knife to force the cut threads upwards. Linear patterns were achieved by scraping a knife along the surface of the satin. The finished effect gives a pattern like the bloom of a peach on one surviving example of the technique, a white satin cloak and doublet

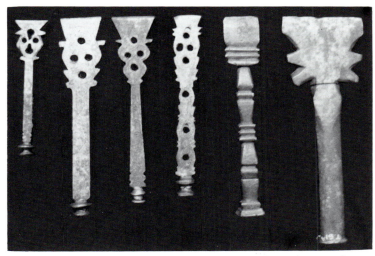

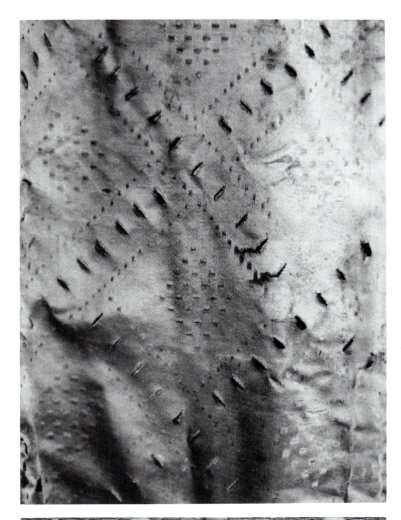

269 *Four cutters for pinking from Seville and two from Bologna (left to right). Late sixteenth century. Victoria and Albert Museum, London*

270 *Satin lining of hanging sleeves from gown in which Pfalzgräfin Dorothea Sabina von Neuberg was buried, 1598. The satin is scored with a trellis design, filled in with tiny pinks. Bayerisches Nationalmuseum, Munich*

271 *Green silk with a woven design resembling the frayed edges of slashing. Early seventeenth century. Whitworth Art Gallery, Manchester*

worn by Karl X Gustavus of Sweden dating from 1654 (Figs 267 and 267a). Few specimens have survived, probably because cutting the warp threads weakened the material. The knives for this work would have had to be razor sharp. Alice and Roger Mountague supplied several pairs of 'Knyves with Sheares' in 1580, 1581 and 1583,[113] which may have been used for this work although two pairs of 'kynves with Sheares in thendes thone guilte thother not guilt Delyverid for Tomasen the woman dwarf' in 1582 are more likely to have been for her use at table, or for closing letters, as Erondell describes.[114]

A number of portraits of Elizabeth show the surface of silk and velvet gowns covered in decorative pinking and slashing (Fig. 268). Pinking, the small cuts up to 6 mm (¼ in.) in size (Fig. 270), might be carried out by the mercer, tailor or embroiderer in a wide variety of patterns with metal cutters (Fig. 269). If the material was pinked or cut by the Queen's tailor or embroiderer, they submitted samples for her approval first, as in one example of 1575 'to Walter Fyshe our Taylour . . . Item for making of two pattrones of wrought vellat cutt billett wise, thone layed with venice golde, thother with silver lase, and one edgid with white Satten, thother with carnacion Satten.'[115] Elizabeth had a plain taffeta gown pinked and cut by Walter Fyshe when it was remodelled in 1565: 'Item for new makinge Pynkynge and cutting alover of a lose gowne of black taphata new lyned with whit sercenet the forequarters new made with black taphata the lyning perfourmed with taphata'.[116] The larger decorative cuts were carried out by the tailor and embroiderer to fit the pattern shapes of the gown or design of the embroidery.

Before any cutting was done the material might be lightly brushed on the back with size or gum arabic to prevent fraying, as in this example where David Smith is entered 'for sysinge

272 'Joan Thornbury, Mrs Hugh Wakeman', panel painting by Hans Eworth, 1566. She wears what is probably a Flanders gown and a white linen handkerchief with a tassel on the corner hangs out of the pocket. Present whereabouts unknown

Cuttinge and purlinge of a Flaunders gowne of Blacke velvet cutt all over with rewes downe righte the gowne for workemanshipp therof xxxs.[117] Sometimes the material would be sufficiently firmly woven not to need sizing. In some cases the soft fringed texture of fraying cuts was sought deliberately; floating threads on the right side of a piece of green silk woven with a double warp are cut to give a similar effect (Fig. 271). Long cuts, seen on the fronts of bodices in the 1570s in several portraits (Fig. 20), were bound round the edge with braid or a narrow hem turned under to make a firm edge, like this example, where they are bound with white satin:

First to Walter Fyshe our Taylour . . . Item for alteringe and newe making of a frenche Gowne with a traine of blak vellat wrought with a very brode garde of blak silke like cheines the same Gowne made into a rounde Gowne ye traine made into slevis and two newe panes in the skyrtes with bodies and two newe partlettes cutt allover with a verye busye cutt and all ye cuttes turned in and edgid with white satten the gowne borderid with a brode border of white taphata the garde of the gowne cutt the bodies, slevis, & two partelettes lyned with blak sarceonett the bodies lyned with canvas and a rolle of bayes in the pleites coverid with sarceonett with Rolles of bent in the slevis coverid with fustian & sarceonett of our great guarderobe.[118]

The term 'stays' has already been mentioned in Chapter VI. It usually appears in the entries for loose gowns and appears to have referred to a strip of material stretching across the back inside, to hold the fullness in position (Fig. 225). There is, however, one entry for Walter Fyshe 'altering of a Frenche

gowne of Blacke Velvet drawne out with sipres trees and making of a newe staie of Fustian of our great guarderobe' in 1562.[119] This was probably to hold the skirt pleats in position but it may be a very early instance of the term describing a supportive lining for a bodice, as it was later used in the seventeenth century. A new stay was put in the same gown in 1563, with three others, but the styles are not specified: 'Firste to Walter Fishe our Tailoure . . . Item for makinge iiij Staies of Taffata for iiij gownes viz one of Black velvet enbrodered with ostriche Fethers an other of gathered sarsenet the iijde of black velvet with Sipers trees and the iiijth of Black velvet enbrodered all over with Satten'.[120] It seems more likely, from the description of taffeta stays, that these were strips stitched behind rows of gathers or pleats as described above. However, a warrant entry for stays stiffened with buckram in 1588 more convincingly indicates their early use as a firm support: 'for making of a loose gowne of ashe colour tufte taphata the grounde silver the bodies lyned and with pockettes and stayes of tawnye taphata the steyes and coller styffenid and the gowne borderid with buckeram all of our great guarderobe'.[121]

'Ventes' were apparently facings for the openings or slits in a garment. Walter Fyshe made 'x paire of ventes of grograyne for x sondry gownes of our great warderobe' in 1565.[122] Presumably these were to replace original ones which were worn or soiled. Often fustian was used for vents,[123] as in this example in 1567:

First to Walter Fyshe our Taylor . . . Item for new makinge of a Do[t]che gowne of black velvet with a spanishe sleve the bodies and slevis lyned with whit Taffata with vents of Fustian in the bodies the plaites lyned with buckeram the skyrtes bordered with whit Taffata the velvet to make the skyrtes being a gowne cut out before of our store of the chardge of Rauphe Hope yeoman of our Warderobe of Robes all the rest of our great warderobe.[124]

Pockets appear to have been plain bags stitched into the side seams of full skirted gowns (Fig. 272) rather than the separate decorative accessories used in the eighteenth century.[125] It is not clear if they were put in Elizabeth's early gowns, but there is an entry in 1573 for Walter Fyshe 'making of twentie Pokettes for xx sundry Gownes'[126] and these may have been to replace earlier ones which had worn out. In 1575 he made pockets for a 'lardge night gown'[127] and a 'large loose gown'[128] as well as for safeguards.[129] These were presumably for carrying handkerchieves (Fig. 272). Pockets often seem to have been made to match or tone with the garment, as in the example of a green velvet safeguard 'the gardes borderid with grene taphata and pockettes of like taphata'.[130] Fyshe made 'Twelve Pockettes of silke grograine: Twelve Pockettes of taphata: and Twelve Pockettes of bridges satten all of our great warderobe'[131] in 1579, presumably to match gowns in these materials and a further 'xlviij Pockettes of grograine taphata & bridges satten for gownes' in 1580.[132] There may have been pockets for kirtles included in this order: Fyshe certainly made one 'pockett for a rounde kyrtell of yellowe taphata' in 1580.[133] William Jones also made large numbers of pockets for a wide variety of gowns.[134]

Early in the reign Walter Fyshe made farthingales as well as gowns, but there must have been so much work that by 1567 there was a separate farthingale maker, whose work is discussed later. The tailors continued to make rolls to support the skirt pleats at the waist and rolls for sleeve heads. When the sleeves widened they needed extra support and these were also made by the tailor. This fashion appears to have originated in

France: in his *Itinerary*, Fynes Moryson wrote 'And they say that the sleeves borne up with whale-bones were first invented to avoid mens familiar touching of their armes'. The following description of a pair of undersleeves made of holland and stiffened with strips of whalebone shows that the early use of bents for stiffening resulted in the word 'bented' being used for 'stiffened' by the end of the century: 'First to William Jones our Taylor . . . Item for making iij paire of verthingale sleves of holland cloth bound with riben, and bented with whales bone of our great warderobe'.[135]

Although whalebone had been used for stiffening the farthingales worn by Mary, Queen of Scots, in 1562,[136] it does not seem to have been used in the Wardrobe of Robes until 1580, when Robert Sibthorpe used it for stiffening Elizabeth's farthingales.[137] William Jones made 'xij Buskes of whales bone and wyer coverid with sarceonet quilted' and Roger Mountague supplied 'one buske of whale bone' in 1586.[138] It was used in increasing amounts for stiffening 'French bodies' and 'petticoat bodies', or corsets. Two examples in the 1590s were both made by William Jones the tailor. The first was 'for makinge of a paire of frenche bodies of Carnacion Taffata Lyned with fustian stiched alover withe whales bone' in 1590 and the second for 'making of a peticoate bodies of orrindge colour Taffata stiched with silke lace alover and bound with lace lined with Fustian and whales bone' in 1593.[139] In 1594 Jones made 'a paire of bodies of spanishe lether spotted allover with flowers and laied about with silver lace lined with Carnacion unshorne velvett' which may have been a leather corset similar to those made in the eighteenth century, which were stiff enough without whalebone.[140]

The embroiderers

The embroiderers worked closely with the tailors, embellishing rich fabrics for the guards which were mounted on the Queen's gowns, sometimes covering the whole surface of a garment (Fig. 273). Guilliam Brallot, William Middleton and David Smith were the Queen's embroiderers at the beginning of the reign. There is a bill for Brallot's work carried out for the Coronation, including the use of gilt spangles,[141] but he does not seem to have worked for the Queen after 1559. Middleton carried out much of the embroidery for the Queen's furnishings (for example he embroidered all the white satin for a bedstead at Windsor Castle)[142] while David Smith carried out most of the embroidery on Elizabeth's gowns. This arrangement seems to have continued amicably until 1569 when John Witton, William Middleton's deputy, and David Smith brought the division of the work to arbitration. William le Grys and Anthony Walker appear to have settled the matter very fairly. Presumably David Smith must have been the better embroiderer as he continued to carry out all the embroidery for the Queen's gowns.

The copie of the Arbitrament for Thenbrauderers
The Award of William le Grys Clarke of the Quenes Majesties Stable and Anthony Walker clarke of her highnes great warderobe in london Arbitratours indifferently elect and Chosen as well on the parte of David Smythe one of the Quenes Majesties Enbrauderers As of the parte of John Witton Enbrauderer and deputie to William Middleton one other enbrauderer to the Quenes majestie for and towchinge the Workmanshipp of Enbraudery of all her highnes offices and other workes for the voydinge of all controverses and

273 *The embroiderer's workshop in Nürnberg, showing the work stretched taut on a frame. Woodcut from 'Eygentliche Beschreibung Aller Stände auff Erden' by Jost Amman and Hans Sachs, 1568. Private collection*

doubtes betwene them have awarded this presente daie beinge the second daie of July Anno undecimo Regine Eliz. etc. Anno Domini 1569 as hereafter enseweth.

Fyrst the said Arbytrators havinge the said Daie and yere called before them the said parties and heringe the allegacions and pro[o]ffes of eyther of them towchinge the workmanshipp of thenbraudery and for the appeasing of all actes that eyther now are moved towchinge the premisses or that might ensue hereafter Arbytrate and order the said daie and yere in maner and Fourme folowinge That is to say That the said David Smythe according to the warde made by John Thomworthe late grome of the Quenes majestyes privie Chamber shall have all thenbraudery of the Quenes majesties Apparell. And also the Said David Smythe and John Witton as towchinge the Stable the workmanshipp shalbe devided into thre partes That is to say The said John witton shall have two partes of all the workmanshipp and the foresaid David Smythe to have one parte of the workmanshipp of the said Stable. And Furthermore it is awarded that all other workmanshipp of Enbraudery towchinge the Gard the Footmen the Littermen and all other workes not Afore mencyoned shalbe equally devided betwene the foresaid David Smythe and the said John witton in maner and Fourme as ys above written. In witnes herof the foresaid Arbitrators to this presente Award have sette their handes and Seales for the daie and yere Fyrst above mencyoned.[143]

John Witton seems to have carried out some further embroidery on the Queen's gowns, as in 1577 there is an entry 'Delyverid to the said David Smyth and John Witton our

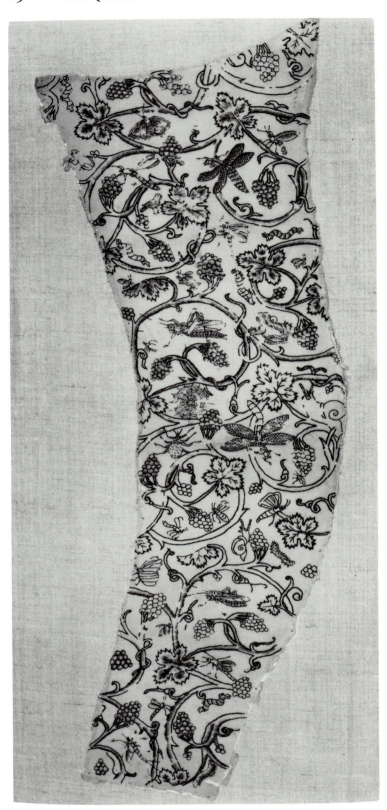

274 *Underside of a white linen sleeve embroidered in black silk with curling sprays of vines, caterpillars, grasshoppers, butterflies, dragonflies, snails, frogs, a cobweb and a spider. c.1600. Victoria and Albert Museum, London (T.11–1950)*

Enbrauderers by them employed upon our said apparell viij yerdes quarter of satten of sundrye colours . . .'[144] and in 1579 another, 'for thre quarters thre nailes of a yerde of carnacion vellat: and thre quarters one naile of a yerde of russet Satten Delyverid to John Witton one other of our Enbrauderers by him employed upon our said apparell of our great

warderobe'.[145] Presumably this work was carried out with David Smith's agreement.

William Middleton makes his last appearance in the warrants in 1581,[146] and David Smith in 1587.[147] David Smith, like Walter Fyshe, left money for the benefit of the poor. Stow records his almshouses in *A Survey of London* published in 1603. They were very close to the site of the Great Wardrobe: 'Touching lanes ascending out of Thames Street to Knightrider Street, the first is [St] Peter's hill; wherein I find no matter of Note, more than certain Almes Houses, lately founded on the west side thereof, by David Smith, Imbroiderer for 6 poore widdowes; whereof each to have 20s. by the yeare'.[148] Further details are given by Strype: 'St Peters Hill, well built and inhabited especially the End next to Old Fishstreet. On this Hill are Alms Houses for six poor Widows, built by David Smith, Embroiderer to Queen Eliz. and called Embroiderers Alms Houses; each having two Rooms, endowed with 3 *l.* per an[num]. After the Fire of London, these Alms Houses were rebuilt by Sir Thomas Fitch'.[149] David Smith also left Woodmonger's Hall, which he had purchased from Edmund Helles, woodmonger, shortly before his death in 1587, to the Mayor and Commonalty on trust for Christ's Hospital.[150]

John Parr's name first appears in the Lady Day warrants of 1581, a year before William Jones.[151] These two men would have built up a similar work routine to that of Walter Fyshe and David Smith during the first half of the reign. Parr continued to work for James I and there are references to him as the 'King's Embroiderer' after 1603.

The embroiderers' equipment and work

The Queen's embroiderers, like the tailors, needed little equipment; a clear working area, embroidery frames, a yardstick, paper or parchment for pricking out their patterns, a pair of shears, small scissors or a knife, an iron, pins, needles, thread, with silks and other materials supplied by the silk-woman. Sample patterns of embroidery were prepared for the Queen to make her choice, as this entry in 1571 demonstrates: 'Delyverid to David Smyth our Enbrauderer One yerde of blak vellat and half a yerde of blak Satten to make pattrons'.[152] The word 'sampler' is also used, as for example, 'Deleveryid to David Smyth our Enbrauderer One yerde of blak vellat and half a yerde of blak Satten to make samplers . . .' in 1571.[153] Smaller pieces of material were used for samples as well; in 1572 he was sent 'One quarter of a yerde of clothe of silver to make pattrons; one half one yerde of orringe colour vellat to make pattrons'.[154] Presumably the discarded samples were used for purses, pin cushions or other small items afterwards; there were a great many of them.

The designs were drawn out on paper or parchment, pricked with a pin, and were then transferred to the material with pounce. This was a fine powder, such as powdered gum sandarac, pipe clay or charcoal, dusted over the perforated pattern sheet to transfer the design to the material beneath.[155] The patterns took a considerable amount of time to prepare but could have been used many times. One was presented to the Queen as a New Year's Gift, 'By Adams Scholemaister to the henchemen a patron of a peire of Slevis';[156] this may have been drawn out by Adams himself, or perhaps purchased from a professional embroiderer (Figs 156 and 274).

The length of material to be embroidered was stretched taut on a frame (Fig. 273). This was paid for as a separate item.

A detailed entry for David Smith in 1563 gives a clear idea of how the cost of the work was divided between labour and materials:

Item to David Smythe our Enbrauderer . . . Item for Enbraudering of a Flaunders gowne of Black velvet wrought allover with a Faire worke with Estriche Fethers and Black Satten made of fyne purled Lace with a Border of Like worke for workemanship thereof — xiiij *li* Item for iiij lb di of purled Lace spente upon the same gown at lxiiijs the lb weight — xiiij *li* viijs Item for j lb di of silke to worke ye same gowne lxs Item for Canvas thred and other necessaries to sett the same in the Frame — vjs viijd.[157]

Another entry shows how much might be spent on altering and enlarging the embroidery on a gown, including the cost of putting it back into the frame for the work to be carried out:

Item to David Smyth oure Enbrauderer for translating and enlarginge the Enbrauderye of a flanders gowne of Blac Velvet wrought allover with a Cutt worke of russet Satten and upon the garde with fyne spanishe Lace and cheyne frendge for workemanship therof xiij*li* vjs viijd. Item for one lb di of spanishe Lace spente upon the same gown at iij*li* the lb weight iiij*li* xs. Item for one pound of spanyshe silke spente upon the same gowne xxxiiijs. Item for canvas threde and other necessaries to set the same in the Frame vjs viijd.[158]

In another detailed entry, this time for a new gown made in 1566, the cost of setting the embroidery in the frame is ten shillings. This increase in price, from six shillings and eight pence in 1563, is due simply to the extra amount of time and work involved in preparing the frame for a gown with a train and large hanging sleeves:

Item to David Smith our Enbrauderer . . . for Enbrauderinge of a Traine Gowne of black velvet with great pendaunt slevis havinge a brode <gard> border of black velvet cut in an antique worke wrought upon whit Taffata with fyne edginge purled lace the gowne cut alover and set with flowres and purles of gold lyned with whit Silver Sarcenet for workmanshipp thereof xvij*li* Item for fyve grosse of edginge purlid Lace at xxxs the grosse vij*li* xs Item for ij poundes of silk lxiiijs Item for x ounces of gold purles spent upon the same gowne at vijs thounce lxxs Item for Cuttinge alover of the same gowne with a small cut xxs Item for Canvas thred and other necessaries to set the same in the Frame xs.[159]

Usually the term 'setting in the frame' is used in the warrants to describe the work of stretching the material taut before commencing embroidery. One reference to John Parr in 1591 uses another term: 'Item for Canvas thred frames and other necessaries employed upon the parcelles before wrytten to set them on the Tentes'.[160]

As well as stretching the material taut in a frame, another preliminary treatment might be needed if the embroiderer was carrying out decorative pinking and cutting. This, as previously mentioned, was to brush the back of the material with size or gum arabic to prevent excessive fraying, as in this example for David Smith '. . . Sizinge and Cutting with a Dyamond Cutt the Lynynge of the forequarters of a gowne, of Blac velvet for workmanshipp therof xs'.[161]

Embroidery was expensive and treated with great care. As we have already seen there are many examples of rich guards, or borders, being transferred to new gowns. In other cases an old ground might be cut away and the embroidery mounted on a new ground, as in this example of 1591: 'Item to John Parr our Embrother . . . for embroderinge before of a paire of hanginge sleves embroidered with dead Trees & other braunches richly wrought with gold silver and colored silkes which were first taken from the old sleves the ground white satten and

275   *Detail of pearls on the black velvet gown in the 'Phoenix' portrait of Queen Elizabeth I in Figure 26. Panel painting by Nicholas Hilliard, c. 1575–76. National Portrait Gallery, London*

afterward embroidered downe upon a new ground of white satten'.[162] Another example dating from 1600 describes embroidery being taken from another doublet but does not describe the ground being cut away. Perhaps these were slips of flowers which were easily detached from the other doublet:

First to William Jones our Taylor . . . Item for making of a doublet of White satten with a gold lace about it, cut and enbrodered and lyned with Sarcenet the bodies stiffened with Canvas and buckram, thenbrauderie taken from another doublet of our store of the chardge of Sir Thomas Gorge Knight gentleman of our warderobe of Roabes the rest of our great warderobe.[163]

Many of the pieces of embroidery for the Queen's gowns were enriched with pearls. Some of these may have been imitation ones made of glass[164] but others were pearls from native oysters and would have needed holes bored through them, for stitching to material (Fig. 275). Theophilus describes how this was done in the twelfth century, and presumably the same technique was used in the sixteenth century:

Pearls are found in shells of the sea and other waters. They are pierced through with a fine steel drill, which is fixed in a wooden shaft and a block of wood [at the top]. On the shaft is a small lead wheel and attached to it is a bar by which it is rotated. If it is necessary for the hole of any pearl to be made larger, a wire is inserted in it together with a little fine sand. One end of the wire is held in the teeth, the other in the left hand, the pearl is moved up and down with the right, and sand is meanwhile applied so that the hole becomes wider. Mother of pearl is also cut up into pieces. These are shaped into pearls with the file — they are most useful on gold — and are polished as above.[165]

The Queen's embroiderers would often incorporate gold-smith's work and jewels into their designs. In one example in 1562 David Smith was employed in 'garnishing of a Whalles head of goldsmythes worke with buttons and Lowpes made of Blewe silk and gold to putt upon a skarf for workemanship therof vjs viij d.'[166] Sometimes the jewels stood on rosettes of cypress or lawn (Fig. 71) such as those worked by John Parr in 1595: 'For drawinge out of a paire of slevis of Tawney satten with copwebb lawne, and for settinge Jewells upon the same, and for making puffinges, of lawne by hand for the Jewells to stand on, beinge tufted with sleve silke and powdered with marygoldes'.[167]

Some of the pieces of work carried out by the embroiders are described in great detail. This scarf made in 1591 must have been an impressive sight for the clerk to describe it so carefully:

Item to John Parr our Enbrauderer . . . for enbrodering of a skarf of white silk Sypers richlie wrought with a brode border both sydes alyke at eche ende scalling Ladders, armed men, scrowles with wordes handes and fethers artyfycyallie wrought with sondrie other devices of venice gold silver and silke of sondrie Colours with a welte on eche syde the same borders lykwise enbrodered and a narrowe border downe both sydes, the same skarf with a brode riche Lace of silver rounde aboute with a riche spangle lace and buttons of silver tufted with silver spangles enryched with silver plate and spangles.[168]

Embroidery was used on a wide variety of accessories as well as on the Queen's gowns. Several examples are given in the warrant for Michaelmas 1594 below, where John Parr carried out work on small delicate items such as coifs and the ends of a pair of garters, as well as embroidery on a larger scale for sleeves and gowns.

Item to John Parr our embrauderer for raysinge up of a paire of bodies of Cloth of silver with cuttes of Carnacion Cloth of gold and enbraudered downe the lace betwene the raysinge. Item for work-manshipp and edginge of a paire of shoes of Clothe of silver lyned with white Taffata, and joyninge the Lyninge and outsyde together. Item for raysinge and tackinge of a paire of wearinge slevis and hanginge slevis of white silke sipres enlarged and raysed upon Carnacion cloth of silver wrought very richlie with purles plates and spangles. Item for raysinge of a nightgowne of Tawney Satten drawne out with lawne, the borders round about the pocket holes and foreventes newe repayred and drawn out with lawne and wroughte as yt was before. Item for makinge of newe facinges coller and lyninges to the slevis of the same gowne of Lawne striped with silver, wrought very richlie with gold spangles in waves and repayeringe then-brauderie of one paire of shoes of Cloth of Silver. Item for enbrauderinge of ij Coyfes of Lawne thone richlie wrought with black Silke and gold, thother with black Silk and silver. Item for repayringe of thenbroderie of a gowne of black satten wrought with Flowers and Leaves of black Satten richlie wrought with gold & silver, set upon Carnacion Satten. Item for raysinge up of a paire of slevis of white

silke sipers upon Carnacion cloth of Silver richlie wrought with silver wormes spangles and purle upon the raysinges. Item for enbrauder-inge of six dozin of flowers richelie wrought with silver plate upon blacke Taffata. Item for enbrauderinge of ij endes of a paire of Garters of ashecolour silke Sipers richelie wrought with Lyllies and hollies of gold silver and silk of sondrie colours. Item for enbrauder-inge of ij muffeler cases of black Taffata richelie wrought with gold silver and silke of sondrie colours. Item for one garter sent to the kinge of Scottes. Item for enbrauderinge of a paire of slevis of white Satten richelie wrought withe gold Twistes plates and spangles, the same cut of [f] and raysed upon whit Cloth of Silver wrought with spangles upon the gowne and tufted with orrendge coloure silke. Item for Canvas Thredd and other necessaries employed upon all the said parcelles to set them on the frames. Item for half one elle of black Taffata, fyve ounces di of silver wormes and two poundes di and thre ounces and half quarter of gold and Silver purles & spangles employed upon the parcelles above wrytten all of our great warderobe.

LMN A garter sent to the kinge of Scottes the garter was not sent but did serve afterwardes for the French king A° xxxviij° RR Eliz.[169]

The skinners

The work of the skinner (Fig. 276) included not only sup-plying, treating and making up furs for lining and decorating mantles, cloaks and gowns, but also keeping them in good repair. He replaced worn or moth-eaten areas and carried out the essential task of regularly airing and beating the furs and fur-trimmed garments to keep them free of dust, moths and fleas.

At the time of the coronation William Jurden 'her Majesties Skynner' was paid 'for Furres and furring of her graces Roabes and others Ciiij^xx^vj li vjs iiijd [£186.6s.4d]'.[170] Adam Bland may have worked for him, as his name appears in the Great Wardrobe accounts at the beginning of the reign together with Katherine Jurden, presumably William's widow, supplying furs for the Queen.[171] Katherine is still listed with Adam in the Accounts made up to Lady Day 1561[172] but by the autumn of the same year Adam Bland was working alone as the Queen's skinner[173] and continued until 1594 when his son Peter took his place by letters patent, dated 30 May of that year.[174]

The warrants for the Blands' work reveal that a considerable variety of furs was used for lining and trimming the Queen's gowns. Adam used quantities of 'Luzarnes',[175] 'Jennetts',[176] 'powderid Armyons',[177] 'lettice',[178] 'Sable skynnes',[179] 'mynkes skynnes',[180] 'squerrills',[181] 'spotted gryzled coney skynes', 'blak and grey coney skynnes',[182] 'callaber',[183] 'mynever',[184] 'gryzeled conney skynnes', 'spotted coney sky-nes', 'ruskyn greye conney skynnes,[185] 'callaber wombes',[186] 'rouse squerilles',[187] 'red lambe skynnes',[188] and 'wolves skynnes'.[189] Sable, ermine and the varieties of coney or rabbit, seem to have been used more frequently than other skins: lettice, lamb and wolf, for example, appear only a few times in the warrants. Bland used sables for making tippets which were worn round the neck and shoulders. There are several entries for these items: one was 'a Typett of three sable skynnes of our store in the chardge of Rauf Hope yeoman of our said Guarderobe of Robes lyned with purple vellat and after with murrey vellat also of our great guarderobe'.[190] Richard Robinson was entered 'for making of a peire of Sables with a perfourmance of Sables', possibly another form of tippet, in 1587.[191] It may have resembled the New Year's gift in 1585 'By the Erlle of Lecester . . . A Sable Skynne the hed and fourre featte of gold fully furnyshed with Dyamondes and Rubyes of sundary sorttes'.[192] Bland also worked on muffs, 'furringe of a

Snufken of heare colour Satten enbrauderid with thre blake Jennett skynnes' in 1583 and 'furring of a Snufkyn of blak vellat furred with fower rusken grey skinnes and edgid with one luzarne skynne' in 1586.[193]

Furs were used to decorate gowns, but they also provided warmth and often might hardly be seen when used as linings. Czar Ivan the Terrible's magnificent gifts of four timbers [bales containing forty skins] of very rich black sables, six well grown white spotted 'luzerance' [lynx] and two gowns of ermines, in 1587,[194] were most acceptable to the Queen, combining opulence with utility. They were doubtless displayed to good effect.

The last warrant for Elizabeth's reign shows that Peter Bland used white fox, white hare, and swan, as well as many of the same varieties of fur as his father. It gives a good example of the type of work carried out each season, throughout the reign:

Item to Peter Bland our said Sisters Skinner for mending the furre of a cloke of perfumed lether with thre sable skinnes and xx^tie Calaber skynnes to performe the same: for mending the furre of a mantle of white and Crimson tufte taphata with xj white foxe skinnes spotted: for mending the furre of a mantell of sky colour damaske with x white foxe skinnes: for edging a traine gowne of tawney satten florished allover with gold with xvj sable skinnes: for furring a muffe of sea greene satten with swanne skinnes & iiij white hare skynnes: for furring a muff of white satten enbrodered allover with gold with six sable skinnes: for making up a paire of sables lyned with carnacion vellat with six sable skinnes of our said store & perfuming them: for a case of white fustian to cary sables in: for mending the furre of a traine gowne of net worke florished allover with gold with two luzarne skinnes emploied thereon: for mending the furre of a traine gowne of tawnie satten enbrodered allover with gold lace with two luzarne skynnes employed thereon: for mending the furre of a traine gowne of peachcolor tissue with thre sable skinnes employed thereon: for mending the furre of a gowne of cloth of silver raysed with carnacion vellat with thre sable skinnes employed thereon: for mending the furre of a cloke of black vellat enbraudered allover with grasshoppers with thre sable skinnes: for mending the furre of a cloke of white satten enbrodered with a performance of powdered Armions: for mending the furre of a cloke of black vellat enbrodered allover with pearle with a performance of powdered Armions: for mending the furre of a loose gowne of watchet satten striped with gold with a performance of powdered armyons: for mending the furr of a cloake of watchet tuft taphata with a performance of powdered armions: for mending the furre of a cloke of orenge color satten striped with gold with a performance of powdred Armions: for mending the furre of a mantle of murrey vellat with a performance of Minever: for mending the furr of a cloke of white satten prented with a performance of powdered Armions: for mending the furr of a cloke of white satten wrought with viij white Cony skinnes: for mending the furr of a mantle of black & purple unshorne vellat with a performance of spotted pure: for mending the furre of a trayne gowne of black satten cut diamondwise, with iij sable skinnes: for mending the furre of a cloke of murrey damaske with sleves garded with vellat with thre sable skynnes: for beating and ayring our said late Sisters Robes and apparrell within the tower of London for himselfe and five men by the space of five daies: for six brushes, six Cardes of our great warderobe.[195]

Elspeth Veale has dealt fully with the background of the fur trade in her book *The English Fur Trade in the Later Middle Ages* and all that is needed here is to give some explanation of the names of the furs used by Adam and Peter Bland. Minsheu discusses them in *The Guide into Tongues* printed in 1617:

Furre . . . commeth of the French fourrér, . . . to line with skinnes. Of Furre we find strange kindes in the statute ann: 24. H[enricus] 8.

276 *A furrier's workshop in Nürnberg. The furrier makes and lines coats, cloaks, hoods, and other garments with such furs as sable, marten, lynx, ermine, polecat, wolf, and fox and from goatskins. Three women's gowns hanging on the rail may be of cloth sent by the tailor for fur linings or trimmings, but it is possible that they are garments made completely by the furrier, possibly lambskin, with the fleece facing the body. Woodcut from 'Eygentliche Beschreibung Aller Stände auff Erden' by Jost Amman and Hans Sachs, 1568. Private collection*

c[hapter] 13. as of sables, which is a rich furre of colour blacke and browne, being the skinne of a beast called a sable, of quantitie between a Polecat, and an ordinarie Cat, and of fashion like a Polecat bred in Russia, but most and the best in Tartaria. Lucerns, which is the skin of a beast so called, being neere the bignesse of a wolfe, of colour between red and browne, something mayled like a Cat, and mingled with blacke spots, bred in Muscovie and Russia, and is a very rich furre. Genets, that is the skin of a beast so called, of bignesse between a Cat and a Wesell, mayled like a Cat, and of the nature of a Cat, bred in Spaine. Whereof there be two kindes, blacke and gray, & the blacke the more pretious furre, having blacke spots upon it hardly to be seen. Foines is a fashion like the Sable, bred in Fraunce for the most part, the top of the furre is blacke, and the ground whitish. Martern, is a beast very like the Sable, the skin something courser, it liveth in all Countries that be not too cold, as England, Ireland and the best be in Ireland. Miniver is nothing but the bellies of Squirrels, as some men say. Others say it is a litle vermine like unto a Wesel, milke white, and commeth from Muscovie. Fitch is that which we otherwise call the Polecat heere in England. Shankes, be the skin of the shanke or legge of a kind of kidde which beareth the furre, that wee call Budge. Calaber is a litle beast in bignesse about the quantite of a squirrel, of colour gray, and bred especially in high Germanie.

'Jennet', or genet, is a type of civet cat, 'Lettice' is the white winter coat of the weasel, and 'foines' the French name of stone

277   *Princess Salome and her attendants wearing hooped skirts, early farthingales. From the retable of St John the Baptist by Pedro Garcia de Benabarre, c. 1470. Museum of Catalan Art, Barcelona*

marten's fur.[196] 'Armions' (ermine) is the winter coat of the stoat, a member of the weasel family: reddish brown in summer, the coat of those found in the North turns white in winter, except the tip of the tail which is always black. Ermine skins were pinked, or slit, for the black tips of the tails, or little pieces of fur from the legs of black lambs, to be stitched in.[197] These little pieces of black fur were called powderings. A warrant entry for Adam Bland 'borderinge of a kyrtle of crymsen vellat with six tymber of Armyons one thowsande pynkes and fowre thowsande powderinges'[198] would seem to describe the arrangement of four little pieces of fur, or powderings, in each pink, or hole, such as those on the ermine for the Coronation and Parliament robes (Fig. 112) familiar from heraldic devices. In another entry Bland furred 'a Cloake of white tufte taphata with thre laces of venice golde and silver employed thereon viij tymber of Armyons tenne tymber of mynever & sixe thowsande pynkes and powderinges'[199] and here there was one tuft of black fur in each pink. This would have given a similar effect to the ermine facings of the cape in Figure 87.

Miniver was made from the white bellies of squirrel skins with an edging of grey and by the mid-sixteenth century it was a cheaper fur than ermine. If all the grey was trimmed off, the fur was a white one described as pured miniver.[200] Miniver is also used in heraldry, the shape of the grey edging of the pelt giving the distinctive shape. When this was removed the squirrel fur probably looked so much like that of the stoat that it was indistinguishable, particularly when black powderings were used on it. The Oxford English Dictionary gives 'pured

miniver, miniver pure' as 'powdered miniver' and states that in modern times the adjective has been misinterpreted as pure white. It seems likely, however, that 'pured miniver' is the correct term for a white squirrel skin with the grey edges trimmed off. The word 'pure' is used by itself in the warrants on several occasions, and it is not clear exactly what this was. The term 'pured' describes fur trimmed or cut down to show one colour only, thus pured gris or grey is the grey fur of the back of the squirrel in winter, without any of the white of the belly.[201] 'Pure' may therefore have been either white or grey squirrel skin. The spotted pure used by Peter Bland may have been imitating ermine.

Great care was taken of the furs and fur-trimmed clothes. Adam Bland supplied quantities of sweet powder each year and this was put into silk bags to lay between the garments. Many of the sweet bags were presented to the Queen as gifts but in 1562 Adam Bland supplied a large order of 'one gross of Crimsen Sarsenet swete Bagges and viij lb of swete powder as well to make swete our Robes and apparell remayning within our Wardrobe of robes as also remayning within oure Tower of London all of our great warderobe'.[202]

It is not quite clear exactly how many men Adam had working with him throughout the reign, but during the summer months in 1590 there were eight men working for a full day beating the furs and another travelling to Windsor for one day, presumably to work on the furs there. This was the equivalent of nine days work for one man on wardrobe care: 'Item to Adam Blande our Skynner . . . Item for the Travell of viij men one daie in beatinge of our Furres and for one mans Chardges of him self and horse to Wyndsoure one daie of our great warderobe'.[203] Peter and five men worked for four days beating and airing the furs during the winter months of 1598–99, the equivalent of twenty-four days work: 'Item to Peter Bland our Skynner . . . for beatinge trymmynge and ayringe of our Robes and Apparell at our pallace at Westminster and our Tower of London, with himself and fyve men by the space of foure dayes of our Greate warderobe'.[204]

A few of the bags used for storage were as rich as the furs they protected. Two particularly splendid ones, in purple velvet and shot taffeta, were enriched with gold and pearl embroidery worked by David Smith:

Item delivered to David Smythe our Enbrauderer . . . certen garnishinges for a Bagge of purple velvett to laye our sables in Enbrodered with gold and pearle with laces Buttons and Tassells to the same made verye richelie with gold and pearle certen garnishinges for a Bagge of chaungeable Taffata to laye oure Sables in Enbraudered with gold and silver with Laces buttons and Tassells richely wrought with gold silver and silk all of our great warderobe.[205]

The farthingale makers and their work

Farthingales, the stiffened underskirts which supported women's kirtles and petticoats to achieve the fashionable line, appear to have been seen first in the 1460s or 1470s[206] (Figs 190, 277). Palencia, a courtier, writes that it was with the intention of concealing the results of an indiscretion that Juana of Portugal, Queen of Castile, adopted the fashion, and her ladies followed suit.[207] Juana died in 1475 and Ruth Matilda Anderson notes in *Hispanic Costume 1480–1530* that she has not found any hooped skirts in this Queen's inventory, but that when the Portuguese Princess Isabel received the Burgundian ambassadors in 1473, she wore a crimson velvet gown with green hoops. Isabel brought five 'verdugadas', each with fourteen hoops, from Portugal when she came to Spain on her marriage.[208] Talavera, Queen Isabel's confessor, disapproved of this fashion and in 1477 wrote 'There is another dress which is very ugly . . . the aforesaid dress greatly exceeds and more than greatly exceeds, the natural proportions, and instead of making women beautiful and well-proportioned, makes them ugly, monstrous and deformed until they cease to look like women and look like bells'.[209] As we have already seen, the fashion for hooped skirts apparently came to England with Katherine of Aragon.[210] Princess Elizabeth wore what seems to be the earliest 'verdingale' recorded in the Royal Wardrobe Accounts in 1545, and it may have been made by Walter Fyshe who was certainly her tailor by 1557.[211] Fyshe made farthingales for the Queen until 1567 as part of his work as her tailor.

The cone-shaped line of the Spanish farthingale may be seen in an engraving of a French woman, dated 1556 (Fig. 178). The hem is caught up a little and the bottom hoop of the farthingale is visible. This moderate size of farthingale was the cause of a number of the Queen's waiting women sitting on the ground at an alfresco supper party in May 1559. An Italian observer of the feast at Whitehall Palace described the scene in the garden, under the long wide gallery on the ground floor, hung with gold and silver brocade. The whole gallery was closed in with wreaths of flowers and leaves scenting the air.

The supper hour having arrived . . . The Queen, having washed her hands, and being at table under her canopy, insisted on having M. de Mountmorency at her little table . . . At the large table all the rest of the French lords and gentlemen sat on one side, and on the other all the ladies, of whom there was no small number, and who required so much space on account of the farthingales they wore that there was not room for all; so part of the Privy Chamber ate on the ground on the rushes, being excellently served by lords and cavaliers, who gave them courage and company at their repast.[212]

The English term verdingale, or farthingale, derived from the 'verdugado' which was so named from the Spanish word 'verdugos' used to describe 'smooth twigs put out by a tree that has been cut or pruned' (coppiced),[213] the original stiffening. However, the hoops which held out the early Spanish farthingale worn in England were probably made of rope; this word is used in the wardrobe warrants and 'osiers', or 'withes', do not appear. Fyshe also seems to have used tightly rolled strips of material to make hoops, to judge from the account of 7½ yards of kersey used 'for the ropes' in 1560.[214] Perhaps real ropes were in general use for stiffening and rolls of kersey were simply an alternative to try and give a softer effect. Strips of cotton, tightly rolled, inserted into tucks forming casings provide a most successful stiffening for one surviving petticoat of about 1855–60 (Fig. 278). There is no reason why this method of stiffening a skirt should not have been used for farthingales. In 1563 Fyshe was entered for 'Takinge oute of ij ropes and newe edginge of a verthingale of crimsen Satten striped with gold'.[215] Here there is no mention of kersey.

Sometimes farthingales were made of stiff material, as well as being stiffened with hoops of rope. Walter Fyshe made 'a varthingale of blacke buckeram the ropes covered with kersey the border benethe covered with black kersey'.[216] The linen was probably coated with some kind of black stiffening agent similar to that used for the interlining of the facings of a velvet gown of about 1610 in the Victoria and Albert Museum.[217] The black kersey used for the border, a light-weight wool cloth, would also have helped to stiffen the hem.

278 *Cotton petticoat with eighteen tucks through which are threaded long strips of cotton, tightly rolled to form hoops. c. 1855–60. Helen Larson collection*

Silk farthingales were more usual for the Queen than those of buckram, but probably did not wear so well as linen. Fyshe was employed in 'new making of a varthingale of purple tufte taffata at iij sondry tymes the ropes covered with kersey' in the winter of 1564–65.[218] Here kersey was used for casings. The ropes were not stiff enough, as later in 1565 he was entered 'for putting in new bent ropes into a verthingale of purple tuft taphata and making it stiffer'.[219] 'Bent ropes' were made of grass of reedy or rush-like character, with stiff stems (Fig. 233). Bent seems to have been used first in 1565. Fyshe may have been experimenting, or perhaps saw a farthingale from Spain or France stiffened in this way and copied it.

Farthingales, like other garments, were frequently altered to keep in fashion. Fyshe was employed in 'makinge larger and settinge in a new back into a verthingale of crimsen Satten and for rippinge the same verthingale againe and takinge out the ropes and makinge it limmerer [more supple] and lyter' in 1565.[220] It is not clear if the ropes were cloth rolls, bents or ropes, but obviously they weighed more than the Queen found comfortable. Fyshe was also employed in 'rippinge of a varthingale of Crimson Tuft Taffata and puttinge in new stiff ropes and thre small Ropes' in 1566.[221] It must have been difficult to make farthingales stiff enough to hold out velvet trained gowns trimmed with fur and jewels, without being uncomfortably heavy, until Sibthorpe first used whalebone in 1580. They were frequently unpicked, or 'ripped'.

A farthingale obviously took a considerable amount of time and skill to make. With an increasing number of clothes being made for the Queen and her women, Walter Fyshe's work in

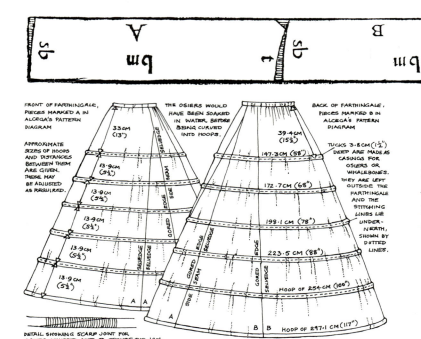

279 (Above) *Verdugada de seda para muger: farthingale of silk for a woman, f. 67 from 'Libro de Geometria, Pratica y Traça', by Juan de Alcega, 1589, Victoria and Albert Museum, London*

280 *Drawings to show the farthingale in Figure 279 when assembled, with tucks for the hoops*

and Bate, would have used pattern shapes similar to those given for the Spanish farthingale in Alcega's *Libro de Geometria, Pratica y Traça* printed in 1589 (Fig. 279):

To cut this silk farthingale one half of the material must be folded over the other half thus making a fold on one side; from the left side, the front [piece A] and then the back [piece B] of the farthingale are cut from a double layer; the rest of the silk should be spread out and doubled full width and then the gores [cuchillos] cut with the widest part of one alongside the narrowest part of the other. It should be noted that the front gores [A] go straight to straight, and the back gores [B] with cross to straight edge, so that the sides will not be on the cross and will not drop. The front of this farthingale has more at the hem than the back. The silk left over may be used for a hem. The length of the farthingale is a bara and a half [49½ inches] and the width round the bottom slightly more than thirteen handspans [palmos], which in my opinion is full enough for this farthingale; if more fullness is required it can be added to this pattern.[232]

The 'bara' was a Castilian measure of 33 inches, so the full length of the farthingale, 49½ inches, (125.7 cm) included an allowance for tucks to be made as casings for ropes, bents or whalebone (Fig. 280). The arrangement of the gores was a practical measure; two edges on the bias, with casings and stiffening across them, would soon sag in wear.[233] It is not clear if the farthingale was made with the hoops outwards, as in the early examples (Figs 277 and 281) or with the casing tucks inside (Fig. 281a).

Robert Sibthorpe spent much of his time in altering and adjusting old farthingales, not always making new ones. He first appears among the warrants in 1571:

Item to Robert Sybthorpe varthingale maker for making of a verthingale of tufte taphata oringe tawny tufte with grene and Ropes of bente bottomed with grene vellat; for making of a Verthingale of fine blak buckeram with Ropes of bente and bottomed with kersey: for making of a Verthingale of tufte taphata blak and grene with Ropes of bente and bottomed with grene vellat wrought with blak lace: and for unrippinge & newe making of a Verthingale of tufte taphata oringe tawnye tufte with grene with bent Ropes all of our greate Guarderobe.[234]

Some of Sibthorpe's work on these farthingales later in the same year may have been due to wear, stiff stems from bent ropes poking through silk taffeta, for example. The black buckram farthingale apparently did not need repairs, being of tougher fabric:

Robert Sybthorpe for undoyinge and newe making agayne and two severall tymes translatinge of a Verthingale of oringe tawny taphata tufte with grene silke with Stuff occupied in the newe making of the

---

this area was taken over by John Bate, who first appears among the warrants in 1567: 'John Bate verthingale maker for making of a verthingale of Crimsin Satten striped edged with Crimsin velvet of our great waredrob'.[222] At the same time he made a purple satin farthingale edged with velvet, altered both, made another 'of Crimsin tuft Taffata edgid with Crimsin velvet of our great warderobe' and supplied 'a hamper to Cary two verthingales in of our great warderobe'. There was another 'wicker Baskett' in 1575[223] but farthingales were not always carried in this way. For example, Robert Sibthorpe made 'a Case of white fryse for verthingalles' in 1572,[224] 'a Case of red buckeram poynted with red rebande' in 1576[225] and 'one Case of yellowe buckeram for a greate Verthingale poynted with lase' in 1582.[226] The points of ribbon and lace (Figs 317 and 318) were to tie across the openings of the cases.

Bate continued to make farthingales for Elizabeth until 1570. In the winter of 1567–68 he was employed in 'translating of a verthingale of white and crymsen taphata tufte with bente Roopes to it at two several tymes: And for making of a verthingale of blak buckeram bottomed with kersey and bente Roopes all of our great Guarderobe'.[227] These farthingales would have received heavy wear and in the following summer Bate made a new buckram farthingale. Fashions were slowly changing and the white and crimson tuft taffeta farthingale was made wider, with an added border of velvet at the hem:

Item to John Bate verthingale maker for making of a verthingale of blak buckeram bottomed with blak kerysey with bent Roopes, silke and ij *d* brode rebande. And for enlarginge of a verthingale of crymsen and white tufte taphata with three yerdes of the same Stuff of our store Receyved of the said Rauf Hope and one elle of crymsen vellat to bottome the same of our greate Guarderobe.[228]

In 1569 Bate made two farthingales of black 'tuke',[229] apparently a type of canvas, which is mentioned in accounts during the late fifteenth and throughout the sixteenth centuries.[230] It was probably similar in texture to buckram.

Bate's last work for the Queen was 'translating of a farthingale of crimsen tufte taphata with newe bent Rope' in 1570.[231] Robert Sibthorpe, the new farthingale maker, worked for the Queen until the end of the reign. He, like Fyshe

281 *Cotton farthingale made from pattern in Figure 279 with six deep tucks holding hoops of osiers on the outside*

281a *The farthingale in Figure 281, with the hoops turned inwards*

282 *Padded rolls, or French farthingales, are being arranged on the wearer. The stitching lines for casings to hold bents or whalebone are clearly shown. Engraving with verses in French and Dutch, c. 1590. Private collection*

same: for undoynge and newe making agayne and once translating of a Verthingale of blak and grene tufte taphata with Stuff occupied in ye newe making of ye same: for translating of a Verthingale of white Satten: for his chardges in mendinge of our verthingalles thre Dayes: And for eightene yerds of greate Bente occupied in the slevis of our Gownes of our greate guarderobe.[235]

It is interesting to note the use of bent for stiffening sleeves as well as farthingales. Bent was also used for sleeve rolls of the type in Figure 25. Typical examples are 'fowre peire of rolls for slevis of bent coverid with white fustian' made in 1574.[236] Four other pairs of rolls made at the same time were 'of cotten coverid with sarceonett'. These were all the work of Walter Fyshe, the tailor.

Bent may have been used from the beginning of the reign, certainly by Walter Fyshe in 1565 and by John Bate thereafter. It was usually described as 'bent ropes'[237] and continued in use together with whalebone from 1580 onwards. In 1572 Robert Sibthorpe provided 26 yards of 'great Bent ropes'[238] and 72 yards of 'great bent' in 1573.[239] This is a typical delivery, with several of 100 yards as, for example, in 1575.[240] It is not clear if 'great' refers to the size of the ropes made from bent, or to the quality of the bent itself, perhaps coarser reeds or rushes. The bent is also described as 'round bottom bent' for a few farthingales from 1576[241] onwards. For example, in 1580 Sibthorpe is employed in 'styffenynge of a verthingale of skye colour taphata the rounde bottom bent coverid with vellat'.[242] This probably meant that the hoop at the hem was circular in cross section. In addition there are several entries for farthingales with round bottom bents 'coverid with vellat with bent', two of the earliest being in 1576.[243] This would seem to indicate that the velvet casing strips were reinforced with bent, probably placed in vertical rows, thus forming a series of rings round the ropes to give extra stiffness. In 1580 Sibthorpe was employed 'fower severall tymes translating and styffenynge of a half verthingale of watchett and strawe colour taphata the bent coverid with like taphata with bent and whalebone to it'.[244] Here the taffeta casings were apparently reinforced with strips of both bent and whalebone. This seems to be the earliest reference to whalebone being used for Elizabeth's farthingales although 'xij bowtis of quhaill horne to be girdis to the

vardingallis the bout v schillingis summa iij pundis . . . Item v balling of quhaill xxxv schillingis' appear in the Queen of Scots' accounts in 1562.[245]

After 1580 whalebone was used in increasing quantities for both 'bodies', or corsets, and sleeve supports as well as farthingales. The warrants do not often specify the exact quantities of whalebone used, typical examples being for 'fower score yerdes of bent and whales bone' in 1582[246] and 'Two hundreth & thirteene yerdes of whale bone & bent' in 1585.[247] However Sibthorpe used only whalebone in 1597 when he altered nine farthingales and was also entered 'for altering & stiffening of vij paier of verthingale slevis with Cxij yardes of whales bone<s> And for iiij^xx vj [86] yards of whales bone delivered to the said William Jones of our great warderobe'.[248] No indication is given of the exact quantity used for individual farthingales.

As we have seen already, Sibthorpe spent much of his time repairing the Queen's farthingales and at first these days were mentioned separately, 'for his chardges in mendinge of our verthingalles thre Dayes'[249] and 'for his charges in mendinge of other verthingalles by the space of foure dayes'[250] in 1571 and 1572. In the Michaelmas warrant of 1572 the distinction is lost, with four new farthingales listed and 'bottomying of a Verthingale of blake taphata: for his chardges vij dayes'.[251] It would seem that the seven days included time for making farthingales as well as altering and mending them.

Sibthorpe spent an increasing amount of time working on the Queen's farthingales: from ten days in the winter of 1572–73[252] and another ten in the summer of 1573[253] it rose to fourteen days in the winter of 1573–74,[254] sixteen days in the summer of 1574,[255] eighteen days each in the winter of 1574–75[256] and summer of 1575,[257] twenty days in the winter of 1575–76,[258] twenty days in the summer of 1576[259] and twenty-four days in the winter of 1576–77.[260] After this the amount of time fluctuates from sixteen days in the summer of 1577[261] to twenty-three days in the summer of 1578[262]dropping to twelve days by the winter of 1580–81,[263] eight days by the summer of 1583[264] and six by the summer of 1585.[265] After Sir Thomas Gorges became Gentleman of the Robes in 1586, the number of days spent by Sibthorpe are not recorded

283 'Queen Elizabeth I'. Illumination from a poem by Georges de la Motthe, a Huguenot refugee, presented to the Queen in 1586. It shows the skirt falling smoothly over padded rolls standing out evenly round the hips. Bodleian Library, Oxford (MS Fr.e.1.)

284 'Mrs Ralph Sheldon', by an unknown artist. English School, c. 1593–95. She wears a black silk damask gown with big sleeves, either bombasted or 'borne out with whalebones' over a kirtle of light brown and pale grey silk, woven in a pattern of acorns, roses and other flowers, with silver metal thread in the weft. The skirt, supported by a half roll, is caught up with a tuck at the front. Private collection

1574 Sibthorpe worked on it again 'undoynge of a verthingale of white Satten and making it longer & bigger and styffenynge it'.[269] In the same warrant he worked on another farthingale, of carnation satin, 'making it lesser and weaker with bent'. In 1575 Sibthorpe is entered for 'styffenynge of a verthingale of strawe colour taphata & byndinge the bent with lase and mendinge the bottom with like colour taphata and bent'.[270] This is probably the farthingale which he altered again later in the same year 'undoyng styffenynge and makinge lesser of a verthingale of strawe colour taphata'.[271] In the winter of 1577–78 he was engaged in 'styffenynge & lyninge in the forepartes of two verthingalles of strawe colour taphata layed on with lase of silke with taphata and bent to it',[272] and later in 1578 'for styffenynge & making lyter of a verthingale of oringe colour taphata two severall tymes the bent coverid with like taphata: for styffenynge of a verthingale of sky colour taphata two severall tymes ye bent coverid with oringe colour vellat, the foreparte lyned three quarters of a yerde depe with like taphata'.[273] In these examples the word 'forepart' refers to the front of the farthingale. The 'stiffening' may be some kind of gum or starch paste brushed over the back of the silk. After the first entry for 'two longe white brushes' in 1575,[274] there are many others in Sibthorpe's warrants. The word 'styffeninge' appears for the first time in 1573.[275]

The first reference to a half farthingale appears in 1580 when Sibthorpe is entered 'for fower severall tymes translatinge and styffenynge of a half verthingale of watchett and strawe colour taphata'.[276] This presumably gave width at the sides and back, leaving the front skirt flat (Fig. 343). Perhaps this evolved from the farthingale 'such as is now used by the French Queen and the Queen of Navarre', sent to Elizabeth by Amyas Paulet in 1577.[277] Some half farthingales were worn with a padded roll tied below the waist to support the fullness of the skirt, thus enlarging the hips. Sibthorpe made 'a half verthingale and a rolle of oringe tawnye & watchett damaske stuffed with cotten woll whale bone & bent' — and there are several other similar entries — in 1581.[278] After this the rolls are entered separately; typical entries include 'making two Rolles of yellowe buckeram with whales bone' in 1585,[279] 'making of thre rolles of hollande clothe with wyers bounde with reben'[280] later in the same year and 'making of a Rolle of starched buckeram with whales bone' in 1586 (Fig. 282).[281] Descriptions do not always make the distinction between fathingale and sleeve rolls, although pairs of rolls would seem to be for sleeves, and are usually made by the tailor. William Jones made 'six payer of Rolles for the ruffes of slevis with bentes coverid with fustian styffenid with buckeram' in 1582.[282] These were presumably to support gathered sleeve-heads, or 'ruffes of the slevis' (Fig. 217).

in the warrants. Judging from the amount of work each half year from 1586 to the end of the reign, it would probably have varied between as little as three days during the summer of 1596,[266] when Sibthorpe newly covered three farthingales of straw colour taffeta, to about twenty days in the summer of 1594,[267] when he made three farthingales, newly covered three others and altered and enlarged three more.

Farthingale shapes were adjusted to suit the changing fashions and, probably, individual gowns. Sibthorpe often carried out alterations to stiffen or to reduce stiffening in farthingales. In 1573 he is entered 'for undoynge of a verthingale of white Satten & making it weaker'.[268] The Queen seems to have changed her mind after wearing it, as in

285 'Lady Throgmorton', by an unknown artist, English School, c. 1600. She wears a doublet, or 'square bodies', and matching petticoat of silk, loosely pleated into a flounce over the semi-circled farthingale. Dents appear in the pleats where the silk is caught with pins underneath. Present whereabouts unknown

286 Costumes for a ballet at the French Court, showing French farthingales stiffened with bents or whalebone, giving the drum shape to the skirt. Watercolour drawing, 1625. Bibliothèque Nationale, Paris

The first 'greate verthingale' appears in the warrants in 1582.[283] It was made of 'orínge colour & purple taphata the bottom bent coveríd with orínge colour vellat with bent and whales bone'. The term 'great' indicated the ever increasing circumference of the Spanish farthingale (Figs 47 and 50). More 'great' farthingales were made, altered and stiffened in the next three years. The last entry seems to be in 1585,[284] after which there are only entries for 'half' farthingales, with an occasional farthingale which is not described as either 'great' or 'half'. The 'great' farthingale with its cone shape and wide hem would have stood out equally all round the body. The drum-shaped farthingale in the Ditchley portrait (Fig. 71) may have been described as a 'half' farthingale, although very large, as it seems to be fairly shallow at the front.

Skirts fall smoothly over padded rolls standing out evenly round the hips during the 1580s (Fig. 283). It seems likely that the flounce recorded in so many paintings of the 1590s and after, evolved from a loose tuck made to shorten the skirt front when worn over a half roll. This stood out at the back and sides and was described as a semi-circled farthingale by Falstaff in Shakespeare's The Merry Wives of Windsor. A skirt made to hang over a complete roll would have to be tucked up for several inches at the front if the other style of roll was worn instead (Fig. 284).

The wheel or drum-shaped farthingale became increasingly popular in the early 1590s. This style had an arrangement of bents and/or whalebone standing out from the waist and possibly hoops round the hem as well. The resultant hard edge (Fig. 106) was often disguised by pinning the skirt at the edge of the frame to make soft pleats (Fig. 285). It has been suggested, from the evidence of a few portraits, that there may sometimes have been a separate pleated flounce, or upper skirt, attached to the bodice, extending to cover the frame edge. This would have given a similar effect to the pinned pleats and a single entry for the 'nether skirts of a petticoat'[285] in the Stowe inventory might tend to support this theory. However, the term appears in the 1570s, before the fashion for the drum-shaped farthingale.[286] There are no surviving specimens to confirm the existence of the separate flounce and cleaning and restoration of pictures has often blurred the evidence. A watercolour drawing of the 'Entrée des Esperducattes' shows dancers wearing French farthingale frames (Fig. 286). They are following Jacqueline, Fairy of the Mad People, in the Ballet des Fées des Forêts de Saint Germain, presented at the Louvre in Paris, on 11 February 1625. Many noblemen at Court and King Louis XIII himself took part in it. The 'Esperducattes' are 'those who are difficult to deceive' and here six male dancers mock the deception practised by women wearing farthingales, revealing the framework beneath on the left. All the dancers wear green bodices decorated with white braid, white scarves and full black sleeves. The farthingale frames are black, probably made of taffeta, and the casings holding whalebones or bents may be seen clearly. The black skirts, probably of taffeta or satin, are carefully arranged in even pleats from the waist to the edge of the farthingale, falling loosely below. This wheel or drum-shaped frame probably developed when rolls padded with cotton, worn over Spanish farthingales, grew too large and heavy for comfort and could not give the extreme width without sagging. If stiffened only with wire, whalebone or bents, large rolls may have been too rounded and springy to give the required line (Fig. 282).

The term 'French farthingale' seems to have been used for both padded roll and drum-shaped farthingale. Mr Starkie's eldest daughter, who was possessed by a spirit in 1597, called out to the Devil: 'My lad, I will have a French farthingale, it shall be finer than thine; I will have it low before and high behind and broad on either side that I may laye mine arms upon it'.[287] The description of this French farthingale is similar to the type worn in Figure 71, which would have been made with a frame of whalebone and/or bents. By 1611 when Cotgrave gave his definition of 'A French Vardingale; or (more properly) the kind of roll used by such women as weare (or are to weare) no Vardingales' and 1617 when Minsheu wrote 'a role to weare under women's gownes a French verdingale', the drum-shaped frame may no longer have been described as specifically French. The warrants for the Wardrobe of Robes during Elizabeth's reign are of no help, as neither farthingales nor rolls are described as a French fashion in them, any more than early farthingales are described as a Spanish fashion. Henry Fitz-Jeoffery writes of 'Your Curles, your Purles, Perriwigs, your Whale bone wheels' in 1617,[288] but does not describe them as a French fashion. Linthicum suggests that the drum-shaped farthingale is an Italian mode, as it is thus designated in a reference to 'farthingales and frounces' in an undated play *Monsieur Thomas* .[289] However, this term does not appear in the warrants, nor do farthingales of this shape appear in Italian paintings of the period.

Cappers, hatters and hoodmakers

Raphael Hammond, the Queen's capper, is listed in the Great Wardrobe Accounts and warrants for the Wardrobe of Robes from the beginning of the reign.[290] At the time of the coronation he was paid 'for making of hattes for the Q: Majesties use xliijs viijd [44s. 8d]'[291] and he worked for her until 1583,[292] when he seems to have retired. Hammond was entitled to wear livery with the other artificers: 'for iij yardes of red clothe to make a coate for the said Raffe hammond and ij yardes of velvet to garde the same For lynyng makinge and enbrauderinge of our lettres of oure great warderobe'.[293] Hammond's title changes a few times before he is finally described as 'capper'. In the Michaelmas warrant of 1562 he appears as 'oure Myllener',[294] in both warrants for 1563 as 'oure haberdasher'[295] and in both warrants for 1564 as 'oure Capper'.[296] The title changes to 'our Hatmaker' in the Lady Day warrant of 1565,[297] but in the next warrant[298] the term 'our Capper' is used again, and he is usually thus described thereafter. It is quite clear from the records that Hammond made hats at the time of Elizabeth's coronation. In 1562 he is entered for making 'iiij ridinge hoodes ij of blac velvet and ij of Blac Taffata Enbrodered with Blac silke ij oz cheyne Frendge for the same hoodes, for making a hatt of Blac velvet enbrodered with black silke lyned with Black Taffata Pynked and for a Felt for the same hatt all of our great warderobe'.[299] The felt would have supported the shape. In 1563 (as 'oure haberdasher') he supplied 'a hatt Band of Damaske gold and for a plume of whit and Blacke Fethers with a Toppe of fyne Egrettes Fethers in it'[300] and, later in the same year, four velvet caps:

for makinge of iiij velvett cappes for pynking the Lynynges, for trymmyng the gold worke with black Sipres of the same cappes. ij fyne black Fethers for the same cappes, for cutting shallower and newe making of a hatt of black velvet for a band of damaske silver and blac silke and for a plume of white & black fethers, with a toppe of white egrettes Fethers all of oure great warderobe.[301]

In 1564, when he is described as 'oure Capper',[302] Hammond altered two hats which had presumably been gifts presented to Elizabeth, 'thone of blac silke and silver wroughte allover with damaske purles of silver thother of red silk and gold'. He put 'Tincell & lace undre the coveringe of the same' and edged 'one of the same hattes with blac Silke and silver And silver purles and silke and silver lace'. He pinked the taffeta linings for both hats and they were decorated with 'ij plumes of Fethers thone white and black thother redd and yellowe withe two toppes of egrettes fethers in them trymed withe silver and spangells of silver'. Hammond also supplied 'two Felttes for the same hattes, and two boxes to putt them in of our great warderobe'. At the same time he made two velvet caps with pinked linings, trimmed with black feathers. As may be seen, he was a skilled craftsman dealing with several types of head-wear and a number of different materials. His work has elements of the crafts of both tailor and silkwoman. It is interesting that the term 'milliner' is used for Hammond in 1562. It appears again at the end of Elizabeth's reign, but is then applied to Richard French,[303] whose work is closely related to that of silkman and silkwoman.

William Cookesbury supplied caps and hats in Hammond's place from 1584,[304] but is not described as 'our capper' at that time. He does not appear to have had livery at first, but is entered as 'one of our artificers' in a warrant for livery at Michaelmas 1586[305] and as 'our capper' in 1587.[306] Deliveries of material, such as nine yards of velvet and eight yards of taffeta to make six caps and two hats in the Lady Day warrant of 1584,[307] were made to Cookesbury until 1587[308] and he is mentioned as having had items delivered to him from Robert Mountague, the silkman, for the Queen's use in 1588[309] but no caps or hats are described. There are no specific entries for him in the warrants for the Wardrobe of Robes from this time until after Elizabeth's death. He then appears in the second warrant of James I's reign as 'our haberdasher' with a very large entry of splendid hats for the new King:

for xvij blacke bever hattes lyned with riche taphata of our store with treble blacke sipers bandes and plumes of blacke fethers to them: one hatte of black bever richlie enbrodered with golde & silver with a band likewise richelie enbrodered & a plume of white feathers to it. one hatte of ashe colour bever lyned with grene taphata with a band enbrodered with venice gold & silver, & a plume of fethers to it. one Cappe of blacke vellat with a plume of white fethers & a byrde of Paradise in it with a band of vellatt to sett Juelles in for our owne wearing. five bever hattes for our said sonne the Prince viz one pynke colour, one purple, one white, & two ashe colour all enbrodered with venice golde & silver, the bands likewise enbrodered with plumes of feathers of sundry colours and Toppes of the byrde of Paradise all lyned with taphata of lyke colour unto the Hattes of our store. one Cappe of blacke vellatt with a band of like vellatt to set Juelles in with a plume of white fethers and a top of the byrde of Paradise and for thre boxes to carrie his said hattes in & for lyning one bever hatt with taphata of our store all the reste of our great warderobe.[310]

Later in the same warrant Cookesbury supplied 'one Hatt of Ashe colour bever lyned with greene taffata, with a band enbraudered and plume of fethers to it'[311] which seems to match one already sent to the King. Perhaps this was for the Prince or Queen Anne, although this is not specified. There were in addition 'two Hatts thone ashe colour thother black felt enbraudered with rich Bands, likewise enbraudered lined with taphata enbraudered and whit fethers. for two black feltes lined with vellat with treble bands of Sipers to them. And two black felts lyned with taffata with treble sipers bandes to them all of our great warderobe'.[312]

Although Cookesbury does not seem to have done very much work in the way of hat or cap making for Elizabeth during the later years of her reign, he continued to work for the Removing Wardrobe of Beds, as in this example in 1595:

Item to William Cookesburye for dying and washinge of seven plumes of fine fethers conteyninge thre skore fethers with twelve fine fethers and three dozen and sixe toppes of egrettes fethers to performe the sayd seven plumes for one bedsteede . . . and for one new plume of fine fethers of divers colours conteyning x single fethers and a fether to make the toppe with six egretts fethers and a bone pipe to it belonging . . . to sett them in.[313]

Hammond was as skilled in working with feathers as Cookesbury. He washed and dyed some elaborate plumes supplied to the Queen's stables in 1567:

Item to Raphaell Hamonde our Capper for makinge of x verye Great plumes of whyte and blewe Fethers for our Cooche and horses and for wasshinge and dyinge of them all trymed with gold silver and spangelles and for trymmynge of xl of the same Fethers with a Chayne lace of venice gold and xij newe whyt Fethers to furnyshe the[m] with all and for makynge and trymmynge them with Gold silver and spangelles and viij Sockettes of Latten and a Cheste to kepe the same plumes in all of our Great Wardrobe.[314]

Although warrant entries for the cappers are not always very detailed, one in 1565 shows how Hammond used feathers decorated with spangles with a top of egret's feathers for trimming the Queen's hats:

Item to Raphaell Hamonde our Hatmaker for mending and lyning of a riche hat with taphata beinge Pinked for a Plumbe of xvj fethers with a tope of egrittes trimmid with a button of damaske golde and for making and trimminge of the same plumbe with venice golde and spangles: for lyning of a hatt of purple taphata pinked: for new making and mendinge of fyve plumbes of fethers belonginge to fyve hattes and for makinge of a velvet cappe lyned with taphata pinked of our great warderobe.[315]

In the same warrant Hammond also made hats for Jack Grene, the Queen's fool, one trimmed with fourteen feathers of assorted colours decorated with silver spangles:

Item for lyninge of ij hattes with crimsin taphata for our said foule with one plume of feathers: for one hate conteyninge xiiij fethers of diverse colours & for making and trimming the same feathers with silver spangles of our great warderobe.[316]

Fairly frequent deliveries of velvet and taffeta were made to Hammond and Cookesbury, such as this one in 1573: 'Delyverid to Raphaell Hammonde our Capper nyne yerdes and a half of blak vellat and fyve yerdes three quarters of blak taphata employed upon eight vellat Cappes One hatt: and one Capp all of taphata'.[317] Unfortunately the warrants do not always specify exactly how many hats and caps were made from the lengths of material and there are only a few entries such as 'for one yerde di of tawny vellat Delyvrid to ye said Raphaell Hammonde to make us a hatte' in 1575[318] which give precise information. One and a half yards (137 cm) of velvet probably twenty inches (50.8 cm) wide would be sufficient to make a hat of the type seen in Figure 288. It seems likely from surviving examples of headwear[319] that all were based on a circular shape darted or gathered into a brim, the cap lying flat on the head (Fig. 221) and the hat raised to form a crown, either with soft fullness (Figs 174 and 194) or pleated

287 'Elizabeth Cornwallis, Lady Kyston, aged 26', by George Gower, 1573. She wears a feather-trimmed black hat with a high crown and jewelled hatband. Formerly at Hengrave Hall, Tate Gallery, London

neatly over a felt or some other stiff foundation (Figs 226 and 289). In 1576 Hammond had a delivery of 6½ yards of velvet and 7½ yards of taffeta 'by him employed upon hats and Cappes for us and in lyninge & turvinge of sundry our hattes & Cappes by him alterid'[320] and in 1579 another 8½ yards of black velvet and 9¼ yards of black taffeta 'by him employed in making of nyne Cappes & turvynge & lyninge of sundrye hattes & Cappes'.[321] The term 'turf' was used for the turn over, turn-up or facing of a cap, hood or hat. In 1592 Greene describes 'a beaver hatte turft with velvet, so quaintly as if he had been some Espagnolo trickt up'.[322] These brim facings would have been replaced when marked with pulling the hat on and off. It is not clear, but Hammond probably used both velvet and taffeta for his 'turvynge'. Repairs were also carried out by the Queen's embroiderer on some occasions: 'for half a yerde of blak vellat one quarter of a yerde of purple Satten and half one yerde of purple taphata Delivered to David Smyth to repayer our enbrauderid hattes'.[323]

Women's hats (Figs 287 and 288) followed the masculine styles which Stubbes roundly condemned in his *Anatomie of Abuses* in 1583:

Wherefore to begin first with their Hattes. Sometimes they we[a]re them sharp on the crowne, peaking up like a sphere, or shafte of a steeple, standing a quarter of a yard above the crowne of their heades, some more, some lesse, as please the phantasies of their mindes. Othersome be flat, and broad on the crowne, like the battlements of a

288 'A young lady called Elizabeth Knollys', panel painting by an unknown artist, English school, 1577. She wears a high-crowned black hat trimmed with a jewelled spray of flowers, feather and hatband of pearls set with jewels. National Trust, Montacute House, Somerset

289 'Sic nobilis femina vel equitant, vel obambulant': in this fashion noble women either ride or walk up and down. The mask

has holes cut for the eyes. The high-crowned hat is trimmed with a wide hatband and a feather. From 'Omnium Poene Gentium Habitus' by Abraham de Bruyn, 1581. Private collection

290 'Mary Tudor', a silver gilt medal by Jacopo da Trezzo, 1555. The side view of a French hood shows a coif tied under the chin and the veil hanging down at the back. British Museum, London

house. An other sort have round crownes, sometimes with one kinde of bande, sometime with an other, nowe blacke, now white, now russet, now red, now greene, now yellowe, now this, nowe that, never content with one colour, or fashion two dayes to an ende . . . Some are of silke, some of velvet, some of taffetie, some of sarcenet, some of wooll, and which is more curious, some of a certaine kind of fine haire, far fetched and deare bought you may bee sure . . . he is no account or estimation amongst men, if hee have not a velvet, or a taffetie Hatte, and that muste bee pincked and cunningly carved of the beste fashion . . . of late there is a new fashion of wearing their Hattes sprung up amongst them, which they father upon the Frenchmen, namely, to weare them without bandes . . . An other sort (as phantasticall as the rest) are content with no kind of Hatt, without a great bunche of feathers of diverse and sundrie colours, peaking on toppe of their heades, not unlyke (I dare not say) Cockscombes.[324]

After 1587 it is not quite clear who made the Queen's caps and hats. John Parr was entered in the Michaelmas warrant for 1602 'for pulling out a hat of gold net, with white tiffany, and sett with large round spangles and hanging spangles and tufted with carnacion silke and on every raising a spangle with a purle in it. tenne ounces di of plates round spangles hanging spangles & purles spent on the same worke'[325] but the maker's name is not given. Perhaps it was a gift, like a number of others, and as Elizabeth, Dowager Lady Russell, pointed out about two which she had presented in 1600, 'though I say it, fine hats'.[326] The Queen wore a considerable variety of headwear, apart from the riding hoods, caps and hats supplied by her cappers. She simply may not have required Cookesbury to make any more, unless what work he did was paid for at the Privy Purse

and the records have not survived. He may well have made all the hats presented to Elizabeth as gifts, as he would have known her head size.

Hoods, French hoods, cornets, biliments or habilliaments, creppins, cauls and coifs are all mentioned in the warrants, but these items were not made by the Queen's cappers. The Ladies and Gentlewomen of the Bedchamber and Privy Chamber seem to have been responsible for both making and arranging a considerable number of them. For example in the Michaelmas warrant of 1568 lengths of four yards each of velvet and satin, three yards of taffeta and two yards of sarsenet, all in black, were delivered to Lady Cobham for the Queen's use 'to make us hoodes and mufflers' while at the same time four yards each of black satin and velvet, three yards of black taffeta and ⅜ yard of crimson velvet were sent to Lady Carewe for more hoods and two yards each of black and orange sarsenet to Dorothy Abington 'to lyne Cawles'.[327] In 1570 four yards of black velvet were delivered to Lady Cobham 'to make habyllyamentes' with two yards of black taffeta to line them [328] and in 1571 four yards of white satin were delivered to Mary Ratcliffe 'to line our Crippens and habilliamentes'.[329] Over the next nine years Mary received further three yard lengths of white satin and in 1578 'six yerdes of Satten white and blak', 'to make us habilliamentes'.[330] Blanche Parry, although in charge of the Queen's books, apparently also helped, as on one occasion 'one yerde half quarter of satten of sundrye colours' was delivered to her ''to be used aboute the attyre of our hedde'.[331] These are typical deliveries throughout the 1560s and 1570s.

291 *Effigy of Dorothy Vernon, wife of Sir John Manners, showing hair piled high in front of a French hood with jewelled billiment, 1584. All Saints Parish Church, Bakewell, Derbyshire*

292 *Side view of effigy in Figure 291, showing veil hanging down at the back*

293 *Effigy of Margaret Tayleboys, wife of Sir George Vernon, showing veil of French hood hanging over the pillow, 1567. All Saints Parish Church, Bakewell, Derbyshire*

It should perhaps be mentioned here that the Queen's women also lined and made mufflers and scarves for her. The mufflers were to wrap round the lower part of the face when on horseback to stop the traveller from breathing very cold air. They might also be used for a protection against dust. A dialogue written in 1591 between two travellers going towards London describes the conditions. The first traveller says 'It is very dustie: the dust doth put out mine eyes'. His companion replies 'Take this taffeta to put before your face, and it will keepe you from the dust and from the sunne'.[332] A mask might also be worn to protect the face (Fig. 289), as Stubbes described:

When thei use to ride abroade, thei have visors made of Velvet . . . wherwith thei cover all their faces, havying holes made in them against their eyes, Whereout they look So that if a man that knew not their guise before, should chaunce to meete one of them he would thinke he met a Monster or a Devil: for face he can see none, but two broade holes aginst her eyes, with glasses in them.[333]

Scarves were used to cover the face and neck as well, but were usually of finer material than the mufflers and often richly embroidered. In some cases plain sarsenet scarves may have been used as an early form of handbag: 'for vij yerdes of doble sarceonett to make Skarfes to carye our necessaries'[334] and 'for thre Skarfes of sarceonett of sundrye colours to carye our necessaryes in'.[335]

As well as all hoods, cauls and habilliaments made and arranged by the Queen's women, there were also professional hood makers working for her. One of the earliest entries among the warrants is for a woman in 1573, 'Ellin Webbe for

making of six whoodes and six Cornettes of Satten and vellat'.[336] A hood, or French hood, may be seen from the front (Figs 4 and 291), from the side (Figs 290, 292 and 293) and from the top (Figs 294 and 295). A cornet according to Randle Holme, was a 'Coif with long Ears, tyed under the Chin, and hanging down deep to the top of the Breast'.[337] The next hood maker mentioned in the warrants is Charles Deberney in 1574 'for making of six whoddes for us'.[338] He appears again in 1575 'for making of six whoddes and six upper habilliamentes lyned with blak Satten'.[339] In the following year he made 'six frenche hoodes: vj Cornettes: and vj Muffelers of vellat lyned with taphata'.[340] Later in 1576 he made 'foure whoddes of vellat lyned with vellat & vj upper habilliamentes of vellat lyned with satten'.[341] A little more detail is given about items in Deberney's next delivery in 1578, 'one whodde one Cornett one upper habilliament of vellat garnesshid with silke sipers with like sipers & vellat for a gyrdell and a Juell of our great guardrobe'.[342] The girdle seems to have been made to match the head-dress. Deberney made his last delivery in 1579 of 'thre whoddes thre upper billementes of vellat with gatherid sipers to them: for making two Muffelers: and for two borders of blak sipers gatherid & rufte with blak bugell buttons of our great guarderobe'.[343] The 'borders' were probably small frills of the type in Figure 38. The 'black bugell buttons' may have been markers to judge the depth of the 'ruffes' or pleats[344] (Fig. 29). Deberney does not seem to have been one of the artificers, entitled to wear livery, but simply supplied his wares to the Wardrobe of Robes.

The next hood supplier is another woman, in 1580: 'Item to Margerett Barney for fower Whoddes fower Cornettes Twelve

294 *Top view of French hood in Figure 293, showing the ruffled edge of the coif beneath*

295 *Another view of French hood in Figure 293*

296 *Detail from Figure 46, showing Queen Elizabeth I wearing a hair net set with pearls, c. 1590. Pollok House, Glasgow*

297 *(Above) 'Queen Elizabeth I', silver medal commemorating the Spanish Armada, 1588. She wears 'an attire for the head', set with jewels. British Museum, London*

billementes & a Crippen Delyverid to the Ladye Leighton to our use' and 'thre Whoddes and Two blak borders Delyverid to Katheryn Newton to our use'.[345] In the Michaelmas warrant for 1583 there is an entry 'to Margerett Sketuze for eight whoddes of vellat (for us) half one elle of serceonett; And for makinge of two upper habilliamentes Delyverid to Brigett Choworthe to our use'.[346] This seems likely to be the same Margaret Barney, now married. She continued to make hoods and other items for the Queen until 1593:[347] her name is spelt variously Sketuse, Schets, Sketts, Sehtz and Schetz. Three hoods she made in 1584 were supplied with 'crymsen sarceonett to wrappe them in Delyverid to Bridgett Chaworthe to our use'.[348] Later in the same year, another two hoods were sent with a box;[349] presumably they were packed in it, to prevent creasing.

Some of the hoods which Margaret made in 1585 were lined with flannel for warmth: 'Item to Margerett Sehtz for fower whoddes of blak vellat with satten sarceonett flanell and vellat to lyne them'.[350] In the same warrant she supplied 'thre Cawles of heare lyned with taphata and for two payer of Rolles Delyverid to Bridgett Carre to our use'.[351] These cauls were nets made of knotted human hair. One decorated with pearls may be seen standing just above the Queen's hair in Figure 296. The rolls delivered to Bridget Carr were probably of tightly packed hair held together inside nets, making foundations to support the natural hair beneath a French hood, or a caul. In 1587 Margaret seems to have altered these four black velvet hoods as well as supplying four new ones and two creppins, which were nets or cauls to cover the hair: 'Item to

298 *A white linen drawn work coif, with additional embroidery in black silk and gold thread with spangles. A ribbon would have been passed through the worked loops at the bottom of the coif to pull it in beneath the hair. Royal Museum of Scotland, Edinburgh*

298a *Detail of drawn work and loops in Figure 298*

298b *Detail of decorative seam on top of coif in Figure 298*

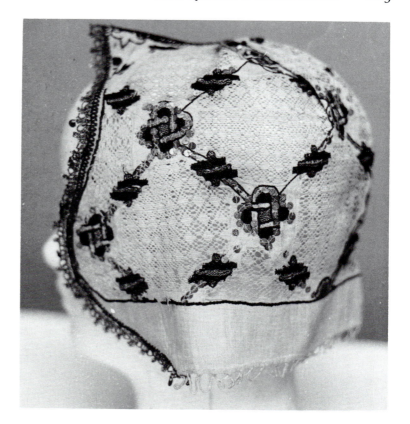

Margerett Schetz for two whoddes of blak vellat with satten & sarceonett, for Two whoddes of blak taphata lyned with satten. for two crippens of venice golde and for altering of iiij whoddes with vellat satten & flanell to perfourme them'.[352] Philip Gawdy described these different styles of head-dress at Court (Fig. 297) in a letter to his sister in 1589:

For the manner of their hoodes at the courte, some weare cripins some weare none. Some weare sattin of all collors with their upper border and some wear none. Some of them weare this daye all these fashions, and the nexte without. So that I fynd nothing more certayne than their uncertaynte, which makes me forbeare to sende you anything further of myne owne devise.[353]

This letter explains why it is so difficult to identify the different parts of women's head-dresses in portraits, particularly when they can only be seen from the front.

In addition to the work of Charles Deberney and Margaret Sketts, Roger Mountague, the silkman supplied cauls, creppins, coifs and riding shadows. Some examples included in 1585 'Sixe fine knotted Cawles wrought with cheine stiche' and 'Two ridinge Shadowes of fine white sipers edgid rounde aboute with golde & silver lase with stringes of golde and silver brede'.[354] In 1586 Mountague supplied 'Two frenche crippens of golde & silver'[355] and also carried out the work of 'translating & mendinge of an attyer for the hed of white nettworke florished with venice silver & for thre oz iij quarters of silver lase to edge the same rounde aboute'.[356] The riding shadows are described by Florio as 'bone graces, shadowes, vailes or launes that women use to weare on their foreheads for the sunne'.[357] The attire for the head was possibly an elaborately arranged veil of network.

In 1587 Mountague supplied 'one thowsande blak Jett bugell droppes for viij doble frenche Creppins of venice silver and venice golde & silver' and 'vj fine white knotted Cawles wrought with cheine stiche'[358] presumably to replace those ordered in 1585 which would have worn out. There were also 'two Coyves of fine hollande cloth wrought allover with blak silke drawen worke overcast & edgid with blak & white silke lase'[359] (Figs 298 and 298a). Later in the same year Mountague supplied 'vj doble Cawles of heare colour stiched cloth lyned with heare colour & blak taphata sarceonett garnished with stringes of heare colour silke lase the stiched cloth for thre of them of our store'[360] and 'two ridinge Shadowes thone of doble white sipers thother of taphata sarceonett both edgid rounde aboute with golde and silver lase with stringes of venice golde and silver breded lase'.[361] The latter were presumably to replace the two shadows ordered in 1585. Mountague was entered for some rather more elaborate shadows in 1599: 'Six chynne shadowes of cutt Lawne gathered in ruffes at the Toppes, edged with silver twiste lace and stringes of haire coloure and white silke haire lacinge riben'.[362] Possibly these were worn for riding too. As they are described as chin shadows they would seem to have covered only chin and neck, where the riding shadow may have been a longer article.

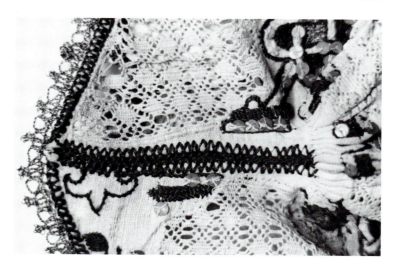

Similar deliveries of creppins, cauls and other items were made in 1588: 'two doble frenche crepens of golde and silver',[363] 'two Cawles of heare wrought with knottes of heare',[364] 'six fine white knotted Cawles wrought with cheine stiche',[365] 'two Cawles of fine nettworke',[366] 'one Coyfe of fine camerike wrought with blak silke edgid with white silke lase',[367] 'one forehed cloth of camerike wrought with blak silke drawne worke edgid with blak and white silke nedle-worke lase',[368] 'Eight doble frenche Crepens of silver and golde & silver'[369] and 'Two single frenche Crepens of silver'.[370] The changing fashions probably account for the fact that, after Margaret Sketts' last order in 1593, Mountague, the silkman, and later Dorothy Speckard, a silkwoman, supplied all the headwear worn by the Queen, with the exception of items presented as gifts. Cauls, coifs and 'attires for the head' in the 1590s were made of network, lawn and other fine materials, delicately arranged and often trimmed with lace and silk braids, all within the province of silkman and silkwoman. Elizabeth favoured wigs dressed increasingly high at the front and these too were within the province of silkman and silkwoman. Roger Mountague, for example, supplied 'vij heads of haire to make attiers, flowers, and other devices for Attiers, Two periwigs of haire' in 1592,[371] 'iij lardge, fayre heddes of heaire iiij perewigges of heaire' in 1595[372] and 'vj faire heddes of heire' in 1601[373] and Dorothy Speckard supplied 'six heades of haire' in 1602[374] and another six in 1603.[375]

The hosiers

Henry Herne is described as 'our hosier' in the warrants for the Wardrobe of Robes from the beginning of the reign[376] until 1592,[377] when he either died or retired. Like the other artificers he was supplied with 'Thre yerdes of red cloth to make hym a Coat and two yerdes of vellat to garde the same, for lyninge making and embrauderinge of our letters all of our great warderobe'.[378] Herne made hose of both cloth and linen, cut on the cross to stretch round the leg, and there are a few examples of silk hose, some of sarsenet and others knitted. An example of the variety of work is given in the warrant for Michaelmas 1562: 'To henry hern oure hosier for makinge xv paire of Clothe hose stitched in the toppes & clockes with an Irishe stitche and lyned in the toppes with Sarsenet xij paire of lynnen hose & ij paire of Silke knytte hose'.[379]

Ralph Abnett, another hosier, supplied hose of the knitted silk variety between 1590[380] and 1597.[381] Apparently he did not make linen hose as between 1592, when Herne stopped supplying them, and 1597 they were made by the Queen's tailor: 'William Jones ... for making of six paire of doble linnen hose of fine hollande clothe of our great Warderobe'.[382] Abnett was not described as 'our hosier' and neither, apparently, did he receive livery. He was followed by Robert Morland, whose first work in 1597 is given in great detail. The latter also took over the making of linen hose from William Jones:

Item to Roberte Morland for seaven payre of newe silke hose of diverse colours, the clockes richelie wroughte withe Gold silver and silke: For scowringe of foure paire of white worsted hose and newe knyttinge them in the feete, the Clockes richelie wrought with gold silver and silke: For scowringe of foure paire of silke hose, the clockes of one paire richelie wroughte with gold silver & silke: For makinge of seaven payre of doble lynnen hose: For plushinge of one

paire of orrendge coloure silke hose, & refresshinge the colours with dyinge: For two paire of newe silke hose made in Gamasshes fasshion: For plushinge of two paire of gamashes, and for eighte paire of newe worsted hose and workinge them richelie in the clockes with gold silver and Silke.[383]

Like Abnett, Morland does not seem to have worn livery and is simply described as 'hosier', not 'our hosier', although in the last warrant of the reign, when the suppliers and craftsmen were paid by James I, he is described as 'our said Sisters hosier'.[384]

Henry Herne supplied the Queen with a few pairs of silk stockings and numerous pairs of both double and single linen hose and cloth hose in regular deliveries from the beginning of the reign until 1577,[385] when worsted knitted stockings from the silkwoman, Alice Mountague, supplanted the cloth variety in the Queen's favour. He seems to have made hose in the sense of both breeches and stockings for men as well: in the Lady Day warrant of 1565 he is entered

for makinge of a payre of Hose of russet clothe for Jacke our said foule with lyninges of lynnen and wollen welted alover: for making of a payre of sloppes of fryse trimmed with red frendge: for making of a paire of botehose of grene clothe trimmed with red silke: for making of a payre of stockinges of grene cloth stiched upon with silke of sondry colors: for makinge of a payre of stockinges of red clothe stiched alover with yellow silke and for makinge of a payre of stockinges of grene clothe trimed with lace of silke of sondry collors with settinge on of red sarceonet lyned with red kersey all of our great warderobe.[386]

The term 'hose' as used in this context probably refers to a pair of trunk hose of russet cloth. They may have resembled the pluderhose worn by a German fool in Figure 299. Slops were large breeches, apparently worn first by clowns and later adopted by fashionable men. Rowlands wrote in 1600:

> When Tarlton clown'd it in a pleasant vaine
> With conceites, did good opinions gaine
> Upon the stage, his merry humours shop,
> Clownes knew the Clowne, by his great clownish slop
> But now th'are gull'd, for present fashion sayes,
> Dicke Tarltons part, Gentlemans breeches plaies:
> In every streete where any Gallant goes,
> The swagg'ring Sloppe, is Tarltons clownish hose.[387]

Thomas Wright gives further evidence of Tarleton's slops being adopted for fashionable wear a year later: 'Sometime I have seen Tarleton play the clowne and use no other breeches than such sloppes or slivings as now many gentlemen weare: they are almost capable of a bushel of wheate; and if they be of sack clothe, they would serve to carrie mawlt to the mill. This absurd, clownish and unseemly attire, only by custome now is not misliked, but rather approved'.[388] Jack's green cloth boothose, provided with the slops, may have been worn with boots, but Cotgrave defines 'Triquehouse' as 'A boot-hose or a thicke hose worne instead of a boot' in 1611.

More detail is given about the trimming for another pair of slops which Herne made for Jack in 1567. There is no indication of the colour used for them, but 'blew and tawny fustian enaples' was used for a hat made at the same time, so presumably they matched:

To the said Henry Herne for makinge of a paire of sloppes for Jack Grene our foole of Fustian of naples with lyninge buckeram and cotton laid over with fourty yardes of Cruell frendge and ij paire of red and grene stockes. One paire of lynnen bootehose trymmed with lace and for ij paire of Cloth hose with lynen lyninges and Cotton and

299 *A German jester. Woodcut from 'Eygentliche Beschreibung Aller Stände auff Erden' by Jost Amman and Hans Sachs 1568. Private collection*

300 *White linen stockings, or hose, with tops embroidered with coloured silks and silver and gold metal thread. Possibly made*

without feet, or removed because they were worn out. Italian, late sixteenth century. Metropolitan Museum of Art (Rogers Fund, 1910), New York

301 *Knitted red silk stockings and silk garters, in which Eleanora of Toledo was buried, 1562. Palazzo Pitti, Florence*

Canvas and pocketes of fustian beinge trymmed with lace alover all of our great Warderobe.[389]

Herne also made some items for another fool in 1572: 'a paire of Canyons lyinge with canvas heare stockes frenge and pockettes for hoyden the foole of our great guarderobe'.[390]

Sixteenth century men's hose consisted of two parts: the tailor usually seems to have made the upper part described by Stubbes in 1583 as 'Hosen, whiche as they be of divers fashions, so are they of sundry names. Some be called Frenche hose, some Gallie and some Venetians'.[391] The hosier made the lower part, which may be variously described as canions, hose, netherstocks or stockings. The work might overlap because, as we have seen, Herne also made slops for fools in the 1560s. The French, trunk or round hose mentioned by Stubbes were of two sorts, one full, round, padded and reaching below mid-thigh, sometimes to the knee, the other style shorter and 'some be paned, cut and drawen out with costly ornamente with Canions annexed, reachying doune below their knees'.[392] The canions made for Hoyden were thigh-fitting extensions of the trunkhose, apparently padded with hair and reaching to the knee. Usually the netherstocks, or stockings, would be pulled up over them and secured with garters. Minsheu described the former as 'Cannions of breeches . . . because they are like cannons of Artillery, or Cans or pots'.

Stubbes commented indignantly on the extravagant fashions in men's stockings, using the term 'netherstocks':

Then have they nether-stockes to these gaie hosen, not of cloth (though never so fine) for that is thought to[o] base, but of Jarnsey, Worsted, Crewell, Silke, Thred, and Suche like, or els[e] at the least of the finest Yearne that can bee got, and so curiously knitte with open

seame downe the legge, with quirks and clocks about the anckles and sometime (haply) interlaced with golde or silver threds, as is wonderfull to behold . . . every one (almost) though otherwise very poore, having scarce fortie shyllinges of wages by the yere will not sticke to have two or three payre of these Silke nether-stockes, or els[e] of the finest Yearne that may bee got, though the price of them be a ryall or twenty shillings, or more . . . for howe can they be lesse: when as the very knitting of them is worth a noble, or a ryall, and some much more. The time hath bene, when one might have clothed all his body well, for lesse then a payre of these nether-stockes will cost.[393]

The word 'hose' was used for women's stockings from the beginning of the reign, although it was only gradually transferred to men's stockings around 1600. The Queen's hose were certainly as fine as any of the netherstocks described by Stubbes. In the early years of the reign Henry Herne supplied hose of cloth, flannel, linen and sarsenet cut on the bias to stretch and fit the leg, with a seam at the back. The shape would have been similar to the pair of footless linen hose in Figure 300. Surviving examples of men's seventeenth century boot hose[394] are cut in the same way, fitting the leg closely below the knee but then flaring out to wide tops. Herne appears in the Great Wardrobe Accounts first in 1560–61 for

scissura xj par Caligar de panno stitched in le Toppes et clocks cum vid irishe stitche et lin[ed] in le toppes cum Taffata ad xxs — xj*li*

Eidem pro ij par Caligarum de flanell ad vj*s* viij*d* — xiij*s* iiij*d*

Eidem pro vij par caligarum de Tel lin[ed] tot de Magna Garderoba Regine precio — x*s*.[395]

These eleven pairs of cloth hose, lined in the tops with taffeta and stitched in the tops and clocks with Irish stitch, two pairs of flannel hose and seven pairs of linen hose, were all supplied tradition said to have belonged to Queen Elizabeth, have taffeta tops.[433]

In the late 1590s another style of stocking appears among the warrants described as 'newe silke hose made in Gamasshes fasshion', as we have already seen, or simply as 'gamashes'. In the following entry in the Michaelmas warrant for 1600 seven pairs are mentioned:

Item to Roberte Morland for makinge vj paire of lynnen hose for thre paire of new silke hose ij paire wroughte richelie with gold silver and silk: Two paire of new worsted hose richelie wroughte with gold silver and silk: One paire of blushe colour gamashes new silke hoses and for plushinge of them, iiij paire of old silk hose scowred and made cleane richelie wroughte with gold silver and silk: sixe paire of old worsted hose scowred and made cleane richelie wrought with gold silver and Silk, two paire of worsted hose made longer in the foote and six paire of old gamashes silke hose scowred and made cleane and for plushinge of them of our great warderobe.[434]

Linthicum suggests that 'gamash' was derived from the French *gamache* and points out that Percyval in 1591 described the Spanish *poloyma* — equivalent of *gamache* — as hose without feet, a description which agrees with Florio's '*scaffoni*; gamaches or upper stockings'.[435] She notes, from a few contemporary literary references which are otherwise not informative, that some gamashes made the leg look larger and others were loose.[436] It may be conjectured that they were a type of leg-warmer. The warrants show that the Queen's gamashes were made of silk and that they had a pile which had to be 'plushed'. It is not clear if this pile was combed up from knitted silk, or if the gamashes were made from bias-cut plush, silk woven with a long pile. However it seems likely that the former technique was used, as a pair of knitted silk stockings supplied by Roger Mountague in 1588 had 'thinside wrought with carnacion in graine sleve silk like into plushe'.[437] They would have been very comfortable, particularly if loose, as the soft silk, which may have been stitched or knotted into place, probably like rows of fringe, would have helped to trap warm air in the folds in the same way as ballet dancers' knitted woollen leg warmers do today. These stockings are listed in the warrant printed below. When tracing the cost of scouring, dyeing and pressing a pair of knitted silk stockings (pro purgacone tinctur et pressing un par Caligarum de serico nexat iijs iiijd) it seemed useful to give the prices of all the items in this large order for Roger Mountague in 1588. However, it takes time to link items in the warrants with the entries in the Great Wardrobe Accounts and considerable space is needed to print them, so only a token example can be given here.

for fyve peire of silke knitt Hose carnacion in graine & other colours wrought at the clockes with venice golde & silver — [at lxvjs viiijd each — xvj li xiijs iiijd].
two paier of plaine silke knitt Hose — [at lvs each — vli xs].
for one payer of silke knitt Hose thinside wrought with carnacion in graine sleve silke like unto plushe — [iiij li xs].
for newe dying [or edging] of fower peire of silke knitt Hose the clockes wrought with venice golde & silver — [xvs the paire — lxs].
for scowring dying & pressing of one peire of silke knitt Hose — [iijs iiijd].
for two peire of garnesey knitt Hose wrought at the clockes with silke — [xxs each — xls].
for two paier of plaine garnesey knitt Hose — [xiijs iiijd each — xxvjs viiijd].
for washing shering & pressing of two peire of garnesey knitt Hose — [ijs vjd each — vs.].[438]

The warrants give no details but it would seem that all the knitted stockings worn by Elizabeth were made by hand. The stocking frame machine invented by the Rev. William Lee in 1589 was only capable of producing coarse gauge stockings.[439] The Queen apparently refused to make Lee a grant of money, or secure him a monopoly, or patent, to encourage his work on the basis that 'I have too much love to my poor people, who obtain their bread by the employment of knitting, to give my money to forward an invention which will tend to their ruin, by depriving them of employment, and thus make them beggars. Had Mr Lee made a machine that would have made silk stockings, I should, I think, have been somewhat justified in granting him a patent for that monopoly, which would have affected only a small number of my subjects, but to enjoy the exclusive privilege of making stockings for the whole of my subjects, is too important to grant to any individual'.[440] Whatever the truth of this, Lee certainly continued to improve his machine. The indenture made between William Lee and George Brooke dated 6 June 1600 records their partnership in 'makinge in a loome or frame All manner of workes usually wrought by knitting needles as in stockinges wastcootes and suche like' and in 'the ventinge selling and uttering of such of the same Artificiall knitt workes'.[441] At this time Lee had still not obtained any 'priviledge graunt or benefitt from the Queenes Majestie' but was obviously still hopeful.

The shoemakers, their equipment and work

Garrett Johnson, the Queen's shoemaker until 1590,[442] had worked for her when she was Princess: 'Garratt Jonson for xij paier of shoes in September [1552] xiiijs'.[443] He was followed by Peter Johnson,[444] presumably his son, who worked for Elizabeth until the end of her reign and then for James I and Anne of Denmark.

William and Rowland Winter were two other craftsmen who made footwear for the Queen. William may have been employed in 1576 because Garrett Johnson could no longer cope with the increasing number of orders each year. In that year Winter made

xij peire of spanishe lether Showes and Pantobles of sundry colours stitched with silke and one peire of Pantobles of oringe colour taphata enbrodered with silke thre peire of theise Showes lyned with taphata all of our great guarderobe.[445]

A glance at Garrett Johnson's entry for the same date shows the kind of pressure he was under:

To Garrett Johnson our Showemaker for making of xiiij peire of vellat Showes Slippers and Pantobles stiched pinked cutt & ravelid lyned with satten scarlett & spanishe lether: thre peire of Slippers of tufte taphata lyned with satten & taphata: one peire of Pantobles & one peire of Showes of lether enbrodered with venice golde the lether of our store lyned with vellat satten & taphata: xxxiij peire of spanishe lether Showes & Pantobles one peire of pantobles being layed with xxiiij yerdes of venice silver twiste: for translating of vj peire of vellat Slippers & Pantobles stiched with silke lyned with Satten & Scarlett: for translating of two peire of tufte taphata Slippers with tufte taphata and blewe taphata to them: and for translating of xxiiij peire of spanishe lether Showes & Pantobles of sundry kindes of colours of our great guarderobe.[446]

'Translating' describes the work of taking an old shoe to pieces and remaking it, cutting out worn sections where necessary.

William Winter's name appears only on this one occasion in 1576. Rowland Winter is entered in the next warrant, perhaps

William's brother or son, unless the clerk made a mistake with the Christian name, entering William instead of Rowland. He was obviously a craftsman skilled in handling fine leathers, as he also made leather jerkins:

Rowland Winter for newemaking of a Jerken of perfumed lether of our store: for making of a Jerken of murrey spanishe lether: for newe making of a Jerken of perfumed lether enbrodered of our store: for newe making of a peire of Showes & Pantobles enbrodered with venice golde and silver of our store: for xv peire of spanishe lether Showes of sundrye colours one peire stiched and lyned with carnacion taphata.[447]

After 1581[448] there are no further entries for Rowland Winter and Garrett Johnson makes all the footwear listed in the warrants until 1590, after which date Peter Johnson takes his place as the Queen's shoemaker. John Parr, the Queen's embroiderer, worked on some of the shoes with Peter Johnson. In 1594, for example, Johnson made 'two paire of shoes of clothe of silver'[449] and Parr is entered 'For edging of a pair of shoes of Clothe of silver and joyninge the owtside and lyninge together beinge white Taffata'.[450] Later in the same year Johnson made another 'paire of Showes of Cloth of Silver'[451] and Parr is listed again 'for workmanshipp and edginge of a paire of shoes of Clothe of silver lyned with white Taffata and joyninge the lyninge and outsyde together'[452] and 'repayeringe thenbrauderie of one paire of shoes of Cloth of Silver'.[453] Other men who worked on the Queen's shoes included 'John Wynneyard . . . for perfumyng of . . . two peire of Showes and two peire of Pantobles of our greate guarderobe' in 1572.[454]

Thomas Dekker's play *The Shoemaker's Holiday*, written in 1598–99, gives a lively account of the shoemaker's trade in the city of London. The characters — Simon Eyre, the master craftsman, Hodge, his foreman, Ralph and Firk, the journeymen, and a boy apprentice — cast light on the organisation of the work carried out by the Queen's shoemakers. Garratt Johnson might have had a similar number of men working for him. June Swann, Keeper of the Shoe Collection at Northampton Central Museum, has records of Northampton shoemakers of the late sixteenth century who took the old medieval maximum of three apprentices at a time, which she thinks presupposes more skilled men than a foreman and two journeymen. Johnson may well have needed more skilled workers to cope with the numbers of shoes ordered by the Queen in the 1570s.

Dekker gives details of the shoemakers' equipment when Firk asks 'Have you all your tools — a good rubbing-pin, a good stopper, a good dresser, your fower sorts of awls, and your two balls of wax, your paring knife, your hand-and-thumb-leathers, and good Saint Hugh's bones to smooth your work?'[455] (Fig. 304). The legend of St Hugh, who became a shoemaker for the love of Winifred and suffered martyrdom with her, leaving his bones 'to all the kind Yeomen of the Gentle Craft' is told by Thomas Deloney in *The Gentle Craft*, published in October 1597. A company of journeymen shoemakers found Hugh's body hanging up and picked clean of flesh. They took the bones and, in order to 'turne them to profit, and avoid suspition' made various tools with them, 'which ever since were called Saint Hughes bones'.[456] Craftsmen producing handmade shoes today still use tools of similar shape. These include bone polishers, preferably made of deer bone.

Other items listed among the warrants for the Wardrobe of Robes included in 1584 'one payer of wedges and a dresser'.[457]

304 *A shoemaker's workshop in Nürnberg. Woodcut from 'Eygentliche Beschreibung Aller Stände auff Erden' by Jost Amman and Hans Sachs, 1568. Private collection*

June Swann points out that although Deloney writes 'St Hugh's bones shall be: First a Drawer and a Dresser, Two wedges, a more and a lesser . . .' no one today seems to know exactly what these tools were, nor how they were used. Dekker mentions 'a good dresser' but not wedges. Miss Swann suggests that a dresser may have been a knife or a hammer for preparing leather, and she has evidence that some early lasts (not yet traced back to the sixteenth century) consisted mainly of a block, plus a wedge front. A pair of these would be needed when shoes were made for right and left feet.

Later in 1584 Johnson supplied 'Two lastes of wodde'.[458] June Swann feels that this refers to two separate styles, perhaps with different toe shapes or with an added heel, otherwise the clerk would have written 'a pair of lasts', one for each foot. She points out that straights, when both shoes were identical, with no difference between right and left, seem to have come in with heels and that there are early straights on Margaret Douglas's effigy in Westminster Abbey, dating from 1578 and on the effigy of Robert Dudley's wife at Warwick, dating from 1588. The new lasts may have replaced old ones which were full of lines of holes from tacks and quite worn out. Alternatively Elizabeth's feet may have spread a little with age, or she may have had corns, and the new lasts were designed to make shoes which would be more comfortable.

Johnson supplied six 'Shooinge hornes' to ease the Queen's shoes onto her feet in 1563[459] and another six in both 1564[460] and 1566.[461] These were presumably made of horn carved to

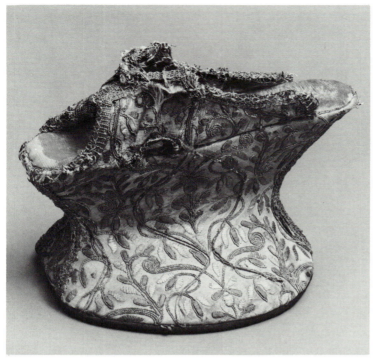

309 *Girl's chopine, òr 'pantoble open at the toe', of silk overlying brown leather embroidered with silver thread. There is a satin sock. English or Italian, c. 1600. Ashmolean Museum, Oxford*

a Maid of Honour, between late 1569 and early 1570, 'iiij paire of calves lether pantobles xiij paire of calves lether shoes iij paire of Spanishe lether shoes And one paire of Calves lether slippers for the said Anne Knowles'.[481] In the next warrant covering the summer of 1570, Johnson made 'ij paire of velvet shoes for the said Anne Knowles, one paire of velvet pantobles xviij paire of calves lether shoes, vij paire of spanish lether shoes and iiij paire of Lether pantobles'.[482] No other gifts of footwear are entered in these Warrants for any of the Queen's servants until 1594 when Peter Johnson made 'iij paire of spanishe Lether shoes corked' for Thomasina, the dwarf.[483]

All the Queen's shoes in the early years of her reign were made of velvet but after Ippolyta had had two pairs of Spanish leather shoes in 1562 and half a dozen pairs in 1563 Elizabeth ventured to try a pair in 1564.[484] She ordered another three pairs in 1565[485] and two more pairs in 1569,[486] still with up to forty pairs of velvet shoes each year. In the warrants for April and September in 1572 the number increases to 'one paire of murrey Spanyshe lether Shoes and ij payre of spanishe Lether Pantobles' and 'viij paire of Spanishe Lether shoos of sondrie colours: Two paire of Spanyshe Lether Shoos Laied on with gold Lace: Two paire of Spanyshe Lether Shoos Laied on with Silver Lace',[487] with a total of thirty-six pairs of velvet shoes, fourteen pairs of velvet slippers and eight pairs of velvet pantobles. By 1575 more Spanish leather than velvet items were ordered for the Queen:

for xxiiij paire of velvett Shoos Slippers and Pantobles stitched with silke Lined with satten and in the Soles with skarlett two paire of Slippers of Tufte Taffata lyned with velvet, xxxiij paire of Spanishe lether shoes and pantobles of sondrie colours and fashions.[488]

From this time until the end of the reign Elizabeth favoured Spanish leather over all other materials for her shoes.

Shoes in the early years of the reign were apparently flat, but heels are mentioned in the warrants occasionally from 1564 onwards:

To Garret Johnson our Showmaker for making twelve pair of velvett Shoes stiched pinked cut & ravelid lyned with satten and in the soles with skarlet corked with velvett raymes stiched with silk viij pair of velvet showes enbrauderid corked with velvet rames stiched with Silke cut and ravelid lyned with satten and in the soles with skarlett four paire of velvet Slippers lyned with skarlet, Six paire of velvet pantobles lyned with Spanish lether One pair of Spanish lether shoes wrought with silke and for translating six pair velvet shoes with vellat to perfourme the heeles.[489]

June Swann points out that 'heels' is a term often used loosely for quarters, the part of the shoe covering the heel, as well as the extension beneath which raises the foot from the ground, but the term 'heels' would describe the type of arched wedges on men's shoes recovered from Henry VIII's flagship, the *Mary Rose*, dating from 1545, and the low wedges seen on the monument of 1549 to Elizabeth, wife of the 2nd Earl of Worcester, in St Mary's Church, Chepstow. Wedges are shown in some of the Queen's portraits (Fig. 307) but high heels and arches are not entered in the warrants until 1595.[490] The earliest monument showing a curve up under the arch known to June Swann is of Mary Carewe in Hascombe Church, Devonshire, dating from 1589 (Fig. 308). The word 'rame' mentioned in this warrant of 1564 appears earlier in 1563. The term today means 'framework', and perhaps this is a reference to the side of the arched wedge. It is not known as a shoemaker's term however, and does not appear in the warrants again after 1572.[491]

Cork was used from the fifteenth century and appears in the warrants from the beginning of Elizabeth's reign. In 1562, for example, there are 'iij paire of corked shoos of velvet lyned throughout with skarlett'[492] and in 1563 'vj paire of velvet Shoos corked, with velvet Rames and the Soles stitched with silke lyned throughout with scarlett ij paire of the said shoos translated lyned with satten'.[493] The cork was used for the whole length of the foot, including the wedge, and the shoe was then soled with leather.

In 1595 Peter Johnson made the first shoes which are described as having high heels and arches:

Peter Jonson for viij payre of Spanishe lether shoes of sondry colours: vj payre of spanyshe lether pantobles of sondry colours, one payre of spanyshe lether shoes with highe heels and arches: One payre of strawe coloure pantables with arches, and layed on with silver lace: for translatinge of one payre of cloth of silver pantobles lyned with white satten: for translating one payre of shoes with highe heeles: and for translating viij payre of shoes and pantobles of our great wardrobe.[494]

In *The Shoemaker's Holiday* Dame Margery asks 'Prithee, let me have a pair of shoes made; cork, good Roger; wooden heel too'.[495] The Queen's high heels were probably made of wood.

Slippers were low, easily slipped-on footwear, without fastenings. Elizabeth usually had about a dozen pairs in plain velvet each year in the 1560s and 1570s. These in the mid and late 1570s are elaborately decorated. In 1578, for example, Rowland Winter made 'Tenne peire of spanishe lether Showes Pantobles and slippers of sundrye colours welted cutt and stiched parte layed with silver lase lyned with scarlett satten and taphata'.[496] There are several references to both velvet and leather footwear 'stitched with sundry stitches' and here the context suggests that the stitching is decorative rather than purely functional. Two pair of 'velvet Shoos fayre enbraudered Lyned with Satten and in the Soles with Skarlett' in 1563[497] may have had large areas completely covered with embroidery: perhaps the terms 'stitched' and 'stitched with sundry stitches' refer to linear patterns. There is certainly a distinction made between 'stitched' and 'embroidered' in the entries from the 1576 warrant for both William Winter and Garrett Johnson, quoted in full earlier.

The word 'welt' has several meanings. June Swann comments that this is the first use of the word 'welted' for footwear that she has seen, but feels that in this context 'welted' refers to a narrow strip of applied trimming and not the method of construction invented around 1500, a narrow strip of leather attaching upper and insole to sole. She points out that slippers were technically slip-on shoes and suggests that these more ornate examples in 1578 may be early thicker-soled shoes. Very few slippers appear in the warrants during the 1580s and early 1590s and the increasing number of pantobles suggests that the Queen wore them instead of slippers at this time. In 1595 Peter Johnson made her

one paire of Slippers of orrendge colour velvet lyned with Skarlet, the soles with Carnacion Velvet, Two paire of Slyppers of Tufte Taffata, the one paire lyned with skarlet and in the soles with carnacion velvet, thother paire lyned with shagge.[498]

Both shoe and slipper uppers were usually lined with satin or Spanish leather and the soles with scarlet, a woollen cloth which would have been both warm and comfortable, gripping the feet like a modern felt insole or sock. The shag lining here, with its looped pile of silk, would have been very soft to wear, and may have been for indoor use.

Pantobles were made with a deep cork sole thickening at the heel with a vamp of velvet, leather or satin over the front of the foot, as far as the instep. Like the modern mule, they had no quarters (upper at the heel). Although made of velvet and other rich materials, pantobles were apparently worn over shoes to keep them out of the mud, as well as on their own. Stubbes described them in 1583:

for shall he not be faine to knock and spurn at every wall stone or poste, to keep them on his feete . . . with their flipping and flapping up and down in the dirte, they exaggerate a mountayne of mire & gather a heape of clay and baggage together, loding the wearer with importable burthen.[499]

Some of Elizabeth's pantobles were made to match her shoes, judging from the descriptions in the warrants, and there are examples with rich decoration. Garrett Johnson made one pair of 'carnacion vellat Pantobles enbroderid with handes and sett with pearle with Twentie pearle to perfourme them' in 1585.[500] The most ornate pairs made by Peter Johnson were 'lether Pantables with spotts of golde' in 1591[501] and 'pantobles of cloth of silver lyned with white satten' in 1598.[502] The latter were so popular that the Queen ordered another two pairs in 1599[503] and one more pair in 1600.[504] These all sound far too beautiful to have been kicked against a wall to keep them on. However, June Swann points out that equally decorative surviving pantobles and Italian chopines show signs of heavy wear.

Peter Johnson made 'iiij paire of pantobles of the new facion layed on with silver lace' in 1591.[505] It is not certain what this new fashion was, unless it is an early reference to arched heels: in 1598 he made 'One paire of Dovecoloure spanyshe lether pantobles laid on with silver lace, with arches in the heeles'.[506] Alternatively the new fashion might have described open toes,

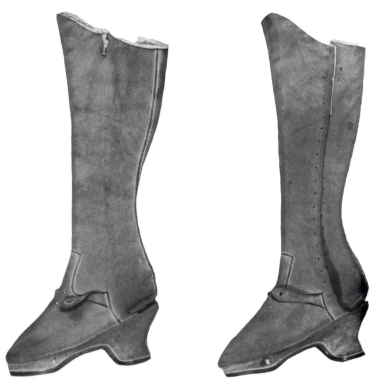

310 *Buskins in soft golden brown leather with a suede finish, by tradition worn by Queen Elizabeth I, c. 1600. Ashmolean Museum, Oxford*

as Johnson made 'two paire of Spanyshe lether pantobles open at the Toes, laid on with silver lace' in 1600.[507]

Some shoes as well as pantobles had cork soles and many writers described all footwear with cork soles as 'corked shoes', without distinguishing between the styles. Puttenham, writing in 1589 described 'These high corked shoes or pantofles which now they call in Spain and Italy shoppini'[508] (Figure 309). The Italian chopine seems to have been much higher than the English variety and the more exaggerated styles do not appear to have been worn in England.

The Queen also wore buskins, boots reaching to the calf or to the knee,[509] in the early years of the reign. Garrett Johnson is entered in the warrant for March 1567 for making 'one paire of buskins of unshorne velvet lyned with Satten and in the soles with skarlet'.[510] He is entered in the same warrant for 'vampinge of a paire of buskins of unshorne velvet', for 'translatinge of a paire of Buskins of unshorne velvet with velvet and Satten to them' and 'for the translatinge of a paire of buskins of plaine black velvet with velvet and Satten to them'. Two more pairs are entered in the warrant for April 1569, 'One paire of buskins of unshorne velvet withe Satten to them. One paire of plaine velvet buskins withe Satten to them. And for new vampinge of the said two paire of buskins with skarlet and Satten to them'.[511]

Johnson's 'new vamping' entered in these warrants, when the part covering the front of the foot was renewed, would have given new life to the velvet buskins, no doubt rubbed and marked with pulling on and off. They probably would have been stained near the sole seam as well. June Swann suggests that alternatively this work might also be carried out for a new fashion. One more pair of buskins was made by Peter Johnson

311 *Detail from Figure 25 showing the brown leather glove with yellow cuffs set with jewels carried by Queen Elizabeth I in the 'Pelican' portrait, c. 1574–75. Walker Art Gallery, Liverpool*

in 1592 'White buskins lyned with orrendge colorid satten and laied on with silver lace':[512] no others are recorded in these warrants. The velvet buskins in the 1560s were presumably used for riding or hunting. The term becomes archaic by the end of the sixteenth century and thereafter is used to describe actors' boots and footwear of the type worn in masques by characters such as the Goddess Diana, the chaste huntress, and Hippolyta, Queen of the Amazons. Queen Elizabeth may have found shoes more comfortable for riding, as these seem to be the only pairs of buskins she ordered. The last pair made in 1592 may well have been worn for a masque. However, there is a pair of boots traditionally known as 'Queen Elizabeth's buskins' at the Ashmolean Museum, Oxford (Fig. 310), which she could have worn at the end of her reign. June Swann feels that the term 'buskins' still describes riding boots as well as theatrical footwear at this time and that the construction at the heel seat is correct. She explains that when heels were first introduced, shoemakers had not invented a way of seaming the upper to the sole all the way round and left a couple of inches hanging loose at the centre back of the heel, as in the Ashmolean pair.

Occasionally the warrants mention styles of footwear from other countries. Garrett Johnson was entered in 1571 for making

one peire of vellat Showes made after the Irishe fation with vellat and Satten occupied in them more then on thother Showes: Twentie and fowre peire of vellat Showes stiched with sundry stiches lyned with satten and in the soles with scarlett: fowre peire of vellat Pantobles lyned with satten and in the soles with scarlett: fowre peire of vellat Slippers lyned with scarlett: for translatinge of thre peire of vellat Showes with newe vellat for the heeles: for translatinge of thre peire of vellat Showes with vellat occupied in the translatinge of them: for vellat occupied in the corked Showes: for thre half civill [Seville] spanyshe lether skynnes thone murrey thother blue and the iij^de

oringe tawnye parte of them made into fyve peire of Showes stiched with silke.[513]

More velvet and satin was used for the shoes made 'after the Irish fashion' than for the other styles, but no other description is given. Spanish leather often appears in the warrants, and here Seville is mentioned specifically as well. Garrett Johnson is also entered 'for translatinge of one paire of shoes of Lether of the French Fashion with new heeles and skarlet in the soles' in 1574,[514] but the description does not tell us exactly what the style was like.

Peter Johnson made 'two paire of Spanish lether shoes of the belony facion' for Elizabeth in 1601 and then, for James I and Anne of Denmark in 1603, 'one paire of showes and pantobles of cloth of gold bound aboute with gold lace for our owne wearing one paire of showes of cloth of gold of Belone facion bounde aboute with gold lace for our said deare wief & two paire of spanishe lether showes for her Belone facion'.[515] 'Belone' may be a clerk's spelling of Boloney, referring to a new style from Bologna, or Polony, a Polish fashion; it cannot describe the material employed, since both cloth of gold and Spanish leather were used for them. It would appear that the term should be 'Polony' as there is a reference to boots and shoes with Polish style heels, among other fashions, in 1615:

But speake, I praie: who ist would gess or skann
Fantasmus to be borne an Englishman?
Hees hatted Spanyard like and bearded to[o],
Ruft Itallyon-like, pac'd like them also:
His hose and doublets Frenche: his bootes and shoes
Are fashond Pole in heeles, but French in toes.
   Oh! hees complete: what shall I descant on?
   A compleate Foole? noe, compleate Englishe man.

Randle Holme offers further details in 1688: 'Shooes according to the fashion of the heels, are some flat and low heeled, or with wooden high heels, broad and narrow; others Leather heels which some term Poloney heels'.[516] Presumably these Polish heels were made from stacked leather.

The warrants for the Wardrobe of Robes were written out by several clerks and detailed descriptions of footwear seem to have depended entirely on the interest and time of the individuals involved. It may simply not have occurred to one clerk to record shoes with high heels, while another would be impressed with the shoemaker's report of a new style and the technical skill involved. Unfortunately the clerks rarely go into the depth of detail we would welcome today.

The glovers

Many portraits of the Queen show her wearing or carrying gloves (Figs 8a, 135, and 311), and it is perhaps surprising that no craftsman working solely as a glover appears among the warrants for the Wardrobe of Robes. It would seem that in the early years of the reign, before large numbers of gloves were presented to Elizabeth at the New Year and on Progresses, John Wynyard, as 'page of our warderobe of our beddes'[517] was responsible for supplying gloves, apparently making them himself. Alice Mountague, the Queen's silkwoman, delivered 'one ounce di quarter and a dram of silke and half an ounce of crimsin silke twyste' to Wynyard 'for our gloves' in 1564[518] and 'x ounces iij quarters di of granado silke and sleve [silke] of sundrie colours, ij ounces of venice gold and silver and ij ounces quarter of gold cheine frendge pyrlid on bothe sydes' to

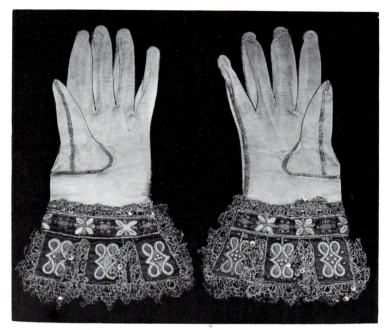

312   Detail from Figure 143 showing the glove with
embroidered scalloped cuff carried by Queen Elizabeth I, c. 1603.
Present whereabouts unknown

313   Leather gloves with embroidered cuffs bordered with
spangled metal bobbin lace, c. 1600. Victoria and Albert
Museum, London (711 and A–1875)

be 'by him employed uppon our gloves and other our
necessaries'[519] in 1565. Wynyard had been provided with
equipment for cutting gloves in 1563:

Item to William hood oure Locksmyth . . . Item delivered to John
Wynyard to oure use one perfumynge panne of Stele ij fyne carvinge
tooles to cutt gloves withall and a fyne lock with a keye for the case of
the perfumyng pan all of oure great warderobe.[520]

The steel perfuming pan was delivered to Wynyard for
another of the duties he undertook as Page of the Wardrobe of
Beds, that of sweetening some of the Queen's leather and fur
lined garments, such as jerkins, loose gowns and cloaks.[521] He
would have perfumed the leather gloves he made for her as
well. Tommaso Garzóni describes the perfumes used for
Spanish gloves:

Spanish gloves are treated with oil of jessamine and with ambergris,
after they have been well washed with a little malmsey wine and
anointed with a little odiferous grease. Or indeed with powder of
cypress, with pomade, with oil of cedar, with oil of benzoin, and with
some grains of musk, with select cinnamon, cloves, storax, nutmeg,
oil of lemon and civet. Or indeed with water of orange flowers and of
musk rose. Or indeed with goat tallow (becco) mixed with oil of
jessamine, of martella, of lemon, camphor, and white lead (biacca).
Or indeed with oil of sweet almonds, roots of white lily, rose water,
oil of musk, oil of fruit stone (spico, spicchio?) white ambergris, oil of
storax, and similar things.[522]

Wynyard would have used the lightest perfumes as Elizabeth
disliked anything too heavy or cloying.[523]

Many of the gloves presented to the Queen were perfumed.
Gifts made at the New Year in 1578 'By the Lady Mary Gray
two peire of swete gloves with fower dosen buttons of golde, in
every one a sede perle'[524] and 'By the Lady Mary Sydney one
peir of perfumed gloves, with twenty four small buttons of
golde, in every of them a small diamond',[525] also give an

example of the type of decoration used on the narrow cuffs,
which may be seen in a number of portraits (Figs 311 and 312).
All three pairs were delivered into the charge of Elizabeth
Knollys who looked after small accessories of this kind.
Another pair of scented embroidered gloves was made part of
a presentation ceremony in the same year when Elizabeth
visited Audley End on a Progress in July. A deputation from
the University of Cambridge attended on her, presenting her
with a book which Cecil had made sure would not be too
strongly perfumed:[526] 'Also with the book the said vice-
chancellour presented a paire of gloves perfumed and garnished with embroiderie and goldsmithe's wourke, price 60s.
and these verses . . .' When the Queen took the gift 'it fortuned
that the paper in which the gloves were folded to open; and hir
Majestie beholding the beautie of the said gloves, as in great
admiration, and in token of hir thankfull acceptation of the
same, held up one of her hands; and then, smelling into them,
putt them half waie upon hir hands'.[527] As they were new, the
leather would have needed slow and careful easing onto the
fingers. It is also possible that Elizabeth may have been
wearing or holding one pair of gloves already, as she had been
travelling: gloves were absolutely essential for protection on
horseback, in summer as well as winter. As we have already
seen, from De Maisse's description in 1597,[528] the Queen
would also wear gloves for warmth in the palace on cold
winter days, not only for travelling.

The number of gloves presented as gifts each year may have
made it unnecessary for John Wynyard to make many after the
mid-1560s, or perhaps Leonard Marshall worked on some of
them. This can only be conjecture as there are apparently no
records of gloves in his name, but he was granted a licence for
life on 30 April 1567:

to work in the occupation of glove making and to keep a shop and to
retain to work under him any person such as others exercising that art

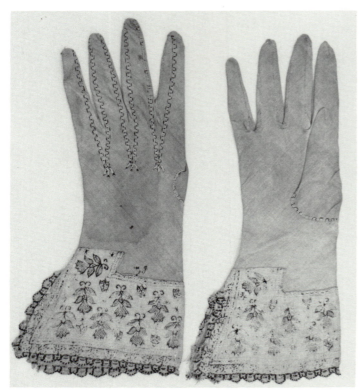

314 *Ivory linen gloves, the cuffs embroidered with black silk, probably for summer wear, c. 1600. Victoria and Albert Museum, London (Cuming Loan 1)*

315 *A pinmaker's workshop in Nürnberg. The pinmaker produces fine, smooth, round-headed pins out of brass wire: he*

also makes clasps for clothing. Woodcut from 'Eygentliche Beschreibung Aller Stände auff Erden' by Jost Amman and Hans Sachs, 1568. Private collection

316 *Brass pin, enlarged to show head, c. 1600. Private collection*

may lawfully retain; notwithstanding Stat. 5 Eliz. providing that no person, except such as then lawfully used certain occupations or had first been an apprentice therein for seven years, should work in those occupations or set to work in the same any man not then a workman or that having been an apprentice would not serve as a journeyman or hired by the year. Marshall, who has served the Queen divers times in the wars as a soldier and lastly as Clerk of the Watch at Newe Haven, has by his industry sufficiently learnt the mistery of glove-making, by means whereof he has obtained his living in time of peace without wandering yearly as others of that vocation have done; and the Queen wishes to encourage others of his sort to learn industrious arts for the better means of orderly living'.[529]

Most of the gloves with deep embroidered cuffs which survive in museum collections date from the early seventeenth century. One pair in the Victoria and Albert Museum shows the depth of cuff seen in portraits around 1600 (Fig. 313). Another pair, probably for summer wear, in fine linen cut on the bias, (Fig. 314) also dates from the last years of Elizabeth's reign.

The pinners

Robert Careles supplied pins for the Queen's use at the time of the coronation: 'Robert Careles pynner for xxiiij[ml] [24,000] pynnes of diverse sortes delivered to the saide wardrobe to her majesties use Liijs iiijd [53s. 4d]'.[530] Although Careles, who 'hathe of longe tyme served us of Pynnes for our owne use', was appointed to the office of 'oure Pynner during his lief' in 1564 and was entitled to 'a fee or wages of Pence by the Day and Twentie and Two shillinges yearlye agaynste the Feast of

Ester for his lyvery as John Pawle Disceased exercysinge the said Rowme hertofore had for the same',[531] his livery is never listed with those for the other artificers among the warrants for the Wardrobe of Robes. The exact number of pence for his daily fee was not given in this draft, but his fees and livery allowance were to be paid by Sir John Mason, Treasurer of the Chamber.

The size of the following order dating from 1565 is typical of others delivered every six months: 'Item to Roberte Careles our Pynner for xviij thousand great verthingale pynnes xx thowsand myddle verthingale Pynnes xxv thowsand great Velvet Pynnes xxx and nyne thowsande smale Velvet Pynnes and xix thowsand Small hed Pynnes all of our great warderobe'.[532]

Great farthingale pins were probably the size of the largest present day pins. They were long and thick, with heads made separately (Fig. 316). They would have been used for pinning deep tucks in farthingales to form casings for whalebone hoops (Fig. 280), for pinning heavy silks into position over the farthingale frame[533] and attaching foreparts. Deep tucks making flounces to hide the hard edge of the farthingale frame may be seen in many portraits (Figs 71 and 285). All these carefully arranged pleats were held with pins. Heavy silks would have needed long or 'great' pins. 'Middle farthingale' pins may have been similar in length to a modern dressmaker's pin, used for pinning light-weight silks into tucks round the edge of the farthingale frame and attaching decorations from the silkwoman to the surface of the gown. The great velvet pins were probably long fine brass pins which could be used on velvet without marking it, and the small velvet pins a shorter variety, perhaps for attaching braids to velvet before stitching; they may also have been used for pinning the sets of ruffs into position.[534] The small head pins were probably used for pinning veils and other fine fabrics.

In the sixteenth century pins were used not only in the process of making clothes, but also when the clothes were being worn; a woman's 'pin money' was intended for that purpose, the pins fastening different parts of the dress together. A portrait of Elizabeth Vernon (Fig. 166) shows a pincushion with both brass and steel pins in it. The 'Pynpillowe of crymsen vellat Delyverid to our use to Dorothey habington one of our Chamberers' would have held the pins needed for Elizabeth's toilet.[535]

The Michaelmas warrant for 1563 gives the prices of various pins:

Item to Robert Careles pynner for xvjm¹ [16,000] great verthingale pynnes at vj _s_ the m¹ [1,000]. xx m¹ [20,000] myddle verthingale pynnes at iiij _s_ the m¹ [1,000].
xx m [20,000] greate vellvet pynnes at ij _s_ viij _d_ m¹ [1,000]. lviij m¹ [58,000] small velvet and hed pynnes at xx _d_ m¹ [1,000] all of our great warderobe.[536]

It is interesting to compare them with another delivery of the same date where used pins have apparently been straightened and the points sharpened for Ippolyta the Tartarian[537] who received many attractive gifts of clothing from Elizabeth:

Item to Robert Careles pynner . . . for one m¹ [1,000] old verthingale pynnes for the said Ipolitane iiij _s_ Item one m¹ [1,000] old myddle verthingale pynnes iij _s_ iiij _d_, one m¹ [1,000] smale verthingale pynnes ij _s_ viij _d_ and iij m¹ [3,000] pynnes at xx _d_ the m¹ [1,000] all of our great warderobe.[538]

The manufacture of pins called for some skill. Harrison records in the early 1570s that 'About that time Englishmen began to make all sort of Pinnes, and at this day they excell all Nations, and it may easily bee proved that straungers have sold Pinnes in this land to the value of threescore thousand pounde a yeere'.[539]

Silkwoman, silkman and milliner

The silkwoman, silkman and milliner who made and supplied so many items for Elizabeth were not listed among the Queen's artificers, nor entitled to livery. The early history of the London silkwomen has been discussed by Marian K. Dale in her article 'The London Silkwomen of the Fifteenth Century'.[540] From the evidence examined she concluded that the 'mistery and craft' of the silkwomen, although not recognised as a separate guild, was pursued on the lines of the craft guilds of male workers. A silkwoman traded in her own right (not merely as her husband's chattel with no separate legal existence of her own) a privilege accorded to the women of London. She took apprentices, who were enrolled before the chamberlain of the City, and trained them in three processes. First, as throwsters, they converted into thread the raw silk imported from Italy where it had been reeled from the cocoon. Secondly, they wove the smaller silk materials such as ribbons, braids and similar trimmings (but not whole cloths). Thirdly, they made up silk goods of various types. In addition to this, Queen Elizabeth's silkwoman and silkman seem to have worked on fine linen as well as silk from 1560 onwards, as we

shall see. They also dealt with the laundering and starching of fine, delicately made items such as lawn sleeves, partlets and veils, certainly from 1578 onwards,[541] and possibly earlier.

Silkwomen in the fifteenth century were of some standing in the City. There are records of them married to knights, aldermen, goldsmiths, and mercers. Anne F. Sutton has given an account of Alice Claver, a London silkwoman in the third quarter of the fifteen century who supplied mantle laces for the coronation of Richard III and Queen Anne.[542] Alice was conveniently married to Richard Claver, a mercer, whose trade included the handling of raw silk and the already thrown Italian silk thread, as well as silver and gold threads of Lucca, Venice and Cyprus, all used by the silkwoman in her craft. The 'mistery and craft' continued to be practised by women until the second half of the sixteenth century. At this time as Harrison records:

And untill the tenth or twelfe yeere of Queene Elizabeth [1568–70], there were but few silke shoppes in London, and those few were onely kept by women, and maide servants, and not by men, so now they are: At which time all the silke shoppes in London had not so much, nor so many sorts of silke, gold or silver threed, nor sorts of silke, gold, or silver threed, nor sorts of silke lace, and gold and silver lace as is at this day in divers particular shopps in Cheapeside, and other places.[543]

Alice Smythe took the place of Marie Wilkinson,[544] silkwoman to Queen Mary, when Elizabeth came to the throne. She is entered in the accounts for the coronation as 'her Majesties Silkewoman for golde, Sylver, Sylke, and Sylkeworke of diverse sortes delivered to the Q: Tayler. And to Raphe Hoope and John Runnyon Officers of the warderobe of the Robes to her graces use as by the particlaryties under there handes dothe appeare xxiij_li_ xviij_s_ v_d_ [£23.18s.5d]'.[545] Between Lady Day and Michaelmas 1562[546] Alice married, unless the change of name can be explained by the employment of a new silkwoman. From 1562 until April 1581 Alice Mountague produced a wide variety of wares for furnishings in the palaces and items for the Stables as well as the Wardrobe of Robes. In the Michaelmas warrant of 1581 Roger Mountague's name appears:[547] Alice may have died or decided to retire. Roger was probably Alice's husband, or some other relative, continuing with the business. He also supplied the Wardrobe of Beds and the Stables as well as the Wardrobe of Robes.

In the early years of Elizabeth's reign the silkwoman was paid by the Great Wardrobe,[548] then from 1567[549] to 1575 by the Privy Purse: there are entries of the following kind in warrants made each half year from Michaelmas 1571 until Lady Day 1575: 'All maner of lace, lawne, buttons and loupes garnishements & silke being employed upon our fore-named Apparell are Receyved at thandes of Alice Mountague our Silkewoman and are payed for by our prevye purse'.[550] On several occasions payments from the privy purse are made specifically 'by thande of Henry Sackeforde esquier'.[551] From 1575 to 1581, she was again paid by the Great Wardrobe.

The contents of the following Lady Day warrant for 1576 are typical of the quantities and variety of items supplied by Alice Mountague each half year:

To Alice Mountague our Silkewoman for
[1] nyne poundes ij oz of silke of sundrye colours:
[2] x oz of lase of venice golde & silver:
[3] ij oz of riche lase of venice golde & silver:

317 *Page from a sample book showing how 'to make a round and hollow poynte' in green and yellow silk, 'to make theise 2 together' and 'to make the flagon bread' in red and white silk, c.1600. Victoria and Albert Museum, London (T.313–1960)*

[4] vj dozen vij peces of hollowe lace of silke of sundry colours tagged:
[5] ij grosse ix dozen of venice rebande poyntes of sundry colours:
[6] xiij grosse of poyntes of spanishe silke of sundry colours:
[7] vj dozen peces of brode poyntinge Rebande of sundrye colours:
[8] vij peces of venice Rebande of sundry colours:
[9] ij peces di of cullen Rebande for key bandes:
[10] iiij peces di of cullen Rebande for gerdelinge:
[11] vj dozen ij yerdes of ij*d* brode spanishe silke Rebande of sundry colours:
[12] iij peces of brode fine white Lawne:
[13] xij fine white paste boardes:
[14] vij dozen of roses made of ashe colour and murrey towers rebande:
[15] one pounde viij oz of fine wier:
[16] xij yerdes of fine blak open lase:
[17] two boultes of blak Thred:
[18] x poundes of white systers Thred:
[19] fyve yerdes di of white flanell:
[20] one Cloute of millen Needles and
[21] one Reame of writinge paper delyverid into thoffice of our said Guarderobe of Robes all of our great guarderobe
[22] Item for xviij very fine heathe brushes delyverid to ye gromes of our prevye Chamber of our great guarderobe.
[23] Item for seven poundes vij oz dimi quarter of venice golde & silver lase:
[24] two ounces quarter di of riche venice lase made of goldesmythes pirle plate and spangelles:
[25] vj oz of frenge of fine venice golde & silver:

[26] one pounde vj oz iij quarters of frenge lase made of jeane satten silke of sundry colours:
[27] thre grosse viij doz di of lase of sundrye sortes & colours made of jean satten silke:
[28] fyve poundes viij oz of granado silke of sundry colours:
[29] xvj peces di of brode poyntinge Rebande of sundrye colours:
[30] iiij dozen of heare lasinge & ii *d* brode Rebande:
[31] thre yerdes of brode venice rebande:
[32] xx dozen of Roses made of ashe colour & murrey rebande:
[33] xiiij yerdes di of brode fine white lawne starched:
[34] xix yerdes of fine blak sipers:
[35] one longe button & loupe made on ye fingers with venice golde and silver:
[36] iij dozen di of venice golde & silver spanishe buttons:
[37] two dozen of fine blak silke spanishe buttons:
[38] for making wider of a kyrtle of grene and white whiped nettworke sett with roses of venice golde white silk sipers & grene and white satten silke:
[39] iij yerdes quarter of silver tyncell:
[40] v yerdes of fine blak stiched lawne wrought allover with knottes of blak granado silke[552]

All these items were 'delyvered to the said Walter Fyshe to be employed upon our said garmentes all of our great guarderobe'. They were followed by a few more items:

Item Delyverid to him more
[1] vij poundes j oz of venice golde & silver lase:
[2] one pounde j oz of spanishe silke of sundrye colours:
[3] two yerdes of fine white starched lawne employed upon three gownes & one kyrtle by us geven as afore all of our great guarderobe.[553]

Alice supplied another large order to William Whittell in the same half year:

Item Delyverid to the said William Whittell to be employed upon our said garments
[1] xj poundes j oz iij quarters of venice golde & silver lase:
[2] ix oz di of riche venice lase made of golde pirle plate & spangelles
[3] one pounde xij oz iij quarters of granado silke of sundry colours:
[4] xvj dozen lase of venice golde & grene silke:
[5] v dozen di of blak satten lase:
[6] iij dozen viij yerdes of fine hearelasing & ij *d* brode rebande
[7] xvij yerdes of brode poyntinge rebande:
[8] thre yerdes of venice rebande:
[9] iiij dozen ix peire of longe buttons & loupes of venice golde bone lase edgid with silver pinkes:
[10] xvij dozen viij buttons of venice golde of silver millen and spanishe:
[11] two yerdes di of blak curled sipers:
[12] viij dozen viij blak spanishe buttons:
[13] for mendinge xij peire of riche buttons & loupes & newe tasselling of them with venice golde & silver:
[14] & for foure peire of riche buttons & loupes garnesshid with goldsmythes pirle pearles & tasselles of venice golde & silver: all of our great guarderobe.[554]

Some other small deliveries of silver lace to Henry Herne and Thomas Ludwell in the same warrant were also paid for by the Great Wardrobe rather than the Privy Purse. These laces of Venice gold and silver may have been bobbin lace made with metal threads (Fig. 322) but there would have been some woven metal thread braids among them. The latter are described below as loom laces in 1576. The Venice ribbon points, Spanish silk points and broad pointing ribbon would have had their ends attached to tags, or aglets, of various sizes

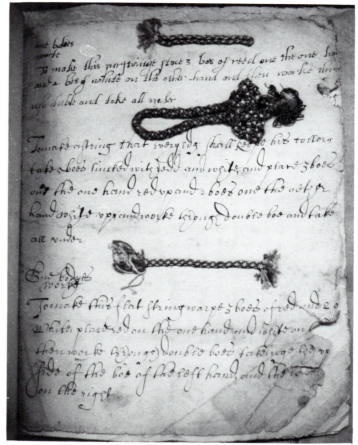

318 *A point made of a strip of satin, the edges turned in once and stitched, with metal tag, or aglet, from a doublet, c. 1615–20. Museo Parmigianino, Reggio Emilia*

319 *Page from a sample book showing how 'to make this purstringe', 'to make a string that every edg shall keepe his collor', and 'to make this flat string', all three in red and white silk, c. 1600. Victoria and Albert Museum, London (T.313–1960)*

320 *(Left) Page from a sample book showing how 'to make a drum poynt', and 'to make the shaft and 4 Crownes' both in red and white silk, and 'to make a 10 boed poynt in a wave', c. 1600. Victoria and Albert Museum, London (T.313–1960)*

321 *Detail from Figure 288 showing a ribbon or braid supporting a jewel, 1577. National Trust, Montacute House, Yeovil*

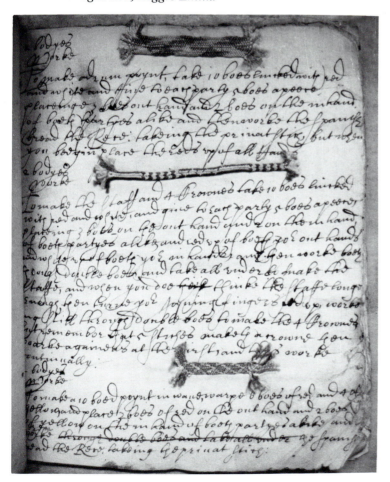

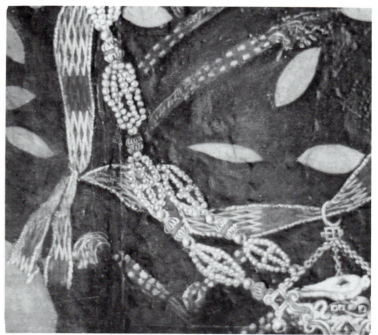

322   *Italian or Spanish gold and silver metal thread bobbin lace with pearls and glass beads, mid-sixteenth century. Monasterio de Pederalbes, Barcelona (inv. no. 115.059)*

by the wardrobe staff. Small metal tags were functional, passing through eyelet holes to attach various pieces of clothing together (Fig. 318): the silkwoman sometimes delivered points and laces already tagged, as in the case of the hollow lace listed above. Large aglets of goldsmiths' work were used for decoration, often tied with ribbon bows (Figs 67 and 324). Hollow lace was worked with silk threads and, as its name implies, was hollow. A cord might be threaded through a length of it, if required, but the example in Figure 317 is pressed flat, to use for points. The double layer gives added strength and firm edges. Laces of this type, made from interlacing silk threads in various patterns (Figs 317, 319, and 320), were used for points, strings or laces to fasten coifs, ruffs, cloaks and other garments, and purse strings. The traditional techniques employed in making these laces are still in use today, in Japan. 'Cullen' ribbon took its name from Cologne and must have been fairly strong, as it was frequently used for girdles and key bands. It may have resembled that in Figure

321 which supports a jewel. 'Towers' ribbon came from Tours and would seem to have been a fairly fine silk, as it was used for decorative roses. Hair lacing ribbon, priced at two pence a yard, was presumably used to bind the hair. The button and loop 'made on ye fingers with Venice golde and silver' may have resembled the loop in Figure 319, although the latter is made with silk threads.

Many items of interest supplied by Alice Mountague appear in other warrants. Colours of threads are not usually specified except for black and white but there are a couple of entries for 'fower ounces of coventrye blewe Thred':[555] Coventry was famous for this blue thread.[556] In addition to the buttons and loops for fastening garments already cited, there are 'vij peire of cloake stringes of venice golde and silver' in 1577 and 'thre dossen peire of Claspes and keepers wroughte with silke' and 'Twentye paire of silver Claspes' in 1578.[557]

Alice supplied wire for stiffening veils and other decorations, for example, 'half a pounde of fine wier' in 1577, 'Two

323   *The knitting needles supplied to Thomasina would have been used for work similar to this glove, which is knitted in beige silk patterned with red, green, yellow and brown, with 'Freuchen Sofia' worked across the back and palm in yellow. Gold thread is used to give the effect of rings on the fingers, c. 1567. Uppsala Cathedral*

324   *'Portrait of an unknown lady aged 43' by an unknown artist, 1567. She wears partlet and sleeves in ivory and pink semi-transparent material, possibly gauze or 'curled sipres', almost revealing her arms. Lord Tollemache, Helmingham Hall, Stowmarket*

poundes of wyer' in 1578 and 'six yerdes of wyer whiped with silke' in 1581:[558] the latter cost 12 pence a yard.[559] Alice made 'a handell for a Fanne of Moriscoworke with venice golde and silver' in 1578,[560] presumably wrapping the metal threads round a wooden base.

In the Michaelmas warrant in 1576 there is an entry for 'six poundes one ounce of riche venice lase made by hande with venice golde silver goldesmythes plate and pipes of golde & silver . . . xxvij li[lbs] of bone lase & loume lase of venice golde & silver of sundrye sortes',[561] descriptions which differentiate between some type of lace made by plaiting the threads in the hands, bobbin lace (Fig. 322) and woven braid. Another 'xiiij li [lbs] j oz quarter of bone lase of venice golde silver goldesmythes plate & spangelles'[562] supplied at the same time had spangles worked into the bobbin lace. In the Lady Day warrant in 1577 there are 'iiij lbs ij oz of passamaine lase and doble wreathe lase of Jeane silke of colours':[563] these two different laces, or braids, were made with silk from Genoa. In the Michaelmas warrant for 1576 Alice also supplied cotton padding, 'xviij li [lbs] of fine white bumbaste', and 'two hundreth of Tronoye Nedelles' and in 1580 there were 'fower payer of knyttinge Nedelles' (Fig. 323) and 'Two peire of

spanishe Gloves' for Thomasina the dwarf.[564] The 'tronoye' (steel) needles would seem to have been a different variety from the 'millen' (Milan) needles already cited. Unfortunately no note is made of their delivery to the particular craftsman, tailor or embroiderer.

Some fine materials (Fig. 324) and occasional lengths of cloth, such as 'lxij yerdes of fyne curle sipers and smothe sipers' and 'Six yerdes quarter of blewe Flanell' supplied in 1577 and 'white Syvework lawne' in 1590 came within the province of the silkwoman and silkman, as well as the more typical 'fyve yerdes of fine white thred networke and two yerdes di of fine lawne wrought richelye with venice golde silver & nettworke' delivered in 1578.[565] Alice also supplied plain lawn and holland, including 'xxiiij elles of holland for oure Laundresse to drie our Partelettes' in 1564.[566] Presumably the delicate partlets were laid out on the linen and patted dry.

The silkwoman's work seems to have expanded considerably during the early years of the reign. Alice employed a woman to mend the Queen's linen in 1563, as in the Lady Day warrant there is this entry: 'Item to a woman for hir wages occupied in the mending of our Ruffes nighte railes and other oure necessaries by the space of vij monthes after xxviij daies

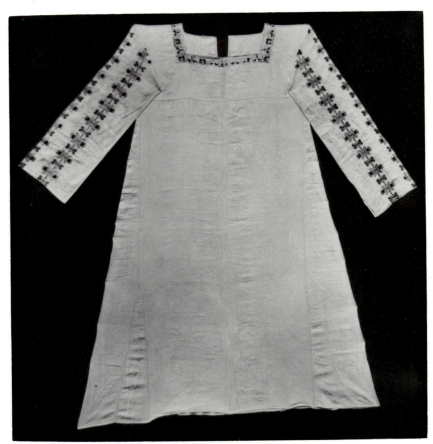

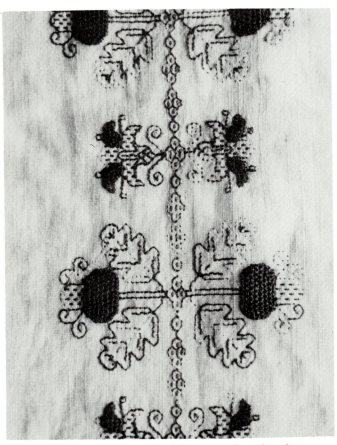

325 *White linen smock with a square neckline, c. 1560–80. Filmer Collection, Gallery of English Costume, Manchester*

326 *Detail of acorns and oak leaves embroidered in black silk in Figure 325*

to the monthe and xx s the monthe vij *li*'.[567] Later in the year she was 'occupied in altering and translating of our partelettes Smockes and other our necessaries by the space of vij monthes after xxviij daies the month vij *li* of our great warderobe'.[568] In 1564 and 1565 the Michaelmas warrants show that Alice's woman was employed again for seven months on the partlets, smocks and 'other our necessaries'.[569] In 1565 ruffs are included as well.[570] She does not appear to be listed separately again, and it is possible that from 1566 onwards at least some of this kind of work was carried out by the Queen's women and their servants. As we have already seen Lady Cobham and the Countess of Shrewsbury both worked on a pair of sleeves as a gift for Elizabeth.[571]

Alice undertook 'hemmynge and edging' partlets and supplied other needlework including 'xxiiij yardes of white Cutt worke for ruffes & xvj yardes di of Broade Cutt worke ruffes for a partelett' and 'xlvij yardes of white Flaunders ruffes purled, iiij white Flaunders worke Bandes Raised' in the summer of 1562.[572] This fine sewing and 'hemmyng, overcasting and edging x yardes of Ruffes for a partelett' in the summer of 1563[573] seems to have led to smock-making and an increasing amount of work of this sort on fine linen by both silkwoman and silkman. Alice for example, is entered for 'making wasshinge & starchinge of half a greate sleve rufte of fine white lawne reyzid verye thicke with small ruffes & stiched under them'[574] and 'for making washing and starchinge of a payer of greate Irishe Slevis' in 1578.[575] Occasionally the material was heavier — 'for working larger of a peire of slevis of flanell with spanishe worke of silke'[576] —but more usually the material was fine and delicate.

Both silkwoman and silkman may have ordered smocks (Figs 325 and 326), ruffs, sleeves, coifs and other items from seamsters,[577] but many of the descriptions give the impression that they carried out the work themselves. Some of the earliest references to particular types of stitches — true stitch, chain stitch, herringbone stitch, drawn work, overcasting and hemming — are found among the warrants for this type of work from silkwoman, silkman and hosier,[578] rather than those for tailor and embroiderer. Alice Mountague, for example, was entered 'for workinge of iiij smockes downe the breaste and aboute the coller with black drawne worke' in 1565[579] and 'for makinge xvj Smockes wrought about the Collers slevis, ruffes and wrist bandes with drawne worke and trew stiche' in 1566,[580] while Roger Mountague supplied 'six fyne white knotted cawles wrought with Chaine stiche' in 1589.[581] He was entered in 1595 'for Cuttinge in peces and settinge together with heringe bone stiche one payre of carnation ingrayne silk Garters, the endes edged with silver lace, hemmed rounde and perfourmed with vj payre of pendaunte buttons of silver twisted with Carnation ingrayne silke'.[582] Unfortunately the warrants do not always give this much detail.

Roger Mountague also made smocks and is entered in 1587 'for drawing and working with blak silke drawen work of vj Smockes one peire of slevis and vj Toothe clothes of hollande cloth the Smockes overcast and edgid with blak & white silke lase & the toothe clothes edgid with golde & silver lase'.[583] The names of other smock-makers appear among the warrants late in the reign. In 1593, for example, there is this entry:

Item to John Robinson for makinge drawinge and workinge and wasshinge of iij Smockes of fine holland clothe with black silke the ruffes and wrestbandes laced with edginge of silke lace And for like makinge and washinge of two nighte Smockes the ruffes wristbands and square beinge edged with lace of our great Warderobe.[584]

327   'Portrait of an unknown lady' by an unknown artist,
English School, c. 1600. She wears a gown trimmed with roses of
gauze or cypress of silkwoman's work, set with jewels.
Metropolitan Museum of Art, New York

328   Detail from Figure 327 of what may be 'pynners on' of
gauze or cypress, pinned to the neck edge of the ruff

Robinson made another three smocks later in the same year.[585] Elizabeth Rogers carried out similar work in 1594: 'For drawinge <and> working and makinge up of fowre smockes of fine holland Clothe with black silke edged with black and white silke bone lace and nedlework lace of our great wardrobe'.[586] In the Lady Day warrant of 1595 she made six more:

Elizabeth Rogers for makinge up, drawinge and workinge with black silk drawenwork of six Smocks of fyne holland cloth edged with black and white silk bonework lace, with two peire of ruffes and wrestbandes of black silk drawenwork likewise edged.[587]

Another six smocks were drawn and worked later in the same year 'with black silke drawneworke . . . of fyne holland cloth the squares and ruffes edged with black silke nedleworke and bone lace'[588] and Elizabeth Rogers was also entered 'for makinge up the same smockes'. The 'square' is the term for the square neckline of a smock (Fig. 325), or, in the case of a high-necked smock, the area of the chest revealed by the square neckline of the gown worn over it.[589]

As we have already seen, Roger Mountague supplied much of the Queen's headwear in the 1580s and 1590s, in the form of cauls, coifs, creppins, 'attires for the head',[590] and wigs[591] as well as items such as chin shadows and riding shadows.[592] He continued to work on exquisite sleeves for the Queen, as had Alice, 'making of a payer of blake stiched Lawne sleevis,

florished with silke and edged at the handes and sydes with blake silke bonelase' in 1583.[593] In the same warrant he was entered 'For wasshinge & starchinge of a vale of starres & for mendinge the same in manye places with new starres of nedleworke and edging the same with silver spangle lase'.[594] He also made a matching 'payer of bodyes of starres edged and seamed with silver spangle Lase' presumably with the 'Two yerdes quarter of fyne white nettworke wrought with starres of Nedleworke' which he supplied at the same time, although this may have been a separate length for some other purpose. Other work of this kind included 'wasshing starching overcasting hemmynge & edginge with one pounde fower oz quarter of brode golde & silver bone lase and carnacion silke in graine of an Apron and a Towell of fine camerike for our Maundie with Tenne peare buttons of golde silver and carnacion in graine silke to garnishe the said Apron & Towell' in 1585.[595] Roger continued to supply quantities of lace, ribbons and braids, sometimes with short descriptions such as 'fower peces two yerdes iij quarters of brode poynting reben and towers reben englishe making'.[596] This 'towers' ribbon was presumably a type of ribbon made in Tours in France, which had been copied in England. In the Michaelmas warrant of 1585, Roger's wares included a wide variety of items including toothcloths, night rails, towels, sheets, 'pillow beres', 'Two pynners on of fine nettworke edgid & bounde with white bone lase and silver lase: one double pynner on of white striped silke sipers thone side edgid & bounde with silver lase, thother side

329   *Needle lace worked with hair in a heraldic design of shields with acorns, oak leaves and flowers in the borders, c. 1600. Victoria and Albert Museum, London (T.44–1962)*

with white bone lase', 'one dozen of long vallopes & one dozen of shorte vallopes all of fine hollande cloth' and 'thre Gyrdelles of blak Jeane silk made on the fingers garnished with buckelles hookes & eyes whiped over with silke'.[597] The 'pillow beres' were pillowcases, the 'pynners on' possibly trimmings for the edge of a gown neckline, to cover the neck edge of a ruff (Figs 327 and 328) or to decorate a headdress. The word 'vallop' does not appear in any dictionary, but as 'vallopes' are usually listed with plain linen items such as sheets, towels and pillow cases among the warrants, it may be conjectured that these were an early form of sanitary protection.

Roger Mountague continued to supply goods in large quantities until 1601. At this time he may have been unable to meet all the requirements of the Court or was thinking about retirement, because a silkwoman, Dorothy Speckard, is also entered in the warrants for the Wardrobe of Robes for an equally large number of items in the Michaelmas warrant of 1601.[598] She produced similar items to those supplied by Roger Mountague, exquisite sleeves, cauls, waistcoats, hand-kerchieves, mantles, veils and also washed and starched items of this kind. Her first order also included 'one fyne sute of Ruffes', 'two chynne ruffes edged with silver', 'a fyne ruffe pynned upon a Frenche wyer with gold net spangled', 'foure paire of fyne Camerick ruffes of Cutworke edged with fyne neadlework purle' and 'Two rebata wyers'.[599] The suit of ruffs consisted of neck and wrist ruffs. The chin ruffs were small ones worn beneath the chin at the same time as a large ruff which bordered the edge of the square neckline; a chin ruff would have hidden the wrinkled skin of advancing years. The ruff pinned to a French wire was ready to wear. The wire was variously described as a supportasse, underpropper or sup-porter: Roger Mountague supplied 'One Supporter of wyer whipped over with silke' in 1588.[600] These supporters would have been circular in shape for a ruff worn with a high necked doublet, or semi-circular to support a ruff standing round a square neckline. The rebato wires were to support smooth standing collars, or rebatoes. Dorothy also made smocks entered in the same warrant, 'for workynge two fyne Smockes in drawne-work with ruffes and wrestbandes and lace to edge them'.[601] As we have already seen, both Alice and Roger Mountague had supplied hose for the Queen, and Dorothy delivered 'one paire of lynen hose wrought with black silke lined with camerick' in 1602,[602] perhaps similar to those in Figure 300 or possibly those in Figure 302.

Among other items to decorate gowns, Dorothy supplied 'cc [200] devises made of heare; xij devices made in hare in maner of peramides: xij devices made in heare in maner of leaves: lx

devices of heare made in maner of globes' in 1602.[603] There were also 'iiij yerdes of heare braid' in the same warrant:[604] this may have been lace of the type in Figures 329 and 330. In the Lady Day warrant for 1603 she is entered for 'Two heare Cawles curiouslie made in workes of haire',[605] 'six heads of heare' and more of the delicately made hair trimmings: 'two hundred devises made of heare in maner of loopes & tuftes: twenty foure yards of heare curle curiously made. twelve yards of round curle made of heare: two hundred devises made of heare in maner of leaves: thre dozen of devices made of black silke and wyer in maner of leaves: twelve devices made of heare in maner of Peramides: twenty foure devices in maner of globes'.[606] Presumably these devices in the form of leaves, pyramids and globes were to match those supplied earlier. Although very little of this work with hair survives, similar effects may be seen in Victorian jewellery, where hair was plaited for bracelets and intricately worked into designs for brooches. Early seventeenth century portraits show long fine strings of plaited hair, looped round the neck or twisted round the wrist, often caught to a ring. The lines in John Donne's poem *The Relique* would seem to show that these were keepsakes and love tokens:

> When my grave is broken up againe
> Some second ghest to entertaine . . .
> And he that digs it, spies
> A bracelet of bright haire about the bone
> Will he not let us alone
> And thinke that there a loving couple lies . . .

Other hair bracelets or laces may have been worn in memory of people who had died.

One entry for Dorothy Speckard's work in the winter of 1602–03 gives the quantity of material used: 'for one mantle with a doble trayne of white copweb lawne Conteyning fortie yards the seames trimed allover with puffs of the same stuff'.[607] The double train may have had two layers, floating free. Another garment in the same warrant had been heavily worn: Dorothy was entered 'for washing & starching a trayne gowne of lawne wrought in gold & silver in maner of peacocks tayles stiched betweene every one, & drawne thorough with gold plate & mending the same being much broken with eight oz of gold plate employed thereon'.[608]

In the Lady Day warrant of 1602, the work of what seems to be another silkman appears, but his trade is not mentioned:

Item to Richard Frenche for making ruffes and repayring a gowne covered with nett and under it done [dun] color satten and two ounces of sprig lace, for making of a dressing with three traynes with

330   *Needle lace worked with hair in a design of acorns and oak leaves, c. 1600. Victoria and Albert Museum, London (T.265–1927)*

331   *The locksmith's workshop in Nürnberg. The locksmith makes locks, keys, bolts, chains, iron chests, grates, weathercocks and many other iron objects. Woodcut from 'Eygentliche Beschreibung Aller Stände auff Erden' by Jost Amman and Hans Sachs, 1568. Private collection*

fortie yardes of stuff, for starching and repayering a fine black mantle set with bugle and making the same up againe. And for six hundreth twentie six yards and a halfe of Tiffanie lawne sipers nett and such like stuff of sondry colors parte striped with gold and silver and employed upon our garments above written and are to be paid for at our great wardrobe.[609]

In the Michaelmas warrant of the same year Richard French is described as 'our Milliner', Roger Mountague as 'our Silkman' and Dorothy Speckard as 'our Silkwoman'.[610] As we have already seen, the title 'milliner' had been used once in 1562 for Raphael Hammond, the Queen's capper. In its original sense the term described a vendor of fancy wares and accessories, especially those which were originally of Milan manufacture, such as 'myllain bonettes' in 1531, ribbons and other trimmings.[611]

The locksmiths and blacksmiths

The post variously described as Locksmith, or Blacksmith, was held by William Hood, 'our Locksmith', at the beginning of the reign[612] and his place was taken by Richard Jeffery, described as 'our Blacksmythe' in the Michaelmas warrant of 1567,[613] where he is listed for three yards of red cloth for his livery coat, 'with two yardes of velvet to gard the same for lyninge makinge and enbraudering of our Lettres all of our great warderob'. John Keyne carried out some work at the same time as Hood. He was paid, among other things 'for a Key and for alteringe the Lock of the robes dore at our Palace of Westminster' in 1562[614] and made 'ij dd [double?] greate stock lockes and the yron work of a greate Chest in our warderobe of Robes at our said Tower of London, one plate Lock and ij spare keyes for the robes Dore at our palace of Westminster' in 1563'.[615] Both Keyne and Gilbert Polson are listed as 'our locksmith' in the Michaelmas warrant of 1566,[616] but this would seem to have been a mistake because Jeffery held the post from 1567 until 1578.[617] Polson appears again, in the Lady Day warrant of 1579[618], supplying the same

type of goods. In the Michaelmas warrant of 1580 there is an entry for 'six yerdes of red cloth to make two Coates thone for Gylberte Polson thother for Arther Myddleton'[619] but although Polson received livery he was not described as 'our locksmith' in the warrants until 1586.[620] Polson's letters patent were made out with those for Thomas Larkin, another locksmith, in 1584.[621]

Precautions against theft of valuable silks and gowns embroidered with gold thread made locks on all doors essential. William Hood produced two keys for an existing lock on the 'wardrobe of robes Dores' in 1564.[622] In 1571 there was a thorough check on security arrangements and Richard Jeffery made 'One greate stocke locke for our Robes Dore at our Mannor at Richemounte with two keyes: for two greate stocke lockes with two keyes for our Guarderobe of Robes at our Mannour of the Stronde: foure fayer keyes for our Robes Dores at our Palloice at Westminster' and 'thre greate doble stocke Lockes with vices and staples to them for our Robes Dores within our Palloice at Westminster and our Tower of London'.[623] In 1575 he made 'one greate stocke locke for our Robes doore at Hamptoncourte with two fayer keyes' and 'one greate plate locke with a counterplate for our Robes dore at Richemounte with thre fayer keyes and staples to the same'.[624] Gilbert Polson made a 'newe plate locke with two keyes for our robes Dore at Westminster' in 1588,[625] so presumably the first one had worn out, or an extra room had been found for the increasing amount of clothing. Jeffery also made 'two newe lockes with keyes and staples for presses in thoffice of our Robes at our Tower' in 1572,[626] and was also responsible for maintenance and repairs, for example putting on 'two padlockes fower lockes for presses: fower boultes for presses with iiij newe boultes and mendinge and oylinge of presse lockes'.[627] Gilbert Polson mended 'the hookes & boultes of xxiij lockes for presses with stapelles to them' in 1580,[628] which gives some idea of their number, and among other similar maintenance jobs was employed in 'mendinge of thre lockes one keye and thre handelles for Standerdes' and 'makinge cleane of tenne keyes for our Robes dores' and

332 *Monkeys 'apeing' the fashion, starching and setting linen ruffs, using setting sticks. Engraving, c. 1570. British Museum, London*

'mendinge the presse Dores of our Guarderobe of Robes within our Tower of London' in 1584.[629]

A wide variety of items was made by the smith both for the use of the other artificers working in the Wardrobe of Robes and for the Queen and her ladies, as well as locks and keys for doors and presses in the Wardrobe of Robes. Elizabeth was fastidious and kept high standards of personal cleanliness. Hentzner noted that at 'Windsor Castle . . . there are worthy of notice here two bathing rooms, cieled and wainscoted with looking-glass'. In 1564 William Hood, 'our Locksmythe', made 'the Iron worke of oure Removinge Bayne'[630] which the Queen took with her when on Progress.

The Queen's shoes were eased onto her feet with steel shoe horns supplied by the smith. Three made by Gilbert Polson in 1567 were 'of stele faire Burnished'.[631] The usual orders were for six at a time: 'to Richarde Jefferye for sixe showing hornes of steele fayre wrought'[632] is a typical entry. Presumably they were given to ladies-in-waiting and being small were easily mislaid, thus accounting for the frequent repeat orders.

Richard Jeffery made several lots of staples 'to drawe Cordes throughe to hange our apparell on in ayringe of them'[633] for the Wardrobe of Robes and also 'one fyer Shovell:

& a fyer forke for our Robes at Westminster'[634] for the fire to air the store. There are many repeat orders for fire irons in all the stores, such as the 'stronge fyer Forke & one fyer Shovell of iron clean fyled' which Gilbert Polson made in 1587.[635] Fire pans were also made for the Queen's use; Gilbert Polson made 'one greate fyer Panne doble bottomed with rolles and pillers of Iron goinge uppon wheeles' in 1588.[636] Similar ones may have been used in the laundry and in the tailor's and embroiderers' workrooms, to heat irons. We have already seen that Hood delivered a steel perfuming pan with a lock and key, and two tools for cutting gloves to John Wynyard in 1563.[637] The locksmiths provided several other sets of tools, such as 'iij paire of fyne compasses with doble Joyntes to lace our gownes withall' in 1565.[638] There is an entry in 1579 for 'Gylberte Powlson for a bodkyn a Hammer a litell Sythye and other Tooles to tagge Poyntes withall clenlye wrought';[639] these were tools for hammering metal tags on the ends of ribbons or laces used for fastening various items of clothing. Thomas Larkin is listed in the great Wardrobe Accounts in 1601

pro iij setting stickes de Chalyb ad iiij*s* — xij*s*
pro le pressinge Iron — vj*s*
pro ij de lez Curlinge bodkins de Chalyb — iij*s* iiij*d*[640]

These setting sticks of 'chalybeate' were tapered metal rods. Entries in the warrants for 'one pressing iron verie well steeled: for one setting stick: one stele bodkin' in 1601[641] and 'one setting stick and one curling iron of steele' in 1602[642] would seem to show that 'chalybeate' was steel rather than iron. The setting sticks were heated in the fire and used to form the characteristic figure-of-eight sets, or pleats, in starched ruffs[643] (Fig. 332). The sticks would have been delivered to the laundress, while the pressing iron might have been for laundress or tailor. The 'curlinge bodkins' and 'curling iron' may have been for setting hair.

The locksmiths supplied some larger items, for example, 'Gylberte Powlson for two curten Rolles being white of tenne foote longe a pece with eye and hookes with skewers . . . Two fyne curten Rolles for Pictures with xxv Rynges fyled white and burnesshid with loopes and vices . . . one foldinge Ladder with ironworke to it'.[644] Measurements were given for the next ladder he made: 'one newe foldinge Ladder of wodde being x foote longe with ironworke to the same'.[645] Polson also supplied ironwork 'for a Hatte Case as joyntes springe vices and plates cleane fyled'.[646]

Animals from foreign countries were novelties. How long they survived in the English climate is uncertain, but some may have had short lives even with the care that would have been lavished on them at Court. In 1562 William Hood 'delivered to the said Dorothie Bradbelt one newe coller of Iron with Joynte Buckles and ij Ringes with swevills & a newe lock to Tye our monkey withall of our great warderobe'.[647] It sounds as if the monkey was fairly lively, as a year later Hood supplied 'a new cheyne of Stele conteyning viij foote longe and a lock with iij Swevills, for our monkey all of our great wardrobe' to Dorothy Broadbelt.[648] Another was delivered to her in 1564, 'one newe longe cheine of Stele for oure monkey with iij swevelles'[649] and later in the same year 'a fyne cheyne for our monkey with a flatt ringe to a joynt and a locke delivered to the lady knowles'.[650] Hood also produced hinges for a cage for the Queen's parrot in 1563[651] and later in the year delivered 'to the said Blaunch parry one newe coller of yron with joyntes made full of holes with haspe and wharle for oure muske catt'.[652] This was followed by 'one longe cheyne with iij Swevelles for oure muske catte'.[653]

The cutlers

The cutler is regularly listed in the warrants for dressing the great bearing sword. There were other swords, daggers and rapiers to be treated as well. John Ayland, the first cutler, appears in the Michaelmas warrant of 1563 as 'our Cutler for dressinge of our greate bearinge Sworde of our great warderobe Item for iij yardes of red cloth to make a coate for the said John Ailand and ij yardes of velvet to garde the same for lyninge makinge and Enbrauderinge of our lettres all of oure great wardrobe'.[654] Ayland's place was taken by Richard Matthew in 1584 where he is listed in the Lady Day warrant for 'makinge cleane of our great bearinge Sworde and mendinge of the pommell: And for making cleane of A Riche Dagger of the chardge of Rauf Hope within our Tower of London'.[655] The latter may have been the dagger which belonged to Edward VI.[656] A bearing sworde is also listed in the Stowe inventory. An entry in the warrant of 1586 shows that Matthew dressed 'two litell bearinge Swordes with

scaberdes of purple vellat,[657] one of which may be that listed in the inventory.[658]

The bearing sword was carried in front of the Sovereign in processions and is described in an account of 1565: 'On Christmas Day, Her Majesty came to Service very richly apparrelled in a Gowne of Purple Velvet, Embroidered with Silver very richly Set with Stones, with a rich Collar Set with Stones, the Earl of Warwick bare the Sword, the Lady Strange the Trayn'.[659]

The coffer-makers

The Queen's clothes were packed into leather covered wooden standards, trunks and coffers. These would have provided protection against mice and damp when the clothes were in store at the Tower and Whitehall. In 1965 this method of storing clothes could still be seen in the attics at Rosenborg Castle in Copenhagen. Heavy wooden chests about six feet long and over two feet deep were arranged on shelves round the walls of the store rooms, and it took at least two men to lift each one. Plans were being made for new museum storage, but the arrangement of the attics at that time, a unique survival from earlier years, must have been very close to that of the Wardrobe of Robes stores in the sixteenth century. Hide leather 'cloth sacks' were also made, presumably for transporting the Queen's clothes from Palace to Palace and on Progresses, although the smaller trunks and coffers would have been used as well. A number of large presses, and standards, or chests, may have been permanent furniture in each Wardrobe store. There were certainly enough at the Tower by 1587 to give Thomas Grene a lot of work: 'for his chardges with his two men by the space of six dayes occupied in lyninge of presses within oure Tower of London with nailes and tape to fasten down the buckeram of oure great guarderobe'.[660]

All the standards, trunks, coffers and leather sacks were made by the Queen's coffer-maker, a post held by the Grene family for many years. Letters patent were made for John and Thomas Grene in 1558 and Thomas continued in service alone after his brother's death in 1565.[661] When he died in 1600[662] his son John took the post and continued to work for King James in 1603.[663] The number of apprentices and journeymen whom the Grenes employed is not known, but on one occasion Thomas Grene covered 'the seate of the chariot wheron the Muzes sate' for the Office of Revels and was paid 'for him & his ij servauntes attendaunce & woorkes doone within this tyme in all xxijs vjd'.[664]

It is difficult to tell the exact size of the various chests and trunks which the Grenes made. The largest seem to have been 'great Standerdes' but no length is given for them. In 1581 Thomas made 'one Standerde of one yerde & half a quarter longe coverid with lether lyned with lynen bounde with iron as lockes Joyntes & handelles'; presumably this was smaller than three 'greate Standerdes of wodde, coverid with hide lether, bounde with iron with lockes joyntes handells & Keyes lyned with canvas', which he made in 1587.[665] It is possible that all the 'great Standards' were about the same size, perhaps five or six feet long, to enable the Queen's gowns to be laid out with little folding.

Trunks would seem to have been used for travelling. Three made in 1574,[666] 1575[667] and 1581,[668] all covered with hide leather and lined with buckram or linen, were an ell long and this may have been the usual size for them. This would certainly have been large enough to hold the robes of the Order of the Garter for the King of Denmark:

to Thomas Grene for two Trunkes coverid with hide lether lyned with buckeram with lockes Joyntes handelles and all other necessaries belonginge to the cariadge of the said Robe to the kinge of Denmarke And one Case of tymber coverid with crymsen vellat lyned with crymsen satten with Ironworke and quiltes of satten to carye a Coller of golde of our said order all of our greate Guarderobe'.[669]

Coffers varied considerably in size, as may be seen from the following examples made by Thomas Grene: 'foure small Cofers being of foureteene ynches the pece coverid with lether lyned with Cotten and lynen cloth with lockes joyntes & handelles to them to put in certayne lettres in the custodye of our trustie and right welbeloved Counsailour Sir William Cicell knight our principall Secretarye' in 1569, 'one lesser Cofer with 'drawinge boxes lyned with cotten for Juelles' in 1577,[670] 'one greate square Cofer coverid with lether bounde with iron & lyned with lynen Delyverid to Charles Smyth keper of our standinge wardrobe within our Castle at wyndesor' in 1578, 'one greate square Cofer Coverid with lether lyned with cotten with lockes & joyntes' in 1581 and 'two greate Cofers of wodde coverid with hide lether lyned with canvas bounde with iron with lockes joyntes handells & squiers' in 1587.[671] Two large coffers, presumably to hold documents, were made in 1570 and here the size is given: 'for two greate Cofers conteyning foure foote & a half large the pece coverid with hide lether lyned with lynen with lockes joyntes handelles and squiers Delyverid to our use to our trustie and right welbeloved Counsailour Sir William Cicell knight our principall Secretarye'.[672]

Some of the warrant entries mention the items of clothing for which the coffers were made. In 1565 William Hood, the locksmith, delivered 'to the said Dorothye Bradbelt to our use one new Haspe with a Doble Joynte and a handell for a coffer to put our slevis and partelets in of our great warderobe'.[673] A few of the coffers were very elaborate. One delivered from George Brideman in May 1574, for the Queen's use, was 'coverid with crymesyn vellat Embroderid with golde, having a garland of cloth of golde embroderid uppon the lyd thereof with the lettres M and R within the said garland';[674] it had belonged either to the late Queen Mary, or to Mary, Queen of Scots. Another, made by John Grene in 1565, had 'tylls and a rome above to put our hattes in covered with leather lyned with cotton bound with yron as lockes joyntes handels and squires'.[675] Another had extra fittings put into it; in the same warrant John was entered for 'the makinge diverse particions within a Jewell coffer to put in Browches, cheynes and girdells in diverse tylles and lyning them with sarcenet and other workmanship therunto'.[676]

Old parchment was used for interlining coffers and cotton wool to pad them. In the Michaelmas warrant of 1564 John Grene used 'six Poundes of fyne Cotton with parchmentes written to set upon coffers with silk lace and garnishing nayles',[677] and in 1565 he made 'One case of tymber covered with leather lyned with lynnen havinge a locke joyntes and handelles to put our lokinge glasse conneglasse and other our necessaries in of our great warderobe . . . xx poundes of cotton woll to stuff the coffer with glasses'.[678] Coffers were not always lined with cotton wool when carrying objects which might be liable to break or spill if bumped. In 1564 John 'delyvered to the said Elizabethe marbery one great Coffer of

333 *Wooden chest or coffer bound with iron, similar to those made by the Grenes. Sixteenth century. The National Trust, Trerice House*

waynscott covered with black fustian enaples garnished with silk riband and garnishing nayles lyned with thick Frise with diverse particians in it to put our swet waters in bound with Iron as locks Joyntes handels and squiers with a case of hide lether to put it in'.[679] Presumably the partitions gripped the bottles or other containers for the 'sweet waters', and the leather outer case acted as a shock absorber.

Delicate objects were stored carefully to avoid damage. In 1575 Thomas Grene made 'one case for a Plume of Fethers coverid with lether lyned with taphata: one Case for a Fanne coveried with lether lyned with red paper',[680] and in 1576 'one boxe being one yerde square coverid with lether lyned with cotten with particions locke handelles and joyntes to laye our Fannes in'.[681] Another case was described in more detail in 1580 'one Case for a Fanne of tymber coverid with lether lyned with taphata with a Quilte of like taphata with Joyntes hookes & eyes';[682] the fans would have rested on these soft surfaces without damage. The fan cases were probably quite shallow and may all have been a yard square, although this can only be conjecture. As we have seen above, hats might be stored in the top of a coffer, above the 'tylles', or drawers, but they might be packed separately, as in 1573 Thomas Grene mended 'a Cap case with a newe keye to it', and fifteen years later he supplied 'one rounde Case for a Hatte coverid with lether lyned with sarseonett with Ironworke to it'.[683] Gilbert Polson made this ironwork, 'for a Hatte Case as joyntes springe vices and plates cleane fyled'.[684] Little detail is given of the metal work on coffers and cases, with a few exceptions such as 'two Cases thone for a Glasse thother for a bottell coverid with crymsen vellat garnesshid with passamaine of venice golde lyned with satten with Joyntes and hookes of copper gilte' and a fan case made in 1583, which was 'coverid with lether with joyntes and hooks of copper lyned with vellat'.[685]

Bags of velvet and other materials, such as 'fyve cases of cotton for v riche petycotes'[686] and 'thre peces of Fustyan for Cases for our riche Garmentes'[687] were made by the tailor to protect many of the garments in store in the Wardrobe of Robes, as we shall see, and it is possible that one or more of these would have been placed inside a 'Cloth sack of hide lether lyned with canvas with braces and laces to it,[688] for travelling. Thomas Grene seems to have made one of the latter fairly regularly each season. Lengths of material and clothes were wrapped in linen, before being put away in the chests and shelved cupboards, or presses. William Dane supplied 'one payer of presse Sheetes of hollande of four bredthes and a half and nyne elles longe for to laye in our Apparell within our Tower of London' and 'one payer of presse Sheetes of hollande of foure bredthes and six elles longe to laye our Apparell within our Mannour at the Stronde in the chardge of John Weste' during the winter of 1567–68, and there are numerous deliveries such as this by James Hewish 'for cccxix elles of hollande cloth to make presse Sheetes & Curtens within our Tower of London'.[689]

Among other items the Grenes also supplied a screen covered with green velvet, coal baskets, candle plates, black jacks, crotchets, hooks and lyor, or tape, for hanging tapestries.[690] One entry in 1581 includes 'eight Buskes', which were presumably made of wood, to stiffen the fronts of 'bodies', or corsets: these were covered by the tailor, 'making Seven Dossen peire of cases of taphata of Sundrye colours, to cover buskes withall of our great guarderobe' and 'makinge of two Dossen payer of cases for buskes of vellat and two Dossen payer of taphata'.[691] The Grenes also made the 'males' or budgets to carry the Queen's letters, at least one a year, more often two. They were usually described in the warrants as 'one Male of blak vellat lyned with satten layed with passamaine lase and frenges of venice golde with braces laces guilt buckelles and a Case of cotten to it' and 'one Male of spanishe lether lyned with cotten with braces laces and guilt buckelles'.[692]

The Grenes also worked with Walter Ripin on the 'close carre' for the Wardrobe of Robes, John, for example, supplying 'One bare hide of Oxe leather to cover our close carre and for lyning the said carre and garnishing yt with riben and nayles within' in 1565.[693] Details are given of Thomas's work on a new one in 1584; 'for coverage of a newe close Carre with hide lether layed underneathe with seare cloth sett on with hobbe nailes lyned with fyne lynen cloth garnished with reben'.[694] The term 'seare cloth' may be linked with the 'searing candle' listed among the necessaries entering the office of the Wardrobe of Robes twice a year and with cerecloth of waxed linen in which embalmed corpses were wrapped; it refers to a waxed cloth impervious to water.

One unusual job carried out by John Grene was to make a cage for the Queen's parrot. In 1563 he 'delivered to Dorothie Bradbelt to oure use one great Cage of Tynker wyar, and plate made strong for a parrot'[695] and with it 'ij pottes of pewter to putt water in thone for oure monkey thother for our parrott . . .' The hinges for the cage were made by William

Hood, the locksmith,[696] and 'Six yerdes of doble grene sarceonett' were delivered 'to make Curtens for a byrdes Cage of nedleworke' in 1574.[697] This may have been for another bird, not necessarily the parrot.

The coach-makers

The wheelwright or coach-maker, as Anthony Silver and Walter Ripin were variously described, did not work exclusively for the Wardrobe of Robes, but Ripin's name appears regularly in the warrants, and should be mentioned as one of the artificers whose work affected that of the Wardrobe staff indirectly. It was he who made the waggons, coaches and other carriages to transport the contents of the Wardrobe of Robes and Wardrobe of Beds when the Queen made her regular moves from Palace to Palace or went on a Progress. Jacob Rathgeb, describing a typical move in 1592, mentioned 300 carts for the bag and baggage and wrote 'for you must know that in England, besides coaches, they use no waggons for the goods, but have only two-wheeled carts, which however are so large that they carry quite as much as waggons, and as many as five or six strong horses draw them'.[698] However, waggons are certainly mentioned in Walter Ripin's letters patent.

The coaches for Elizabeth's personal use were made during the early years of her reign by Anthony Silver, wheelwright.[699] He was followed in 1569 by Walter Ripin, described as a wheelwright in the first warrant,[700] but thereafter as a coach-maker.[701] In 1573 Walter Ripin 'Cochemaker' was appointed to the 'office of maker of all our Coches close carres charettes and wagons'.[702] His fee was 'twelve pence by the Daie of good and lawfull money of England quarterlie' and he was allowed yearly 'three yardes of read cloth for his Lyverie Coate of twelve shillinges the yarde, two yardes of blac velvet to garde the same coats of eightene shillinges the yarde and eight yardes of frize at twelve pence the yarde for the Lynynge therof with the makinge and enbraunderinge of the Lettres of E and R upon the said Liverie Coate'.[703] He also had leave to take up timber and have it carried as 'shalbe thought mete and nedefull'. This was endorsed with a note of reversion for Thomas Walker in May 1603 when James I came to the throne.[704] The provision of transport came under the Stables department within the Great Wardrobe, except for one constantly recurring item listed in the warrants for the Wardrobe of Robes; this was 'our close carre'. Four new ones were made between 1574 and 1586[705] and frequent repairs were carried out. Gilbert Polson is entered as 'mendinge of a Locke to our close Carre & makinge a newe keye' in 1583.[706] Details are given in 1578 'for making of a cloase Carre with tymberworke and ironworke therunto belonginge coverid with hide lether sett on with hobbe nailes & lyned with lynen & seare cloth paynted with fyne golde byse & oyle colours'[707] and of mending one in 1585 'with cloutes nailes lycor pyncers hammer and other necessaries'.[708]

The 'close carre' was kept in good repair and it was the job of the Serjeant Painter to paint the coat of arms and other decorations on it; Nicholas Lyzarde is listed in 1569 'for payntinge and gildinge of our close Carre with our Armes lettres beastes and Badges'.[709] William Hearne 'our serjeannte paynter' painted and gilded 'our said close Carr with our Armes Beastes Badges Lettres and Cognizaunces layed on with Oyle fyne golde byse and other colours verye richelye' in 1574.[710] In 1576 he was entered for 'mendinge the payntinge of our close Carre and layinge the carriadge in oyle'[711] and in 1579 'for payntinge of the Cariadges and wheeles of our said cloose Carre'.[712] Thomas Gower painted the car with 'our beastes badges & Armes with fyne byse golde and oyle colours'[713] in 1582 and it was painted again by George Gower in 1584.[714]

Von Wedel describes two empty coaches following the Queen's coach when he watched a procession in 1585.[715] The first was embroidered with gold and silver; the second was 'studded with nails of gold' and would seem to have been this 'close carre'. Its use can only be conjectured but, as there was a spare coach (presumably in case the Queen's coach broke down), it may have housed spare gowns and accessories for her, if she wished to ride on horseback. The term 'close' means 'enclosed, shut in', and the 'close carre' may simply have been a windowless carriage for transporting clothes, but it may also have carried a 'close-stool', a chamber utensil enclosed in a stool or box. This would have made a travelling convenience to which the Queen and her ladies could retire on long journeys, rather than using the earth closets of any neighbouring houses, or retreating into hedgerows, with the attendant risk of damaging expensively embroidered silk gowns. In the Lady Day warrant of 1565 there are descriptions of four close stools: 'to John Grene our Coffermaker for making four close stowles covered with black Velvet enbrauderid upon and garnished with riben and gilt nayles the seates and laythes covered with skarlet fringed with Silk and golde and iiij Pannes of pewter with cases of lether lyned with canvas to put them in delivered to katherine Astlye to our use of our great wardrobe'.[716]

Wardrobe care and storage

It can have been no easy task to care for Elizabeth's gowns, slowly increasing in number with each year's gifts and items made in the Wardrobe of Robes. There was one permanent store in use throughout the reign, at the Tower of London, another at the Palace of Whitehall at Westminster, from the late 1560s onwards, with one more at Somerset Place, or 'Strondehouse', between 1568 and 1572 and the store at the Office of the Wardrobe of Robes, which seems to have come into use during the 1580s. All of them would have needed constant supervision to avoid damage to the fabrics from damp, mildew, mice, moths and dust. As we have seen, the coffer-makers supplied stout wooden chests, or standards, coffers, trunks and hide leather cloth-sacks to protect the clothes both in store and when travelling.

The skinner mended, perfumed, trimmed and beat the furs to keep them in condition and free of moth, as has already been described. The Yeoman of the Robes would have organized the continual movement and airing of the garments which would have been carried out by the Grooms and Pages of the Robes. Fires were lit to air the store rooms and prevent damp, and the warrants record increasing quantities of fuel. 'One Lode of coles to Ayre our saide apparell within our said Tower of London' was used in 1562.[717] In the Lady Day warrant of 1569 Adam Blande supplied 'one loade of Coales to Ayer our Robes and Apparell within our said Tower' and two more loads were delivered later in the same year 'employed in ayring of our Robes and Apparrell within our Tower of London, Westm[inster] and Strondehouse . . .'[718] In 1570 another two

loads of coal were used at the Tower and Westminster and one load of coal 'to ayer our Apparell remayning in chardge within our manor at the Stronde'.[719] By 1572 six loads were needed at the Tower and Westminster with one load to 'our Manner at the Stronde' at Lady Day and another load at Michaelmas, for John West, presumably at the Strand.[720] Three loads of coal are a regular delivery each half year from Adam Bland until the Michaelmas warrant of 1586 when two loads of coal were ordered, with two thousand billets for wood fires.[721] It is difficult to know which would be the cleaner fuel; coal gives out smoke, and wood produces ash which settles in a fine dust all over the room. However, the stores were obviously kept dry and all the clothes were hung out over lines to be aired.

Richard Jeffery, the Queen's Blacksmith, made 'xij staples to drawe Ropes thorowe' in 1572,[722] 'six staples to drawe Cordes throughe to hange our apparell on in ayringe of them' in 1574,[723] 'vj staples to drawe cordes throughe to ayer our Robes on' in 1575[724] and another six staples in 1576.[725] 'Six boultes of stronge Cordes to ayer our Apparell withall' are entered in the warrants in 1584.[726] Presumably pairs of staples were set opposite each other, embedded in the walls, with the ropes stretched taut between them to take the weight of the garments, which, in the case of the ermine lined parliament robes, would have been considerable.

Quantities of sweet powder were used to 'laye amongst our Roobes and apparrell'; eight pounds are entered in 1564,[727] supplied by Adam Bland the skinner, six pounds in April 1568,[728] eight pounds in October of the same year, with another two pounds sent to Somerset Place.[729] The amounts fluctuated; nineteen pounds were used in 1570,[730] eighteen pounds in 1571[731] and twenty-four pounds in 1584.[732] The deliveries of powder may have included some packages of fuller's earth to clean grease out of skins, wool and fur, as well as pulverised orris root with a fragrant odour like that of violets and damask powder, perfumed with damask roses, to smell sweet. The scented powder would have been placed in sweet bags to lay among the clothes. This is explained in an entry in the Michaelmas warrant of 1571, 'to John Wynne-yarde for one Dossen of silke Bagges with a twiste of golde and silke lyned with lether; Two dossen of large fustian Bagges with a lase of Thred: and two dossen of lesser Bagges all being perfumed with Amber Muske Syvett and stufte with perfumed Cotten and sweete powder all of our greate Guarderobe'.[733] These sweet bags were stored in a wooden box until they were required, to preserve the perfume. In the Lady Day warrant of 1565 John Grene, 'our Coffermaker . . . delivered to the said John Winniarde one great case to put in swete bages made of white wode covered with crimsin Velvet lyned with crimsin Sarceonet quilted by thimbrawderer and garnished with riben and gilt nayles all of our great warderobe'.[734]

As we have seen, a number of different perfumes were used for the Queen's clothes. John Wynyard supplied two pounds of 'damaske powder fyne' and one pound of coarse damask powder for perfuming a gown, a cloak, two pairs of shoes and two pairs of pantobles in 1572 and in the Michaelmas warrant of 1579 he is entered 'for perfumynge of eighte Gownes & fower Fannes with muske Civett and amber gryse: and for Two poundes of fyne perfumed Powder with muske civett and other drugges of our great warderobe'.[735] Another order in 1581 gives more details of items of clothing which were perfumed individually: 'to John Whynneyarde for perfumynge of our parliament Robes one gowne with a traine: sixe other gownes at sundrye tymes: for kepinge & trymming of fower spanishe skynnes and thre cordevante skynnes & a half: and for one pounde of white Powder perfumed with muske, sivett and other needefull Stuff'.[736] Any garments trimmed or lined with fur or made of leather might smell unpleasant. The curing treatment in England was still rather primitive in the sixteenth century. Sweet powder may also have helped to keep away moth as well as making the clothes smell pleasant. William Turner comments in his *Herbal*, printed in 1568: 'The Citrone appel . . . is thought to save clothes from beyng gnawed of mothes, if it be layd amongst clothes',[737] but there is no evidence that this treatment was used in the Wardrobe of Robes.

It would seem that as well as using press sheets, many pieces of clothing were individually wrapped to keep them from dust in the stores of the Wardrobe of Robes, to judge from the large number of bags supplied each year. These were usually made by the tailor. They range from items such as 'a Cloake bagge of blak vellat striped with lase of blak silke and lyned with russet Satten'[738] and 'a Cloake bagge of blak vellat layed over with golde lase and lyned with satten'[739] (almost as rich as the garments they protected) which would have been quite literally for cloaks, to 'a Case of buckeram for a greate frenche Gowne of blak vellat with a garde enbraudered with golde. And for another Case of buckeram for a Cloake'.[740] These buckram cases were more practical, as they could have been laundered frequently. It is not clear if 'sixe Cloake bagges of myllen [Milan] fustian lyned with buckeram'[741] were washable, but items such as 'a Case of blak Cotten for a Gowne of blak taphata . . . a Case for the bodies and slevis and a border aboute a Gowne of white Satten of white Cotten',[742] 'twentie Cases of Cotten viz sixe for french Gownes: eight for Petycoates and sixe for Cloakes: for one Case of fustian for a lose Gowne and another Case of fustian for a Cloake',[743] 'xxiiij Cases of Dowlas viz fyve for french Gownes: ix for Petycoates: vj for forepartes: & iiij for rounde Gownes'[744] and 'a Case of Dowlas for the garde of a foreparte'[745] would doubtless have been laundered at regular intervals.

The Queen's clothes were kept sweet smelling, free of moth, dust and damp in store, and portraits show how her elaborately embroidered gowns of velvet and satin were protected from touching the skin, and consequent soiling. Linen smocks were worn beneath 'bodies' and gowns, with linen ruffs, and linen wrist ruffs or turn-back cuffs, all of which were washable. Some of this laundry was dealt with by the silkwoman, as we have seen, and some by the Queen's laundress. Elizabeth Smith occupied the latter post at the beginning of the reign, when she was described as 'Laundres for the Quenes majesties table stuffe' in a warrant for livery at the time of the coronation.[746] It is not clear if this is the same woman who laundered the Queen's partlets in 1564 when Alice Mountague supplied 'xxiiij elles of holland for our Laundresse to drie our Partelettes'.[747] Later in 1564 the name is given as Smithson. She seems to have carried out minor repairs and replaced laces, as well as laundry work. Alice Mountague, the silkwoman, 'delivered to Elizabeth smithson our laundres to our use three ounces di of silke iiij ounces of bone lace of gold and silke of colors for ij Pillowbeares xij Pair of partlet laces of gold and silver six pair of Partelet laces of gold silver and silke: Once ounce of fyne Sisters thred: half a yarde of fyne laune: half a hundred of nedels seven yardes of Ruffes of laune for a partelet wrought with black spanish worke and edgid with gold bone lace: Six yardes of ruffes of laune for a partelett being wrought over[t]wharte with a cheverne of carnacion silke the ruffes

334 *A brush maker's workshop in Nürnberg. The brush maker manufactures brushes of all qualities for all purposes, from gold-mounted hairbrushes to brushes for scouring glasses. Woodcut from 'Eygentliche Beschreibung Aller Stände auff Erden' by Jost Amman and Hans Sachs, 1568. Private collection*

edgid with gold lace and six yardes of ruffes of laune for a partelett being hemmed edged and overcast with gold and carnacion silk lace all of our great warderobe'.[748]

Anne Twiste took Elizabeth Smithson's place in 1576.[749] There is an entry for 'Twelve elles of hollande cloth Delyverid to Anne Twiste our Laundres to carye and drye our lynen in' in the Michaelmas warrant of 1580[750] and another twelve ells of holland cloth were delivered to her in 1583, 'to our use to folde and carrye our clothes in of our great Guarderobe'.[751] James Hewish supplied another twelve ells to her in 1585[752] without specifying the use to which the linen was put, and twelve more in 1587 'to make bagges to carye our lynen in'.[753] In the Lady Day warrant of 1588 'Twelve elles of hollande cloth to foulde clothes upon'[754] were entered for Anne's use with a further twelve ells later in the same year 'to make bagges to cary our lynnen in'.[755] It is clear from these entries that the Queen's laundress dealt with some delicate embroidered linen garments such as partlets, ruffs and smocks, as well as table linen, although both the Queen's silkwomen and silkman undertook laundering of fine embroidered veils and other items,[756] which would have required more skill.

The tailor would often unpick and remodel the Queen's gowns, taking out linings stained with perspiration and putting in new ones. Marks on rich fabrics could have been disguised, if not completely removed. Cleaning methods seem to have been confined mainly to rubbing, brushing and beating the clothes. Regular deliveries of necessaries to the Office of the Wardrobe of Robes included 'Three dossen of Brusshes: Two dossen of rubbinge Brushes' (Fig. 334) and 'one yerde of cloth to make rubbing clothes'.[757] No detail is given of the method which Walter Fyshe used for 'takinge oute the staines of a foreparte of cloth of golde'[758] nor how William Jones worked on a foreparte of cloth of silver 'gettinge out the staines' and 'Dressing & getting oute the staines oute of xlviij yerdes of satten'[759] but there were certainly efficient ways of cleaning hangings and carpets. Letters patent were issued on 12 January 1585 to James Burton and Segar Drase, 'scowrers of Arras', who

have of late invented and devised a new kinde of makinge Cleene of hanginges and Carpettes much fayrer than heretofore hath bynne donne by any others, the proof wherof we have seene in some hanginges of our owne. We let you theruppon to understand that we have not only receyved the said James and Segar in to our service for this purpose But also are pleased to geve unto them for ther service to be donne unto us at all tymes when they shalbe therunto requyred, the Fee of iiijd by the day duringe ther naturall lyves . . . And our further pleasure ys that they shall have for every stick of Tapistry beinge made Cleane viijd. And for every stick of Turkey worke being made Cleane xd . . . and . . . have given and graunted unto the said James and Segar and unto them of ther Servauntes and assignes onlie free pryveledge for the makinge Cleane of all maner of hanginges and Carpettes and other thinges whatsoever beinge of Arres or Tapastrie . . . during the terme of xij years. prohibitinge and straightlie upon our highe displeasure Commaundinge all mayiors, Justices of Peace, Shreffes bayliefes Constables, hedboroughes [head burghers?] and all other our officers whatsoever to ayde and assyst the said James and Segar or ther assignes as often as nede shall requyre to make Searche fynde out and see that no other persons do in any otherwyse intermeddle with the same duringe the said terme of xij yeares. And that all such as shall offend herein after warnynge geven them to be Commytted to pryson untill our Further pleasure be knowne.[760]

It is obvious that Burton and Drase had discovered some highly effective cleaning process. Whether these methods of cleaning could also have been used on clothes is uncertain, but regular brushing would have removed surface dust. This must have taken a considerable amount of time, as the work would have had to be done carefully to avoid damaging decorative braids and embroidery. The job was probably carried out by the Groom and Page of the Robes at the same time as the skinner beat the furs trimming the garments. The increasing number of clothes led to the employment of an extra member of staff in 1583, Robert Pamplin, 'brussher of our Robes'.[761] He was paid 'for his travell and paynes by the space of half one yere past thre poundes of our greate guarderobe' and the same for the following half year until 1585 when he was paid five pounds 'for his travell and paines in mendinge and alteringe of our Garmentes by the space of one half yere past'.[762]

It seems that Pamplin's increased duties included some laundry work. In the Michaelmas warrant of 1587 he is entered 'for wasshinge and starchinge of xlij peire of slevis. xxiij Rolles . & xxvj yerdes of hollande cloth. for wasshinge and starchinge of xliiij peces of narrowe cuttworke to drawe oute Gownes conteyning xxx yerdes: for wasshinge and starchinge of one foreparte and one face for a Gowne of lawne cuttworke: for making of ix Curtens of hollande cloth and for his travell and paynes one half yere past fyve poundes all of our greate Guarderobe'.[763] It was probably this work that earned Pamplin promotion to the post of Page of the Robes in the spring of 1588.[764] Around this time Richard Nightingale was promoted to Groom of the Robes[765] from the post of Yeoman of the Male.[766] His work as Groom is entered in the Lady Day warrant of 1588:

beating and ayring of our Robes & apparell with two thowsande billets. Two loades of Coales. Two poundes of Powder. six peces of Frenche buckeram. Two dossen of Brusshes. one dossen of rubbinge brusshes and for making of eight peire of presse Sheetes the cloth of our stores threst of our greate guarderobe'.[767]

Roger Earle became 'Brussher of our Robes',[768] but for his 'travayles and paynes by the space of one half yere paste' he was only paid fifty shillings. Pamplin must have been a capable and hardworking man; by 1598 he was Groom of the Robes[769] and was appointed Yeoman of the Robes in 1603,[770] when James I came to the throne. Roger Earle was followed by John Banghe in 1594,[771] Raffe Holland in 1597[772] and George Eagle in 1600,[773] but none of these four seems to have carried out alterations and laundry work in the same way as Robert Pamplin.

Notes

1 PRO, LC5/49, ff. 213–14.
2 Cloth woven from irregularly coloured wools, see *Linthicum*, p. 61.
3 PRO, LC5/49, f. 286. Arthur Middleton was expelled. See note 38.
4 For examples of deliveries from Dane see PRO, LC5/33, f. 16, warrant dated 20 Oct. 1562 and BL, Egerton 2806, f. 50, warrant dated 28 Sept. 1572, and from Hicks and Ferrars see PRO, LC5/37, f. 236, warrant dated 28 Sept. 1601.
5 PRO, LC5/32, f. 325, dated Anno 5 Mary (between 6 July 1557 and 5 July 1558).
6 PRO, AO1, Roll 1, Bundle 2339.
7 BL, Add. 5751 A, f. 57, warrant for deliveries dated 24 Sept. 1559.
8 *Cal. Pat. Rolls Eliz.*, 1558–60, 1, pt. 7, p. 354, dated 7 January 1560.
9 PRO, LC5/32, f. 291. For detailed account of George Lovekyn, see Anne F. Sutton, 'George Lovekyn, Tailor to Three Kings of England, 1470–1504' in *Costume* 15, 1981, pp. 1–12. For Richard Gibson see W. R. Streitberger, 'The Development of Henry VIII's Revels Establishment', in *Medieval English Theatre*, 7, no. 2, pp. 84–94.
10 See Chapter VI, note 36. The last mention of Fyshe among the warrants is in BL, Egerton 2806, f. 174v, warrant dated 6 April 1582.
11 *Feuillerat*, John Arnold's appointment, p. 72; Walter Fyshe's appointment, p. 73.
12 *Cal. Pat. Rolls, Eliz.*, 1572–75, VI, p. 226, no. 1205, and *Feuillerat*, p. 73.
13 BL, Egerton 2806, f. 174v, warrant dated 6 April 1582.
14 PRO, LC5/32, f. 272, letters patent of Edward Kirkham 'for keeping of all vestures and apparell of the Revells', dated 28 April 1586.
15 *Feuillerat*, p. 16.
16 *Haynes, State Papers*, 1, p. 368.
17 HMC *Hatfield, Salisbury MSS* (1883) pt. 1, p. 361, no. 1184. Report dated 20 August 1568.
18 *Williams, Platter*, p. 198.
19 See Chapter V, note 18. The run of New Year's Gift Rolls is incomplete, so the gift cannot be checked.
20 See Chapter V, note 10.
21 PRO, Brudenell, f. 422, 10 Sept. 1578, proved in 1585.
22 *Feuillerat*, p. 13.
23 Ibid.
24 *Cunningham, Revels Accounts*, p. 136, undated but probably for December 1578 as other accounts for the Amazons masque near it are dated between 20 and 28 December 1578.
25 See Chapter VII, note 41.
26 See note 21.
27 *Clode, Merchant Taylors*, pt. 1, p. 239, and *Clode, Memorials*, p. 479.
28 *Stow*, 1, p. 181.
29 Payments to Edward Jones for the late Queen Mary's clothes appear in the first warrant of Elizabeth's reign in 1559, PRO, LC9/53, f. 13v.
30 *Records of the Merchant Taylors, Index to Freemen 1530–1929*, Guildhall Library, London.
31 *Clode, Merchant Taylors*, II, p. 342.
32 Ibid., pp. 343–44.
33 BL, Egerton 2806, f. 73, warrant dated 14 Oct. 1574.
34 Ibid., f. 80v, warrant dated 13 April 1575.
35 Ibid., f. 99, warrant dated 14 April 1576.
36 Ibid., f. 107v, warrant dated 26 Sept. 1576. For full details see Chapter V, note 128.
37 PRO, LC5/49, f. 217, Richard Nightingale was promoted to Groom of the Robes by letters patent dated 18 July 1588. See BL, Egerton 2806, f. 197, warrant dated 12 April 1587 and f.226, warrant for livery dated 7 Nov. 1587, for Nightingale as Yeoman of the Male; f.235v, warrant dormant for livery dated 20 May 1588, for Nightingale as Groom.
38 PRO, LC5/49, f. 286, certificate dated 3 Nov. 1594.
39 BL, Egerton 2806, ff. 89, 89v, warrant dated 28 Sept. 1575.
40 Ibid., f. 96v, warrant dated 14 April 1576.
41 Ibid., f. 105v, warrant dated 26 Sept. 1576.
42 Ibid., f. 114, warrant dated 12 April 1577, possibly the doublet listed in *Arnold, Lost from HMB*, p. 78, no. 369.
43 Ibid., f. 185v, warrant dated 20 April 1583.
44 Ibid., f. 140v, warrant dated 10 April 1579.
45 HMC *Hatfield, Salisbury MSS*, II, p. 3, no. 6, confession dated 15 January 1572.
46 *Moryson, Itinerary*, Part III, Book 4, Chapter II, p. 180.
47 BL, Egerton 2806, f. 73, warrant dated 14 Oct. 1574.
48 *Cennini*, p. 104.
49 *Alcega*, examples on ff. 74, 74v, 75, 75v, 76v.
50 *Cennini*, pp. 106–07.
51 BL, Egerton 2806, f. 62v, warrant dated 20 Oct. 1573.
52 Garsault, *L'Art du Tailleur* (1769), quoted in *Arnold, Patterns 1660–1860*, p. 5.
53 *Cunningham, Revels Accounts*, p. 37. Christmas 1572.
54 BL, Egerton 2806, ff. 132v, warrant dated 26 Sept. 1578 and f. 154, warrant dated 12 April 1580. 'Mett yards' and 'mett ells' for the Wardrobe of Robes were usually supplied by Robert Sibthorpe, the farthingale maker.
55 Ibid., f. 184v, warrant dated 20 April 1583.
56 Cited in *OED*, Thomas Wilson, *The Arte of Rhetorique*, (1553), p. 83b; Francis Robinson, *A Glossary of words used in the neighbourhood of Whitby* (1876).
57 Thomas Dekker, *The Seven Deadly Sinnes of London* (1606), p. 31.
58 BL, Egerton 2806, f. 137v, warrant dated 10 April 1579 (two pairs); f. 158, warrant dated 28 Sept. 1580 (two pairs); f.184v, warrant dated 20 April 1583 (one pair) and f. 190, warrant dated 26 Sept. 1583 (one pair).

59 Ibid., f. 195, warrant dated 12 April 1584.
60 Ibid., f. 200v, warrant dated 27 Sept. 1584; f. 223, warrant dated 26 Sept. 1587; f. 235, warrant dated 27 Sept. 1588.
61 Ibid., f. 233, warrant dated 27 Sept. 1588.
62 Ibid., ff. 60, 60v, warrant dated 20 Oct. 1573.
63 Ibid., f. 159, warrant dated 28 Sept. 1580.
64 PRO, LC5/37, f. 14, warrant dated 14 April 1594.
65 Ibid., f. 73, warrant dated 28 Sept. 1595.
66 PRO LC9/91, f. 9v, 1600–01.
67 *Harrison*, pt. II, (1878), p. 34.
68 BL, Egerton 2806, f. 145v, warrant dated 12 Oct., 1579; f. 197, warrant dated 12 April 1584; f. 224, warrant dated 26 Sept. 1587.
69 Cited in *OED*, William Caxton, *The Foure Sonnes of Amyon* (1489), vii, 173.
70 *Arnold, Patterns*, p. 17, Fig. 100 and p. 66.
71 *Anderson, Hispanic Costume*, p. 253, note 128.
72 Cited in *OED*, Claudius Hollyband, *The Treasurie of the French Tong* (1580).
73 *Arnold, 'Neckwear'*, pp. 111–13.
74 The transparent wax is almost invisible in the examples I have examined.
75 BL, Egerton 2806, f. 166v, warrant dated 6 April 1581: see also f. 106 warrant dated 26 Sept. 1576, for delivery of 'two bundelles of browne paper'.
76 PRO, LC5/33, f.4, warrant dated 20 Oct. 1562.
77 BL, Egerton 2806, f. 29, warrant dated 4 April 1571; f. 34v, warrant dated 24 Sept. 1571.
78 Ibid., f. 44v, and f. 45, warrant dated 28 Sept. 1572.
79 Ibid., f. 59v, warrant dated 20 Oct. 1573.
80 Ibid., f. 72, warrant dated 14 Oct. 1574.
81 Ibid., f. 79v, warrant dated 13 April 1575. The 'slevis of buckeram' may have been sleeve supports, rather than patterns. This is not clear from the description.
82 Ibid., f. 137, 137v, warrant dated 10 April 1579.
83 Ibid., f. 151, warrant dated 12 April 1580.
84 Ibid., f. 170, warrant dated 25 Sept. 1581.
85 Ibid., f. 111v, warrant dated 12 April 1577.
86 Ibid., f. 151, warrant dated 12 April 1580.
87 Ibid., f. 137v, warrant dated 10 April 1579.
88 Ibid., f. 77, warrant dated 13 April 1575.
89 PRO, LC5/33, ff. 124–25, warrant dated 16 April 1565.
90 BL, Egerton 2806, f. 102, warrant dated 26 Sept. 1576.
91 Ibid., f. 125, warrant dated 12 April 1578.
92 Ibid., f. 201, warrant dated 27 Sept. 1584.
93 Ibid., f. 225v, warrant dated 26 Sept. 1587.
94 PRO, LC5/37, f. 10, warrant dated 12 April 1594.
95 BL, Egerton 2806, f. 2v, warrant dated 14 April 1568.
96 Ibid., f. 58v, warrant dated 20 Oct. 1573.
97 Ibid., f. 26v, warrant dated 14 Oct. 1570.
98 Ibid., f. 157, warrant dated 28 Sept. 1580.
99 Ibid., f. 95, warrant dated 14 April 1576.
100 See note 118.
101 BL, Egerton 2806, f. 137, warrant dated 10 April 1579.
102 Ibid., f. 163v, warrant dated 6 April 1581.
103 Ibid., f. 78v, warrant dated 13 April 1575.
104 T. S. Willan, *Studies in Elizabethan Foreign Trade* (1959), p. 254 and p. 76; see also p. 240 for source of the accounts.
105 PRO, LC5/37, f. 59, warrant dated 10 April 1595. For calico see *Linthicum*, pp. 104–05.
106 BL, Egerton 2806, f. 12v, warrant dated 26 April 1569.
107 Ibid., f. 16v, warrant dated 6 Oct. 1569.
108 Ibid., f. 34v, warrant dated 24 Sept. 1571.
109 Ibid., f. 163v, warrant dated 6 April 1581.
110 PRO, LC5/36, f. 119, warrant dated 27 Sept. 1589.
111 For examples see BL, Egerton 2806, f. 116v, warrant dated 27 Sept. 1577 ('cutt and raste'); f. 163v, warrant dated 6 April 1581 ('razed and pinked'); also Stowe inventory f. 60v/66 and f. 57/16.
112 PRO, LC5/37, f. 22, warrant dated 27 Sept. 1594.
113 BL, Egerton 2806, f. 156, warrant dated 12 April 1580, supplied by Alice; f. 172v, warrant dated 15 Sept. 1581, supplied by Roger; f. 188, warrant dated 20 April 1583, supplied by Roger.
114 See Chapter V, note 182.
115 BL, Egerton 2806, f. 77, warrant dated 18 April 1575.
116 PRO, LC5/33, ff. 143–44, warrant dated 20 Oct. 1565.
117 Ibid., f. 55, warrant dated 4 May 1563.
118 BL, Egerton 2806, f. 79, warrant dated 13 April 1575.
119 PRO, LC5/33, ff. 3–4, warrant dated 20 Oct. 1562.
120 Ibid., ff. 63–64, warrant dated 2 Nov. 1563.
121 BL, Egerton 2806, f. 227v, warrant dated 3 April 1588.
122 PRO, LC 5/33, f. 143, warrant dated 20 Oct. 1565.
123 See *Arnold, Patterns*, fig. 371, pp. 120, 121, for vents in a gown faced with olive-green, twill-weave wool.
124 PRO, LC5/34, f. 22, warrant dated last day of Sept. 1567.
125 A woman's silver camlet boned bodice and matching petticoat of c. 1660–65 at the Museum of Costume, Bath, has a pocket set in the side seam of the petticoat.
126 BL, Egerton 2806, f. 53, warrant dated 1 April 1573.
127 Ibid., f. 80, warrant dated 13 April 1575.
128 Ibid., f. 87v, warrant dated 28 Sept. 1575.
129 Ibid., ff. 86, 88, warrant dated 28 Sept. 1575.

130 Ibid., f. 86.
131 Ibid., f. 144v, warrant dated 12 Oct. 1579.
132 Ibid., f. 152, warrant dated 12 April 1580.
133 Ibid., f. 151, warrant dated 12 April 1580.
134 For examples see PRO, LC5/36, f. 133, warrant dated 18 May 1590.
135 For 'sleeves borne up with whale-bones' see *Moryson, Itinerary*, Part III, Book 4, Chapter 2, p. 177; for verthingale sleeves see PRO, LC5/37, f. 190, warrant dated 8 April 1600.
136 See note 245.
137 BL, Egerton 2806, f. 158v, warrant dated 28 Sept. 1580.
138 Ibid., f. 213 and f. 217, warrant dated 27 Sept. 1586.
139 PRO, LC5/36, f. 133, warrant dated 18 May 1590; f. 251, warrant dated 10 May 1593.
140 PRO, LC5/37, f. 9, warrant dated 12 April 1594. See also Chapter VI, notes 235 and 236, for 'a peire of bodies of sweete lether' in 1579 and eighteenth century leather corsets.
141 PRO, LC5/49, f. 339.
142 BL, Egerton 2806, f. 8, warrant dated 14 April 1568.
143 PRO, LC5/32, f. 315, dated 2 July 1569.
144 BL, Egerton 2806, f. 115v, warrant dated 12 April 1577.
145 Ibid., f. 148v, warrant dated 12 Oct. 1579.
146 Ibid., f. 167, warrant dated 6 April 1581.
147 Ibid., f. 222, warrant dated 12 April 1587.
148 *Stow*, II, p. 16.
149 *Strype*, III, p. 229.
150 *Stow*, II, note on p. 359.
151 BL, Egerton 2806, f. 167v, warrant dated 6 April 1581; f. 174v, warrant dated 6 April 1582.
152 Ibid., f. 33v, warrant dated 4 April 1571.
153 Ibid., f. 36v, warrant dated 24 Sept. 1571.
154 Ibid., f. 42v, warrant dated 9 April 1572.
155 See *OED* and S. F. A. Caulfield and B. C. Saward, *The Dictionary of Needlework* (1882, facs. ed. 1972) for further details.
156 New Year's Gift Roll 1562, BL, Harl. Roll V18, printed in *Progr. Eliz.*, I, p. 118.
157 PRO, LC5/33, f. 54, warrant dated 4 May 1563.
158 Ibid., ff. 72–73, warrant dated 2 Nov. 1563.
159 Ibid., f. 173, warrant dated 25 March 1566.
160 PRO, LC5/36, f. 189, warrant dated 27 Sept. 1591.
161 PRO, LC5/33, f. 55, warrant dated 4 May 1563.
162 PRO, LC5/36, f. 177, warrant dated 10 June 1591.
163 PRO, LC5/37, ff. 190–91, warrant dated 8 April 1600.
164 *Princely Magnificence*, p. 66, cat. no. 57.
165 C. R. Dodwell (trs.) *Theophilus: The Various Arts* (1961), p. 171. Manuscript probably written between 1110 and 1140, not later than 1150.
166 PRO, LC5/33, f. 17, warrant dated 20 Oct. 1562.
167 PRO, LC5/37, f. 71, warrant dated 28 Sept. 1595.
168 PRO, LC5/36, f. 188, warrant dated 27 Sept. 1591. 'Both sydes alyke' means 'reversible', ie., double-sided embroidery.
169 PRO, LC5/37, f. 21, warrant dated 27 Sept. 1594.
170 PRO, AO1, Roll 1, Bundle 2339.
171 PRO, LC9/53, f. 18, Anno Primo 1558–59, 1559–60, but dates are not apparently in sequence as see f. 15v, Walter Fyshe warrant 16 April Anno Secundo (1560). William Jurden is listed as 'oure skynner' in BL, Add. 5751A, f. 57, Signet warrant dated 24 Sept. 1559.
172 PRO, LC9/54, f. 20, Michaelmas 1560–Michaelmas 1561.
173 Ibid., f. 33v.
174 PRO, LC5/49, ff. 285–86, dated 30 May 1594.
175 For example BL, Egerton 2806, f. 5, warrant dated 14 April 1568.
176 For example, ibid., f. 18v, warrant dated 6 Oct. 1569.
177 For example, ibid., f. 23v, warrant dated 12 April 1570.
178 For example, ibid.
179 For example, ibid., f. 31v, warrant dated 4 April 1571.
180 For example, ibid., f. 23v, warrant dated 12 April 1570.
181 For example, ibid., f. 55v, warrant dated 1 April 1573.
182 For example, ibid., f. 48, warrant dated 28 Sept. 1572; f. 55v, warrant dated 1 April 1573.
183 For example, ibid., f. 55v, warrant dated 1 April 1573.
184 For example, ibid., f. 55, warrant dated 1 April 1573.
185 For example, ibid., f. 67, warrant dated 14 April 1574; f. 125, warrant dated 12 April 1578.
186 For example, PRO, LC5/36, f. 144, warrant dated 28 Sept. 1590.
187 For example, BL, Egerton 2806, f. 195v, warrant dated 12 April 1584.
188 For example, ibid., f. 214, warrant dated 27 Sept. 1586.
189 For example, ibid., f. 153v, warrant dated 12 April 1580.
190 Ibid., f. 56, warrant dated 1 April 1573.
191 Ibid., f. 225v, warrant dated 26 Sept. 1587.
192 New Year's Gift Roll 1585, Folger Z.d.16.
193 BL, Egerton 2806, f. 193, warrant dated 26 Sept. 1583; f. 220, warrant dated 12 April 1586.
194 See Chapter V, note 37.
195 PRO, LC5/37, f. 285, warrant dated 18 May 1603.
196 *Veale*, p. 23.
197 *Veale*, p. 32.
198 BL, Egerton 2806, f. 47v, warrant dated 28 Sept. 1572.
199 Ibid., f. 55, warrant dated 1 April 1573.
200 *Veale*, pp. 23, 24, 29, 137, 138.
201 *OED*.
202 PRO, LC5/33, f. 8, warrant dated 20 Oct. 1562.
203 PRO, LC5/36, f. 144, warrant dated 28 Sept. 1590.
204 PRO, LC5/37, f. 162, warrant dated 30 March 1599.
205 PRO, LC5/33, f. 48, warrant dated 4 May 1563.
206 *Anderson*, p. 208.
207 Ibid.
208 Ibid.
209 Quoted in *Waugh, Corsets*, p. 23.
210 See Chapter VI, note 80.
211 See Chapter VI, note 83.
212 *CSP Venetian*, VII, 1558–80, p. 92. Letter describing the events of 24 May, from Il Schifanoya to the Castellan of Mantua, dated 30 May 1559.
213 *Anderson*, p. 208.
214 See Chapter VI, note 84.
215 PRO, LC5/33, f. 40, warrant dated 4 May 1563.
216 Ibid., f. 125, warrant dated 16 April 1565.
217 See *Arnold, Patterns*, p. 52, fig. 377.
218 PRO, LC5/33, f. 125, warrant dated 16 April 1565.
219 Ibid., ff. 144–45, warrant dated 20 Oct. 1565.
220 Ibid., f. 144.
221 Ibid., f. 166, warrant dated 25 March 1566.
222 Ibid., f. 189–90, warrant dated 10 Feb. 1567.
223 BL, Egerton 2806, f. 90, warrant dated 28 Sept. 1575.
224 Ibid., f. 48v, warrant dated 28 Sept. 1572.
225 Ibid., f. 106, warrant dated 26 Sept. 1576.
226 Ibid., f. 179v, warrant dated 28 Sept. 1582.
227 Ibid., f. 4v, warrant dated 14 April 1568.
228 Ibid., f. 10, warrant dated 16 Oct. 1568.
229 Ibid., f. 15, warrant dated 26 April 1569.
230 *OED*.
231 BL, Egerton 2806, f. 23, warrant dated 12 April 1570. He made a farthingale for Anne Knolles, f. 27v, warrant dated 14 Oct. 1570.
232 *Alcega*, p. 67 and *Arnold, Patterns*, p. 7, figs 27, 28.
233 *Arnold, Patterns*, p. 124 for Castilian bara and p. 7 for arrangement of gores.
234 BL, Egerton 2806, f. 32, warrant dated 4 April 1571.
235 Ibid., f. 37v, warrant dated 24 Sept. 1571.
236 Ibid., f. 66v, warrant dated 14 April 1574.
237 PRO, LC5/33, f. 144–45, warrant dated 20 Oct. 1565.
238 BL, Egerton 2806, f. 48v, warrant dated 28 Sept. 1572.
239 Ibid., f. 56v, warrant dated 1 April 1573.
240 Ibid., f. 81v, warrant dated 13 April 1575.
241 Ibid., f. 106, warrant dated 26 Sept. 1576.
242 Ibid., f. 154, warrant dated 12 April 1580.
243 Ibid., f. 106, warrant dated 26 Sept. 1576.
244 Ibid., f. 158v, warrant dated 28 Sept. 1580.
245 *Robertson, Inventaires*, p. xxviii.
246 BL, Egerton 2806, f. 176v, warrant dated 6 April 1582.
247 Ibid., f. 205, warrant dated 16 April 1585.
248 PRO, LC5/37, f. 111, warrant dated 8 July 1597.
249 BL, Egerton 2806, f. 37v, warrant dated 24 Sept. 1571.
250 Ibid., f. 42v, warrant dated 9 April 1572.
251 Ibid., f. 48, warrant dated 28 Sept. 1572.
252 Ibid., f. 56v, warrant dated 1 April 1573.
253 Ibid., f. 62, warrant dated 20 Oct. 1573.
254 Ibid., f. 68, warrant dated 14 April 1574.
255 Ibid., f. 73v, warrant dated 14 Oct. 1574.
256 Ibid., f. 81v, warrant dated 13 April 1575.
257 Ibid., f. 90, warrant dated 28 Sept. 1575.
258 Ibid., f. 97v, warrant dated 14 April 1576.
259 Ibid., f. 106, warrant dated 26 Sept. 1576.
260 Ibid., f. 113, warrant dated 12 April 1577.
261 Ibid., f. 119v, warrant dated 27 Sept. 1577.
262 Ibid., f. 132v, warrant dated 26 Sept. 1578.
263 Ibid., f. 166v, warrant dated 6 April 1581.
264 Ibid., f. 191, warrant dated 26 Sept. 1583.
265 Ibid., f. 209, warrant dated 27 Sept. 1585.
266 PRO, LC5/37, f. 103, warrant dated 28 Sept. 1596.
267 Ibid., f. 22, warrant dated 1 Sept. 1594.
268 BL, Egerton 2806 f. 62, warrant dated 20 Oct. 1573.
269 Ibid., f. 67v, warrant dated 14 April 1574.
270 Ibid., f. 81v, warrant dated 13 April 1575.
271 Ibid., f. 90, warrant dated 28 Sept. 1575.
272 Ibid., f. 125v, warrant dated 12 April 1578.
273 Ibid., f. 132v, warrant dated 26 Sept. 1578.
274 Ibid., f. 81v, warrant dated 13 April 1575.
275 Ibid., f. 56v, warrant dated 1 April 1573.
276 Ibid., f. 158v, warrant dated 28 Sept. 1580.
277 See Chapter VI, note 75.
278 BL, Egerton 2806, f. 166, warrant dated 6 April 1581.
279 Ibid., f. 203v, warrant dated 16 April 1585. Made by William Jones.
280 Ibid., f. 208, warrant dated 27 Sept. 1585. Made by William Jones.
281 Ibid., f. 214v, warrant dated 27 Sept. 1586. Made by Robert Sibthorpe.
282 Ibid., f. 178v, warrant dated 28 Sept. 1582.
283 Ibid., f. 176v, warrant dated 6 April 1582.
284 Ibid., f. 209, warrant dated 27 Sept. 1585.
285 Stowe inventory, f. 60v/71.
286 See notes 101, 102.
287 *Harrison, Description of England*, quoted in E. Sitwell, *The Queens and the Hive*, p. 471.
288 Quoted in *Waugh, Corsets*, p. 33.
289 See *Linthicum*, p. 181.
290 For example, PRO, LC9/54, f. 24, Michaelmas 1560–Michaelmas 1561.
291 PRO, AO1/Roll 1, Bundle 2339.
292 BL, Egerton 2806, f. 186, warrant dated 20 April 1583.
293 PRO, LC5/33, f. 51, warrant dated 4 May 1563. This appears to be the earliest entry for his livery.
294 Ibid., f. 15, warrant dated 12 Oct. 1562.
295 Ibid., f. 51, warrant dated 4 May 1563 and f. 70, warrant dated 2 Nov. 1563.

296 Ibid., f. 90, warrant dated last day of May 1564 and f. 115, warrant dated 27 Sept. 1564.
297 Ibid., f. 129, warrant dated 16 April 1565.
298 Ibid., f. 150, warrant dated 20 Oct. 1565.
299 Ibid., f. 15, warrant dated 12 Oct. 1562.
300 Ibid., f. 51, warrant dated 4 May 1563.
301 Ibid., f. 70, warrant dated 2 Nov. 1563.
302 Ibid., f. 90, warrant dated last day of May 1564.
303 PRO, LC5/37, f. 274, warrant dated 27 Sept. 1602.
304 BL, Egerton 2806, f. 198v, warrant dated 12 April 1584.
305 Ibid., f. 218v, warrant dated 27 Sept. 1586.
306 PRO, LC5/49, f. 213, and BL, Egerton 2806, f. 226, warrant dormant for liveries dated 7 Nov. 1587.
307 BL, Egerton 2806, f. 198v, warrant dated 12 April 1584.
308 Ibid., f. 224, warrant dated 26 Sept. 1587.
309 Ibid., f. 230v, warrant dated 3 April 1588.
310 PRO, LC5/37, f. 314, warrant dated 28 Sept. 1603.
311 Ibid., f. 323.
312 Ibid.
313 Ibid., f. 51, warrant dated 18 Feb. 1595. Here Cookesbury is described as 'Fether maker'.
314 PRO, LC5/34, f. 26, warrant dated last day of Sept. 1567.
315 PRO, LC5/33, f. 129, warrant dated 16 April 1565.
316 Ibid. See note 386 for hose and slops for Jack Grene, the Queen's fool, in the same warrant.
317 BL, Egerton 2806, f. 57, warrant dated 1 April 1573.
318 Ibid., f. 84v, warrant dated 13 April 1575.
319 *Arnold, Patterns*, pp. 31–34, 93–94.
320 BL, Egerton 2806, f. 98, warrant dated 14 April 1576.
321 Ibid., f. 148, warrant dated 12 Oct. 1579.
322 Robert Greene, *A disputation betweene a hee conny-catcher and a shee conny-catcher* (1592).
323 BL, Egerton 2806, f. 74v, warrant dated 14 Oct. 1574.
324 *Stubbes*, 1583 edn, pp. 21v, 22.
325 PRO, LC5/37, f. 272, warrant dated 27 Sept. 1602. See also John Parr 'tacking of a hatt of Tiffany lawne and raysing yt on a nother lawne and enbrawdering yt, with two ounces of pynched plate & hanging spangles', f. 178, warrant dated 28 Sept. 1599.
326 See Chapter V, note 32.
327 BL, Egerton 2806, f. 10, warrant dated 16 Oct. 1568.
328 Ibid., f. 26v, warrant dated 14 Oct. 1570.
329 Ibid., f. 33, warrant dated 4 April 1571.
330 For example, ibid., f. 41v, warrant dated 9 April 1572; f. 55, warrant dated 1 April 1573; f. 74v, warrant dated 14 Oct. 1574 (two yards); f. 82, warrant dated 13 April 1575; for 'Satten white and black', f. 126v, warrant dated 12 April 1578; f. 148, warrant dated 12 Oct. 1579; f. 159v, warrant dated 28 Sept. 1580.
331 Ibid., f. 159v, warrant dated 28 Sept. 1580.
332 W. Stepney, *The Spanish Schoole-master* (1591), p. 32.
333 *Stubbes*, 1583 edn, p. 42v. Randle Holme noted 'A Mask . . . This is a thing that in former times Gentlewomen used to put over their Faces when they Travel to keep them from Sun burning; it covered only the Brow Eyes and Nose, through the holes they saw their way; the rest of the face was covered with a Chin-cloth. Of these Masks they used them either square with a flat and even top, or else the top cut with an half round; they were generally made of Black Velvet. The second form of Mask is the Visard Mask, which covers the whole face, having holes for the eyes, a case for the Nose, and a slit for the mouth, and to speak through; this kind of Mask is taken off and put on in a moment of time, being only held in the Teeth by means of a round bead fastned on the inside over against the mouth'. *Holme, Academy*, III, p. 13.
334 BL, Egerton 2806, f. 120, warrant dated 27 Sept. 1577.
335 Ibid., f. 128, warrant dated 12 April 1578.
336 Ibid., f. 57, warrant dated 1 April 1573.
337 *Holme, Academy*, III, p. 98.
338 BL, Egerton 2806, f. 68v, warrant dated 14 April 1574.
339 Ibid., f. 82, warrant dated 18 April 1575.
340 Ibid., f. 98, warrant dated 18 April 1576.
341 Ibid., f. 107, warrant dated 26 Sept. 1576.
342 Ibid., f. 127, warrant dated 17 April 1578.
343 Ibid., f. 140, warrant dated 10 April 1579.
344 See Chapter II, 'Phoenix' and 'Siena Sieve' portraits.
345 BL, Egerton, 2806, f. 160, warrant dated 28 Sept. 1580.
346 Ibid., f. 191, warrant dated 26 Sept. 1583.
347 PRO, LC5/36, ff. 264–65, warrant dated 28 Sept. 1593.
348 BL, Egerton 2806, f. 196v, warrant dated 12 April 1584.
349 Ibid., f. 201, warrant dated 27 Sept. 1584.
350 Ibid., f. 209v, warrant dated 27 Sept. 1585.
351 Ibid.
352 Ibid., f. 224, warrant dated 26 Sept. 1587.
353 Quoted in *Linthicum*, p. 224.
354 BL, Egerton 2806, f. 205v, warrant dated 16 April 1585.
355 Ibid., f. 215v, warrant dated 27 Sept. 1586.
356 Ibid., f. 216, warrant dated 27 Sept. 1586.
357 John Florio, *A worlde of wordes, or most copious and exact dictionarie in Italian and English* (1598).
358 BL, Egerton 2806, f. 220v, warrant dated 12 April 1587.
359 Ibid.
360 Ibid., f. 224, warrant dated 26 Sept. 1587.
361 Ibid., f.224v, warrant dated 26 Sept. 1587.
362 PRO, LC5/37, f. 164, warrant dated 30 March 1599.
363 BL, Egerton, 2806, f. 229v, warrant dated 3 April 1588.
364 Ibid., ff. 229v, 230.
365 Ibid., f. 230.
366 Ibid.
367 Ibid.
368 Ibid.
369 Ibid., f. 233, warrant dated 27 Sept. 1588.
370 Ibid.
371 PRO, LC5/36, ff. 212–13, warrant dated 6 June 1592.
372 PRO, LC5/37, f. 90, warrant dated 29 April 1595.
373 Ibid., f. 222, warrant dated 1 April 1601.
374 Ibid., f. 257, warrant dated 19 April 1602.
375 Ibid., f. 288, warrant dated 18 May 1603.
376 PRO, LC9/54, f. 23, Michaelmas 1560–Michaelmas 1561.
377 PRO, LC5/36, f. 221, warrant dated 28 Sept. 1592.
378 BL, Egerton 2806, f. 188, warrant dated 20 April 1583. An early entry for this livery is in PRO, LC5/33, f. 13, warrant dated 20 Oct. 1562.
379 PRO, LC5/33, f. 13, warrant dated 20 Oct. 1562.
380 PRO, LC5/36, f. 136, warrant dated 18 May 1590.
381 PRO, LC5/37, f. 111, warrant dated 8 July 1597.
382 PRO, LC5/36, f. 253, warrant dated 10 May 1593.
383 PRO, LC5/37, f. 119, warrant dated 11 April 1597.
384 Ibid., f. 289, warrant dated 18 May 1603.
385 BL, Egerton 2806, f. 119, warrant dated 27 Sept. 1577.
386 PRO, LC5/33, f. 128, warrant dated 16 April 1565.
387 S. Rowlands, *The Letting of Humours Blood in the Head-Vaine*, (1600), epigram 30.
388 Thomas Wright, *The Passions of the Minde in Generall* (1601), quoted in *Harrison*, p. 246.
389 PRO, LC5/33, f. 197, warrant dated 10 Feb. 1567.
390 PRO, LC5/34, f. 171, warrant dated 9 April 1572. See also BL, Egerton 2806, f. 43.
391 *Stubbes*, 1583 edn., p. 25v; 1585 edn., p. 23v.
392 Ibid.
393 Ibid., 1583 edn., pp. 26, 26v; 1585 edn., pp. 24, 24v. For jersey spinning and knitting see Chapter VI notes 293–96.
394 Illustrated in J. L. Nevinson, 'New Material for the History of XVIIth Century Costume in England', *Apollo*, XX (1934), Fig. VI, p. 317.
395 PRO, LC9/54, f. 23.
396 Ibid., f. 36.
397 *Stow, Annales*, p. 867, quoted in *Anderson*, p. 70.
398 Hewel, *History of the World*, quoted in *Progr. Eliz.*, I, p. xlii.
399 New Year's Gift Roll 1562, printed in *Progr. Eliz.*, I. p. 118.
400 New Year's Gift Roll 1563, PRO, C47/3/38.
401 PRO, LC5/33, f. 89, warrant dated 31 May 1564.
402 Ibid., f. 147, warrant dated 20 Oct. 1565.
403 BL, Egerton 2806, f. 10v, warrant dated 16 Oct. 1568.
404 Ibid., f. 31v, warrant dated 4 April 1571.
405 Ibid., f. 66v, warrant dated 14 April 1574.
406 Ibid., f. 115, warrant dated 12 April 1577.
407 Ibid., f. 120v, warrant dated 27 Sept. 1577.
408 *Progr. Eliz.*, II, p. 144. For discussion of jersey and garnesey yarn see Chapter VI notes 293–96.
409 *Progr. Eliz.*, II, p. 145.
410 BL, Egerton 2806, f. 173, warrant dated 15 Sept. 1581.
411 Ibid., f. 181, warrant dated 28 Sept. 1582.
412 Ibid., f. 192, warrant dated 26 Sept. 1583.
413 Ibid., f. 197v, warrant dated 12 April 1584.
414 Ibid., f. 206, warrant dated 16 April 1585.
415 Ibid.
416 Ibid., f. 216v, warrant dated 27 Sept. 1586.
417 Ibid., f. 230v, warrant dated 3 April 1588.
418 Ibid., f. 234, warrant dated 27 Sept. 1588.
419 *Minsheu, Dialogues*, p. 2.
420 See note 383.
421 BL, Egerton 2806, f. 31v, warrant dated 4 April 1571.
422 Ibid., f. 223v, warrant dated 26 Sept. 1587.
423 See Chapter VI, p. 110, where the Lady Ri-Mellaine apparently wears socks under her stockings.
424 Robert Latham and William Matthews (eds). *The Diary of Samuel Pepys* (1971), 4, p. 140, note 1, 15 May 1663.
425 BL, Egerton 2806, f. 142, warrant dated 10 April 1579.
426 Ibid., f. 173, warrant dated 15 Sept. 1581.
427 Ibid.
428 Ibid., f. 181, warrant dated 28 Sept. 1582.
429 Ibid., f. 224v, warrant dated 26 Sept. 1587.
430 Ibid., f. 192, warrant dated 26 Sept. 1583.
431 Ibid., f. 234, warrant dated 27 Sept. 1588.
432 Ibid., f. 206, warrant dated 16 April 1585.
433 Illustrated in Lord David Cecil, *Hatfield House* (1973), p. 20.
434 PRO, LC5/37, f. 213, warrant dated 28 Sept. 1600.
435 *Linthicum*, p. 259.
436 Ibid.
437 BL, Egerton 2806, f. 230v, warrant dated 3 April 1588.
438 Ibid. See also PRO, LC5/36, f. 67 for the same entry. The prices have been taken from LC9/79, f. 11. The entry in Egerton 2806 reads 'for new dying of fower peire of silke knitt Hose', while LC5/36 and LC9/79 give 'new edging'. Further work of linking prices with warrant entries is now in progress.
439 Gravenor Henson, *History of the Framework Knitters* (1831, reprint 1970), p. 43.
440 Ibid., p. 45. The story of Lee is briefly recorded by Stow and Aubrey.
441 The whole document is given in full in E. W. Pasold, 'In search of William Lee', *Textile History*, vol. 6, 1975, pp. 7–17.
442 BL, Egerton 2806, f. 144, warrant dated 28 Sept. 1590.
443 *Smythe, Household Expenses*, p. 43.
444 PRO, LC5/36, f. 173, warrant dated 10 June 1591.
445 BL, Egerton 2806, f. 106v, warrant dated 26 Sept. 1576.
446 Ibid., ff. 106, 106v.
447 Ibid., f. 113v, warrant dated 12 April 1577.

448 Ibid., f. 173v, warrant dated 15 Sept. 1581.
449 PRO, LC5/37, f. 13, warrant dated 12 April 1594.
450 Ibid., f. 14.
451 Ibid., f. 23, warrant dated 27 Sept. 1594.
452 Ibid., f. 21.
453 Ibid., f. 22.
454 BL, Egerton 2806, f. 50, warrant dated 28 Sept. 1572.
455 Dekker, sc. IV, line 83, p. 109.
456 Ibid., p. 107, note 49 for this extract from Thomas Deloney, The Gentle Craft, c. 1597–98.
457 BL, Egerton 2806, f. 196, warrant dated 12 April 1584.
458 Ibid., f. 205, warrant dated 16 April 1585.
459 PRO, LC5/33, f. 49, warrant dated 4 May 1563.
460 Ibid., f. 89, warrant dated last day of May 1564.
461 Ibid., f, 170, warrant dated 25 March 1566.
462 See notes 631 and 632.
463 PRO, LC5/33, f. 214v, warrant dated 27 Sept. 1586.
464 PRO, LC5/34, f. 210, warrant dated 20 May 1573.
465 BL, Egerton 2806, f. 202v, warrant dated 27 Sept. 1584.
466 PRO, LC5/33, f. 13, warrant dated 20 Oct. 1562; BL, Egerton 2806, f. 48v, warrant dated 28 Sept. 1572. It might be assumed that the 'cutting irons' were for cutting out the various sections of the shoe, but June Swann points out that they are not mentioned in Deloney's list of shoe tools in 1597 and doubts that they go back that far. She feels that irons for pinking could be correct.
467 Dekker, sc. I, lines 239–47, p. 97.
468 PRO, LC5/33, f. 13, warrant dated 20 Oct. 1562.
469 Ibid., f. 49, warrant dated 4 May 1563.
470 J. Heywood, Proverbs and Epigrammes (1562). I am indebted to Miss June Swann for this reference.
471 John Higgins, The nomenclator or remembrancer of Adrianus Junius (1585).
472 PRO, LC5/33, f. 149, warrant dated 20 Oct. 1565.
473 Ibid., f. 170, warrant dated dated 25 March 1566.
474 Linthicum, p. 253.
475 PRO, LC5/33, f. 128, warrant dated 16 April 1565.
476 Muriel St Claire Byrne (ed.) The Lisle Letters, vol. 2 (1981) pp. 433–34.
477 June Swann suggests that quartered shoes had ceased to be an innovation and the term was dropped from the descriptions of the Queen's shoes. Possibly the term 'quarter shoes' here describes parti-coloured footwear for the Fool.
478 PRO, LC5/33, f. 149, warrant dated 20 Oct. 1565.
479 Ibid., f. 197, warrant dated 10 Feb. 1567.
480 PRO, LC5/34, f. 94, warrant dated 6 Oct. 1569.
481 Ibid., f. 109, warrant dated 12 April 1570.
482 Ibid., f. 125, warrant dated 14 Oct. 1570.
483 PRO, LC5/37, f. 23, warrant dated 27 Sept. 1594.
484 PRO, LC5/33, f. 114, warrant dated 27 Sept. 1564.
485 Ibid., f. 149, warrant dated 20 Oct. 1565.
486 PRO, LC5/34, f. 81, warrant dated 26 April 1569. The same warrant entry is in BL, Egerton 2806, f. 15, of the same date.
487 PRO, LC5/34, f. 169, warrant dated 9 April 1572 and f. 195, warrant dated 28 Sept. 1572.
488 Ibid., f. 308, warrant dated 28 Sept. 1575.
489 PRO, LC5/33, f. 114, warrant dated 27 Sept. 1564.
490 PRO, LC5/37, f. 73, warrant dated 28 Sept. 1595.
491 PRO, LC5/34, f. 195, warrant dated 28 Sept. 1572.
492 PRO, LC5/33, f. 13, warrant dated 20 Oct. 1562.
493 Ibid., f. 49, warrant dated 4 May 1563.
494 PRO, LC5/37, f. 73, warrant dated 28 Sept. 1595.
495 Dekker, sc. x, line 33, p. 136.
496 BL, Egerton 2806, f. 132v, warrant dated 26 Sept. 1578.
497 PRO, LC5/33, f. 49, warrant dated 4 May 1563.
498 PRO, LC5/37, f. 62, warrant dated 10 April 1595.
499 Stubbes, 1583 edn, p. 27; 1585 edn, p. 28.
500 BL, Egerton 2806, f. 205, warrant dated 16 April 1585.
501 PRO, LC5/36, f. 173, warrant dated 10 June 1591.
502 PRO, LC5/37, f. 130, warrant dated 29 March 1598.
503 Ibid., f 165, warrant dated 30 March 1599.
504 Ibid., f. 213, warrant dated 28 Sept. 1600.
505 PRO, LC5/36, f. 187, warrant dated 27 Sept. 1591.
506 PRO, LC5/37, f. 150, warrant dated 27 Sept. 1598.
507 Ibid., f. 213, warrant dated 28 Sept. 1600.
508 Quoted in Linthicum, p. 248.
509 OED gives further details of the early use of the word.
510 PRO, LC5/34, f. 16, warrant dated 28 March 1567.
511 Ibid., f. 81, warrant dated 26 April 1569. The same warrant entry is in BL, Egerton 2806, f. 15.
512 PRO, LC5/36, f. 211, warrant dated 6 June 1592.
513 BL, Egerton 2806, f. 37, warrant dated 24 Sept. 1571. The same warrant entry is in PRO, LC5/34, f. 153, where Seville is given as 'cyvill'.
514 PRO, LC5/34, f. 237, warrant dated 14 April 1574. The same warrant entry is in BL, Egerton 2806, f. 67v.
515 PRO, LC5/37, f. 237, warrant dated 28 Sept. 1601; ibid., f. 313, warrant dated 28 Sept. 1603.
516 William Goddard, A Neaste of Waspes (1615), quoted in Harrison, I, p. lxix; Holme Academy, III, p. 14.
517 PRO, LC5/33, f. 148, warrant dated 20 Oct. 1565.
518 Ibid., f. 89, warrant dated last day of May 1564.
519 Ibid., f. 148, warrant dated 20 Oct. 1565.
520 Ibid., f. 72, warrant dated 2 Nov. 1563.
521 BL, Egerton 2806, f. 147v, warrant dated 12 Oct. 1579, for examples of perfuming gowns and fans; ibid., f. 167v, warrant dated 6 April 1581, for Parliament robes and gowns; Stowe inventory, f. 69v/70 for a cloak.
522 Tommasso Garzóni, La Piazza Universale (1616), passage dated to 1560 by Gay, quoted in Anderson, p. 255, note 202.

523 Progr. Eliz., II, p. 110, records that in 1578 a book presented to the Queen should have 'no savour of spyke, which commonly bookbinders did seek to add, to make their books savour well; for that her Majesty could not abide such a strong scent'.
524 New Year's Gift Roll, 1578, Soc. of Antiquaries MS 537, printed in Progr. Eliz., II, p. 65.
525 Ibid., p. 72.
526 See note 523.
527 Progr. Eliz., II, pp. 112–13.
528 See Chapter I, note 68. For descriptions by Hentzner and Platter of the Queen wearing gloves, see ibid., notes 74 and 75, and full quotations in text.
529 Cal. Pat. Rolls, Eliz., 1566–69, IV, p. 18, no. 79.
530 PRO, AO1, Roll 1, Bundle 2339, 1559. The abbreviation ml is for mille, Latin for 1,000.
531 PRO, LC5/32, f. 60, warrant dated Sept. 1564, no day given.
532 PRO, LC5/33, f. 150, warrant dated 20 Oct. 1565.
533 See Arnold, Patterns, pp. 11, 12.
534 Arnold, 'Neckwear', p. 114.
535 BL, Egerton 2806, f. 79v, warrant dated 13 April 1575.
536 PRO, LC5/33, ff. 70, 71, warrant dated 2 Nov. 1563.
537 See Chapter V, notes 160, 161.
538 PRO, LC5/33, f. 71, warrant dated 2 Nov. 1563.
539 Harrison, pt. II, (1878), p. 34.
540 M. K. Dale, 'The London Silkwoman of the Fifteenth Century' in Economic History Review, IV (1933), pp. 324–35.
541 Egerton 2806, f. 128, warrant dated 12 April 1578.
542 Anne F. Sutton, 'Alice Claver, silkwoman of London and maker of mantle laces for Richard III and Queen Anne' in The Ricardian, vol. 5, no. 70 (Sept. 1980).
543 Harrison, pt. II, (1878), p. 36.
544 PRO, LC9/52, f. 27 and PRO, LC9/53, f 14v.
545 PRO, AO1, Roll 1, Bundle 2339. The account of Sir Richard Sackville for the coronation of Queen Elizabeth.
546 PRO, LC9/55, ff. 12 and 23.
547 BL, Egerton 2806, f. 172, warrant dated 15 Sept. 1581.
548 PRO, LC9/55, f. 12 and f. 23, 1561–62.
549 Alice Mountague's name, work and prices appear in almost all the Great Wardrobe Accounts until 1581, with the exception of PRO, LC9/59, Michaelmas 1566–Michaelmas 1567 and LC9/61, Michaelmas 1568–Michaelmas 1569. The book for 1569–70 is missing. PRO, LC9/62, Michaelmas 1570–Michaelmas 1571, the Michaelmas 1571 entry for Alice is not in this book.
550 BL, Egerton 2806, f. 43, warrant dated 9 April 1572. See also f. 38v, warrant dated 24 Sept. 1571; f. 47v, warrant dated 28 Sept. 1572; f. 55, warrant dated 1 April 1573; f. 63, warrant dated 20 Oct. 1573; f. 69, warrant dated 14 April 1574; f. 73, warrant dated 14 Oct. 1574; f. 80v, warrant dated 13 April 1575. Ibid., f. 91 and 92v, warrant dated 28 Sept. 1575, is the first where Alice is paid 'at our great guarderobe'.
551 Ibid., f. 63 warrant dated 20 Oct. 1573.
552 Ibid., f. 99, 99v, warrant dated 14 April 1576.
553 Ibid., f. 99v.
554 Ibid.
555 Ibid., f. 149, warrant dated 12 Oct. 1579.
556 Linthicum, p. 28, note 2; p. 100, note 1.
557 BL, Egerton 2806, f. 115, warrant dated 12 April 1577; f. 127v, warrant dated 12 April 1578; f. 134, warrant dated 26 Sept. 1578.
558 Ibid., f. 115, warrant dated 12 April 1577; f. 134v, warrant dated 26 Sept. 1578; f. 168v, warrant dated 6 April 1581.
559 PRO, LC9/77, f. 14.
560 BL, Egerton 2806, f. 134v, warrant dated 26 Sept. 1578.
561 Ibid., f. 108, warrant dated 26 Sept. 1576. Santina Levey points out that from other quotations the exact meaning of the term 'loom lace' is not clear.
562 Ibid.
563 Ibid. f. 114v, warrant dated 12 April 1577.
564 Ibid., f. 108, warrant dated 26 Sept. 1576; f. 160v, warrant dated 28 Sept. 1580.
565 Ibid., f. 114v, 115, warrant dated 12 April 1577; PRO, LC5/36, f. 147, warrant dated 28 Sept. 1590; BL, Egerton 2806, f. 128, warrant dated 12 April 1578.
566 PRO, LC5/33, f. 88, warrant dated 31 May 1564.
567 Ibid., f. 45, warrant dated 4 May 1563.
568 Ibid., f. 66, warrant dated 2 Nov. 1563.
569 Ibid., f. 111, warrant dated 27 Sept. 1564; f. 147, warrant of 20 Oct. 1565.
570 Ibid., f. 147, warrant dated 20 Oct. 1565.
571 Chapter V, note 21.
572 PRO, LC5/33, f. 9, warrant dated 20 Oct. 1562.
573 Ibid., f. 66, warrant dated 2 Nov. 1563.
574 BL, Egerton 2806, f. 128, warrant dated 12 April 1578.
575 Ibid., f. 134v, warrant dated 26 Sept. 1578.
576 Ibid., f. 128, warrant dated dated 12 April 1578.
577 For references to a seamster's shop and work, see Middleton, Dekker, II, i, p. 33.
578 For 'Irishe stiche' see note 396 and full quotation in text.
579 PRO, LC5/33, f. 147, warrant dated 20 Oct. 1565.
580 Ibid., f. 168, warrant dated 25 March 1566.
581 PRO, LC5/36, f. 122, warrant dated 27 Sept. 1589.
582 PRO, LC5/37, ff. 74, 75, warrant dated 28 Sept. 1595.
583 BL, Egerton 2806, f. 224, warrant dated 26 Sept. 1587.
584 PRO, LC5/36, f. 255, warrant dated 10 May 1593.
585 Ibid., f. 264, warrant dated 28 Sept. 1593.
586 PRO, LC5/37, f. 15, warrant dated 12 April 1594.
587 Ibid., f. 63, warrant dated 10 April 1595.
588 Ibid., f. 73, warrant dated 28 Sept. 1595.
589 For further information about squares, see Arnold, 'Smocks and Shirts', p. 95. The term 'square' is also used for jewellery, see Arnold, 'Sweet England's Jewels', p. 35.

590 See notes 355–56, 358–60, 363–67, 369–70.
591 See notes 371–72.
592 See notes 354, 361–62.
593 BL, Egerton 2806, f. 186v, warrant dated 20 April 1583.
594 Ibid.
595 Ibid., f. 205v, warrant dated 16 April 1585.
596 Ibid., f. 187, 187v, warrant dated 20 April 1583.
597 Ibid., f. 210, warrant dated 27 Sept. 1585.
598 PRO, LC5/37, f. 235, warrant dated 28 Sept. 1601.
599 Ibid.
600 Arnold, 'Neckwear', pp. 120–23; BL, Egerton 2806, f. 233, warrant dated 27 Sept. 1588.
601 PRO, LC5/37, f. 235, warrant dated 28 Sept. 1601.
602 Ibid., f. 257, warrant dated 19 April 1602.
603 Ibid., ff. 273–74, warrant dated 27 Sept. 1602.
604 Ibid., f. 274, warrant dated 27 Sept. 1602.
605 Ibid., f. 287, warrant dated 18 May 1603.
606 Ibid., f. 288, warrant dated 18 May 1603.
607 Ibid.
608 Ibid.
609 Ibid., f. 258, warrant dated 19 April 1602.
610 Ibid., ff. 272–74, warrant dated 27 Sept. 1602.
611 OED.
612 PRO, LC5/33, f. 15, warrant dated 20 Oct. 1562.
613 PRO, LC5/34, f. 26, warrant dated last day of Sept. 1567.
614 PRO, LC5/33, f. 13, warrant dated 20 Oct. 1562.
615 Ibid., f. 49, warrant dated 4 May 1563.
616 PRO, LC5/33, ff. 194 and 197, warrant dated 10 Feb. 1567. This is the Michaelmas warrant for 1566, late.
617 BL, Egerton 2806, f. 126, warrant dated 12 April 1578.
618 Ibid., f. 140v, warrant dated 10 April 1579.
619 Ibid., f 160v, warrant dated 28 Sept. 1580.
620 Ibid., f. 215, warrant dated 27 Sept. 1586. Here he is described as 'our Smyth'.
621 PRO, LC5/49, ff. 283–85, letters patent dated 7 Nov. 1584.
622 PRO, LC5/33, f. 91, warrant dated last day of May 1564.
623 BL, Egerton 2806, f. 32v, warrant dated 4 April 1571; f. 37v, warrant dated 24 Sept. 1571.
624 Ibid., f. 81v, warrant dated 13 April 1575.
625 Ibid., f. 228v, warrant dated 3 April 1588.
626 Ibid., f. 48v, warrant dated 28 Sept. 1572.
627 Ibid., f. 120, warrant dated 27 Sept. 1577.
628 Ibid., f. 154v, warrant dated 12 April 1580.
629 Ibid., f. 201v, warrant dated 27 Sept. 1584; f. 196v, warrant dated 12 April 1584.
630 PRO, LC5/33, f. 91, warrant dated last day of May 1564.
631 Ibid., f. 194, warrant dated 10 Feb. 1567.
632 BL, Egerton 2806, f. 42v, warrant dated 9 April 1572.
633 For example, ibid., f. 68, warrant dated 14 April 1574 and f. 81v, warrant dated 13 April 1575.
634 Ibid., f. 81v.
635 Ibid., f. 221v, warrant dated 12 April 1587.
636 Ibid., f. 234v, warrant dated 27 Sept. 1588.
637 PRO, LC5/33, f. 72, warrant dated 2 Nov. 1563.
638 Ibid., f. 154, warrant dated 20 Oct. 1565.
639 BL, Egerton 2806, f. 148, warrant dated 12 Oct. 1579.
640 PRO, LC9/91, f. 9v, dated 28 Sept. 1601.
641 PRO, LC5/37, f. 237, warrant dated 28 Sept. 1601.
642 Ibid., f. 259, warrant dated 19 April 1602.
643 Arnold, 'Neckwear', pp. 114–15.
644 BL, Egerton 2806, f. 140v, warrant dated 10 April 1579.
645 Ibid., f. 223v, warrant dated 26 Sept. 1587.
646 Ibid., f 228v, warrant dated 3 April 1588.
647 PRO, LC5/33, f. 15, warrant dated 20 Oct. 1562.
648 Ibid., f. 71, warrant dated 2 Nov. 1563.
649 Ibid., f. 91, warrant dated last day of May 1564.
650 Ibid., f. 118, warrant dated 27 Sept. 1564.
651 Ibid., f. 51, warrant dated 4 May 1563.
652 Ibid., f. 71, warrant dated 2 Nov. 1563.
653 Ibid., f. 91, warrant dated last day of May 1564.
654 PRO, LC5/33, f. 72, warrant dated 2 Nov. 1563.
655 BL, Egerton 2806, f. 198v, warrant dated 12 April 1584. Possibly the bearing sword listed in Stowe inventory f. 94/[3].
656 Stowe inventory, f. 7v/[11].
657 BL, Egerton 2806, f. 215, warrant for the whole year dated 27 Sept. 1586.
658 Stowe inventory, f. 94/[1].
659 BL, Add. 4712, f. 24v, dated 24 Dec. 1565. Note says taken from MS Lib. W.Y. 193 in the College of Arms.
660 BL, Egerton 2806, f. 223v, warrant dated 26 Sept. 1587.
661 PRO, LC5/49, f. 353, letters patent for John and Thomas Grene dated 17 April 1558; ibid., ff. 158–59, warrant for livery for Thomas dated 24 Oct. 1565. Also see note 683.
662 Ibid., f. 240, warrant for livery dated 21 Nov. 1600.
663 PRO, LC5/37, f. 318, warrant dated 28 Sept. 1603.
664 Feuillerat, p. 158.
665 BL, Egerton 2806, f. 171v, warrant dated 15 Sept. 1581; ibid., f. 220v, warrant dated 12 April 1587.
666 Ibid., f. 74, warrant dated 14 Oct. 1574.
667 Ibid., f. 90v, warrant dated 28 Sept. 1575.
668 Ibid., f. 171v, warrant dated 15 Sept. 1581. Another example, also an ell long, is not lined, ibid., f. 120, warrant dated 27 Sept. 1577.
669 Ibid., f. 182, warrant dated 28 Sept. 1582. Presumably these coffers were waterproof, but details are not always given. However, in 1564 two coffers were made to carry Garter robes to 'oure said brother the Frenche kinge' which were 'of

white wood covered with cerecloth and lether with a covering of hide lether to defend the water lined doble with white Frize bound with yron as Lockes joyntes handells and Squires with girdles of lether to carie on hors[e]bac[k] the said robes', PRO, LC5/33, f. 90, warrant dated last day of May 1564.
670 BL, Egerton 2806, f. 16, warrant dated 26 April 1569; ibid., f. 119v, warrant dated 27 Sept. 1577.
671 Ibid., f. 127, warrant dated 12 April 1578; ibid., f. 166v, warrant dated 6 April 1581; ibid., f. 223v, warrant dated 26 Sept. 1587. Stamped leather might be used to cover coffers, as for 'one cofer of whit wood with diverse tills in it covered with lether Prentid bound with Iron with lockes joyntes handells and squiers with a case of lether to put it in', PRO, LC5/33, f. 114, warrant dated 27 Sept. 1564.
672 BL, Egerton 2806, ff. 24, 24v, warrant dated 16 April 1570.
673 PRO, LC5/33, f. 130, warrant dated 16 April 1565.
674 BL, Add. 5751A, f. 87, no. 32, warrant dated 19 May 1574.
675 PRO, LC5/33, f. 150, warrant dated 20 Oct. 1565.
676 Ibid.
677 Ibid., f. 115, warrant dated 27 Sept. 1564.
678 Ibid., f. 149, warrant dated 20 Oct. 1565.
679 Ibid., f. 115, warrant dated 27 Sept. 1564.
680 BL, Egerton 2806, f. 90v, warrant dated 28 Sept. 1575.
681 Ibid., f. 106v, warrant dated 26 Sept. 1576.
682 Ibid., f. 154v, warrant dated 12 April 1580.
683 Ibid., f. 62, warrant dated 20 Oct. 1573, where John is incorrectly listed instead of Thomas. This error is noted in PRO, LC5/34, f. 195, 'Thomas Grene named in the warrant that was signed by the quene by the name of John Grene'. Ibid., f. 228v, warrant dated 3 April 1588.
684 Ibid., f. 228v, warrant dated 3 April 1588.
685 Ibid., f. 133, warrant dated 26 Sept. 1578; ibid., f. 185v, warrant dated 20 April 1583.
686 PRO, LC5/33, f. 38, warrant dated 4 May 1563.
687 BL, Egerton 2806, f. 191v, warrant dated 26 Sept. 1583.
688 For example ibid., f. 196, warrant dated 12 April 1584.
689 Ibid., f. 6, warrant dated 14 April 1568; ibid., f. 225v, warrant dated 26 Sept. 1587, see PRO, LC5/36, f. 56 for same entry, where '319' is written more clearly.
690 For example, BL, Egerton 2806, f. 16, warrant dated 26 April 1569; ibid., f. 19, warrant dated 6 Oct. 1569; ibid., ff. 81v, 82, warrant dated 13 April 1575; ibid., f. 90v, warrant dated 28 Sept. 1575.
691 Ibid., f. 166v, warrant dated 6 April 1581; ibid., f. 182v, warrant dated 20 April 1583; ibid., f. 189, warrant dated 25 Sept. 1583.
692 For example ibid., f. 201, warrant dated 27 Sept. 1584; ibid., f. 205, warrant dated 16 April 1585.
693 PRO, LC5/33, f. 150, warrant dated 20 Oct. 1565.
694 BL, Egerton 2806, f. 196, warrant dated 12 April 1584.
695 PRO, LC5/33, f. 50, warrant dated 4 May 1563.
696 Ibid., f. 51.
697 BL, Egerton 2806, f. 74v, warrant dated 14 Oct. 1574.
698 Rye, p. 14. Rathgeb was private secretary to Frederick Duke of Wirtemberg, and visited England with him in August 1592, keeping a record of his travels.
699 PRO, LC5/49, ff. 351–52, letters patent dated May 1559.
700 Ibid., f. 19v, warrant dated 6 Oct. 1569.
701 As for example ibid., f. 27, warrant dated 14 Oct. 1570.
702 LC5/49, ff. 323–24, letters patent dated 24 Sept. 1573.
703 Ibid.
704 CSP Dom. Eliz. Add. 1566–79, p. 453, no. 29, dated 24 Sept. 1573, with note of reversion in May 1603.
705 BL, Egerton 2806, f. 68, warrant dated 14 April 1574; ibid., f. 133v, warrant dated 26 Sept. 1578; ibid., f. 196, warrant dated 12 April 1584; ibid., f. 215, warrant dated 27 Sept. 1586.
706 Ibid., f. 186, warrant dated 20 April 1583.
707 Ibid., f. 133v, warrant dated 26 Sept. 1578.
708 Ibid., f. 209v, warrant dated 27 Sept. 1585.
709 Ibid., f. 19v, warrant dated 6 Oct. 1569.
710 Ibid., f. 68, warrant dated 14 April 1574.
711 Ibid., f. 107, warrant dated 26 Sept. 1576. Also see ibid., f. 98, warrant dated 14 April 1576.
712 Ibid., f. 140v, warrant dated 10 April 1579.
713 Ibid., f. 176v, warrant dated 6 April 1582.
714 Ibid., f. 196, warrant dated 12 April 1584.
715 Chapter I, note 53.
716 PRO, LC5/33, ff. 128–29, warrant dated 16 April 1565. For examples of close stools see R. W. Symonds 'Of Jakes and Close Stools', in The Connoisseur, vol. 129–30, 1952, pp. 86–91.
717 Ibid., f. 8, warrant dated 20 Oct. 1562.
718 BL, Egerton 2806, f. 15, warrant dated 26 April 1569; ibid., f. 18v, warrant dated 6 Oct. 1569.
719 Ibid., f. 23v, warrant dated 12 April 1570; ibid., f. 28, warrant dated 14 Oct. 1570.
720 Ibid., f. 48, warrant dated 28 Sept. 1572; ibid., f. 49v, warrant dated 28 Sept. 1572.
721 Ibid., f. 214v, warrant dated 27 Sept. 1586.
722 Ibid., f. 48v, warrant dated 28 Sept. 1572.
723 Ibid., f. 68, warrant dated 14 April 1574.
724 Ibid., f. 81v, warrant dated 13 April 1575.
725 Ibid., f. 98, warrant dated 14 April 1576.
726 Ibid., f. 202v, warrant dated 27 Sept. 1584.
727 PRO, LC5/33, f. 110, warrant dated 27 Sept. 1564.
728 BL, Egerton 2806, f. 5, warrant dated 14 April 1568.
729 Ibid., f. 10v and f. 11, warrant dated 16 Oct. 1568.
730 Ibid., f. 23v, warrant dated 17 April 1570 (10 lb); ibid., f. 27 (8 lb for Tower and Whitehall), f. 28 (1 lb for Somerset Place), warrant dated 14 Oct. 1570.
731 Ibid., f. 31v, warrant dated 4 April 1571 (8 lb); ibid., f. 37, warrant dated 24 Sept. 1571 (10 lb).

732 Ibid., f. 195v, warrant dated 12 April 1584 (12 lb); ibid., f. 200v, warrant dated 27 Sept. 1584 (12 lb).
733 Ibid., f. 38, warrant dated 24 Sept. 1571.
734 PRO, LC5/33, f. 129, warrant dated 16 April 1565.
735 BL, Egerton 2806, f. 50, warrant dated 28 Sept. 1572; f. 147v, warrant dated 12 Oct. 1579.
736 Ibid., f. 167v, warrant dated 6 April 1581.
737 William Turner (Dean of Wells), *The first and seconde partes of the herbal of William Turner . . . corrected and enlarged with the thirde parte lately gathered.* (Cologne, 1568) pt. 2, p. 50.
738 BL, Egerton 2806, f. 35v, warrant dated 24 Sept. 1571.
739 Ibid., f. 214, warrant dated 27 Sept. 1586.
740 Ibid., f. 8, warrant dated 14 April 1568.
741 Ibid., f. 36, warrant dated 24 Sept. 1571.
742 Ibid., f. 45, warrant dated 28 Sept. 1572.
743 Ibid., f. 88v, warrant dated 28 Sept. 1575.
744 Ibid., f. 116v, 117, warrant dated 27 Sept. 1577.
745 Ibid., f. 122, warrant dated 12 April 1578.
746 See Chapter VII, note 93, extract in text and Figure 256.
747 PRO, LC5/33, f. 88, warrant dated last day of May 1564.
748 Ibid., ff. 111–12, warrant dated 27 Sept. 1564.
749 BL, Egerton 2806, f. 92v, warrant dated 28 Sept. 1575 and PRO, LC5/49, f. 186, warrant for livery dated 9 April 1576. See also *Progr. Eliz.*, I, pp. 270–71, for payments 'to Mrs Taylor, the Quenes Laundresse, for her wages, at £4 per annum for one yere ended at the Annunciation of our Lady, 1568, with £6 paid for her livery gown £10. os. od' and another £4 in 1569. It is not clear if Elizabeth Smithson had married and continued to be described under her maiden name in some places, as in BL, Egerton 2806, f. 83, warrant dated 13 April 1575, or if this was a second laundress.
750 BL, Egerton 2806, f. 159v, warrant dated 28 Sept. 1580.
751 Ibid., f. 193, warrant dated 26 Sept. 1583.
752 Ibid., f. 209, warrant dated 27 Sept. 1585.

753 Ibid., f. 221v, warrant dated 12 April 1587.
754 Ibid., f. 229, warrant dated 3 April 1588.
755 Ibid., f. 234v, warrant dated 27 Sept. 1588.
756 See notes 574, 575, 584, 594, 595 and 608.
757 For example BL, Egerton 2806, f. 23, warrant dated 12 April 1570; ibid., f. 164v, warrant dated 6 April 1581; ibid., f. 235, warrant dated 27 Sept. 1588.
758 Ibid., f. 162, warrant dated 6 April 1581.
759 Ibid., f. 227v and f. 229, warrant dated 3 April 1588.
760 PRO, LC5/49, f. 314, letters patent dated 12 Jan. 1585 and PRO, LC5/32, f. 270, another copy. For details of early methods of cleaning tapestries see Wendy Hefford, 'Bread, brushes and brooms: aspects of tapestry restoration in England, 1660–1760', in *Acts of the Tapestry Symposium, November 1976,* (Fine Arts Museums of San Francisco, 1979) pp. 65–75.
761 BL, Egerton 2806, f. 196v, warrant dated 12 April 1584.
762 Ibid., f. 207, warrant dated 16 April 1585.
763 Ibid., f. 225v, warrant dated 26 Sept. 1587.
764 Ibid., f. 235v, warrant dormant for liveries dated 20 May 1588, see also PRO LC5/49, f. 217, dated 19 May 1588.
765 Ibid.
766 Ibid., f. 226, warrant dormant for liveries dated 7 Nov. 1587. See also PRO, LC5/49, f. 213, another copy.
767 Ibid., f. 229, warrant dated 3 April 1588.
768 Ibid., f. 235, warrant dated 27 Sept. 1588.
769 PRO, LC5/49 f. 235, 'a certificate of alteration of thofficers of the Robes', dated 7 Nov. 1598, where Richard Nightingale is Yeoman, Robert Pamplyn, Groom, and Thomas Horne, Page. See Chapter VII note 70.
770 PRO, LC5/49, f. 244, warrant for livery dated 27 July 1603, where Robert Pamplyn is Yeoman, Thomas Horne, Groom, and Raffe Holland and Thomas Ellis, Pages.
771 PRO, LC5/37, f. 24, warrant dated 27 Sept. 1594.
772 Ibid., f. 120, warrant dated 11 Sept. 1597.
773 Ibid., f. 214, warrant dated 28 Sept. 1600.

IX

Editor's Note on the Transcripts of the Stowe and Folger Inventories and Extracts from New Year's Gift Rolls, and Warrants for the Wardrobe of Robes

Transcripts

The editorial principles governing the transcription of the following manuscripts and all manuscript extracts used in this book were adopted with the primary aim of presenting the material as clearly and economically as possible. Recent rises in the cost of paper, typesetting, and proof reading make any attempt at following the original layout of the manuscript prohibitive; photographic reproductions of the original manuscripts can in any case be obtained relatively cheaply by those who wish to study handwriting and the finer linguistic details. A completely modernized version of the transcription, involving the normalization of spelling, capitalization, and punctuation appropriate for some historical documents would have removed the variations in spelling of technical and other terms which are of significance to costume and textile historians. A compromise has therefore been reached which I hope will meet the needs of general readers as well as those with a particular interest in costume, embroidery design, or textiles.

Spelling

I have retained the original spelling throughout, silently extending most abbreviations and contractions; in almost all cases the word is given in full by the same scribe in another part of the manuscript and where there are variations in the spelling the most common form has been used. A certain number of normalizations have been adopted for the ease of the reader. The capital letter F is used instead of ff. It is, perhaps, unnecessary to explain that certain letters, for example u and v, i and j, i or ie and y, c, and t, were interchangeable at this period. I have resorted to modern usage with u and v for eyes accustomed to the distinction between the vowel and the consonant, thus 'euery' is given as 'every'. I have also distinguished between i and j so that, for example, 'Maiestie' is shown as 'Majestie'. There seemed to be less of a problem with the interchangeable i or ie and y, and I have therefore left words like 'ladie', 'sylke', 'wyre' in their original form. The c/t interchange occurs in words like 'carnation' which also appears as 'carnacion' and in its contracted form as 'carnaçon'. The short line or tittle made over a letter, or letters, indicates that the following letter has been omitted, in this case the i. I have silently extended all such contractions, and left any alternative spelling, thus 'façon' is extended to 'facion' and is left as 'fasshyon' where written in this form. I have left the few examples of the old English thorn, 'y' for 'th' in 'ye' instead of 'the' where these occur; this was a standard contraction which persisted until the end of the seventeenth century. One common contraction still in use today, the ampersand, &, has been retained. Mr for Master is printed as Mr and silently extended when used for a title eg., Master of the Great Wardrobe. Mrs, Mris, Mres for Mistris/Mistress is printed as Mrs, retaining the word when given in full, with all the variations of spelling. Sr, sometimes written Syr, is silently

Warrants for the Wardrobe of Robes

The records for the Wardrobe of Robes at the beginning of the reign have to be pieced together from several manuscript sources, but from 1560 onwards warrants authorizing payment for tailors, embroiderers and other craftsmen working for the Wardrobe of Robes were made out every six months, against Michaelmas (Feast of St Michael, 29 September) and Lady Day (Feast of the Annunciation, 25 March) with only one exception during Elizabeth's reign. This was in 1586 when the warrants were made out at the end of a twelve month period, dated 27 September.[3] At this time Sir Thomas Gorges was taking over as Gentleman of the Robes from Ralph Hope, Yeoman of the Robes, and there would have been a lot of extra work for the clerks. The words 'of our great guarderobe' following most of the warrant entries indicate that the materials were from the Great Wardrobe store near Baynard's Castle. Other materials 'of our store receyved of George Brideman Keeper of our Palloice at Westminster' had been stored at Whitehall.

The method of preparing warrants has been described in Chapter VII. Extracts detailing the work carried out on the Queen's clothes have been taken from various copies of the particular warrants and used for comparison with items in the Stowe and Folger inventories. The copies presumably made for the Lord Chamberlain's Office are written in a series of books 31.1 cm (12¼ inches) × 21.6 cm (8½ inches) running from Michaelmas 1562 to Michaelmas 1603 (PRO, LC5/33–37). They are written by a number of different scribes in hands varying from court and neat round secretary to cramped, heavily inked, secretary, which is not easy to read, as no guide lines were used. Occasionally the paper is of poor quality, rather like blotting paper, and the ink shows through to the reverse side making the writing even more difficult to read (Fig. 335). The books are bound in vellum stiffened with card.

A book of copies of particular warrants from 1567 to 1585, made for the use of the Office of the Wardrobe of Robes, is now preserved in the British Library, Egerton MS2806. It was at one time in the collection of Sir Thomas Phillipps at Middle Hill and is numbered 'Phillipps MS 8853' in the front. A note on the flyleaf records the British Museum's purchase from Quaritch on 10 July 1896. The manuscript is 38.7 cm (15¼ inches) × 29.8 cm (11¾ inches) and written in a variety of secretary hands in varying degrees of legibility on paper which is of better quality than that used for the other copies of warrants. It is watermarked with a type of pot with a handle. The pages were folded lengthwise to give margin widths as a writing guide. There are no ruled or scored lines and the scribes have used the grain of the paper to a certain extent, to guide their hands. However, the writing is quite often crooked and the lines unevenly spaced. The book was probably bound in the nineteenth century, but part of the original vellum cover is retained on the title page.

Clothes entered in the warrants could have been made at any time during the preceding six months, starting from the date of the previous warrant. The Michaelmas warrants therefore show clothes made and altered for wear during the spring and summer months, while Lady Day warrants list clothes for autumn and winter. The Queen examined the warrants first, as she had done when Princess with the household accounts.[4] She then put her signature to them, to authorize payment, shortly after they were prepared, wherever the Court might be, at 'Croidon', 'Our Mannour at Grenewich', 'our Palloice within

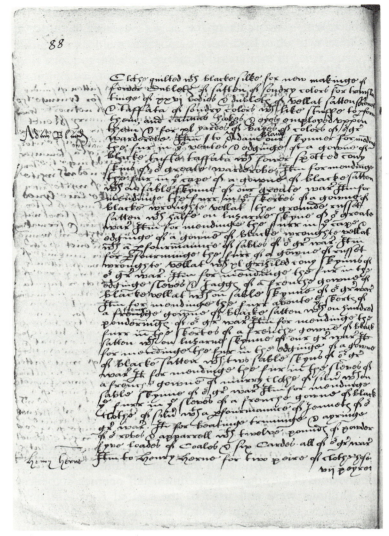

335   *Extract from a copy of a warrant for the Wardrobe of Robes dated 27 September 1577. Public Record Office, London, (LC5/35, f.88)*

our Honor of Hamptoncourte', 'Nonesuche', 'our Mannour of Otelandes', 'our Mannour at Readinge', 'Ricott', 'our Mannour at Richemounte', 'our Mannour at St James', 'our Mannour at Stronde', 'our Palloice of Westminster', 'our Castle at Wyndesor' or 'our Mannour at Woddestocke'. Warrants for the linen and clothes for poor women at the Royal Maundy are marked (M) in the following list.

Dates and places where warrants for the Wardrobe of Robes were made out to be signed by the Queen, taken from PRO, LC9/53–55, BL, Egerton 2806 and PRO, LC5/33–37. In a few cases she did not sign the warrants to authorize payment for several weeks.

12 November	1559 Westminster	
[Payments for clothes for the late Queen Mary]		
1 April	1560 Westminster	(M)
16 April	1560 Westminster	
last day of November	1560 Westminster	
20 March	1561 Westminster	(M)
10 April	1561 Westminster	
20 October	1561 St James's	
8 March	1562 Westminster	(M)

25 April	1562	Westminster
20 October	1562	Hampton Court
1 April	1563	Westminster (M)
4 May	1563	Westminster
2 November	1563	Windsor
24 March	1564	Windsor (M)
last day of May	1564	Richmond
27 September	1564	St James's
1 March	1565	Westminster (M)
16 April	1565	Westminster
20 October	1565	Westminster
10 March	1566	Greenwich (M)
25 March	1566	Greenwich
10 February	1567	Westminster

[This is the Michaelmas warrant for 1566 but there was a long delay in completing and signing it].

10 March	1567	Westminster (M)
28 March	1567	Westminster
last day of September	1567	Windsor
20 March	1568	Westminster (M)
14 April	1568	Greenwich
16 October	1568	Windsor
10 March	1569	Westminster (M)
26 April	1569	Westminster
6 October	1569	Windsor
6 March	1570	Hampton Court (M)
12 April	1570	Hampton Court
14 October	1570	Windsor
21 February	1571	Westminster (M)
4 April	1571	Westminster
24 September	1571	Richmond
10 March	1572	Westminster (M)
9 April	1572	Westminster
28 September	1572	Windsor
27 January	1573	Somerset Place, Strand. (M)
1 April	1573	Greenwich
20 October	1573	Greenwich
24 February	1574	Hampton Court (M)
14 April	1574	Greenwich
14 October	1574	Hampton Court
31 January	1575	Hampton Court (M)
13 April	1575	St James's
28 September	1575	Woodstock
last day of February	1576	Westminster (M)
14 April	1576	Westminster
26 September	1576	Reading
9 February	1577	Hampton Court (M)
12 April	1577	Westminster
27 September	1577	Windsor
7 February	1578	Hampton Court (M)
12 April	1578	Greenwich

26 September	1578	Richmond
12 March	1579	Westminster (M)
10 April	1579	Westminster
12 October	1579	Greenwich
21 February	1580	Westminster (M)
12 April	1580	Westminster
28 September	1580	Richmond
18 February	1581	Westminster (M)
6 April	1581	Westminster
15 September	1581	Greenwich
10 March	1582	Greenwich (M)
6 April	1582	Greenwich
28 September	1582	Windsor
20 February	1583	Richmond (M)
20 April	1583	Greenwich
26 September	1583	Oatlands
22 March	1584	Westminster (M)
12 April	1584	Westminster
27 September	1584	Oatlands
19 March	1585	Greenwich (M)
16 April	1585	Greenwich
27 September	1585	Nonsuch
12 February	1586	Greenwich (M)

No Lady Day Warrant in 1586

27 September	1586	Windsor
21 February	1587	Greenwich (M)
12 April (Signed 28 May)	1587	Greenwich
26 September (Signed 7 November)	1587	Richmond
30 March	1588	Greenwich (M)
3 April	1588	Greenwich
27 September	1588	St James's
20 February	1589	Westminster (M)
3 April	1589	Westminster
27 September	1589	Richmond
9 April	1590	Greenwich (M)
18 May	1590	Greenwich
28 September	1590	Windsor
18 February	1591	Greenwich (M)
10 June	1591	Greenwich
27 September	1591	Oatlands
8 March	1592	Westminster (M)
6 June	1592	Greenwich
28 September	1592	Rycote
9 March	1593	St James's (M)
10 May	1593	Croydon
28 September	1593	Windsor
12 February	1594	Hampton Court (M)
12 April	1594	Greenwich
27 September	1594	Greenwich

12 April	1595 Westminster	(M)
10 April	1595 Westminster	
28 September	1595 Nonsuch	
7 February	1596 Richmond	(M)
29 April	1596 Greenwich	
28 September	1596 Greenwich	
Last day of January	1597 Westminster	(M)
8 July	1597 Westminster	
11 September	1597 Westminster	
22 February	1598 Westminster	(M)
29 March	1598 Westminster	
27 September	1598 Nonsuch	
30 March	1599 Richmond	(M)
30 March	1599 Richmond	
28 September	1599 Nonsuch	
12 February	1600 Richmond	(M)
8 April	1600 Richmond	
28 September	1600 Oatlands	
10 March	1601 Westminster	(M)
1 April	1601 Westminster	
28 September	1601 Richmond	
4 February	1602 Westminster	(M)
19 April	1602 Greenwich	
27 September	1602 Oatlands	
18 May	1603 Tower of London [signed by James I]	

Description of Stowe and PRO inventories

Two inventories were made of the contents of the Wardrobe of Robes remaining in the Tower of London, at Court and in the Office of the Wardrobe of Robes near Baynard's Castle in 1600. There are two copies of the larger of these inventories, which lists the contents of the Wardrobe of Robes remaining in the Tower of London and at Court. Apparently only one copy survives of the second inventory, now in the Folger Shakespeare Library, Washington, DC, which gives the items remaining in the Office of the Wardrobe of Robes near Baynard's Castle at this time. No second copy is mentioned, although it seems likely that there would have been one. It is not known if any other inventories were made in 1600 which are now missing, perhaps for Somerset Place — 'our mannour in the Stronde' — or other stores.

The copy of the main part of the inventory printed here, Stowe 557 in the British Library, is 42 cm (16½ inches) × 28 cm (11 inches) with a writing area on each page of approximately 30.4 cm (12 inches) × 17.8 cm (7 inches) (Fig. 337). The duplicate copy, LR 2/121, now among the Land Revenue Miscellaneous Books in the Public Record Office, is a fraction larger. Originally the two books would have been the same size, but both were rebound in the nineteenth century and the BL copy again, in 1981. The paper used for both manuscripts is watermarked with a bunch of grapes (Fig. 336). Each page is faintly scored with lines as a guide for writing.

The description of the contents of the inventory appearing in the front of both copies explains that one, signed by the hands

of the Commissioners, Lord Buckhurst, Lord Hunsdon, Sir John Fortescue, and Sir John Stanhope, was to remain in the Office of the Wardrobe of Robes and the other, signed by Sir Thomas Gorges, was to be kept by Lord Buckhurst in his capacity as Lord High Treasurer of England, presumably at the Office of the Exchequer.

The Stowe inventory must be the former manuscript, though not signed by the Commissioners, nor the date filled in. However it was obviously kept in the Wardrobe of Robes. The nature of the margin notes scribbled in between 1600 and 1604 shows that they were written by Wardrobe staff carrying out the usual checks and recording the transfer of items from one store to another (Figs 416 and 439).

The PRO inventory is signed by Lord Buckhurst, not Sir Thomas Gorges. At first he put his signature 'T. Buckhurst' at the foot of every folio, both recto and verso, but by the end of the section of mantles, he signed only the recto side of the remaining folios. Most items are illegibly initialled in the right margin with what is probably 'Rem' for 'remaining' and a few are marked 'x' in the left margin, close by the entry. This is, no doubt, the copy of the inventory which was kept in the Office of the Exchequer, a permanent record of the contents of the Wardrobe of Robes in 1600. It was never used for checking, and the items are not numbered. There are no preliminary pages with notes, as in the Stowe inventory, and the page numbers are given by the original scribe, on the recto of each folio. The folio numbers of the two manuscripts are therefore different, f. 2 in the PRO inventory being f. 5 in the Stowe inventory, for example.

Three folios 31.8 cm (12½ inches) × 20.5 cm (8 inches) and nineteen folios 39 cm (15⅜ inches) × 26 cm (10¼ inches) are bound in at the back of the PRO inventory. These list various items of clothing and linen, some in the charge of Mr Zachary Bethell, and may be 'the Lynnen which hath beene much worne' and 'Remnantes of Stoffes of sondry Kindes' mentioned in the Commission of 1619. Lack of space prevents the inclusion of this transcript here.[5] One folio 24.7 cm (9¾ inches) × 19.3 cm (7⅝ inches) and four folios 33.6 cm (13¼ inches) × 20.9 cm (8¼ inches) are bound into the back of the Stowe inventory. They list the succession of Masters of the King's Great Wardrobe, written by a clerk in 1706.

How did the Stowe inventory pass from the safekeeping of the Wardrobe of Robes? After James I came to the throne, Sir Thomas Gorges may have taken it for his wife Helena, whom Elizabeth affectionately called 'the good Lady Marquess'. Perhaps one of the staff of the Wardrobe of Robes removed it after Elizabeth's gowns had been dispersed, either sold or cut up for the use of Anne of Denmark and her women. At all events, according to notes written in the front of the inventory, it eventually passed into the hands of Sir Simeon Stewart and was sold at auction, at his seat in Hampshire in May 1779, to Sir John Cullom, Bart. The latter afterwards sold it to Mr Craven Ord, an antiquary. During the period of Ord's ownership, John Nichols transcribed some extracts and printed them in Volume I of the first edition of The Progresses of Queen Elizabeth in 1785. In 1790 Ord gave the inventory to Thomas Astle who recorded the gift in the front.

Thomas Astle, antiquary and palaeographer, died in 1803 and left his collection of manuscripts by will to the Marquis of Buckingham for £500. If the offer had been declined, the British Museum would have enjoyed the right of purchase at the same price. However, the Marquis accepted the offer and built a gothic room at Stowe to house the collection. The inventory remained in the Stowe Book Room until 1849. The entire collection was then put up for sale, but was purchased privately by the Earl of Ashburnham for £8,000. Finally his son sold the manuscripts to the British Library in 1883, where they have remained ever since.[6]

The Stowe and Folger inventories printed here do not include the contents of the New Year's Gift Rolls of 1601, 1602 and 1603, nor do they list any new gowns made after 1600. There was probably a book to record all these items which has not yet been found. Entries from copies of particular warrants for the Wardrobe of Robes and the New Year's Gift Rolls have been linked to many of the items in these inventories to give the date of entry into the Wardrobe, the donor of the gift, or the name of tailor and embroiderer. Some gowns remained unaltered from the day they were presented, occasionally not made up. Others were renovated and furs replaced several times, sometimes as much as ten years later. Each of these extracts has been quoted in full for purposes of comparison. There were many other entries which might have been matched up, but the descriptions were insufficiently detailed to be certain that they were correct.

The Stowe and PRO duplicate copies of the inventory list the contents of the Wardrobe of Robes in 1600 at the Court and Whitehall (items headed with the initial C) and at the Tower of London (items headed with the initial T). Some clothes and personal jewels which belonged to King Edward VI and Queen Mary are entered first. Those for Queen Elizabeth consist of 99 mantles and veils with Coronation, Mourning, Parliament, and Garter Robes, 102 French gowns, 67 round gowns, 100 loose gowns, 126 kirtles, 135 foreparts (numbered 136 in error), 125 petticoats, 96 cloaks, 31 cloaks and safeguards, 13 safeguards, 43 safeguards and jupes, 85 doublets, 18 lap mantles, 43 pieces of material, mostly silks, 27 fans, 9 pairs of pantobles and 128 items of personal jewellery, including sets of buttons. When added to the items in the Folger inventory the total is over 1,900 pieces of clothing and jewels. To this should be added the unknown total number of gowns presented at the New Year and on Progresses between 1601 and 1603, together with all the clothes made in the Wardrobe of Robes during these three years. It still seems unlikely, however, that this would have amounted to the 2,000 gowns 'with all things else answerable' mentioned by Chamberlain in 1603, unless by 'gowns' he also meant mantles, petticoats, cloaks, and safeguards.

The various categories of garments appear to have been entered in sequence according to the value and type of material from which they were made, and then by the date of their arrival in the Wardrobe of Robes within each of these groups. Silks woven with gold and silver threads were the most expensive sort and were listed first, followed by velvets, satins, cypress, taffeta, network, stitched cloth, and lawn. A similar sequence is given in an 'Act of Apparel' of 1597[7] where 'Cloth of gold or sylver tissued' then 'Silke of colour purple' were first on the list, not to be worn under the degree of Countess. They were followed by 'Cloth of gold, Cloth of sylver, Tincelled sattyn, Sattyns brauncht with sylver or gold, Sattyns striped with sylver or gold, Taffaties brauncht with sylver or gold, Taffaties with gold or sylver groundes, Tinseld taffaties tuft or plaine, Tinseld cipresses, Cipresses flourisht with sylver or gold, Gold or sylver chamblets, Networkes wrought with sylver or gold, Tabines brauncht or wrought with sylver or gold, Or any other silke or cloth mixt or embrodered with perle, gold or sylver'; these were not to be worn under the

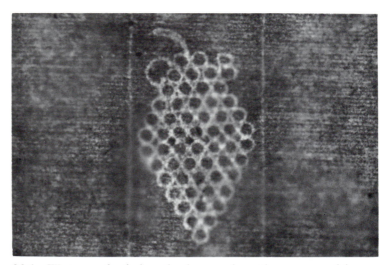

336 *Watermark of a bunch of grapes from the paper used for both the Stowe inventory in the British Library, London, and the duplicate copy in the Public Record Office, London*

degree of Baronness. Lists of materials used at Elizabeth's coronation[8] are arranged in a similar way. A few items in the Stowe inventory are out of sequence, perhaps because they had been mislaid and were added as and when Wardrobe staff located them. Occasional descriptions of 'cloth of gold tissued with silver', 'satin tissued with gold' and 'vellat tissued with gold' appear among the French gowns, round gowns, loose gowns, kirtles, petticoats, and cloaks. Four yards of this very expensive material, 'Clothe of Tishewe the ground golde and Tyshewe sylver'[9] were purchased in 1558 for a new bodice and sleeves for the kirtle for Elizabeth's coronation and the looped pile of both this and the earlier 'clothe of golde tissued with golde and silver' used for the rest of the kirtle and mantle may be seen clearly in Hilliard's miniature (Fig. 87). Here, and in some other instances, where the word 'tissue' is used in conjunction with 'raised', it would seem that the clerks are describing a looped pile of metal thread. Natalie Rothstein points out that the term 'tissue' has a technical meaning: 'In order to manage large patterned and heavy fabrics especially those with gold and silver used in great quantities the weaver had to have two warp systems: the lampas structure. The threads of one warp were controlled by the figure harness of the drawloom and they were pushed up or down as required by the pattern. A second warp was necessary to bind all the patterned and brocaded wefts. This double warp structure was called a 'tissue' in English.'[10] Entries for 'a gowne of peach-colour Tissued velvet'[11] and 'a Jupp of ashcolour Taffata tissued'[12] in 1595 and 'a highe bodied gowne of dove colour tissued taffata'[13] in 1601 would seem to show the use of the word 'tissued' in this sense, and without metal threads.

Handwriting in the Stowe and PRO inventories

The whole of the Stowe inventory is written in a small round secretary hand, with the titles and 'Firste' in each section in an engrossing hand, imitating black letter print. The same style is followed for the duplicate inventory in the Public Record Office, but this volume was probably the work of another scribe. The writing seems to be neater and more consistent and there are fewer corrections. There are minor differences in spelling between the two manuscripts, which are consistent throughout, for example 'demi sleeves' in the Stowe inventory and 'demy sleeves' in the PRO copy.

The two manuscripts would need to be examined side by side, by a handwriting expert, to be certain of the hands. It is likely, however, that there were two scribes and that they would have checked each other's work on completion. Some of the alterations in the Stowe inventory are very close to the original hand but may be the work of the scribe who wrote out the PRO copy.

Alterations, additions and margin notes in the Stowe inventory show how this manuscript was used for checking in the same way as the inventory of Henry VIII's jewels stored in the 'Secret Juelhous in the Tower of London', which was made in the third year of Edward VI's reign.[14] Two copies usually seem to have been made of warrants and inventories, for different departments. In the case of the PRO and Stowe inventories, the former, as we have seen, was kept as a permanent record of the contents of the Wardrobe of Robes in 1600. The latter was used by the officers of the Wardrobe of Robes to record the condition and movement of various items to and from the stores. When the Stowe and PRO inventories were prepared almost every item was headed by a 'C' or 'T' decoratively written in an engrossing hand, to indicate if it was at Court, in the store at the Palace of Westminster at Whitehall, or in the Wardrobe Tower at the Tower of London (Figs 337 and 416). The contents of the Wardrobe of Robes were checked against the Stowe inventory in 1603, probably when James I's officer went through the stores. The initials 'c' and 't' were hastily written in the right margin to show where each item was at that time (Figs 337 and 416). Sometimes a second 'c' or 't' was written beside the first letter, which was then usually, although not always, cancelled by striking it through. This presumably indicated either that the garment was still there or that it had been moved again. Occasionally there is a small cross in the left margin beside the number of the garment and beside each entry in the right margin there is a firm black dot. These were also checking marks. The dots also appear throughout the jewels section (ff. 95–104) where there are no 'c' or 't' marks (Fig. 439): these jewels were in the charge of Katherine Howard, Countess of Nottingham, and Mary Ratcliffe. No doubt they kept a daily check on jewels worn by the Queen.

Most of the margin notes in the Stowe inventory are almost illegible (Figs 416 and 439). Many appear to have been scribbled while the clerk was standing up, apparently with the book propped against the wall of the store-room to steady it. The men checking the clothes were probably working in the normal cramped conditions of any large wardrobe store. Each garment would have been lifted out of a great wooden chest or standard, and removed from the bag protecting it, for close inspection 'at the view', as it is described in some of the notes in the inventory.

Alterations to entries in the Stowe inventory are carried out much more neatly. Often there are only a few words in each hand for the purposes of comparison and it is sometimes difficult to be certain which one was employed, as the ink varies, as well as the size of pen. The following groupings have been attempted to give some idea of the number of people involved and the amount of checking carried out on the contents of the Wardrobe of Robes between 1600 and 1604. In a few cases the margin notes recording the transfer, re-use or gift of certain gowns and jewels are dated.

Key to hands used in margin notes and alterations in the Stowe inventory

H 1   The original scribe and/or another clerk who wrote in a very similar hand, using a finer pen, checking the MS very soon after it was written, correcting small details, for example 'satten' changed to 'caffa' (f. 77v/24) 'ravelled' changed to 'frenged' (f. 78/32). There are over thirty minor corrections in these hands and it is difficult to distinguish between them. In cases where slight alterations have obviously been made by the original scribe I have simply indicated the nature of the alteration in the text.

H 2   Several additions and alterations made by another small neat secretary hand, checking the MS not long after it was written, undated.

H 3   Ten notes made by a hand mainly checking jewels and materials, undated.

H 4   Twelve notes made by a hand checking pearls and noting the issue of fabrics, undated.

H 5   Three notes made by a neat hand recording lost pieces of jewellery, undated.

H 6   Two notes made by a neat hand recording the re-use of fur, undated.

H 7   A neat hand recording the re-use of one lot of fur and two lengths of material, undated.

H 8   Two notes in a hurried hand, recording items lost, and one alteration undated.

H 9   The almost illegible hand of the scribe who checked the location of every item in the inventory putting 'c' or 't' in the right margin, probably in 1603. He made over sixty notes between 1600 and 1603 for deliveries to the Jewel House and items given away, many of them dated.

H10   The hand recording nine gifts made by the Queen, mainly to Helena, the 'Lady Marques' of Northampton, five initialled 'tg' by her second husband, Sir Thomas Gorges, Gentleman of the Wardrobe of Robes, and four of them dated. The initials are underlined with a flourish resembling an S.

H11   Eighteen notes in a bold hand recording some items moved to the Bedchamber and two taken for the use of King James I in 1603.

H12   The hand recording twelve receipts of jewels from Mrs Ratcliffe, undated.

H13   The hand recording five items sent to the Queen, undated, possibly Queen Anne of Denmark, rather than Queen Elizabeth.

H14   A neat hand noting three lots of jewels, one with Lady Scudamore and two taken by Sir George Hume for the use of King James I. This is similar to H11.

H15   The hand recording four lots of jewels received by Sir Thomas Gorges from Mrs Mary Ratcliffe in May 1603.

H16   'Rem' an abbreviation of 'remaining' written beside almost every item in the MS in the left margin, starting on 22 June, 1603, with a detailed check of lost and broken jewels on 30 January, 1604. It is not clear if this is Old Style or New Style date, so 1604 may be 1605.

H17   One of the owners of the MS before Thomas Astle, possibly Mr Craven Ord.

H18   Thomas Astle, antiquarian and palaeographer to whom Craven Ord gave the manuscript in 1790.

Description of Folger inventory

This manuscript book, a companion to Stowe 557, measures approximately 32.4 cm (12⅞ inches) × 20.5 cm (8¹/₁₆ inches). It was formerly Phillipps MS 27476 in the collection at Middle Hill and was purchased by Quaritch at the Phillipps sale at Sothebys on 10 June 1896. Presumably Mr Folger bought the manuscript from Quaritch although no invoice for it has been traced. The volume was previously bound in vellum and was rebound at the Folger Library in 1962 with its present half-leather binding. The paper is watermarked with a crowned shield enclosing the letter B and beneath is a scroll with the words NICHOLAS LEBE. It appears to be closest to *Briquet* no. 8079.

It is not certain if there were two copies of the Folger inventory. No second copy is mentioned on f. 1, although it is likely that there would have been one. It has neither margin notes for checking, as does the Stowe inventory, nor signatures by Lord Buckhurst, as in the PRO inventory. It may have been prepared after the Stowe and PRO inventories had been completed, and perhaps its contents should have been included with them. The manuscript gives details of all clothes remaining in the Office of the Wardrobe of Robes in 1600. It lists four items belonging to Queen Mary and then for Elizabeth, 2 robes, 26 French gowns, 14 round gowns, 27 loose gowns, 23 kirtles, some with doublets, 58 foreparts, some with doublets, 27 petticoats, 1 lap mantle, 41 cloaks, some with safeguards, 38 doublets including some cases and coverings and 4 fans. At the back are listed a few items taken as fees and all the jewels lost by the Queen since 1586, at which time Sir Thomas Gorges was appointed Gentleman of the Robes.

The Folger inventory is written in a small neat secretary hand, possibly by the same scribe who wrote the PRO inventory, with either a change of hand or a change of pen for ff. 11/21–11ᵛ/25. Here, again, the manuscripts would need to be examined by a handwriting expert to be certain of the hands. Originally this manuscript may have been the same size as the other inventories but, as Giles Dawson notes, it has been badly damaged. Part of his report is given here.

Report made on Folger MS V.b.72, by Giles Dawson, 25 May 1962

Before this MS was taken apart and restored (by Robert Lunow) much of it was unreadable because of crude repairs made probably early in this century but perhaps in the nineteenth. The MS was then put into a quite satisfactory plain vellum binding. The need for repairs had been urgent: from long exposure to damp and mildew all the leaves had become spongy and extremely delicate. Luckily the worst damage had occurred in the wide margins, where certain areas disintegrated before repairs could be made. In a good many leaves this disintegration and total destruction of the paper ate into the text, sometimes rather extensively.

The old repairs consisted of sticking (with a tenacious adhesive) some kind of strong tissue over the margins and other soft and weak parts of the leaves. The tissue, doubtless transparent enough when it was applied, had since yellowed and darkened to such a degree that reading through it was always difficult, in some places impossible.

When the Folger binder began the restoration he found that in places it was impossible to remove the mending tissue without removing also the writing under it. The tissue was much stronger than the spongy paper, and both tissue and adhesive resisted soaking, while the weak paper did not. Still, most of the tissue could be lifted safely except where the old paper was weakest. In these places it proved impossible to lift the tissue without skinning off the written surface.

In two respects the final results were less than wholly satisfactory: (1) In a good many places small patches of tissue had to be left. These now appear as dark areas with fairly sharp outlines (well exemplified on ff. 1–3) that much reduce the legibility of the underlying writing. Here and there a letter or two or even a whole word was, despite the binder's care and skill, lifted and lost...

Before the restoration was begun a microfilm was made, and it turned out that the writing covered with mending tissue showed up much better than in the MS itself. [Note: this film was used for the transcript printed here. J.A.].

When the old repairs were made the sheets were separated, so that our binder found them all disjunct. He discarded two of the leaves, numbered 21 and 22, because they were blank and badly decayed. All the other leaves he washed, sized with a gelatine solution, strengthened at the margins with Japanese tissue, and finally covered on both sides with silk chiffon, using rice starch paste.

Notes

1 For guidance in reading and transcribing documents and manuscripts from 1500–1650, see *Dawson, Kennedy-Skipton*, pp. 3–26 and 129, also *Denholm Young, Handwriting*, pp. 77–84.
2 See *Arnold, Patterns*, pp. 124–25 for tables of measurements and metric conversions.
3 See BL, Egerton 2806, f.212v and PRO, LC5/36, f.7, warrant dated 27 Sept. 1586, and Chapter VII, note 101, with full quotation in text.
4 'Thaccumpte of Thomas Parry Esquyer' for 1551–52 with 26 folios each bearing the signature of the Princess and countersigned by Sir Walter Buckler, then her Chamberlain, is noted in *Progr. Eliz.*, I, p. vii, and a full transcript given in *Smythe, Household Expenses*.
5 I hope to publish this transcript at a later date.
6 *Collins*, p. 8.
7 *Egerton Papers*, pp. 247–52.

8 For details of the coronation robes see Chapter III and *Arnold, 'Coronation Portrait'*, pp. 727–29; for other 'Clothes of Tishewe clothes of golde Sylver and Tyncell Velvet Satten Damask and other kindes of Sylkes' used for the coronation', ibid., pp. 735–41. Similar materials used for the clothes in the portrait of *Elizabeth I when Princess*, see Chapter II and Figures 17, 18 and 19.
9 PRO, E101/429/4, see *Arnold, 'Coronation Portrait'*, p. 735.
10 Personal communication in a letter dated 1 August 1985. I am very grateful to Miss Natalie Rothstein for her help.
11 PRO, LC5/37, f.57, warrant dated 10 April 1595.
12 Ibid., f.69, warrant dated 28 Sept. 1595.
13 Ibid., f.231, warrant dated 28 Sept. 1601.
14 See *Collins*, pp. 237–39 for description of the two copies of this inventory, BL, Add. MS 46, 348, and MS 29 in the Library of the Society of Antiquaries of London. Also see *Arnold, 'Sweet England's Jewels'*, p. 31.

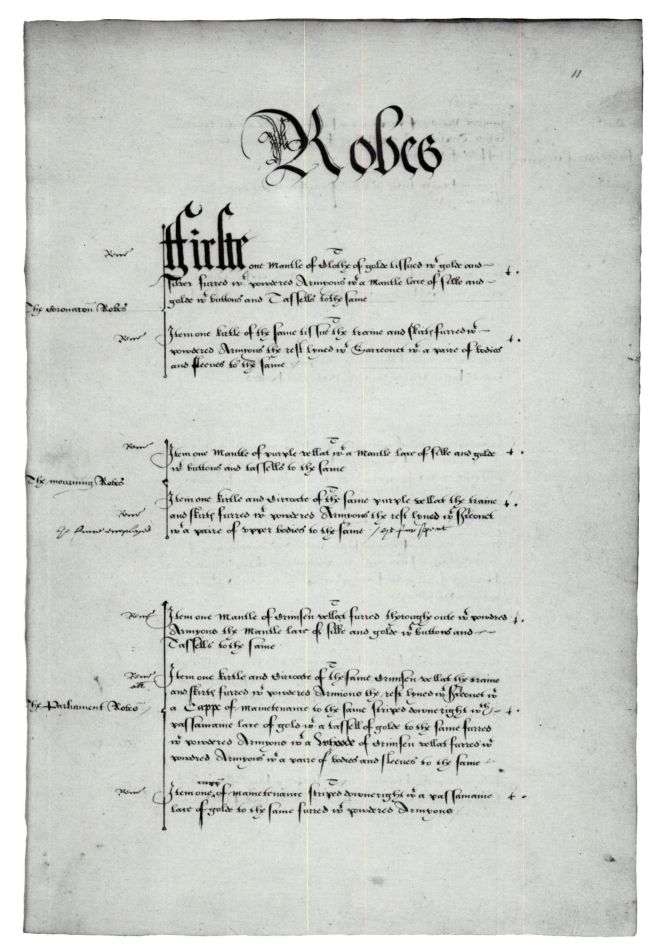

337 Folio *11 from the Stowe inventory, listing the Coronation robes, mourning robes and*
Parliament robes (reduced in size). British Library, London (Stowe 557)

X

The Inventory Made in July 1600 of all Clothes, Silks and Personal Jewels remaining in the Wardrobe of Robes at the Tower of London and within the Court at the Palace of Whitehall, Westminster, and other Royal Residences

MSS Stowe 557 in the British Library and LR2/121 in the Public Record Office, London

The Stowe Inventory

Inside cover

Strype's Ecclesiastical Memorials Vol I Appendix p. 172. Lady Brian in her letter to Lord Cromwell says that the Lady Elizabeth after her mother & Anne had been put to death had neither cloaths nor necessaries.

Many curious particulars concerning the Princess Elizabeth during the reign of her sister Queen Mary are to be found in Mr T. Warton's life of Sir Thomas Pope printed for Cadell in 1780 8ᵛᵒ

Note written after 1790 by Thomas Astle.

ff. 1, 1ᵛ, 2

[No entries]

f. 2ᵛ

Extract (by Philip Hills Esq A.D. 1800) from a Manuscript in Colchester Castle Library intitled 'A Diarian Discourse or Ephemeridia Narration by Sir Symonds D'Ewes of Stowe Hall Com: Suffolk'. N.B.

This M.S. is only a part of Sir Symonds D'Ewes's Diary the original of which is in the Harleian Library No. [no number given]

'AD 1620 January 21 King James consumed that mighty Mass of Treasure left by Queen Elizabeth, without bettering any Man, except a few beggerlye Scots, and gave away that inestimable Wardrobe for charitye preserved by all His Ancestors, to one onlye Scott, namely Erle of Dunbar(¹) who breaking those venerable Robes of ancient Kings and wickedlye transporting them into the Low Countrys, sold them for above One Hundred Thousand Pounds'.

The above account may be true when we attend to the description of the Robes Jewells etc in this Book.

(¹)George Hume of Manderstoun, one of the great favourites of King James the 1st — In 1590 he was knighted & constituted Master of the King's Wardrobe — In 1601 he was made Lord High Treasurer of Scotland — He accompanied King James into England in 1603 — On the 7th of July 1604 he was created an English Peer, by the title of Lord Hume of Berwick — On March 3rd, 1605 he was dignified by the

Title of the Earl of Dunbar. In 1609 he was made a Knight of the Garter — He died January 29th, 1611 & was buried at Dunbar. See his Epitaph & several particulars concerning him in Crawford's Lives of the Great Officers of State in Scotland page 397.

LMN £100,000. Notes written after 1790 by Thomas Astle.

f. 3

This Book belonged to Sir Simeon Stewart and was sold by Auction at his seat in Hampshire in May 1779 to ⟨ . . . . ⟩ [[Sir John Cullum Bart afterwards to Mr Craven Ord who placed it in 1790 in my M.S. Library. T. Astle.]]

Note written after May 1779 by the previous owner of the MS. Deletion and addition after 1790 by Thomas Astle.

The Booke of all suche Robes Apparell Silkes Jewells and other stuffe in the chardge of Sir Thomas Gorg knight gentleman of her majesties wardrobe of Robes

The title of the book cut from the original vellum cover, stuck onto the centre of the page.

This book contains an account of all the Robes, Apparel Silks, Jewels &tc. of Queen Elizabeth in the charge of Sir Tho. Gorges Knight Gentleman of the Wardrobe, taken by virtue of the Queen's Commission dated July 4th 42 Eliz AD 1600 directed to Thos. Lord Buckhurst Lord High Treasurer of England, George Lord Hunsdon Lord Chamberlain of the Queen's Houshold, Sir John Fortescue Knight Chancellor & under-Treasurer of the Exchequer & Sir John Stanhope Knight Treasurer of Her Majesty's Chamber or to any Three of them of which the Lord Treasurer or Lord Chamberlain to be one

It appears by a Note at the end of this Book that all the Jewels &tc therein mentioned were by Sir Tho. Gorges Knight delivered into the charge of Mrs Mary Ratcliffe May 28th 1603, 2 months & 4 Days after the accession of King James the 1st. In the presence of Edwd. Carye, Thos. Knyvett. Francis [no surname given].

Note written after 1790 by Thomas Astle.

ff. 3ᵛ, 4

[No entries]

f. 4ᵛ

A Booke of all suche Garments Jewelles Silkes and other stuffe garnishmentes of golde pearle and stone and also of dyvers stones of severall natures and workemanship as are remayninge in the Offyce of the Gardrobe of Robes the   day of Julie in the xlijth yeare of the raigne of our soveraigne Ladie Elizabeth by the grace of god of Englande Fraunce and Irelande Queene Defender of the faith etc: And now in the Chardge of Sir Thomas Gorges knight gent of the Robes, At which tyme the right Honorable Thomas Lorde Buckhurste Lorde highe Threasorer of Englande George Lorde Hunsdon Lorde Chamberlaine of her Majesties house [hold] Sir John Fortescue knighte Chauncellor and under threasorer of Thexchequer and Sir John Stanhope knighte Threasorer of her highnes Chamber by vertue of her highnes Commission under the greate Seale of Englande bearing date the iiijth daie of Julie in the saide xlijth yere of her highnes raigne to them or to anye three of them (whereof the Lorde Threasorer or Lorde Chamberlaine to bee allwaies one) in that behalf directed. did repaire to the saide Garderobe of the Robes as well within the Courte as at the Tower of London and whitehall and there did take a perfecte Survey of all such Robes garmentes and Jewells and other parcells as at that tyme were there founde to remaine. According to whiche Survey they have Caused to be written twoe severall Bookes the one of whiche Bookes is subscribed with the handes of the saide Commissioners and remayneth for a Chardge to the saide

Office of the Robes. the other is subscribed by the saide Sir Thomas Gorges knight and remaineth with the saide Lorde Threasorer.

'xxvij', for the day of July is given in PRO, LR2/121 and Folger, V.b.72. The space is left in BL, Stowe 557, but not filled in. LMN by Thomas Astle 'Taken by Commission dated July 4, 42 Eliz. A.D. 1600'.

f. 5

Robes late Kinge Edwarde the vj th

The items listed between ff. 5–10 were used by Elizabeth's brother Edward and her sister Mary. No attempt has been made to link any clothing with warrant entries for the work of tailors and embroiderers before November 1558.

[1]   Firste one Robe of clothe of silver lyned with white satten of thorder of ⟨the⟩ St Michell with a brode border of enbroderie with a wreathe of venice golde and the skallop shell and a frenge of the same golde and a small border aboute that, the grounde beinge blew vellat embrodered with halfe Moones of silver with a whoode and a Tippet of Crymsen vellat with a like enbroderie, the Tippet perished in one place with Ratts and a Coate of Clothe of silver with demi sleeves with a frenge of venice golde.

Loc. 'T', 't'. LMN in H16 'Rem xxijnd Junij Anno primo R.Ris Jacobi primi 1603'.

[2]   Item one kirtle of Crymsen vellat lyned with white Taphata for the order of the garter.

Loc. 'T', ⟨'c'⟩, 't'. LMN in H11 'delivered to ye Kinges taylor'. LMN in PRO, LR2/121 'Issued to the kings taylor'.

[3]   Item a kirtle of Crimsen vellat lyned with white sarceonet with a border rounde aboute of Mynnever powdered with Armyons with a whoode of the same vellat furred with mynnever and powdered ⟨with⟩ Armyons for the parliamente Robe.

Loc. 'T', 't'. LMN in H16 'Rem'. LMN in H11 'Kinge Edwardes'.

f. 5ᵛ

Apparell

[1]   Item one Gowne of purple [cloth of] golde tissue with a brode garde of purple vellat enbrodred with venice golde and with wreathes of purles of damaske golde edged with vellat unlyned.

Loc. 'T', 't' LMN in H16 'Rem'.

[2]   Item one gowne of blacke vellat with a brode garde of blacke vellat enbrodred with purles of silver and fower wreathes of the same edged with vellatt unlyned.

Loc. 'T', 't'. LMN in H16 'Rem'.

[3]   Item one gowne of Crimsen satten enbrodered allover with purles of damaske golde edged with Crimsen satten with a short stocke sleeve unlyned.

Loc. 'T', 't'. LMN in H16 'Rem'.

[4]   Item one frocke of clothe of golde reized and tissued with golde and silver with a billament lace of venice golde lyned with blacke vellatt.

Loc. 'T', 't'. LMN in H16 'Rem'.

[5]   Item one frocke or Cassocke of Clothe of silver reized with golde and silver tissue and greene vellat edged with vellat and lyned with satten.

Loc. 'T', 't'. LMN in H16 'Rem'.

[6]   Item one frocke of clothe of silver chequered with redd silke like birdes eies with demisleeves with a cutt of Crymsen vellat pursled on with silver lined with Crimsen vellat.

Loc. 'T', 't'. LMN in H16 'Rem'.

f. 6

[7]   Item one Coate of clothe of silver enbrodered allover with purles of damaske golde with twoe great wreathes of silver lyned with Taphata.

Loc. 'T', 't'. LMN in H16 'Rem'.

[8]   Item one rydinge Coate of Crimson vellatt enbrodered with a brode border rounde aboute of gold of venice, and small borders downeright the flower of the worke with purles of Damaske golde lined with vellatt.

Loc. 'T', 't'. LMN in H16 'Rem'.

[9]   Item one Coate with demisleeves of Crimsen Satten enbrodered allover with a twiste of golde and a border of Crimson vellat enbrodered with golde and pulled out with tincell lyned with vellat.

Loc. 'T', 't'. LMN in H16 'Rem'.

[10]   Item one rydinge Coate of purple Taphata stronge downeright with small cheines like a flagon cheine of silver and guilt on either side a wreathe of venice golde cut and lyned with golde sarceonet and vellat.

Loc. 'T', 't'. LMN in H16 'Rem'. The word 'stronge' means 'strung' here.

[11]   Item one Jerkine of Clothe of silver with longe cutts downeright bounde with a Billament lace of venice silver and blacke silke lined with Satten.

Loc. 'T', 't'. LMN in H16 'Rem'.

[12]   Item one Dublet of Crimson Satten allover enbrodered with venice golde cut and pulled out with tincell Sarceonet with a paire of hose of Crimson satten enbrodered with venice golde.

Loc. 'T', 't'. LMN in H16 'Rem'.

338 *Detail of dagger from Figure 339, with a bunch of tassels hanging from it*

339 *'Edward VI when Prince of Wales', panel painting attributed to William Scrots, c. 1546. He wears a russet satin gown with hanging sleeves. It is trimmed with velvet guards in a deeper shade of russet, embroidered with gold thread, lined with lynx. The white satin doublet beneath is embroidered and slashed, with puffs of linen shirt pulled through on the sleeves. It is decorated with broad guards of yellow satin embroidered with couched gold thread. The pendent jewel incorporates the Prince of Wales's crown and feathers. Royal Collection. Reproduced by Gracious Permission of Her Majesty the Queen*

[13] Item one Dublet and a paire of hose of Crimsen satten enbrodered with borders downerighte of venice silver and parte of the borders stitched with purple silke.

Loc. 'T', 't'. LMN in H16 'Rem'.

f. 6ᵛ

[14] Item one Dublet of purple Taphata and a paire of hose of purple vellat st[r]onge overthwart with small cheines like a flagon cheine of silver guilt and a wreathe overthwarte of the same.

Loc. 'T', 't'. LMN in H16 'Rem'. For 'st[r]onge' see f. 6/10 above.

f. 7

Jewelles

[1] Firste one Brouche of golde with a small Table Rubie in it and divers personages.

[2] Item one Brouche of golde with fower personages and three diamondes in it.

[3] Item one Brouche of golde of St Paule with a Table Diamonde and twoe small Table Rubies.

[4] Item fiftie and twoe paire of Aglets of golde enameled of sondrie sorts.

[5] Item eightene Buttons and eightene paire of Aglets of golde three square enameled blacke.

[6] Item three dozen of buttons and three dozen paire of Aglets of golde three square enameled white.

[7] Item three and twentie dozen and seaven paire of verie small Aglets of golde of sondrie sortes.

f. 7ᵛ

[8] Item fower dozen and eight buttons and fower dozen and eight paire of Aglets of golde made like unto poynted diamondes enameled blacke.

[9] Item fower dozen and six buttons and fower dozen and six paire of Aglets of golde made like unto pointed diamondes enameled white.

[10] Item one poynarde the hafte Ivorie with an open pomell the hafte striped downe with golde with a knife the hafte of golde the locker and Chape of golde havinge a pece of the Chape broken of[f] with a Tassell of blew silke and a skaberde of leather.

[11] Item one Dagger the hafte hilt and pomell of Crystall garnished with golde the shethe of Steele wrought Damaskine worke the locker Chape and garnishment in the middeste of golde havinge therin fower Rubies and fower Emerodes great and smale wantinge the biggest Emerode in the locker, havinge a Tassell of venice golde garnished with pearles and fower perles pendant lackinge one Button upon the Crosse.

340 'Mary Tudor', by Antonio Mor, c. 1554. She wears a velvet French gown with matching partlet lined with embroidered linen. The wide sleeves are turned back, caught behind the upper arm. Forepart and matching under-sleeves are in patterned silk woven with two sizes of looped silver metal thread. Museo del Prado, Madrid

f. 8
Gownes late Queene Maries

[1] Firste one Frenche gowne of purple Clothe of golde lyned with purple Taphata with wide sleeves to the same.

Loc. 'T', 't'. LMN in H16 'Rem'.

[2] Item one frenche gowne of purple Clothe of silver lined with purple Taphata with wide sleeves to the same.

Loc. 'T', 't'. LMN in H16 'Rem'.

[3] Item one riche gowne of Crimson Satten embrodered with purled golde and set with garnets with wide sleeves to the

same turned up with Murrey vellat allover enbrodered with purled golde and set with pearle lacking sondrie great and small pearle in the border of the traine and sleeves and five roses of garnets in the traine. the pearle taken of[f].

Loc. 'T', 't'. LMN in H16 '{Less} p(ear)le' and 'Rem'. RMN in H4 'pearll taken offe'. In PRO, LR2/121 these are the original scribe's addition, using a different pen.

[4] Item one Frenche gowne of crimsen vellat edged with pur⟨ple⟩led golde hemmed on both sides the edge with pearle taken of[f].

Loc. 'T', 't'. LMN in H16 'Rem'.

[5] Item one frenche gowne of blacke vellat with an edge of purle and pipes of golde the wide sleeves turned up allover with like purle and pipes lackinge parte of the pipes on the sleeves and in the border.

Loc. 'T', 't'. LMN in H16 'Rem'.

[6] Item one frenche gowne of riche golde tissue with a border of purple satten allover enbrodered with purles of damaske golde and pearle lined with purple Taphata ⟨lackinge sondrie⟩ with small pearle taken of[f].

Loc. 'T', 't'. LMN in H16 'Rem'. Alison Carter suggests that this may have been the gown worn by Mary for her wedding on 25 July 1554 together with the kirtle listed in f. 9ᵛ/[11]; See Carter, 'Mary Tudor's Wardrobe', p. 16.

f. 8ᵛ

[7] Item one loose gowne of purple wrought vellat with Satten grownd the worke fourmed downe with venice golde and with a border enbrodered with golde and Silver the sleeves lackinge.

Loc. 'T', 't'. LMN in H16 'Rem'.

f. 9
Kirtells

[1] Firste one kirtle of Crimsen vellatt the foreparte embroidered with golde and set with pearle lyned with Taphata lacking sixetene greate pearle and verie manye small pearle ⟦the pearle taken of[f]⟧ ⟦since⟧

Loc. 'T', 't'. LMN in H16 'Rem'. Additions in H2 and H4. In PRO, LR2/121 'the p(ear)le taken off' is in another hand.

[2] Item one kirtle of purple vellatt the foreparte embroidered with golde and set with pearle lyned with Crimsen Taphata with another traine to the same embrodered like the foreparte unlined lacking fiftie fower of the greatest pearle and sondrie small p(ear)le — ⟦the pearle taken of[f]⟧ ⟦since⟧

Loc. 'T', 't'. LMN in H16 'Rem'. Additions in H2 and H4.

[3] Item one kirtle of greene vellat the foreparte embroidered with golde Lyned with Crimsen Taphata.

Loc. 'T', 't'. LMN in H16 'Rem'.

[4] Item one french Kirtle of purple cloth of sylver braunched and raized with silver tissue lyned with Blewe Taphata.

Loc. 'T', 't'. LMN in H16 'Rem'.

[5] Item one Kirtle of Crimsen Satten embroidered with damask purle and venice golde and set with pearle with a rounde traine of like embrodere lyned with Crimsen Taphata both set with fortye fower small Buttons of golde in each a small pearle lacking twelve of the pearle and the

foreparte cut in the topp a quarter of a yarde in length ⟨lackinge many of⟩ the pearle ⟨taken of⟩ ⟦and buttons⟧ ⟦pearll & buttons taken of[f] since⟧.

Loc. 'T', 't'. LMN in H16 'Rem'. Deletions in H2 and additions in H2 and H4.

f. 9ᵛ

[6] Item one kirtle of purple Satten the foreparte embroidered with venice golde and lyned with redd kersey.

Loc. 'T', 't'. LMN in H16 'Rem'.

[7] Item one foreparte of blacke cloth of golde embrodered with venice golde.

Loc. 'T', 't'. LMN in H16 'Rem'.

[8] Item one french kirtle thouteside of rich cloth of golde tissue the inside of Crimsen cloth of golde edged with a passamaine lace of golde.

Loc. 'T', 't'. LMN in H16 'Rem'.

[9] Item one french kirtle of purple clothe of sylver raized with sylver tissue lyned with Crimsen Taphata.

Loc. 'T', 't'. LMN in H16 'Rem'.

[10] Item one french kirtle of murrey cloth of tissue golde and silver let downe with murrey Satten edged with vellat and lined with Crimsen Taphata.

Loc. 'T', 't'. LMN in H16 'Rem'.

[11] Item one rounde Kirtle of golde tissue with a brode border embrodered with damaske silver and some pearle the hinder parte white satten lyned with white Taphata ⟦the pearle taken of[f]⟧

Loc. 'T', 't'. LMN in H16 'Rem'. Addition in H2. See f. 8/[6].

[12] Item one kirtle of Crimsen Satten the foreparte embrodered with a lozenge knott of venice golde lace and sett with pearle lyned with Crimsen Taphata — ⟦the pearle taken of[f]⟧

Loc. 'T', 't'. LMN in H16 'Rem'. Addition in H2.

[13] Item one french kirtle of purple cloth of golde tissue let downe with purple Satten and lyned with Crimsen Taphata.

Loc. 'T', 't'. LMN in H16 'Rem'.

f. 10

[14] Item one foreparte of a kirtle of white vellatt allover enbrodered with venice golde and set with small turquesses garnets and ⟨ragged pearle⟩ set in the border ⟦pearll taken of[f]⟧

Loc. 'T', 't'. LMN in H16 'Rem'. Deletion and addition in H4.

f. 10ᵛ

[No entries]

341 *The 'Siena Sieve' portrait of Queen Elizabeth I, by an unknown artist, c. 1580. The Queen wears a black French gown 'with high bodies', a fine white silk wired veil, and holds a sieve, symbol of chastity. Pinacoteca di Siena*

f. 11

Robes [Queen Elizabeth]
The Coronation Robes

[1A] Firste one Mantle of Clothe of golde tissued with golde and silver furred with powdered Armyons with a Mantle lace of silke and golde with buttons and Tassells to the same.

[2A] Item one kirtle of the same tissue the traine and skirts furred with powdered Armyons the rest lyned with Sarceonet with a paire of bodies and sleeves to the same.

These two items are bracketed together. Loc. 'T', 't' for both. LMN in H16 'Rem' for both.

Described as the Robes of Estate in PRO, LC5/32, f. 237, these were first worn by Mary Tudor at her coronation in 1553. Elizabeth used both mantle and kirtle, with a new bodice for the kirtle, at her coronation in 1559. The robes are shown in the 'Coronation' miniature by Nicholas Hilliard (Fig. 87) and the 'Coronation' portrait at the National Portrait Gallery (Fig. 86). For further details see Chapter III

The mourning Robes

[3A] Item one Mantle of purple vellat with a Mantle lace of silke and golde with buttons and tassells to the same

[4A] Item one kirtle and Circoate of the same purple vellat the traine and skirtes furred with powdered Armyons the rest lyned with sarceonet with a paire of upper bodies to the same. ⟦the fur spent⟧

These two items are bracketed together. Loc. 'T', 't' for both. LMN in H16 'Rem' for both. LMN beside [4A] in H16 'the same employed'. Addition in H9; in PRO, LR2/121 this reads 'the furre employed'. These would appear to be the 'Robes of purple vellat' worn at the coronation (PRO, E101/429/3, f.2ᵛ, printed in J. Arnold, 'The "Coronation" Portrait of Queen Elizabeth I', *The Burlington Magazine*, CXX, November 1978, p.735). For further details see Chapter III.

The Parliament Robes

[5A] Item one Mantle of Crimsen vellat furred throughe oute with powdred Armyons the Mantle lace of silke and golde with buttons and Tassells to the same.

[6A] Item one kirtle and Circoate of the same Crimsen vellat the traine and skirtes furred with powdered Armions the rest lyned with sarceonet with a Cappe of Mainetenance to the same striped downeright with passamaine lace of gold with a tassell of golde to the same furred with powdered Armyons with a whoode of Crimsen vellat furred with powdred Armyons with a paire of bodies and sleeves to the same.

These two items are bracketed together. Loc. 'T', 't' for both. LMN in H16 'Rem' for both. LMN in H16 {'all'}. The Parliament Robes at the Coronation were, apparently, those worn by Queen Mary. For further details see Chapter III

[7A] Item one capp of mainetenance striped downeright with a passamaine lace of golde to the same furred with powdered Armyons.

This second cap of maintenance is bracketed with 5A and 6A above. Loc. 'T', 't'. LMN in H16 'Rem'. The cap of maintenance was formerly worn as a symbol of official dignity and later carried before the sovereign in procession. The fur was kept in good order: 'for mendinge the furre of our parliament Robe with kyrtle Cyrcoate a whodde and two Cappes of maintenance every of them perfourmed with powderid armyons of our great guarderobe'. (Warrant 16 April, 27 Eliz. 1585. BL, Egerton 2806, f.204ᵛ).

f.11ᵛ

Robes for the order of the garter

[8A] Item one Mantle of purple vellat for thorder of the Garter lyned with white Taphata with mantle lace of purple silke and golde and tassells of the same.

[9A] Item one frenche kirtle with bodies of crimsen vellat laide with a lace of venice golde.

These two items are bracketed together. Loc. 'C', 'c' for both. LMN in H16 'Rem' for both. The robes are illustrated in Figure 114. For further details see Chapter III.

1 Item one Mantle of venice golde silver and Murrey silke laide rounde aboute with a passamaine lace of venice golde silver and flat silver.

Loc. 'T', 't'. LMN in H16 'Rem'.

2 Item one Mantle of Carnacion and purple unshorne vellat in waves furred throughout with Mynnever spotted.

Loc. 'T', 't'. LMN in H16 'Rem'.

3 Item one Mantle of watchet Satten striped with golde edged aboute with a pincked lace of venice golde faced before with one pane of watchet vellat striped with silver lyned with watchet sarceonet.

Loc. 'T', 't'. LMN in H16 'Rem'. This would appear to have been in the Wardrobe of Robes since 1576, when an alteration was carried out: 'First to Walter Fyshe our Taylour . . . Item for alteringe of a Mantle of watchett satten striped with golde sent oute of Fraunce newe lyned afore with white satten striped with silver of our great guarderobe.' (Warrant 14 April, 18 Eliz. 1576. BL, Egerton 2806, f.93ᵛ).

4 Item one Mantle of tawnye satten bordered with an enbroderie of venice golde and silver and enbrodered allover with bias Cloudes and spangles of like golde faced with white Satten razed with a border enbrodered with like golde.

Loc. 'T', 't'. LMN in H16 'Rem'. This item was a New Year's gift: 'By the Countes of Shrewsbury, a mantyll of tawny satten enbrawdred with a border of Venice golde and silver, lyned with white taphata, and faced with white satten. Delivered to the foresaid Rauf Hoope.' (New Year's Gift Roll, 21 Eliz. 1579. Folger, Z.d.15, printed in *Progr. Eliz.*, II, p.251).

5 Item one Mantle of blacke silke networke with a traine enbrodred allover with flowers or knotts of venice golde and silver bounde aboute with a lace of like golde and silver lyned with blacke Sarceonet.

Loc. 'T', ⟨'C'⟩, 't'. LMN in H16 'Rem'. Details of payment are given: 'First to Walter Fyshe our Taylour . . . Item for making of a mantell of black nett worke with a trayne embrauderid allover with Flowers of golde and silver and bounde aboute with a lase of golde and Silver lyned with black sarceonett and the Coller lyned with buckeram Eightene yardes of the said nett worke of our store of the chardge of the said Rauf Hope the rest of the nett worke payed for by henry Sackforde Esquier, the sarceonett buckeram and making of our greate guarderobe.' (Warrant 4 April, 13 Eliz. 1571. BL, Egerton 2806, f.30ᵛ).

6 ⟨Item one Mantle of blacke networke striped with silver and owes with silver and bounde aboute with a small bindinge lace of like silver with a traine.⟩

Loc. 'T', ⟨'C'⟩, 't'. LMN in H16 'Rem'. RMN in H9 'geven' and the whole item is struck through by the same hand. In PRO, LR2/121 the item has not been cancelled.

f.12

7 Item one Mantle of blacke networke edged with a lace of venice silver upon the seames.

Loc. 'T', ⟨'C'⟩, 't'. LMN in H16 'Rem'.

8 Item one vale of heare colour networke florished with golde threedes and spangles.

Loc. 'T', 't'. LMN in H16 'Rem'.

9 Item one Mantle of white networke striped like waves of like networke florished with silver.

Loc. 'T', ⟨'C'⟩ 't'. LMN in H16 'Rem'.

10 Item one Mantle of tawney networke with tufts of like silke florished with Silver.

Loc. 'T', ⟨'C'⟩ 't'. LMN in H16 'Rem'.

11 Item one Mantle of aishcolour sleve silke networke and golde with a traine.

Loc. 'T', 't'. LMN in H16 'Rem'.

12 Item one vale of white networke florished with golde twist and spangles.

Loc. 'T', 't'. LMN in H16 'Rem'.

13 Item one Mantle of blacke networke of silke bounde aboute with a passamaine lace of blacke silke

Loc. 'T', 't'. LMN in H16 'Rem'.

14 Item one Mantle of white lawne or networke striped set with tufts of black silke and spangles of silver.

Loc. 'T', ⟨'C'⟩, 't'. LMN in H16 'Rem'. This was a New Year's gift: 'By the Barronesse Lumley a Mantle of white striped lawne set with tuftes & spangles of black sylke. Delivered to the forsaid Rauf hope. (New Year's Gift Roll, 26 Eliz. 1584. BL, Egerton 3052, printed in *Costume*, 9, 1975, p.28).

15 Item one Mantle of blacke networke florished with silver and striped ⟨to⟩ with lace.

Loc. 'T'. ⟨'C'⟩, 't'. LMN in H16 'Rem'. Deletion in H1.

f.12ᵛ

16 Item one Mantle of blacke networke florished allover with golde and spangles like waveworke.

Loc. 'T', ⟨'C'⟩, 't'. LMN in H16 'Rem'.

17 Item one Mantle without a traine of tawnye networke richelye florished with venice golde and silver like starres and Crossebillets bounde aboute with a lace of venice golde.

Loc. 'T', ⟨'C'⟩, 't'. LMN in H16 'Rem'.

18 Item one vale of blacke networke florished with venice silver like flagonworke and enbrodered allover with roses

342 'Queen Elizabeth I', panel painting by an unknown artist, c. 1590. The Queen wears an embroidered veil. The wide, shallow cutwork ruff, bordered with lace and open at the front, is similar to that in Figure 44. The frills at the ends of the smock sleeves are pulled out carefully to show the embroidery. Ampleforth College, York, on loan from Lord Deramore

343 'Queen Elizabeth I', by an unknown artist, c. 1580. The Queen wears a wired gauze or net veil. The embroidered frills at the ends of the smock sleeves are turned down over her wrists. Tacked to the ends of the sleeves are a pair of white linen cuffs edged with bobbin lace. Present whereabouts unknown

of venice golde silver and silke of Colours of silkewomans worke.

Loc. 'C', 't'. LMN in H16 'Rem'.

19 Item one Irishe Mantle of Murrey networke florished with venice golde silver and silver plate like waves with a deepe frenge of venice golde and silver aboute the Coller and downe before.

Loc. 'C', 't'. LMN in H16 'Rem'. This was a New Year's gift: 'By Sir John Parrett . . . And two Irishe mantles the one murry . . . laced with silver lace and freindge. The mantles delivered to John Whinyard.' (New Year's Gift Roll, 31 Eliz. 1589. BL, Lansd. Roll 17, printed in *Progr. Eliz.*, III, p. 10). Further information about this and other Irish mantles is given in J. Arnold, 'Jane Lambarde's Mantle' in *Costume*, 14, 1980, pp. 62–63.

20 Item one Mantle of blacke silke networke striped with silver and garnished with tuftes of damaske silver.

Loc. 'C', 't'. LMN in H 16 'Rem'.

21 Item one Mantle of white networke diamondewise wrought like small Cob-webb roundell worke laide with silver plate.

Loc. 'T', 't'. LMN in H16 'Rem'.

22 Item one Mantle of blacke networke florished with venice silver in waves Diamondewise.

Loc. 'C', 't'. LMN in H16 'Rem'.

23 Item one Mantle or loose gowne of aishColour networke florished with venice golde and silver plate billetwise with owes of golde and silver and a threede of like gold and silver like flames.

Loc. 'C', 't'. LMN in H16 'Rem'. This was probably a gift as it does not appear among the warrants for the Wardrobe of Robes before this entry: 'First to William Jones our Taylour . . . Item for alteringe of a Mantell of ashe colour nettworke and making of new sleevis and wynges perfourmed with like stuff of our great Guarderobe.' (Warrant 26 Sept, 25 Eliz. 1583. BL, Egerton 2806, f. 190).

f. 13

24 Item one Mantle of white networke striped with small silver threds diamonde-wise and small tufts of silver and spangles downe the seames.

Loc. 'C', 't'. LMN in H16 'Rem'.

25 Item one Mantle of silver networke.

Loc. 'C', 't'. LMN in H16 'Rem'.

26 〈Item one mantle of white net cutt and florished with venice silver and owes〉.

Loc. 'C', 't'. LMN in H16 'Rem'. RMN in H9 'geven'. The whole item is struck through by the same hand.

27 Item one Mantle of white net striped with a white stripe and tufte allover with white silke tufts.

Loc. 'C', 't'. LMN in H16 'Rem'.

28 Item one Mantle with a traine of pale pincke coloured networke florished allover

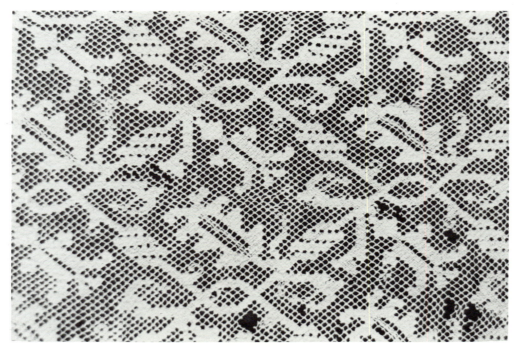

344 *Detail from a band of fine white linen lacis, or knotted net, made on the diagonal, described in the inventories as 'networke diamondewise wrought'. Victoria and Albert Museum, London (1132–1875)*

with silver like Esses and branches Billet-wise.

Loc. 'C', 't'. LMN in H16 'Rem'.

29 Item one Mantle of tawney ⟦or Russet⟧ networke florished with golde allover in braunches billetwise and some golde plate.

Loc. 'C', 't'. LMN in H16 'Rem'. Addition in H3.

30 Item one Mantle of white net tufte with peache Colour silke and striped with silke.

Loc. 'C', 't'. LMN in H16 'Rem'.

31 ⟨Item one Mantle of white net enbrodered allover with silver and owes like wheate eares and Compas poynted waves⟩.

Loc. 'C', 't'. LMN in H16 'Rem'. RMN in H9 'geven'. The whole item is struck through by the same hand. In PRO, LR2/121 the item has not been cancelled.

32 Item one Mantle of pincke Colour net striped with silver or Copper.

Loc. 'C', 't'. LMN in H16 'Rem'.

f. 13ᵛ

33 Item one Mantle of white networke florished allover with branches of silver and starres of golde, lyned.

Loc. 'C', 't'. LMN in H16 'Rem'.

34 Item one vale of white net striped with silver diamondewise.

Loc. 'C', 't'. LMN in H16 'Rem'.

35 Item one vale of striped networke florished with Carnacion silke and some owes.

Loc. 'C', 't'. LMN in H16 'Rem'.

36 Item one Mantle with a traine of blacke networke striped with three stripes of blacke silke diamondewise.

Loc. 'C', 't'. LMN in H16 'Rem'.

37 Item one Mantle of white networke florished with silver plate diamondewise.

Loc. 'C', 't'. LMN in H16 'Rem'.

38 Item one Mantle of white networke tufte up (pe/pon) with a net of venice silver Diamonde wise and silver spangles without a traine.

Loc. 'C', 't'. LMN in H16 'Rem'.

39 Item one Mantle of aishcolour Taphata with twoe Burgonyon gardes enbrodered allover with golde upon lawne lyned with white Taphata sarceonet and set thoroughoute with ragged pearle.

Loc. 'C', 't'. LMN in H16 'Rem' and '{less} p(ear)le'. RMN in H9 'The pearle taken of[f] for the kinges use the 24 of aprill at Whithall 1603'. The description of a mantle made in 1591 is very close to this item. Burgundian guards were presumably made in Burgundy or purchased from a merchant of Burgundy. They appear on the Queen's clothes as early as 1561 (J. Arnold, *Lost from Her Majesties Back*, 1980 p. 22). Those listed here may have replaced the original 'riche borders' of 1591. The embroidery is given as venice silver instead of gold, but this may be a scribe's error. The work of both tailor and embroiderer are recorded: 'First to

William Jones our Taylour … Item for makinge of a Mantle with a trayne of ashecolor taffeta embroidered alover & set with pearles, lyned with sarcnet of our great warderobe'. (Warrant 10 June, 33 Eliz. 1591. PRO, LC5/36, f. 168). 'Item to John Parr our Embrother … Item for embroderinge of a Mantle of ashe colour taffata beinge cutt and wrought alover with a wave of venice silver and powthered with pearles betwene the waves representinge haile havinge two riche borders sett on downe before and round about the trayne of our store'. (Warrant 10 June, 33 Eliz. 1591. PRO, LC5/36, f. 176).

40 Item one Mantle of white ⟨Taphata⟩ ⟦Tyffanye⟧ striped with venice silver and orenge Colour silke.

Loc. 'C', 't'. LMN in H16 'Rem'. Alteration in H1. Same alteration made in PRO, LR2/121, but in another hand.

f. 14

41 Item one Mantle of blacke stitched cloth enbrodered allover with a border of Roses Cloudes and Daizeis of venice golde silver and silke lyned with white Sarceonet.

Loc. 'C', 't'. LMN in H16 'Rem'.

42 Item [one] Mantle of russet stitched Clothe with xxj paire of small Agglets of golde and one Aglett.

Loc. 'C', 't'. LMN in H16 'Rem' and 'xxxvj aglettes less ij'. In PRO, LR2/121 'and one Aglett' and 'xxi paire of' are struck out and 'xxxvi' written in.

43 Item one vale of heare colour stitched Clothe or networke striped with silver plate lace downe the seames.

Loc. 'C', 't'. LMN in H16 'Rem'.

44 Item one Vale of Murrey stitched Clothe wrought overthwart with silver and spangles.

Loc. 'C', 't'. LMN in H16 'Rem'.

45 Item one vale of Tawney stitched clothe striped Downeright with venice golde pincked lace.

Loc. 'C', 't'. LMN in H16 'Rem'.

46 Item one Mantle of aish Colour stitched clothe striped with gold lace on the seames without a Traine.

Loc. 'C', 't'. LMN in H16 'Rem'.

47 Item one Mantle of blacke stitched Clothe edged with a bone lace of small pearle and bugle and five fishes of Mother of pearle one set with small Emerodes and garnets.

Loc. 'C', 't'. LMN in H16 'Rem'.

48 Item one Mantle of white stitched Cloth seamed Downe with one lace of venice golde without a Traine.

Loc. 'C', 't'. LMN in H16 'Rem'.

f. 14ᵛ

49 Item one Mantle of blacke stitched clothe florished and seamed with venice silver.

Loc. 'C', 't'. LMN in H16 'Rem'. This was a New Year's gift 'By the Barronesse Talbott widdowe A mantle of black stitch cloth florished and seamed with venis silver. Delivered to the Roabes'. (New Year's Gift Roll, 31 Eliz. 1589 BL, Lansd. Roll 17, printed in *Progr. Eliz.*, III, p. 7). This may be the item listed in 1602, for 'Dorethie Speckard our silkewoman for … washyng and starching a Mantle of stiched cloth florished with silver taking it asonder, mending it, and making the same up againe'. (Warrant, 19 April, 44 Eliz. 1602. PRO, LC5/37, f. 257).

50 Item one Mantle of white stitched clothe florished in some places with a small threed of venice golde and silver.

Loc. 'T', 't'. LMN in H16 'Rem'.

51 Item one Mantle of blacke stitched Clothe seamed with a lace of venice silver.

Loc. 'C', 't'. LMN in H16 'Rem'.

52 Item one Mantle of blacke stitched Clothe striped with golde bounde about with a small plate lace of golde and a lace upon the seames.

Loc. 'C', 't'. LMN in H16 'Rem'.

53 Item one Mantle of aishcolour stitched clothe florished with oaken leaves of golde and silver bounde aboute with a plate lace of venice golde silver and owes.

Loc. 'C', 't'. LMN in H16 'Rem'.

54 Item one Mantle of blacke stitched Clothe with workes diamondwise in squares wrought with thredes of venice golde like knotts edged and the seames laide on with a small plate lace.

Loc. 'C', 't'. LMN in H16 'Rem'.

55 Item one Mantle of blacke stitched clothe florished allover Diamondewise with a threede of venice golde and starres and owes in the Myddest.

Loc. 'C', 't'. LMN in H16 'Rem'.

56 Item one Mantle of aishecolour stitched Clothe florished with venice golde and owes.

Loc. 'C', 't'. LMN in H16 'Rem'.

f. 15

57 Item one Mantle of white stitched clothe florished with white silke edged with venice silver.

Loc. 'C', 't'. LMN in H16 'Rem'.

58 Item one Mantle of blacke stitched clothe striped with silver bounde aboute with a lace of venice silver.

Loc. 'C', 't'. LMN in H16 'Rem'.

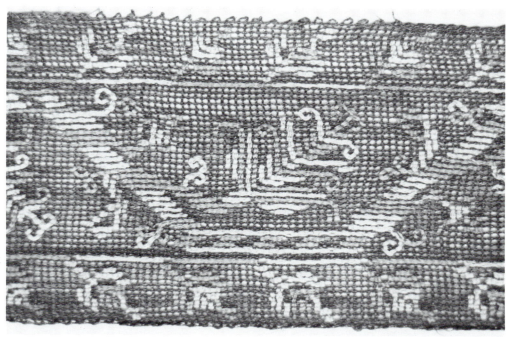

345 *Border of blue burato, the ground a woven gauze resembling hand knotted net, darned with yellow and cream silk, possibly 'networke enbrodered allover'. Victoria and Albert Museum, London (638–1893)*

59 Item one Mantle with a Traine of blacke stitched clothe striped downerighte.

Loc. 'C', 't'. LMN in H16 'Rem'.

60 Item one Mantle of white stitched cloth enbrodered with venice silver and owes of silver cut in open cuts billetwise.

Loc. 'C', 't'. LMN in H16 'Rem'.

61 Item one Mantle of white Sipers tufted with heare colour silke with a small passamaine lace of like colour silke and venice silver.

Loc. 'C', 't'. LMN in H16 'Rem'.

62 Item one Mantle of white Sipers seamed with purle golde and spangles.

Loc. 'C', 't'. LMN in H16 'Rem'.

63 Item one vale of blacke stitched ⟨clothe⟩ Sipers florished with silver and spangles striped with silver lace called fryse.

Loc. 'C', 't'. LMN in H16 'Rem'.

64 Item one Mantle of white striped sipers edged with silver purled edginge.

Loc. 'C', 't'. LMN in H16 'Rem'.

f. 15ᵛ

65 Item one Mantle of ⟨aishcolored sipers⟩ ⟦or heare colour networke⟧ tackt up in risinge cutts with some smale plate of silver.

Loc. 'T', 't'. LMN in H16 'Rem'. Alteration in H2. This alteration is not made in PRO, LR2/121.

66 Item one Mantle of white curled Sipers with tufts of silver downe the seames.

Loc. 'C', 't'. LMN in H16 'Rem'. This item was a New Year's gift: 'By Mr Richarde Frenche, one mantell of white curled cypres, with tuftes of silver down the seames. Deljvered to the Robes.' (New Year's Gift Roll, 42 Eliz. 1600. Printed in *Progr. Eliz.*, III, p. 458).

67 Item one square vale of white Damaske worke lawne with small tuftes one the edge.

Loc. 'T', 't'. LMN in H16 'Rem'.

68 Item one Mantle of white lawne cutt florished with golde and spangles edged with a bonelace of venice golde.

Loc. 'C', 't'. LMN in H16 'Rem'.

69 Item one Mantle of Lawne cutworke with roses and oken leaves with a little blacke silke therin.

Loc. 'T', 't'. LMN in H16 'Rem'. This item was a New Year's gift: 'By the Lady Marques of Northampton A mantle of Lawne Coutworke with Roses and Oken leves with A Lyttle blacke Sylke in yt. Delivered the foresaid Raulfe Hope'. (New Year's Gift Roll, 27 Eliz. 1585. Folger, Z.d.16).

70 Item one Mantle of lawne cutworke florished with silver cutte like crosse Billetts.

Loc. 'C', 't'. LMN in H16 'Rem'. This item was a New Year's gift: 'By the Countes of Commberland. A Mantle of Lawne Coutworke floryshed with Sylver. Delivered Raulfe Hope'. (New Year's Gift Roll, 27 Eliz. 1585. Folger, Z.d.16).

346 *Cream silk sprang of Near Eastern origin, eighteenth century. This technique may have been the 'knitworke' used for mantles. Victoria and Albert Museum, London (T.19–1933)*

71   Item one Mantle of Lawne cutworke with halfe Moones.

Loc. 'T', 't'. LMN in H16 'Rem'.

72   Item one Mantle of lawne cut with tufts of Murrey or tawney silke.

Loc. 'C', 't'. LMN in H16 'Rem'.

73   Item one Vale of Lawne pintched up striped with a small lace of golde and owes of Golde.

Loc. 't'. LMN in H16 'Rem'. This was a shared New Year's gift: 'By the Lorde Hounsdon Lorde Chamberlein parte of a valle of Lawne pynched up striped with a small Passament of venus golde and Owes of golde. Delivered to the said Sir Tho: Gorges' and 'By the Baronesse Hunsdon parte of a vaylle of Lawne pynched up striped with a small lace of Venus golde and Owes. Delivered to the said Sir Thomas Gorges'. (New Year's Gift Roll, 30 Eliz. 1588. BL, Add. 8159).

f. 16

74   Item one Mantle of lawne cutworke in squares with little Roses cut up (pe/pon) with golde plate and owes seamed with a small purle lace of venice golde.

Loc. 'T', 't'. LMN in H16 'Rem'.

75   Item one Mantle of white stitched lawne striped overthwarte with silver plate bounde aboute with a plate lace of silver.

Loc. 'C', 't'. LMN in H16 'Rem'.

76   Item one Mantle of white lawne florished allover with venice silver.

Loc. 'C', 't'. LMN in H16 'Rem'.

[77   Item 78 should be entered as 77. This is a scribe's error in numbering. There are only 98 mantles not 99.]

78   Item one Mantle of white lawne cut and turned in enbrodered alover with workes of silver like pomegranetts roses honiesocles and acornes.

Loc. 'C', 't'. LMN in H16 'Rem'.

79   Item one Mantle of lawne cut oute and florished with silver plate.

Loc. 'C', 't'. LMN in H16 'Rem'.

80   Item one Mantle of white lawne cut and florished with silver and tufts of silke of colour de Roie.

Loc. 'C', 't'. LMN in H16 'Rem'.

81   Item one Mantle of heare colour silke knitworke florished with plates and starres of Silver.

Loc. 'C', 't'. LMN in H16 'Rem'.

82   Item one Mantle of knitworke florished allover with venice silver like Roses and Leaves.

Loc. 'C', 't'. LMN in H16 'Rem'.

83   Item one Mantle withoute a traine of white knitworke flourished with a twiste of venice silver and spangles.

Loc. 'C', 't'. LMN in H16 'Rem'.

f. 16ᵛ

84   Item one vale ⟦or mantle⟧ of white knitworke florished with silver.

Loc. 'C', 't'. LMN in H16 'Rem'. Addition in H1.

85   Item one Mantle or vale of white Tiffyney tufte with orange colour silke downe the ⟨sleeves⟩ ⟦seames⟧.

Loc. 'C', 't'. LMN in H16 'Rem'. Alteration in H2.

86   Item one Mantle of white Tiffeney striped with silver thredes and small tufts of silver downe the Seames.

Loc. 'C', 't'. LMN in H16 'Rem'.

87   Item one Mantle of white silver striped tiffeney with small silver frenge aboute and tufts of silver and spangles downe the seames.

Loc. 'C', 't'. LMN in H16 'Rem'. This item was a New Year's gift: 'By Mr Carmarden one Mantell of white tyffany stryped with silver with tuftes on the seames of venice silver and

spangles. Delivered to the Robes'. (New Year's Gift Roll, 41 Eliz. 1599. Folger, Z.d.17).

88   Item one Mantle of white tiffeney striped with silver tufted with orenge colour silke bounde aboute with a lace of venice silver.

Loc. 'C', 't'. LMN in H16 'Rem'.

89   Item one vale or Mantle of tawney tiffeney striped with silver and small silver tufts on the seames.

Loc. 'C', 't'. LMN in H16 'Rem'.

90   Item one Mantle of white tiffeney striped with silke and golde with small tufts of golde and spangles downe the seames.

Loc. 'C', 't'. LMN in H16 'Rem'. This item was a New Year's gift: 'By the Lady Leighton one Mantell of tyffany stryped with silke & golde with small tuftes of venyce golde with spangles downe the seames. Delivered to the Robes'. (New Year's Gift roll, 41 Eliz. 1599. Folger, Z.d.17).

91   Item one Mantle of tiffeney striped with golde and white stripes and pincked ⟦or orenge⟧ colour silke and tufts of orenge colour downe the seames.

Loc. 'C', 't'. LMN in H16 'Rem'. Addition in H1. This item was a New Year's gift: 'By the Lady Hawkyns one Mantell of tyffany striped with golde and white silke with small tuftes of Orenge colored silke. Delivered to the Robes'. (New Year's Gift Roll, 41 Eliz. 1599. Folger, Z.d.17).

92   Item one Mantle of white tiffeney striped with silver and tufte with silver downe the seames.

Loc. 'C', 't'. LMN in H16 'Rem'.

f. 17

93   Item one Mantle of white tiffeney striped with silver ⟨and tuftes on⟩ ⟦and tuftes downe⟧ the seames of silver and spangles and white stripes of silke.

Loc. 'C', 't'. LMN in H16 'Rem'. Alteration in H2.

94   Item one Mantle of Tiffeney striped with silver.

Loc. 'C', 't'. LMN in H16 'Rem'. This item was a New Year's gift: 'By the Lord Henry Howarde one Mantle of Tyffanye stryped with sylver. Delivered to the Robes'. (New Year's Gift Roll, 41 Eliz. 1599. Folger, Z.d.17).

95   Item one Mantle of white striped tiffeney in workes like cloudes of golde owes allover.

Loc. 'C', 't'. LMN in H16 'Rem'.

96   Item one Mantle with a traine of tiffeney or striped clothe with branches seamed with small tufts of venice silver and spangles.

Loc. 't'. LMN in H16 'Rem'.

97 Item one Mantle of silver tincell printed and bounde aboute with a passamaine lace of silver.

Loc. 'C', 't'. LMN in H16 'Rem'.

98 Item one Mantle withoute a traine of blacke Networke faire florished over with a twiste of venice golde like starres.

Loc. 'T', 't'. LMN in H16 'Rem'.

99 Item one Mantle of white Tyffeney striped with silver like plate cut and tackt allover with rising Cutts and small tufts of silver thredde and spangles of sylver.

Loc. 't'. LMN in H16 'Rem'.

f. 17ᵛ

[No entries].

f. 18

Frenche Gownes

1 Firste one Frenche ⟨gold⟩ gowne of purple cloth of golde wrought with roses and hoinesocles with a Jagge of clothe of silver striped with purple silke lined with yellowe Sarceonet.

Loc. 'T', 't'. LMN in H16 'Rem'. It seems likely that the following description is of this gown when it was made in 1576: 'First to Walter Fyshe our Taylour . . . Item for making of a frenche Gowne with a longe traine of purple cloth of golde the bodie made with a high Coller and great pendaunte slevis of the spanishe facion lyned with yellowe satten with great doble Jagges the gowne edgid with yellowe satten & lyned with yellowe sarceonett the gowne with a Jagge of cloth of silver striped with purple silke with rolls of bent coverid with fustian in the slevis drawne oute with fine white Lawne the cloth of golde and cloth of silver of our store receyved of George Brideman keper of our Palloice at Westminster savinge thre yerds di of cloth of gold with threste of the stuff for the same gowne of our great guarderobe'. (Warrant 14 April, 18 Eliz. 1576. BL, Egerton 2806, ff. 93ᵛ, 94). It was altered six years later: 'Item to William Jones our Taylour . . . for translatinge and enlarginge of the sides of a gowne of purple cloth of golde with like stuff to perfourme it of our great guarderobe'. (Warrant 6 Apil, 24 Eliz. 1582. BL, Egerton 2806, f. 175).

2 Item one frenche gowne of purple cloth of golde tissue bounde aboute with a lace of venice golde and silver edged with Sables.

Loc. 'T', 't'. LMN in H16 'Rem'. The original warrant for making this gown gives full details of the tailor's work and materials used: 'Item to William Jones our Taylour for making of a frenche gowne of purple cloth of golde tyssue bounde aboute with a lase of venice golde and silver edgid aboute with strawe colour satten and lyned with strawe colour sarceonett the bodies lyned with sackecloth and styffened with buckeram with buckeram aboute the skyrtes and toppes of the slevis and bentes in the slevis coverid with fustian with a Rolle of bayes in the pleites the tyssue of our store within our Guarderobe of Robes all threste of our great guarderobe'. (Warrant 6 April, 24 Eliz. 1582. BL, Egerton 2806, f. 174ᵛ). The Queen may have put on a little weight, as the gown was altered and enlarged shortly after it was made, probably at the same time as the French gown above. 'Item to William Jones our Taylour . . . for alteringe and enlarginge the sides of a gowne of purple cloth of golde tyssue with like stuff to perfourme it of our great guarderobe.' (Warrant 6 April, 24 Eliz. 1582, BL, Egerton 2806, f. 175). The gown was altered again, to keep in fashion, nine years later: 'First to William Jones our Taylour . . . Item for alteringe and pecinge longer of a payre of bodyes for a gowne of purple cloth of gold tishew furred with sables with a plate lace of venice gold & silver perfourmed with like tishew & sarcnet and for pecinge longer of a paire of forbodyes with a coller to the same gowne of white satten cutt and tacte up sett with gold oes, laced alover with gold lace, performed with like satten and sarcnet of our great warderobe'. (Warrant 10 June, 33 Eliz. 1591. PRO, LC5/36, f. 169).

3 Item one coveringe for a frenche gowne of gold plate with tufts of peache colour silke.

Loc. 'T', 't'. LMN in H16 'Rem' and 'less the Bodies'.

4 Item one frenche gowne of russet clothe of golde bounde aboute with a lace of venice silver with a coveringe [[for a frenche gowne]] of white Lawne cutworke raized up with silver plate and spangles Diamonde wise.

Loc. 'T', ⟨'C'⟩'t'. LMN in H16 'Rem'. Addition in H2.

5 Item one frenche gowne of blacke clothe of gold bordered rounde aboute with a brode border Indented wise enbrodered within the same like wilde Fearne brakes upon Lawne and golde plate.

Loc. 'C', 'c'. LMN in H16 'Rem'. It seems likely that the following description is of this gown when it was altered in 1582: 'First to William Jones our Taylour . . . Item for alteringe of a payer of bodies and makinge them open before and enlarginge the slevis and sides of a gowne of blak cloth of golde with bentes coverid with fustian with like stuff and taphata to perfourme it of our great guarderobe'. (Warrant 28 Sept., 24 Eliz. 1582. BL, Egerton 2806, f. 178ᵛ). The following may be an alternative bodice, made in 1588: 'First to William Jones our Taylour . . . Item for makinge a peire of bodyes & sleeves of blacke stitched cloth for a gowne of blacke clothe of gold . . .' (Warrant 27 Sept., 30 Eliz. 1588. BL, Egerton 2806 f. 231ᵛ).

f. 18ᵛ

6 Item one coveringe for a gowne of venice golde silver and blacke silk Networke.

Loc. 'T', ⟨'C'⟩ 't'. LMN in H16 'Rem'. This item was a New Year's gift: 'By the Barronesse Howard A covering of A gowne of black nettwork faire florished over with venis gold.

347 *Detail from a band of lacis made with a decorated mesh, known as 'mezza mandolina', possibly the 'networke' used for 'coverings'. Victoria and Albert Museum, London (T.229–1913)*

Delivered to the Roabes'. (New Year's Gift Roll, 31 Eliz. 1589. BL, Lansd. Roll 17, printed in *Progr. Eliz.*, III, p. 6).

7 Item one traine gowne of golde and silver Chamblet with workes allover like lardge braunches.

Loc. 'C', 'c'. LMN in H16 'Rem'.

8 Item one traine gowne of aishcolour clothe of golde with a faire border downe before enbrodered with silver.

Loc. 'C', 'c'. LMN in H16 'Rem'. Probably a gift to the Queen, as it does not appear among the warrants until this entry: 'Fyrste to William Jones our Tayloure . . . Item for alteringe and makinge new bodies and enlarginge the slevis of a gowne of ashecolour Cloth of gold the bodies beinge new lyned with Sarcenet and stiffened with Canvas and buckeram with a silver lace about of our greate warderobe'. (Warrant 28 Sept., 43 Eliz. 1601. PRO, LC5/37, f. 231).

9 Item one frenche gowne of cloth of silver with braunches of watchet and orenge colour silke tissued with golde garded with aishcolour tapheta laide with networke enbrodered with Cyphers flower de Luces and Crownes of venice golde.

Loc. 'T', 't'. LMN in H16 'Rem'. Probably a gown made in 1579: 'First to Walter Fyshe our

348 *Iris, or fleur-de-lis, detail from a polychrome embroidered white satin panel, probably part of a skirt, c. 1600. Victoria and Albert Museum, London (T.138–1981)*

Taylour ... Item for making of a frenche Gowne of tyssue garded with ashe colour taphata enbroderid with venice golde layed upon with nettworke the gowne lyned with strawe colour sarceonett the ruffes with buckeram and fustian to sett in the Rolles of bent the tyssue of our store Receyved of George Brideman keper of our Palloice at Westminster threste of our greate warderobe'. (Warrant 12 Oct., 21 Eliz. 1579. BL, Egerton 2806, f. 144).

10   Item one frenche gowne of clothe of silver striped with golde with workes of aish colour silke embroidered rounde aboute with ostridge feathers of venice golde and blacke silke.

Loc. 'T', 't'. LMN in H16 'Rem'. The gown was a New Year's gift: 'By Sir Fraunces Walsingham principall secretary a Gowne of Russet clothe of silver stryped wythe golde and a border of Feathers. Delivered to the foresaid

Rauf Hoope.' (New Year's Gift Roll, 23 Eliz. 1581. Eton Coll. BLA 18 192).

11   Item one frenche gowne of clothe of silver enbrodered with a brode border like pillers and Essefirmes of venice golde.

Loc. 'T', 't'. LMN in H16 'Rem'. This is probably a gown made in 1595: 'Fyrste to William Jones our Tayloure ... Item for makinge of a highebodyed gowne with a trayne of white cloth of Silver, with a gold lace aboute, the bodies and slevis enbraudered with pillers and esse firmies with a border of the same, the skirtes of the gowne Lyned with Sarcenet, the bodies Lyned with Canvas and buckeram and stiffened with the same and lyned with Sarcenet of our great warderobe'. (Warrant 10 April, 37 Eliz. 1595. PRO, LC5/37, f. 58). Embroidery at the hemline would easily get soiled and part of it was replaced in 1598: 'Item to John Parr our enbrauderer for enbrauderinge of peramides and esse firmies wrought upon murrey Satten with purles plates Spangles and venice stuffe being voided out and enbraudered on the hinder parte of a traine gowne of Cloth of Silver with fyve ounces of purles plate and spangles'. (Warrant 29 March, 40 Eliz. 1598. PRO, LC5/ 37, f. 129). In this entry the 'pillers' are described as 'peramides'.

12   Item one Frenche gowne of blacke Cloth of silver with a border of Venice golde and silver upon orenge colour satten like branches of flowers lined with orenge colour Taphata Sarcenet.

Loc. 'C', 't'. LMN in H16 'Rem'. This gown was probably a gift, as it does not appear among the warrants until this entry: 'Item to John Parr our Enbrauderer ... For enlardginge & repayringe of the enbraudery in the skirtes and forebodies of a gowne of black Cloth of Silver wrought with sondrie flowers upon Orrendge Tawny Satten'. (Warrant 28 Sept., 32 Eliz. 1590. PRO, LC5/36, f. 145).

f. 19

13   Item one frenche gowne of heare colour cloth of silver with workes edged with a plate lace of venice golde the sleeves lined with cloth of silver Chamblet prented with a paire of sleeves of cloth of golde cut in risinge panes.

Loc. 'T', 't'. LMN in H16 'Rem'. This gown was a New Year's gift: 'By Sir Thomas Layton knight A french gowne of Here colored Cloth of sylver with workes edged with a plate Lace of venis golde the Sleves Lyned with Cloth of Sylver prynted with a payre of sleves of Cloth of Golde cut in Rysing paynes. Delivered to Raf hope'. (New Year's Gift Roll, 27 Eliz. 1585. Folger, Z.d.16). Eight years later William Jones carried out work to bring it into fashion again 'alteringe and pecinge longer the bodies of a gowne of haire colour cloth of silver laced with gold lace and lined with Sarcenet of our great Warderobe'. (Warrant 10 May, 35 Eliz. 1593. PRO, LC5/36, f. 250).

14   Item one Frenche gowne of silver chamblet allover laide overthwarte with gardes of blacke satten cut in works laide

with twists of venice golde and silver owes with a border of blacke vellat richelie enbrodered with venice golde and silver the bodies and sleeves of like enbrawderie with a paire of sleeves of like silver chamblet enbrodered with owes of golde allover lyned with white sarceonet.

Loc. 'T', 't'. LMN in H16 'Rem'.

15   Item one Coveringe for a french gowne of silver plate with tuftes and knotts of blacke silke.

Loc. 'T', 't'. LMN in H16 'Rem'.

16   Item one frenche gowne of orenge colour and white cloth of silver branches bounde aboute with a plate lace of venice golde and silver and tufts of tawneye silke.

Loc. 'C', 'c'. LMN in H16 'Rem'.

17   Item one frenche gowne of silver Chamblet bounde aboute with a lace of Venice golde.

Loc. 'C', 'c'. LMN in H16 'Rem'.

18   Item one highe bodied gowne with a traine of blacke clothe of silver with a border wrought aboute with silver lace.

Loc. 'C', 't'. LMN in H16 'Rem'. The gown was made in 1592: 'First to William Jones our Tailor for makinge of a highe bodied gowne, with a traine of black cloth of Silver, with a border wrought about with silver lace, the bodies and sleves laced alover with like lace, cutt in paines, lyned with clothe of gold printed, the bodies stiffened with Canvas, buckeram, hooks and eyes, the traine lined with sarcenett, & edged about with like cloth of gold, & pocketts of Taffata the cloth of gold of our store, of the chardge of Thomas Knivett esquier keper of our Pallace at westminster, the rest of our great warderobe'. (Warrant 6 June, 34 Eliz. 1592. PRO, LC5/36, f. 207).

19   Item one Frenche gowne of Silver chamblet laide aboute with a plate lace of venice golde.

Loc. 'C', 't'. LMN in H16 'Rem'. This is possibly a gown listed among the warrants for 1591, although identification cannot be definite without a more detailed description: 'Fyrste to William Jones our Taylour ... Item for makinge of a highe bodied gowne with a Traine of Silver Chamblet laced with venice gold lace, the bodies stiffened with Canvas and buckeram with hookes and eyes, pockettes of Taffata, buckeram to laye aboute the Traine and lyned with Sarcenet of our great warderobe'. (Warrant 27 Sept., 33 Eliz. 1591. PRO, LC5/36, f. 182).

f. 19ᵛ

20   Item one Frenche gowne with a traine of silver chamblet wrought with trees and birdes of venice golde, silver and silke of sondrie Colours.

Loc. 'C', 'c'. LMN in H16 'Rem'.

21   Item one traine gowne of peach colour clothe of silver tissued with golde

and silver in workes like feathers or braunches.

Loc. 'C', 'c'. LMN in H16 'Rem'.

22 Item one traine gowne of pincke colour silver Chamblet enbolster allover with silver like halfe Moones, sonnes and starres.

Loc. 'C', 'c'. LMN in H16 'Rem'.

23 Item one frenche gowne of carnacion tissue bounde aboute with a passamaine of venice golde edged with Sables.

Loc. 'T', 't'. LMN in H9 'delivered by the lord chamberlayns command to John baker upholster for the Kings use'. It seems likely that this is a gown which was trimmed with sables in 1583, perhaps for winter wear: 'Item to Adam Blande our Skynner . . . for edginge the bodyes sleevis and Jagges of a gowne of carnacion cloth of silver with sixe sables skynnes of our great guarderobe'. (Warrant 26 Sept., 25 Eliz. 1583. BL, Egerton 2806, f. 190ᵛ). The fur may have been attacked by moth and some of it was replaced in 1588: 'Item to Adam Blande our Skynner for mendinge the furre of a Gowne of carnacion cloth of silver tyssue with fower sable skynnes of our store of the chardge of the said Thomas Knyvett'. (Warrant 3 April, 30 Eliz. 1588. BL, Egerton 2806, f. 228). The material would have been of good quality and John Green probably used it for covering stools.

24 Item one frenche gowne of tawney vellat cut allover edged rounde aboute with a double wreath lace of blacke silke the bodies and sleeves laced thicke allover with like lace.

Loc. 'T', 't'. LMN in H16 'Rem'. Decorative cuts in the velvet would have shown the lining. Here black has been changed for white: 'First to Walter Fyshe our Taylour . . . Item for alteringe and newe lyninge of the skyrtes of a frenche Gowne of tawnye vellat cutt sometyme lyned with blak sarceonett the same taken oute and white sarceonett layed in the white sarceonett being in the same gowne before threste of our greate warderobe'. (Warrant 28 Sept., 22 Eliz. 1580. BL, Egerton 2806, f. 157). The white lining had been used previously and may have got shabby, as it was replaced in the following year: 'First to Walter Fyshe our Taylour . . . Item for lyninge of a traine gowne of tawnye vellat cutt allover lyned with white sarceonett of our great guarderobe'. (Warrant 6 April, 23 Eliz. 1581. BL, Egerton 2806, f. 162ᵛ).

25 Item one french gowne of blacke vellat with a garde embroidered longe with bugle like pipes.

Loc. 'C', 'c'. LMN in H16 'Rem'.

26 Item one frenche gowne of blacke vellat enbrodered allover with branches of bugles greate and small.

Loc. 'C', 'c'. LMN in H16 'Rem'. This gown was probably a gift, as it does not appear among the warrants before this entry: 'First to Walter Fyshe our Taylour . . . Item for alteringe and making longer of the traine of a frenche gowne of blak vellatt enbroderid over with braunches of bugell the lyninge perfourmed with sarceonett of our great warderobe'. (Warrant 10 April, 21 Eliz. 1579. BL, Egerton 2806, f. 137). The term 'peire of ruffes', lined with buckram, possibly refers to gathered sleeveheads: 'First to Walter Fyshe our Taylour . . . Item for making of a peire of ruffes for a frenche gowne of blak vellat enbroderid with bugell lyned with buckeram of our great guarderobe.' (Warrant 6 April, 23 Eliz. 1581. BL, Egerton 2806, f. 163ᵛ).

27 Item one french gowne of blacke vellat enbrodered allover with wormes of silke of sondrie colours cut upon white Sarceonet stained.

Loc. 'C', 't'. LMN in H16 'Rem'. This gown was probably a gift. Two alterations were carried out within six months, 'First to Walter Fyshe our Taylour . . . Item for alteringe and newe making of a frenche gowne of blak vellat with wormes the vellat cutt oute like the skallop lyned with white sarceonett colorid with a worke of oringe colour stayned like Clowdes of our great warderobe' and then 'for alteringe of a frenche gowne of blak vellat with wormes the pendaunte slevis newe lyned with oringe colour satten rased ye gowne edgid with like colour satten of our greate warderobe'. (Warrant 12 April, 22 Eliz. 1580. BL, Egerton 2806, ff. 150ᵛ, 151).

f. 20

28 Item one frenche gowne of heare colour vellat richlie enbrodered with venice golde silver and ragged seede pearle like a dead Tree.

Loc. 'T', 't'. LMN in H16 'Rem'. This seems to be a gown which twice had work carried out on it in 1581: 'First to Walter Fyshe our Taylour . . . Item for making of the nether partes of a frenche gowne of heare colour vellat enbrauderid allover verye richelye lyned with white sarceonett the Jagges lyned with cloth of silver the vellat of our store receyved of the said Thomas Knevett, threste of our greate guarderobe'. (Warrant 6 April, 23 Eliz. 1581. BL, Egerton 2806, f. 164). Later in the same year Fyshe made 'a payer of newe forebodies for a frenche gowne of heare colour vellat enbroderid lyned with sarceonett & canvas of our great guarderobe'. Warrant 15 Sept., 23 Eliz. 1581. BL, Egerton 2806, f. 169ᵛ).

29 Item one frenche gowne of blacke vellat bounde aboute with a lace of blacke silke.

Loc. 'C', 'c'. LMN in H16 'Rem'. This seems likely to be a gown which was remade in 1571, although the description is not detailed enough to identify it with certainty: 'First to Walter Fyshe our Taylour . . . Item for new making of a French Gowne of black vellat wrought aboute with lase the gowne lyned with black sarceonett the slevis drawen oute with lawne with Rolles of bentes in the slevis and a Rolle of buckeram in the playtes the bodyes lyned with canvas the neither partes of the gowne of our store Receyved of the said Rauf Hope the vellat to make newe bodyes and slevis and to alter the gowne of our greate guarderobe'. (Warrant 4 April, 13 Eliz. 1571. BL, Egerton 2806, f. 31).

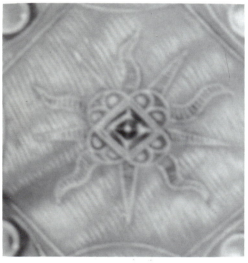

349 *Sun-in-splendour, detail from a polychrome embroidered white satin panel, probably part of a skirt, c. 1600. Victoria and Albert Museum, London (T.138–1981)*

350 *Sun-in-splendour embroidered in gold thread on white satin, detail from Figure 52, c. 1588–89. by kind permission of the Marquess of Tavistock and the trustees of the Bedford Estates, Woburn Abbey*

30 Item one frenche gowne of heare colour vellat laide aboute with a lace of blacke silke and twoe satten wreathe laces the bodies enbrodred allover with like lace.

Loc. 'C', 'c'. LMN in H16 'Rem'. This gown was made in 1582: 'Item to William Jones our Taylour . . . for making of a frenche gowne of heare colour vellat with two paire of bodies lyned with canvas buckeram & taphata the skyrtes borderid with buckeram and taphata the toppes of the slevis styffenid with buckeram with bentes coverid with fustian and Rolles of cotten in the pleites eleven yerdes di of the vellat of our said store owte of thoffice of our said guarderobe of robes all threst of our great guarderobe'. (Warrant 6 April, 24 Eliz. 1582.

351 *Detail from a christening procession, possibly of Edward Fortunatus, son of Princess Cecilia of Sweden and the Marquess of Baden, on 30 September 1565, in the Royal Chapel at the Palace of Westminster. Queen Elizabeth, the godmother, wears a French gown, the train borne by the Lady Margaret Clifford. The Queen and many of her attendant ladies wear cauls, an Italian fashion. The College of Arms, London (MS 6, f.77v)*

BL, Egerton 2806, f. 175ᵛ). Jones carried out more work on it later in the same year, 'alteringe of a payer of bodies & makinge them open before and a paire of slevis for a gowne of heare colour vellat with thre lases the lyninge perfourmed with taphata of our great guarderobe'. (Warrant 28 Sept., 24 Eliz. 1582. BL, Egerton 2806, f. 178ᵛ).

31 Item one frenche gowne of pawle colour vellat with a brode border of decaied trees of venice golde silver and silke with pendaunte sleeves lyned with white Satten enbrodered with like workes.

Loc. 'T', 't'. LMN in H16 'Rem'. This was probably a gift as it does not appear among the warrants until this entry: 'Fyrst to William Jones our Taylour . . . Item for alteringe and pecinge longer the bodies of a gowne of Paule colour velvet enbraudered with deade Trees, and for alteringe and enlarginge the hanginge slevis and new lynynge them with Tawney Sarcenet and Lawne floryshed with Silver and spangles and perfourmed with Lyke stuff of our great warderobe'. (Warrant 28 Sept., 32 Eliz. 1590. PRO, LC5/36, f. 141). The next year Jones carried out some more work on the sleeves, changing the appearance of the gown 'alteringe of a paire of hanginge sleves of pawle colour velvet embroidered and new lyninge them with white satten embroidered of our great warderobe'. (Warrant 10 June, 33 Eliz. 1591. PRO, LC5/36, f. 170). The first linings were replaced later in the year, and Jones carried out further work 'alteringe and pecinge longer of a paire of bodyes and new lyninge of a paire of hanginge sleves, for a gowne of paule color velvet embroidered, the lyninge in the sleves taken out of them before of our great warde-robe'. (Warrant 10 June, 33 Eliz. 1591. PRO, LC5/36, f. 168). Ten years later Jones made the gown ready for the Queen to wear again 'alteringe and enlardinge a gowne of paule colour velvet . . . of our great warderobe'. (Warrant 28 Sept., 43 Eliz. 1601. PRO, LC5/37, f. 231).

32 Item one frenche gowne of pale colour vellat with twoe borders of venice golde enbrodered with owes edged with white satten.

Loc. 'C', 't'. LMN in H16 'Rem'.

33 Item one frenche gowne of blacke uncut vellat enbrodered allover with knotts and tufts of blacke silke.

Loc. 'C', 'c'. LMN in H16 'Rem'. This was probably a gift and extra embroidery was needed: 'Item to John Parr our Embrother . . . Item for augmentinge of the embrodery of a gowne of blacke unshorne velvet wrought with knottes of black silke lace'. (Warrant 10 June, 33 Eliz. 1591. PRO, LC5/36, f. 176).

34 Item one frenche gowne of heare colour vellatt cut curiouslie lined with Carnacion plushe ⟨made of a peece of stuff geven anno xxxᵐᵒ r(eg)ne E(lizabethae)⟩.

Loc. 'C', 'c'. LMN in H16 'Rem'. The last part has been deleted by underlining in H1. William Jones used the material two years after it was given to the Queen: 'for makinge of a highe bodyed gowne with a traine of hare colour vellat lyned with Carnacion plushe, the bodies stiffened with Canvas and buckeram, the bodies Lyned with Sarcenet and pockettes of Taffata, the velvet of our Store, the rest of our great warderobe'. (Warrant 18 May, 32 Eliz. 1590. PRO, LC5/36, f.133).

35 Item one frenche gowne of blacke vellat laide with lace the sleeves of blacke networke tacked up(pe/pon).

Loc. 'C', 'c'. LMN in H16 ⟨'Rem'.⟩ RMN in H9 'geven'.

f. 20ᵛ

36 ⟨Item one frenche gowne of blacke pincked vellat with some tufts bounde aboute with blacke silke lace⟩.

Loc. 'C', 'c'. LMN in H16 ⟨'Rem'.⟩ RMN in H9 'geven'. The whole item is struck through by the same hand.

37 Item one traine gowne of blacke wrought vellatt the grounde golde the bodies and downe before in risinge puffs of silver embroidered.

Loc. 'C', 'c'. LMN in H16 'Rem'.

38 Item one gowne of the french fashion of black satten enbrodered allover with blacke striped vellatt lyned with blacke Taphata faced and edged with sables.

Loc. 'T', 't'. LMN in H16 'Rem'. This gown was probably a gift as it does not appear among the warrants until this entry: 'Item to Adam Blande our Skynner . . . for mendinge the furre of a frenche gowne of blak satten embroderid allover with striped vellat with a perfourmance of Sables of our great warderobe. (Warrant 28 Sept., 22 Eliz. 1580. BL, Egerton 2806, f. 158ᵛ).

39 Item one strieght bodied gowne with a traine of white Satten embroidered allover with damaske golde and with a border of damaske golde enbrodered upon Crimson vellat lyned with Serceonet ⟦wythowt slyvis⟧.

Loc. 'T', 't'. LMN in H9 'geven by Queen the 10 of {May} 1601'. Addition in H9(?). In PRO, LR2/121 RMN reads 'no sleeves to this gowne'. Illegible signature {'R. Pamplyn'}. This may be one of the oldest gowns remaining in the Wardrobe of Robes in 1600. The warrants give details of embroidery which may have been for this gown, carried out in 1566 'Item to David Smith our Enbrauderer . . . Item for enbrauder-inge of a Traine Gowne of whit Satten garded with Crimsen velvet and wrought alover very Richly with flagon Chayne of gold and silver purles of diverse sortes for workmanshipp therof lxx li. Item for xxviij pound waight of flagon Chayne and purles of gold and silver spent upon the same gowne at iiij li the pound waight One hundred and xii poundes Item for ij pound waight of yelow and whit silk spent upon the same gowne iiij li Item for Canvas thred and other necessaries to set it in the frame xs'. (Warrant 25 March, 8 Eliz. 1566. PRO, LC5/33, f. 172). There is a warrant to Walter Fyshe six years later: 'for altering and newe making of a frenche Gowne of white Satten embroidered allover with golde lyned with white sarceonett the bodies newe made and lyned with canvas & the slevis enlarged & drawen oute with lawne the garde of the bodies & slevis enlarged with crymsen vellat of our great guarderobe'. (Warrant 28 Sept., 14 Eliz. 1572. BL, Egerton 2806, f. 44ᵛ).

40 Item one french gowne of blacke satten with a traine with three gardes of blacke vellat enbrodered with golde and silver and furred with powdred Armyons and lyned with white sarceonet.

Loc. 'T', 't'. LMN in H16 'Rem'.

41 Item one frenche gowne of blacke satten with a brode garde enbrodered with a worke like unycornes.

Loc. 'T', 't'. LMN in H16 'Rem'. The embroidered guard had already been used once before the gown was made in 1571: 'First to Walter Fyshe our Taylour . . . Item for making of a french gowne of blacke satten with a garde of blacke vellat enbrauderid like unicornes being taken from a gowne of black vellat of our store of the chardge of Raufe Hope yeoman of our guarderobe of Roobes the gowne lyned and ye sleves drawen out with asshe colour sarceonett of our said store the slevis also drawen out with white sarceonett the gardes perfourmed with blacke vellat the bodies lyned with canvas the playtes with buckerom a Rolle of cotten and Rolls of bentes and fustian in the slevis of our great guarderobe.' (Warrant 4 April, 13 Eliz. 1571. BL, Egerton 2806, f. 29ᵛ). There is a warrant four years later for Fyshe, 'for lyninge of a frenche Gowne of blak Satten with a garde enbrodered with unicornes lyned with ashe colour taphata the syse drawne oute with ashe colour and oringe colour sarceonett of our great guarderobe'. (Warrant 28 Sept., 17 Eliz. 1575. BL, Egerton 2806, f. 85ᵛ). Fyshe made a new bodice five years later so that the gown might be worn again: 'for making of a payer of bodies of blak satten for a gowne enbroderid like unicornes lyned with ashe colour taphata of our greate warderobe.' (Warrant 28 Sept., 22 Eliz. 1580. BL, Egerton 2806, f. 158).

42   Item one Frenche gowne of blacke satten cut and pincked allover with a garde of blacke vellatt embrodered with venice golde like three borders of leaves of raized worke.

Loc. 'T', 't'. LMN in H16 'Rem'.

43   Item one frenche gowne of blacke Satten with a verie brode garde enbrodered with an enbroderie like Artichockes with leaves of blacke Satten and venice golde and silver upon Carnacion satten.

Loc. 'T', 't'. LMN in H9 'geven to mrs hide by the Quene the 7 of march 1600'. Signature 'Luce Hyde'. The gown was probably a gift to the Queen as it does not appear among the warrants before this entry: 'Item Delyverid to David Smyth our Enbrauderer . . . One yerde quarter of blak Satten and one yerde of blak taphata, employed upon a Gowne enbroderid like Artichoughes'. (Warrant 20 Oct., 15 Eliz. 1573. BL, Egerton 2806, f. 62ᵛ). Walter Fyshe was engaged in work upon it two years later: 'alteringe and enlarginge the bodies & slevis of a frenche gowne of blak satten with a garde enbroderid like artichoughes of our great guarderobe'. (Warrant 28 Sept., 17 Eliz. 1575. BL, Egerton 2806, f. 88ᵛ). He was employed again, in 1576, 'lyninge of a frenche gowne of blak satten with a garde enbroderid like Artichoves lyned with blak sarceonett of our great guarderobe'. (Warrant 26 Sept., 18 Eliz. 1576. BL, Egerton 2806, f. 101ᵛ). In 1582 William Jones worked on the gown twice, to keep it in the latest fashion: 'for alteringe of a gowne of blak satten enbroderid with artichockes of our great guarderobe'. (Warrant 6 April, 24 Eliz. 1582. BL, Egerton 2806, f. 175) and 'for alteringe of a gowne of blak satten enbroderid with artichouches the skyrtes made wider layed under the garde with cloth of golde the bentes in the slevis coverid with fustian and styffenid with buckeram with pockettes of taphata with like stuff cloth of golde taphata & sarceonett to perfourme it of our great guarderobe'. (Warrant 28 Sept., 24 Eliz. 1582. BL, Egerton 2806, f. 179).

f. 21

44   Item one spanishe gowne of tawney Satten with a riche border embrodered with venice golde and silver like a garde lyned with white sarceonet.

Loc. 'T', 't'. LMN in H16 'Rem'. The rich border is described as being 'like a garde' and this item may be a gown made by Walter Fyshe in 1576, where the guard had been used before: 'for making of a spanishe Gowne of tawnye satten with a verye great pendaunte sleve with doble Jagges in the syse and small skyrtes to the bodies the gowne lyned with white sarceonett & edgid with white satten the slevis lyned with white satten cutt and raste allover & lyned undernethe with white sarceonett the small skyrtes edgid with white satten the gowne partlelye garded with a garde taken from a Gowne of tawnye satten of our store Receyved of Blaunche Pary one of the gentilwomen of our prevye Chamber xviij yerdes di of satten towards the making of the same gowne exchaunged for so muche murrey satten of our store the satten to performe the same gowne of our great guarderobe'. (Warrant 14 April, 18 Eliz. 1576. BM, Egerton 2806, f. 95).

45   Item one frenche gowne of tawney Satten with a garde enbrodered like knotts and snailes and a fewe bugle.

Loc. 't'. LMN in H16 'Rem'. The guard here may have been removed from this earlier gown: 'First to Walter Fyshe our Taylour . . . Item for alteringe of a traine gowne of blak wrought vellat with a garde enbroderid like snailes with two peire of bodies & two peire of slevis one of the peire of bodies with a highe coller and great spanishe slevis lyned with lawne the same taken oute & newe lyned with blak sarceonett the gowne borderid with like sarceonett thother slevis edgid with white taphata ye same taken oute & newe edgid with blak taphata newe lyned & drawne oute with blak sarceonett of our great guarderobe.' (Warrant 14 April, 18 Eliz. 1576. BL, Egerton 2806, f. 95ᵛ).

46   Item one frenche gowne of white Satten striped with golde laide with three laces of venice silver and black silke withoute bodies.

Loc. 'T', 't'. LMN in H16 'Rem'. This gown was based on an old kirtle. Walter Fyshe was entered in the warrant 'for making of the hinder quarters with a traine for a frenche gowne of white satten striped with golde layed with thre lases of venice golde silver and blak silke borderid with blak sarceonett the satten to make the hinder parte & traine of our store of the chardge of the said George Brideman and the forequarters being a rounde kyrtle of our store threste of our greate guarderobe'. (Warrant 26 Sept., 20 Eliz. 1578. BL, Egerton 2806, ff. 129ᵛ, 130).

47   Item one frenche gowne of heare colour satten embrodered allover with owes and tufts of knitworke with a verie brode garde of tawney satten embrodered with flowers of Venice golde and knitworke.

Loc. 'T', 't'. LMN in H16 'Rem'. Walter Fyshe is listed in 1579 'for making of the skyrtes of a gowne of heare colour satten enbroderid allover with a verye brode garde of tawneye

352   Detail of a snail worked in crimson silk on a white linen smock, c. 1600. Victoria and Albert Museum, London (T.2–1956)

satten coverid with lawne enbroderid with golde lyned with white sarceonett the satten of our store Receyved of the said Rauf Hope. The lawne Receyved of Marye Scudemore threste of our greate warderobe'. (Warrant 12 Oct., 21 Eliz. 1579. BL, Egerton 2806, f. 144). The next year he was employed in 'making of a payer of ruffes for a frenche gowne of heare colour satten enbroderid allover the ruffes lyned with white taphata buckeram & sarceonett of our great warderobe'. (Warrant 12 April, 22 Eliz. 1580. BL, Egerton 2806, f. 151). The gown was brought into fashion again, eight years later, by William Jones. He was employed in 'alteringe of a gowne of heare colour satten enbroderid allover with a broade border of tawny satten enbrodered aboute and perfourmed with like stuffe of our great guarderobe'. (Warrant 27 Sept., 30 Eliz. 1588. BL, Egerton 2806, ff. 231, 231ᵛ).

48   Item one frenche gowne of Cloudie colour Satten garded with heare colour vellat embrodered with knottes and gal-troppes of venice golde onlie before covered with blacke taphata cutte.

Loc. 'C', 'c'. LMN in H16 'Rem'. The work in making this gown was shared by two men. Walter Fyshe was entered in the warrant 'for making of the skyrtes of a frenche gowne of clowdye colored satten garded with heare colour vellat enbroderid with knottes and galtropes borderid with white sarceonett of our greate warderobe'. (Warrant 12 Oct., 21 Eliz. 1579. BL, Egerton 2806, f. 144ᵛ). At the same time Arthur Middleton carried out the work of 'making of a payer of bodies of clowdye colour satten the slevis being rufte thicke thone ruffe vellat thother satten lyned with sarceonett canvas hookes & eyes with a perfourmance of vellat'. (Warrant 12 Oct., 21 Eliz. 1579. BL, Egerton 2806, f. 146ᵛ). William Jones made an alternative bodice for this gown in 1587: 'a payer of highe bodies of clowdie colour satten with a garde of heare colour vellat enbroderid lyned with canvas & sarceonett of our great guarderobe'. (Warrant 26 Sept., 29 Eliz. 1587. BL, Egerton 2806, f. 223).

49   Item one frenche gowne of heare colour Satten snipte and cut upon white sarceonet enbroderid allover with a plate lace of venice golde and a border of venice golde and silver purle and owes.

Loc. 'T', 't'. LMN in H16 'Rem'.

353 *'Portrait of an unknown lady', by a follower of Antonio Mor, c. 1565–70. She wears a French gown in red velvet trimmed with gold bobbin lace. Partlet and tight-fitting under-sleeves are both in white linen embroidered with gold and silver metal thread. They are covered with semi-transparent 'mezza mandolina', a type of netting, loose over the arms, and fitting closely over the partlet. The edge can just be seen behind the ruff and neckband. Museo del Prado, Madrid*

354 *Detail of gold and silver bobbin lace bordering a chalice veil, Spanish or Italian, mid-sixteenth century. It is worked with seed pearls and glass beads in the design. Monasterio de Pederalbes, Barcelona (115.060)*

50 Item one frenche gowne of blacke satten with a brode garde of black vellat enbrodered with venice golde and silver the bodies and sleeves of vellat likewise embroidered with flowers and knottes lined with Carnacion sarceonett.

Loc. 'C', 't'. LMN in H16 'Rem'.

51 Item one frenche gowne of blacke Satten prented and enbrodred with leaves of heare colour Satten.

Loc. 'C', 'c'. LMN in H16 'Rem'. The work on this gown was probably divided in the same way as for item 48, possibly to get it made quickly. Walter Fyshe carried out the work of 'making of the nether partes of a frenche gowne of blak printed satten enbroderid with leaves of heare colour satten lyned with blak sarceonett the satten of our store of the chardge of Rauf Hope yeoman of our guarderobe of Robes and the heare colour satten of our store of the chardge of Thomas Knevett keper of our Palloice of Westminster the rest with fower yerdes of like prented satten all of our greate guarderobe'. (Warrant 6 April, 23 Eliz. 1581. BL, Egerton 2806, f. 163ᵛ). Another tailor,

William Whittell, may have made the bodice, as he worked on over forty during this half year; the warrants are not clear on this point. William Jones carried out some work on the gown in the following year, 'alterynge the Jagges of the slevis of a gowne of blak satten enbroderid with leaves of heare colour satten with bentes in the slevis coverid with fustian stiffenid with buckeram with taphata to the bentes of our great guarderobe'. (Warrant 28 Sept., 24 Eliz. 1582. BL, Egerton 2806, f. 179). Jones worked on it again, over ten years later, 'Alterynge and pecinge longer of a paire of bodies of black Satten enbrodered with leaves of haire colour Satten bugles and lawne with black silk lace about it the bodies lined with Sarcenet of our great Warderobe'. (Warrant 10 May, 35 Eliz. 1593. PRO, LC5/36, f. 253).

f. 21ᵛ

52 Item one french gowne of Murrey satten cut with a skallop cut and laide with a lace of venice golde Chevernewise allover.

Loc. 'T', 't'. LMN in H16 'Rem'. Walter Fyshe is listed in 1581 'for makinge of a frenche Gowne of murrey satten with greate pendaunte

slevis layed allover with golde lase chevernewise and cutt betwene the lases with skallope cutt lyned with white sarceonett the ruffes lyned with paste bourde the slevis lyned with ashe colour satten enbrauderid allover the lase and the lyninge for the slevis of our store taken from a frenche gowne of white satten threst of our greate guarderobe'. (Warrant 6 April, 23 Eliz. 1581. BL, Egerton 2806, f. 162ᵛ).

53 Item one gowne of horsefleshe colour Satten enbrodered allover with owes cut with small cuts with a brode lace aboute it of venice golde the longe sleeves lined with clothe of golde the gowne lined with orenge colour sarceonett.

Loc. 'T', 'c'. LMN in H16 'Rem'.

54 Item one frenche gowne of orenge colour Satten striped with silver garded with a verie brode garde of Tawney Satten cut enbrodered with venice golde silver Damaske golde purle and Spangles.

Loc. 'C', 't'. LMN in H16 'Rem'. This was a New Year's gift, 'By Sir Fraunses Walsingham Knight principall secretary a frenche gowne of oringe tawny satten stryped with silver garded with a very brode garde of Tawny Satten cut enbradored with venice golde sylver damaske gold purll and spangles. Delivered to the foresaid Rauf hope.' (New Year's Gift Roll, 26 Eliz. 1584. BL, Egerton 3052, printed in *Costume* 9, 1975, p. 29).

55 Item one frenche gowne of Carnacion satten striped with golde and silver bounde aboute with a passamaine lace of venice golde And a coveringe of blacke networke florished with golde and silver.

Loc. 'T', 't'. LMN in H16 'Rem'. The gown did not have a covering when it was first made: 'First to William Jones our Taylour . . . Item for making of a Gowne of carnacion satten striped with golde and silver the bodyes lyned with serceonet and canvas borderid with serceonett the bentes coverid with taphata the stryped satten of our store of the chardge of Thomas Knevett esquier Keeper of our Palloice at Westmester all the rest of our great guarderobe.' (Warrant 26 Sept., 25 Eliz. 1583. BL, Egerton 2806, f. 189ᵛ). In 1588 Jones made 'a coveringe of blak stiched cloth for a paier of bodies for a frenche gowne of carnacion striped satten of our great guarderobe'. (Warrant 3 April, 30 Eliz. 1588. BL, Egerton 2806, f. 227). Later that year he is listed 'for enlarginge the sides of the trayne of a gowne of carnacion satten stripte with golde & silver covered with a networke florished with golde and silver perfourmed with like stuffe of our great guarderobe'. (Warrant 27 Sept., 30 Eliz. 1588. BL, Egerton 2806, f. 231ᵛ). Jones carried out more work on this gown in 1590 'enlardginge the sydes of the traine of a gowne of Carnation Satten striped with gold and Silver with gold lace newe bordered with Sarcenet and perfourmed with Satten and Sarcenet of our great warderob'. (Warrant 28 Sept., 32 Eliz. 1590. PRO, LC5/36, f. 142).

56 Item one frenche gowne of blacke Satten with a brode garde of blacke vellat cut upon white Satten fourmed with a lace of golde and silver edged with Sables.

Loc. 'T', 't'. LMN in H16 'Rem'. The gown was trimmed with sables by Adam Bland. This work is listed separately from that of 'Walter Fyshe our Taylour for making of a frenche gowne of blak satten with a brode garde of blak vellat enbroderid with venice golde & silver the vellat cutt oute and layed underneth with white satten with a payer of greate pendaunte slevis of blak vellat cutt lyned with white satten, the garde for the skyrtes perfourmed with vellat the gowne lyned with white sarceonett the garde and slevis taken from a spanyshe gowne of blak vellat that was layed underneth with murrey satten the olde bodies made into Jagges of our great warderobe'. (Warrant 12 April, 22 Eliz. 1580. BL, Egerton 2806, f. 150ᵛ). Bland is entered in a warrant in 1584 'for mending the furre of a gowne of blak satten perfourmed with two sable skynnes of our great guarderobe'. (Warrant 27 Sept., 26 Eliz. 1584. BL, Egerton 2806, f. 200ᵛ).

57 Item one frenche gowne of russet satten florished with leaves of silver bounde aboute with a passamaine of venice golde with pendaunte sleeves lined with ⟨white⟩ clothe of silver and wearing sleeves of clothe of silver cut in risinge panes of cloth of golde and silver.

Loc. 'T', 't'. LMN in H16 'Rem'. This was a New Year's gift 'By Sir Fraunses Waullsingham knight prynsipall Secretary. A French gowne of Russett Satten Floryshed with Leves of Sylver bound A boute with A passamayn of venis golde with pendante Sleves Lyned with Cloth of Sylver & A payer of wering Sleves of Cloth of Sylver Cutt in Risinge paynnes of Cloth of golde and Sylver. Delivered Raulf hope'. (New Year's Gift Roll, 27 Eliz. 1585. Folger, Z.d.16).

58 Item one french gowne of blacke satten prented laide with an open lace of golde edged with Carnacion plushe.

Loc. 'C', 'c'. LMN in H16 'Rem'.

f. 22

59 Item one french gowne of tawney satten embroidered allover with knottes sonnes and Cloudes of golde silver and silke furred with luzarnes

Loc. 'T', 't'. LMN in H16 'Rem'. The gown was probably a gift, as it does not appear among the warrants until this entry. 'Item to John Parr our Embrother . . . Item for enlardginge of the embrodery of a paire of forebodies & trayne of a gowne of tawny satten richly wrought, with cloudes sunnes and other devices, allso for embroideringe of new Jagges to the same'. (Warrant 10 June, 33 Eliz. 1591. PRO, LC5/36, ff. 176, 177). Parr carried out more work in 1598 'enbrauderinge of a border aboute the hinder parte of the skirte of a Traine gowne of Tawney Satten wroughte with Clowdes and sondry devises in colours withe four ounces quarter of purles plates and spangles'. (Warrant 29 March, 40 Eliz. 1598. PRO, LC5/37, f. 130). Almost as much work was carried out again by Parr later in the year, when he was entered in the warrant 'For enbrauderinge of a border, aboute the hinder parte, of the skirte, of a Traine gowne, of Tawney Satten, richlie wrought with Clowdes and sonnes and sondry devices in Colours, with iiij ounces of purles, plates and spangles spent theron'. (Warrant 27 Sept., 40 Eliz. 1598. PRO, LC5/37, f. 148). William Jones renovated the gown so that it could be worn again in the following year and is entered 'for alteringe and makinge up againe a gowne of Tawnye Satten enbraudered with gold and silver and furred of our great warderobe'. (Warrant 30 March, 41 Eliz. 1599. PRO, LC5/37, f. 161).

60 Item one Frenche gowne of blacke Satten cut embroidered allover with a small lace of venice golde and silver in squares embroidered within them with slippes of sondrie sortes and owes the border embrodered with feathers and Essefirmes the sleeves lyned with white satten cut and razed enbrodered with slippes of Venice golde.

Loc. 'T', 't'. LMN in H16 'Rem'. This gown was probably a gift as it does not appear among the warrants until this entry: 'First to Walter Fyshe our Taylour . . . for settinge in of two newe panes into a frenche Gowne of blak satten cutt and enbrauderid allover with venice golde & silver the lyninge and edginge perfourmed with white satten of our great guarderobe'. (Warrant 6 April, 24 Eliz. 1582. BL, Egerton 2806, f. 174ᵛ).

61 Item one frenche gowne of blacke satten prented with a brode garde embrodered with a satten twiste and bugle.

Loc. 'C', 'c'. LMN in H16 'Rem'.

62 Item one frenche gowne of blacke satten prented alover laide aboute with a lace of silver the sleeves lyned with peache coloure plushe.

Loc. 't'. LMN in H16 'Rem'. RMN in H2 {ownce cast}.

63 Item one frenche gowne of heare colour Satten florished with silver like peares bounde aboute with silver lace.

Loc. 'C', 'c'. LMN in H16 'Rem'.

64 Item one frenche gowne of tawnie tissued satten with bindinge lace of venice silver and plate withoute a traine.

Loc. 'C', 't'. LMN in H16 'Rem'.

65 Item one frenche gowne of blacke satten prented laide over with a lace of venice golde and silver plate like waves and set with owes and flowers alover the pendaunte sleeves lined ⟨and⟩ with prented clothe of silver.

Loc. 'C', 'c'. LMN in H16 'Rem'. This was probably a gift, as it does not appear among the warrants until this entry: 'Fyrste to William Jones our Tayloure . . . Item for alteringe and pecinge Longer of a gowne of black Satten wrought with gold and silver lace lyke waves performed with Lyke stuffe of our great warderobe'. (Warrant 28 Sept., 34 Eliz. 1592. PRO, LC5/36, f. 219).

f. 22ᵛ

66 Item one frenche gowne of orenge colour Satten [[or spanishe Taphata]] florished with silver beinge in parcelle [[now remayninge in six peces charged amonge the silkes]].

Loc. 'T', 't'. LMN in H16 'Rem'. First addition in H1, second addition in H4. See f. 90/[42].

67 Item one frenche gowne of blacke Cipers lined with blacke taphata edged with bugle and silke lace with rondles.

Loc. 'C', 'c'. LMN in H16 'Rem'.

68 Item one frenche gowne of Aishe colour Cipers with a brode garde embrodered with flowers and leaves of venice golde silver and silke lyned with orenge colour taphata.

Loc. 'T', 't'. LMN in H16 'Rem'. Walter Fyshe is entered in a warrant of 1575 'for making of a frenche Gowne with a longe traine of ashe colour sipers with a sleve made very

355 *'Portrait of an unknown lady', by Antonio Mor, c. 1575. She wears a black French gown with a semi-transparent partlet. The edge of the smock neckline can be seen round the square neckline, beneath the partlet. Detachable sleeves are embroidered with gold spangles and flowers of pink and green silk which stand away from the surface. The carcanet of jewels round her neck is made 'en suite' with the girdle. Museo del Prado, Madrid*

longe to stande in ruffes alonge tharme the bodies made with cuttes the gowne with a garde wrought with venice golde silver & silke of colours the gowne lyned with oringe colour taphata with a rolle of bayes in the pleites coverid with sarceonett & rolles in the slevis coverid with fustian and sarceonett xxvj yerdes of sipers of our store and threste of the sipers to make the gowne Receyved of Alice Mountague our Silkewoman threste of the Stuff of our great Guarderobe'. (Warrant 13 April, 17 Eliz. 1575. BL, Egerton 2806, f. 80). Two years later Fyshe was employed in 'alteringe and newe making of the skyrtes of a french gowne of ashe colour sipers'. (Warrant 27 Sept., 19 Eliz. 1577. BL, Egerton 2806, f. 116). Thirteen years later there is another entry among the warrants: 'Item to John Parr our Enbrauderer ... For enlarginge

the enbraudery of a paire of Slevis for a gowne of Ashe colour Sipers richlie wrought with sondry Flowers of gold and silver'. (Warrant 28 Sept., 32 Eliz. 1590. PRO, LC5/36, f. 145).

69   Item one french gowne of blacke Cypers cut allover diamondewise edged with taphata laide with lace and a fewe bugle.

Loc. 'C', 'c'. LMN in H16 'Rem'. Walter Fyshe is entered in a warrant of 1577 'for making of a frenche Gowne with a traine of blak Sipers lased allover with blak silke lozenge facion the lozenges cutt diamonde wise the cuttes doble edgid with taphata and thedginge snipte the snippes stitched downe one in anothers defalte: every bredthe of the sipers sett

together with borders of knottes made of blak silke lase the gowne lyned with taphata & a rolle of bayes, & buckeram in the pleites of our great guarderobe'. (Warrant 12 April, 19 Eliz. 1577. BL, Egerton 2806, f. 111). Fyshe carried out further work on the gown in 1581 'making of a peire of Ruffes for a frenche gowne of blak sipers cutt allover with a lozenge cutt edgid with blak taphata the ruffes lyned with buckeram cotten and sarceonett and rolles of bent coverid with fustian of our greate guarderobe'. (Warrant 6 April, 23 Eliz. 1581. BL, Egerton 2806, ff. 162ᵛ, 163).

70   Item one frenche gowne of blacke Cypers embrodered like waves allover lined with blacke Sarceonet.

Loc. 'C', 'c'. LMN in H16 'Rem'.

71   Item one frenche gowne of blacke Taphata with a faire golde embrodered with venice golde and silver like frutige cut allover and lyned with white sarceonet.

Loc. 'T', 't'. LMN in H16 'Rem'. This gown was probably a gift, as it does not appear among the warrants until this entry: 'First to Walter Fyshe our Taylour ... Item for alteringe enlarginge & settinge in of foure panes into the slevis of a frenche gowne of blak taphata with a garde enbroderid like frutige the panes cutt byas edgid with white satten and lyned with white sarceonett of our great guarderobe.' (Warrant 26 Sept., 18 Eliz. 1576. BL, Egerton 2806 f. 101ᵛ).

72   Item one frenche [gowne] of blacke Taphata cut and striped with lace of blacke silke and golde powdered with owes lined with white Taphata cut in panes allover.

Loc. 'C', 'c'. LMN in H16 'Rem'.

f. 23

73   Item one Frenche gowne of blacke pincked tufte Taphata laide about with plate lace of venice silver with buttons and loupes of like silver the bodies and sleeves cut allover sett with owes of silver.

Loc. 'T', 't'. LMN in H16 'Rem'.

74   Item one frenche gowne of blacke and heare colour tufte Taphata striped with tuftes of like silke and owes in them bounde aboute with a passamaine of venice golde.

Loc. 'C', 'c'. LMN in H16 'Rem'. This gown was probably a gift, as it does not appear among the warrants until this entry: Fyrste to William Jones our Tayloure ... Item for alteringe and pecinge longer of iij peire of bodies, one of heaire coloure and black Tufte Taffata set with owes & Lace with gold lace ... Canvas buckeram hooks and eyes of our great warderobe. (Warrant 28 Sept., 34 Eliz., 1592. PRO, LC5/36, f. 220).

75   Item one frenche gowne of black tufte Taphata striped allover with a plate lace embroidered and buttons of like silver plate.

Loc. 'T', 't'. LMN in H16 'Rem'.

76 Item one frenche gowne of aish colour Taphata cut and enbrodred allover with sondrie flowers and slippes of venice golde silver and silke in longe panes bounde with a passamaine lace of venice golde tackte up lyned with silver Chamblett striped with Carnacion Silke.

Loc. 'C', 'c'. LMN in H16 'Rem'. William Jones is entered in a warrant of 1590 'for makinge of a highe bodyed gowne of Ashe colour Taffata cut in rysinge Cuttes and tact up bound about with a lace of Carnacion Silke gold and Silver and spangles the bodies and slevis lyned with lawne and Sarcenet, the bodies stiffened with Canvas buckeram hook and eyes to the same, the hanginge slevis, facinge and Stomacher lyned with Silver Chamblet covered with lawne, floryshed with Silver and bound with Silver lace, the skirtes bordered with Taffata all of our great Warderobe'. (Warrant 28 Sept., 32 Eliz. 1590. PRO, LC5/36, f. 142). Jones worked on it again 'alteringe and pecinge longer the bodies of a Gowne of ashcolor Taffata, lined with silver Chamblet striped with Carnacion, the gowne beinge with tuckes of the same Taffata, bound with gold lace of our great warderobe'. (Warrant 28 Sept., 37 Eliz. 1595. PRO, LC5/37, f. 67). Six years later he was employed in 'alteringe a gowne of ashe colour Taffata, the hanginge slevis lyned with Lawne, silver Chamblett & Sarcenet of our great warderobe'. (Warrant 28 Sept., 43 Eliz. 1601. PRO, LC5/37, f. 231).

77 Item one Frenche gowne of blacke silke networke wrought with venice golde and silver with twoe small laces of venice golde and silke aboute it lyned with tawnie Taphata.

Loc. 'T', 't'. LMN in H16 'Rem'.

78 Item one coveringe for a Frenche gowne of heare colour silke networke florished allover with silver set upon a gowne of blacke satten prented edged with a passamaine lace of venice silver and black silke with ⟨twoe paire of bodies⟩ drawne out with orenge colour tawnie sarceonet and owes of silver and sylke.

Loc. ⟨'T'⟩, 't'. LMN in H16. Deletion in H1.

f. 23ᵛ

79 Item one Coveringe for a Frenche gowne of blacke silke silver and gold networke with spangles like Mailes with an edginge lace of gold and silver with spangles.

Loc. 'T', 't'. LMN in H16 'Rem'. This was a New Year's gift: 'By the Lorde Wynsor A Coveringe for a frenche gowne of blacke sylke sylver and gold networke wyth Spangles. Delivered to the foresaid Rauf hope'. (New Year's Gift Roll, 26 Eliz. 1584. BL, Egerton 3052, printed in Costume 9, 1975, p. 28).

80 Item one Coveringe for a Frenche gowne of blake networke florished allover with venice golde and spangles with bone lace of like golde.

Loc. 'C', 't'. LMN in H16 'Rem'.

356 Detail from Figure 327 showing jewels set on what may be 'roses of cipers' or gauze. These stand away from the surface of bodice and sleeves which are 'cut chevronwise' for decoration, c. 1600. Metropolitan Museum of Art, New York

357 Detail from Figure 16 showing jewels set on cutwork bows above two bands of gold metal braid which decorate the front of the bodice, c. 1585. National Trust, Trerice House, Cornwall

81 Item one Coveringe of blacke networke seamed and laced aboute with venice silver and blacke Sylke.

Loc. 'C', 't'. LMN in H16 ⟨'Rem'⟩ and in H8(?) {Wasted}. RMN in H4 'Eaten with Rattes'.

82 Item one frenche gowne of blacke networke embroidered allover with Bugle lined with ⟨heare⟩ ⟦white⟧ ⟨colour sarceonet⟩ {white}.

Loc. 'C', 'c'. LMN in H16 'Rem'. Alterations in H2. Illegible word in H8(?).

83 Item one frenche gowne of blacke silke networke of twoe sortes florished with venice golde lyned with white sylver Chamblet.

Loc. 'C', 'c'. LMN in H16 'Rem'. This was a New Year's gift: 'By Sir Thomas Cecill A French gowne of black silke nettworke of two sortes florished with venis gold and lyned with white Chamlett. Delivered at the Roabes'. (New Year's Gift Roll, 31 Eliz. 1589. BL, Lansd. Roll 17, printed in Progr. Eliz., III, p. 10).

84 Item one Coveringe for a frenche gowne of blacke networke powdered allover with feathers and slippes of venice Silver.

Loc. 'C', 'c'. LMN in H16 'Rem'.

358 *Detail from a satin panel 'embroidered with snails, leaves and antiques' in applied velvet, satin and couched cord, c. 1600. Victoria and Albert Museum, London (T.22–1947)*

85 Item one Frenche gowne of white lawne embrodered allover with Roses of Cipers and Bugle lyned with blacke Taphata.

Loc. 'C', 'c'. LMN in H16 'Rem'. The work of making this gown was divided between two men, probably for speed: 'First to Walter Fyshe our Taylour ... Item for making of the nether skyrtes of a frenche gowne of fine white lawne enbroderid allover with bugells & sipers sett allover with Roses of sipers lyned with taphata the winges lyned with buckeram & cotten drawen oute with sipers and lawne undernethe, the lawne being a vale of our store threste of our greate warderobe'. (Warrant, 10 April, 21 Eliz. 1579. BL, Egerton 2806, ff. 137, 137ᵛ). William Whittell was responsible 'for making of a peire of bodies slevis Jagges and winges of white lawne for a gowne enbrodered with black silke and bugells lyned with sarceonett canvas hookes & eyes'. (Warrant 10 April, 21 Eliz. 1579. BL, Egerton 2806, f. 138ᵛ). In 1595 William Jones carried out the work of 'alteringe pecinge longer, enlarginge and makinge up newe againe of a gowne of white Lawne enbraudered with blacke Sipers and bugles, lyned with Black Taffata of our great warde-robe'. (Warrant 10 April, 37 Eliz. 1595. PRO, LC5/37, f. 59).

86 Item one Coveringe for a Frenche gowne of white lawne cutworke three square lozenges set upon a gowne of blacke Clothe of golde edged with a passamaine lace of venice golde lined with blacke sarceonett.

Loc. 'C', 't'. LMN in H16 'Rem'.

f. 24

87 Item one Coveringe for a frenche gowne of lawne cutworke florisht with venice golde and spangles in cutworke like Roses.

Loc. 'T', 't'. LMN in H16 'Rem'. This was probably a New Year's gift: 'By the Countes of Penbroke Junior A Covering of A gowne of Lawne Coutworke, floryshed with venis golde. Deliverid Raufe hope'. (New Year's Gift Roll, 27 Eliz. 1585. Folger, Z.d.16).

88 Item one Coveringe for a frenche gowne of lawne embroidered allover with Fountaines, Snailes, swordes and other devices upon silver Chamblet prented.

Loc. 'T', 't'. LMN in H16 'Rem'. This was a New Year's gift: 'By Mr Foulke Grevell A Covering for a French gowne of Lawne Imbraudered with Fountaynnes snakes and swordes all over. Delivered to Rauf hope'. (New Year's Gift Roll, 27 Eliz. 1585. Folger, Z.d.16). Both snails and snakes are seen in Elizabethan embroidery, and the difference between these two entries may simply be a scribe's error, or the snakes may be among the 'other devices'.

89 Item one Coveringe for a frenche gowne of lawne florished with silver bordered ⟨with⟩ and striped downe the bodies and sleeves with venice golde and blacke sylke.

Loc. 'C', 'c'. LMN in H16 'Rem'. Deletion in H1.

90 Item one Coveringe for a french gowne of lawne embroidered alover with flowers of venice golde and blacke silke edged rounde aboute with a plate lace of venice golde and blacke silke.

Loc. 'C', 'c'. LMN in H16 'Rem'.

91 Item one coveringe of white Lawne cut like leaves striped thicke with plate laces of golde silver and spangles.

Loc. 'T', 't'. LMN in H16 'Rem'.

92 Item one Coveringe of Lawne cut with spotts of blacke silke seamed and laced aboute with silver and blacke silke.

Loc. 'C', 'c'. LMN in H16 'Rem'.

93 Item one traine gowne of lawne cutworke like roses and leaves florished with venice silver and lyned with pincke colour Taphata.

Loc. 'C', 'c'. LMN in H16 'Rem'.

94 Item one french gowne of peache colour Curle edged with a plate lace of Silver.

Loc. 'C', 'c'. LMN in H16 'Rem'. This gown was probably a gift, as it does not appear among the warrants until this entry: 'First to William Jones our Taylour ... Item for alteringe and newe making of a gowne of peache colour silke curle the lase taken of & sett in againe perfourmed with like stuf of our great guarderobe'. (Warrant 26 Sept., 29 Eliz. 1587. BL, Egerton 2806, f. 223). The next year Jones was entered in a warrant 'for alteringe and new makinge of a highe bodyed gowne with a Trayne of peache colour silke curle striped with lase of our stores the bodyes & sleeves lyned with sarceonet and stiffened with buckeram with Damaske to line the skyrtes of our great guarderobe'. (Warrant 27 Sept., 30 Eliz. 1588. BL, Egerton 2806, f. 231ᵛ). He carried out more work in 1592 'alteringe and pecinge longer of iij paire of bodies ... the third peachecolour Curle laced with silver lace perfourmed with lyke stuffe Canvas buckeram hooks and eyes of our great warderobe'. (Warrant 28 Sept., 34 Eliz. 1592. PRO, LC5/36, f. 220).

f. 24ᵛ

95 Item one frenche gowne of Carnacion Capha striped with golde and silver edged with the same stuffe.

Loc. 'T', 't'. LMN in H16 'Rem'.

96 Item one french gowne of russet stitched cloth richlie florished with golde and silver lyned with orenge colour taphata and hanginge sleeves lyned with white Taphata embroidered with Antiques of golde and silke of sondrie colours called China worke.

Loc. 'C', 'c'. LMN in H16 'Rem'. This may be a gown listed in a warrant of 1595, although there is insufficient detail to be certain: 'First to William Jones our Taylour ... Item for makinge up agayne a gowne of russett stiched clothe florished with gold and silver plate with carnacion and gold lace aboute it beinge new lined with Sarcenet of our great warderobe'. (Warrant 28 Sept., 37 Eliz. 1595. PRO, LC5/37, f. 67).

97 Item one Coveringe for a frenche gowne of blacke stitched Clothe florished

with venice golde and silver and some owes.

Loc. 'T', 'c'. LMN in H16 'Rem'. This was a New Year's gift: 'By the Barrones Hunsdon. A peire of bodies for the Covering of a gowne of black stitcht Cloth florished with gold and some Owes. Delivered to the Roabes' and 'By the Lord Hunsdon Lord Chamberleyne the nether skertes of the Coveringe of a gowne black stitcht cloth florished with gold and some Owes, Delivered to the Roabes'. (New Year's Gift Roll, 31 Eliz 1589. BL, Lansd. Roll 17, printed in *Progr. Eliz.*, III, pp. 5, 6).

98 Item one ⟨french⟩ highe bodied gowne with a traine of blacke stitched Cloth wrought with golde and silver edged and faced with Luzarnes.

Loc. 'T', 't'. LMN in H16 'Rem'. Deletion in H1. William Jones is entered in a warrant of 1592 'for makinge of a highe bodied Gowne, with a traine of black stiched clothe, wrought with gold and silver, and embrothered with flowers of gold and silver, laced with gold and silver, the bodies stiffened with Canvas and buckeram, hooks and eies, lyned with Taffata and sarcenet the traine lyned with Taffata, and pocketts of Taffata, the sticht clothe of our store as afore, the rest of our great warderobe. (Warrant 6 June, 34 Eliz. 1592. PRO, LC5/36, f. 207).

99 Item one Coveringe for a frenche gowne of heare colour stitched Cloth florished with venice golde and silver laide downe the seames with golde and silver lace.

Loc. 'T', 't'. LMN in H16 'Rem'.

100 Item one traine gowne of Claie colour or Issabella colour cloth of silver with borders verie faire embroidered like leaves of Carnacion Silke.

Loc. 'C', 'c'. LMN in H16 'Rem'.

101 Item one Coveringe for a french gowne of blacke stitched cloth florished with venice golde like flames and starres of silver Betweene.

Loc. 'C', 't'. LMN in H16 'Rem'.

102 Item one french gowne of aish colour ⟨cloth of⟩ sylver Chamblet with a traine to take of and on.

Loc. 'C', 'c'. LMN in H16 'Rem'. Deletion in H1.

[Two unnumbered folios, blank on both sides]

f. 25

Round Gownes

1 Firste one Rounde gownde of peache colour cloth of golde tissued with gold bounde with silver lace.

Loc. 'C', 't'. LMN in H16 'Rem'. 'gownde' is a scribe's error.

2 Item one rounde gowne of cloth of silver wrought with purple and yellowe

359 *Detail of a pomegranate embroidered with black silk and enriched with gold thread, on white linen, c. 1585–90. Royal Museum of Scotland, Edinburgh*

silke laide aboute and downerighte with a brode passamaine lace of venice golde and silver with buttons and loupes of like golde silver pipes and small seede p(ear)le.

Loc. ⟨'C'⟩, ⟨'T'⟩, 't'. LMN in H16 'Rem'.

3 Item one rounde gowne of strawe colour clothe of silver bounde with a lace of venice silver with workes like pomegranetts.

Loc. 'T', 't'. LMN in H16 'Rem'. This gown was probably a gift as it does not appear among the warrants until this entry: 'Fyrste to William Jones our Tayloure ... Item for alteringe the bodies and enlardginge of a gowne of strawe colour Cloth of Silver & borderinge the skirtes with Taffata of our greate warderobe'. (Warrant 27 Sept., 36 Eliz. 1594. PRO, LC5/37, f. 18).

4 Item one rounde gowne of Clothe of silver prented bounde aboute with a plate lace of venice golde.

Loc. 'C', 'c'. LMN in H16 'Rem'.

5 Item one rounde gowne of aish-colour clothe of silver the borders and bodies prented bounde aboute with a bindinge lace of venice silver.

Loc. 'C', 'c'. LMN in H16 'Rem'.

6 Item one rounde gowne of white Cloth of Silver with workes of yellowe silke like flies wormes and Snailes.

Loc. 'C', 'c'. LMN in H16 'Rem'.

f. 25ᵛ

7 Item one rounde gowne of silver Chamblet covered over with heare colour Cipers embroidered rounde aboute with a

brode border of flowers of golde silver and silke and flames of fire.

Loc. 'C', 'c'. LMN in H16 'Rem'.

8 Item one rounde gowne of Silver Chamblet garded bias wise allover with heare colour Satten.

Loc. 'C', 'c'. LMN in H16 'Rem'. This gown was probably a gift, as it does not appear among the warrants until this entry: 'First to William Jones our Taylour ... Item for alteringe pecinge longer and enlarginge of a Gowne of silver Chamblet enbraudered with gardes of haire colour satten and silver, and lined with Carnation Sarcenett performed with like stuffe and Sarcenet of our great warde-robe'. (Warrant 28 Sept., 37 Eliz. 1595. PRO, LC5/37, f. 67).

9 Item one rounde gowne of silver Chamblett embroidered allover with son-drie flowers and devises of venice golde silver and silke of sondrie Colours the sleeves embroidered like leaves and vines.

Loc. 'C', 'c'. LMN in H16 'Rem'.

10 Item one rounde gowne of silver Chamblet or tabine frenged billetwise and a brode border downe before with leaves of ⟦Carnacion⟧ silke and silver.

Loc. 'C', 'c'. LMN in H16 'Rem'. This gown was probably a gift, as it does not appear among the warrants until this entry: 'Fyrste to William Jones our Tayloure ... Item for alteringe and newe makinge up againe of a gowne of silver Chamblet enbraudered with leaves, with a silver lace about yt, the bodies newe stiffened with Canvas and buckeram the gowne newe Lyned with Taffata of our great Warderobe'. (Warrant 10 April, 37 Eliz. 1595, PRO, LC5/37, f. 58).

360 *Embroidery design of a salamander in flames of fire drawn out on a piece of linen, not worked, c. 1600. Victoria and Albert Museum, London (T.88–1925)*

11 Item one rounde gowne of white silver Chamblet covered over with white stitched Clothe embroidered upon with owes of venice silver like Sonnes, knotts and droppes.

Loc. 'C', 'c'. LMN in H16 'Rem'.

12 Item one rounde gowne of silver Chamblet covered with a coveringe of Cobweb lawne florished with venice silver like peramides.

Loc. 'C', 'c'. LMN in H16 'Rem'.

13 Item one rounde gowne of heare colour silver Chamblet covered over with blacke net like Copwebb.

Loc. 'C', 'c'. LMN in H16 'Rem'.

14 Item one rounde [[gowne]] without sleeves of black vellat embrodered all over with flowers and grashopers of venice golde silver and silke.

Loc. 'T', 't'. LMN in H16 'Rem'.

f. 26

15 Item one rounde gowne with hanginge sleeves of blacke unshorne vellat laide allover with a small wier of golde like skallop shells and set with owes and embroidered with a garde and dyvers borders with flowers embossed with golde silver silke and with ragged pearls.

Loc. 'T', 't'. LMN in H9 'at Whithall the 16th of december 1602'. Signature 'Frauncis Cobham of Kildare'. This gown was a New Year's gift: 'By therle of Warwick, a gowne with hanging sleeves of black vellat alover with small wyer of golde lyke Scallop Shelles, set with Spangilles, enbrawdred with a garde with sondry byrdes and Flowers enbossed with golde Silver and Silke, set with seede perle. Delivered

to Rauf Hoope.' (New Year's Gift Roll, 20 Eliz. 1578. Soc. of Antiquaries MS 537, printed in *Progr. Eliz.*, II, p. 66). The gown was altered before it was given to the Countess of Kildare and paid for when James I came to the throne: 'First to William Jones our said Sisters Taylor ... Item for altering & new making up againe a high bodied gowne of black uncutt vellat given by our said Sister unto the Countesse of Kildare, and of the chardge of the said Sir Thomas Gorges knight, with an enbrodered gard about with pearles with a performance of vellat and sarcenet to make new bodies and enlarge the skirts, & for making a paire of wering sleves of white satten cut in Snippes & raised upon silver chamblet and sarcenet, the bodies stiffened with canvas and buckram of our great warderobe'. (Warrant 18 May, 1 James 1603. PRO, LC5/37, f. 283). Extra embroidery was carried out at the same time: 'Item to John Parr our said sisters enbrauderer ... for enbrodering and enlardginge of a gowne of black vellat uncutt richlie wrought allover with skallopes of venice golde rounde spangells and purles the bodies newe embrodered and the skirtes enlardged with thre yardes of bordering newe wrought with pearle golde purles plates and rounde spangels and coloured silkes with CLtie [150] pearle and vj oz di of purle and round spangels spente theron'. (Warrant 18 May, 1 James 1603. PRO, LC5/37, f. 284).

16 Item one rounde gowne of peache colour vellat tissued with golde like ostridge feathers bounde with a lace of venice silver.

Loc. 'T', 't'. LMN in H16 'Rem'.

17 Item one rounde gowne of heare colour vellat with a spangle lace of venice golde and silver and tufts of Carnacion silke.

Loc. 'C', 'c'. LMN in H16 'Rem'. The warrant for making this gown gives full details

of the tailor's work and materials used: 'Fyrste to William Jones our Taylour ... Item for makinge of a highe bodied gowne of hare colour velvet laced about with a spangle lace of Venice golde silver and Carnacion silke set with buttons and tassells billett wyse of lyke spangle lace, the bodies drawne out with lawne stiffened with Canvas, buckeram hookes and eyes, lyned with Sarcenet and buckeram to lay aboute the skirtes and bordered with Sarcenet and pocketes of Taffeta, the hanginge slevis lyned with Silver Chamblett and Covered over with lawne, set with gold plate of our great warderobe'. (Warrant 27 Sept., 33 Eliz. 1591. PRO, LC5/36, f. 182).

18 Item one rounde gowne of blacke vellat with xviij tene lardge buttons embrodered with p(ur)le of sondrie sortes.

Loc. 'C', 'c'. LMN in H16 'Rem'.

19 Item one rounde gowne of the Irish fashion of orenge tawney Satten cut and snipte garded thicke overthwarte with aishcolour vellat embroidered with venice golde and spangles.

Loc. 'T', 't'. LMN in H16 'Rem'. This gown was probably a gift as it does not appear among the warrants until this entry: 'First to Walter Fyshe our Taylour ... Item for alteringe and enlarginge of ye slevis of a gowne of oringe colour satten of the Irishe facion the gardes perfourmed with ashe colour vellat and lyned with ashe colour sarceonett of our great guarderobe'. (Warrant 26 Sept., 18 Eliz. 1576. BL, Egerton 2806, f. 102ᵛ). William Jones carried out some unspecified work on it seven years later 'alteringe of a gowne of oringe colour satten garded with ashe colour vellat of our great Guarderobe'. (Warrant 26 Sept., 25 Eliz. 1583. BL, Egerton 2806, f. 189ᵛ). He worked on it again in 1590 'alteringe and newe makinge up of a gowne of Orrendge Coloure Satten garded alover with ashecoloure velvet enbraudered and new makinge the bodies stiffened with Canvas and buckeram and Lyned with Sarcenet with stuffe to perfourme yt of our great warderobe'. (Warrant 28 Sept., 32 Eliz. 1590. PRO, LC5/36, f. 141).

20 Item one gowne with bodies and sleeves of white satten laide over with a passamaine of venice golde and silver chevernwise lyned with strawe colour sarceonet.

Loc. 'T', 't'. LMN in H16 'Rem'. This was a New Year's gift: 'By the Countes of Shrewesbury a gowne of white Satten leyed on with pasmane of golde chevernewyse lyned with Strawe collored Sarceonet. Delivered to Rauf Hoope'. (New Year's Gift Roll, 20 Eliz. 1578. Soc. of Antiquaries MS 537, printed in *Prog. Eliz.*, II, p. 67). Walter Fyshe was engaged in work upon it three years later: 'alteringe and makinge newe of a payer of slevis for a rounde gowne of white satten layed allover with lase of golde and silver chevernewise perfourmed with like satten and lyned with yellowe sarceonett of our great guarderobe'. (Warrant 15 Sept., 23 Eliz. 1581. BL, Egerton 2806, f. 169ᵛ).

21 Item [one] rounde gowne of heare colour satten with three gardes of Carnacion plushe with three laces of venice ⟨silke⟩ silver with pendaunte sleeves likewise lined.

Loc. 'C', 'c'. LMN in H16 'Rem'. The warrant for making this gown gives details of the tailor's work and materials used. 'Flushe' is occasionally used instead of 'plush', but these may be scribe's errors: 'First to William Jones our Taylour . . . Item for making of a Gowne of heare colour satten with thre lases of venice silver aboute it and thre gardes of carnacion flushe the bodies stiffenid with canvas bayes & buckeram & buckeram to laye aboute the skyrtes lyned with carnacion sarceonett the slevis lyned with carnacion flushe the bentes coverid with taphata of our great guarderobe'. (Warrant 27 Sept., 28 Eliz. 1586. BL, Egerton 2806, f. 212ᵛ). Eight years later, he worked on it again 'alteringe and pecinge longer the bodies of a gowne of heaire colour satten with Carnacion plushe of our greate Warderobe'. (Warrant 27 Sept., 36 Eliz. 1594. PRO, LC5/37, ff. 20, 21). Jones carried out further work to keep the gown in fashion: 'alteringe of a gowne of heaire coloure Satten and pecinge longer the bodies, with three silver laces about, the hanginge slevis new lyned with Carnacion Plushe, and thre gardes about the skirtes, the bodies lyned and bordered with Sarcenett of our great warderobe'. (Warrant 29 April, 38 Eliz. 1596. PRO, LC5/37, f. 87).

22 Item one rounde gowne of white satten richelie embroidered with venice golde and silke like hopes and hoinesuckles lyned with Carnacion Taphata.

Loc. 'T', 't'. LMN in H16 'Rem'.

f. 26ᵛ

23 Item one rounde gowne of yellowe Satten cut and lined with blacke sarceonet wrought allover with shorte staves billetwise with flate silver with a like passamaine.

Loc. 'T', 't'. LMN in H9 'at Whit hall the 18 of december 1602'. Signature 'Susanna Veare'. This seems to be New Year's gift, originally described as a kirtle and doublet. 'By the Countes of Shrewisbury a kirtell and a Doublet of yellowe Satten cut lined with blake sarceonet wrought allover with shorte Staves of purlid Silver with a like passamaine. Deliverid to the saide Rauf hoope.' (New Year's Gift Roll, 7 Eliz. 1565. BL, Add.4827). It appears to have been altered for the Queen before this final alteration thirty-seven years later, although no detailed description can be linked with it: 'First to William Jones our said Sisters Taylor . . . Item for altering and new making up againe of a highe bodied gowne of straw color satten given by our said Sister to the Lady Susan Vere of the Charge of the said Sir Thomas Gorges knight, cutt allover with performance of satten and sarcenet to make new bodies and enlarge the skirts stiffened with canvas and buckram of our great warderobe'. (Warrant 18 May, 1 James 1603. PRO, LC5/37, f. 283). Extra embroidery was carried out at the same time so that the gown would be in the latest fashion: 'Item to John Parr our said sisters enbrauderer . . . for

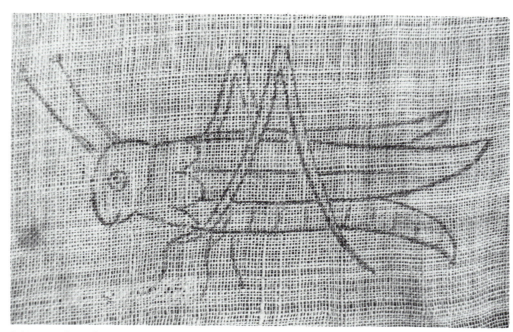

361 *Embroidery design of a grasshopper drawn out on a piece of linen, not worked, c. 1600. Victoria and Albert Museum, London (T.88–1925)*

enbraudering and enlarging a gowne of yellow satten cut & sett with crosse billets of silver lace allover with flowers of silver at eche end of every billet with silver purle & pulling out the bodies & sleves with white tiffany with iiij oz di of flowers & two oz di of purle spent thereon'. (Warrant 18 May, 1 James 1603. PRO, LC5/37, f. 284).

24 Item one rounde gowne of orenge colour Satten prented edged and bounde aboute with a passamaine lace of venice silver.

Loc. 'C', 'c'. LMN in H16 'Rem'. This was probably a gift, as it does not appear among the warrant until this entry: 'Fyrste to William Jones our Tayloure . . . Item for alteringe of a rounde gowne of orrendge colour Satten printed with a Silver lace about yt and newe borderinge the same with Sarcenet of our great warderobe'. (Warrant 28 Sept., 34 Eliz. 1592. PRO, LC5/36, f. 219).

25 Item one rounde gowne of blacke Satten prented cut and set alover with owes of golde with a brode border cut and tacked up laide on each side of the border with a lace of golde and silver laide under the border with oreng colour Taphata the sleeves and bodies turned oute with orenge colour plushe.

Loc. 'C', 'c'. LMN in H16 'Rem'. This was probably a gift, as it does not appear among the warrants until this entry: 'Fyrste to William Jones our Tayloure . . . Item for alteringe of a gowne of black Satten set on with owes alover newe faced and edged rounde about with orrendge Coloure plushe, and for enlardginge of a paire of slevis of white Satten of our great Warderobe'. (Warrant 27 Sept., 36 Eliz. 1594. PRO, LC5/37, f. 21).

26 Item one rounde gowne of orenge colour Satten laide allover with lace of

venice silver like waves the bodies sleeves and border rounde aboute of orenge colour or Lion colour tawney Satten Chevernewise.

Loc. 'T', 't'. LMN in H16 'Rem'.

27 Item one rounde gowne of Isabella colour Satten cut in snippes and raised up set with silver spangles.

Loc. 'C', 'c'. LMN in H16 'Rem'.

28 Item one rounde gowne of heare colour Satten wrought with branches of silver like Cloudes droppes and ⟨flowers⟩ feathers laide about with a brode bonelace of venice golde.

Loc. 'T', 't'. LMN in H16 'Rem'. Alteration in H1.

29 Item one rounde gowne of Beasar colour Satten with workes of silver like gynney wheate and braunches.

Loc. 'C', 'c'. LMN in H16 'Rem'.

30 Item one rounde gowne of aishcolour Satten florished with silver like flames Raine bowes and droppes set allover with golde owes with a Traine made to it.

Loc. 'C', 'c'. LMN in H16 'Rem'.

f. 27

31 Item one rounde gowne of white Satten embrodered allover the bodies sleeves and downe before and a small border rounde aboute of venice silver like globes with an Indented skirte.

Loc. 'T', 't'. LMN in H16 'Rem'. This was probably a gift, as it does not appear among the warrants until this entry: 'Fyrste to William Jones our Tayloure . . . Item for alteringe of a

362 *Detail of filberts, or hazelnuts, and pansies used for embroidery on a sleeve, from the 'Portrait of a lady called Elizabeth Throckmorton'. Painting by an unknown artist, c. 1585–90. The work was probably in black silk on white linen. Present whereabouts unknown*

white Satten gowne enbraudered alover with globes of Silver and enlardginge the bodies & slevis with Satten with a silver lace about yt, the bodies newe stiffened with Canvas and buckeram perfourmed with lyk stuff and Sarcenet of our great warderobe'. (Warrant 10 April, 37 Eliz. 1595. PRO, LC5/37, f. 58).

32 Item one rounde gowne of aish-colour Taphata cut in risinge cutts and tackt up bounde aboute with a lace of Carnacion silke golde silver and spangles.

Loc. 'C', 'c'. LMN in H16 'Rem'.

33 Item one rounde gowne of the Irishe facion of orange colour Taphata cut and embroidered with spangles with gardes of murrey Taphata embroidered with silver lyned with white sarceonet with a paire of sleeves of Lawne of the Irish facion embroidered with silver owes and knotts of silver plate.

Loc. 'C', 'c'. LMN in H16 'Rem'.

34 Item one rounde gowne of heare colour tufte taphata the grounde silver laide aboute with a plate lace of golde and silver.

Loc. 'C', 'c'. LMN in H16 'Rem'.

35 Item one rounde gowne of Dove or Turtle colour spanish taphata florished allover with golde silver and silke of sondrie Colours.

Loc. 'C', 'c'. LMN in H16 'Rem'.

36 Item one rounde gowne of blacke Taphata cut allover in risinge snippes and laide overthwarte with silver plate.

Loc. 'C', 'c'. LMN in H16 'Rem'.

37 Item one rounde [gowne] of partridge colour taphata with a brode border enbrodred with golde and silver like peramides and cut and tackt up with a kirtle under it of silver Chamblet painted in waves fishes and Rockes.

Loc. 'C', 'c'. LMN in H16 'Rem'.

38 Item one rounde gowne of tawney Cypers embroidered alover with a small twist of venice silver and owes of silver laide underneath with silver Chamblett.

Loc. 'C', 'c'. LMN in H16 'Rem'.

f. 27ᵛ

39 Item one rounde gowne of white Sipers laide upon silver chamblet with some embroiderie of golde like branches of flowers or Nutts.

Loc. 'C', 'c'. LMN in H16 'Rem'.

40 Item one rounde gowne of blacke networke florished with golde and silver in workes laide aboute with golde lace.

Loc. 'C', 'c'. LMN in H16 'Rem'.

41 Item one rounde gowne of pale pincke colour networke florished all over with golde the bodies and border downe before embroidered with golde and silver like peramides and wheate Eares.

Loc. 'C', 'c'. LMN in H16 'Rem'.

42 Item one rounde gowne of white networke florished allover with Silver like grapes and vine leaves and laide under it with white golde Chamblett.

Loc. 'C', 'c'. LMN in H16 'Rem'.

43 Item one rounde gowne of lawne cut and snipte with small silver plates upon aishcolour silver Chamblet.

Loc. 'C', 't'. LMN in H16 'Rem'.

44 Item one rounde gowne of lawne cutworke florished allover with venice silver diamondewise laid upon orenge colour taphata.

Loc. 'C', 'c'. LMN in H16 'Rem'.

45 Item one rounde gowne of lawne embroidered allover with golde and silver with workes like Peramides and grapes ⟨striped with silver and frenged like Esses⟩.

Loc. 'C', 'c'. LMN in H16 'Rem'. Deletion in H1.

46 Item one rounde gowne of white Tabine tissued with golde like dropes and a rounde worke billetwise cut with frenge of white silke.

Loc. 'C', 't'. LMN in H16 'Rem'.

47 Item one rounde gowne of white Tabine striped with silver the sleeves bodies and border garnisht with spangles.

Loc. 'C', 'c'. LMN in H16 'Rem'. This was a New Year's gift: 'By the Lady Walsingham widowe one rounde gowne of white Tabynne striped with silver the sleeves bodyes and border garnished with Spangles. Delivered to the Robes'. (New Year's Gift Roll, 40 Eliz. 1598. PRO, C47/3/40).

f. 28

48 Item one rounde gowne of silver Tabine with workes of orenge tawney silke like great Esses and branches with brode buttons of tawnye silke and silver downe before embroidered.

Loc. 'C', 't'. LMN in H16 'Rem'.

49 Item one rounde gowne of silver Tabine with workes like small Esses with frenge billetwise with a border downe before like fearne brakes embroidered with golde.

Loc. 'C', 'c'. LMN in H16 'Rem'.

50 Item one rounde gowne of golde tabine with tufts of meale colour vellat like Droppes and flames in threes.

Loc. 'T', 't'. LMN in H16 'Rem'.

51 Item one rounde gowne of silver tincell striped with silke and small workes with a small border rounde aboute it like vyne leaves and flames of tawney [silke] embroidered with Silver.

Loc. 'C', 'c'. LMN in H16 'Rem'.

52 Item one rounde gowne of Dove colour Capha with workes of golde and orenge colour silke like Raine bowes Cloudes and droppes and flames of fire.

Loc. 'C', 'c'. LMN in H16 'Rem'.

[53] Item one rounde gowne of Chesnut colour Satten Cut allover.

Loc. 'C', 't'. LMN in H16 'Rem'.

54 Item one rounde gowne of Russet wrought vellat the grounde silver cut a sonder allover and set together with a lace of venice golde silver and russet silke cheverne fashion lyned with orenge colour Taphata.

Loc. 'T', 't'. LMN in H16 'Rem'.

55 Item one rounde Gowne of clothe of silver wrought with Carnacion silke like flames of fire.

Loc. 't'. LMN in H16 'Rem'.

f. 28ᵛ

56 Item one rounde gowne of Tawnye vellat laide with fower laces of venice golde bordered with yellowe sarceonet.

Loc. 'C', 't'. LMN in H16 'Rem'.

57 Item one rounde gowne of Isabella colour cloth of sylver with works of orenge colour like vyne leaves and grapes with a border downe before.

Loc. 'C', 'c'. LMN in H16 'Rem'.

58 Item one Rounde gowne of white tuft Taphata the grounde sylver with Buttons downe before of silver Enbroderers worke.

Loc. 'C', 'c'. LMN in H16 'Rem'.

59 Item one Rounde gowne of white cloth of sylver with a Traine to take of and on with a border downe before of sylver Chamblet raized up with white Satten enbrodered with sylver like skallops and bounde aboute with silver lace.

Loc. 'C', 'c'. LMN in H16 'Rem'.

60 Item one Rounde gowne of white silver tabine with worke like flames and frenged Crosse billettwise laide aboute with golde lace.

Loc. 'C', 'c'. LMN in H16 'Rem'.

61 Item one Rounde gowne of golde Chamblett like droppes and flames of silver raized worke.

Loc. 'C', 'c'. LMN in H16 'Rem'.

62 Item one Rounde gowne of Claie colour Taphata laide upon with lawne Cutworke florished with venice silver twist and owes.

Loc. 'C', 'c'. LMN in H16 'Rem'.

63 Item one Rounde gowne of white cloth of sylver with a brode Border downe before of white Satten enbrodered with golde & Sylver owes Cut and snipt and raized up.

Loc. 'C', 'c'. LMN in H16 'Rem'.

f. 29

64 Item one Rounde gowne of russet Satten florished with gold and sylver with buttons and loopes of venice golde and sylver and bounde aboute with a lace of like silver edged with fawne colored plush.

Loc. 'C', 'c'. LMN in H16 'Rem'.

65 Item one rounde gowne of white silver Tincell striped with small corded silver bounde aboute with a sylver lace.

Loc. 'T', 't'. LMN in H16 'Rem'.

66 Item one rounde gowne of blacke tuft Taphata the grounde silver garnished with lace Buttons and loupes of venice

363 *Detail of a vine leaf embroidered with black silk and enriched with gold thread, on white linen, c. 1585–90. Royal Museum of Scotland, Edinburgh*

golde faced with oreng colour satten cut and lyned with sarceonet.

Loc. 'C', 'c'. LMN in H16 'Rem'.

67 Item one rounde gowne of heare colored raized mosseworke enbrodered allover with leaves pomegranets and men.

Loc. 'T', 't'. LMN in H16 'Rem'. This may be connected with a cloak (f. 71ᵛ/96) and a jacket (f. 85/84) which are similar in design, also with 'heare colored raized mosseworke'.

f. 29ᵛ

[No entries]

f. 30

Loose Gownes

1 Firste one loose gowne of plaine purple vellat laide with bonelace of venice golde silver and silke thinside beinge unshorne vellat white spotted blacke.

Loc. 'T', 't'. LMN in H16 'Rem'. Walter Fyshe is entered in a warrant in 1572 'for making of a night Gowne thouteside plaine purple vellat thinside unshorne vellat white spotted with blak layed with bone lase of golde silver and silke the slevis layed very thicke with like lase the coller lyned with canvas and pockettes of purple taphata the vellat to make the Gowne of our store Receyved of George Brydeman keper of our Palloice at Westminster threst of our greate guarderobe'. (Warrant 9 April, 14 Eliz. 1572. BL, Egerton 2806, f. 41ᵛ). William Jones worked on it in 1592 'alteringe of a night gowne of purple unshorne velvet the insyde black and whit and makinge newe slevis and Jagges laced alover with golde silver and black Silk lace of our great Warderobe'. (Warrant 28 Sept., 34 Eliz. 1592. PRO,

LC5/36, f. 218). The gown must have received considerable wear, as in the following year he is entered again 'for making of a paire of new Slevis and Jagges for a loose gowne of plaine purple velvet thinside unshorne velvet spotted black and white laced alover with gold silver and black silke lase of our great Warderobe'. (Warrant 28 Sept., 35 Eliz. 1593. PRO, LC5/36, f. 259).

2 Item one gowne of Carnacion vellat striped with silver bordered aboute with a lace of venice golde and silver faced with white unshorne vellatt powdered [[with black set with Owes lyned with ashe couloured sarcenet]].

Loc. 'C', 't'. LMN in H16 'Rem'. Addition by H2. In PRO, LR2/121 this is part of the original entry.

3 Item one loose gowne of Carnacion vellat with longe sleeves laide aboute with buttons and loupes of venice golde silver and spangles the sleeves lined with white vellat embrodred slightlie with venice golde owes and tufts of Carnacion silke.

Loc. 'T', 't'. LMN in H16 'Rem'.

4 Item one loose gowne of blacke vellat striped with white and blacke silke embroidered rounde aboute with wheate eares of venice golde and silver faced with white Satten razed.

Loc. 'T', 't'. LMN in H16 'Rem'.

5 Item one loose gowne of pale Carnacion vellat furred with Squerrills and faced with Sables.

Loc. 'C', 'c'. RMN in H11 'Bed chamber'.

6 Item one loose gowne of strawe colour vellat with a plate lace of Silver.

Loc. 'T', 't'. LMN in H16 'Rem'.

f. 30ᵛ

7 Item one loose gowne of Bee colour vellatt uncut and cutt in ⟨stripes⟩ ⟦slippes⟧ embrodered with silver owes and silke of colors with a small border of like embroderie.

Loc. 'C', 't'. LMN in H16 'Rem'. Alteration in H2.

8 Item one loose gowne of Carnacion vellatt cut and uncut embrodred with venice silver like Ostridge feathers.

Loc. 'T', 't'. LMN in H16 'Rem'.

9 Item one loose gowne of tawney wrought vellat the oute side, the inside Carnacion unshorne vellatt bounde aboute with a billament lace buttons and loopes of venice golde and plate lace.

Loc. 'T', 't'. LMN in H16 'Rem'. This was a New Year's gift: 'By the Erlle of Lece[s]tor Lorde Stuard of the Household A Nytegowne of Tawny wrought vellat one the oute syde the Insyde being Carnation unshorne vellat bound A boute with a Byllimentt Lace and Buttons and Louppes of venis golde and plate Lace. Delivered Raulfe hope yeoman of the Robes'. (New Year's Gift Roll, 27 Eliz. 1585. Folger, Z.d.16).

10 ⟨Item one loose ⟦gowne⟧ of tawnye wrought vellatt Satten grounde bounde aboute with a plate lace of venice golde and silver faced with aishcolour and orenge colour spotted plushe⟩.

Loc. 'T', 't'. LMN in H16 'Rem'. RMN in H9 'bed chamber'. The item is cancelled by striking out. This gown was a New Year's gift: 'By the Countes of Shrewesbury A gowne of Tawny wrought vellatt satten ground bound Aboute with a plate Lace of venis gold and Sylver Fased with Ashe colored and Orring tawny Fringed sylke spotted with Buttens and Loopes of venis golde and Sylver. Delivered Raulfe Hope. (New Year's Gift Roll, 27 Eliz. 1585. Folger, Z.d.16).

11 Item one loose gowne of blacke Satten embrodered allover with roses and paunceis and a border of oken leaves roses and paunceis of venice golde silver and silke with a face likewise embrodered.

Loc. 'T', 't'. LMN in H16 'Rem'.

12 Item one loose gowne of tawney Satten cut and embrodered all over with leaves and flowers of venice golde faced with Satten like heare colour cut and embrodered allover.

Loc. 'T', 't'. LMN in H16 'Rem'. This was a New Year's gift: 'By Sir Frauncis Waulsingham, Pryncipall Secretary, a night gowne of tawney satten, all over enbraderid, faced with satten like heare collour. Delivered to the forsaid Rauf Hope'. (New Year's Gift Roll, 21 Eliz. 1579.

Folger, Z.d.15, printed in *Progr. Eliz.*, II, p. 257).

13 Item one loose gowne of white Satten faced with orenge colour satten embrodered allover with Friers knotts and roses in branches of venice golde and tawney Silke and cut with a slight border of venice silver and orenge colour Sylke.

Loc. 'T', 't'. LMN in H16 'Rem'.

f. 31

14 Item one loose gowne of Crimsen Satten laide aboute with a passamaine lace of venice golde and silver faced with white Taphata lyned with white sarceonet.

Loc. 'C', 'c'. LMN in H16 'Rem'. RMN in H9 'bed Chamber'. This was probably a gift, as it does not appear among the warrants until this entry: 'Fyrst to William Jones our Tayloure . . . Item for alteringe a lose gowne of Crimsin Satten the faces newe lyned with Taffata and Sarcenet being Cutt and Tuft of our great warderobe'. (Warrant 28 Sept., 42 Eliz. 1600. PRO, LC5/37, f. 207).

15 Item one loose gowne of carnacion satten razed allover throughoute with Minnever furred, edged rounde about with powdered Armyons.

Loc. 'C', 'c'. LMN in H16 'Rem'. This was a joint New Year's gift (cf. f. 24ᵛ/97): 'By the Barronesse Hunsedon parte of a Nyte gowne of Carnation Satten rased furred thorowe out with mynyver and edged Rownde aboute with powdered Armyons. Delivered to the foresaid Rauf hope'. (New Year's Gift Roll, 26 Eliz. 1584. BL, Egerton 3052, printed in *Costume*, 9, 1975, p. 28). Her husband, Lord Hunsdon, gave the other part (ibid.).

16 Item one gowne of russet Satten striped with golde lyned with unshorne vellat spotted white and blacke.

Loc. 'C', 't'. LMN in H16 'Rem'. This was a New Year's gift: 'By Sir Thomas Layton knight a Nightgowne of Russett Satten stryped with golde lyned with unshorne vellatt spotted white and blacke' No delivery was noted. (New Year's Gift Roll, 26 Eliz. 1584. BL, Egerton 3052, printed in *Costume* 9, 1975, p. 29).

17 Item one loose gowne of orenge colour satten prented laide aboute with bonelace of venice silver faced with tawny plush lined with sarceonet.

Loc. 'C', 'c'. LMN in H16 'Rem'.

18 Item one loose gowne of blacke prented satten cut and tuft laide with bonelace of venice golde and blacke silke faced with blacke taphata Cut and set with small owes.

Loc. 'C', 'c'. LMN in H16 'Rem'.

19 Item one loose gowne of horseflesh colour satten prented laide aboute with a brode open lace of venice golde lined with white plushe.

Loc. 'C', 'c'. LMN in H16 'Rem'.

20 Item one loose gowne of white satten embrodered allover with golde owes and cut allover lined with white sarceonett.

Loc. 'T', 't'. LMN in H16 'Rem'.

21 Item one loose gowne of blacke Satten prented faced and garded rounde aboute with three gardes of orenge colour plushe and three laces of silver.

Loc. 'C', 'c'. LMN in H16 'Rem'. This was a New Year's gift: 'By the Countys of Shrewsburye a gowne of blacke satten prynted faced and garded rounde aboute with three gardes of Oringe colloured Flushe and three passama[n]e Laces of venis silver. Delivered to the said Sir Thomas Gorges'. (New Year's Gift Roll, 30 Eliz. 1588. BL, Add.8159). 'Flush' is occasionally used instead of 'plush', but these may be scribe's errors.

f. 31ᵛ

22 Item one loose gowne of aishcolour Satten cut and embrodered allover with golde owes and faced with white Satten the face likewise embrodered with waves.

Loc. 'T', 'c'. LMN in H16 'Rem'.

23 Item one loose gowne of Tawney Satten cut allover the sleeves and border embrodered with a lace and owes of silver and drawne oute with Lawne.

Loc. 'C', 'c'. LMN in H16 'Rem'.

24 Item one loose gowne of Claie colour Satten prented laide with a brode plate lace of venice silver faced with white plushe.

Loc. 'C', 'c'. LMN in H16 'Rem'.

25 Item one loose gowne of heare colour Satten prented and pincked laide about with twoe brode passamaine laces of venice silver lined with Carnacion plushe.

Loc. 'T', 't'. LMN in H16 'Rem'.

26 Item one loose gowne of tawney Satten prented the sleeves embrodered with a plate lace of venice golde like knotts furred with mynnever and faced with heare colour plushe.

Loc. 'c'. LMN in H16 'Rem'.

27 Item one loose gowne of peach colour or Murrey Satten cut and tufte allover with a border embrodered with venice golde silver and watchet Sylke.

Loc. 'C', 'c'. LMN in H16 'Rem'.

28 Item one loose gowne of Drakes colour Satten cut and tufted laide on the seames and rounde aboute with twoe laces of venice silver faced and edged with white plushe.

Loc. 'C', 'c'. LMN in H16 'Rem'. This was probably a gift, as it does not appear among the warrants until this entry. 'First to William Jones our Tailor . . . Item for Alteringe of a night gowne of drakes colour satten, laced with silver

364 *'Portrait of a lady possibly of the Wentworth family', panel painting attributed to Hans Eworth, 156[5]. She wears a black velvet 'loose', or 'Flanders' gown, the guards embroidered with gold thread and couched gold cord, bordered round the edges with a thick fringe of black silk and gold thread. Forepart and sleeves are in deep pink silk embroidered in a trellis design with red silk and pearls. Both neck and wrist ruffs are edged with red and gold plied cord, which holds the figures-of-eight in shape. The black velvet hat is trimmed with a hatband of a double row of pearls, gold buttons set with rubies and pearls, and pink and white feathers. Tate Gallery, London*

365 *Detail from Figure 364. The hanging sleeves of the loose gown, decorated with diagonally placed guards and fringe, can just be seen behind her arms*

lace, the bodies new lined with Fustian of our great warderobe'. (Warrant 6 June, 34 Eliz. 1592. PRO, LC5/36, f. 209). Jones worked on it again, six years later 'alteringe a Gowne of drakes coloure Satten new faced, the slevis lyned and edged aboute with white plushe of our great warderobe'. (Warrant 29 March, 40 Eliz. 1598. PRO, LC5/37, f. 129).

f. 32

29 Item one loose gowne of tawnye Satten prented embroidered with silver owes faced and edged with white plushe.

Loc. 'T', 't'. LMN in H16 ⟨'Rem'⟩. RMN in H9 'geven'.

30 Item one loose gowne of peache colour Satten tissued with silver in workes like feathers laide about with silver lace.

Loc. 'C', 't'. LMN in H16 'Rem'.

31 Item one loose gowne of white Satten the sleeves snipte and cutte havinge twoe open laces of venice golde aboute it.

Loc. 'C', 't'. LMN in H16 'Rem'.

32 Item one loose gowne of white Satten prented embroidered alover with a plate of venice golde and owes.

Loc. 'T', 't'. LMN in H16 'Rem'.

33 Item one loose gowne of peache colour Satten ⟨embroidered allover⟩ florished with silver laide aboute with a brode plate lace of venice golde faced and edged with white plushe.

Loc. 'T', 't'. LMN in H16 'Rem'. Alteration in H1. This was probably a gift as it does not appear among the warrants until this entry: 'First to William Jones our Taylour . . . Item for new facinge and edginge of a gowne of peache colour satten printed with white plushe, the sleves lyned with like plushe, of our great warderobe. (Warrant 10 June, 33 Eliz. 1591. PRO, LC5/36, f. 169). He worked on it again, two years later 'alteringe of a night gowne of peache colour tishued Satten beinge [lyned] with white Plushe of our great warderobe'. (Warrant 10 May, 35 Eliz. 1593. PRO, LC5/36, f. 253).

34 Item one loose gowne of white Satten embroidered allover with owes with a brode plate lace of venice golde faced and edged with powdered Armyons.

Loc. 'T', 't'. LMN in H16 'Rem'.

35 Item one loose gowne of ladie Blushe Satten laide with a bonelace of venice golde and silver with spangles with buttons downe before of the same lace.

Loc. 'C', 'c'. LMN in H16 'Rem'.

36 Item one loose gowne of white stitched Satten embroidered allover with owes and bordered rounde aboute with borders like peramydes of venice golde plate and owes.

Loc. 'T', 't'. LMN in H16 'Rem'.

f. 32ᵛ

37 Item one loose gowne of aishcolour Satten pincked in tufts allover and laide with twoe silver laces.

Loc. 'C', 'c'. LMN in H16 'Rem'.

366 *A knot made from narrow gold braid, possibly 'a true-love knot of passmane lace of venice gold', on a piece of dark green printed, or stamped velvet, c. 1600. Museo de Valencia de Don Juan, Madrid*

38   Item one loose gowne of Carnacion satten aboote striped with silver laide aboute with a silver frendge lace and spangles.

Loc. 'C', 'c'. LMN in H16 'Rem'.

39   Item one loose gowne of blacke tufte Taphata laide with lace buttons and loopes of venice golde furred throughe with Sables.

Loc. 't'. LMN in H16 'Rem' and in H6 'Sables employed'. RMN in H7 'ye sables imploied on divers thinges longe since'. In PRO, LR2/121 'the sables taken out'. The warrant for making this gown gives details of the tailor's work and materials used: 'First to Walter Fyshe our Taylour . . . Item for making of a night Gowne of blak tufte taphata layed with lase buttons and loupes of venice golde the bodies slevis and coller lyned with murrey sarceonett and pockettes of like sarceonett with a steye of fustian and canvas to lyne the coller the ruffes of the slevis lyned with buckeram and the Gowne vented about with buckeram all of our great guarderobe'. (Warrant 12 April, 12 Eliz. 1570. BL, Egerton 2806, f. 22). The fur was put in at the same time: 'Item to Adam Bland our Skynner for furringe of a night Gowne of blak tufte taphata layed with lase of venice golde

furred with the furre of two forequarters of Sables taken owte of a Gowne of our store and foureteene sable Skynnes being of the chardge of the said Rauf Hope And one hundreth and Thirtye sable skynnes of our store Receyved of George Brydeman keper of our Palloice at Westm(inster) and fourtye and six mynkes skynnes employed upon the slevis of the same Gowne of our great guarderobe'. (Warrant 12 April, 12 Eliz. 1570. BL, Egerton 2806, f. 23ᵛ). When the fur got shabby, parts were replaced: 'Item to Adam Blande our Skynner for mendinge the furre of a gowne of blak tufte taphata layed aboute with lase of blak silke and golde with two sable skynnes of our greate warderobe'. (Warrant 10 April, 21 Eliz. 1579. BL, Egerton 2806, f. 138). Five years later he carried out more work 'mendinge the furre of a gowne of blak tufte taphata with one sable skynne of our great guarderobe'. (Warrant 27 Sept., 26 Eliz. 1584. BL, Egerton 2806, f. 200ᵛ).

40   Item one loose gowne of blacke tufte Taphata edged with a bonelace of blacke silke frenged with silke and faced with taphata pincked.

Loc. 't'. LMN in H16 'Rem'.

41   Item one loose gowne of blacke tufte Taphata laide rounde about with a brode plate lace of venice silver faced with plushe of sondrie Colours.

Loc. 'T', 't'. LMN in H16 'Rem'.

42   Item one loose gowne of blacke tufte taphata laide downerighte with an open lace of silver and Carnacion silke faced with lawne cutworke florished with silver and Carnacion silke tufts.

Loc. 'T', 't'. LMN in H16 <'Rem'>. RMN in H9 'bed chamber'. This was probably a gift, as it does not appear among the warrants until this entry: 'First to William Jones our Taylour . . . Item for Alteringe of a night gowne of black tuft Taffata with a lace of Silver and Carnacion Silke and new lainge in the Slevis and facing of lawne Cutworke of our Store the rest of our great Warderobe'. (Warrant 28 Sept., 35 Eliz. 1593. PRO, LC5/36, f. 260).

43   Item one loose gowne of aishcolour tufte taphata embrodered with owes allover.

Loc. <'T'>, 't'. RMN in H11 'bede chamber'.

44   Item lose gowne of aishcolour tufte taphata the grounde silver furred with Callaber.

Loc. 'C'. RMN in H11 'bede chamber'. The warrant for making this gown gives details of the tailor's work and materials used; 'First to William Jones our Taylour . . . Item for making of a loose gowne of ashe colour tufte taphata the grounde silver the bodies lyned and with pockettes and stayes of tawnye taphata the steyes and coller styffenid and the gowne borderid with buckeram all of our great guarderobe'. (Warrant 3 April, 30 Eliz. 1588. BL, Egerton 2806, f. 227ᵛ). The fur was put in at the same time: 'Item to Adam Blande our

Skynner . . . for furringe of the said gowne of ashe colour tufte taphata with tenne tymber & fower skynnes of callaber of our great guarderobe'. (Warrant 3 April, 30 Eliz. 1588. BL, Egerton 2806, f. 228). Apparently Blande put in some sables as well, 'laying in a furre of sables into a gowne of ashe colour tufte taphata the grounde silver with seven tymber and seven skynnes of callaber of our great guarderobe'. (Warrant 3 April, 30 Eliz. 1588. BL, Egerton 2806, f. 228). The sables seem to have been taken out again, as later that year Blande is entered 'for mendinge the furre of a gowne of ashe colour tufte taphata the grounde silver with fowerteene callaber skynnes of our great guarderobe'. (Warrant 27 Sept., 30 Eliz. 1588. BL, Egerton 2806, f. 232).

f. 33

45   Item one loose gowne of aishcolour tufte taphata the grounde silver faced and edged with heare colour plushe.

Loc. 'T', 't'. LMN in H16 'Rem'.

46   Item one loose gowne of white tufte Taphata the grounde silver florished allover with owes of silver.

Loc. 'C', 'c'. LMN in H16 'Rem'. This was probably a gift as it does not appear among the warrants until this entry: 'First to William Jones our Taylor for altering and enlarging the sides of a loose gowne of white tuft taffeta the grounde silver performed with like stuff and sarcenet of our great Warderobe', (Warrant 8 April, 42 Eliz. 1600. PRO, LC5/37, f. 190).

47   Item one loose gown of blacke taphata with Compas lace of blacke silke and silver with a braided lace with a plate on either side.

Loc. 'T', 't'. LMN in H16 'Rem'. The warrant gives details of the tailor's work and materials used: 'First to Walter Fyshe our Taylour . . . Item for makinge of a large loose Gowne of blak taphata with compas lase of blak silke & silver & a brayed lase with a plate on ether side the greate lase the slevis lased allover verye thicke windinge like waves & doble Jagges in the syse lased with like lase the gowne with a staye of ye same taphata borderid with like taphata the border up the ventes & half the forequarters belowe at the skyrtes lased with the same lase the cape lyned with taphata & canvas & pockettes of taphata of our greate guarderobe'. (Warrant 28 Sept., 17 Eliz. 1575. BL, Egerton 2806, f. 87ᵛ).

48   Item one loose gowne of black taphata with a border of twoe plate laces of venice golde and silver.

Loc. 'C', 't'. LMN in H16 'Rem'. This was a New Year's gift: 'By Mrs Skydmore a gowne of blacke Taffata with a border of ij plate laces of venys golde and sylver. Delivered to the foresaid R. hope'. (New Year's Gift Roll, 26 Eliz. 1584. BL, Egerton 3052, printed in *Costume*, 9, 1975, p. 30).

49   Item one loose gowne of blacke taphata with a brode border embrodered with a cheine lace of venice golde and tuftes of white Sylke.

Loc. 'C', 'c'. LMN in H16 'Rem'. This was a joint New Year's gift (cf. f. 31/15): 'By Mrs Skudeamore parte of a loose gowne of black taffety with a border ymbrodered with A Chayne lace of venis gold and tuftes of white silke. Delivered to the Roabes'. (New Year's Gift Roll, 31 Eliz. 1589. BL, Lansd. Roll 17, printed in *Progr. Eliz.*, III, p. 11). Her husband, John Scudamore, gave the other part (ibid., p. 13).

50 Item one loose gowne of blacke taphata pincked Chevernewise embrodered rounde aboute with a border of flowers of silke of sondrie colours some owes.

Loc. 'C', 'c'. LMN in H16 'Rem'.

51 Item one loose gowne of aishcolour taphata pincked with a border embroidered with venice silver orenge colour and murrey silke.

Loc. 'C', 'c'. LMN in H16 'Rem'.

52 Item one loose gowne of spanishe taphata wrought with golde and silver with leaves and flowers of silke of sondrie Colours and a paire of hanginge sleeves.'

Loc. 'T', 't'. LMN in H16 'Rem'.

f. 33ᵛ

53 Item one loose gowne of partridge colour taphata cut and lyned with orenge colour sarceonet.

Loc. 'C', 'c'. LMN in H16 'Rem'.

54 Item one loose gowne of pinked colour taphata called Maiden blushe.

Loc. 'C', 'c'. LMN in H16 'Rem'.

55 Item one loose gowne of aishe or Dove colour Taphata the sleeves coller and border embroidered with leaves of venice ⟨silver⟩ golde.

Loc. 'C', 'c'. LMN in H16 'Rem'. Alteration in H1. This was a joint New Year's gift (cf. f. 33/49).: 'By the Lady Scudamore, parte of a loose gowne of ashe-colored taffeta, the sleves, coller, and border, embrothered with leaves of Venyce golde. Delivered to the Robes'. (New Year's Gift Roll, 42 Eliz. 1600. Printed in *Progr. Eliz.*, III, p. 452). Her husband, Sir John Scudamore, gave the other part (ibid. p. 454). The Queen probably wore the gown several times, as soon as it was given to her, as William Jones is entered in a warrant in the spring of 1600 'for altering and new lyning with white sarcenet of a loose gowne of ashcolour taffeta imbrodered with gold of our great warderobe'. (Warrant 8 April, 42 Eliz. 1600. PRO, LC5/37, f. 190).

56 Item one loose gowne of peache colour silke networke florished with venice golde and bounde aboute with a passamaine of venice silver lyned with white Sarceonet.

Loc. 'T', 't'. LMN in H16 'Rem'.

57 Item one loose gowne of Murrey Networke florished with golde bounde on the seames and rounde aboute with a plate lace of venice golde lined with tawnye Sarceonett.

Loc. 'T', 't'. LMN in H16 'Rem'.

58 Item one loose gowne of tawney striped networke florished allover with thredes of golde and silver bounde with a passamaine lace of venice silver unlyned.

Loc. 'T', 't'. LMN in H16 'Rem'.

59 Item one loose gowne of white networke florished with silver plate Diamondwise bounde with a Billiamentt lace of venice silver.

Loc. 'T', 't'. LMN in H16 'Rem'.

60 Item one loose gowne of russet networke with workes.

Loc. ⟨'T'⟩, 't'. LMN in H16 'Rem'. This was probably a gift, as it does not appear among the warrants before this entry: 'First to William Jones our Taylor ... Item for alteringe and newe makinge up agayne of a gowne of russett nett enbraudered with gold and silver, beinge newe faced to the foot with Sarcenet of our great warderobe'. (Warrant 28 Sept., 37 Eliz. 1595. PRO, LC5/37, f. 68).

f. 34

61 Item one loose gowne of blacke networke florished with leaves of venice golde silver and some plate.

Loc. 'T', 'c'. LMN in H16 'Rem'.

62 Item one loose gowne of blacke networke florished with workes allover of golde and silver and bindinge lace and a bonelace of gold and silver.

Loc. 'C', 't'. LMN in H16 'Rem'.

63 Item one loose gowne of ⟨white⟩ ⟦tawnie⟧ networke striped with silver the seames tufted with silver and spangles.

Loc. 'C', 't'. LMN in H16 'Rem'. Alteration in H1.

64 Item one loose gowne of white networke florished with threedes of golde and tufts of tawnie silke.

Loc. 'C', 't'. LMN in H16 'Rem'.

65 Item one loose gowne of blacke networke florished allover with silver like braunches and roses.

Loc. 'C', 'c'. LMN in H16 'Rem'. This was a New Year's gift: 'By the Barones {Deleware} one louse gowne of blacke Networke florished all over with braunches like roses of Venyce silver and owes. Delivered to the Robes'. (New Year's Gift Roll, 41 Eliz. 1599. Folger, Z.d.17).

66 Item one loose gowne of aishcolour networke florished with venice golde and silver like feathers allover.

Loc. 'C', 'c'. LMN in H16 'Rem'.

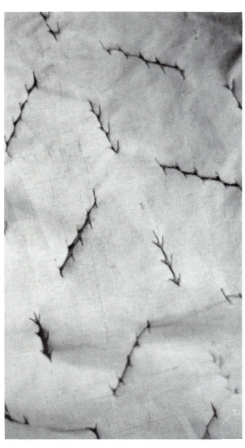

367 *Satin lining of a cloak 'cut and pinked chevernwise', c. 1610–20. Victoria and Albert Museum, London (T.378–1898)*

67 Item one loose gowne of blacke Networke florished allover with venice golde and silver like Feathers.

Loc. 'C', 'c'. LMN in H16 'Rem'. This was a New Year's gift: 'By the Barronnes of Hunsdon, wydowe, one loose gowne blacke of networke, florished all over with Venyce golde and silver lyke feathers. Delivered to the Robes'. (New Year's Gift Roll, 42 Eliz. 1600. Printed in *Progr. Eliz.*, III, p. 450).

68 Item one loose gowne of blacke Networke florished with silver and edged with silver lace.

Loc. 'T', 't'. LMN in H16 'Rem'.

f. 34ᵛ

69 Item one loose gowne of orenge colour Damaske with twoe great gards and three small and a small breade lace of venice silver faced with blacke unshorne vellatt.

Loc. 'C', 'c'. LMN in H16 'Rem'. This was probably a gift as it does not appear among the warrants until this entry: 'First to William Jones our Taylour ... Item for alteringe of a loose Gowne of orenge collour Damaske perfourmed with like stuf and the lyninge perfourmed with serceonett of our great guarderobe'. (Warrant 20 April, 25 Eliz. 1583. BL, Egerton 2806,

371, 372 *Slips of honeysuckle and rose, two details from the top of a white linen smock embroidered with polychrome silks in a design incorporating rainbows, clouds and flowers, c. 1585–1600. Whitworth Art Gallery, Manchester*

making of a gatherid kyrtle of blewe golde baudeken welted with blewe vellat layed with a lace of carnation silke and golde lyned with blewe taphata the stuff to make the kyrtle of our store Receyved of the said Rauf Hope threst of our greate guarderobe'.' (Warrant 6 Oct., 11 Eliz. 1569. BL, Egerton 2806, f. 17).

11 Item one rounde kirtle of blacke clothe of silver wrought like roses and hoinesocles with a plate lace of silver lyned with white sarceonett and frenged with golde and silver.

Loc. 't'. LMN in H16 {'cast'}. RMN in H4 'not seen at the vewe'.

12 Item one frenche kirtle of clothe of silver striped overthwart with Carnacion silke with workes of watchet silke with a lace of venice golde flate Damaske silver and blacke Sylke.

Loc. 'T', 't'. LMN in H16 'Rem'.

13 Item one frenche kirtle and a traine of blue clothe of silver embroidered all over with venice golde with a small garde of blacke vellat embrodered with golde and silver lyned with blacke sarcenet.

Loc. 'T', 't'. LMN in H16 'Rem'. This was a joint New Year's gift: 'By the Lady Cheyny, the trayne of a French kyrtill of blewe cloth of silver, enbrawdred al over with Venice golde, with a small garde of black vellat, enbrawdred with golde and silver, and lyned with blac sarceonet' and 'By the Lord Cheyny, a fore parte and a peir of boddys of a Frenche kyrtill of blewe cloth of silver, enbrawdred al over with Venice golde, with a small garde of black vellat, enbrawdred with Venice golde and silver, and lyned with black sarceonet. Delivered to Rauf Hoope'. (New Year's Gift Roll, 20 Eliz. 1578. Printed in *Progr. Eliz*, II, pp. 70, 71).

f. 38

14 Item one frenche kirtle with a traine of clothe of silver wrought with yellowe

and peache colour silke laide with bone lace of venice golde silver and spangles lyned underneathe with white Taphata.

Loc. 'T', 't'. LMN in H16 'Rem'. Originally the kirtle was lined with black taffeta: 'First to Walter Fyshe our Taylour . . . Item for making of a frenche kyrtle with a traine of cloth of silver wrought with yellowe and peache colour silke layed with bone lase of venice golde and silver with spangelles lyned underneathe with blak taphata lett downe with white satten and lyned with blak sarceonett the cloth of silver of our store of the chardge of George Brideman keper of our Palloice at Westminster threste of our greate guarderobe'. (Warrant 26 Sept., 20 Eliz. 1578. BL, Egerton 2806, f. 129).

15 Item one rounde kirtle of prented clothe of silver with a plate lace of venice gold and Crymsen silke.

Loc. 'C', 't'. LMN in H16 'Rem'. This was a New Year's gift: 'By the Counties of Lincollne A Rounde Kyrtille of Clothe of Silver prynted with a passamayne of plate golde Unlyned. Delivered to the foresaid Rauf Hoope'. (New Year's Gift Roll, 23 Eliz. 1581. Eton Coll. BLA 18 192.)

16 Item one rounde kirtle of strawe colour clothe of silver with one brode and a narrowe lace of venice silver.

Loc. 'C', 'c'. LMN in H16 'Rem'.

17 Item one rounde kirtle of Carnacion clothe of silver wrought with branches of honiesuccles with pomegranets bounde with golde lace.

Loc. 'T', 't'. LMN in H16 'Rem'.

18 Item one rounde kirtle of white clothe of silver bounde aboute with a lace of venice golde.

Loc. 'T', 't'. LMN in H16 'Rem'.

19 Item one rounde kirtle of white clothe of silver Chevernd with bluncket

with lace of golde and spangles buttons and loopes.

Loc. 'T', 't'. LMN in H16 'Rem'.

20 Item one kirtle of plaine Clothe of silver with workes bounde with golde lace.

Loc. 'T', 't'. LMN in H16 'Rem'.

21 Item one rounde kirtle of aishe colour clothe of ⟨silver⟩ ⟦golde⟧ branched laide with silver lace.

Loc. 'C', 'c'. LMN in H16 'Rem'. Alteration in H2.

f. 38ᵛ

22 Item one rounde kirtle of Synamon colour clothe of silver with workes like ⟨strip⟩ slippes.

Loc. 'C', 'c'. LMN in H16 'Rem'.

23 Item one rounde kirtle of aishe colour clothe of silver with workes like feathers and Cockell shells.

Loc. 'C', 'c'. LMN in H16 'Rem'.

24 Item one rounde kirtle of Clothe of silver with grapes vines and vyne leaves of sondrie coloured Silke.

Loc. 'C', 'c'. LMN in H16 'Rem'.

25 Item one rounde kirtle of white cloth of silver with works like branches of feathers wheate eares and flames of fier of sondrie colours.

Loc. 'C', 'c'. LMN in H16 'Rem'.

26 Item one rounde kirtle of clothe of silver tissued like flames and droppes of venice golde.

Loc. 'C', 'c'. LMN in H16 'Rem'.

27 Item one round kirtle of clothe of silver with workes of golde like slippes and feathers.

Loc. 'C', 'c'. LMN in H10 'tg geven by Hir majestie [to] Lady Marques'. The initials are those of Sir Thomas Gorges. Cf. f. 37ᵛ/7, f. 39/34, f. 59ᵛ/55 and f. 60ᵛ/69.

28 Item one rounde kirtle of Clothe of silver wrought with branches of sylke of sondrie colours like vyne leaves and grapes.

Loc. 'T', 't'. LMN in H16 'Rem'.

29 Item one rounde kirtle of Dove colour Cloth of silver with a border downe before with slippes of seede p(ear)le.

Loc. 'C', 'c'. LMN in H16 'Rem'.

f. 39

30 Item one rounde kirtle of white clothe of silver with workes and striped with golde and silkes of sondrie ⟨sorts⟩ coloours.

Loc. 'C', 'c'. LMN in H16 'Rem'.

31 Item one rounde kirtle of skie colour clothe of silver with workes like Cloudes and starres.

Loc. 'C', 't'. LMN in H16 'Rem'.

32 Item one rounde kirtle of clothe of silver prented downe before and rounde aboute like Peramydes.

Loc. 'C', 't'. LMN in H16 'Rem'.

33 Item one rounde kirtle of Clothe of silver striped overthwarte and tissued with venice golde like Cheines and Corded betwene.

Loc. 'C', 't'. LMN in H16 'Rem'.

34 Item one rounde kirtle of clothe of silver tissued with golde and silver in braunches of Gynney wheate eares.

Loc. 'C', 'c'. LMN in H10 'tg geven by hir majestie [to] Lady marques'. The initials 'tg' are those of Sir Thomas Gorges. Cf. with f. 37ᵛ/37, f. 38ᵛ/27, f. 59ᵛ/5 and f. 60ᵛ/69.

35 Item one rounde kirtle of Isabella colour clothe of silver prented downerighte in spaces like grapes and leaves.

Loc. 'C', 'c'. LMN in H10.

36 Item one rounde kirtle of white clothe of silver with workes like droppes and braunches of flame colour silke with knotted buttons of venice silver downe before.

Loc. 'C', 'c'. LMN in H16 'Rem'. Apart from the colour, which may have been a scribe's error, this description is close to a New Year's gift: 'By Sir William Knolles Comptroller of her Majesties houshoulde one rounde kyrtell of orange colored cloth of silver like droppes and braunches with knotted buttons of venyce silver downe before. Delivered to the Robes'. (New Year's Gift Roll, 41 Eliz. 1599. Folger, Z.d.17).

37 Item one rounde kirtle of clothe of silver with braunches and flowers of sylke of sondrye colours.

Loc. 'T', 't'. LMN in H16 'Rem'.

f. 39ᵛ

38 Item one rounde kirtle of white Cloth of Sylver bounde aboute with a lace of venice golde and seaven buttons like the birdes of Arabia embrodered downe before.

Loc. 'C', 'c'. LMN in H16 'Rem'. This was a joint New Year's gift: 'By the Barronnes Audeley, parte of a rounde kyrtell of white cloth of silver bound about with a lace of Venyce golde, and seven buttons like birds. Delivered to the Robes'. Her husband, Lord Audley, gave the other part, with the description of buttons 'lyke the birdes of Arabia' (New Year's Gift Roll, 42 Eliz. 1600. Printed in *Progr. Eliz.*, III, pp. 450–51).

39 Item one rounde kirtle of white clothe of silver like slippes of trees of orenge colour silke with eight buttons embrodered like Coronets of sylver.

Loc. 'C', 'c'. LMN in H16 'Rem'. This was a New Year's gift: 'By Sir William Knowlys, Comptroller of her Maiesties Howsholde, one rounde kirtell of ashe-colored cloth of silver lyke slyppes of trees of orenge-color silke with 8 buttons, embrothered like coronetts. Delivered to the Robes'. (New Year's Gift Roll, 42 Eliz. 1600. Printed in *Progr. Eliz.*, III, p. 453). The difference in colour was presumably a scribe's error.

40 Item one rounde kirtle of blacke vellatt with a brode bugle lace.

Loc. 'C', 't'. LMN in H16 'Rem'.

41 Item one rounde kirtle of plaine blacke vellat with a cheine frenge lace.

Loc. 'C', 'c'. LMN in H16 'Rem'. Walter Fyshe is entered: 'for making of a rounde kyrtell of blak vellat layed with cheine frenge lase borderid with sarceonett of our great guarde-robe'. (Warrant 12 April, 22 Eliz. 1580. BL, Egerton 2806, f. 151ᵛ).

42 Item one rounde kirtle of white Satten the foreparte laide allover with pipes of Damaske golde and ⟨bounde⟩ bordered with like pipes and a passamaine lace aboute The border lined with white sarceonet.

Loc. 'T', 't'. LMN in H16 'Rem'.

43 Item one rounde kirtle of white satten cut and pincked allover stript downerighte with a lace of venice golde and blacke Sylke.

Loc. 'T', 't'. LMN in H16 'Rem'.

44 Item one rounde kirtle of Carnacion Satten netted over with Carnacion Silke Silver and Spangles like gardes the hinder parte bordered with a like border of like stuf lyned with Carnacion ⟨Satten⟩ ⟦sarsenet⟧.

Loc. 'T', 't'. LMN in H16 'Rem'. Alteration in H3.

45 Item one frenche kirtle of white Satten cutt allover enbrodered with hopes flowers and Cloudes of venice golde sylver and sylke.

Loc. 'T', 't'. LMN in H16 'Rem'.

f. 40

46 Item one rounde kirtle of Carnacion Satten prented striped with silver laide with a plate lace of venice silver and buttons and loopes of like silver downe before.

Loc. 'C', 't'. LMN in H16 'Rem'.

47 Item one rounde Kirtle of aishe colour Satten striped with silver with a brode plate lace of venice golde.

Loc. 'C', 'c'. LMN in H16 'Rem'. This was probably a gift, as it does not appear among the warrants until this entry: 'First to William Jones our Taylour . . . Item for enlarginge the sides of a kyrtell of ashe colour satten striped with silver perfourmed with like satten and sarceonett to perfourme the borderinge of our great guarde-robe'. (Warrant 28 Sept., 24 Eliz. 1582. BL, Egerton 2806, f. 179).

48 Item one rounde kirtle of orange colour satten cutt and raveled striped with lace of venice silver lined with white sarceonett.

Loc. 'C', 't'. LMN in H16 'Rem'. This was a New Year's gift: 'By the Countes Lenneox A kyrtle of Orraynge Tawny Satten cut and lyned with white sarceonett laide all over with passamayne of Sylver. Delivered to the foresaid Rauf Hope'. (New Year's Gift Roll, 23 Eliz. 1581. Eton Coll. BLA 18 192). William Jones renovated it thirteen years later 'newe border-inge with taffata of a round kirtle of orrendge Colour satten cut of our great warderobe'. (Warrant 27 Sept., 36 Eliz. 1594. PRO, LC5/37, f. 18).

49 Item one rounde kirtle of strawe colour Satten rewed with silver with a passamaine lace of venice silver aboute it.

Loc. 'T', 't'. LMN in H16 'Rem'.

50 Item one rounde kirtle of tawney Satten striped with silver and tuftes of white silke like faggotts.

Loc. 'C', 'c'. LMN in H16 'Rem'.

51 Item one rounde kirtle of white satten cutt allover set withe tuftes of Carnacion silke and owes laide aboute with a brode plate lace of venice ⟨golde⟩ ⟦sillver⟧ and Carnacion silke.

Loc. 'C', 'c'. LMN in H16 'Rem'. Alteration in H2. This was a gift: 'By the Lady Marques of Northampton a rounde kyrtill of white Satten cut alover set with knottes of carnacion Silke and Spangilles and bounde abought with a

373 *Detail of dog-rose, or possibly eglantine, embroidered in black silk and enriched with gold thread, on white linen, c. 1585–90.*
Royal Museum of Scotland, Edinburgh

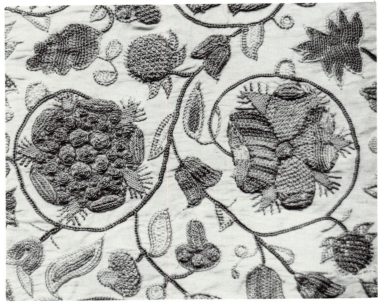

374 *Detail of a Tudor rose, a pansy, strawberries, acorns and leaves, embroidered with polychrome silks and enriched with gold thread, on white linen, c. 1600. Burrell Collection, Glasgow*

brode plate lace of venice golde and carnacion Sylke. Delivered to the forsaid Rauf Hope'. (New Year's Gift Roll, 26 Eliz. 1584. BL, Egerton 3052, printed in *Costume* 9, 1975, p. 28).

52 Item one rounde Kirtle ⟨of⟩ and a dublet of white satten cutt tackt upp with a small passamaine of venice golde and silke striped.

Loc. 'T', 't'. LMN in H16 'Rem'.

53 Item one kirtle of white Satten cutt allover striped overthwart with a plate lace of venice golde lyned with blacke Taphata Sarcenett.

Loc. 'C', 'c'. LMN in H16 'Rem'. This was a new Year's gift: 'By the Barrones Dakers. A kertle of white Satten Cout all over & stryped over T[h]wart with a plate Lace of venis golde and Lyned with blacke Taffatay. Delivered the forsaid Raulfe hope'. (New Year's Gift Roll, 27 Eliz. 1585, Folger, Z.d.16).

f. 40ᵛ

54 Item one kirtle and a dublet of Carnacion Satten cutt in snippes striped bias allover and rounde aboute with one ⟨lace⟩ plate lace of venice silver lyned with white sarceonett.

Loc. 'C', 'c'. LMN in H16 'Rem'. Deletion in H1.

55 Item one rounde kirtle of Claie colour satten or terrsigillata enbrodred allover with flowers of venice silver and blacke silke.

Loc. 'C', 't'. LMN in H16 'Rem'.

56 Item one rounde kirtle of Carnacion satten cut and striped with lace embrodered allover with shrimpes of golde and silver.

Loc. 'T', 't'. LMN in H16 'Rem'. This was probably a gift as it does not appear among the warrants until this entry: 'Fyrst to William Jones our Taylour . . . Item for alteringe and newe borderinge with Taffata a kirtle of Carnacion Satten enbraudered with Shrimpes of our great warderobe'. (Warrant 28 Sept., 32 Eliz. 1590. PRO, LC5/36, f. 142).

57 Item one rounde kirtle of Carnacion Satten striped with golde bounde aboute with Silver lace.

Loc. 'C', 'c'. LMN in H16 'Rem'. This was a New Year's gift: 'By the Baronesse Cobham a Rownde kertill of Carnation Satten striped with golde and bounde aboute with a lace of silver. Delivered to the said Sir Tho: Gorges'. (New Year's Gift Roll, 30 Eliz. 1588. BL, Add.8159).

58 Item one rounde kirtle of white Satten enbrodered with a slight border like a ryver of the sea and slightlie embrodered allover with plate Esses of plate golde with a deepe golde frendge.

Loc. 'T', 't'. LMN in H16 'Rem'.

59 Item one rounde kirtle of orenge colour Satten laced allover with silver lace like flagonworke.

Loc. 'C', 'c'. LMN in H16 'Rem'.

60 Item one rounde kirtle of tawnye Satten prented embrodered allover with venice golde and Silver plate like waves and tufts of Tawnye Sylke.

Loc. 'T', 't'. LMN in H16 'Rem'.

61 Item one rounde kirtle of white Satten cutt allover and enbrodered with a border of Silver plate striped downe with like embroderye like Peramydes.

Loc. 'C', 'c'. LMN in H16 'Rem'.

f. 41

62 Item one rounde kirtle of aishe or Dove colour Satten cutt and printed enbrodered allover with owes lyned with strawe colour sarceonet.

Loc. 'C', 'c'. LMN in H16 'Rem'. The description is not very detailed, but this may be a kirtle which was in the Wardrobe of Robes by 1586. 'First to William Jones our Taylour . . . Item for making of a Traine for a rounde kyrtell of ashe colour satten prented like globes bounde aboute with golde lase & lyned with strawe colour sarceonett of our great guarde-robe'. (Warrant 27 Sept., 28 Eliz. 1586. BL, Egerton 2806, f. 213ᵛ).

63 Item one rounde kirtle of Isabella colour Satten with a faire border embrodered with Silver like vyne leaves and grapes.

Loc. 'C', 'c'. LMN in H16 'Rem'.

64 Item one rounde kirtle of white Satten embrodered allover with slippes of flowers with a brode border rounde about and before like pillers rounde aboute with grapes.

Loc. 'C', 'c'. LMN in H16 'Rem'.

65 Item one rounde kirtle of white Satten tufte and enbrodered allover with sondrie wormes and flies with a border like Peramydes rounde aboute and downe before.

Loc. 'C', 'c'. LMN in H16 'Rem'. This was a New Year's gift: 'By Sir Edward Dyer one rounde kertle of white satten tuft imbrothered all over with sundry wormes and flyes with a border like p(er)amodes rounde about and downe before. Delivered to ye Robes'. (New Year's Gift Roll, 40 Eliz. 1598. PRO, C47 3/40).

375   Detail of a 'peramyde', or spire, acorns and oak leaves, embroidered in gold and silver thread and green silk, on a man's white linen nightcap, c. 1600. Gallery of English Costume, Platt Hall, Manchester

376   Slips of flowers, a river of the sea, rainbows, clouds and drops, detail from the top of a linen smock embroidered with polychrome silks, c. 1585–1600. Whitworth Art Gallery, Manchester

66   Item one rounde kirtle of white Satten enbrodered allover with a worke like flames pescods and pillars with a border likewise enbrodred with Roses.

Loc. 'C', 'c'. LMN in H10 'geven by hir majestie the 16 of aprill 160 '[space left]. Signature 'A. Walsingham'. This item was a New Year's gift: 'By Sir Edward Dyer one rounde kirtell of white satten embrothered all over like flames with a brode border imbrothered like Roses. Delivered to the Robes'. (New Year's Gift Roll, 41 Eliz. 1599. Folger, Z.d.17).

67   Item one rounde kirtle of white Satten enbrodered with a faire border rounde aboute and downeright in fower places with workes like vynes and vyne leaves slightlye enbrodered with Sylver.

Loc. 'C', 'c'. LMN in H16 'Rem'.

68   Item one rounde kirtle of white Satten tufte enbrodered allover like Esses of golde owes and a border embrodered like peramydes and flames. And one Dublet of Silver tyncell enbrodered with puffs like leaves of lawne florished with Silver plate and Spangles.

Loc. 'C', 'c'. LMN in H16 'Rem'. This was a New Year's gift: 'By the Lady Egerton, one rounde kyrtell of white satten, cutt and embrothered all over like esses of Venyce golde, and a border embrothered like peramydes; and one doublet of silver chamlett, embrothered with puffes lyke leaves, florished with silver. Delivered to the Robes'. (New Year's Gift Roll, 42 Eliz. 1600. Printed in Progr. Eliz., III, p. 452).

f. 41ᵛ

69   Item one rounde kirtle of white Satten embroidered with a runninge worke like ⟨Peramydes⟩ ⟦pances⟧ honyesuccles and frutage with a verye faire border rounde about and downe before with like enbroderie of golde silver and Silke of dyvers colours.

Loc. 'C', 'c'. LMN in H16 'Rem'. Alteration in H2.

70   Item one rounde kirtle of Satten beinge white embroidered alover with golde owes in works like Peramydes and Crownes.

Loc. 'C', 'c'. LMN in H16 'Rem'.

71   Item one rounde kirtle of tawnye Satten embroidered allover with braunches called Maple Trees of venice golde and Sylke.

Loc. 'T', 't'. LMN in H16 'Rem'.

72   Item one rounde gathered kirtle of Carnacion tufte taphata the grounde white laide with Silver plate lace.

Loc. 'C', 'c'. LMN in H16 'Rem'. Walter Fyshe was employed in making this 'rounde gatherid kyrtle of carnacion tufte taphata the grounde white layed with silver plate lase and borderid with carnacion sarceonett of our great warderobe'. (Warrant 28 Sept., 22 Eliz. 1580. BL, Egerton 2806, f. 157ᵛ).

73   Item one rounde kirtle of Carnacion tufte taphata the grounde Sylver buttoned looped and bounde about with a passamaine lace of venice golde.

Loc. 'T', 't'. LMN in H16 'Rem'. This was probably a gift as it does not appear among the warrants until this entry: 'First to William Jones our Taylour . . . Item for alteringe and inlarging of a round kirtle of carnacion tuft taffata, the ground silver with a gold lace about it, performed with like stuffe & sarcnet of our great warderobe'. (Warrant 10 June, 33 Eliz. 1591. PRO, LC5/36, f. 171).

74   Item one rounde kirtle of orenge colour tufte taphata the grounde Sylver with workes like pomegranetts with buttons byas wise downe before made of Silver lace with a lace of Silver rounde aboute.

Loc. 'C', 'c'. LMN in H16 'Rem'.

75   Item one rounde kirtle of heare colour tufte taphata the ground Silver with workes like pomegranets and Artichoques.

Loc. 'C', 'c'. LMN in H16 'Rem'.

76   Item one rounde kirtle of pincke colour tufte Taphata the grounde Silver with buttons of Silver like Peramydes downe before.

Loc. 'C', 'c'. LMN in H16 'Rem'.

f. 42

77   Item one rounde kirtle of strawe colour Taphata cut with a slight border of venice Silver like Cloudes.

Loc. 'C', 'c'. LMN in H16 'Rem'.

78   Item one kirtle of white Taphata cut and raveled bounde with golde lace.

Loc. 'T', 't'. LMN in H16 'Rem'.

79   Item one rounde kirtle of pincke colour spanishe Taphata striped with threds of Sylver overthwarte and cut betwene.

Loc. 'C', 'c'. LMN in H16 'Rem'.

80   Item one rounde kirtle of silver Chamblet striped in sondrye places with a

small plate lace of venice golde bounde aboute with a passamaine of venice golde lyned with white Sarceonett.

Loc. 'C', 'c'. LMN in H16 'Rem'. This was a New Year's gift: 'By the Countes of Lincoln a rounde kyrtill of Silver Chamlet striped in sundry places with a smaule plate lace of venice golde, and bounde abought with a like plate lace. Delivered to the forsaid Rauf Hope.' (New Year's Gift Roll, 26 Eliz. 1584. BL, Egerton 3052, printed in *Costume* 9, 1975, p. 28).

81   Item one kirtle of orenge colour golde Chamblet bounde with silver lace.

Loc. 'C', 'c'. LMN in H16 'Rem'.

82   Item one rounde kirtle of white silver Chamblet laide rounde aboute with a brode plate lace of venice golde edged with a small lace of venice golde.

Loc. 'C', 'c'. LMN in H16 'Rem'.

83   Item one rounde kirtle of white silver Chamblet bounde aboute with a faire golde lace and frenged with like golde.

Loc. 'C', 'c'. LMN in H16 'Rem'.

84   Item one kirtle of orenge colour sylver Chamblet with Flames.

Loc. 'C', 'c'. LMN in H16 'Rem'.

f. 42ᵛ

85   Item one rounde kirtle of sylver Chamblet or Tabine striped overthwarte with venice silver frendge and white sylke with a brode billiament lace and a bindinge lace of venice golde rounde aboute the skirts.

Loc. 'C', 'c'. LMN in H16 'Rem'.

86   Item one rounde kirtle of sylver Chamblet or Tabyne frenged overthwarte with white sylke and workes of peache colour sylke like feathers.

Loc. 'C', 'c'. LMN in H16 'Rem'.

87   Item one rounde kirtle of Mayden blush Sylver Chamblet.

Loc. 'C', 'c'. LMN in H16 'Rem'.

88   Item one rounde kirtle of white Sylver chamblet bounde [with] silver lace.

Loc. 'C', 'c'. LMN in H16 'Rem'.

89   Item one rounde kirtle of Beasar [[colour]] Silver Chamblet with embrodered golde buttones downe before.

Loc. 'C', 'c'. LMN in H16 'Rem'. Addition in H2.

90   Item one rounde kirtle of silver Chamblet or Tabyne with flowers of golde silver and sylke of sondrie colours.

Loc. 'C', 'c'. LMN in H16 'Rem'. This was a New Year's gift: 'By the Barronnes Chandoes, widowe, one rounde kyrtell of silver chamlett

or tabyne, with flowers of golde, silver and silke of sondrye colors. Delivered to the Robes'. (New Year's Gift Roll, 42 Eliz. 1600. Printed in *Progr. Eliz.*, III, p. 451).

91   Item one rounde kirtle of aish colour and white Damaske bounde aboute with a passamaine of venice golde.

Loc. 'T'. 't' LMN in H16 'Rem'. This was a New Year's gift: 'By Mrs Chaworthe a Rownde kyrtle of ashecollored and white damaske bownde aboute with a passamayne of venys golde and Carnation silke. Delivered to Ra. hope'. (New Year's Gift Roll, 26 Eliz. 1584, BL, Egerton 3052, printed in *Costume* 9, 1975, p. 30).

92   Item one kirtle of skie colour Damaske bounde with a lace of golde and Carnacion Sylke.

Loc. 'C', 'c'. LMN in H16 'Rem'.

f. 43

93   Item one rounde kirtle of white Damaske bounde with golde lace.

Loc. 'C', 'c'. LMN in H16 'Rem'. This gown may be one made as the Queen's 'best gown' for the Maundy ceremony. There are a number of entries for similar gowns among the warrants. These three examples were all made by William Jones: 'a rounde kyrtell of white damaske bounde with lase and borderid with tawnye taphata of our great Guarderobe'. (Warrant 28 Sept, 24 Eliz. 1582. BL, Egerton 2806, f. 179), 'a rounde kyrtell of white damaske with a golde lase borderid with taphata the Damaske being a traine of our store threste of our great guarderobe'. (Warrant 27 Sept., 28 Eliz. 1586. BL, Egerton 2806, f. 213ᵛ) and 'a rounde kirtle of white damaske bound about with gold lace bordered with Sarcenet of our great warderobe'. (Warrant 28 Sept., 32 Eliz. 1590. PRO, LC5/36, ff. 142, 143). Another six examples, almost identical in description, date from 1591 (Warrant 27 Sept., PRO, LC5/36, f. 184), 1592 (Warrant 6 June, ibid., f. 208), 1592 (Warrant 28 Sept., ibid., ff. 219–20), 1593 (Warrant 10 May, ibid., f. 250), 1593 (Warrant 28 Sept., ibid, f. 259) and 1595 (Warrant 10 April, PRO, LC5/37, f. 58). See chapter III for further discussion of the Maundy ceremony.

94   Item one rounde kirtle and a Dublet of Carnacion Capha wrought with silver like flowers bounde aboute with a lace of venice golde under a Coveringe of peacockes tailes.

Loc. 'C', 'c'. LMN in H16 'Rem'.

95   Item one rounde kirtle of white Capha striped with golde.

Loc. 'C', 'c'. LMN in H16 'Rem'.

96   Item one rounde kirtle of white Capha or tiffeny ‹cut and› tuft striped with Silver.

Loc. 'C', 'c'. LMN in H16 'Rem'. Deletion in H1.

97   Item one rounde kirtle of white China Capha Damaske bounde aboute with a passamaine lace of venice golde.

Loc. 'C', 'c'. LMN in H16 'Rem'. RMN in H11 ‹'bede chamber'›. This was a New Year's gift in 1600: 'By Mistriss Mary Ratclyffe, one rounde kyrtell of white china damaske bound about with passamyne lace. Delivered to the Robes'. (New Year's Gift Roll, 42 Eliz. 1600. Printed in *Progr. Eliz.*, III, p. 455).

98   Item one rounde kirtle and a Dublet of white Lawne striped with sylver or striped tiffenye.

Loc. 'C'. LMN in H10 'geven the 26 of october at Richmount 1602'. Signature 'R. Pamplyn'.

99   Item one rounde kirtle of lawne enbrodered allover like waves of the sea and fishes of sylver and silke.

Loc. 'C', 'c'. LMN in H16 'Rem'.

100   Item one rounde kirtle of lawne cut in workes like [[flowers &]] frutage florished with sylver plate.

Loc. 'C', 'c'. LMN in H16 'Rem'. Addition in H2. This was a New Year's gift: 'By the Lady Harrington, one rounde kyrtell of lawne cut in workes like flowers and frutage, laide upon blacke cypress tufted. Delivered to the Robes.' (New Year's Gift Roll, 42 Eliz. 1600. Printed in *Progr. Eliz.*, III, p. 453).

f. 43ᵛ

101   Item one rounde kirtle of networke florished with ‹venice› sylver owes and some spangles.

Loc. 'C', 'c'. LMN in H16 'Rem'.

102   Item one rounde kirtle of white Networke florished allover with twisted venice golde and silver.

Loc. 'C', 'c'. LMN in H16 'Rem'.

103   Item one rounde kirtle of blacke networke florished allover with golde and sylver owes and sylver tufts and enbrodered with silver buttons downe before.

Loc. 'C', 'c'. LMN in H16 'Rem'.

104   Item one rounde kirtle of white stitched clothe with workes enbrodered allover with sylver twists and sylver owes.

Loc. 'C', 'c'. LMN in H16 'Rem'.

105   Item one rounde kirtle of [[silver]] Tabyne ‹cloth of sylver› cut billetwise ‹upon› with peache colour silke with flames of venice golde betweene.

Loc. 'C', 'c'. LMN in H16 'Rem'. Alterations in H2.

106   Item one rounde kirtle of sylver Tabyne with workes of heare colour and aish colour sylke.

Loc. 'C', 'c'. LMN in H16 'Rem'.

377 *Slips of honeysuckle and gillyflowers, or pinks, embroidered in black silk on white linen, edged with gold thread, c. 1585–1600. Present whereabouts unknown*

107 Item one rounde kirtle of silver Tabyne wrought with slippes of venice golde sylver and Carnacion sylke.

Loc. 'C', 'c'. LMN in H16 'Rem'.

108 Item one rounde kirtle of white Tabyne with workes of white frendge Chevernewise.

Loc. 'C', 'c'. LMN in H16 'Rem'.

f. 44

109 Item one kirtle of pincke colour Tabyne with knotted buttons of sylver downe before.

Loc. 'C', 'c'. LMN in H16 'Rem'.

110 Item one rounde kirtle of white Tabine with some sylver and workes like braunches Diamondewise and white tufts Dyamondewyse.

Loc. 'C', 'c'. LMN in H16 'Rem'.

111 Item one rounde kirtle of blacke sylver Tabyne with workes like Esses of blacke silke frendge and enbrodered ⟨like globe⟩ ⟦with gowld⟧ buttons downe before.

Loc. 'C', 'c'. LMN in H16 'Rem'. Alterations in H2.

112 Item one rounde kirtle of white silver tabyne rewed overthwart with gold like a twiste and small crosse billets of white frenge like small Esses.

Loc. 'C', 'c'. LMN in H16 'Rem'.

113 Item one rounde kirtle of sylver Tabine with slippes of white silke like vellatt and tufts of Carnacion sylke and some golde.

Loc. 'C', 'c'. LMN in H16 'Rem'. This was a New Year's gift: 'By the Countesse of Oxenforde, one rounde kyrtell of silver tabynne, with slyppes of white silke like vellat, and tuftes of carnacon silke, with some golde. Delivered to the Robes'. (New Year's Gift Roll, 42 Eliz. 1600. Printed in *Progr. Eliz.*, III, p. 446).

114 Item one rounde kirtle of sylver Tabyne with starres and droppes of golde tissued.

Loc. 'C', 'c'. LMN in H16 'Rem'. This was a New Year's gift: 'By the Lord Cobham one rounde kyrtell of silver tabyne, with starres and droppes of gold tyssued. Delivered to the Robes'. (New Year's Gift Roll, 42 Eliz. 1600. Printed in *Progr. Eliz.*, III, p. 450).

115 Item one rounde kirtle of white tabine in squares of sylver and white tufts with longe buttons of venice silver lace downe before.

Loc. 'C', 't'. LMN in H16 'Rem'. This was a New Year's gift: 'By the Barronnes Ryche, one rounde white kirtell of tabyne in squares of silver and white tuftes. Delivered to the Robes'. (New Year's Gift Roll, 42 Eliz. 1600. Printed in *Progr. Eliz.*, III, p. 451).

116 Item one rounde kirtle of orenge colour tabine with slippes and lozenges of aishecolour silke with a border downe before like holye berrie leaves.

Loc. 'C', 'c'. LMN in H16 'Rem'. This was a joint New Year's gift: 'By Sir Henry Gyllforde, parte of a rounde kyrtell of orenge-colored tabyne, with slyppes and lozenges of ashe-color silke, with a border downe before like hollybery leaves. Delivered to the Robes'. Lady Guildford, his wife, gave the other part (New Year's Gift Roll, 42 Eliz. 1600. Printed in *Progr. Eliz.*, III, pp. 452, 454).

f. 44ᵛ

117 Item one rounde kirtle of sylver Tyncell striped with golde and knotted buttons downe before of venice golde.

Loc. 'C', 'c'. LMN in H16 'Rem'. This was a New Year's gift: 'By the Barronnes Lomley, one rounde kyrtell of silver tynsell stryped with golde and knotted buttons. Delivered to the Robes'. (New Year's Gift Roll, 42 Eliz. 1600. printed in *Progr. Eliz.*, III, p. 451).

118 Item one kirtle and a Dublet of blacke striped Copper Tiffenye with a brode border downe before and the bodies Cutt and tackt upp garnished with venice golde in tufts.

Loc. 'C', 'c'. LMN in H16 'Rem'. This was a New Year's gift: 'By the Lady Newton, one doublett and a kyrtell of blacke stryped tynsell with a brode border downe afore, and the bodyes cutt and tacked upp, garnished with Venyce golde. Delivered to the Robes'. (New Year's Gift Roll, 42 Eliz. 1600. Printed in *Progr. Eliz.*, III, p. 453).

119 Item one rounde kirtle of white knitworke with tufts allover with pincke colour Sylke.

Loc. 'C', 'c'. LMN in H16 'Rem'. This was a New Year's gift: 'By the Lady Leighton, one kyrtell of white knyttworke, tufted all over with pincke-colored silke. Delivered to the Robes'. (New Year's Gift Roll, 42 Eliz. 1600. Printed in *Progr. Eliz.*, III, p. 452).

378 *White silk embroidered with a lily, sea monster, flying bird and butterfly in polychrome silks, detail from Figure 129, possibly 1599. National Trust, Hardwick Hall, Derbyshire*

[120] Item one rounde ⟨gowne⟩ kirtle of strawe colour taphata ruft upp thicke allover with lace of venice silver and spangles.

Loc. 'T', 't'. LMN in H16 'Rem'.

121   Item one kirtle of Carnacion Cloth of silver bounde with a lace of venice silver and spangles.

Loc. 'C', 't'. LMN in H16 'Rem'.

122   Item one kirtle of white Satten cut and prented laide with faire knott buttons downe before bounde aboute with a golde lace.

Loc. 'C', 'c'. LMN in H16 'Rem'.

123   Item one rounde kirtle of Dove colour or peach colour golde Chamblett bounde aboute with a binding lace of venice golde.

Loc. 'C', 'c'. LMN in H16 'Rem'. This item was probably a gift, as it does not appear among the warrants until this entry: 'First to William Jones our Taylor . . . Item for altering and bordering, two kyrtells thone of black taphata striped with gold, thother of peach-color and gold chamblet of our great warderobe'. (Warrant 27 Sept., 44 Eliz. 1602. PRO, LC5/37, f.271).

124   Item one Rounde [[kirtle]] of white ⟨kirtle⟩ Capha Satten rewed with gold with twoe small plate laces aboute it.

Loc. 'C', 'c'. LMN in H16 'Rem'. Alterations in H1 and H2.

f. 45

125   Item one Rounde kirtle of peach colour cloth of sylver with works of Pomegranetts and Pyne ap[p]les.

Loc. 'C', 'c'. LMN in H16 'Rem'.

126   Item one Rounde kirtle of cloth of sylver tissued with golde and silver like Blasing starres grapes and slippes of flowers.

Loc. 'C', 'c'. LMN in H16 'Rem'.

f. 45ᵛ

[No entries]
[One unnumbered folio, blank on both sides].

f. 46

Forepartes

1   First one foreparte and a Dublet of purple clothe of golde striped with golde and sylver edged with a passamaine of golde.

Loc. 'T', 't'. LMN in H16 'Rem'. This was a New Year's gift: 'By Mrs Dale a Dublate and a foreparte of purple Cloth of golde striped with golde and silver & edged with passamayne of golde. Delivered to the foresaid R. Hope'. (New Year's Gift Roll, 26 Eliz. 1584. BL, Egerton 3052, printed in *Costume* 9, 1975, p. 30).

2   Item one foreparte of orenge colour prented cloth of golde with a plate lace of venice golde and sylver.

Loc. 'T', 't'. LMN in H16 'Rem'. This was a New Year's gift: 'By Mrs Dale a Doblate and a gathered foreparte of Orrenge Collored golde prented. Delivered to the foresaid Rauf Hoope'. (New Year's Gift Roll, 23 Eliz. 1581. Eton Coll. BLA 18 192).

3   Item one foreparte of a kirtle and a Dublet of cloth of sylver embrodered allover with Damaske golde purle.

Loc. 'T', 't'. LMN in H16 'Rem'. This was a New Year's gift: 'By the Countes of Bedford a foreparte of a kirtill of cloth of Silver Enbrawdred alover with damaske golde purle. Delivered to the forsaid Rauf Hope'. (New Year's Gift Roll, 26 Eliz. 1584. BL, Egerton 3052, printed in *Costume* 9, 1975, p. 28).

4   Item one foreparte of clothe of sylver embrodered allover with Rainebowes cloudes flames of fyre and sonnes of sylke and sondrye Colours.

Loc. 'C', 't'. LMN in H16 'Rem'.

5   Item one foreparte of cloth of sylver laide aboute with a passamaine lace of golde.

Loc. 'C', 't'. LMN in H16 'Rem'. Mrs Dale obviously found that forepartes made accept-

able gifts, see nos. 1 and 2, above: 'By Mrs Dalle one foreparte of clothe of silver, laide about with a passamaye lace of venis golde. Delivered to the said Sir Tho: Gorges'. (New Year's Gift Roll, 30 Eliz. 1588. BL, Add. 8159).

6   Item one faire foreparte of clothe of Sylver embrodered allover with flowers and leaves of sondrie sorts and colours of sylke golde and sylver set with sondrye seede p(ear)le and bigger ragged pearle in manye places.

Loc. 'C', 't'. LMN in H16 'Rem'.

f. 46ᵛ

7   Item one foreparte of a kirtle of blacke vellat allover embrodered with purles and pipes of Damaske golde.

Loc. 'T', 't'. LMN in H16 'Rem'. This was a New Year's gift: 'By the Countes of Shrewisburye Oone foreparte of a kyrtell and a placarde of blak vellat allover enbrauderid with pipes and purles of Damaske golde. Delyverid to the said Rauf Hope'. (New Year's Gift Roll, 10 Eliz. 1568. Soc. of Antiquaries MS 538).

8   Item one forepart of blacke vellat embroidered allover with ragged pearle and purle of Damaske golde lackinge dyvers pearle.

Loc. 'T', 't'. LMN in H16 'Rem'.

9   Item one foreparte of russet unshorne vellat the grounde blacke embrodered allover with venice golde and some verie small seede p(ear)le bounde aboute with a passamaine lace of venice golde and russet silke.

Loc. 'T', 't'. LMN in H16 'Rem'. This was a New Year's gift: 'By Mr William Cornwallis, a foreparte of blacke vellat wrought with braunches of Russet vellat unshorne and garnisshed with smale seede perle. Delivered to the said Rauf Hoope'. (New Year's Gift Roll, 23 Eliz. 1581. Eton Coll. BLA 18 192).

10   Item one foreparte of a kirtle of white satten embrodered allover with venice golde like Rondles ⟨of⟩ and Crymsen sylke with flowers within the rondells.

Loc. 'T', 't'. LMN in H16 'Rem'. This was a New Year's gift : 'By the Lady Cobham a foreparte of a kyrtell of white Satten allover enbrauderid with venice golde like Roundelles. Delyverid to the said Rauf Hope'. (New Year's Gift Roll, 10 Eliz. 1568. Soc. of Antiquaries MS 538).

11   Item one foreparte of white Satten embrodered allover like frutige of venice golde silke and silver glisteringe.

Loc. 'T', 't'. LMN in H16 'Rem'.

12   Item one verie faire foreparte of peache colour Satten embrodered allover with a faire border embrodered with sondrie beastes and fowle of venice golde and sylke lyned with greene Sarceonet.

Loc. 'T', 't'. LMN in H16 'Rem'.

13   Item one foreparte of Murrey Satten allover embroidered with beasts of venice golde and sylver frenged with like golde and Sylke.

Loc. 'T', 't'. LMN in H16 'Rem'.

14   Item one verie large forepart of white Satten striped allover bias with a passamaine of venice golde and sylver like waves.

Loc. 'T', 't'. LMN in H16 'Rem'.

f. 47

15   Item one gathered foreparte of russet Satten enbroidered allover with roses and flowers of venice golde and sylver lyned with taphata sarcenet.

Loc. 'T', 't'. LMN in H16 'Rem'.

16   Item one foreparte of purple Satten cut Diamondewise embroidered with venice golde drawne out with lawne set with seede pearle and damaske golde lyned with yellowe Taphata.

Loc. 'T', 't'. LMN in H16 'Rem'. This was a New Year's gift: 'By the countes of Bedford a feyer foreparte of a kyrtill of purple Satten alover enbrawdered with venice golde cut diamonde fashon drawen owte with lawnde set with sede perle and lyned with yelow taphata. Delivered to Rauf Hoope'. (New Year's Gift Roll, 19 Eliz. 1577. PRO, C47 3/39).

17   Item one gathered foreparte of strawe colour satten cut and razed allover laide with a riche lace of venice golde and sylver lyned with white Sarceonett.

Loc. 'T', 't'. LMN in H16 'Rem'.

18   Item one foreparte and a paire of sleeves of white satten embroidered with braunches and trees of damask golde with twoe gardes of blacke vellatt upon the foreparte embroidered with golde sylver and sylke with pearle lyned with tawnye sarceonett.

Loc. 'T', 't'. LMN in H16 'Rem'. This was a New Year's gift: 'By the Countes of Warwyck, a fore parte and a peir of Sleves of white Satten, enbrawdred with branches and trees of Damaske golde, two gardes of black vellat, upon the fore parte enbrawdred with golde Silver and Sylke set with seede perle, and lyned with tawney Sarceonett. Delivered to Rauf Hoope'. (New Year's Gift Roll, 20 Eliz. 1578. Soc. of Antiquaries MS 537 printed in *Progr. Eliz.*, II, p. 67).

19   Item one lardge gathered foreparte of yellowe Satten embroidered with venice sylver with roses of twiste of sylver lyned with strawe colour sarceonet.

Loc. 'T', 't'. LMN in H16 'Rem'.

20   Item one foreparte of Murrey satten embroidered with flowers of venice golde silver and silke lyned with orenge colour tawney sarceonett.

Loc. 'T', 't'. LMN in H16 'Rem'.

21   Item one foreparte of white satten embroidered with flowers of venice sylver and some Carnacion sylke with twoe borders of blacke vellat enbroidered with venice golde and seede p(ear)le lyned with Carnacion taphata.

Loc. 'T', 't'. LMN in H16 'Rem'. This was a New Year's gift: 'By the Countes of Oxford, a foreparte of a kyrtyll of white satten enbrawdred with flowers of silver and two borders of golde and sede perle enbrawdred upon black vellat. Delivered to the foresaid Rauf Hoope'. (New Year's Gift Roll, 21 Eliz. 1579. Folger, Z.d.15, printed in *Progr. Eliz.*, II, p. 251).

f. 47ᵛ

22   Item one foreparte of white Satten embroidered with blacke sylke and golde with twoe faire borders of venice golde and seede pearle embrodred upon blacke vellat.

Loc. 'T', 't'. LMN in H16 'Rem'. This was a New Year's gift: 'By the Countes of Bedford, a foreparte of white satten, enbrawdred with black sylke and golde, with two feyer borders of Venice golde and sede pearle enbrawdred. Delivered to the foresaid Rauf Hoope'. (New Year's Gift Roll. 21 Eliz. 1579. Folger, Z.d.15, printed in *Progr. Eliz.*, II, p. 251).

23   Item one foreparte of orenge colour Satten cut and embroidered with knotts of venice sylver like Trueloves garded with twoe brode borders of orenge colour vellat laide with one brode lace and twoe narrowe laces of venice golde and sylver.

Loc. 'T', 't'. LMN in H16 'Rem'. This was probably a gift as it does not appear among the warrants until this entry: 'First to Walter Fyshe our Taylour . . . Item for lengthenynge of a foreparte of oringe colour satten embroderid over with knottes of silver the lyninge perfourmed with white sarceonett of our greate warderobe'. (Warrant 12 Oct., 21 Eliz. 1579. BL, Egerton 2806, f. 145).

24   Item one foreparte of heare colour satten rufte allover in waves of stitched lawne and laide with plate lace of sylver guilt lyned with tawnye sarceonet.

Loc. 'T', 't'. LMN in H16 'Rem'. This was probably a gift as it does not appear among the warrants until this entry: 'to Walter Fyshe our Taylour . . . Item for lyninge of a gatherid foreparte of heare colour satten with tawnye sarceonett of our great warderobe'. (Warrant 12 April, 22 Eliz. 1580. BL, Egerton 2806, f. 151).

25   Item one foreparte of white satten pincked with a garde of purple satten embroidered with flowers of venice golde and sylver.

Loc. 'T', 't'. LMN in H16 'Rem'. This was a New Year's gift: 'By Mr Dyer, a foreparte of white satten, with a brode garde of purple satten, enbraudered withe Venice golde, silver and sede pearle, unlyned. Delivered to the foresaid Rauf Hope'. (New Year's Gift Roll, 21 Eliz. 1579. Folger, Z.d.15, printed in *Progr. Eliz.*, II, p. 262).

379   *Memorial brass to Cyssel Arundell, c. 1578. She wears an embroidered forepart with narrow ruff and large sleeveheads following the French fashion. St Mawgan in Pydar, Cornwall*

26   Item one foreparte of white and tawnye satten embroidered allover with venice golde and silver in panes the white enbroidered with flowers.

Loc. 'T', 't'. LMN in H16 'Rem'. This was a New Year's gift: 'By Mr Beinedicke Spenolle, a foreparte of white and tawnie satten, al over faire enbrauderid with golde and silver . . . The foreparte with Rauf Hope'. (New Year's Gift Roll, 21 Eliz. 1579. Folger, Z.d.15, printed in *Progr. Eliz.*, II, p. 262).

27   Item one foreparte of crymosin satten embroidered allover verie richly with venice gold.

Loc. 'T', 't'. LMN in H16 'Rem'. The description does not give much detail, but it may be the earliest New Year's gift to remain in the Wardrobe of Robes in 1600: 'By Spynnolla a Straunger oone foreparte of a kirtell and a paire of sleves wrought all over with golde and silke like into a Cawle upon Crymsen Satten with a partelett of like work'. (New Year's Gift Roll, 1 Eliz. 1559. Rylands Lib. Eng. MS 117). Twenty years later Walter Fyshe was entered in a warrant 'for alteringe and newemaking of a foreparte of crymsen satten embroiderid allover with venice golde made longer with a payer of slevis of like workemanship of our store Receyved of Blanche Parye and perfourmed by our Enbrauderer frengid with venice golde and

 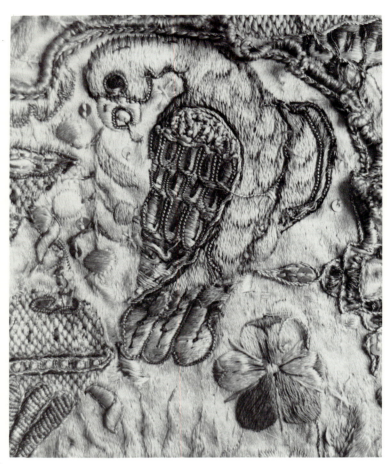

380, 381 Strawberries and flowers, and a parrot holding a spray of berries and leaves, with a pansy below, two details from a polychrome embroidered white satin panel, probably part of a skirt, c. 1600. Victoria and Albert Museum, London (T.138–1981)

crymsen silke lyned with white sarceonett of our greate warderobe'. (Warrant 12 Oct., 21 Eliz. 1579. BL, Egerton 2806, f. 144ᵛ).

28 Item one foreparte ⟨of⟩ and a Dublet of white Satten enbrodered allover with Rainebowes of venice gold and spangles.

Loc. 'T', 't'. LMN in H16 'Rem'.

f. 48

29 Item one foreparte of orenge colour Satten laide allover with a white cutworke set with spangles and a brode passamaine lace of venice golde and sylver on the neather parte.

Loc. 'T', 't'. LMN in H16 'Rem'.

30 Item one foreparte of tawnie satten garded thicke with white satten snipt Chevernewise laide with a small Cheine lace of venice golde.

Loc. 'T', 't'. LMN in H16 'Rem'.

31 Item one foreparte of white Satten embroidered allover with bugles made like flowers upon stalkes within knotts.

Loc. 'T', 't'. LMN in H16 'Rem'.

32 Item one foreparte of orenge colour Satten embroidered with ostridge feathers of venice sylver and knotts of like Sylver.

Loc. 'C', 't'. LMN in H16 'Rem'. This item was probably a gift. When it was relined, the Queen had a pair of sleeves made to match it. First to William Jones our Taylour . . . Item for makinge of a paire of dublett slevis of orrindge colour Satten enbrodered alover bound with silver lace lined with Sarcenett and for new lininge of a forparte of like Satten and Sarcenet embroidered with fethers and lined with Sarcenett of our great warderobe. (Warrant 10 May, 35 Eliz. 1593. PRO, LC5/36, f. 252).

33 Item one foreparte of heare colour Satten embroidered allover with flowers and leaves like beane blossoms with a traile of seede pearle and a small border of like pearle.

Loc. 'T', 't'. LMN in H16 'Rem'.

34 Item one forepart of blacke Satten embroidered allover with Ostridge feathers of sondrye colours and a border of like feathers set with verye small seede p(ear)le.

Loc. 'T', 't'. LMN in H16 'Rem'.

35 Item one foreparte of blacke Satten cut and embroidered allover with spangles and twiste lace of venice golde and Sylver like waves.

Loc. 'T', 't'. LMN in H16 'Rem'.

f. 48ᵛ

36 Item one foreparte of white Satten embroidered allover with straweberreis and leaves with a brode garde of heare colour Satten likewise embroidered lined with heare colour Taphata.

Loc. 'T', 't'. LMN in H16 'Rem'. The description is not detailed enough to identify it with certainty, but the following gift was also embroidered with strawberries: 'By the Barronesse Wylleby the Lordes wyfe a foreparte of white Satten enbradored with pescoddes frogges & strabury flowers with a border of strawe collored satten enbradored with golde lyned with strawe collored Taphata. Delivered to the foresaid Rauf Hoope'. (New Year's Gift Roll, 23 Eliz. 1581. Eton Coll. BLA 18 192).

37 Item one foreparte of white Satten embroidered allover with branches of hoinesuckles and Jellyflowers and some greene Sylke.

Loc. 'C', 't'. LMN in H16 'Rem'.

38 Item one foreparte of a kirtle of white Satten embroidered allover with golde plate and redd roses set with verie small seede pearle in them lackinge manye pearles.

382, 383   *A thunderbolt, strawberries and a squirrel and a little bird eating strawberries with an iris below, two details from a polychrome embroidered white satin panel, probably part of a skirt, c. 1600. Victoria and Albert Museum, London (T.138–1981)*

Loc. 'C', 't'. LMN in H9 at Whit hall the 16 of December 1602'. Signature 'Frauncis Cobhame of Kildare'.

39   Item one foreparte of white satten embrodered allover with flowers of venice golde and Sylke of sondrie colours in Compas knotts lined with white sarceonett.

Loc. 'C', 't'. LMN in H16 'Rem'.

40   Item one foreparte of whyte Satten cut enbrodered allover Chevernewise with venice golde with a border of plate lace and other flowers of like golde and sylver lyned with Carnacion sarceonet.

Loc. 'C', 't'. LMN in H16 'Rem'.

41   Item one foreparte of a kirtle of white Satten allover embroidered with greate braunches of venice golde and silver and silke of sondrie colours antique worke with a faire border of the same stuffe with a small frendge of venice golde and sylver.

Loc. 'C', 't'. LMN in H16 'Rem'. This was a New Year's gift: 'By the Lorde Taulbott a foreparte of a kertle of white Satten alover embroidered with greate braunches of venys golde silver and Sylke of sondrye Collers with a fayre border of the same Stuff with a smale Frynge of Venis golde & silver. Delivered to the

forsaid Rauf hope'. (New Year's Gift Roll, 26 Eliz. 1584. BL, Egerton 3052, printed in *Costume* 9, 1975, p. 28).

42   Item one foreparte of white satten embroidered with Daffadillies of venice golde and other flowers.

Loc. 'T', 't'. LMN in H16 'Rem'.

f. 49

43   Item one foreparte of white Satten covered with blacke stitched cloth florished Chequerwise with golde and Carnacion sylke and owes.

Loc. 'T', 't'. LMN in H16 'Rem'.

44   Item one foreparte and a Dublett of Carnacion Satten cut laide Chevernewise with plate Lace of Sylver.

Loc. 'C', 't'. LMN in H16 'Rem'. This was a New Year's gift: 'By Mr Newton a foreparte of a kyrtell of carnasion satten cut and layd chevernewyse wyth a plate lase of Sylver. Delivered to the forsaid Ra. hope.' (New Year's Gift Roll, 26 Eliz. 1584. BL, Egerton 3052, printed in *Costume* 9, 1975, p. 30).

45   Item one foreparte of purple Satten embroidered allover richelie with venice golde silver purle and pearle.

Loc. 'T', 't'. LMN in H16 'Rem'.

46   Item one foreparte of white Satten embroidered with an Eglantine tree spreadinge allover and flowers and leaves of venice golde and Silke.

Loc. 'T', 't'. LMN in H16 'Rem'. This was a New Year's gift: 'By the Erlle of Penbroke A forparte of white Satten enbraudered with Eglentyne flowers and other Leves. Delivered to the forsaid Raulf hope'. (New Year's Gift Roll, 27 Eliz. 1585. Folger, Z.d.16).

47   Item one foreparte of white Satten embroidered allover with flowers and leaves of venice golde and damaske golde purled garnished with Sondrie pearle in the myddest of the roses unmade lackinge manie pearle.

Loc. 'T', 't'. LMN in H16 'Rem'. This was a New Year's gift: 'By the Countes of Bathe A forparte of A kertle of white Satten unmade embrawdered all over with flowers and Leves of venis golde and Damaske purlle wrethed garnished with sundery perlles in the Myddest of the Flowers. Delivered Raulf hope'. (New Year's Gift Roll, 27 Eliz. 1585. Folger, Z.d.16).

48   Item one foreparte of Satten of sondrie colours embroidered with the twelve signes of venice golde sylver and sylke of sondrie colours unmade.

Loc. 'T', 't'. LMN in H16 'Rem'. This was a joint New Year's gift: 'Barrones Hounsdon

384 *An insect, possibly a wasp, embroidered in black silk, from a white linen shirt, c. 1585–1600. Museum of Costume, Bath*

385 *A lion, detail from a polychrome embroidered white satin panel, probably part of a skirt, c. 1600. Victoria and Albert Museum, London (T.138–1981)*

parte of A forparte of A kertle of Satten of Dyvers Colors embraudered with the twelve Synnes with golde sylver & Sylke of dyvers Colers unmade. Delivered the forsaid Raulfe hope'. (New Year's Gift Roll, 27 Eliz. 1585. Folger, Z.d.16) and 'By the Lorde of Hounsdon parte of A Forparte of A kertle of Satten of sundery Colers Imbraudered with the Twelve Synnes of venis golde Sylver & Sylke of sundery Colers un made. Delivered the forsaid Raulf hope'. (New Year's Gift Roll, 27 Eliz. 1585. Folger, Z.d.16). The embroidery of the signs of the Zodiac does not seem to have found favour with the Queen. The description in the inventory was taken from Lord Hunsdon's entry, and the forepart was, apparently, never made up and worn.

49 Item one foreparte and a paire of sleeves of orenge colour Satten cut upon white.

Loc. 'T', 't'. LMN in H16 'Rem'.

50 Item one foreparte of white Satten embroidered allover with Murrey Satten Set with seede pearle and bigger pearle lackinge manye pearle.

Loc. 'C', 't'. LMN in H16 'Rem'. This forepart may have been made from a New Year's gift which was presented 'By the Countes of Bedford A kertle of white Satten all over Embrawdered with Murrey satten sett with sede perlles and bygger perlles. Delivered to Raulfe hope'. (New Year's Gift Roll, 27 Eliz. 1585. Folger, Z.d.16).

f. 49ᵛ

51 Item one foreparte of white Satten embroidered verie faire with borders of the sonne Mone and other signes and plannetts of venice golde silver and Silke of

sondrie colours with a border of Beastes beneath likewise embroidered.

Loc. 'C', 't'. LMN in H16 'Rem'.

52 Item one foreparte of white Satten embroidered allover with a runninge worke like potts and within them Jellieflowers lined with yellowe sarceonett.

Loc. 'T', 't'. LMN in H16 'Rem'.

53 Item one foreparte of white Satten embroidered allover verie faire like Seas with dyvers devyses of Rockes shippes and fishes embroidered with venice golde sylver and silke of sondrye colours garnished with some seede pearle.

Loc. 'C', 't'. LMN in H16 'Rem'.

54 Item one foreparte of white Satten embroidered allover with paunceis little Roses knotts and a border of Mulberies pillers and pomegranets of venice golde Sylver and sylke of sondrye Colours.

Loc. 'C', 't'. LMN in H16 'Rem'.

55 Item one foreparte of white Satten embroidered overthwart and downe right with venice golde and Carnacion silke in spaces and flowers betweene them with a brode Border likewise embroidered.

Loc. 'C', 't'. LMN in H16 'Rem'.

56 Item a forepart of peach colour Satten embroidered allover verie faire with dead trees flowers and a Lyon in the Myddest garded with manye pearles of sondrye sortes.

Loc. 'C', 't'. LMN in H16 'Rem'.

57 Item one foreparte of orenge colour Satten cut and embroidered allover with a worke ⟦chevernewise and compasse knotts of venice silver and black silk with many Owes with a network plated and with spangles⟧.

Loc. 'T', 't'. LMN in H16 'Rem'. Addition in H2.

f. 50

58 Item one foreparte of Tawnye Satten cut embroidered overthwarte with slight embroderye of venice golde sylver and owes like knotts.

Loc. 'T', 't'. LMN in H16 'Rem'.

59 Item one foreparte of white Satten embroidered allover with spiders flies and Roundells with Cobwebbs of venice golde and tawnye sylke.

Loc. 'C', 't'. LMN in H16 'Rem'.

60 Item one foreparte of yellowe Satten embroidered allover with honiesuckles flowers and a runninge worke of venice silver and blacke silke.

Loc. 'T', 't'. LMN in H16 'Rem'.

61 Item one foreparte of Carnacion Satten embroidered with a slieght traile of honysuccles of venice golde and sylver with a lawne cut striped downeright with a plate lace of golde and Spangles.

Loc. 'T', 't'. LMN in H16 'Rem'.

62 Item one foreparte of greene Satten covered allover with Networke of sondrie colours.

Loc. 'T', 't'. LMN in H16 'Rem'.

386, 387   *A slip of vine, caterpillars, insects and birds, two details from a large panel of white ribbed silk with an additional weft of silver threads, embroidered with polychrome silks, said to have belonged to Blanche Parry, c. 1590–1600. The Church of St Faith, Bacton*

63   Item one foreparte and a ⟨paire of⟩ sleeves of white Satten netted over with a riche worke of venice sylver golde and spangles one sleeve wantinge the foreparte verie narrowe.

Loc. 'T', 't'. LMN in H16 'Rem' and 'less j sleve'.

64   Item one foreparte of peache colour Satten embrodered allover with Networke of colours with a passamaine lace of venice golde.

Loc. 'T', 't'. LMN in H16 'Rem'.

65   Item one foreparte of white Satten embroidered with roses acornes and other flowers allover with Nedleworke with a Nedleworke border of sondrye Beasts and trees of venice golde sylver and sylke of sondrye colours.

Loc. 'T', 't'. LMN in H16 'Rem'.

f. 50ᵛ

66   Item one foreparte of white Satten covered with lawne with men and fowles of venice golde and plate golde.

Loc. 'C', 't'. LMN in H16 'Rem'.

67   Item one forepart of orenge colour Satten cut and raveled slightlie embrodered allover Chevernewise with a threede of venice sylver and blacke silke and a brode border likewise embroidered with a networke florished with sylver.

Loc. 'T', 't'. LMN in H16 'Rem'.

68   Item one foreparte of Carnacion Satten laide over with a networke florished with a plate of sylver and blacke silke in Compas knotts.

Loc. 'T', 't'. LMN in H16 'Rem'.

69   Item one foreparte of Carnacion Satten covered with network of blacke silke and golde bounde aboute with a golde lace with Beasts flowers and skalloppe shells of lawne.

Loc. 'C', 't'. LMN in H16 'Rem'. William Jones was entered in a warrant in 1585 'for making of a foreparte carnacion satten coverid with nettworke of blak silke & golde bounde aboute with a golde lase and borderid with buckeram of our greate guarderobe' (Warrant 27 Sept., 27 Eliz. 1585. BL, Egerton 2806, f. 208).

70   Item one foreparte of Carnacion Satten covered with networke of lawne like knotts and beasts of blacke silke.

Loc. 'C', 't'. LMN in H16 'Rem'.

71   Item one foreparte of orenge colour Satten covered with cutworke of lawne with threedes of silver.

Loc. 'C', 't'. LMN in H16 'Rem'.

72   Item one foreparte and a Dublet of Carnacion Satten with a lawne Cutworke with flower Deluces garnished with owes.

Loc. 'T', 't'. LMN in H16 'Rem'.

73   Item one foreparte of Murrey Satten with a network of flowers and Men with Bowes of venice golde.

Loc. 'T', 't'. LMN in H16 'Rem'.

f. 51

74   Item one foreparte of white Satten with three bonelaces of golde and sylver.

Loc. 'C', 't'. LMN in H16 'Rem'.

75   Item one foreparte of heare colour Satten covered with blacke networke florished downeright and overthwart Chevernewise with venice sylver and small roses.

Loc. 'T', 't'. LMN in H16 'Rem'.

76   Item one foreparte of white Satten enbrodered allover with roses pauncies and Pomegranets and other workes with a small plate lace and some blacke silke lyned with Sarceonet with a border richlie embroidered with Beastes of sondry sorts flowers and fruites of silke and golde.

Loc. 'C', 't'. LMN in H16 'Rem'.

77   Item one foreparte of greene Satten embroidered allover with sylver like beastes fowles and Fishes.

Loc. 'T', 't'. LMN in H16 'Rem'.

78   Item one foreparte of white Satten cut embrodered allover with flowers of golde silver and sylke of sondry colours within Compas knotts of plate lace and blacke sylke.

Loc. 'T', 't'. LMN in H16 'Rem'.

79   Item one foreparte of white Satten embrodered allover with venice golde sylver and Carnacion silke in squares and flowers Chevernewise unmade.

388 *Slip of borage(?), detail from silk in Figure 386, c.1590–1600. The Church of St Faith, Bacton*

Loc. 'T', 't'. LMN in H16 'Rem'. This was a New Year's gift: 'By the Lorde Talbott a foreparte of white satten Imbrothered all over with Venus golde silver and Carnation silke in Squarres. Delivered to the said Sir Tho: Gorges'. (New Year's Gift Roll, 30 Eliz. 1588. BL, Add.8159).

80 Item one foreparte of white Satten cut and enbrodered with owes laide allover with a plate lace of venice golde like poynted ⟦waves⟧ overthwart and Downeright.

Loc. 'C', 't'. LMN in H16 'Rem'.

f. 51ᵛ

81 Item one foreparte of white Satten cut and embrodered allover with a Mosse worke of lardge flowers within a plate lace like waves.

Loc. 'C', 't'. LMN in H16 'Rem'.

82 Item one foreparte of white Satten embrodered allover with a faire worke of flowers leaves and such like of venice golde silver and silke of sondrie colours.

Loc. 'C', 't'. LMN in H16 'Rem'.

83 Item one foreparte of Carnacion Satten laide allover with lawne cutworke florished with golde spangles and tuftes of white silke like fagotts.

Loc. 'T', 't'. LMN in H16 'Rem'.

84 Item one foreparte of white Satten enbrodered allover with frutige of venice golde silver and silke of sondrie colours

and a brode border of like worke with a Traile of Carnacion silke wrought like Mosse.

Loc. 'C', 't'. LMN in H16 'Rem'.

85 Item one foreparte of white Satten embroidered allover with Paunicies and Peramides and a border of frutidge and birdes of venice golde silver and silke of sondrie colours.

Loc. 'T', 't'. LMN in H16 'Rem'.

86 Item one foreparte of white Satten enbrodered allover richelie with venice golde silver and Silke and a verie brode border of like embroderie.

Loc. 'T', 't'. LMN in H16 'Rem'.

87 Item one foreparte of Tawnie Satten embrodered allover with sondrie Devises of sunne beames and Cloudes.

Loc. 'T', 't'. LMN in H16 'Rem'.

f. 52

88 Item one foreparte of white Satten cut in knotts enbrodered allover with venice golde and silver of wier worke like greene Mosseworke and beastes of sondrie facions upon braunches.

Loc. 'T', 't'. LMN in H16 'Rem'.

89 Item one foreparte of white Satten enbrodered allover with Roses and flowers of venice golde silver and silke of sondrie colours.

Loc. 'T', 't'. LMN in H16 'Rem'.

90 Item one foreparte of white Satten enbrodered allover with a worke of venice golde and therein burridge flowers Roses and honiesuccles.

Loc. 'T', 't'. LMN in H16 'Rem'.

91 Item one forepart with a paire of wearinge sleeves and hanginge sleeves of white satten cut snipt and rufte up with borders betweene overthwart of plate like knotts and some owes of golde and silver.

Loc. 'T', 't'. LMN in H16 'Rem'.

92 Item one foreparte gathered of Lawne Chequered with golde wrought with purple silke laide with lace of venice golde and silver.

Loc. 'T', 't'. LMN in H16 'Rem'.

93 Item one foreparte of Lawne embrodered with flowers of golde silver and silke of sondrie colours most like harts and lyned with blewe sarceonett.

Loc. 'T', 't'. LMN in H16 'Rem'.

94 Item one foreparte of Lawne embrodered with Bees and sondrie wormes lyned with white Taphata.

Loc. 'C', 't'. LMN in H16 'Rem'.

95 Item one foreparte of Lawne cutworke florished with threedes of venice golde and sylver.

Loc. 'T', 't'. LMN in H16 'Rem'.

f. 52ᵛ

96 Item one foreparte of Lawne wrought with roses of white Sypers florished with plate lace of golde and spangles.

Loc. 'C', 't'. LMN in H16 'Rem'.

97 Item one foreparte of a kirtle of Lawne embrodered allover with venice golde sylver blacke redd greene and Carnacion silke like beasts and foules.

Loc. 'C', 't'. LMN in H16 'Rem'. This was probably a New Year's gift: 'By the Lorde Hunsedon A foreparte of A kyrtill of Lawne all over enbraudered with golde. Delivered to the foresaid Rauf Hoope'. (New Year's Gift Roll, 23 Eliz. 1581. Eton Coll. BLA 18 192).

98 Item one foreparte of Lawne cutworke in knots with flowers of golde sylver and silke of sondrie colours lined with horseflesh colour Satten unmade with some garnetts.

Loc. 'T', 't'. LMN in H16 'Rem'.

99 Item one foreparte of white Lawne striped with silver plate and pufte up in Rolles.

Loc. 'C', 't'. LMN in H16 'Rem'. This was a New Year's gift: 'By Mr Stanhoppe a foreparte of a kertle of Lawne Cutwourke striped with silver plate and puffed up like Rolles. Delivered to the said Sir Tho: Gorges'. (New Year's Gift Roll, 30 Eliz. 1588. BL, Add.8159).

100 Item one foreparte and a paire of sleeves of Lawne cutworke striped overthwarte with a plate of golde and a waveworke of like skallop lined with tawnie satten bound with a plate lace of venice golde.

Loc. 'T', 't'. LMN in H16 'Rem'.

101 Item one foreparte and a Dublet of lawne cutworke garnished with golde plate in rewes and wreathed rolles in spaces Diamondewise and garnished with spangles and owes upon whit Satten.

Loc. 'C', 't'. LMN in H16 'Rem'.

102 Item one forepart of Lawne cutworke like leaves with plate and spangles in risinge puffes.

Loc. 'C', 't'. LMN in H16 'Rem'.

103 Item one foreparte of white striped golde Lawne florished with venice golde and garnished with sondrie flowers of sylkewomans work.

Loc. 'C', 't'. LMN in H16 'Rem'.

f.53

104 Item one foreparte of Lawne Cutworke florished with golde and silver owes upon sylver Chamblet.

Loc. 't'. LMN in H16 'Rem'.

105 Item one foreparte of Lawne cutwork florished with a threedde of venice golde and silver with a bonelace of venice golde and silver on the skirte.

Loc. 't'. LMN in H16 'Rem'.

106 Item one foreparte of purple Taphata set with Roses of whit Cipers and Cheines betweene of venice golde with a brode passamaine of venice golde unmade and unlined.

Loc. 'T', 't'. LMN in H16 'Rem'. This was a New Year's gift: 'By the Lady Mary Vere a fore parte of purple Taphata set with Roses of white sipers and cheynes betwene of venice golde with a brode pasmane of golde unlyned and unmade. Delivered to Rauf hoope'. (New Year's Gift Roll, 20 Eliz. 1578. Soc. of Antiquaries MS 537, printed in *Progr. Eliz.*, II, p. 72). This apparently did not find favour with the Queen, as it was still unlined and unmade in 1600.

107 Item one foreparte of Carnacion Taphata embrodered allover with Pauncies and leaves.

Loc. 'T', 't'. LMN in H16 'Rem'.

108 Item one foreparte of a kirtle of blacke Taphata laide over⟨th⟩ with networke wrought allover with venice golde silver and spangles Diamondewise.

Loc. 'C', 't'. LMN in H16 'Rem'.

109 Item one foreparte of tawnye taphata with a knitworke of golde sylver and spangles.

Loc. 'T', 't'. LMN in H16 'Rem'.

110 Item one foreparte of Bluncket Taphata covered with a networke of Roses Jellieflowers of golde silver and silke.

Loc. 'T', 't'. LMN in H16 'Rem'.

[111] Scribe's error, item 111 is not listed. There is no extra garment in the PRO inventory.

112 Item one foreparte of orenge colour taphata embrodered upon with Lawne cutworke in knotts of white sylke like fagotts.

Loc. 'T', 't'. LMN in H16 'Rem'.

f.53ᵛ

113 Item one verie lardge foreparte of blacke networke with Cheineworke of venice golde and Crimsen silke and set with spangles with a border of leaves of like golde and silke thedge indented lyned with white taphata.

Loc. 'T', 't'. LMN in H16 'Rem'.

114 Item one foreparte of Networke chaungeable embrodered with roses and flowers of venice golde silver and silke lyned with Crimsen sarceonet.

Loc. 'T', 't'. LMN in H16 'Rem'. This was a New Year's gift: 'By the Lady Hawarde Junior a foreparte of Networke changeable enbrawdred with Flowers like Roses of golde Silver and Sylke, and lyned with crymsen Taphata. Delivered to Rauf hope'. (New Year's Gift Roll, 20 Eliz. 1578. Soc. of Antiquaries MS 537, printed in *Progr. Eliz.*, II, p. 71).

115 Item one foreparte of Networke florished with venice golde spangles and plate of golde like starres Diamondewise with stitched cloth lyned with Murrey sarceonet.

Loc. 'T', 't'. LMN in H16 'Rem'.

116 Item one foreparte of networke ⟨florished⟩ of Murrey silke florished with golde and silver lyned with strawe colour and white sarceonet.

Loc. 'T', 't'. LMN in H16 'Rem'. This was a New Year's gift: 'By Mr Newton a Foreparte of murrye lawne netwourke flourisshed all over with venis golde and silver lyned with Strawe collour and white Sarsonett. Delivered to the said Sir Tho: Gorges'. (New Year's Gift Roll, 30 Eliz. 1588. BL, Add.8159).

117 Item one foreparte of white networke like Roundles and buttons florished with venice golde and owes laide upon purple Satten and lyned with white sarceonet.

Loc. 'T', 't'. LMN in H16 'Rem'. This was a New Year's gift: 'By the Barronesse Rich A fore parte of white nettworke like Rundells and buttons florished with Venis gold and Owes layde upon purple satten and lined with white sarsenett. Delivered to the Roabes'. (New Year's Gift Roll. 31 Eliz. 1589. BL, Lansd. Roll 17, printed in *Progr. Eliz.*, III, p. 7).

118 Item one forepart of white Tincell netted allover wroughte with white roses of lawne with a passamaine of purled golde and silver upon blewe ⟦lyned with white taffeta⟧.

Loc. 'T', 't'. LMN in H16 'Rem'. Addition in H2. This was a New Year's gift: 'By the Countes of Warwike a foreparte of a kirtell of white Tincell allover wrought with whit Roses of lawne with a passamaine of purlid golde and silver upon blewe lined with white Taphata And a rounde kirtell and a Doublet ... Delivered to the said Rauf hoope'. (New Year's Gift Roll, 7 Eliz. 1565. BL, Add.4827). The round kirtle and doublet are listed in the Folger inventory, f. 6ᵛ/7.

119 Item one foreparte of silver Tincell covered with Lawne and set allover with spangles and Butterflies and wormes of silke of sondrye colours.

Loc. 'C', 't'. LMN in H16 'Rem'.

389 *Detail of a cockerel worked in crimson silk on a white linen smock, c.1600. Victoria and Albert Museum, London (T.2–1956)*

f.54

120 Item one forepart of knitworke florished with venice golde and tuffes of Carnacion and watchet silke unlyned.

Loc. 'T', 't'. LMN in H16 'Rem'.

121 Item one foreparte of knitworke florished thicke with spangles of golde.

Loc. 'T', 't'. LMN in H16 'Rem'. This was a New Year's gift: 'By Mr Skydmour A Forparte of white knytworke Floryshed thick with Spangles. Delivered to Rauf Hope'. (New Year's Gift Roll, 27 Eliz. 1585. Folger, Z.d.16).

122 Item one foreparte of white knitworke garnished with plate silver.

Loc. 'C', 't'. LMN in H16 'Rem'.

123 Item one foreparte of white cutworke like roses with a small silver twiste laide diamondewise lyned with silver Chamblet prented.

Loc. 'C', 't'. LMN in H16 'Rem'.

124 Item one foreparte of white cutworke plated diamondeswise with silver ⟦or gowld⟧ plate.

Loc. 'C', 't'. LMN in H16 'Rem'. Addition in H2.

125 Item one foreparte of Needleworke of silke of sondrie colours like flowers lyned with ⟨Murrey⟩ silver Tincell.

Loc. ⟨'T'⟩, 't'. LMN in H16 'Rem'. Alteration in H2.

126 Item one foreparte of Needleworke of silke of sondrie colours like roundles with roses within them lyned with Tincell.

Loc. 'T', 't'. LMN in H16 'Rem'.

127 Item one foreparte of blacke Taphata sarceonet covered with white Lawne with roses of Cipers and some tufts of venice golde and Spangles.

Loc. 'C', 't'. LMN in H16 'Rem'.

f. 54ᵛ

128 Item one foreparte of white sarceonet covered with blacke knitworke embrodered allover with a cheine lace of blacke and greene silke with Roses and honiesuccles of Carnacion silke and silver.

Loc. 'T', 't'. LMN in H16 'Rem'.

129 Item one foreparte of blacke stitched clothe florished with golde like globes lyned with carnacion Satten.

Loc. 'T', 't'. LMN in H16 'Rem'.

130 Item one foreparte of blacke stitched cloth embrodered allover with a twiste of golde and sylver billetwise with leaves laide underneath with tincell and lyned with Carnacion Satten.

Loc. 'T', 't'. LMN in H16 'Rem'. This was a New Year's gift: 'By Mrs Wolley a foreparte of a kertill of blacke stitch clothe Imbrothered all over with a twist of Venus golde and silver layde uppon Tynsell and lyned with Carnation Taffata. Delivered to the said Sir Tho: Gorges'. (New Year's Gift Roll, 30 Eliz. 1588. BL, Add. 8159).

131 Item one foreparte of stitched cloth plated diamondewise in puffes in Cinques of Needleworke.

Loc. 'T', 't'. LMN in H16 'Rem'.

132 Item one foreparte of Cipers embrodered allover with Grapes and leaves of verie small seede pearle and silke of sondrie colours laide underneath with orenge colour Satten lyned with white sarceonet edged with silver lace.

Loc. 'T', 't'. LMN in H16 'Rem'.

133 Item one foreparte of aishe colour Cypers embrodered with sondrie Devises verie faire and Lyons of golde plate.

Loc. 'C', 't'. LMN in H16 'Rem'.

134 Item one foreparte of silver Chamblet verie faire embrodered with golde silver and silke of sondrye colours.

Loc. 'T', 't'. LMN in H16 'Rem'.

135 Item one foreparte of silver Chamblet raized up(pe/pon) allover with workes like leaves embrodered verie richelie.

Loc. ⟨'T'⟩ 'C', 't'. LMN in H16 'Rem'.

f. 55

136 Item one foreparte of silver Chamblet embrodered allover with venice Sylver and owes like leaves and Garlandes.

Loc. 'C', 't'. LMN in H16 'Rem'.

f. 55ᵛ

[No entries]
[One unnumbered folio blank on both sides]

f. 56

Peticoates

1 Firste one Peticoate of Carnacion golde chamblet prented with a ⟨brode⟩ border Crimson Satten embrodered with sondrie Devises.

Loc. 'T', 't'. LMN in H16 'Rem'.

2 Item one Peticoate of golde Chamblet embrodered wth a brode border of Peramydes and flowers betweene them of golde silver and colored silke and owes of golde and silver.

Loc. 'C', 'c'. LMN in H16 'Rem'. This was a New Year's gift: 'By the Lady Southwell one Peticoate of gold chamlett imbrothered with a brode border of p(er)amodes and flowers between them. Delivered to the Robes'. (New Year's Gift Roll, 40 Eliz. 1598. PRO, C47 3/40).

3 Item one Peticoate of silver Chamblet or tabine with works and frenged billetwise with three brode bone laces of venice golde and Spangles.

Loc. 'C', 'c'. LMN in H16 'Rem'.

4 Item one Peticoate of white Chamblet striped with silver prented with a border of six brode bone laces of venice golde and silver plate striped allover brode arroweheaddwise with a lesse lace of like venice golde and silver plate.

Loc. 'T', 't'. LMN in H16 'Rem'. RMN in H9 'bed border'. This was a New Year's gift: 'By the Barrones Dakers A petticote of white chamlett striped with silver printed with A border of vj broade bone laces of venis gold and silver plate and striped all over broade arrowehedwyse, with a lesse lace of like venis gold & silver plate. Delivered to the Roabes'. (New Year's Gift Roll, 31 Eliz. 1589. BL, Lansd. Roll 17, printed in *Progr. Eliz.*, III, p. 6).

5 Item one Peticoate of blacke cloth of silver wrought with blacke white and yellowe silke with a brode border made of bone lace of venice golde and spangles like waves.

Loc. 'T', 't'. LMN in H16 'Rem'.

f. 56ᵛ

6 Item one Peticoate of cloth of silver wrought with Carnacion and yellowe silke with twoe gardes of greene Satten laide with purple lace of golde silver and some small pearle.

Loc. 'T', 't'. LMN in H16 'Rem'.

7 Item one Peticoate of strawe colour cloth of silver with five open laces aboute laide upon watched Taphata.

Loc. 'C', 't'. LMN in H16 'Rem'. The scribe has written 'watched' instead of 'watchet' in this entry.

8 Item one Peticoate of watchet vellat with a brode border embrodered with sondrie flowers of golde and silke of sondrie colours.

Loc. 'T', 't'. LMN in H16 'Rem'.

9 Item one Peticoate of orenge colour vellat prented set with silver owes striped alloverthwart with an open lace of silver.

Loc. 'T', 't'. LMN in H16 'Rem'.

10 Item one Peticoate of Carnacion Satten allover embrodered with golde and silver with a border set with [[seede]] pearles and frenged with golde and silke.

Loc. 'C', 't'. Addition in H2. LMN in H9 'gevene by the Quene the 10 of May at {Richmount} 1601'. Signature 'R. Pamplyn'.

11 Item one Peticoate of purple Satten cut and set with flowers of venice golde embrodered with a small border of golde and silver and frenged with like golde and silver and lyned with Sarceonet.

Loc. 'T', 't'. LMN in H16 'Rem'. This is one of the oldest garments remaining in the Wardrobe of Robes in 1600. The warrant for embroidery gives details of the cost of materials and workmanship: 'Item to David Smyth our Enbrauderer for enbrodering of a peticote of purple satten allover with small flowers of gold and Silver purles lyned with purple gold Sarcenet for workemanship thereof xliij s iiij d. Item for viij oz di of gold and silver purles spente upon the same peticote at vj s viij d thounce lvj s viij d. Item for iij oz of Silke to worke the same peticote withall at ij s thounce vj s'. (Warrant 20 Oct., 4 Eliz. 1562. PRO, LC5/33, ff. 16, 17).

12 Item one Peticoate of Crimson Satten embrodered allover with venice golde and flowers of greene silke.

Loc. 'T', 't'. LMN in H16 'Rem'. This was probably a gift, as it does not appear among the warrants until this entry. 'Fyrste by William Jones our Taylour ... Item for alteringe of a petycoate of Crimsen satten enbraudered alover with venice gold, and makinge a paire of bodies of Crimsen Satten Lyned with Changable Taffata of our great warderob'. (Warrant 27 Sept., 33 Eliz. 1591. PRO, LC5/36, f. 185).

13 Item one Peticoate of Carnacion Satten allover embrodered richlie with venice golde sylver and sylke.

Loc. 'C', 'c'. LMN in H16 'Rem'.

f. 57

14 Item one Peticoate of watchet or blewe Satten embrodered allover with

390 *A woman, possibly Spanish, said to be in North Africa, working on a cushion on her lap. Her skirt is tucked up, perhaps for coolness. She wears a farthingale stiffened with 'ropes of kersey' or some other material, threaded through tucks as in Figures 278, 280 and 281. Her chopines stand on the floor. Engraving by Jan Cornelisz Vermeyen, 1545. Rijksmuseum, Amsterdam*

391 *'Portrait of an unknown lady', painting attributed to William Segar, c.1593–95. She wears what is probably a doublet of white linen embroidered with black silk and gold thread, the tabbed skirts outlined with gold braid. The petticoat is of white ribbed silk with additional silver metal thread in the weft, possibly 'silver chamblet', patterned with tiny black ermine tails, either woven, embroidered or painted. The deep tuck at the front is pinned to the farthingale beneath. Both black velvet loose gown and doublet are decorated with enamelled buttons. Sabin Galleries Limited. London*

flowers and beastes of venice golde silver and silke like a wildernes.

Loc. 'T', 't'. LMN in H16 'Rem'.

15 Item one Peticoate of Carnacion satten allover embroidered skallop facion of bone lace with flowers in them with venice golde and silver set with spangles frenged with like golde and silke lyned with greene sarceonet.

Loc. 'T', 't'. LMN in H16 'Rem'. This was a New Year's gift: 'By Benedicke Spinula a peticoat of carnation Satten allover embrodered with venice golde & silver sett with spangles frenged with a smale freng of like golde & silver lyned with grene sarceonett. Delivered to Rauf Hoope'. (New Year's Gift Roll, 19 Eliz. 1577. PRO, C47/3/39).

16 Item one Peticoate of white Satten razed and edged with a brode embroderie of divers colours.

Loc. 'T', 't'. LMN in H16 'Rem'. This was a New Year's gift: 'By the Lady Margret Countes of Darby, a petticote of white Satten, reysed and edged with a brode embrawdery of Divers collours. Delivered to Rauf Hoope, yoman of the Roobes'. (New Year's Gift Roll, 20 Eliz. 1578. Soc. of Antiquaries MS 537, printed in *Progr. Eliz.*, II, p. 65).

17 Item one Peticoate of yellowe Satten laide allover like waves with a passamaine of venice silver and tawnye silke frenged with silver and silke lyned with tawnie Sarceonett.

Loc. 'T', 't'. LMN in H16 'Rem'. This was a New Year's gift: 'By the Lorde Cobham a petticote of yelow Satten leyed allover with a pasmane of Silver and tawnye sylke frenged with Silver and sylke and lyned with tawny Serceonet. Delivered to Rauf hoope'. (New Year's Gift Roll, 20 Eliz. 1578. Soc. of Antiquaries MS 537, printed in *Progr. Eliz.*, II, p. 70).

18 Item one Peticoate of Tawney Satten razed allover with fower borders of embroderie of venice silver and ⟨gardes of⟩ with Lypes lyned with orenge colour sarceonet.

Loc. 'C', 'c'. LMN in H16 'Rem'. This was a New Year's gift: 'By the Lady Dacres of the South a pettycote of Tawny Satten reysed with iiij borders of enbrawdery Silver and golde with hoopes lyned with orenge collored Sarceonet. Delivered to Rauf hope'. (New Year's Gift Roll, 20 Eliz. 1578. Soc. of Antiquaries MS 537, printed in *Progr. Eliz.*, II, p. 71). The embroidery motif is given here as 'hoopes', but this apparently should be 'lypes'. The embroidery with lips should be compared with f. 93/1 where a pair of pantobles are embroidered with hands and eyes.

19 Item one Peticoate of Watchet Satten laide allover with a bone lace of venice golde and silver and gardes of passamaine

392   *Slip of gillyflower, pink or carnation, detail from the top of a white linen smock embroidered with polychrome silks, c. 1585–1600. Whitworth Art Gallery, Manchester*

393   *Detail of gillyflower, pink or carnation, embroidered in straw on crimson velvet, early seventeenth century. Museo Parmigianino, Reggio Emilia*

of like golde and silver bounde aboute lyned with yellowe Taphata.

Loc. 'T', 'C' written on top of each other, 't'. LMN in H16 'Rem'. This was a New Year's gift: 'By Benedic Spynnala a petticote of watchet Satten leyed alover with pasman lace of golde and sylver and Flowers with viij gardes of pasman of golde and Silver rownde abowte it lyned with yelo Taphata. Delivered to Rauf hoope'. (New Year's Gift Roll, 20 Eliz. 1578. Soc. of Antiquaries MS 537, printed in *Progr. Eliz.*, II, p. 78).

20   Item one Peticoate of White Satten embroidered allover with Roses of venice golde and plate lace with three gardes likewise Embroidered.

Loc. 'T', 't'. LMN in H16 'Rem'. This was a New Year's gift: 'By the Lady Barones Morley, a pettycote of white satten all over embrawdred with roses of golde; and 3 gards likewyse enbrawdred, lyned with white satten, and frenged with sylke and golde. Delivered to the forsaid Rauf Hope'. (New Year's Gift Roll, 21 Eliz. 179. Folger, Z.d.15, printed in *Progr. Eliz.*, II, p. 255).

f. 57ᵛ

21   Item one Peticoate of Carnacion Satten embroidered with pauncies and flowers of silke of sondrie colours with a brode border made with laces and twist of golde and silver and spangles.

Loc. 'T', 't'. LMN in H16 'Rem'. This was a New Year's gift: 'By the Lady Crofts, a peticote of carnation satten, enbrawderid with flowers of silke of sondry collours. Delivered to the same Rauf Hoope'. (New Year's Gift Roll, 21 Eliz. 1579. Folger, Z.d.15, printed in *Progr. Eliz.*, II, p. 256).

22   Item one Peticoate of yellowe Satten embroidered allover with dropps and with a brode border of venice sylver purle and twiste lyned with Carnacion Taphata sarceonet.

Loc. 'T', 't'. LMN in H16 'Rem'.

23   Item one peticoate of white Satten embroidered with a deepe border of Trees of venice golde silver and greene silke lined with Murrey sarcenet.

Loc. 'T', 't'. LMN in H16 'Rem'.

24   Item one peticoate of peach colour satten embroidered verie faire with flowers of venice golde silver and silke of divers colours.

Loc. 'C', 'c'. LMN in H16 'Rem'. This was a New Year's gift: 'By therle of Hertford a pettycote of peche collored Satten embrawdred alover verey Feyer with Flowers of venice golde Silver and Sylke of divers collors. Delivered to Rauf Hope Yoman of the robes'. (New Year's Gift Roll, 26 Eliz. 1584. BL, Egerton 3052, printed in *Costume* 9, 1975, p. 28).

25   Item one peticoate of Horseflesh colour satten embroidered allover with twists of venice golde and sylver.

Loc. 'T', 't'. LMN in H16 'Rem'.

26   Item one peticoate of bluncket Sat-ten allover embroidered with a small twiste of venice golde the border aboute it with like enbroderie and frenged with golde and silver.

Loc. 'T', 't'. LMN in H16 'Rem'. This was a New Year's gift: 'By Mr Wolley a pettycote of Blunkett Satten alover enbradored with a smale

Twiste of venys gold and iij borders about yt of lyke enbradere and frenged with golde and sylver. Delivered to Ra. hope'. (New Year's Gift Roll, 26 Eliz. 1584. BL, Egerton 3052, printed in *Costume* 9, 1975, p. 30).

27   Item one peticoate of Murrey Satten wrought with golde and three brode borders of white Satten embroidered with venice sylver and purle.

Loc. 'T', 't'. LMN in H16 'Rem'. This was New Year's gift: 'By Mr Dyer a pettycote of murre satten wrought with golde and iij brode borders of white satten enbradored with venyce gold silver and purle. Delivered to Ra. Hope'. (New Year's Gift Roll, 26 Eliz. 1584. BL, Egerton 3052, printed in *Costume* 9, 1975, p. 30).

f. 58

28   Item one peticoate of watchet Satten embroidered allover with knots of lace of venice sylver and tufts of sylke.

Loc. 'C', 't'. LMN in H16 'Rem'. This was a New Year's gift: 'By Mr Dyer A pettycoate of watched Satten Imbraudered all over with knottes of Lace of venis Sylver with tuftes of sylke of Colers. Delivered to Raufe hope'. (New Year's Gift Roll, 27 Eliz. 1585. Folger, Z.d.16).

29   Item one peticoate of orenge colour Satten embroidered allover with a twiste of venice silver owes with fower borders of watchett satten enbroidered like leaves lyned with watchet sarceonet.

Loc. 'T', 't'. LMN in H16 'Rem'.

30   Item one peticoate of Murrey satten allover embroidered with Esses of venice silver and golde and the border beneath

embrodered with beasts and fowles of like golde and silver lyned with yellow taphata.

Loc. 'T', 't'. LMN in H16 'Rem'.

31 Item one peticoate of Carnacion satten embroidered allover with satten and venice sylver billetwise with three <broders> borders of white satten embrodered with venice [[gold]] sylver and silke lyned with Carnacion sarceonet.

Loc. 'T', 't'. LMN in H16 'Rem'. Addition in H2.

32 Item one peticoate of strawe colour satten with knots of venice silver and watchet sylke with owes and tufts of like silke with five laces of plate & silver.

Loc. 'T', 't'. LMN in H16 'Rem'.

33 Item one peticoate of white Satten cut laide Chevernwise with a golde plate lace and fyve open laces of golde and plate <lace> lyned with strawe colour sarceonet.

Loc. 'T', 't'. LMN in H16 'Rem'.

34 Item one peticoate of orenge colour satten cut striped overthwart with a small lace of venice sylver and five brode laces of sylver and plate.

Loc. 'C', 't'. LMN in H16 'Rem'. This was probably a gift, as it does not appear among the warrants until this entry: 'Fyrste to William Jones our Tayloure . . . Item for alteringe of a petycoat of Orrendge colour Satten laced alover with Silver lace, newe lyned with Sarcenett of our greate warderob'. (Warrant 28 Sept., 34 Eliz. 1592. PRO, LC5/36, f. 218).

f. 58ᵛ

35 Item one Peticoate of white satten embroidered allover with blacke flies with a border of fountaines and Trees embrodered rounde aboute it and waves of the Sea.

Loc. 'T', 't'. LMN in H16 'Rem'.

36 Item one peticoate of Sea water greene Satten embroidered allover with flowers like Lilliepotts of [[gold]] silver and sylke.

Loc. 'T', 't'. LMN in H16 'Rem'. Addition in H2. This was a New Year's gift: 'By the Countys of Lyncolne Widdowe A Peticoate of Sea water greene Satten Imbrothered all over with Flowers in lillye pottes of venus golde, silver and silke. Delivered to the said Sir Thomas Gorges'. (New Year's Gift Roll, 30 Eliz. 1588. BL. Add.8159).

37 Item one Peticoate of heare colour Satten embroidered allover with leaves of golde silver and silke and a brode border enbrodered with flowers birdes and a fewe seede pearle.

Loc. 'C', 'c'. LMN in H16 'Rem' <'Rem'>. This was a New Year's gift: 'By the Countys of Bedforde A peticoate of heare colloured Satten Imbrothered all over with leaves of Venus golde silver and silke with a Broade Border

394 *Detail of gillyflower, pink or carnation, embroidered with black silk and enriched with gold thread, on white linen, c. 1585–90. Royal Museum of Scotland, Edinburgh*

Imbrothered with Flowers Byrdes and a fewe pearles. Delivered to the saide Sir Tho: Gorges'. (New Year's Gift Roll, 30 Eliz. 1588. BL, Add.8159).

38 Item one Peticoate of sea water greene Satten embroidered allover with knotts and Trees like holly bushes of golde silver and silke.

Loc. 'T', 't'. LMN in H16 <'Rem'> and in H9 'geven by her majesties commandment the 3 of Aprell'. Signature 'R. Pamplyn'. This was a New Year's gift: 'By Mr Wolley one of her majesties Secretaries a Peticoate of Sea water greene satten Imbrothered all over with knottes and Trees like holly Busshes of venus golde silver and silke. Delivered to the said Sir Tho: Gorges'. (New Year's Gift Roll, 30 Eliz. 1588. BL, Add.8159).

39 Item one Peticoate of Carnacion Satten embroidered allover with venice golde and Silver with a narrowe border likewise embroidered.

Loc. 'T', 't'. LMN in H16 'Rem'. This was a New Year's gift: 'By the Countys of Comberlande a Peaticote of Carnation Satten Imbrothered all over with venus golde and silver with a narrowe Border likewise Imbrothered. Delivered to the said Sir Tho: Gorges'. (New Year's Gift Roll, 30 Eliz. 1588. BL, Add.8159).

40 Item one Peticoate of Carnacion Satten embroidered with a plate and purles of golde and a border embroidered with pearle.

Loc. 'T', 't'. LMN in H16 'Rem'. This was a New Year's gift: 'By the Ladye Walsingham a peticoate of Carnation satten Imbrothered all over with a plate and purles of golde, and a

broade Border fayre Imbrothered. Delivered to the said Sir Tho: Gorges'. (New Year's Gift Roll, 30 Eliz. 1588. BL, Add.8159).

41 Item one Peticoate of Carnacion Satten embroidered with a brode garde or border of antiques of flowers and fishes of venice golde silver and sylke and allover with a twiste of venice golde.

Loc. 'C', 't'. LMN in H16 'Rem'. This was a joint New Year's gift: 'By the Countesse of Ormount parte of a petticote of Carnacon satten ymbrodered with a broade garde or border of Antickes of flowers and fishes of venis gold silver and all over with a twist of venis gold. Delivered to the Roabes'. The other part was given by her husband, the Earl of Ormond (New Year's Gift Roll, 31 Eliz. 1589. BL, Lansd. Roll 17, printed in *Progr. Eliz.*, III, pp. 2, 3).

42 Item one Peticoate of white Satten quilted allover with knotts of venice golde and silver with some plates with fower borders embroidered with Jellieflowers and roses of venice golde.

Loc. 'T', 't'. LMN in H16 'Rem'. This was a New Year's gift: 'By Mr Dyer, a petticote of white satten quilted all over with venis gold and silver with some plates with iiij borders embroidered with gillyflowers and Roses of venis gold and lyned with white sarsenett. Delivered to the Robbes'. (New Year's Gift Roll, 31 Eliz. 1589. BL, Lansd. Roll 17, printed in *Progr. Eliz.*, III, p. 12).

f. 59

43 Item one Peticoate of Dove colour Satten embroidered with a twiste of venice silver and syxe small borders embroidered with flowers of like silver.

Loc. 'C', 'c'. LMN in H16 'Rem'.

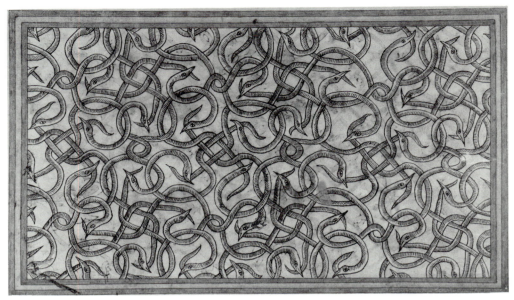

395 *Design of interlaced snakes, or serpents, detail from page 253ᵛ of Thomas Trevelyon's 'Miscellany', a book of embroidery patterns, 1608. This may have been used for the Queen's petticoat of white satin 'embroidered allover slightlie with snakes of venice golde'. Folger Shakespeare Library, Washington, D.C.*

44   Item one Peticoate of heare colour Satten cut laced bias with venice silver and Carnacion silke lace and fyve border laces of silke and sylver.

Loc. 'T', 't'. LMN in H16 'Rem'.

45   Item one Peticoate of Crimsen satten richelie embroidered allover with squares of plate and purle of Damaske golde and roses of venice ⟦golde silver and silke⟧.

Loc. 'T', 't'. LMN in H16 'Rem'. Addition in H2.

46   Item one Peticoate of whyte Satten embroidered allover slightlie with snakes of venice golde silver and some owes with a faire border embroidered like Seas Cloudes and Raine bowes.

Loc. 'T', 't'. LMN in H16 'Rem'.

47   Item one peticoate of Carnacion Satten tissued with sylver bounde aboute with tufted silver lace.

Loc. 'C', 't'. LMN in H16 'Rem'.

48   Item one peticoate of Issabella colour satten prented and cut laide allover with a lace of venice silver in waves and beneath with fyve brode and fower narrowe laces of venice silver and plate.

Loc. 'C', 'c'. LMN in H16 'Rem'.

49   Item one peticoate of Claie colour Satten embroidered allover with roses and grapes with three brode borders likewise embroidered.

Loc. 'C', 'c'. LMN in H16 'Rem'.

f. 59ᵛ

50   Item one Peticoate of heare colour Satten embroidered allover with a small twiste of silke and golde like knotts Diamondewise with starres in the myddest and a brode border embroidered with flowers and Beastes and a traile of seede pearle.

Loc. 'C', 'c'. LMN in H16 'Rem'.

51   Item one Peticoate of peache colour Satten embroidered allover with a faire brode border of like embroderie of venice golde sylver and silke.

Loc. 'T', 't'. LMN in H16 'Rem'.

52   Item one Peticoate of heare colour Satten embroidered allover with wormes and Butterflies and with a faire border likewise embroidered and some pearle in it.

Loc. 'C', 't'. LMN in H16 'Rem'.

53   Item one Peticoate of white Turquye Satten embroidered allover with a twiste of venice golde and owes like knotts.

Loc. 'T', 't'. LMN in H16 'Rem'.

54   Item one Peticoate of white Satten embroidered allover with stalkes of vyne leaves and grapes and honyesuccles of venice golde silver and Sylke.

Loc. 'C', 'c'. LMN in H16 'Rem'.

55   Item one Peticoate of Murrey Satten faire embroidered allover and a broade border of flowers of venice golde silver and Silke.

Loc. 'T', 't'. RMN in H10 'tg gevene by hir majestie [to] Lady marques. The initials 'tg' are those of Sir Thomas Gorges. Cf. f. 37ᵛ/7, f. 38ᵛ/27, f. 39/34 and f. 60ᵛ/69.

56   Item a Peticoate of white Satten embroidered allover with venice golde &

Silver with a faire border and frenge of venice golde set within thedge.

Loc. 'T', 't'. LMN in H16 'Rem'.

57   Item one Peticoate of Carnacion Satten embroidered allover with a worke like roses and other flowers.

Loc. 'T', 't'. LMN in H16 'Rem'.

f. 60

58   Item one Peticoate of white Satten embroidered allover like peramydes and flowers of venice golde and silke.

Loc. 'C', 't'. LMN in H16 'Rem'.

59   Item one Peticoate of pincke colour Satten embroidered allover with workes of roses grapes and leaves and ⟨fower⟩ three borders aboute of like embroderie.

Loc. 'T', 'c'. LMN in H16 'Rem'.

60   Item one Peticoate of white Satten embroidered allover with braunches of venice golde and silke of sondrie colours with a faire border rounde aboute.

Loc. 'T', 't'. LMN in H16 'Rem'.

61   Item one Peticoate of white Satten embroidered allover with venice golde silver and silke of dyvers colours with a verie faire border of pomegranetts pyne aple trees frutidge and the nyne Muses in the same border.

Loc. 'C', 'c'. LMN in H16 'Rem'.

62   Item one Peticoate of white Satten embroidered with venice golde silver and silke of dyvers colours like frutidge and silver owes and watchet silke like starres and three borders likewise embroidered.

Loc. 'C', 'c'. LMN in H16 'Rem'.

63   Item one Peticoate of white Satten embroidered allover with a runninge worke of roses and three brode borders likewise embroidered with flowers of sondrie kindes of venice golde silver and silke of colours.

Loc. 'C', 'c'. LMN in H16 'Rem'.

64   Item one Peticoate of pincked colour Satten embroidered allover with venice golde having three borders of venice golde likewise embroidered.

Loc. 'C', 't'. LMN in H16 'Rem'.

f. 60ᵛ

65   Item one Peticoate of white Satten enbroidered allover with leaves and flowers of venice golde and silke and three borders likewise embroidered all the leaves beinge greene.

Loc. 'T', 't'. LMN in H16 'Rem'.

66   Item one peticoate of Claie colour Satten razed with a brode border of venice silver plate like peramydes.

396   *A woman representing Astrology, with the sun, crescent moon, stars and an armillary or celestial sphere, detail from a polychrome embroidered white satin panel, probably part of a skirt, c. 1600. Victoria and Albert Museum, London (T.138–1981)*

397   *Detail from Queen Elizabeth's petticoat in Figure 129. Painting by an unknown artist, possibly 1599. The white silk is embroidered here with a snake, flowers, whale, butterfly and kingfisher. National Trust, Hardwick Hall, Derbyshire*

Loc. 'C', 't'. LMN in H10 'gevene by hir majestie at grenwich the 12 of May 1602'. Signature 'R. Pamplyn'. This was a New Year's gift: 'By the Lady Walsingham one Peticoate of clay coloured satten rased with a broade border of Venis silver plate like a p(er)umedes. Delivered to the Robes'. (New Year's Gift Roll, 40 Eliz. 1598. PRO, C47/3/40).

67   Item one peticoate of Mayden blush Satten embrodered allover with flowers and devyses of venice golde and silver like arches & peramydes.

Loc. 'C', 'c'. LMN in H16 'Rem'. This was a New Year's gift: 'By Sir William Knolles Comptroller of her Majesties househoulde one Peticoate of maidenblushe satten imbrodered all over with flowers and devises of Venis golde and silver. Delivered to the Robes'. (New Year's Gift Roll, 40 Eliz. 1598. PRO, C47/3/40).

68   Item one peticoate of Isabella colour satten embrodered allover with braunches of silver owes and three brode borders of silver.

Loc. 'C', 'c'. LMN in H13 'Sent to the quene'. This margin note probably refers to Queen Anne of Denmark rather than Queen Elizabeth. This was a joint New Year' gift: 'By the Lady Elizabeth Somerset wief to Sir Henry Gilford parte of a Petticote of Clay colored satten embrothered all over with branches of owes & three brode borders of venyce silver. Delivered to the Robes. (New Year's Gift Roll, 41 Eliz. 1599. Folger, Z.d.17). Her husband gave the other part. 'Isabella' was also described as clay colour, cf. f. 24ᵛ/100, and flaxseed colour cf. f. 37ᵛ/9.

69   Item one peticoate of Carnacion Satten embrodered allover with a worke like Cloudes and Peramydes.

Loc. 'C'. RMN in H10 'tg gevene by hir majestie [to] Lady marques'. The initials tg are those of Sir Thomas Gorges. Cf. f. 37ᵛ/7, f. 38ᵛ/27, f. 39/34 and f. 59ᵛ/55. This was a New Year's gift: 'By the Lady Walsingham widowe one pettycoate of Carnacyon satten embrothered all over like Clowdes hopes and peramydes. Delivered to the Robes'. (New Year's Gift Roll, 41 Eliz. 1599. Folger, Z.d.17).

70   Item one peticoate of white Satten embrodered allover with twiste of golde and a brode border of golde and silke like pyneap[p]les frutidge and ⟨peramides⟩ ⟦paunceis⟧.

Loc. 'C', 'c'. LMN in H16 'Rem'. Alteration in H2.

71   Item one Nether skirts of a peticoate of white Satten embrodered alover like fountaines and flowers with a brode border likewise embrodered.

Loc. 'C', 't'. LMN in H16 'Rem'. This was a New Year's gift: 'By Sir Thomas Jarratt the Nether skirtes of a pettycote of white satten embrothered all over like fountaynes and flowers with a broade border likewise embrothered. Delivered to the Robes'. (New Year's Gift Roll, 41 Eliz. 1599. Folger, Z.d.17).

72   Item one Peticoate of white Satten embrodered allover with trailes of golde twiste and garlandes of coloured silke and golde with a faire border embrodered like frutidge.

Loc. 'C', 't'. LMN in H16 'Rem'. This was a New Year's gift: 'By the Counteis of Southampton widowe one Pettycoate of white satten embrodered all over with trayles of golde twysted and garlandes of Colored silke and golde with a faire border ymbrothered lyke frutage. Delivered to the Robes'. (New Year's Gift Roll, 41 Eliz. 1599. Folger, Z.d.17).

f. 61

73   Item one peticoate of white Satten cut and tufted embrodered allover like starres of golde and Carnacion silke in tufts with three borders like buttons.

Loc. 'C', 't'. LMN in H16 'Rem'. This was a New Year's gift: 'By the Lady Harington one pettycote of white satten cut & tufted embrothered all over like starres of golde owes & Carnacion silke tuftes. Delivered to the Robes'. (New Year's Gift Roll, 41 Eliz. 1599. Folger, Z.d.17).

74   Item one peticoate of white Satten embrodered allover with flies and braunches with a faire broade border enbrodered like Cloudes Sunbeames and Rockes.

Loc. 'C', 'c'. LMN in H16 'Rem'. This was a New Year's gift: 'By the Lady Walsingham, widowe, one pettycote of white satten, embrothered all over with flyes and branches, with a broade border. Delivered to the Robes'. (New Year's Gift Roll, 42 Eliz. 1600. Printed in *Progr. Eliz.*, III, p. 453).

398   *Detail of pansy, embroidered with black silk and enriched with gold thread, on white linen, c. 1585–90. Royal Museum of Scotland, Edinburgh*

75   Item one peticoate of Claie colour Satten embroidered allover with braunches of silver and a broade border embroidered in some places like Cloudes and ⟨frear⟩ fearne brakes.

Loc. 'C', 'c'. LMN in H16 'Rem'. This was a joint New Year's gift: 'By the Lady Walsingham, junior, parte of a pettycote of clay-color satten, embrothered all over with branches of silver. Delivered to the Robes'. (New Year's Gift Roll, 42 Eliz. 1600. Printed in *Prog. Eliz.*, III, p. 453). Her husband, Sir Thomas Walsingham, gave the other part.

76   Item one peticoate of white Satten enbrodered allover like grapes and pyne aples and a verie brode border likewise faire enbrodered.

Loc. 'C', 'c'. LMN in H16 'Rem'. This was a New Year's gift: 'By Sir Edward Dyer one pettycote of white satten embrothered all over like grapes and pyne-apples and a very broade border likewise embrothered. Delivered to the Robes'. (New Year's Gift Roll, 42 Eliz. 1600. Printed in *Prog. Eliz.*, III, p. 454).

77   Item one Peticoate of white Satten embrodered allover like feathers and billetts with three broade borders faire embrodered with snakes and frutidge.

Loc. 'C', 't'. LMN in H16 'Rem'. This was a New Year's gift: 'By Mr Frauncis Bacon, one pettycote of white satten embrothered all over like feathers and billets, with three brode borders, faire embrothered with snakes and frutage. Delivered to the Robes'. (New Year's Gift Roll, 42 Eliz. 1600. Printed in *Prog. Eliz.*, III, p. 457).

78   Item one peticoate of white Satten embrodered allover with peramydes pillers

and Muses in cloudes with a faire broade border embroidered like clouds and pavillions of venice golde silver and silke of sondrie colours.

Loc. 'T', 't'. LMN in H16 'Rem'.

79   Item one peticoate of white Satten embroidered allover with Rockes fishes and such like with a broade border like cloudes Seas fishes and Rockes of venice golde silver and silke of sondrie colours.

Loc. 'T', 't'. LMN in H16 'Rem'.

f. 61ᵛ

80   Item one Peticoate of white Satten embroidered allover with a runninge worke of venice golde and silke and golde owes with three borders of roses Pauntsies and peramydes.

Loc. 'T', 't'. LMN in H16 'Rem'.

81   Item one Peticoate of watchet Satten embroidered allover with Rainebowes and cloudes with a broade border embroidered like pillers and grapes wyndinge upon braunches.

Loc. 'T', 't'. LMN in H16 'Rem'.

82   Item one peticoate of spanishe Taphata of colours with twoe gardes of white Satten embroidered with flowers and leaves of golde silver and silke.

Loc. 'T', 't'. LMN in H16 'Rem'.

83   Item one Peticoate of Carnacion Taphata embroidered allover with a twist of venice silver.

Loc. 'T', 't'. LMN in H16 'Rem'. This was a New Year's gift: 'By the Baronesse Paggett Care

one peaticoate of Carnation Taffata Imbrothered all over with Twist of venus silver and a Dublett of white satten cut all over in leaves and lyned with Carnation Flusshe. Delivered to the said Sir Tho: Gorges'. (New Year's Gift Roll, 30 Eliz. 1588. BL, Add.8159). The doublet seems to be that entered in the Folger inventory, f. 16/32, where 'Flusshe' is spelt 'plushe'.

84   Item one peticoate of Carnacion Taphata embroidered with a broade border of venice golde and allover with a twiste of like golde.

Loc. 'T', 't'. LMN in H16 'Rem'. This was a New Year's gift: 'By the Ladye Longe a peticoate of Carnation Taffata Imbrothered with a broade Border of Venus golde silver and silke and all over with a Twist of like golde. Delivered to the said Sir Tho: Gorges'. (New Year's Gift Roll, 30 Eliz. 1588. BL, Add.8159).

85   Item one Peticoate of white Taphata sarceonet embroidered allover like leaves of venice golde and Carnacion sylke.

Loc. 'C', 't'. LMN in H16 'Rem'.

86   Item one peticoate of spanishe Taphata Chaungeable striped with silver tufted with Carnacion and bluncket sylke.

Loc. 'C', 'c'. LMN in H16 'Rem'.

87   Item one peticoate of heare colour Taphata sarceonet embroidered allover with twist of venice golde and some owes.

Loc. 'C', 't'. LMN in H16 'Rem'. The PRO inventory gives 'with a twiste'.

[88] Scribe's error, item 88 not listed. There is no extra garment in the PRO inventory.

f. 62

89   Item one peticoate of strawe colour Taphata sarceonet embroidered allover with a twiste of venice silver and watchet silke and silver owes.

Loc. 'T', 'c'. LMN in H16 'Rem'.

90   Item one Peticoate of strawe colour sarceonet quilted allover and frenged with venice silver and blewe silke.

Loc. 't'. LMN in H16 'Rem'. This was a New Year's gift: 'By Mrs Abyngdon a petycoate of sarceonet quilted lined with white Flannell and frenged with venice golde and blewe silke. Deliverid to the said Rauf hoope'. (New Year's Gift Roll, 7 Eliz. 1565. BL, Add.4827).

91   Item one peticoate of Carnacion sarceonet quilted with fyve borders of greene silke and owes of golde.

Loc. 'T', 't'. LMN in H16 'Rem'.

92   Item one Peticoate of white sarceonet embrodered allover with a Cordaunte of golde and three narrowe borders likewise embroidered with golde and some blewe silke like flowers.

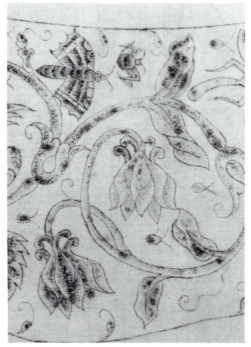

399 *Moth and columbines, detail from white linen sleeve embroidered in black silk in Figure 156. Victoria and Albert Museum, London*

400 *Detail of daffodil embroidered with black silk and enriched with gold thread, on white linen, c. 1585–90. Royal Museum of Scotland, Edinburgh*

Loc. 'T', 'c'. LMN in H16 'Rem'. This was a New Year's gift: 'By Sir Thomas Layton Capitayne of Garnesey one peticoate of white Sarsonet Imbrothered all over with a Cordaunt of venus golde, and three narrowe Borders likewise Imbrothered with Venus golde and some blewe silke like Flowers. Delivered to the said Sir Tho: Gorges'. (New Year's Gift Roll, 30 Eliz. 1588. BL, Add.8159).

93 Item one peticoate of white sarceonet embroidered rounde aboute with a broade border like Eglantine flowers and allover embroidered with a twiste of venice golde and powderings of Carnacion silke.

Loc. 'T', 'c'. LMN in H16 'Rem'. This was a New Year's gift: 'By Sir Thomas Layton Capteine of Garnsey A petticote of white sarsnett Imbrodered round about with a broade border like Eglantyne flowers and all over ymbrodered with a twist of venis gold and powderinges of Carnation silke. Delivered to the Roabes'. (New Year's Gift Roll, 31 Eliz. 1589. BM, Lansd. Roll 17, printed in *Progr. Eliz.*, III, p. 9). Sir Thomas's gift in the previous year (f. 62/92) must have found favour with the Queen.

94 Item one peticoate of white taphata sarceonet enbrodered allover with leaves of venice golde and Carnacion silke and owes and greene leaves in the border.

Loc. 'C', 't'. LMN in H16 'Rem'.

95 Item one peticoate of white sarceonet embroidered allover with venice golde and silver and silke like roses and feathers.

Loc. 'T', 't'. LMN in H16 'Rem'.

96 Item one peticoate of white sarceonet embroidered allover with a twiste of venice golde and Carnacion silke.

Loc. 'C', 'c'. LMN in H16 'Rem'. This was a New Year's gift: 'By Sir Thomas Leighton one Peticoate of white Sercionet imbrothered all over with carnation silke and golde. Delivered to the Robes'. (New Year's Gift Roll, 40 Eliz. 1598. PRO, C47/3/40).

f. 62ᵛ

97 Item one peticoate of white sarceonet embroidered allover with a small twiste of venice golde of a runninge worke like Daffadillies.

Loc. 'C', 't'. LMN in H16 'Rem'.

98 Item one Peticoate of white sarceonet quilted enbrodered allover with venice golde sylver and orenge colour silke.

Loc. 'T', 't'. LMN in H16 'Rem'.

99 Item one Peticoate of pale or Claie colour sarceonet embroidered allover with silver and a broade border likewyse embroidered with Candellstickes of venice golde upon sea greene silke.

Loc. 'C', 't'. LMN in H16 'Rem'.

100 Item one Peticoate of white sarceonet quilted allover with a small threede of venice golde and silke of colours with flowers and feathers embroidered with Carnacion watchet and grene silke with three borders rounde aboute embroidered with pauncies roses and pillers.

Loc. 'C', 't'. LMN in H16 'Rem'.

101 Item one Peticoate of white sarceonet embroidered allover with a runninge worke of venice silver and Carnacion silke twist with a border likewise embroidered.

Loc. 'C', 't'. LMN in H16 'Rem'.

102 Item one Petycoate of white sarceonet embroidered allover with Sonnes and Cloudes of golde and silver and a brode border rounde aboute with venice golde silver and silke of sondrie colours.

Loc. 'T', 't'. LMN in H16 'Rem'.

103 Item one Petycoate of white sarceonet embroidered allover with carnacion and blewe silke and silver with an Indented skirte.

Loc. <'T' 'C'>, 't'. LMN in H16 'Rem'.

f. 63

104 Item one Petycoate withoute bodies of white sarceonet embroidered allover with venice sylver plate and some Carnacion silke like Columbynes.

Loc. 'C', 't'. LMN in H16 'Rem'. This was a New Year's gift: 'By the Earle of Cumberland, one pettycote of white sarcenett, embrothered all over with Venyce silver plate, and some carnacon silke like colombines. Delivered to the Robes'. (New Year's Gift Roll, 42 Eliz. 1600. Printed in *Progr. Eliz.*, III, p. 446).

105 Item one Petycoate of white sarceonet embroidered allover with venice golde silver and silke of sondrie colours

401, 402   *Six trees with the sun behind them, and a flagon with dolphins at the base, two details from a polychrome embroidered white satin panel, probably part of a skirt, c. 1600. Victoria and Albert Museum, London (T.138–1981)*

like peramides with three borders likewise embrodered.

Loc. 'T', 't'. LMN in H16 'Rem'. This was a New Year's gift: 'By the Barronnes Chandoes Knowlys, one pettycote of white sarcenett, embrothered all over with Venice gold, silver and silke of dyverse colors like peramydes, with three borders likewise embrothered. Delivered to the Robes'. (New Year's Gift Roll, 42 Eliz. 1600. Printed in *Progr. Eliz.*, III, p. 451).

106   Item one Petycoate of withoute bodies of sarceonet embrodered allover with a twiste of venice silver and owes like true loves Indented in the skirte.

Loc. 'T', 't'. LMN in H16 'Rem'. This was a New Year's gift: 'By the Barronnes Sheiffeilde Stafforde, one pettycote without bodyes of sarcnet, embrothered all over with a twyste of Venyce silver and owes. Delivered to the Robes'. (New Year's Gift Roll, 42 Eliz. 1600. Printed in *Progr. Eliz.*, p. 451). The scribe should have deleted 'of' in the first line.

107   Item one Petycoate of pale pincke colour sarceonet embrodered allover with a twiste of venice golde and heare colour

silke with three borders embroidered with roses and paunceis of venice golde and silke.

Loc. 'C', 't'. LMN in H16 'Rem'. This was a New Year's gift: 'By the Baronnes Katheryn Cornewalles one pettycote of pyncke Colored sarcenet embrothered all over with a Twiste of venyce golde. Delivered to the Robes'. (New Year's Gift Roll, 41 Eliz. 1599. Folger, Z.d.17).

108   Item one Petycoate of beasar colour sarceonet embroidered allover with vyne leaves and grapes with three borders embroidered like flames of venice golde.

Loc. 'C', 'c'. LMN in H16 'Rem'.

109   Item one Peticoate of orenge colour tufte Taphata the grounde sylver with sixe plate laces of venice silver.

Loc. 'C', 'c'. LMN in H9 'geven to M[r]s Hide the 7 of January 1602 by the Quene'. Illegible signature {'Luce Hide'}.

110   Item one Petycoate of whyte tufte Taphata the grounde silver with fyve broad spangle laces of venice silver set upon orenge colour Taphata.

Loc. 'C', 't'. LMN in H16 'Rem'. RMN in H11 {'bed chamber'}.

f. 63ᵛ

111   Item one Petycoate of Murrey tufte taphata the grounde silver with three broade plate laces with spangles set upon Bluncket Taphata.

Loc. 'T', 't'. LMN in H16 'Rem'.

112   Item one Petycoate of white tufte Taphata the grounde silver with three bone laces of venice golde and sylver set upon orenge tawnie taphata.

Loc. 'C', {'c'}. RMN in H11 'bede chamber'. This was a New Year's gift: 'By Sir Edward Hobby one Peticoate of white tuft taffata the grounde silver with three boane laces of Venis gold and silver sett upon Carnation silke. Delivered to the Robes'. (New Year's Gift Roll, 40 Eliz. 1598. PRO, C47/3/40).

113   Item one Petycoate of watchet plush striped with golde lace.

Loc. 'T', 't'. LMN in H16 'Rem'.

114 Item one Peticoate of white and orenge colour plush striped overthwarte with venice sylver lace.

Loc. 'T', 't'. LMN in H16 'Rem'. This was a New Year's gift: 'By the Baronesse Dakers a Peticoate of white and Oring tawny Flusshe striped with lace of venus silver over thwarte. Delivered to the said Sir Tho: Gorges'. (New Year's Gift Roll, 30 Eliz. 1588. BL, Add.8159). 'Flusshe' is either an alternative way of spelling 'plushe' or a scribe's error in copying the entry. It is spelt in this way four times in the Gift Roll of 1588, cf. f. 61ᵛ/83, f. 63ᵛ/14, f. 31/21.

115 Item one Peticoate of whyte watchet and Carnacion plush cut in triangle lozenges and a bonelace betweene them of golde and silver havinge syxe broade bone laces on the border of like golde and sylver.

Loc. 'T', 't'. LMN in H16 'Rem'. This was a New Year's gift: 'By Mr Dyer one peticoate of white watched and Carnation plus[h]e cut in tryangles lozenges. And a Boune Lace betweene them of venis golde and silver having six broade bone laces on the border of like golde and silver. Delivered to the said Sir Tho: Gorges'. (New Year's Gift Roll, Anno 30 Eliz. 1588. BL, Add.8159).

116 Item one Peticoate of Aish colour silke plush with golde and sylver.

Loc. 'T', 't'. LMN in H16 'Rem'.

117 Item one Petycoate of heare colour Capha like golde flames laide with [[iiij⟨five⟩]] ⟨syxe⟩ brode ⟨bone laces of⟩ venice silver plate lace.

Loc. 'C', 'c'. LMN in H16 'Rem'. Alterations in H4. This was a New Year's gift: 'By the Barrones Cobham A petticote of haire Cullored Caffa laide with vj laces of venis silver with plate. Delivered to the Roabes'. (New Year's Gift Roll, 31 Eliz. 1589. BL, Lansd. Roll 17, printed in *Progr. Eliz.*, III, p. 6). The printed version gives 'faire' instead of 'haire'.

118 Item one petycoate of Crymson Capha florished with sylver with fyve broade passamaine laces of venice golde sylver and watchet sylke.

Loc. 'T', 't'. LMN in H16 'Rem'. This was a New Year's gift: 'By Mr Henry Brooke a petticote of Carnation Capha florished with silver with fyve broade passamayn laces of gold silver and watched silke. Delivered to the Roabes'. (New Year's Gift Roll, 31 Eliz. 1589. BL, Lansd. Roll 17, printed in *Progr. Eliz.*, III, p. 13).

f. 64

119 Item one Peticoate of Carnacion stitched clothe florished with venice silver and silver spangles.

Loc. 'T', 't'. LMN in H16 'Rem'.

120 Item one Petycoate of lawne wrought allover with sondrie Beasts flowers and birdes of venice golde silver and

silke of sondrie colours with twoe borders of like embroderye.

Loc. 'C', 't'. LMN in H16 'Rem'.

121 Item one Peticoate of Carnacion silke networke florished with venice sylver and sylver owes.

Loc. 'T', 't'. LMN in H16 'Rem'.

122 Item one Petycoate of sylver Tabyne with workes of purple tufte Taphata in braunches with a border of sylver Chamblet laide with fyve sylver laces upon orenge colour Taphata tufted and raveled.

Loc. 'T', 't'. LMN in H16 'Rem'. This was a New Year's gift: 'By Mr Warberton A pettycote of silver tabyne with workes of purple Tuftaffeta in braunches. Delivered to the Robes'. (New Year's Gift Roll, 41 Eliz. 1599. Folger, Z.d.17).

123 Item one petycoate withoute bodies of silver Tyncell wrought in squares like Castell walls with a border of Trees of greene silke needleworke and other devyses like waves.

Loc. 'T', 't'. LMN in H16 'Rem'. This was a New Year's gift: 'By the Countes of Darby, wydowe, one pettycote without bodyes, of silver tynsell, wrought in squares, with a border of trees of grene sylke needleworke. Delivered to the Robes'. (New Year's Gift Roll, 42 Eliz. 1600. Printed in *Progr. Eliz.*, III, p. 447).

124 Item one petycoate of whyte Tyncell striped with three brode laces of golde and sylver with tufts of watchet and Carnacion sylke.

Loc. 'C', 'c'. LMN in H16 'Rem'. This was a New Year's gift: 'By the Lord Henry Howard, one pettycote of white tynsell stryped with three brode laces of golde, with tuftes of watchet and carnacion silke. Delivered to the Robes'. (New Year's Gift Roll, 42 Eliz. 1600. Printed in *Progr. Eliz.*, III, p. 450).

125 Item one petycoate of aishcolour China Taphata enbrodered allover like Oaken leaves and slippes of venice ⟨of⟩ golde sylver and sylke of sondrye colours.

Loc. 'C', 'c'. LMN in H16 'Rem'. This was a New Year's gift: 'By the Barronnes Katheryn Cornewalleis, one pettycote of ashe-colored China taffeta, embrothered all over like oaken leaves and ackhornes, and slyppes of Venyce golde, silver, and silke. Delivered to the Robes'. (New Year's Gift Roll, 42 Eliz. 1600. Printed in *Progr. Eliz.*, III, p. 451).

f. 64ᵛ

[No entries]
[One unnumbered folio, blank on both sides].

f. 65
Cloakes

1 Firste one Cloake of blacke clothe of golde with a passamaine lace of golde

lyned with strawe colour tufte taphata the grounde sylver.

Loc. 'C', 'c', 't'. LMN in H16 'Rem'.

2 Item one Cloake of clothe of golde with workes of tawnie silke bounde aboute with a bindinge lace of sylver and lyned with Carnacion plushe.

Loc. 'C', 'c', 't'. LMN in H16 'Rem'.

3 Item one Cloake beinge shorte of cloth of golde striped set with spangles with twoe gardes enbrodered with leaves of venice ⟨lyned⟩ golde lyned with purple Sarceonett.

Loc. 'T', 't'. LMN in H16 'Rem'. Alteration in H1.

4 Item one rounde Cloake of aish colour cloth of golde laide aboute with a lace of silver lyned with peach colour plush.

Loc. 'C', 'c', 't'. LMN in H16 'Rem'.

5 Item one rounde cloake of blacke cloth of golde with buttons and loopes on thone side of venice golde and blacke silke lined with whyte Satten prented.

Loc. 'C', ⟨'c'⟩, 't'. LMN in H16 'Rem'. This was a New Year's gift: 'By Mr Wolley one of her majesties Secretaries A Round Cloke of black Cloth of gold, with buttons and lowpes on thinside of venis golde and black silke. Delivered to the Robbes'. (New Year's Gift Roll, 31 Eliz. 1589. BL, Lansd. Roll 17, printed in *Progr. Eliz.*, III, p. 12).

6 Item one Cloake of Dove colour cloth of golde bounde aboute with a byndinge lace of venice sylver plate lyned with white Satten prented laide with loopes of venice sylver.

Loc. 'C', ⟨'c'⟩, 't'. LMN in H16 'Rem'.

f. 65ᵛ

7 Item one Cloake of peach colour Cloth of golde tissued with golde lined with white plush bounde aboute with silver lace.

Loc. 'C', 'c', 't'. LMN in H16 'Rem'.

8 Item one cloake of cloth of golde striped with tissued golde and lined with aish colour Satten florished with sylver like flames and set with buttons of open worke of seede p(ear)le and golde downe the fore vents.

Loc. 'C', 'c', 't'. LMN in H16 'Rem'.

9 Item one cloake of cloth of sylver wrought with purple and yellowe silk striped downeright and laide aboute with a brode passamaine lace of venice golde and sylver with buttons and loopes of like golde and sylver pipes and seede p(ear)le lyned with orenge tawnye Satten laide with like lace.

Loc. 'T', 't'. LMN in H16 'Rem'.

10   Item one shorte Cloake of sylver Bawdekyn with leaves of purple silke and golde garded with Crimson vellat embrodered with silver lyned with Crymson unshorne vellat.

Loc. 'T', 't'. LMN in H16 'Rem'.

11   Item one Cloake of white prented clothe of sylver edged with passamaine lace of venice golde lyned with strawe colour vellat stayned.

Loc. 'C', 'c', 't'. LMN in H16 'Rem'.

12   Item one Dutch Cloake of cloth of sylver prented laide with three plate laces of golde lyned with watchet satten striped with golde.

Loc. 'C', 't'. LMN in H16 'Rem'.

13   Item one Cloake of Cloth of Sillver straw colour lined with tufted Taphata.

Loc. 'C', 't'. LMN in H16 'Rem'. This may have been a cloak altered in 1595, which was then newly lined with satin but must have been relined again, with taffeta, before 1600: 'First to William Jones our Taylor ... Item for alteringe pecinge longer, and new lyninge with white Satten, a Cloke of strawcolour cloth of Silver with a silver lace aboute, performed with like stuffe of our great warderobe'. (Warrant 28 Sept., 37 Eliz. 1595. PRO, LC5/37, f. 69).

f. 66

14   Item one Cloake of russet cloth of Sylver striped [[layd]] with three silver laces with an Indented Jagge bounde with silver lace lyned with peach colour Satten raized.

Loc. 'T', 't'. LMN in H16 'Rem'. Alteration in H3. Walter Fyshe is listed in 1575 'for making of a Cloake of russett tyncell striped with gold & silver cutt rounde about with an Indented Jagge & bounde aboute with a passamayne lase of venice silver and a silver lase aboute the Cloake lyned with white wrought unshorne vellat layed on thinside aboute the Jagge with a small plate lase of blak silke & golde and another lase of blak silke and golde layed aboute thinside the coller lyned with canvas ye tyncell of our store of the chardge of Rauf Hope yeoman of our Guarderobe of Robes threst of our great guarderobe'. (Warrant 28 Sept., 17 Eliz. 1575. BL, Egerton 2806, f. 86ᵛ).

15   Item one shorte Cloake of blacke cloth of silver laide rounde with a passamaine of venice golde lined with orenge colour plush.

Loc. C', 'c', 't'. LMN in H16 'Rem'. This was a New Year's gift: 'By the Lady Hennage one shorte Cloke of black Cloth of silver layde round about with A Passamayne, before with buttons and lowpes of like lace of venis gold and silver lyned with white plushe. Delivered to the Roabes'. (New Year's Gift Roll, 31 Eliz. 1589. BL, Lansd. Roll 17, printed in *Prog. Eliz.*, III, p. 8). The lining was changed in 1593: 'First to William Jones our Taylour ... Item for new lininge of a Cloke of black clothe of silver, with

orringe colour plushe of our great warderobe'. (Warrant 10 May, 35 Eliz. 1593. PRO, LC5/36, f. 253).

16   Item one rounde Cloake of Iron colour or blacke cloth of sylver bounde aboute with a lace of venice golde and blacke sylke lined with striped tufte Taphata.

Loc. 'C', 'c', 't'. LMN in H16 'Rem'.

17   Item one Cloake of flame colour Cloth of sylver lyned with whyte plush bounde aboute with a Sylver lace.

Loc. 'C', 'c', 't'. LMN in H16 'Rem'.

18   Item one Cloake of blacke clothe of Sylver with workes like harts flames and slippes lyned with sylver Chamblet prented.

Loc. 'C', 'c', 't'. LMN in H16 'Rem'.

19   Item one Cloake of white clothe of Sylver striped downerighte half waies with golde open lace lyned with silver chamblet.

Loc. 'T', 't'. LMN in H16 'Rem'.

20   Item one Cloake of cloth of sylver with workes of flowers akornes and peasecoddes of silke of sondrie colours.

Loc. 'C', 'c', 't'. LMN in H16 'Rem'. This may be a cloak which was lined in 1595: 'First to William Jones our Taylor ... Item for lyninge a cloke of Cloath of Silver with flowers of silke of sondry colours, with white Taffata being tufted alover of our great warderobe'. (Warrant 28 Sept., 37 Eliz. 1595. PRO, LC5/37, f. 69).

21   Item one Cloake of Isabella colour clothe of silver lined with white plushe.

Loc. 'C', 'c', 't'. LMN in H16 'Rem'.

f. 66ᵛ

22   Item one Cloake of Isabella colour cloth of sylver like waves lyned with white silver Chamblet cut and tufte billetwise bounde about with a passamaine lace of venice golde.

Loc. 'C', 'c', 't'. LMN in H16 'Rem'.

23   Item one Cloake thoute side Claie colour cloth of silver prented and thinside peach colour plush with golde and Sylver therin.

Loc. 'C', 't'. LMN in H16 'Rem'.

24   Item one Cloake of peach colour cloth of Silver lyned with aish colour unshorne vellat.

Loc. 'C', 'c', 't'. LMN in H16 'Rem'. This was a New Year's gift: 'By Sir Edward Hobby one Cloke of peach colored cloth of silver lyned with Ashe colored unshorne velvett. Delivered to the Robes'. (New Year's Gift Roll, 41 Eliz. 1599. Folger, Z.d.17).

25   Item one Cloake of greene wrought vellat laide with borders rounde aboute and downeright of venice golde.

Loc. 'T', 't'. LMN in H16 'Rem'.

26   Item one Cloake of purple vellat thinside beinge fryzed vellat spotted white and russet laide on with faire borders downerighte and rounde aboute of venice golde.

Loc. 'T', 't'. LMN in H16 'Rem'. This was made in 1567: 'First to Walter Fyshe our Taylor ... Item for makinge of a Cloake of purple velvet thinside beinge fryzed velvet spotted whyte and russet Layed on with iij brode laces of gold and iiij narrowe laces aboute the Cloake and striped Downe right with like laces the velvet of our store of the Chardge of the said George Brydeman and the lace of our store Taken from a Cloake of swete lether the rest of our Great warderobe. Item for makynge of a Case of Red beyes for the same Cloake of our great warderobe'. (Warrant last day of Sept., 9 Eliz. 1567. PRO, LC5/34, f. 23).

27   Item one shorte Cloake of blacke vellat with a brode border richlie embrodered with leaves and flowers of venice golde silver and silke like frutige lined with Cloth of silver striped with Dyvers colours.

Loc. 'T', 't'. LMN in H16 'Rem'.

28   Item one Cloake of tufte vellat orenge colour and white garded with Murrey Taphata laide with bone lace of venice golde & sylver.

Loc. 'T', 't'. LMN in H16 'Rem'.

29   Item one Dutch Cloake of Cloth of sylver verie faire enbrodered with golde purle upon Lawne like vyne leaves and wormes with buttons and loopes of like stuffe.

Loc. 'T', 't'. LMN in H16 'Rem'.

f. 67

30   Item one Cloake of purple vellat the grounde white satten with a narrowe border of venice golde striped downe and rounde aboute with six buttons of golde enameled like half Moones with greate loopes of venice golde garnished with pearle (one button lackinge).

Loc. 'T', 't'. LMN in H16 'Rem'. Walter Fyshe was entered in 1575 'for making of a Cloake of purple vellat the grounde white satten striped downeright & with a border buttons & loupes taken from a Cloake of purple satten lyned with lawne striped with golde ye coller lyned with canvas of our great guarderobe'. (Warrant 28 Sept., 17 Eliz. 1575. BL, Egerton 2806, f. 88). He worked on it again three years later, 'altering and newe lyninge of a Cloake of purple vellat the grounde satten lyned with white taphata pinked of our great guarderobe'. (Warrant 26 Sept., 20 Eliz. 1578. BL, Egerton 2806, f. 129ᵛ).

403 *Slip with flower and pea-pods, or, peasecods, worked in crimson silk on a white linen smock, c. 1600. Victoria and Albert Museum, London (T.2–1956)*

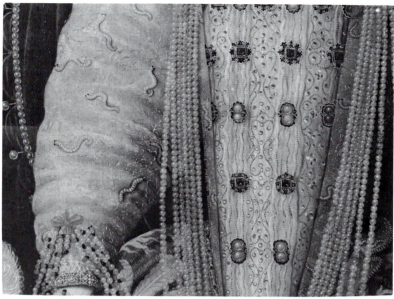

404 *Silkworms and mulberry leaves embroidered in white silk and gold and silver thread on white satin sleeves, detail from Figure 413. Painting by an unknown artist, c. 1600. The Collection at Parham Park*

31 Item one Cloake of wrought vellat watchet and blewe laide with a brode bone lace of venice golde and silver furred with powdered Armions.

Loc. 'C', 'c', 't'. LMN in H16 'Rem'. This may be a cloak which appears in the warrants in 1570, but there is insufficient detail to identify it with certainty: 'Item to Adam Blande our Skynner . . . for leyinge in a furre of powderid Armyons into a shorte Cloake of wrought vellat like gardes the Armyons of our store Receyved of the said Rauf Hope and a perfourmaunce of armyons and powderinges and two thowsand pynkes of our great guarderobe'. (Warrant 12 April, 12 Eliz. 1570. BL, Egerton 2806, f. 23ᵛ). Blande cleaned the fur six years later when he was entered 'for skowringe of a furre of powderid armyons and leyinge in the same into a Cloake of watchett wrought vellat with iiij tymber of armyons & Twelve hundreth pinkes & powderinges to perfourme the same of our great guarderobe'. (Warrant 14 April, 18 Eliz. 1576. BL, Egerton 2806, ff. 97, 97ᵛ).

32 Item one Dutche Cloake of blacke vellat with a broade garde of venice golde and sylver byas with an Indented Jagge garnished with like lace faced with russet unshorne vellatt.

Loc. 'T', 't'. LMN in H16 'Rem'.

33 Item one Dutche Cloake of blacke vellat embroidered allover with flowers and grashoppers of venice golde silver and silke lyned with tawnie sarceonet furred with Sables.

Loc. 'T', 't'. LMN in H16 'Rem'. This may be a cloak which appears in the warrants in 1579, but there is insufficient detail to identify it with certainty: 'Item to Adam Blande our Skynner . . . Item for fasinge of a Cloake of blak vellat enbroderid allover fased with thirtye and fyve

sable skynnes of our store and two Sable skynnes of our greate wardrobe'. (Warrant 10 April, 21 Eliz. 1579. BL, Egerton 2806, ff. 138, 138ᵛ). The grasshopper motif makes it fairly certain that this is the cloak which was repaired in 1602: 'Item to Peter Bland our skynner . . . for mending the face and edging of a cloake of black velvet embroidered allover with gold and grassehoppers, with one sable skynne to the cape and edging'. (Warrant 27 Sept., 44 Eliz. 1602. PRO, LC5/37, ff. 271, 272). The fur was treated again in the following year: 'Item to Peter Bland our said Sisters Skinner . . . for mending the furre of a cloke of black vellat enbroidered allover with grasshoppers with thre sable skins'. (Warrant 18 May, 1 James 1603. PRO, LC5/37, f. 285).

34 Item one Dutche Cloake of tawnie vellate laide with twoe brode laces of venice golde and silver plate with buttons and loopes of like lace lyned with white Satten striped with golde and silver.

Loc. 'C', 't'. LMN in H9 'bed chamber'. RMN in H9 'bed chamber'.

35 Item one Cloake of peache colour vellat laide with three brode laces of venice silver and buttons and loopes of like silver lyned with Carnacion unshorne vellat spotted white.

Loc. 'C', <'c'>. LMN in H10 'geven by hir majestie the 5 of october 1601'. Signature 'A. Walsingham'. This was a New Year's gift: 'By Mr Stanhop A Cloke of Peache Colored vellatt Layd with thre brode Lases of venis Sylver buttons and Louppes of Lyke Sylver and Lyned with Carnation unshorne vellatt spotted with white. Delivered to Rauf hope'. (New Year's Gift Roll, 27 Eliz. 1585. Folger, Z.d.16).

36 Item one rounde Cloake of blacke vellat with a brode border cut bounde

aboute with a lace of venice sylver lyned with whyte Satten prented.

Loc. 'C', 'c', 't'. LMN in H16 'Rem'. See f. 69/60 note.

f. 67ᵛ

37 Item one Cloake of paul colour yellat embroidered allover with pauncies roses and other flowers of venice golde sylver and silke with a border likewise embroidered lyned with white Satten prented.

Loc. 'C', 't'. LMN in H16 'Rem'. See f. 69/60 note.

38 Item one Dutch Cloake of blacke vellat bounde aboute and striped with aish colour silke and golde lace the sleeves garded with tufts of aish colour silke and lxxvj buttons of golde knotts faste untyed lyned with aish colour plush.

Loc. 'T', 't'. LMN in H16 'Rem'.

39 Item one Cloake of blacke vellat with three passamaine laces of venice golde with longe and shorte strippes of like lace lyned with blacke taphata cut and raveled.

Loc. 'C', 'c', 't'. LMN in H16 'Rem'.

40 Item one Cloake of blacke vellat lyned with blacke plush.

Loc. 'C', 'c', 't'. LMN in H16 'Rem'.

41 Item one rounde Cloake of blacke vellat embroidered allover (savinge one quarter of a yearde in depth on the shoulders) verie faire with venice golde silver and peacockes feathers in colours garnished with seed pearle and other

405 *Two dragonflies pulling a beetle in a net, detail from a polychrome embroidered white satin panel, probably part of a skirt, c. 1600. Victoria and Albert Museum, London (T.138–1981)*

pearles (whereof the most parte are lackinge) furred through out with powdered Armyons.

Loc. 'T', 't'. LMN in H16 'Rem'.

42 Item one Cloake of blacke vellat laied with a lace of blacke silke like waves.

Loc. 'C', 'c', 't'. LMN in H16 'Rem'. This was probably a gift as it does not appear among the warrants until this entry: 'First to Walter Fyshe our Taylour . . . Item for alteringe and making shorter of a Cloake of blak vellat layed with blak silke lase like waves of our great warderobe'. (Warrant 10 April, 21 Eliz. 1579. BL, Egerton 2806. f. 137).

43 Item one rounde Cloake of Carnacion vellat edged with small seede p(ear)le and a rowe of bigger pearle in the myddest and garnished with xxiij^tie buttons and loopes of like seede p(ear)le and bugle lyned with whit plush.

Loc. 'C', 'c', 't'. LMN in H16 'Rem'. This was probably a gift as it does not appear among the warrants until this entry: 'First to William Jones our Taylor . . . Item for altering and new lyning with white plush of a Cloake of Carnacion velvet with pearle buttons of our greate Warderobe'. (Warrant 8 April, 42 Eliz. 1600. PRO, LC5/37, f. 190).

f. 68

44 Item one rounde Cloake of paule colour Carnacion vellat laide rounde aboute with a lace and loopes of sylver lyned with white plushe.

Loc. 'C', 'c', 't'. LMN in H16 'Rem'.

45 Item one longe Cloake of Murrey vellat with a border rounde aboute

wrought with a small cheine lace of venice sylver and one rowe on eche side ⟨with⟩ of buttons and loopes of like sylver furred with Mynnever throughoute and rusken gray paned.

Loc. 'T', 't'. LMN in H16 'Rem'. This was a New Year's gift: 'By the Countesse of Lyncoln widdowe A longe Cloake of murry velvett with a border round aboute of a small Cheyne lace of venis silver and two Rowes of buttons and lowpes of like silver furred thorough with mynnyover and Calloper like myll pykes. Delivered to the Roabes'. (New Year's Gift Roll, 31 Eliz. 1589. BL, Lansd. Roll 17, printed in *Progr. Eliz.*, III, p. 3).

46 Item one Cloake of purple vellat laide aboute and striped downe like waves of tufte lace of venice golde furred throughe with Callaber spotted.

Loc. 'T', 'c', 't'. LMN in H16 'Rem'.

47 Item one Cloake of tawnie uncut ⟦vellat⟧ with braunches of tawnie unshorne vellat and wrought with golde the grounde golde and lyned with white Plush.

Loc. 'C', 'c', 't'. LMN in H16 'Rem'. Addition in H1.

48 Item one Cloake of blacke wrought vellat the grounde golde with a byndinge lace of venice sylver aboute lyned with aishcolour plush.

Loc. 'C', 'c', 't'. LMN in H16 'Rem'.

49 Item one Cloake of Crymson vellat with a faire border of silver like peramydes lyned with Carnacion Tabyne the grounde silver with workes like squares and slippes.

Loc. 'C', 'c', 't'. LMN in H16 'Rem'.

50 Item one Cloake of Murrey damaske garded with three gardes of blacke vellatt laide with lace of venice golde with a brode face and edge of Sables and furred with Callaber the sleeves lyned with Crymson Sarceonet.

Loc. 'T', 't'. LMN in H16 'Rem'. This is one of the earliest items still remaining in the Wardrobe of Robes in 1600 and was probably a gift, as it does not appear among the warrants until this entry: 'First to Walter Fyshe our Taylor . . . Item for blak velvet to gard a Cloke of murrey Damaske the slevis lined with Crimsen Sarcenet of our great warderobe'. (Warrant 28 March, 9 Eliz. 1567. PRO, LC5/34, f. 13). Adam Bland was entered in the same year 'for Furringe of a Cloke of murrey Damask with one furre of Sables and mynkes of our store in the Chardge of the said Rauph hope and more employed upon the Coller and edginge viij Sable Skynnes of our store receyved of the said george brydeman and to performe the same Cloke One Tymber of mynkes of our great warderobe'. (Warrant 28 March, 9 Eliz. 1567. PRO, LC5/34, f. 15). Fifteen years later Blande worked on the cloak again: 'mendinge the furre of a Cloke of murrey Damaske with a

performance of Mynkes and one sable skynne of our great guarderobe'. (Warrant 28 Sept., 24 Eliz. 1582. BL, Egerton 2806, f. 179^v).

f. 68^v

51 Item one Cloake of blacke damaske laied with lace of venice golde silver and silke lyned with orenge colour vellat laide aboute with a passamaine lace of venice golde and silver.

Loc. 'C', 't'. LMN in H16 'Rem'.

52 Item one Cloak of Crymson Taphata razed with white and yellowe silke garded with greene vellat lyned with the same.

Loc. 'T', 't'. LMN in H16 'Rem'. This is one of the earliest items still remaining in the Wardrobe of Robes in 1600. The material was a gift from Lady Knollys and the cloak was made by 'Walter Fyshe our Taylor . . . Item for makynge of a Cloake of Crymsin Taffata reysed with whyte and yelowe silke garded with Grene velvet and lyned with same the Coller lyned with Canvas the Stuffe to make the Cloake receyved of the Lady Knolles all the rest of our Great warderobe'. (Warrant last day of Sept., 9 Eliz. 1567. PRO, LC5/34, f. 24). Nine years later it was renovated: 'Item to Arther Middleton . . . for alteringe and enlarginge of a Cloake of tufte taphata the grounde crymsen reyzid with yellowe the lyninge performed with grene vellat and the garde performed with like vellat and crymsen taphata'. (Warrant 26 Sept., 8 Eliz. 1576. BL, Egerton 2806, f. 104^v).

53 Item one Cloak of aishcolour Taphata laide aboute with twoe bone laces of venice golde lyned with yellowe Taphata.

Loc. 'C', 't'. LMN in H16 'Rem'.

54 Item one Cloake of blacke Taphata laide aboute and striped with lace of venice golde and sylver wrought with pipes and p(ur)le with a Jagge wrought byas with passamaine lace of venice golde and silver lyned with greene cloth of golde and sylver.

Loc. 'T', 't'. LMN in H16 'Rem'.

55 Item one Cloak of pynk colour Taphata with braunches and flowers of Colored sylkes lyned with white plush.

Loc. 'C', 'c', 't'. LMN in H16 'Rem'. This was a New Year's gift: 'By the Barones Hunsden Junior one Cloake of Taffeta with braunches & flowers lyned with white plushe. Delivered to the Robes'. (New Year's Gift Roll, 41 Eliz. 1599. Folger, Z.d.17).

56 Item one shorte Cloake of blacke tufte Taphata striped and laide rounde aboute with an open lace of venice golde and sylver lyned with watchet plush.

Loc. 't'. LMN in H16 'Rem'.

57 Item one rounde Cloake of black tufte Taphata furred with Callaber.

Loc. 'T', 't'. LMN in H16 'Rem'.

58 Item one Cloake of blacke tufte Taphata the grounde golde tufte with heare colour sylke lyned with heare colour plush.

Loc. 'C', 't'. LMN in H16 'Rem'.

f. 69

59 Item one shorte Cloake of perfumed Leather enbrodered with three small borders of venice golde sylver and crimsen silke faced and edged with Sables and furred with Callaber.

Loc. 'T', 't'. LMN in H16 'Rem'. This was probably a gift, as it does not appear among the warrants until this entry: 'Item to Adam Blande our Skynner for mendinge the furre of a Cloake of lether with one sable skynne, & half a Tymber of callaber of our greate guarderobe'. (Warrant 6 April, 23 Eliz. 1581. BL, Egerton 2806, f. 165ᵛ). He worked on it again in the following year 'mendinge the furre of a Cloake of perfumed lether with a pefourmance of calaber and Sables of our great guarderobe'. (Warrant 28 Sept., 24 Eliz 1582. BL, Egerton 2806, f. 179ᵛ). Three years later Blande was again entered 'for mendinge the furre of a Cloake of perfumed lether with a perfourmance of callaber of our great guarderobe'. (Warrant 27 Sept., 27 Eliz. 1585. BL, Egerton 2806, f. 209). This seems to be the same cloak that was treated again eighteen years later by Peter, probably Adam's son: 'Item to Peter Bland our said Sisters Skinner for mending the furre of a cloke of perfumed lether with thre sable skinnes and xxᵗⁱᵉ Calaber skynnes to performe the same'. (Warrant 18 May, 1 James 1603. PRO, LC5/37, f. 285).

60 Item one Cloak of perfumed Leather striped downerighte and laide with lace of venice golde and sylver set with small buttons like skallop shells upon a brode border lyned with aish colour Satten cut and pincked with like buttons and loopes.

Loc. 'T', 't'. LMN in H16 'Rem'. This was probably a gift. There is an entry for lining a leather cloak with taffeta which may refer to this one before the satin lining was put in: 'Fyrste to William Jones our Taylour . . . Item for alteringe & newe Lyninge of iij Clokes two of velvet lyned with printed satten the thirde of perfumed lether lyned with taffata Cut and tufted & sarcenet of our great Warderobe'. (Warrant 27 Sept., 33 Eliz. 1591. PRO, LC5/36, f. 185). The two velvet cloaks may be f. 67/36 and f. 67ᵛ/37.

61 Item one heare colour Satten embroidered allover with venice golde silver and sylke like Cloudes wormes and beastes lyned with prented clothe of sylver.

Loc. 'C', 't'. LMN in H16 'Rem'. Walter Fyshe is entered in a warrant in 1579 'for making of a Cloake of heare colour satten enbroderid allover with venice golde silver and silke being taken from a Cloake of our store of crymsen satten and the enbrauderie perfourmed lyned with prented cloth of silver of our store Receyved of the said George Brideman the satten of our store Receyved of Rauf Hope

yeoman of our warderobe of Robes threste of our greate wardrobe'. (Warrant 12 Oct., 21 Eliz. 1579. BL, Egerton 2806, f. 144).

62 Item one shoulder Cloake of Carnacion prented Satten furred with Minkes and edged with powdered Armyons.

Loc. 'C'. RMN in H11 'bed chamber'. This was probably a gift, as it does not appear among the warrants until this entry: 'Item to Adam Blande our Skynner . . . for mending the furre of a Cloake of carnacion satten prented with a perfourmance of powderid armyons of our great guarderobe'. (Warrant 27 Sept., 28 Eliz. 1586. BL, Egerton 2806, f. 214).

63 Item one Dutch Cloake of white Satten allover embroidered with venice golde with three borders like fryers knotts lyned with strawe colour and ⟨blewe⟩ [[whit]] Changeable Taphata.

Loc. 'T', 't'. LMN in H16 'Rem'. Alteration in H2. This was a New Year's gift: 'By the Barrones Cobham a Du[t]che Cloke of white Satten alover enbradored with venys gold with iij borders enbradored lyke fryers knottes lyned with strawcollored and blew changeable Taphata. Delivered to the foresaid Rauf hope'. (New Year's Gift Roll, 26 Eliz. 1584. BL, Egerton 3052, printed in *Costume* 9, 1975, p. 28).

64 Item one Dutche Cloake of white stitched Satten with twoe small laces of venice golde furred throughe with white Conye.

Loc. 'T', 't'. LMN in H16 'Rem'.

65 Item one Cloake of tawnye Satten the shoulders embroidered like a Cloude with Sonnebeames and Rainebowes the rest embroidered with Hawthorne trees Essefirmes Cyphers hopes and other devyses with a narrowe border likewise embrodered set with viijᵗʰ sleight buttons of golde lyned with white Satten prented

Loc. 'C', 'c', 't'. LMN in H16 'Rem'. This was probably a gift, as it does not appear among the warrants until this entry: 'First to Walter Fyshe our Taylour . . . Item for alteringe newe makinge and makinge longer of a Cloake of tawnye satten enbroderid allover bounde aboute with venice golde lase lyned with white satten prented the coller lyned with buckeram of our great guarderobe'. (Warrant 15 Sept., 23 Eliz. 1581. BL, Egerton 2806, f. 170). Eighteen years later William Jones was entered 'for alteringe a Cloke of Tawny Satten enbraudered and newe lyninge yt with white Satten printed of our great warderobe'. (Warrant 28 Sept., 41 Eliz. 1599. PRO, LC5/37, f. 176).

f. 69ᵛ

66 Item one Dutche Cloake of orenge colour Satten striped with golde with a garde of blacke Taphata sarceonet laide with a brode bone lace of venice golde and silver furred with Mynnever and faced with powdered Armyons.

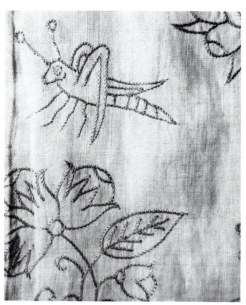

406 *Detail of a grasshopper and filberts, or hazel nuts, worked in crimson silk on a white linen smock, c. 1600. Victoria and Albert Museum, London (T.2–1956)*

Loc. 'T', 't'. LMN in H16 'Rem'. William Jones was entered in 1586 'for making of a Dou[t]che Cloake of orange satten striped with silver with a garde of blak taphata and thre laces of venice golde & silver the cloake furred & the slevis lyned with sarceonett the coller stiffenid with canvas & buckeram & buckeram to laye aboute it the satten of our store of the chardge of Thomas Knyvett esquier keper of our Palloice at Westminster threst of our great guarderobe'. (Warrant 27 Sept., 28 Eliz. 1586. BL, Egerton 2806, f. 213). Sixteen years later it was renovated: 'Item to Peter Bland our Skynner . . . for mending the furr of a cloke of orendge color satten with a performance of powdered Armions'. (Warrant 19 April, 44 Eliz. 1602. PRO, LC5/37, f. 256). The difference between gold and silver stripes was probably a scribe's error.

67 Item one rounde Cloake of aish colour Satten embroidered with a brode border of roundells and squares of golde and Carnacion silke and sondrie flowers of like golde silver and silke lyned with Carnacion tufte taphata cut and uncut striped.

Loc. 'C', 'c', 't'. LMN in H16 'Rem'.

68 Item one longe Robe like a Cloake of aishcolour Satten striped with golde lyned with strawe colour Taphata tufte.

Loc. 'C', 'c', 't'. LMN in H16 'Rem'. This was a New Year's gift: 'By Mr Broucke one longe Robe like a cloke of Ashe colloured satten striped with golde lyned with strawe coloured Taffata tufte. Delivered to the said Sir Tho: Gorges'. (New Year's Gift Roll, 30 Eliz. 1588. BL, Add.8159).

69 Item one Cloake of Dove colour Satten covered with russet Networke

407 *Detail of flowers, butterfly and caterpillar or 'worm', embroidered in black silk, enriched with gold thread, on a white linen forehead cloth, c. 1600. Victoria and Albert Museum, London (T.26–1975)*

florished with venice golde and silver lyned with Carnacion plush bounde with a lace of venice golde.

Loc. 'C', 'c', 't'. LMN in H16 'Rem'.

70   Item one Cloake of plaine white Satten embroidered with three gardes rounde aboute with venice golde silver cheeflie greene silke and a fewe small seede pearle the Coller and facinge likewise embroidered furred with powdered Armyons.

Loc. 'T', 't'. LMN in H16 'Rem'. Although the description is not detailed enough to identify this cloak with certainty, it seems to be one that was perfumed in 1593: 'Item to John Winyard for perfuminge of a Cloke of white satten furred with powdered Armions with muske Civitt and Ambergrize emploied upon it of our great warderobe'. (Warrant 28 Sept., 35 Eliz. 1593. PRO, LC5/36, f. 264).

71   Item one longe Sea Cloake of heare colour Satten laide in sondrye places with buttons and loopes of venice golde plate and blewe silke and some owes lyned with aish colour plush.

Loc. 'T', 't'. LMN in H16 'Rem'.

72   Item one Cloake of white Satten prented furred throughe with Mynnever and edged with powdered Armyons.

Loc. 'T', 't'. LMN in H16 'Rem'.

f. 70

73   Item one Cloake of white Satten prented embrodered allover with Butterflies and wormes of golde sylver and silkes of sondrye colours with a faire border of like embroderie.

Loc. 'C', 'c', 't'. LMN in H16 'Rem'.

74   Item one Cloak of Murrey silke Networke wrought allover with silke of

sondrie colours like steepels with a brode [[passamaine]] of venice golde and silver passamaine lace, lyned with watchet Taphata.

Loc. 'C', 't'. LMN in H16 'Rem'. Addition in H2.

75   Item one Cloake of blacke silke Networke florished with golde and sylver lyned with hearecolour Satten and Carnacion plush.

Loc. 'C', 'c', 't'. LMN in H16 'Rem'. This was a New Year's gift: 'By the Baronesse Talbot widowe a Cloake of blacke silke netwourke flourisshed with golde and silver lyned with Strawe colloured Taffata and Carnation flushe. Delivered to the said Sir Thomas Gorges'. (New Year's Gift Roll, 30 Eliz. 1588. BL, Add.8159).

76   Item one Cloake of white Networke florished with silver and silver spangles both sides alike.

Loc. 't'. LMN in H16 'Rem'.

77   Item one Cloake of white Networke embroidered with venice golde silver small twiste and owes of golde and sylver lyned with white cloth of silver prented like waves and leaves.

Loc. 'C', 't'. LMN in H16 'Rem'.

78   Item one Cloake of blacke Network florished with venice golde and bounde with a lace of venice silver.

Loc. 'C', 't'. LMN in H16 'Rem'. This was a New Year's gift: 'By Sir Thomas Leighton, one cloke of blacke networke, florished with Venyce golde, bounde with a lace of Venice silver. Delivered to the Robes'. (New Year's Gift Roll, 42 Eliz. 1600. Printed in *Progr. Eliz.*, III, p. 454).

79   Item one Cloak of Skarlett with twoe laces buttons and loopes of silver and golde lined with Carnacion Taphata pincked.

Loc. 'C', 'c', 't'. LMN in H16 'Rem'. this may be a cloak which was lined with white taffeta in 1594 and relined before 1600 with carnation taffeta: 'Fyrste to William Jones our Tayloure . . . Item for newe Lyninge of a Cloke of skarlet with whit Taffata printed and Cut alover of our great Warderobe'. (Warrant 27 Sept., 36 Eliz. 1594. PRO, LC5/37, f. 19).

80   Item one Cloake of Skarlet with twoe faire laces of golde and sylver lyned with greene vellatt.

Loc. 'C', 'c', 't'. LMN in H16 'Rem'. This cloak was altered in 1576: 'Item to William Whittell . . . for translatinge of a Cloake of scarlett the lyninge perfourmed with grene vellat'. (Warrant 26 Sept., 18 Eliz. 1576. BL, Egerton 2806, f. 105ᵛ).

f. 70ᵛ

81   Item one Cloake of orenge colour silke Chamblet striped with silver the lyninge of white Satten embroidered allover with honiesuckles and other flowers of venice golde silver and silke.

Loc. 'C', 't'. LMN in H16 'Rem'.

82   Item one Cloake of sylver Chamblet florished with slippes of flowers of golde and silke of sondrie colours lined with maiden blushe satten prented.

Loc. 'C', 'c', 't'. LMN in H16 'Rem'.

83   Item one Cloake of aishcolour grograine with a brode garde cut and frenged laide about the cutts with a small breade lace of venice golde lyned with strawe colour cloth of silver.

Loc. 'C', 't'. LMN in H16 'Rem'.

84   Item one Dutch Cloake of orenge colour grograine laide rounde aboute with a small lace of sylver like gardes lyned with clothe of Sylver with workes of orenge colour silke.

Loc. 'T', 'C' written on top of each other, 't'. LMN in H16 'Rem'. This was probably a gift, as it does not appear among the warrants until this entry: 'Fyrste to William Jones our Taylour . . . Item for alteringe pecinge longer & newe makinge of a du[t]che Cloke of Orrendge Colour silke grograine laced with silver lace, the slevis enlarged and peced longer lyned with Cloth of Silver of our great warderob'. (Warrant 27 Sept., 33 Eliz. 1591. PRO, LC5/36, f. 185).

85   Item one shorte Cloake of blacke stitched Cloth florished with silver striped with owes laide upon heare colour Taphata sarceonet lyned with white plush.

Loc. 'C', 'c', 't'. LMN in H16 'Rem'.

86   Item one shorte Cloake of white stitched cloth florished with venice golde silver and some Carnacion silke allover, laide upon with white Taphata and lyned with white plushe.

Loc. 'T', 't'. LMN in H16 'Rem'. This was a New Year's gift: 'By Mr Bruncker one shorte

Cloke of white sticht Cloth florished all over with venis gold silver and some Carnation silke layde upon white taffety and lyned with white plushe ... Delivered to the Robbes'. (New Year's Gift Roll, 31 Eliz. 1589. BL, Lansd. Roll 17, printed in *Progr. Eliz.*, III, p. 12).

87 Item one Cloak of blacke stitched cloth like leaves florished with venice golde and sylver lyned with white Satten prented with buttons and loops of venice golde, powdered with blacke silke.

Loc. 'C', 'c', 't'. LMN in H16 'Rem'.

f. 71

88 Item one Cloake of tawnie stitched cloth florished with golde and golde owes lyned with sylver Chamblet and bound with golde lace.

Loc. 'C', 't'. LMN in H16 'Rem'.

89 Item one Cloake of white stitched cloth garnished with owes and tufts of orenge colour silke.

Loc. 'C', 't'. LMN in H16 'Rem'.

90 Item one Cloake of blacke stitched cloth florished with venice golde and sylver lyned with silver Chamblet prented.

Loc. 'C', 't'. LMN in H16 'Rem'.

91 Item one Cloak of blacke knitworke florished with venice sylver and sylver owes lyned with aish colour plush.

Loc. 'C', 'c', 't'. LMN in H16 'Rem'.

92 Item one Cloake of blacke knitworke florished with venice golde and silver like ragged staves and small owes lyned with cloth of silver prented.

Loc. 'C', 't'. LMN in H16 'Rem'.

93 Item one Cloak of Sylver Tabyne with workes like slippes of aish colour silke.

Loc. 'C', 'c', 't'. LMN in H16 'Rem'.

94 Item one Cloake of blacke vellat embroidered with twoe borders of braunches of pearle lyned with blacke cloth of Sylver [[lackinge many pearll]].

Loc. 'C', 'c, 't'. LMN in H16 'Rem'. Addition in H4. Part of the material for this cloak was a gift from Lady Drury: 'First to Walter Fyshe our Taylour ... Item for making of a Cloake of blak vellat enbroderid with two borders of braunches of pearle lyned with oringe colour cloth of silver the color lyned with canvas the cloth of silver of our store Receyved of the Ladye Drurye all threst of our greate warderobe'. (Warrant 10 April, 21 Eliz. 1579. BL, Egerton 2806, f. 137).

f. 71ᵛ

95 Item one shorte Cloake of blacke vellat lyned with heare colour plush and set with ix paire of loopes of pearle.

Loc. 'C', 'c', 't'. LMN in H16 'Rem'.

96 Item one Cloake of heare colour raized Mosseworke embroidered like stubbes of dead Trees set with xiiij^ene buttons embroidered like Butterflies with fower pearles and one Emerode in a pece lyned with Cloth of sylver prented.

Loc. 'T', 't'. RMN in H9 'Lady Shrewesbery'. Cf. f. 85/84 for what seems to be a matching jacket, with the margin note 'Lady Shrowsbery', and with f. 29/67 for a round gown.

[One unnumbered folio, blank on both sides]

f. 72

Cloakes and Saufegardes

1 Firste one Cloake and a Saufegarde of cloth of golde with braunches of silke of sondrie colours the Cloake lyned and the saufegarde edged with white plushe.

Loc. 'C', 't'. LMN in H16 'Rem'.

2 Item one Cloake and a Saufegarde of purple and yellowe cloth of Sylver like leaves striped downerighte with a lace of carnacion silke venice golde and flate damaske sylver lyned with white Satten the saufegarde but bordered with like satten.

Loc. 'T', 't'. LMN in H16 'Rem'.

3 Item one Cloake and a Saufegarde of cloth of silver with braunches of watchet and orenge colour silke laide aboute with a lace of venice golde silver and spangles set with buttons and loopes of like lace the Cloake lyned with Orenge colour Satten razed.

Loc. 'T', 't'. LMN in H13 'Sent to the quene'.

4 Item one Cloake and Saufegarde of Carnacion vellat embroidered with a slight border of flowers and leaves of venice golde and sylver the Cloak lyned with white Satten striped with golde with buttons and loops of lace of venice golde and sylver.

Loc. 'C', <'c'>, 't'. LMN in H16 'Rem'.

5 Item one dutch Cloake and a Saufegarde of blacke vellat with tufts of heare colour silke lined with heare colour sarceonet The Cloake lyned with heare colour Taphata tufte.

Loc. 'C', <'c'>, 't'. LMN in H16 'Rem'.

f. 72ᵛ

6 Item one rounde Cloake and a Saufegarde of uncut sea water vellatt garnished with lace buttons and loopes of silver.

Loc. 'C', 't'.

7 Item one Cloake and a Saufegarde of heare colour vellat laide rounde aboute and striped downerighte and buttons in the forequarter of brode passamaine lace of venice golde and silver plate the Cloak lined with prented cloth of silver the saufegarde lined with white sarcenet.

408 *Detail of a butterfly worked in crimson silk on a white linen smock, c. 1600. Victoria and Albert Museum, London (T.2-1956)*

Loc. 'C'. RMN in H9 <'geven'>. This was a New Year's gift: 'By Sir Fraunces Walsingham principall Secretary A Cloke and A Savegard of haire Cullored velvett laide Round aboute and striped downe righte and lowpes in the fore quarters of a broade passamayn lace of venis gold and silver plate the Cloke lyned with printed cloth of silver and the savegard lyned with white sarsenett, and a doublett ... Delivered to the Roabes'. (New Year's Gift Roll, 31 Eliz. 1589. BL, Lansd. Roll 17, printed in *Progr. Eliz.*, III, p. 9). See f. 82/36 for the doublet. The printed version gives 'faire' instead of 'haire' coloured.

8 Item one Cloake and saufegarde of heare colour vellat uncut and cut in workes striped and laced downerighte with lace of golde & silver.

Loc. 'C', 'c', 't'. LMN in H16 'Rem'.

9 Item one Dutch Cloake and a saufegarde of blacke wroughte vellat set with owes of golde laide with a lace of venice golde and silver.

Loc. 'C', 'c', 't'. LMN in H16 'Rem'.

10 Item one Cloake & a saufegarde and a Hatt of black Taphata enbrodered allover with droppes of venice golde blacke silke and spangles.

Loc. 't'. LMN in H16 'Rem'. This was probably a gift as it does not appear among the warrants until this entry: 'First to Walter Fyshe our Taylour ... Item for alteringe and enlarging of a Saufegarde of blak taphata enbrodered with droppes of golde lyned with oringe colour & blak sarceonett of our great guarderobe'. (Warrant 28 Sept., 17 Eliz. 1575. BL, Egerton 2806, f. 87ᵛ).

11 Item one Dutch Cloake and a saufegarde of Celestiall coloure Taphata garded allover with like Taphata laide with silver lace The Cloak havinge but three gardes lyned with like Taphata.

Loc. 'C', 'c' 't'. LMN in H16 'Rem'.

410 *'Peramides', or spires, embroidered in polychrome silks and gold thread on white satin, detail from Figure 150. Painting by an unknown artist, c. 1603. The Viscount Cowdray, Cowdray Park*

cut with fower borders downeright of small clouded sylver lace like Esses.

Loc. 'C', 'c'. LMN in H16 'Rem'.

8 Item one Juppe and Saufegarde of peach color cloth of silver enbrodered upon with white lawne faced with white satten prented.

Loc. 'C', 't'. LMN in H16 'Rem'.

9 Item one Juppe and Saufegard of aishcolour cloth of Silver with works of wheate eares and droppes with buttons upon the sleeves and downe before with owes of gold and Carnacion silke.

Loc. 'C', 'c'. LMN in H16 'Rem'. These items were probably a gift as they do not appear among the warrants until this entry: 'First to William Jones our said Sisters Taylor . . . Item for altering a Juppe & Safegard of ashe color cloth of silver new faced & edged with carnacion plush bordered with taphata of our great warderobe'. (Warrant 18 May, 1 James 1603. PRO, LC5/37, f. 283).

10 Item one Juppe and Saufegarde of Cloth of sylver with workes of orenge colour silke like vyne leaves and grapes with a border downe before and downe the sleeves of buttons of lawne wrought with venice sylver and Carnacion sylke.

Loc. 'C', 'c'. LMN in H16 'Rem'.

11 Item one Juppe and Saufegarde of brasell colour cloth of silver with a lace of gold and silver with spangles upon Carnacion satten.

Loc. 'C', 'c'. LMN in H16 'Rem'.

12 Item one Juppe and Saufegarde of pale colour vellat laid round aboute with a brode lace of golde and sylver with buttons and loopes of like lace the bodie faced with white satten prented and lyned with white sarceonet.

Loc. 'C', 't'. LMN in H16 'Rem'.

13 Item one Juppe and Saufegard of aish colour vellat laide aboute with a brode

lace of sylver with buttons and loopes of like lace faced with plush of orenge colour and aish colour.

Loc. 'C', 'c'. LMN in H16 'Rem'.

f. 77

14 Item one Juppe and Saufegarde of peache colour unshorne vellatt the Juppe laide allover with plate lace buttons and loopes of venice golde faced with prented clothe of sylver the saufegarde laide rounde aboute with lace alike.

Loc. 'T', 't'. LMN in H16 'Rem'.

15 Item one Juppe and Saufegarde of heare colour vellatt laide aboute and garnished with knotte buttons and loopes of venice sylver edged rounde with Carnacion plushe laide with a lace of venice silver.

Loc. 'C', 'c'. LMN in H16 'Rem'. These items were probably a gift, as they do not appear among the warrants until this entry: 'First to William Jones our Tayloure for alteringe of a Jupp of hairecolour velvitt with a silver lace about and pecinge longer and enlarginge the slevis perfourmed with like stuffe and Sarcenett of our great Warderobe'. (Warrant 12 April, 36 Eliz. 1594. PRO, LC5/37, f. 7). Jones carried out more work in the following year: 'alteringe and pecinge longer of a Jupp of hairecolour velvet with a silver lace lyned with Carnacion Sarcenet and faced with Carnacion plushe of our great warderobe'. (Warrant 10 April, 37 Eliz. 1595. PRO, LC5/37, f. 58). Cf. with f. 77ᵛ/22 for 'Compas knotte buttons'.

16 Item one Saufegarde and Juppe of willowe colour vellatt laide aboute and garnished with buttons and loopes of lace of venice golde and sylver faced with orenge colour plushe.

Loc. 'T', 't'. LMN in H16 'Rem'. These items were probably a gift, as they do not appear among the warrants until this entry: 'First to William Jones our Tayloure . . . Item for Alteringe of a Jupp of willow colour velvett and pecinge it longer perfourmed with like stuffe the forequarters new lined with sarcenett of our great warderobe'. (Warrant 12 April, 36 Eliz. 1594. PRO, LC5/37, f. 9).

17 Item one Juppe and Saufegarde of Murrey vellatt embroidered downe before with workes like knotts with lyons and other beastes within them with a bone lace of venice golde aboute lyned with watchet Taphata cut skallopewise.

Loc. 'T', 't'. LMN in H16 'Rem'.

18 Item one Juppe and Saufegarde of aishe diste colour vellat laide aboute with an open lace of venice golde and silver buttons and loopes of like lace.

Loc. 'C', 'c'. LMN in H16 'Rem'.

19 Item one Juppe and Saufegarde of orenge colour or marigolde colour vellat cut and uncutt the sleeves and downe

before garnished with a lace of venice sylver like Essefirmes and laide aboute with twoe plate laces of venice silver.

Loc. 'C', 'c'. LMN in H16 'Rem'. These items were probably a gift, as they do not appear among the warrants until this entry: 'First to William Jones our Taylor for altering a Jup and Savegard of Orenge color uncut velvet new facing them with white plushe and new bordering the safegard with sarcenet of our great warderobe'. (Warrant 19 April, 44 Eliz. 1602. PRO, LC5/37, f. 255).

20 Item one Juppe and Saufegarde of pale colour vellatt embroidered allover with a thredd of sylver and some owes Diamondewise and tuftes of white sylke in the myddest edged with white plushe.

Loc. 'C', 'c'. LMN in H16 'Rem'.

f. 77ᵛ

21 Item one Juppe and Saufegarde of russet Satten florished with silver laide aboute with twoe golde laces with a narrowe face of heare colour plushe.

Loc. 'C', 'c'. LMN in H16 'Rem'.

22 Item one Juppe and Saufegarde of peach colour Satten prented laide with a faire lace of golde and silver and Compas knotte buttons and with white plushe.

Loc. 'C', 'c'. LMN in H16 'Rem'. These items were probably a gift, as they do not appear among the warrants until this entry: 'First to William Jones our Tayloure ... Item for alteringe and pecinge longer of a Jupp of peachcolour Sattin faced with white plushe the savegard edged round about with white plushe perfourmed with like stuffe and sarcenett of our great warderobe'. (Warrant 12 April, 36 Eliz. 1594. PRO, LC5/37, f. 9).

23 Item one Juppe and Saufegarde of Murrey Satten embrodered allover verie faire with venice golde silver and silke.

Loc. 'T', 't'. LMN in H16 'Rem'.

24 Item one Juppe and Saufegarde of Isabella colour ⟨Satten⟩ ⟦caffa⟧ braunched with silver like feathers laide with a faire lace of golde and sylver.

Loc. 'C', 'c'. LMN in H16 'Rem'. Alteration in H2.

25 Item one Juppe and Saufegarde of white Satten prented allover and Cutt the sleeves and border downe before sett with leaves embrodered and raized.

Loc. 'C', 'c'. LMN in H16 'Rem'.

26 Item one Juppe and Saufegarde of Dove colour satten embrodered allover with flowers of venice golde silver and silke.

Loc. 'T', 't'. LMN in H16 'Rem'.

27 Item one Juppe and Saufegarde of pincke or Dove colour Satten embrodered allover with venice sylver like grapes and vine leaves.

Loc. 'C', 'c'. LMN in H16 'Rem'.

f. 78

28 Item one Juppe and Saufegarde of Claie colour Satten embroidered allover with silver in workes like Peramides right and contrarie.

Loc. 'C', 'c'. LMN in H16 'Rem'.

29 Item one Juppe and Saufegarde of aishe colour Taphata cut and snipte like gardes laide with a ⟨brode⟩ ⟦binding⟧ lace of venice golde and owes lyned with orenge colour sarceonett.

Loc. 'C', 't'. LMN in H16 'Rem'. Alteration in H2.

30 Item one Juppe and Saufegarde of aishe colour or Dove colour Taphata cutt and embroidered allover downeright in waves like leaves of silver plate and a small twiste of venice silver.

Loc. 'T', 't'. LMN in H16 'Rem'.

31 Item one Juppe and Saufegarde of white Taphata embroidered allover and cutt allover with a border of like embroderie with slippes and flowers of venice golde and silke of sondrie colours set with owes.

Loc. 'C', 'c'. LMN in H16 'Rem'. RMN in H2[?] '£98·10·6¾ £12·19·7½'. This note was written with a very fine pen and is hardly visible.

32 Item one Juppe and saufegarde of white Taphata or Tabine striped with golde cut and ⟨raveled⟩ ⟦frenged⟧ betwene.

Loc. 'C', 'c'. LMN in H16 'Rem'. Alteration in H1.

33 Item one Juppe and Saufegarde of sande colour spanish Taphata with works of silke of sondrie colours tissued with gold and silver with buttons of open worke downe before and upon the sleeves.

Loc. 'C', 'c'. LMN in H16 'Rem'.

34 Item one Juppe and Saufegarde of heare colour tuft Taphata the grounde silver the upper p(ar)te lyned and the skirttes edged with white plushe.

Loc. 'C', 'c'. LMN in H16 'Rem'. These items were probably a gift, as they do not appear among the warrants until this entry: 'Fyrst to William Jones our Tayloure ... Item for alteringe a Jupp and a safegard of heaire colour tuft Taffata new faced the slevis newe lyned with white plushe and the skirtes edged aboute of our great warderobe'. (Warrant 29 March, 40 Eliz. 1598. PRO, LC5/37, f. 128).

f. 78ᵛ

35 Item one Juppe and Saufegarde of Palme colour tufte Taphata the grounde golde and orenge colour lyned with white sarceonett.

Loc. 'C', 'c'. LMN in H16 'Rem'.

36 Item one Juppe and Saufegarde of white tufte Taphata the grounde sylver striped downeright with golde lace and twoe in a place.

Loc. 'C', 'c'. LMN in H16 'Rem'. These items were probably a gift, as they do not appear among the warrants until this entry: 'First to William Jones our Taylor ... Item for altering a Jupp and a safegarde of white tuft taffeta the ground silver enlarged with like stuff and sarcenet of our great warderop'. (Warrant 8 April, 42 Eliz. 1600. PRO, LC5/37, f. 190).

37 Item one Juppe and Saufegarde of pincke colour tufte Taphata the grounde silver with knotted buttons of venice golde.

Loc. 'C', 'c'. LMN in H16 'Rem'.

38 Item one Juppe and Saufegarde of heare colour Capha like golde flames of fire and garnished with buttons loupes and lace of venice silver lyned with white plushe.

Loc. 'C', 'c'. LMN in H16 'Rem'. This was a New Year's gift: 'By the Countesse of Shrewsbury A safegard with a Jhup or gaskyn Coate of haire Cullored satten like flames of fire of gold and garnished with buttons loupes and lace of venis silver. Delivered to the Roabes'. (New Year's Gift Roll, 31 Eliz. 1589. BL, Lansd. Roll 17, printed in *Progr. Eliz.*, III, p. 3). The printed version gives 'faire' instead of 'haire' coloured. The difference between capha and satten is a scribe's error.

39 Item one Saufegarde and Juppe of Lawne enbrodered allover with starres of venice silver and wheate Eares of venice golde bounde with a lace of venice silver.

Loc. 'C', 'c'. LMN in H16 'Rem'. These items were probably a gift, as they do not appear among the warrants until this entry: 'Fyrste to William Jones our Tayloure ... Item for alteringe and newe makinge up againe of a Juppe of lawne enbruadered with starres, and laced with Silver lace, lyned with Lawne of our great warderobe'. (Warrant 28 Sept., 34 Eliz. 1592. PRO, LC5/36, f. 218). He worked on these garments again three years later 'alteringe and newe makinge up agayne a Jupp and Safegard of lawne with starrs of Silver beinge enbraudered with a silver lace aboute of our great warderobe'. (Warrant 28 Sept., 37 Eliz. 1595. PRO, LC5/37, f. 68). This embroidery appears again in an entry for laundry in 1601, but the safeguard has apparently been altered, as it is here described as a round kirtle. This may, however, be a scribe's error: 'Item to Dorothie Speckard our Silkwoman ... for washing starching and mending a round kirtell and Jup of lawne wrought with starres and wheate Eares and mending the same with iij quarters of a yard of starched lawne employed upon pecing the Jup & coller ... All which said parcelles were delyvered to the ladies and gentlewomen of our privie chamber and are to be paid for at our great warderobe'. (Warrant

28 Sept., 43 Eliz. 1601. PRO, LC5/37, f. 236). Dorothy Speckard charged 60 shillings for her work (PRO, LC9/91, f. 20ᵛ).

40   Item one Juppe and Saufegarde of white lawne cut in snippes and spangles in thende of the snippes lined with silver Chamblet.

Loc. 'C', 't'. LMN in H16 'Rem'. These items were probably a gift, as they do not appear among the warrants until this entry: 'Fyrste to William Jones our Tayloure … Item for alteringe and newe making of a Juppe of lawne lyned with Silver Chamblett and for enlarginge the slevis and settinge in newe stayes of Taffata perfourmed with lyke stuffe of our great Warderobe'. (Warrant 28 Sept., 34 Eliz. 1592. PRO, LC5/36, ff. 217, 218). Ten years later both items were laundered, a specialist job, as they had to be unpicked and made up again. The silver chamblet lining was not washable: 'Item to Dorethie Speckard our silkewoman … for washing and starching a Jup and savegard of lawne cutt and sett with owes of silver and spangles and making the same up againe'. (Warrant 19 April, 44 Eliz. 1602. PRO, LC5/37, f. 258).

41   Item one Juppe Saufegarde of Dove colour grograine faire embroidered allover with gold silver and silke of sondrie colours with a border enbrodered like hollye.

Loc. 'T', 't'. LMN in H16 'Rem'.

f. 79

42   Item one Juppe and Saufegarde of Isabella colour Curle with a raized worke of venice silver downe before and allover the sleeves.

Loc. 'C', 'c'. LMN in H16 'Rem'. This was probably a gift, as it does not appear among the warrants until this entry: 'First to William Jones our Taylor … Item for alteringe a Jupp of claycolour curle and making newe stayes of Taffata to the same of our great warderobe'. (Warrant 28 Sept., 37 Eliz. 1595. PRO, LC5/37, f. 70). 'Isabella colour' was also described as 'clay colour', cf. f. 24ᵛ/100.

43   Item one Juppe and Saufegarde of aish colour networke florished allover with small thredds of venice golde and silver and some plate and owes billetwise.

Loc. 'C', 'c'. LMN in H16 'Rem'.

f. 79ᵛ

[No entries]
[One unnumbered folio, blank on both sides]

f. 80

Dublettes

1   Firste one Jaquett of Isabella colour clothe of golde with workes like flames and feathers of silver embroidered like snailes and seede pearle.

Loc. 'C', 'c'. LMN in H16 'Rem'.

2   Item one Dublet of blacke clothe of golde with dogges of silver.

Loc. 'C', 'c'. LMN in H16 'Rem'.

3   Item one Dublet of clothe of silver embroidered with oaken leaves of blacke silke and sonnes.

Loc. 'C', 'c'. LMN in H16 'Rem'. This would seem to be a doublet made in 1586, although the oak leaves are here described as trefoils: 'First to William Jones our Taylour … Item for making of a Dublett of cloth of silver enbroderid with traifoiles and Sonnes lyned with blak sarceonett stiffenid with canvas & bayes of our great guarderobe'. (Warrant 27 Sept., 28 Eliz. 1586. BL, Egerton 2806, f. 213ᵛ).

4   Item one Dublett of white clothe of silver prented with a wave worke and laide with a lace of venice golde and silver with buttons of like lace and tassells at thende.

Loc. 'C', 'c'. LMN in H16 'Rem'. The warrant for making this doublet gives details of the materials used : 'First to William Jones our Taylor … Item for makinge a dublet of whit cloth of silver printed alover, with a gold and silver lace aboute, and sett on with buttons and tassells, the bodies stiffened with canvas and buckeram hookes and eyes, the bodies new lyned with Sarcenet, the lininge of the slevis beinge perfourmed with Taffata of our great warderobe'. (Warrant 28 Sept., 37 Eliz. 1595. PRO, LC5/37, f. 69).

5   Item one Jaquet of white cloth of sylver embroidered in spaces downeright in the bodies and sleeves with golde silver and sylke of Peramides and Pillers byaswise.

Loc. 'C', 'c'. LMN in H16 'Rem'.

6   Item one Dublet of silver Chamblet set allover with golde spangles golde owes and peach colour silke.

Loc. 'C', 'c'. LMN in H16 'Rem'.

f. 80ᵛ

7   Item one Dublet of silver Chamblet raized in little rysing snippes of white Satten and sylver plate and spangles upon sylver twiste.

Loc. 'C', 'c'. LMN in H16 'Rem'.

8   Item one Dublett of sylver Chamblet striped overthwarte with silver plate lace and lawne cut in snippes and sylver spangles.

Loc. 'T', 't'. LMN in H16 'Rem'. This was a New Year's gift: 'By the Lady Hobby one doublet of silver chamlett striped overthwarte with a silver plate Lace & lawne cutt in snipps & silver spangles. Delivered to the Robes'. (New Year's Gift Roll, 40 Eliz. 1598. PRO, C47/3/40).

9   Item one Dublett of sylver Chamblett embroidered upon like leaves of like sylver Chamblet with owes and spangles.

Loc. 'C', 'c'. LMN in H16 'Rem'. This was a New Year's gift: 'By the Baronnes Boroughe one Doublet of silver chamblett embrothered upon like leaves of like sylver chamblett with owes and spangles. Delivered to the Robes'. (New Year's Gift Roll, 41 Eliz. 1599. Folger, Z.d.17).

10   Item one Dublett of silver Chamblett covered with nett of silver and blacke silke in tuftes.

Loc. 'C', 'c'. LMN in H16 'Rem'.

11   Item one Dublett of peach colour Satten embroidered allover with venice golde like flowers.

Loc. 'T', 'C' written on top of each other, 't'. LMN in H16 'Rem'. This was a New Year's gift: 'By the Lorde Ryche A Dublet of peche collored Satten enbradored alover with venys gold & sylke. Delivered to the foresaid Rauf hope'. (New Year's Gift Roll, 26 Eliz. 1584. BL, Egerton 3052, printed in Costume 9, 1975, p. 28).

12   Item one Dublett of blacke Satten embroidered with feathers and small seede pearle.

Loc. 'C', 'c'. LMN in H16 'Rem'. This was a New Year's gift: 'By Mrs West A Doblett of blacke Satten enbraudered with Fethers of golde and Sylver and smaull sede perlles. Delivered to Rauf hope'. (New Year's Gift Roll, 27 Eliz. 1585. Folger, Z.d.16). Six years later William Jones is entered 'for alteringe of a dublet of black satten embroidered like fethers & enlarginge the sleves with satten & sarcnet of our great warderobe'. (Warrant 10 June, 33 Eliz. 1591. PRO, LC5/36, f. 171). He worked on it again four years later 'alteringe and pecinge longer of a dublet of black Satten with fethers enbraudered with gold and Silver, with a gold and Silver lace about yt perfourmed with lyke Stuffe and Sarcenet of our great warderobe'. (Warrant 10 April, 37 Eliz. 1595. PRO, LC5/37, f. 59).

13   Item one Dublett of white Satten embroidered allover with flowers of venice golde silver and silke Chevernewyse.

Loc. 'C', 'c'. LMN in H16 'Rem'. This was a New Year's gift: 'By Mr John Norris A Doblett of white Satten Imbraudered all over byas with Flowers of venis gold Sylver and Sylke. Delivered to Raufe hope'. (New Year's Gift Roll, 27 Eliz. 1585. Folger, Z.d.16). Here 'chevronwise' is given as 'bias'.

14   Item one Dublet of peach colour Satten embroidered allover with roses and other flowers of venice golde drawen out with lawne.

Loc. 'C', 't'. LMN in H16 'Rem'. This was a New Year's gift: 'By the Erlle of Hertff[ord] A Doblett of pechcolored satten enbrawdered with Roses of venus golde and Sylke. Delivered the foresaid Raulf hope'. (New Year's Gift Roll, 27 Eliz. 1585. Folger, Z.d.16). Six years later 'William Jones was entered 'for alteringe pecinge longer and newe makinge up of a dublet of peachecolour Satten enbraudered and drawne out with lawne of our great Warderobe'. (Warrant 27 Sept., 33 Eliz. 1591. PRO, LC5/36, f. 185).

15   Item one Dublet of white Satten embrodered allover with Jellyflowers and other flowers of venice golde and silke.

Loc. 'T', 'C' written on top of each other, 'c'. LMN in H16 'Rem'.

f. 81

16   Item one Dublet of orenge colour Satten cut striped byas wise with a small lace of venice sylver lyned with white sarceonett.

Loc. 'C', 't'. LMN in H16 'Rem'.

17   Item one Dublett of white Satten cut striped byaswise with a plate lace of golde lyned with yellowe sarceonett.

Loc. 'T', 't'. LMN in H16 'Rem'. This was a New Year's gift: 'By Mrs Skydmore a Doblate of white satten striped with golde lyned with yellowe serseonett. Delivered to the foresaid Rauf Hoope'. (New Year's Gift Roll, 23 Eliz. 1581. Eton Coll. BLA 18 192).

18   Item one Dublett of Carnacion Satten embroidered like waves with a swellinge lace of venice silver and a small twiste with owes of silver.

Loc. 'T', 't'. LMN in H16 'Rem'. This was a New Year's gift: 'By the Lorde Winsor A Dublate of carnacion Satten with waves of sylver lase & spangelles Laide betwixte. Delivered to the foresaid Rauf Hoope'. (New Year's Gift Roll, 23 Eliz. 1581. Eton Coll. BLA 18 192). Ten years later more embroidery was carried out: 'Item to John Parr our Enbrauderer . . . Item for enlarginge of thenbrauderie of a paire of slevis and bodies for a dublet of Carnacion Satten wrought alover lyke waves enbossed and richelie wroughte with venice silver'. (Warrant 27 Sept., 33 Eliz. 1591. PRO, LC5/36, ff. 188, 189).

19   Item one Dublett of white Satten embroidered allover with sondrie fruites and flowers of venice golde silver and silke of sondrye Coloures.

Loc. 'C', 'c'. LMN in H16 'Rem'.

20   Item one Dublet of Carnacion Satten embroidered allover with hollye leaves and hopes sett with small seede pearle.

Loc. 'T', 't'. LMN in H16 'Rem'. The description is not very detailed, but this is probably a New Year's gift: 'By the Barronesse Morley A Doblate of Carnation Satten allover enbradored with hoopes and Flowers of Golde and garnished withe riche seede perles. Delivered to the foresaid Rauf Hoope'. (New Year's Gift Roll, 23 Eliz. 1581. Eton Coll. BLA 18 192).

21   Item one Dublett of Carnacion and heare colour Satten cutt in skallop cut embroidered with owes and a small Cheine of sylver.

Loc. 'C', 'c'. LMN in H16 'Rem'.

22   Item one Dublet of white Satten cut striped byas with a lace of golde.

Loc. 'C', 't'. LMN in H16 'Rem'.

411   *Detail from 'Lady Clopton of Kentwell Hall' in Figure 229, showing her black velvet doublet embroidered with triangles and curving drops in gold thread, with a covering of finest white cobweb lawn or silk. Yale Center for British Art, Paul Mellon Collection, New Haven, Connecticut*

23   Item one Dublett of white Satten cut with a blacke Satten wreath lace and a plate of golde with small owes.

Loc. 't'. LMN in H16 'Rem'.

f. 81ᵛ

24   Item one Dublett of tawnye Satten cut upon Tyncell laide allover with russet silke and golde lace Indented wise.

Loc. 'T', 't'. LMN in H16 'Rem'.

25   Item one Dublett of Carnacion Satten covered with networke of golde and aishe colour silke with a passamaine lace of golde and spangles.

Loc. 'T', 't'. LMN in H16 'Rem'.

26   Item one Dublet of white Satten embroidered allover with flowers flies and wormes of golde silver and silke of sondrie colours and a vale or loose gowne of blacke networke florished with golde.

Loc. 't'. LMN in H16 'Rem'.

27   Item one Dublett of strawe colour Satten cut and lyned with cloth of silver embroidered upon with knotts Roses and sonnes of venice golde and silver.

Loc. 'T', 't'. LMN in H16 'Rem'.

28   Item one Dublett of Carnacion Satten cut and embroidered allover with Roses and Leaves of venice golde and silver.

Loc. ⟨'T', 'C'⟩, 't'.

29   Item one Dublett of orenge colour Satten cut and tackt up(pe) laide with silver owes lyned with peache colour grograine.

Loc. 'c'. LMN in H16 'Rem'.

30   Item one Dublett of strawe colour Satten cut and prented tackte up(pe) and sett with owes of sylver lyned with white sarceonett.

Loc. ⟨'T'⟩, 'c'. LMN in H16 'Rem'.

31   Item one Dublet of Carnacion and white satten cut in panes Chevernewise set with owes striped with a lace of golde ⟨and sylver⟩.

Loc. 'C', 'c'. LMN in H16 'Rem'.

32   Item one Dublet of peach colour Satten covered with lawne Cutt worke florished with golde owes.

Loc. 'T', 't'. LMN in H16 'Rem'.

412   *Castle or fortress, detail from a polychrome embroidered white satin panel, probably part of a skirt, c. 1600. Victoria and Albert Museum, London (T.138–1981)*

413   *'Portrait of an unknown lady', painting by an unknown artist, c. 1600. A detail of the embroidery is given in Figure 404. The stomacher is embroidered with silver thread and silver*

spangles, with panels of white cypress striped with silver thread caught down with enamelled buttons set with rubies, diamonds and pearls. The petticoat is in brown silk with an additional weft of gold threads and a woven pattern of yellow ochre feathers and flowers. It seems to be the same sitter in Figure 327, with the identical jewel but different clothes. The Collection at Parham Park

f. 82

33   Item one Dublett of Carnacion Satten embroidered with golde silver and sylke of sondrie colours.

Loc. 'C', 'c'. LMN in H16 'Rem'. This was a New Year's gift: 'By the Baronesse Lumley a dublett of Carnation Satten Imbrothered with venus golde, silver and silke of divers cullours. Delivered to the said Sir Thos: Gorges'. (New Year's Gift Roll, 30 Eliz. 1588. BL, Add.8159).

34   Item one Dublett of white Satten embroidered allover with golde silver and Carnacion silke with squares and flowers Chevernewise.

Loc. 'C', 'c'. LMN in H16 'Rem'. This appears to have been a New Year's gift: 'By the Baronesse Talbott Junior one dublett unmade of white satten Imbrothered all over with venus Golde, Silver and Carnation silke in Squares. Delivered to the said Sir Tho: Gorges'. (New Year's Gift Roll, 30 Eliz. 1588. BL, Add.8159).

35   Item one Dublett of white Satten embroidered allover like Cloudes verie faire skallop facion with flowers and fruites of venice golde silver and silke betwene them.

Loc. 'C', 'c'. LMN in H16 'Rem'. This was a New Year's gift: 'By Sir Roberte Sydney A dooblett of white satten embrodered all over like Cloudes very faire of Scallopp fashion with flowers and fruites of venis gold silver and silke betwene them. Delivered to the Roabes.' (New Year's Gift Roll, 31 Eliz. 1589. BL, Lansd. Roll 17, printed in *Progr. Eliz.*, III, p. 10).

36   Item one Dublet of white Satten cut embroidered allover with owes of venice golde and striped byas with a passamaine lace of venice golde and plate.

Loc. 'C', 'c'. LMN in H16 'Rem'. This was a New Year's gift: 'By Sir Fraunces Walsingham principall Secretary A Cloke and A savegard . . . and a doublett of white satten Cutt & ymbrodered all over with Owes of venis gold, and striped over[t]whart with a passamayn of venis golde and plate. Delivered to the Roabes'. (New Year's Gift Roll, 31 Eliz. 1589. BL, Lansd. Roll 17, printed in *Progr. Eliz.*, III, p. 9). See f.72ᵛ/7 for the cloak and safeguard. The printed version gives 'Esses' instead of 'Owes'.

37   Item one Dublet of heare colour Satten covered over with a blacke stitched cloth florished with venice golde silver owes and verie litle Buttons of venice golde and silver lyned with white sarceonett.

Loc. 'T', 't'. LMN in H16 'Rem'.

38   Item one Dublet of aish colour Satten covered over with russett Networke florished with venice golde silver and owes lyned with Carnacion sarceonet.

Loc. 'T', 't'. LMN in H16 'Rem'.

39   Item one Dublet of white Satten cut and embroidered allover with a running worke of flowers and fruites of sondrie sorts of venice golde silver and silke and silver owes set on with blewe

Loc. 'C', 'c'. LMN in H16 'Rem'.

40   Item one Dublet of Sea water greene Satten cut and enbrodered allover with flowers of venice golde silver and silke of sondrie colours and sorts drawen out with lawne.

Loc. 'T', 't'. LMN in H16 'Rem'.

f. 82^v

41   Item one Dublet of white Satten cut and snipte allover striped overthwarte ⟨byas⟩ with a plate lace of venice golde and lyned with silver Chamblet.

Loc. 'C', 'c'. LMN in H16 'Rem'. Deletion in H1. This was a New Year's gift: 'By the Barrones Cobham. A Doblett of white Satten Cout Ruft up & stryped over T[h]wart with A smaull passamayn lace of venis gold and Sylke. Delivered the forsaid Raulfe hope'. (New Year's Gift Roll, 27 Eliz. 1585. Folger, Z.d.16). Lord Cobham gave the Queen a matching round kirtle at the same time, but this does not seem to have been entered in the Inventory in 1600.

42   Item one Dublet of white Satten laide upon with a lawne cutt in rysing puffes embroidered with owes of silver and bounde with a lace of venice silver.

Loc. 'T', 't'. LMN in H16 'Rem'.

43   Item one Dublet of Isabella colour Satten cut and snipte covered with white Lawne cutworke garnished with silver plate.

Loc. 'C', 'c'. LMN in H16 'Rem'.

44   Item one Dublett of white Satten embroidered allover in shorte panes with golde twiste and owes razed up like wreathes upon silver chamblett and the panes lyned with Carnacion sarceonett.

Loc. 'C', 'c'. LMN in H16 'Rem'.

45   Item one Dublett of white Satten cut allover and embroidered with golde plate like Esses three in a place and some golde owes.

Loc. 'T', 't'. LMN in H16 'Rem'.

46   Item one Dublett of blacke Satten cut allover diamondewise drawen out with Cobbewebbe lawne and embroidered allover with braunches of seede pearle.

Loc. 'C', 'c'. LMN in H16 'Rem'.

47   Item one Dublet of white Satten embroidered like Seas with fishes Castles and sonne beames of venice golde silver and silke of sondrie colours.

Loc. 'T', 't'. LMN in H16 'Rem'.

48   Item one Dublet of white Satten cut in open workes richlie embroidered with venice golde silver and silkes of sondrie colours like beasts of dyvers sorts.

Loc. 'C', 'c'. LMN in H16 'Rem'.

f. 83

49   Item one Dublett of white Satten cut allover in small rysing panes embroidered allover with golde plate, twiste of gold and tufts of oreng colour silke and golde owes laide under with silver Chamblet.

Loc. 'C', 'c'. LMN in H16 'Rem'.

50   Item one Dublet of Maiden Blush colour Satten embroidered with knotts of blacke silke and silver owes with a Covering of lawne cut in spaces.

Loc. 'C', 't'. LMN in H16 'Rem'.

51   Item one Dublet of white Satten cut and embroidered allover like knotts and Roses drawen oute with Cobwebbe lawne.

Loc. 'C', 'c'. LMN in H16 'Rem'.

52   Item one Dublet of white Satten cut and embroidered upon with leaves and garlandes of silke needleworke.

Loc. 'C', 'c'. LMN in H16 'Rem'.

53   Item one Dublet of white Satten cut and snipte allover laide with golde lace raized up(pe/pon) and set with owes.

Loc. 'T', 'c'. LMN in H16 'Rem'. William Jones was entered in 1584 'for making of a Dublett of white satten cutt, layed with golde spangell lase lyned with sarceonett styffenid with canvas buckeram & bayes all of our great guarderobe'. (Warrant 27 Sept., 26 Eliz. 1584. BL, Egerton 2806, f. 199^v).

54   Item one Dublet of white Satten embroidered allover with silver cut with snippes and raized up(pe/pon) in puffes laide under with silver Chamblet.

Loc. 'C', 'c'. LMN in H16 'Rem'.

55   Item one Dublet of white Satten cut in rysing Indentes embroidered with plates of silver and small silver owes and wormes.

Loc. 'C', 'c'. LMN in H16 'Rem'.

56   Item one Dublet of white Satten cut and snipte downerighte with venice golde and sylver.

Loc. 'C', 'c'. LMN in H16 'Rem'. This was a New Year's gift: 'By Mr Foucke Grivell one doublet of white satten cutt and snipped downe right with Venis golde and silver. Delivered to the Robes.' (New Year's Gift Roll, 40 Eliz. 1598. PRO, C47/3/40).

57   Item one Dublet of white Satten embroidered allover with grapes and vyne leaves raized up laide under with silver Chamblett.

Loc. 'C', 'c'. LMN in H16 'Rem'.

f. 83^v

58   Item one Dublett of white Satten embroidered allover in rysing puffes of Roses and Leaves of coloured silke laide under with silver Chamblett with golde owes.

Loc. 'C', 'c'. LMN in H16 'Rem'.

59   Item one Dublett of white Satten embroidered and raized upon like flies and leaves of venice silver garnished with knitworke.

Loc. 'C', 't'. LMN in H16 ⟨'Rem'⟩. This was a New Year's gift: 'By the Barronnes Hunsdon, junior, one doublet of white satten, embroidered and razed upon like flyes, and leaves of Venyce silver, and garnished with white knyttworke. Delivered to the Robes.' (New Year's Gift Roll, 42 Eliz. 1600. Printed in *Progr. Eliz.*, III, p. 450).

60   Item one Dublett of white Satten cut snipt and raized upp(e/pon) with owes of venice golde.

Loc. 'C', 'c'. LMN in H16 'Rem'.

61   Item one Dublet ⟨unmade⟩ of white Satten embroidered allover like snakes wounde togeather richlie wrought with venice silver with puffes of Lawne embrodered with venice silver like wheate Eares.

Loc. 'C', 'c'. LMN in H16 'Rem'. Deletion in H1. This was a joint New Year's gift: 'By the Countes of Shrewesbury, junior, parte of a doublet, unmade, of white satten, embrothered all over like snakes wounde together, of Venyce silver, richly wrought and puffes of lawne embrothered with Venice silver like wheate eares. Delivered to the Robes'. (New Year's Gift Roll, 42 Eliz. 1600. Printed in *Progr. Eliz.*, III, p. 447). Her husband, the Earl of Shrewsbury, gave the other part. Work was carried out on the doublet three years later: 'Item to John Parr our said sisters enbrauderer . . . for drawing forth a doublet of white satten wrought allover with snakes & wheat eares of silver the wheat eares cutt of and set upon new lawne'. (Warrant 18 May, 1 James 1603. PRO, LC5/37, ff. 284, 285).

62   Item one Dublet of white Satten cut and raized up(pe/pon) like Lillies with silver and orenge colored silke drawen out with white Cipers.

Loc. 'C', 'c'. LMN in H16 'Rem'.

63   Item one Dublet of white Satten cut and raized up(pe/pon) like Crownes embrodered with silver owes and plate and drawen oute.

Loc. 'C', 'c'. LMN in H16 'Rem'.

64   Item one Dublet of white Satten striped with gold glisteringe.

Loc. 'T', 't'. LMN in H16 'Rem'.

65   Item one Dublet of blacke Taphata embroidered allover with trees of Hawthorne of venice golde and greene silke.

Loc. 'T', 't'. LMN in H16 'Rem'.

66   Item one Dublet of Carnacion taphata sarceonet covered with Lawne Cutworke in compasses and tufts of white silke set with owes and spangles of golde.

Loc. 'T', 't'. LMN in H16 'Rem'.

f. 84

67   Item one Dublet of orenge colour Taphata covered with white Nettworke slightlie florished with knotts of silver and golde and knotts of threedd.

Loc. 'T', 't'. LMN in H16 'Rem'.

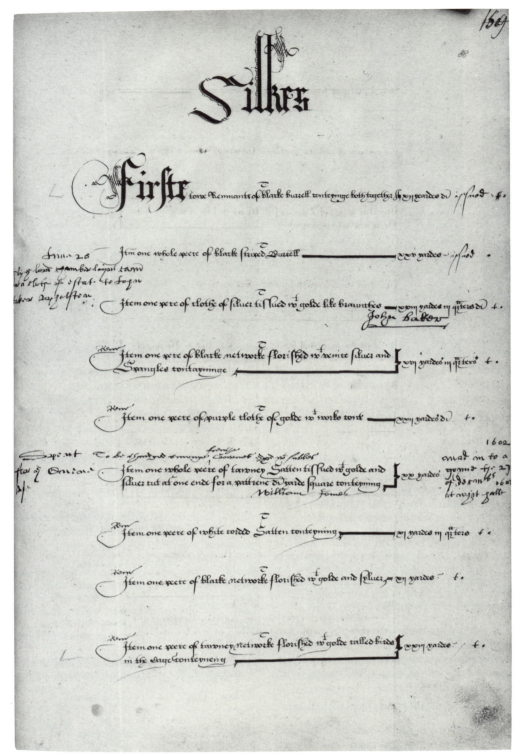

416   *Folio 88 from the Stowe inventory, listing silks in store. British Library, London (Stowe 557)*

[5]   Item one peece of purple clothe of golde with works conteyning —— xxij yardes di

Loc. 'T', 't'. LMN in H16 'Rem'.

[6]   Item one whole peece of tawney Satten tissued with golde and silver cut at one end for a pattrene di yarde square conteyning —— xx yardes

Loc. 'T'. LMN in H9 'Spent for ye Quenes use'. RMN in H9 'mad in to a gowne the 27 of december 1602 at whit halle'. Signature 'William Jones'. NAE in H3 'To be chardged amonge frenche Gownes {lynd} with sables'. Jones made 'a highbodied gowne of tawney tissued satten with a gold lace about furred with sables & lyned with sarcenet the bodies stiffened with canvas & buckeram, the tissued satten of our store of the charge of the said Sir Thomas Gorges knight the rest of our great warderobe'. (Warrant 18 May, 1 James I, 1603. PRO, LC5/37, f. 283).

[7]   Item one peece of white corded Satten conteyning —— xj yardes iij quarters

Loc. 'T', 't'. LMN in H16 'Rem'.

[8]   Item one peece of blacke Networke florished with golde and sylver —— xij yardes

Loc. 'T', 't'. LMN in H16 'Rem'.

[9]   Item one peece of tawney Networke florished with golde called birds in the Cage conteyneng —— xxiij yardes

Loc. 'T', 't'. LMN in H16 'Rem'.

f. 88ᵛ

[10]   Item one peece of strawe colour India Canvas conteyning vj yardes

Loc. 'T', 't'. LMN in H16 'Rem'.

[11]   Item one peece of watchet Satten with flowers of silver tissue conteyning xxj yardes di

Loc. 'T', 't'. LMN in H16 'Rem'.

[12]   Item twoe peeces of Turquey silke striped with silke of colours the moste blewe and redd contayninge —— vj yardes di

Loc. 'T', 't'. LMN in H16 'Rem'.

[13]   Item twoe handekercheifes like Barbers aprones

Loc. 'T', 't'. LMN in H16 'Rem'.

[14]   Item twoe Remnants of blacke Satten florished with flowers of golde and silver contayning ——xiiij yardes di

Loc. 'T', 't'. LMN in H16 'Rem'.

[15]   Item one peece of white braunched Capha conteyning —— x yardes

Loc. 'T', 't'. LMN in H16 'Rem'.

[16]   Item three peeces of Baudekin of sondrye colours each peece contayning vij yardes —— xxj yardes

Loc. 'T', 't'. LMN in H16 'Rem'.

[17]   Item one peece of Carnacion grograine florished with golde conteyning ——ix yardes

Loc. 'T', 't'. LMN in H16 'Rem'.

[18]   Item ⟨one⟩ three whole peeces of Crimsen grograine florished with golde either of them conteyning eight yards a peece or therabouts —— xxiiij yardes

Loc. 'T', 't'. LMN in H16 'Rem'. Deletion in H1.

f. 89

[19]   Item one peece of purple Baudekyn with sondrie workes in it conteyning —— vij yardes di di quarter

Loc. 'T', 't'. LMN in H16 'Rem'.

[20] Item twoe peeces of Carnacion China Chapha either of them contayning Nyne yardes —— xviij yardes

Loc. 'T', 't'. LMN in H16 'Rem'. 'Chapha' is a scribe's error for 'Capha'.

[21] Item twoe shoulder Mantles & one forepart ⟨of white taphata called⟩ China worke embrodered allover with sondrie fowles and beasts of silke of sondrie colours

Loc. 'T', 't'. LMN in H16 'Rem'. Deletion in H1.

[22] Item one peece of white China Satten embrodered allover with beasts birds and flowers of silke of sondrie colours contayning in lenght twoe yards di di quarter in breadth iij quarters of a yarde —— twoe yardes di di quarter

Loc. 'T', 't'. LMN in H16 'Rem'.

[23] Item one peece of blacke stitched clothe florished with starres and owes of venice golde and silver contayning ——xx yardes

Loc. 'T', 't'. LMN in H16 'Rem'.

[24] Item one peece of Murrey or pale colour vellatt contayning —— xxiiij yardes

Loc. 'T', 't'. LMN in H16 'Rem'.

[25] Item one Remnant of Drakes colour cloth of golde contayning —— x yardes

Loc. 'T', 't'. LMN in H16 'Rem'.

[26] Item one peece of pale rushe colour cloth of sylver contayninge xix yardes 3 quarters

Loc. 'T', 't'. LMN in H16 'Rem'.

[27] Item xix Remnants of white silke Curle contayninge in the whole Ciiij yardes

Loc. 'T'. RMN in H4 'issued all'.

f.89ᵛ

[28] Item one peece of blacke stitched clothe embrodered upon with venice golde silver˙ and golde owes contayninge ——⟨xv⟩ xiiij yardes

Loc. 'T'. RMN in H9 'spent & issued in d(. . . . .)'.

[29] Item one peece of pale orenge colour clothe of silver with workes like Pyneaples and Artichoughes contayning —— xxv yardes di

Loc. 'T', 't'. LMN in H16 'Rem'.

[30] Item one whole peece of clothe of silver tissued with sylver and raized with Carnacion vellatt —— xxiiij yardes quarter

Loc. 'T', 't'. LMN in H9 'June 18 Delyverid by ye lorde chamberlayns command for a clothe of estat to John baker upholster[er] & for

417 *Detail of yellow silk woven with a cream pattern, enriched with gold and silver wire (much of which has disintegrated) and a raised pile in two sizes of looped gold and silver thread. Victoria and Albert Museum, London (T.111–1910)*

chayres stoles & cusshions to John gren cofer maker 1603'. Signatures 'John Baker' and 'Johne gren'. This would have been for the coronation of James I, on Monday, 25 July 1603.

[31] Item one Remnant of white stitched clothe florished with venice silver and silver spangles contayning —— ⟨one yarde iij quarters⟩ xiij yardes

Loc. 'T', 't'. LMN in H16 ⟨'Rem'⟩. Deletion in H1. RMN in H9 'spent'.

[32] Item one peece of Cloth of sylver with flowers of sylke of sondrie colours contayning —— xvij yardes

Loc. 'T', 't'. LMN in H16 'Rem'.

[33] Item one peece of Dove colour Cloth of tissue with workes of wheat Eares horse shoes and flower de luces contayning —— xxv yardes

Loc. 'T', 't'. LMN in H9 'June 18 delyvered by ye lorde chamberlayns command for a clothe of estate to John baker upholster[er] & for chayres stoles & cussyenes to John grene coffermaker 1603'. Signatures 'John Baker' and 'Johne gren'. This would have been for the coronation of James I.

[34] Item one Remnant of cloth of sylver raized with vellat tissued with golde sylver and silke of sondrie colours —— ij yardes quarter

Loc. 'T', 't'. NAE in H9 'delivered to John baker by the lord chamberlayns command June the 20 for ye sam[e] stat[e]'. Signature 'John Baker'. Presumably this was for the same cloth of estate for the coronation.

[35] Item one peece of cloth of sylver tissued with golde sylver and unshorne vellat in workes of sondrie colours contayning —— xvij yardes

Loc. 'T', 't'. LMN in H9 'June 26 delivered by ye lord chamberlayns command for a clothe of estat to John baker upholster[er]'. Signature 'John Baker'. This would have been for the coronation of James I.

f.90

[36] Item one peece of white Tiffanye contayning —— lx yardes

Loc. 'T', 't'. LMN in H16 'Rem'.

[37] Item one Remnant of orenge colour and aishe colour golde and sylver Chamblett with workes like flagon worke contayning —— xv yardes di

Loc. 'T', 't'. LMN in H16 'Rem'.

[38] Item one peece of white riche clothe of silver tissue in gardes contayning —— viij yardes iij quarters

Loc. 'T', 't'. LMN in H9 'June 18 delivered by the lord chamberlyns command for stoles chayres & cussyons to John Baker upholster[er] & John Grene cofermaker 1603'. Signatures 'John Baker' and 'Johne gren'. This would have been for the coronation of James I.

[39] Item one peece of cloth of gold tissued cut into squares conteyning ——xiiij yardes di

Loc. 'T', 't'. LMN in H9 'June 11 delivered by the lord chamberlyns command for stoles chayres & cussyons to John baker upholster[er]

418 *Fan with black, red, yellow, and white feathers, detail from Figure 215, c.1575. National Portrait Gallery, London*

419 *White ostrich feather fan, the gold handle set with a ruby, pearls and diamonds, detail from Figure 64, c.1590–92. Toledo Museum of Art, Ohio*

420 *Fan with pink feathers, the gold handle set with rubies and pearls, detail from Figure 218, c.1580–85. Private collection*

& John Grene cofermaker 1603'. Signatures 'John Baker' and 'Johne gren'.

[40] Item one Remnant of Spanishe Taphata florished with golde and sylke of dyvers colours conteyninge —— x yardes quarter

Loc. 'T', 't'. LMN in H16 'Rem'.

[41] Item one Remnant of aishe colour cloth of sylver with feathers and other workes contayning —— x yardes

Loc. 'T', 't'. LMN in H16 'Rem'.

[42] ⟨Item six whole breadthes of orenge colour Spanish Taphata florished with sylver sometymes made into a gowne and nowe remaines in peeces⟩

Loc. 't'. RMN in H7 'vacat quia entred amongst french gownes'. The whole item is cancelled by striking through. Cf. f. 22ᵛ/66.

[43] Item one pece of white thredd knitworke set with a fewe spangles of sylver contayning —— v yardes di

RMN in H7 'Imploied' and ⟨'ymploied since the'⟩.

f.90ᵛ

[No entries]

f.91

Fannes

In this section the ink of 'Rem' is slightly deeper in colour from 'delivered xxx° Januarii 1604' and was written at a different time. It is not clear if this is Old Style or New Style date, so 1604 may be 1605. Each item is marked with a small cross by the number, except no. 3. These are checking marks of some kind.

1 Firste ⟨one Fanne of white feathers⟩ with a handle of golde garnished with fower faire diamondes twoe faire Rubies twoe small diamondes and seaven rocke Rubies and one Emerode with a faire looking glasse garnished with golde sett with three small table Rubies with a redd and white Rose in the middest enameled with a Septer and a Crowne over it in the handle thereof ⟨in a Case of blacke vellatt laide with a passamaine of venice golde⟩ And one verie little laver of silver guilte with a spoute the handle broken.

Loc. 'C', 'c'. LMN in H16 'Rem' and 'delivered xxx° Januarii 1604. less the white rose'. The deletions are made by underlining the words.

2 Item one ⟨Fanne of blacke feathers⟩ with a handle of golde enameled blacke the upper parte dyvers colours.

Loc. 'C', 'c'. LMN in H16 'Rem' and 'delivered xxx° Januarii 1604'. The deletion is made by underlining the words. This probably means that the feathers have disintegrated as the handle is intact. Cf. with f.91/1, 4, f.91ᵛ/6, 7, f.92ᵛ/22, 23.

3 Item one Fanne of white feathers with a handle of golde havinge twoe snakes wyndinge aboute it garnished with a ball of diamondes in the ende and a Crowne on each side within a paire of winges garnished with diamondes lacking vj diamonds.

Loc. 'C', 'c'. LMN in H11 'Taken by the Kinges majestie the 19 of may 1603'.

4 Item ⟨one Fanne of white feathers with Carnacion feathers curled⟩ The handle of Aggatt garnished with golde.

Loc. 'C', 'c'. LMN in H16 'delivered xxx° Januarii 1604'. The deletion is made by underlining the words.

5 Item one Fanne of Carnacion white and orenge colour feathers with a handle of Cristall garnished slightlie with golde enameled.

Loc. 'C', 'c'. LMN in H16 'Rem' and 'delivered xxx° Januarii 1604'.

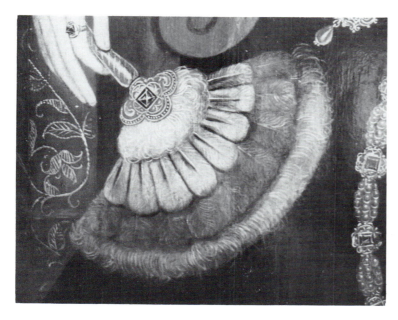

f.91ᵛ

6 Item ⟨one Fanne of feather of divers colours⟩ the handle of golde with a Beare and a ragged staffe on both sides and a looking glasse on thoneside.

Loc. 'C', 'c'. LMN in H16 'Rem' and 'delivered xxx° Januarii 1604'. The deletion is made by underlining the words.

7 Item one Fanne ⟨of white feathers with painted feathers⟩ the handle of Jeatt garnished with golde slightlie and xvj verie small sparks of diamondes.

Loc. 'C', 'c'. LMN in H16 'Rem' and 'delivered xxx° Januarii 1604'. The deletion is made by underlining the words.

8 Item one Fanne of the feathers of the Birde of Paradise and other colored feathers thone set with six small starres and one great starre set with iiijᵒʳ little Saphires the handle of sylver guilte.

Loc. 'C', 'c'. LMN in H16 'Rem' and 'delivered xxx° Januarii 1604'.

9 Item one handle of Cristall garnished with golde and a worde enameled.

Loc. 'C', 'c'. LMN in H16 'Rem' and 'delivered xxx° Januarii 1604'.

10 Item one handle of golde enameled set with small Rubies and Emerodes lacking x stones with a shipp under saile on thone side.

Loc. 'C', 'c'. LMN in H16 'Rem' and 'delivered xxx° Januarii 1604'.

11 Item one handle of christall garnished with sylver guilte with a worde within the handle.

Loc. 'C', 'c'. LMN in H16 'Rem' and 'delivered xxx° Januarii 1604'.

12 Item one ⟨Fanne of white and tawney feathers⟩ set in a handle of golde with the Beare and the ragged staffe.

Loc. 'C', 'c'. LMN in H16 'Rem' and 'delivered xxx° Januarii 1604'. The deletion is made by underlining the words.

13 Item one handle of Cristall garnished with golde with a devise under the Christall painted.

Loc. 'C', 'c'. LMN in H16 'Rem' and 'delivered xxx° Januarii 1604'.

f.92

14 Item one handle of golde with a shell of Mother of pearle.

Loc. 'C', 'c'. LMN in H16 'Rem' and 'delivered xxx° Januarii 1604'.

15 Item one handle of a Fanne of golde enameled greene with a hope on thoneside and xxᵗⁱᵉ Diamondes small and pointed on the other side wanting v diamondes.

Loc. 'C', 'c'. LMN in H16 'Rem' and 'delivered xxx° Januarii 1604'.

16 Item one Fanne of white peacockes feathers with the handle of golde enameled white and greene wreathed.

Loc. 'C', 'c'. LMN in H16 'Rem' and 'delivered xxx° Januarii 1604'.

17 Item one ⟨Fanne of feathers with a⟩ handle of sylver guilte ⟨and wrought⟩ ⟦chased⟧.

Loc. 'C', 'c'. LMN in H16 'Rem' and 'delivered xxx° Januarii 1604'. Addition in H3. The deletions are made by underlining the words.

18 Item one handle of Cristall garnished with golde enameled with a sea one bothe sides and a Shippe on each side with a pommell enameled white with Pomaunder.

Loc. 'C', 'c'. LMN in H16 'Rem' and 'delivered xxx° Januarii 1604'.

19 Item one Fanne of Swanne downe with a Maze of greene vellatt embrodered

421 *Fan with red and white feathers, detail from Figure 46, c. 1590. Pollok House, Glasgow*

422 *Fan with white feathers, the gold handle set with diamonds, detail from Figure 102, c. 1585–90. Lord Tollemache, Helmingham Hall, Stowmarket*

423 *Fan with curled white feathers, detail from Figure 129, c. 1599. The National Trust, Hardwick Hall, Derbyshire*

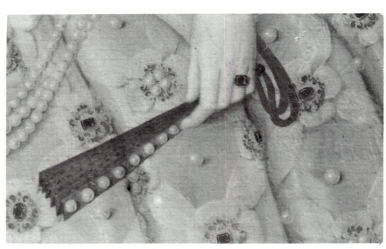

424   *Folding fan decorated on both guardsticks with five pearls, each set on a tuft of red silk, detail from Figure 71, c. 1592–94. National Portrait Gallery, London*

425   *Folding fan, possibly of pinked leather, the guardsticks decorated with pearls. Details from Figure 74, c. 1592–1600. Pitti Palace, Florence*

with seede p(ear)le and a verie small Cheine of silver guilte and in the middest a border on both sides of seede pearle sparks of Rubies and Emerodes and therein a Monster of golde the head and Breast of Mother of pearle the handle of Cristall.

Loc. 'T', 'c'. LMN in H16 'Rem' and 'delivered xxx° Januarii 1604'. This was a New Year's gift. 'By the Countesse of Bath, a Fanne of Swanne downe with a maze of greene velvett, ymbrodered with seed pearles and a very small chaine of silver gilte and in the middest a border on both sides of seed pearles sparkes of Rubyes and Emerodes and therein a monster of gold the head and breaste mother of pearles ... Delivered the Fanne to the Roabes'. (New Year's Gift Roll, 31 Eliz. 1589. BL, Lansd. Roll 17, printed in *Progr. Eliz.*, III, p. 4).

20   Item one Fanne of sondrie colored feathers with a handle of Agath garnished with sylver guilte.

Loc. 'C', 'c'. LMN in H16 'Rem' and 'delivered xxx° Januarii 1604'. This was a New Year's gift: 'By A gentleman unknowne A Fanne of sundry Cullored Fethers with A handle of Aggeth garnished with silver gilte. Delivered to the Roabes'. (New Year's Gift Roll, 31 Eliz. 1589. BL, Lansd. Roll 17, printed in *Progr. Eliz.*, III, p. 13).

21   Item one Fanne of sylkewomans worke with a handle of golde enameled.

Loc. 'C', 'c'. LMN in H16 'Rem' and delivered xxx° Januarii 1604'.

f.92ᵛ

22   Item one ⟨Fanne of white feathers⟩ with a handle of silver guilte like an Anker.

Loc. 'C', 'c'. LMN in H16 'Rem' and 'delivered xxx° Januarii 1604'.

23   Item ⟨one Fanne of white feathers⟩ with a handle of Cristall slightlie garnished with golde and set with ix sparks of Emerodes [[ij bigger ones loste]].

Loc. 'C', 'c'. LMN in H16 'Rem' and 'delivered xxx° Januarii 1604'. RMN in H3 'one loste'. Addition in H3.

24   Item one Fanne of orenge colour Satten cut allover upon silver Tincell with a handle of golde enameled white and grene and set with a starre of diamondes one each side and three half moones on each side set with sparks of Rubies with a Globe in thende of it garnished with some sparks of Rubies.

Loc. 'C', 'c'. LMN in H16 'Rem' and 'delivered xxx° Januarii 1604'.

25   Item one handle of Elitropia garnished with golde set with Sparks of diamondes Rubies and sixe small pearles lacking one diamonde.

Loc. 'C', 'c'. LMN in H16 'Rem' and 'delivered xxx° Januarii 1604'. NAE in H16 'broken'.

26   Item one handle of Cristall slightlie garnished with golde and some pearle.

Loc. 'C', 'c'. LMN in H16 'Rem broken' and 'delivered xxx° Januarii 1604'. NAE in H16 'broken'.

27   Item one handle of Aggatt and garnished with golde and pearles and some sparks of Rubies.

Loc. 'C', 'c'. LMN in H16 'Rem' and 'delivered xxx° Januarii 1604'.

f.93

Pantobles

1   Firste one paire of Pantobles of Carnacion vellat enbrodered with handes and eies set with a border of pearle of sondrie sorts.

Loc. 'C', 'c'. This was a New Year's gift: 'By the Barronesse Shandowes Dowager a paire of Slippers of Carnacion vellat enbraudered withe a border of perle and handes and Eyes enbraydered. Delivered to the Roobes by Charles Smyth'. (New Year's Gift Roll, 23 Eliz. 1581. Eton Coll. BLA 18 192). The slippers were apparently translated to pantobles.

2   Item one paire of Pantobles of cloth of silver embroidered with a Mill.

Loc. 'T', 'c'.

3   Item one paire of Pantobles of wyllowe colour vellatt embroidered with purle of silver.

Loc. 'T', 'c'.

4   Item one paire of Pantobles of heare colour vellat embroidered with seede pearle.

Loc. 'C', 'c'.

5   Item one paire of Pantobles of silke needleworke like Roses the grounde sylver.

Loc. 'C', 'c'.

6   Item one paire of Pantobles of peach colour vellatt embroidered allover with venice gold and seede p(ear)le.

Loc. 'C', 'c'.

7   Item one paire of Pantobles of peach colour Chamblet embroidered with seede pearle and some stone in Collets of small valewe.

Loc. 'C', 'c'.

f.93ᵛ

8   Item one paire of Pantobles of orenge colour vellatt enbrodered upon with Essefirmes and other knotts of seede pearle and some ragged p(ear)le.

Loc. 'T', 'c'.

9   Item one paire of Pantobles of aish colour vellatt embroidered with fyves of seede p(earl)le.

Loc. 'T', 'c'.

[One unnumbered folio, blank on both sides]

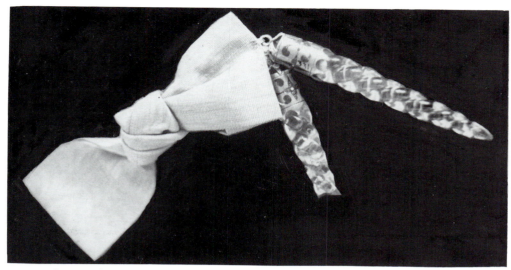

426 (above) Glass or crystal aglets, one broken, with modern ribbon, c. 1600. Skokloster Slott

427 Gold armlet, enamelled, and set with rubies and diamonds, detail from Figure 25, c. 1574–75. Walker Art Gallery, Liverpool

f. 94

Sondrie Parcells

[1] Firste one little bearinge Sworde with a pommell and hiltes of Iron guilte.

Loc. 'C'. LMN in H16 'Rem'.

[2] Item one parte of a furre of Sables for a night gowne.

Loc. 'T'. LMN in H16 'Rem'.

[3] Item one bearing Sworde the handle hiltes and pommell of silver guilte the skabberde garnished with like sylver guilte.

Loc. 'C'. LMN in H16 'Rem' and in H3 'at Courte'.

[4] Item one Sworde with a pommell of sanguinnarie.

Loc. 'C'. LMN in H16 'Rem'.

[5] Item one Canapie of Crimson Capha damaske (to carrie over one) striped with lace of venice golde and sylver the handle Mother of p(ear)le.

Loc. 'C'. LMN in H16 'Rem'. This may be an early parasol as it apparently had only one handle. Jeremy Farrell notes that in his researches the earliest mention of what he takes to be a parasol occurs in *Robertson, Inventaires de la Royne d'Escosse* for 1561 (p.33) where it is described a 'a cannabie of crammosie satine' with 'mony litle paintit buttonis all serving to bear to mak a schaddow afoir the Quene.' This and another reference for 1565 to a 'petit pavillion' (p. 156) were thought to be parasols by Robertson (p.xx).

[6] ⟨Item one paire of Lawne sleeves of Cutworke⟩.

Loc. 'C'. This item has been deleted by striking through.

[7] Item one Bagg of white Satten embroidered one both sides with sondrye personages.

Loc. 'C'. LMN in H16 'Rem'.

[8] Item fower luzarnes skines.

Loc. 'T'. LMN in H16 'Rem'.

f. 94ᵛ

[9] Item fyve paire of Sable skines.

Loc. 'T'. LMN in H9 'spent'.

[One unnumbered folio, blank on both sides]

f. 95

Jewells

In this section each item is marked with a small cross in the left margin, except 45, 56, 57 and 58, which have a single stroke. 75 and 76 have neither cross nor stroke. These are checking marks of some kind.

[1] Firste in Collettes of golde in everie Collet one Ballas one being broken ——xxiij

Loc. 'C'. LMN in H16 'Rem'.

[2] Item in buttons of golde with fyve pearles in each button —— xxij

Loc. 'C'. LMN in H16 'Rem' and 'xxij'. RMN in H5 'one lost'.

[3] Item in small Agletts of golde —— xlvj paire

Loc. 'C'. LMN in H16 'Rem xlviij paire {dd} xlvj paire delivered xxx° Januarii Anno Primo RRⁱˢ Jacobi etc 1604 To Mr {Robert Jessi}. RMN in H5 'iiij lost'.

[4] Item one Cappe ⟨and⟩ bande of Goldesmythes worke conteyninge eight pearles in a peece —— vj peeces

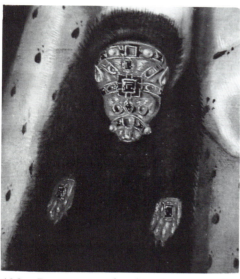

428 Fur tippet with rubies for eyes and diamonds on the feet, similar to the 'Sable Skynne the hed and fourre feate of gold fully furnyshed with Dyamondes and Rubyes' given to Elizabeth by the Earl of Leicester in 1585. Detail from Figure 391, c. 1593–95. Sabin Galleries Ltd, London

Loc. 'C'. LMN in H16 'Rem', 'less ij pearles' and 'delivered xxx° Januarii 1604'.

[5] Items in Buttons of golde furnished with small pearle in three Rowes called Suger loafe Buttons —— xlij

Loc. 'C'. LMN in H16 'Rem' and 'delivered xxx° Januarii 1604'.

[6] Item one Brouche of golde with a small Aggatt and a Cyrcle of xv sparks of Rubies and xij sparkes of Diamondes.

Loc. 'C'. LMN in H16 'Rem' and 'delivered xxx° Januarii 1604'.

[7] Item in Aglettes ⟦of golde⟧ enameled white and redde —— CCiiijˣˣ [280] paire

Loc. 'C'. Addition in H2.

429 *Jewel 'of golde like a Peramides' set with diamonds and pendent pearls, detail from Figure 129, c. 1599. National Trust, Hardwick Hall, Derbyshire*

430 *Gold jewel with enamelled figures and 'antiques', set with rubies and diamonds. A pendent pearl hangs below, detail from Figure 215, c. 1575. National Portrait Gallery, London*

431 *Pendent jewel and collar of state set with pearls, detail from Figure 102. The gold jewel, with two figures and a daisy, is set with a diamond and a pendent pearl, c. 1585–90. Lord Tollemache, Helmingham Hall, Stowmarket*

[8]   Item in Buttons of sylver like Roses —— Cxlvj

Loc. 'C'. LMN in H16 'Rem', 'delivered xxx° Januarii 1604' and 'delivered Cxliiij', 'less ij'.

f.95ᵛ

[9]   Item in Aglettes garnished with small garnettes —— ij paire

Loc. 'C'. LMN in H16 'Rem' and 'delivered xxx° Januarii 1604'.

[10]   Item in faire lardge Aglettes of golde enameled and wreathed aboute with small pearle and one bigger pearle in thende —— xxxᵗⁱᵉ paire

Loc. 'C'. LMN in H16 'Rem'.

[11]   Item one Jewell of golde enameled blacke with xxviijᵗⁱᵉ pearles eight small table Rubies one Rose of Rubies and one table diamonde in the myddest.

Loc. 'C'. LMN in H16 'Rem'.

[12]   Item one small Jewell of golde like a white Lyon with a flie one his side standing upon a base or foote garnished with twoe Opalls twoe verie little pearles fyve Rubies one Rubie pendant and twoe little shorte cheines on the backe of the Lyon.

Loc. 'C'. LMN in H16 'Rem' and 'delivered xxx° Januarii 1604'.

[13]   Item one Jewell of golde like an Angell the bodie Mother of p(ear)le the winges garnished with sparks of Diamondes and Rubies and twoe antiques like horses under it garnished with like sparkes of Rubies and two Diamondes.

Loc. 'C'. LMN in H16 'Rem' and 'delivered xxx° Januarii 1604'.

[14]   Item one Jewell of golde like a Mounte of Diamondes in sixe Rowes and a lozenged diamonde in the myddest.

Loc. 'C'. LMN in H16 'Rem' and in H14 'Taken to the Courte for the kinges Majestie by Sir George Hume knight'.

[15]   Item one Jewell of golde like a Ring artillerie crossewise garnisht with sparkes of diamondes one triangle diamonde in the top and three small pearles pendaunt aboute the Jewell.

Loc. 'C'. LMN in H16 'Rem' and delivered xxx° Januarii 1604'.

[16]   Item one Jewell of golde set with vij ⟨Diamondes⟩ Emerodes one diamonde small sparkes of Rubies three verie little pearles pendaunt with a Rocke of Mother of p(ear)le and a Bucke under it.

Loc. 'C'. LMN in H16 'Rem' and 'delivered xxx° Januarii 1604', 'less j pearle'.

f.96

[17]   Item one Jewell like a frogg of Agatt with three diamondes & one Rubie on the head with a pendaunt of fower sparkes of diamonde standing upon a flower de luce of golde garnished with sparkes of Rubies and twoe small pearles pendaunt lacking one diamond.

Loc. 'C'. LMN in H16 'Rem' and 'delivered xxx° Januarii 1604', 'less one diamonde & the pendaunte and one pearle pendaunte' and in H11 'the pendaunte taken of[f] and set to the Juell like a pellicane'.

[18]   Item one Fearne braunche of golde having therin a Lyzarde a Ladye Cowe and a Snaile.

Loc. 'C'. LMN in H16 'Rem' and 'delivered xxx° Januarii 1604'.

[19]   Item one Bodken of golde with a harrowe garnished with sparkes of Diamondes and one small pearle pendaunte.

Loc. 'C'. LMN in H16 'Rem' and 'delivered xxx° Januarii 1604'.

[20]   Item one Jewell of golde made fower square garnished with a border of sparkes of Diamondes and set within with eight Rubies iiijᵒʳ diamondes and a true love of diamondes in the middest.

Loc. 'C'. LMN in H16 'Rem'.

[21]   Item one Jewell of golde like a double rounde knott garnished with Rubies fower small pearles and fower diamondes.

Loc. 'C'. LMN in H16 'Rem', in H3 'midle dimonde loste' and in H16 'less a diamonde in the mydle'.

[22]   Item one Jewell of golde like a Peramides garnished with sparkes of Diamondes and Rubies, one bigger Rubie in the foote fower p(ear)les and one bigger pearle pendaunt. One feather of three sprigges of pearle of sondrie bignes.

Loc. 'C'. LMN in H16 'Rem' and 'delivered xxx° Januarii 1604'.

[23]   Item one Jewell of golde like a triangle made like a powch garnished with sparkes of diamondes and Rubies and twoe small Opalles lacking twoe, and over it a roundell of Opalles with a starre of Diamondes within it.

Loc. 'C'. LMN in H16 'Rem' and 'delivered xxx° Januarii 1604'.

[24]   Item one Jewell of golde like a knott garnished with sparkes of litle Diamondes and a verie litle p(ear)le pendaunte.

432 *Black enamelled gold jewel, set with three table-cut rubies and one diamond, two triangle diamonds and a pointed diamond, pinned to a sleeve. Detail from Figure 46, c.1590. Pollok House, Glasgow*

433 *Pendant (enlarged) designed as a sleeve end with wrist ruff and crystal hand, second half of sixteenth century. Museo Lazzaro Galdiano, Madrid*

Loc. 'C'. LMN in H16 'Rem' and 'delivered xxx° Januarii 1604'.

f.96ᵛ

[25] Item in small buttons with faces of Aggatt [[or camewes]]. —— xviij.

Loc. 'C'. LMN in H16 'Rem' and 'delivered xxx° Januarii 1604'. Addition in H3.

[26] Item one little Brouch enameled like a grene leafe with a Butterflie.

Loc. 'C'. LMN in H16 'Rem' and 'delivered xxx° Januarii 1604'.

[27] Item in slight buttons of golde enameled like Paunceis with verie small pearle one in each Button lacking three pearle —— lxv

Loc. 'C'. LMN in H16 'Rem' and 'delivered xxx° Januarii 1604'.

[28] Item one little Crane of golde.

Loc. 'C'. LMN in H16 'Rem' and 'delivered xxx° Januarii 1604'. This may have been a New Year's gift in 1585, although there is not enough detail to identify it with certainty: 'Item a juell of golde, like a crane, the body garnished with opalls standing upon three smale rubies and two smale dyamonds, and a very smale perle pendante. Geven by the Barones Burley'. (*Progr. Eliz.*, II, p.426).

[29] Item in buttons of golde vij with Rubies and vj with diamondes —— xiij

Loc. 'C'. LMN in H16 'Rem' and 'delivered xxx° Januarii 1604'.

[30] Item one flower of golde like a Pauncey having three Rubies and twoe Emerodes in it.

Loc. 'C'. LMN in H16 'Rem' and 'delivered xxx° Januarii 1604'.

[31] Item one litle flower of golde with a Course pearle like a peare with a border of fine sparkes of Rubies a little diamonde and a Rubie pendaunte.

Loc. 'C'. LMN in H16 'Rem' and 'delivered xxx° Januarii 1604'.

[32] Item in pomaunder buttons like acrones with seede pearle xxxvj in twoes.

Loc. 'C'. LMN in H16 'Rem' and 'delivered xxx° Januarii 1604'. These were a New Year's gift: 'By the countes of Warwyck thre Dosen of Buttons of golde being Acorns. Delivered to the Lady Howarde'. (New Year's Gift Roll, 19 Eliz. 1577. PRO, C47 3/39).

[33] Items in Buttons like pressed harts —— Lxxvj

No Loc. given. LMN in H16 'Rem Lxxiij' 'delivered xxx° Januarii 1604,' 'delivered lxxv'. RMN in H8 'these lost'.

[34] Item in Buttons like Lyzarnes enameled grene —— iiijˣˣ xij [92]

Loc. 'C'. LMN in H16 'Rem'.

[35] Item in Buttons with shells of Mother of pearle —— Cxvj

Loc. 'C'. LMN in H16 'Rem'.

f.97

[36] Item one Jewell of golde like a Crosse bowe garnished with diamondes.

Loc. 'C'. LMN in H11 'Taken by the Kinges majestie the 19 of may 1603'. This may have been given to Anne of Denmark, see Fig. 120.

[37] Item one Jewell of golde with a flie and a spider in it upon a Rose.

Loc. 'C'. LMN in H16 'Rem' and 'delivered xxx° Januarii 1604'. This may have been a New Year's gift in 1573 although there is not enough

detail to identify it with certainty: 'Item, a fayre flower of golde, having thearin a spider and a flye of agathe; and garnished with rubyes, dyamondes, and emeraldes, with one perle pendaunte, having a scorpion on the one side thearof, the flye being loose. Given by therle of Ormounde'. (*Progr. Eliz.*, I, p.323).

[38] Item a hand⟨le⟩ holding a hollie Bushe of golde enameled.

Loc. 'C'. LMN in H16 'Rem' and 'delivered xxx° Januarii 1604'.

[39] Item one little honiesuckle of golde with twoe little Rubies.

Loc. 'C'. LMN in H16 'Rem' and 'delivered xxx° Januarii 1604'.

[40] Item one little leafe of golde with a graspe in it.

Loc. 'C'. LMN in H16 'Rem' and 'delivered xxx° Januarii 1604'. A graspe is the handle or fluke of an anchor, but it is possible, in this context, that the word may be an abbreviation of grasshopper.

[41] Item one greene hawthorne braunch of golde.

Loc. 'C'. LMN in H16 'Rem' and 'delivered xxx° Januarii 1604'. This may have been a New Year's gift in 1587 although there is not enough detail to identify it with certainty: 'Item a Branche of Golde being an Hathorn, the flowers fully garneshed with very smale garnett and A smale Triangled Diamonde in it'. (BL, Add.5751A, f.215).

[42] Item one bunch of flowers of golde.

Loc. 'C'. LMN in H16 'Rem' and 'delivered xxx° Januarii 1604'.

[43] Item one little leafe of Mother of pearle with a little Saphire in it.

Loc. 'C'. LMN in H16 'Rem' and 'delivered xxx° Januarii 1604'.

 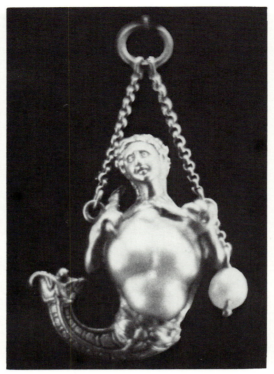 

434a, b, c *Pendent ship of mother of pearl and gold, with a little dog on board. Pendent merman with a baroque pearl used for his chest. Pendent galloping horse, a baroque pearl used for the main part of the body. All three jewels hang from gold chains, second half of the sixteenth century. Museo Lazzaro Galdiano, Madrid*

[44]   Item in Buttons of golde with pearles like starres —— xij

Loc. 'C'. LMN in H16 'Rem' and 'delivered xxx° Januarii 1604'.

[45]   Item one Jewell of golde like a sprigge of fyve garnished with sparkes of diamondes and a Sune of a Rubie graven the beames garnished with sparkes of diamondes and Rubies.

Loc. 'C'. LMN in H9 'delivered to ye Juell house'. RMN in H16 'chardge after with Mrs Ratclif'.

[46]   Item one flower of golde with a sunne and a dog under it garnished with sparkes of Diamondes one double p(ear)le pendaunt and twoe little pearles lacking the biggest diamonde.

Loc. 'C'. LMN in H16 'Rem' and 'delivered xxx° Januarii 1604'.

[47]   Item one flower of golde garnished with fyve small Rubies and three small diamondes like a bunch of Hawthorne.

Loc. 'C'. LMN in H16 'Rem' and 'delivered xxx° Januarii 1604', 'less a diamonde'.

f.97ᵛ

[48]   Item in rounde Buttons of white and blacke Aggatt —— xlij & ij withoute stalks

Loc. 'C'. LMN in H16 'Rem' and 'delivered xxx° Januarii 1604'.

[49]   Item in Buttons with Camewes —— xviij

Loc. 'C'. LMN in H16 'Rem' and 'delivered xxx° Januarii 1604'.

[50]   Item in Buttons like Tortoises with one pearle in a peece —— v

Loc. 'C'. LMN in H16 'Rem' and 'delivered xxx° Januarii 1604'. See J. Arnold, *Lost from Her Majestie's Back*, no. 173 for similar buttons lost at Bath in 1574.

[51]   Item in Buttons like Tortoises enameled greene with a half pearle in each —— vj

Loc. 'C'. LMN in H16 'Rem' and 'delivered xxx° Januarii 1604'.

[52]   Item in longe Buttons of golde set with pearles of sondrie sortes and bignes garnished with sparkes of Rubies and a bigge p(ear)le upon the topp of each Button —— xviij

Loc. 'C'. LMN in H16 'Rem' and 'delivered xxx° Januarii 1604'.

[53]   Item in Buttons of golde enameled with Crosses of sondrie colours and small flowers aboute them —— xxiij

Loc. 'C'. LMN in H16 'Rem'.

[54]   Item in Buttons of golde enameled redd set with fyve pearles and fower sparkes of Emerodes in each button lacking twoe pearles and one Emerode —— xiij

Items 53 and 54 are bracketed together. Loc. 'C'. LMN in H16 'Rem', 'delivered xxx° Januarii 1604' and 'less iij pearle'.

[55]   Item in Buttons of seede pearle one Rowe of bigger pearle and a small garnett in the middest —— xvij

Loc. 'C'. LMN in H16 'Rem' and 'delivered xxx° Januarii 1604'.

[56]   Item in Buttons of golde with one diamonde and fower small diamondes aboute it —— one.

Loc. 'C'.

[57]   Item in Buttons of golde with one small diamonde in each —— vij

Items 56 and 57 are bracketed together. Loc. 'C'. LMN in H12 'Re(turne)d Mrs Radclif'.

f.98

[58]   Item in Buttons of golde with twoe pearles in a peece —— vij

Loc. 'C'. LMN in H12 'Re(turne)d Mrs Radclif'. RMN in H15 'Memorandum these iijᵉ last parcelles were retourned to Mrs Rattliffes chardge the xxviijth of Maye 1603 in the presence of us'. Signatures 'Tho. Knyvett', 'Fra. Goston'.

[59]   Item in Buttons of golde like Roses with small sparkes of Rubies and one sparke of a diamonde in the middest —— xv

Loc. 'C'. LMN in H16 'Rem' and 'delivered xxx° Januarii 1604'.

435 *A jewel which may be a sieve, with an inscription on the rim, 'A terra il ben mal dimora in sella', detail from Figure 60, c. 1590. National Trust, Charlecote Park, Warwickshire*

436 *Chains of jewels including armillary or celestial spheres, detail from Figure 20, c. 1575. By courtesy of Reading Borough Council*

[60] Item one little Brouch of golde garnished with one Emerode three sparkes of diamondes three sparks of Rubies and other smaller sparkes of Rubies with three sprigges of golde garnished with sparks of Rubies.

Loc. 'C'. LMN in H16 'Rem' and 'delivered xxx° Januarii 1604'.

[61] Item one Jewell of golde like an Irish darte garnished with fower small diamondes.

Loc. 'C'. LMN in H16 'Rem' and 'delivered xxx° Januarii 1604'. This seems to be the jewel delivered to the Queen at Rycote in 1592, a gift from one of Sir Henry Norris's sons, see Chapter IV, note 31.

[62] Item one Jewell of golde garnished with sparkes of diamondes and Rubies and a Salamander in the middest.

Loc. 'C'. LMN in H16 'Rem', 'delivered xxx° Januarii 1604' and 'less a diamonde'. Although opals are not mentioned in the description, this may have been a New Year's gift in 1577: 'Item, a juell of golde, being a table, thearin is a salamaunder of ophalles, garnished with 18 smale dyamondes, and a pendaunte with ophales and rubyes. Geven by Mr. Thomas Heneage, Threasorour of the Chamber'. (*Progr. Eliz.*, II, p. 53).

[63] Item in Buttons of golde each set with one Rubie and fower small pearles —— xxiiij[or]

Loc. 'C'. LMN in H16 'Rem xxiiij' and 'delivered xxx° Januarii 1604 ⟨less j⟩'.

[64] Item one set of Buttons of golde enameled having fyve small pearle in each —— xvj

Loc. 'C'. LMN in H16 'Rem' and 'delivered xxx° Januarii 1604'.

[65] Item fower small Buttons of golde having in each one small Diamonde fyve buttons of golde having in each one Rubie And Tenne buttons of golde having in each fyve small pearles in all —— xix

Loc. 'C'. LMN in H16 'Rem' and 'delivered xxx° Januarii 1604', 'less j diamonde'.

f. 98[v]

[66] Item one Jewell like a rocke garnet slightlie garnished with a Ryme of golde on the outeside.

Loc. 'C'. LMN in H16 'Rem' and 'delivered xxx° Januarii 1604'.

[67] Item in Buttons of golde set with one small Rubie and fower pearles in each —— xxiiij

Loc. 'C'. LMN in H16 'Rem', 'xxiiij ⟨less j⟩', 'delivered xxx° Januarii 1604' and 'delivered xxiiij'.

[68] Item one ⟨garnet cut⟩ [[or glasse]] table wise set in open golde worke withoute foil.

Loc. 'C'. LMN in H16 'Rem' and 'delivered xxx° Januarii 1604'. Deletion made by underlining the words. Addition in H3.

[69] Item one Jewell of golde like a sprigg ⟨of feathers⟩ garnished with sparkes of ⟨diamondes⟩ Rubies and Emerodes and a small white face of Agatt in the middest thereof.

Loc. 'C'. LMN in H16 'Rem' and 'delivered xxx° Januarii 1604'.

[70] Item one Jewell of golde like three Doves the border garnished with fower sparkes of Rubies and three pearles.

Loc. 'C'. LMN in H16 'Rem' and 'delivered xxx° Januarii 1604'.

[71) Item ⟨one Cappe of blacke vellat with a bande havinge⟩ Ten buttons of golde whereof fyve are set with Cynques of sparkes of diamondes and fower small pearle in a peece. thother fyve with fower sparkes of rubies and one pearle in a peece And xviij small buttons of golde with fower small pearles in a peece And fyve buttons of golde garnished with sparkes of diamondes Rubies and pearle ⟨in the feather⟩.

Loc. 'C'. LMN in H16 'Rem the Juell' and 'delivered xxx° Januarii 1604'. Deletion made by underlining the words.

[72] Item in Buttons of golde each set with fower pearles and one garnet in the middest —— x[en]

Loc. 'C'. LMN in H16 'Rem' and 'delivered xxx° Januarii 1604'.

437 *Gold and enamelled jewel with a pelican, daisies, roses, and fleur-de-lis, set with a pointed diamond and sparks of rubies and diamonds. Detail from Figure 30, c. 1583–84. Private collection*

f. 99

[73]   Item in Buttons of golde like small Mulletts or starres garnished with small sparkes of Rubies [[& some p(ear)le some with p(ear)le & some with Rubies]] ——xxviij

Loc. 'C'. LMN in H16 'Rem' and 'delivered xxx° Januarii 1604'. Addition in H3.

[74]   Item in Buttons of golde with opalls and twoes of pearle —— xiiij

Loc. 'C'. LMN in H16 'Rem', 'delivered xxx° Januarii 1604' and 'less ij opalls'.

[75]   Item in Buttons set with shells of Mother of p(ear)le lacking ij pearles —— lxj

RMN in H15 'chardged before as parcell of {a} cxvj fol.'.

[76]   Item pearle of sondrie sortes and bignes taken from a french gowne of blacke cloth of golde.

LMN in H16 'delivered to Mrs Radlyf'.

[77]   Item in Buttons of golde [[like knottes]] having one pearle in a [[eache]] Button ⟨taken from a rounde gowne of tawnie Satten⟩ —— xxxiij

LMN in H16 'Rem' and 'delivered xxx° Januarii 1604, less some pearle'. Additions in H2. The deletion is made by underlining the words.

f. 99ᵛ

[No entries]

f. 100

Jewells   Receaved by Sir Thomas Gorges Knight of the charge of the Ladie Katherine Howarde Countesse of Nott[ingham]

In this section each item is marked with a small cross in the left margin, except 19, which has a single stroke. These are checking marks of some kind.

[1]   Firste in greate rounde Buttons of golde enameled with sondrye colours each set with small sparkes of Rubies and one pearle in the middest called great Bucklers —— lxxij

Loc. 'C'. LMN in H16 'Rem'.

[2]   Item in small buttons of golde enameled with sondrie colours one with a sparke of a diamonde an other with a Rubie and one with a pearle called small Bucklers lacking three pearles —— [[⟨lx⟩ iiijˣˣ ix [99] whereof in the handes of the Ladye Scudamore]]

Loc. 'C'. LMN in H16 'Rem' and 'iiijˣˣ vj. less iij'. RMN in H9 '⟨22⟩ 22 iij lost of those the Lady Scydmore had'. Addition in H14.

[3]   Item one Brouch of golde set with eight small diamondes and sparkes of diamondes in the myddest.

Loc. 'C'. LMN in H16 'Rem'.

[4]   Item one Jewell of golde like a Circle of Pauncies Dasies and other flowers garnished with sparkes of diamondes and Rubies havinge therin a Butterflie of mother of pearle garnished with sparkes of Rubies and a Crabbe holding the same.

Loc. 'C'. LMN in H16 'Rem', 'delivered xxx° Januarii 1604' and 'less ij litell Roses on the border'. The device of a crab and butterfly appears in Geffrey Whitney's *A Choice of Emblemes*, see Chapter IV, notes 26 and 27.

[5]   Item one Jewell of golde like a Butterflie with doble winges of mother of pearle the bodie set with sixe small diamondes with a pearle pendaunte.

Loc. 'C'. LMN in H16 'Rem' and 'delivered xxx° Januarii 1604'.

f. 100ᵛ

[6]   Item one Jewell of golde like a Pellican garnished with diamondes of sondrie sortes and bignes under her feete three Rubies and a triangle diamonde with three small shorte cheines and a knobbe garnished with sparkes of diamondes and Rubies.

Loc. 'C'. LMN in H16 'Rem' and in H14 'Taken to the Courte for the kinges Majestie by Sir George Hume knight'.

[7]   Items in Buttons of golde with twoe pearles in a peece —— viij

Loc. 'C'. LMN in H16 'Rem'.

[8]   Item in Buttons of golde with one diamonde in a peece —— vij

Loc. 'C'. LMN in H16 'Rem'. These buttons should probably be with those listed in f. 102/1.

[9]   Item in Buttons of golde with shells of Mother of pearle —— Cxxij

Loc. 'C'. LMN in H16 'Rem'.

[10]   Item one Jewell of golde like a frogg garnished with diamondes.

Loc. 'C'. LMN in H16 'Rem' and 'delivered xxx° Januarii 1604'.

[11]   Item in Buttons of golde with ragged staves and trueloves of Diamondes lacking the diamondes of one Button —— xiij

Loc. 'C'. LMN in H16 'Rem'. These may have been a gift from the Earl of Leicester in 1580, originally on a black velvet cap, 'a bande abowte it with 14 buttons of golde garnished with dyamonds, being raged staves and truelove knots, garnished with rubyes and dyamondes'. (*Progr. Eliz.*, II, p. 289).

[12]   Item in Buttons of golde enameled having sixe pearles twoe sparkes of diamondes and twoe sparkes of Rubies in each —— xx

Loc. 'C'. LMN in H16 'Rem' and 'delivered xxx° Januarii 1604'.

[13]   Item in Buttons with fower pearles in a peece —— ij

LMN in H15 'Rem' and 'delivered xxx° Januarii 1604'.

[14]   Item in Buttons enameled with one small Emerode in the middest lacking three Emerodes —— xltie

Loc. 'C'. LMN in H16 'Rem' and 'delivered xxx° Januarii 1604'.

[15]   Item in Buttons with one small pearle enameled —— xljtie

Loc. 'C'. LMN in H16 'Rem' and 'delivered xxx° Januarii 1604'.

f. 101

[16]   Item one feather with Emerodes [[Rubies]] and pearle

Loc. 'C'. LMN in H16 'Rem' and 'delivered xxx° Januarii 1604'. Addition in H1.

[17]   Item in lardge Aglettes of golde enameled overthwart —— xvij paire

Loc. 'C'. LMN in H16 'Rem' and 'delivered xxx° Januarii 1604'.

[18]   Item in Buttons of golde with vij sparks of diamondes in each —— xxiiij

LMN in H16 'Rem', 'less xij sparks of diamondes'.

[19]   Item in Buttons of golde enameled with ragged staves either of them set with one great Diamonde twoe lesser diamondes twoe sparkes of diamondes and eight small Rubies lacking therof three of the greater diamondes one Collet and all one of the lesser diamondes Collett and all and three Rubies —— xvij

Loc. 'C'. LMN in H16 'Rem', 'delivered xxx° Januarii 1604'. 'less one bigger diamonde' and 'With the kings Majestie'.

f. 101ᵛ

[No entries]

f. 102

Jewells Receaved by Sir Thomas Gorges Knight of Mrs Marye Radcliffe

In this section each item is marked with a single stroke except 15, 26, 31 and 32. These are checking marks of some kind.

[1] Firste in Buttons of golde each set with one diamonde of sondrie cutts and bignes viz of the first sorte xxiiijᵒʳ of the seconde sorte xlij of the thirde sorte xviij lacking twoe diamondes of the iiijᵗʰ sorte xxxiij and of the vᵗʰ sorte tenn In all —— Cxxvij

Loc. 'C'. LMN in H9 'delivered to ye Juell house'. RMN in H9 'iij lost be ye {earle} of {essexe} & one by the Quene'. These were probably in the large group entered in the 1587 inventory of Queen Elizabeth's jewels delivered into the custody of Mrs Mary Ratcliffe: 'Item buttons of golde with diamondes one lacking a stone Clxxiij [173]'. (BL, Royal App. 68, f. 25). Forty six are now missing or listed elsewhere.

[2] Item in buttons of golde each set with one Rubie of sondrie bignes wherof the first sortes xxxiiij (lacking one Rubie) of the seconde sorte xij and of the thirde sorte iiij In all —— lᵗⁱᵉ

Loc. 'C'. LMN in H9 'delivered to ye Juell house'. RMN indecipherable. These were in the 1587 inventory of Queen Elizabeth's jewels delivered into the custody of Mrs Mary Ratcliffe: 'Item buttons of golde with Rubies one lacking a stone lv [55]'. (BL, Royal App. 68, f. 25). Five are now missing or listed elsewhere.

[3] Item in Buttons of golde called Trueloves each set with fower pearle viz of the firste sorte lxxviij of the seconde sorte xj of the thirde sorte xxx and of the fourthe sorte xxviij In all —— Cxlvij

LMN in H9 'delivered to ye Juell house'. RMN in H9 '{ten} be ye erle of {esshye} & one by ye Quene'. These were in the 1587 inventory of Queen Elizabeth's jewels delivered into the custody of Mrs Mary Ratcliffe: 'Item buttons with trueloves of pearle, one lacking one pearle Clij [152]'. (BL, Royal App. 68, f. 25). Five are now missing or listed elsewhere.

[4] Item in Buttons of golde knotted with three pearles in a peece —— lxv

Loc. 'C'. LMN in H9 'delivered to ye Juell house'. RMN in H9 'one lost by the quene'. These were in the 1587 inventory of Queen Elizabeth's jewels delivered into the custody of Mrs Mary Ratcliffe: 'Item in Buttons with three pearles knotted, wherof Six broken and one lackinge a pearle lxxij [72]'. (BL, Royal App. 68, f. 25). Seven are now missing or listed elsewhere.

[5] Item in Buttons of golde called Peascoddes with three pearles in a peece —— Cxxxᵗⁱᵉ

Loc. 'C'. LMN in H9 'delivered to ye Juell house'. These were in the 1587 inventory of Queen Elizabeth's jewels delivered into the custody of Mrs Mary Ratcliffe: 'Item buttons of golde like Pescoddes with three pearles in a peece lacking one pearle Cxxxj [131]'. (BL, Royal App. 68, f. 25ᵛ). One is now missing or listed elsewhere.

[6] Item in Buttons of golde enameled with dyvers colours in each a diamondes —— ⟨x⟩xxiiijᵒʳ

Loc. 'C'. LMN in H9 'delivered to ye Juell house'. These were in the 1587 inventory of Queen Elizabeth's jewels delivered into the custody of Mrs Mary Ratcliffe: 'Item buttons of golde enameled with diverse colors eache with a diamonde xxiiijᵗⁱᵉ [24]'. (BL, Royal App. 68, f. 25ᵛ).

f. 102ᵛ

[7] Item in buttons of golde enameled with dyvers colours in each a Rubie —— xxiiij

Loc. 'C'. LMN in H9 'delivered to ye Juell house'. RMN in H9 'iiij rubies lost'. These were in the 1587 inventory of Queen Elizabeth's jewels delivered into the custody of Mrs Mary Ratcliffe: 'Item buttons of golde enameled with diverse colors each with a Rubie xxiiijᵗⁱᵉ [24]'. (BL, Royal App. 68, f. 25ᵛ).

[8] Item in buttons of golde like Tortoyses in each one a pearle ——iiijᶜ iiijˣˣ xiiij [494]

Loc. 'C'. LMN in H12 'Re(turn)ed to Mrs Radclif'. These were in the 1587 inventory of Queen Elizabeth's jewels delivered into the custody of Mrs Mary Ratcliffe: 'Item buttons with Tortoyses with one pearle in a pece CCCCiiijˣˣ xiiij [494]'. (BL, Royal App. 68, f. 25ᵛ). In 1582 460 of them were used to decorate the border of a black velvet train (J. Arnold, 'Lost from Her Majesties Back', no. 354). See f. 97ᵛ/50.

[9] Item a Jewell of golde like a harte fullie garnished with diamondes and a roundell aboute it fullie garnished with diamondes with a pendaunte of three meane pearles lacking one diamonde.

Loc. 'C'. LMN in H9 'delivered to ye Juell house'. This was a New Year's gift in 1587 but the donor's name is not known: 'Item a Juell of golde like a harte fullie garnished with Dyamondes with a rondle rounde aboute also fullie garnished with dyamonds with a pendant of thre meane pearles'. (BL, Add. 5751A, f. 212ᵛ).

[10] Item one little flower of golde fullie garnished with Rubies twoe small Opalls and three small pearles.

Loc. 'C'. LMN in H9 'delivered to ye Juell house'.

[11] Item one Jewell of golde having twoe handes thone holding a sworde

438 *Jewel of an enamelled rose set with a diamond at the centre of a collar of state, and a jewel with a gold phoenix enamelled red, rising from a pyre set with a ruby, detail from Figure 26. National Portrait Gallery, London*

thother a Trowell both garnished with sparkes of diamondes and betweene the handes a garnishment of Opalles.

Loc. 'C'. LMN in H9 'delivered to ye Juell house'. This was a New Year's gift in 1587 but the donor's name is not known: 'Item a Juell of golde having too handes, thone holding a Sworde, the other a Trowell, the sworde and Trowell garnished with small sparks of Dyamonds & betweene the too handes A garnishment of small Opaules with A Sonne hanging over'. (BL, Add. 5751A, f. 213ᵛ). See Chapter IV, notes 23, 24 and 25.

[12] Item one Jewell of golde like a halfe Moone garnished with sparkes of diamondes and over it a Crowne and one verie little pearle pendaunte.

Loc. 'C'. LMN in H9 'delivered to ye Juell house'. This was a New Year's gift in 1587, but the donor's name is not known: 'Item a Jewell of golde lyke A halfe Moone garnished with sparcks of Dyamonds, and over it A Crowne, with a Pendant of A Dyamonde Tryangled with ij Lytle Fishes, and a small pearle pendant. RMN 'less ye pendaunt & ij fyshes'. (BL, Add. 5751A, f. 215ᵛ).

[13] Item one Flower of golde with fyve table diamondes and a border of diamondes of sondrie cuttes and bignes and a fowle pearle pendaunte.

Loc. 'C'. LMN in H9 'delivered to ye Juell house'. RMN in H9 (?) 'Delyvered in to ye Juell house'.

f. 103

[14] Item in peeces of golde with one Rubie or a knott enameled parcell of a Cheine and a girdell —— Ciiij

Loc. 'C'. LMN in H9 'delivered to ye Juell house'. RMN in H5 '12 loste'.

439 *Folio 102 from the Stowe inventory listing jewels, with a number of margin notes. British Library, London (Stowe 557)*

[15] Item in pearle upon a thride wayeng lace thride and all —— xv oz di di quarter.

Loc. 'C'. LMN in H11 'delivered to Mrs Ratclif'.

[16] Item one Flower of golde having a Saphire withoute foile in the middest one diamonde one Rubie one Emerode and a verie fowle pearle pendaunte.

Loc. 'C'. LMN in H9 'delivered to ye Juell house'. RMN in H11 'now (.....) to the ballyfes'.

[17] Item one faire lardge Jewell of golde like a half Moone garnished with sparkes of diamondes about the same a roundell garnished with sparkes of Rubies over it fyve shorte Sprigges garnished with sparkes of Rubies in the middest therof a flower de luce with fyve small diamondes underneath one table Rubie fower small diamondes And twoe half Circles garnished with sparkes of Rubies.

Loc. 'C'. LMN in H11 'Delyvered to the Juell house'. RMN in H15 'Retourned to Mrs Rattliffes chardge from whome it was delivered'.

[18] Item one Jewell of golde enameled blacke with v table Rubies in the middest fowre small Rubies and iij small diamondes on the border with vij spriges garnished with sparkes of diamondes and Rubies.

Loc. 'C'. LMN in H12 'Re(turne)d to Mrs Radclif'.

[19] Item one Jewell of golde garnished with Jacintes with twoe pearles and three

spригges garnished with like Jacintes lacking one Jacinte.

Loc. 'C'. LMN in H12 'Re(turne)d to Mrs Radclif'.

[20] Item one Jewell of golde the lower p(ar)te set with viij small Rubies iij Opalls with a Harte over it garnished with small Rubies and one Opall in the middest and a Crowne over it garnished with sparkes of diamonde and three Opalles pendaunte.

Loc. 'C'. LMN in H9 'Delyvered to ye Juell house'. This was a New Year's gift in 1595, but the donor's name is not known: 'Item one Jewell of golde made like an Alter and a Harte over it with a Crowne over it all garnished with small Rubyes fower fayer opalles & thre opalles pendaunt'. (BL, Add. 5751A, f. 237).

f. 103ᵛ

[21] Item one Jewell of golde with one table ⟨Rubie⟩ diamonde in the middest three small diamondes in the border fower small table Rubies one flower de luce of diamondes and three sprigges twoe garnished with sparkes of diamondes and one with sparkes of Rubies.

Alteration in H2.

[22] Item one small Jewell of golde with twoe triangle diamondes twoe little diamondes, one long table Rubie in the middest and three pearles pendaunte.

Loc. 'C'.

[23] Item one Jewell of golde havinge therin a Garnett or Dublet set aboute with halfe pearle and three sprigges with some pearle and sparkes of Garnetes therein. ⟦(. . .) broken⟧

Loc. 'C'. LMN in H12 'Re(turne)d Mrs Radclif'. Items 21, 22 and 23 are bracketed together. Addition in H12.

[24] Item in Buttons of golde each set with one Rubye parcell of an Habillimente —— xvj

Loc. 'C'. LMN in H11 'delivered to mrs Ratliff by Sir thomas gorge may 16, 1603, Whit hall'.

[25] Item in greate p(ear)les set in Crampions of golde —— xᵉⁿ

Loc. 'C'. LMN in H11 'delivered the x of may by Sir thomas gorge 1603'.

[26] Item in pearles upon a paire of sleeves and a stomacher of cloth of sylver embrodered like Arches.

Loc. 'C'.

[27] Item one Jewell of golde like a Deasye and small flowers aboute it garnished with sparkes of diamondes and Rubies with her Majesties picture graven within a Garnet And a sprigge of three branches garnished with sparkes of Rubies one pearle in the topp and a small pendaunte of sparkes of diamondes.

Loc. 'C'. LMN in H9 'delivered to the Juell house'. RMN in H9 'the pearle lost', 'the pendant lost'. This was a New Year's gift in 1593, but the donor's name is not known: 'Item a Jewell of golde like a Daysie and smale flowers abowte it garnished with sparcks of Dyamonds and Rubyes, with Her Majesties Picture graven within a Garnet: And a Sprigge of iij branches garnished with Sparcks of Rubyes, one perle in the Topp, and ⟦a⟧ Small Pendants of Sparcks of Dyamonds'. (BL, Add. 5751A, f. 229).

f. 104

[28] Item one Jewell of golde with a border of eight small diamondes one Rocke Rubie in the middest and one pearle pendaunte.

Loc. 'C'. LMN in H12 'Re(turne)d Mrs Radclif'. RMN in H4 'pearll lost' and H16 'less the pearle'.

[29] Item one Jewell of golde like a Snake wounde togeather garnished with small Opalles and Rubies.

Loc. 'C'. LMN in H12 'Re(turne)d to Mrs Radclif'. This may be the jewel worn by the Queen on her left sleeve in the 'Rainbow' portrait, Fig. 140.

[30] Item one Flower of golde with a braunch of flowers moste enameled watchet garnished with sparkes of garnets and small pearle and one small diamonde in the foote.

Loc. 'C'. LMN in H12 'Re(turne)d to Mrs Radclif'.

[31] Item one Jewell of ⟦gold⟧ garnished with sparkes of diamondes and Rubies like a sonne with fyve sprigges three with diamondes and twoe with Rubies with a Sonne graven in a Stone in the middest thereof.

Loc. 'C'. LMN in H12 'Re(turne)d Mrs Radclif'. RMN in H9 'charge before ⟨6⟩ 7 {loose} (. . . . . . .)'.

[32] Item one Flower of golde garnished with diamondes Rubies and ⟨small Emerodes⟩ with a Flower de luce of diamondes in the middest.

LMN in H12 'Re(turne)d Mrs Radclif'. RMN in H9 'charge be fore ⟨6⟩ the other less —— 1'. Deletion by striking through the words.

Memorandum all the Jewelles before mentioned were receaved by Sir Thomas Gorges knight of Mrs Mary Ratcliffe were by him delivered over into the chardge of the said Mrs Ratliffe the xxviijth of Maye 1603 in the presence of us
Edwa: Carye   Tho: Knyvett   Fra: Goston

Memorandum in H15 with signatures of Edward Carey, Francis Goston and Thomas Knyvett.

'N.B. Queen Elizabeth obit 24th March 1602/3. The delivery here mentioned was made 28 May 1603 after the accession of King James I'. Pencilled note in Thomas Astle's hand made in c. 1800.

XI

The Inventory
Made in July 1600 of all Clothes remaining in the Office of the Wardrobe of Robes at Blackfriars, with a List of Personal Jewels lost since 1586

MS V.b.72 in the
Folger Shakespeare Library,
Washington, DC

The Folger Inventory

f. 1

Mensis Julii anno regni Regine Elizabeth' xlij^{do} 1600

A Booke of all suche Robes apparell and garmentes remayninge within thoffice of her highnes warderobe of Robes, surveied, viewed and laide apart, by vertue of her highnes Comission under the greate Seale of Englande bearing date the iiijth daie of Julie in the saide xlijth yeare of her Majesties raigne and directed unto the right honorable Thomas Baron of Buckhurst Lorde highe Thre(asore)r of Englande, George Baron of Hunsdon lorde Chamberlayn of her Majesties house-(hold), Sir John Fortescue knight, Chauncellour of thexchequer and Sir John Stanhop knight, Threasorer of her Majesties Chamber. And alsoe of all suche Jewells and other parell as by the saide Comissioners are founde to bee loste by her Majestie and to bee wantinge since the tyme that the saide Robes and Jewells have been comitt(ed) to the truste and Custodie of Sir Thomas Gorges knight.

Apparell late {Queene Maries}

[1] Firste one French Gowne of black Satte[n] (..........) with blacke vellat lyned with Tawney Taph[ata] (.....) edged with Sables.

Edges of page are torn away.

[2] Item one French gowne of blacke Satten lyned (.....) with white Taphata and edged with luzarnes.

Edges of page are torn away.

f. 1^v

[3] Item one loose gowne of blacke vellat laide on with a brode passamaine lace of golde and silver and twoe small laces on either side.

[4] Item a Placarde or foreparte of a kirtle of purple cloth of golde.

f. 2

Robes [Queen Elizabeth]

[1] Firste a kirtle for the Parliament Robe of Crymsen vellatt lyned in the bodies and sleeves with white Sarceonett.

[2] Item one Mantle of white stitch cloth seamed downe with one lase of venice golde with a Traine.

Frenche Gow{nes}

[1] Firste a gowne of black Satten after the french fashion garded with vellat and lyned with Taphata faced and edged with Sables cut all over and sett with tufts of black silke.

[2] Item one gowne with a traine of the french fashion of black vellatt embrodered all over with unshorne vellatt and lyned with Taphata.

[3] Item one straight bodied gowne of black pincked vellat with twoe cloude lases of venice silver and orange colour silke, with Roses of aishe Colour Rybon the bodies and the sleeves of like lace, like double Bowes bordered with orenge Coloure Taphata.

f. 2^v

[4] Item one Frenche gowne with a traine of white satten pinked and cutt all

440 *'Queen Elizabeth I', by an unknown artist, c. 1590–95. The Queen wears what appears to be a doublet, or 'pair of bodies' with matching stomacher, embroidered with pearls and set with jewels. Her petticoat is embroidered in a linear curving design incorporating flowers and leaves, set with pearls. The fine silk veil is wired and edged with small pearls. Present whereabouts unknown*

441 *Detail of 'white gold chamblet' sleeve in Figure 64, c. 1590–92. Lilies, strawberries, eglantine, honeysuckle, daisies, daffodils, pansies, acorns and gillyflowers, or pinks, are embroidered in polychrome silks within a strapwork pattern enriched with pearls, on a ribbed silk with an additional weft of gold thread. Toledo Museum of Art, Ohio*

over striped downe right with a bonelace of venice golde.

[5] Item one French gowne of black clothe of Silver with workes, the bodies and sleeves wrought all over with lace of venice golde and silver, and twoe like laces about the skirtes edged with Jennetes.

[6] Item one Coveringe for a French gowne with bodies and sleeves of white lawne bordered aboute with twoe small Crowne laces of venice golde.

[7] Item one Frenche gowne of Tawnye Birle laid with a brode passimaine lace of venice golde and Spangles.

Paper badly damaged here.

[8] Item one French gowne of Carnacion cloth of silver with an indented Jagg bounde with a passamaine lace of venice golde and black silke furred with Luzarnes.

This was a New Year's gift: 'By the Lorde Howarde A Gowne with a Trayne of Carnation

Clothe of silver layde with a Passamayne of golde and black silke. Delivered to Rauf Hoope'. (New Year's Gift Roll, 19 Eliz. 1577. PRO, C47/3/39).

[9] Item one Frenche gowne of black vellat cutt all over embroidered with peaches and pyne apples of {venice} golde and silver.

[10] Item one French gowne of black vellatt embroidered with a small traile of black silke twiste.

Loc. 'C'.

[11] Item one Frenche gowne of black vellatt cut all{over}, lyned with white Sarceonet with a shorte {traine} edged with black Satten.

[12] Item one french gowne of black vellatt bounde aboute with a passamaine lace of venice silver with watchet plushe in it.

[13] Item one Frenche gowne of Tawnye or lyon colour {satten} striped with

golde bounde aboute with a lace of {venice} silver the hanginge sleeves lyned with clothe of Sat{ten}.

This may have been a New Year's gift. Walter Fyshe is entered for two alterations in 1581 'alteringe and makinge longer wasted of a peire of bodies for a frenche gowne of tawnye satten striped with golde the lyninge of the bodies performed with canvas of our great guarderobe' and 'alteringe the Jagges and hangynge slevis of a frenche gowne of tawnye satten striped with golde the Jagges newe wyred of our great guarderobe'. (Warrant 15 Sept., 23 Eliz. 1581. BL, Egerton 2806, ff. 169ᵛ–170). He worked on it again in the following year 'newe making of a frenche gowne of tawnye satten striped with golde cutt allover with longe pendaunte slevis hangynge open the Jagges newe wyred and lyned with prented cloth of silver lased with venice silver lase the bodies lyned with white sarceonett of our greate guarderobe'. (Warrant 6 April, 24 Eliz. 1582. BL, Egerton 2806, f. 174ᵛ).

f. 3

[14] Item one Frenche gowne with high bodies of black tuft Taphata striped with

442   *Detail from an embroidered valance, c. 1588–90. The lady wears similar clothes to those in Figure 189, with wide ruff open at the front. Her forepart is richly embroidered, with a deep guard, and she carries a large muff. Victoria and Albert Museum, London (T.134–1913)*

443   *Detail from a green satin sleeve embroidered with couched green cord, green bugle beads, French knots and tufts of green silk, c. 1600. Victoria and Albert Museum, London (225–1893)*

golde and silver laide about with a passamaine of venice golde lyned with white Taphata Sarceonet edged with luzarnes.

This was a New Year's gift: 'By the Countes of Shrewesbury a frenche gowne with high boddies of black Tufte Taphata striped with golde and silver layd abought with a pasment of venice golde lyned with white Taphata or sarceonet. Delivered to the forsaid Rauf Hope'. (New Year's Gift Roll, 26 Eliz. 1584. BL, Egerton 3052, printed in *Costume* 9, 1975, p. 30). Fifteen years later William Jones was entered 'for alteringe a gowne of black Tuft Taffata striped with gold and silver beinge furred, and the slevis enlarged with lyke stuff and Sarcenet of our greate warderobe. (Warrant 30 March, 41 Eliz. 1599. PRO, LC5/37, ff. 160, 161).

[15]   Item one French gowne of black Siet bounde with a billament lace lyned with Sarceonet with a white networke bounde with black silke and silver lace.

The original warrant of 1584 gives details of William Jones's work: 'making of a gowne of blak syett with two peire of highe bodies & one peire of square bodies with billement lase lyned with sarceonett the bodies stiffenid with canvas and bayes with bentes in the slevis coverid with taphata and lyned with sarceonett of our great guarderobe'. (Warrant 27 Sept., 26 Eliz. 1584. BL, Egerton 2806, f. 199ᵛ).

[16]   Item one French gowne of Russet Satten silvered with a border of heare coloure Satten embroidered with Twysts of venice golde and silver and owes of golde

and silver the bodies and sleeves allover embrodered with like stuff the gowne lyned with strawe colour Sarceonet faced with Sables.

Loc. 'C'. This may have been a New Year's gift. In 1592 William Jones is entered 'for alteringe and pecinge longer the bodies of the gowne of russett Satten woven with Silver and embrodered alover and enlarginge the slevis laced about with golde lace furred with Sables perfourmed with lyk stuffe & Sarcenet of our great warderob. (Warrant 28 Sept., 34 Eliz. 1592. PRO, LC5/36, f. 220).

[17]   Item one French gowne of heare colour cloth of silver printed, having a spangle lace rounde aboute it in workes billetwise in the bodies and sleeves (the lace emploied upon a gowne of heare coloured vellatt.

This may have been a New Year's gift. In 1589 William Jones was entered for 'alteringe of a gowne of hare colour cloth of Silver printed and makinge of a paire of hanginge slevis to yt cut and tacte up, lyned with Silver Tincell and holland clothe covered over with lawne of our greate warderobe'. (Warrant 27 Sept., 31 Eliz. 1589. PRO, LC5/36, f. 119).

[18]   Item one French gowne of Russet Capha bounde about with a passamaine lace of venice silver and a smale lace of like silver and spangles the bodies and sleeves cut like Essefirmes likewise bounde.

[19]   Item one French gowne of aishcolour Satten prented with hoapes in spaces

the sleeves cut embroidered with hoapes of golde bounde with a lace of venice golde.

Loc. 'C'.

[20]   Item one Frenche gowne of aishe colour Satten striped with goldé bounde with lace of Silver and Carnacion silke with buttons and loopes of silke and Silver.

f. 3ᵛ

[21]   Item one French gowne of printed cloth of silver bounde about with a passamaine lace of venice golde with a Traine to take of[f] and on.

[22]   Item one French gowne of black Taphata pinked and cutt with a garde embroidered with black Satten cut upon white lawne striped embroidered with venice golde.

[23]   Item one Frenche gowne of blacke wrought vellat tissued with golde bounde about with a lace of venice golde and blacke silke furred with Sables.

Loc. 'C'.

[24]   Item one French gowne of paule Colour vellatt uncut, cut like flowers and cut in panes with buttons like knottes of Venice silver.

Loc. 'C'. This may have been a New Year's gift. In 1601 William Jones was entered 'for alteringe and enlardginge a gowne of paule colour velvet, and enlardginge a paire of slevis of Carnacion Satten with a silver lace of our great warderobe'. (Warrant 28 Sept., 43 Eliz. 1601. PRO, LC5/37, f. 231).

[25] Item one French gowne of aishe Colour vellat bounde about with silver lace.

Loc. 'C'.

[26] Item one Frenche gowne of blacke cloth of golde with {laid} pearle upon it.

This may be a gown listed as 'high bodied', in a warrant of 1589 which gives details of William Jones's work: 'makinge of a highe bodied gowne with a trayne of black cloth of gold embrodered with pearle with a byndinge lace the bodies stiffened with Canvas and buckeram and buckeram to lay aboute yt the gowne lyned with Sarcenet and pockettes of taffata the Cloth of gold of our Store of the Chardge of the said Thomas Knyvett the rest of our greate warderobe. (Warrant 3 April, 31 Eliz. 1589. PRO, LC5/36, f.99). This is possibly the same gown which John Parr worked on two years later, 'repayringe & augmentinge of the embroiderie of a gowne of blacke wrought cloth of gold, richly wrought with pearle alover in the bodyes and sleves, havinge a brode border downe the forevents & a narrowe border about the skirtes & traine the bodyes and trayne beinge enlardged, and the pearle ripped of[f] and new supplied againe, allso for rippinge of the great powderinge pearle from the flowers, wormes, and sprigges of the forebodyes, back, sleves, forventes, and trayne and makinge them sutable agayne, allso for embroderinge of a new Collor to the same gowne'. (Warrant 10 June, 33 Eliz. 1591. PRO, LC5/36, f. 176). This seems to be the same gown which Parr worked on again six years later. The pearls here are threaded on silver wire: 'Item to John Par our Enbrauder ... Item for repairing thenbraudery of the slevis bodies backe & ventes of a gowne of blacke Cloth of gold, richlie wrought with perles threddded ⟨with⟩ on silver wyer, and for making new puffines of lawne by hand, enbrauderinge on the same, with an ounce di di quarter of wier spent theron'. (Warrant 8 July, 39 Eliz. 1597. PRO, LC5/37, f. 110).

f. 4
Rounde Gownes

[1] Firste one straight bodied gowne of black vellat all over cut upon white Sarceonet and embroidered with purles of Damaske golde like starres with a border of white Taphata embroidered with a cut of black vellatt.

Walter Fyshe remodelled this gown in 1570 'altering and newe makyng of a Frenche gowne of black Vellatt cutt upon whyte Tyncell sercenitt and sett all over with purles of Venyce gold And for making the same gowne into A round gowne the pleytes lyned with buckerame and with whyte sercenitt upon the same with a perfourmaunce of black Vellatt to edge the same about the skyrtes of our great guarderobe'. (Warrant 14 Oct., 12 Eliz. 1570. BL, Egerton 2806, f. 25ᵛ).

[2] Item one rounde gowne of clothe of Silver prented bounde about with a passamaine lace of venice silver and a Covering for it of venice golde Carnacion and watchet silk knetworke.

[3] Item one Dutch gowne of Murrey Taphata Sarceonet covered with network Florished allover with venice golde silver and Spangles with a passamaine lace of like gold and silver.

[4] Item one rounde gowne of cloth of golde prented bounde about with a passamaine lace of venice golde with a paier of bodies and sleeves a partlet and a paier of ruffes [of] like stuff.

[5] Item one rounde gowne of Tawnye Satten cut laide with passamaine lace of venice golde like Compas knottes with buttons of the same lyned with yellowe Sarceonet.

This was a New Year's gift: 'By the countes of Shrewsbury a gowne of tawny Satten leyed with a pasmayn lace of venice golde and buttons of the same lyned with yelow Serceonet. Delivered to Rauf Hope'. (New Year's Gift Roll, 19 Eliz. 1577. PRO, C47/3/39).

[6] Item one rounde gowne of black Taphata pin{ked} welted with three weltes of black vellatt.

[7] Item one rounde gowne of fygured Satten striped with threedes of golde with a binding lace of venice golde.

[8] Item one rounde gowne of black wrought vellatt with a brode lace of venice golde and silver lyned with changeable Sarceonet.

f. 4ᵛ

[9] Item one rounde gowne of Carnacion Satten golde and Russet silke cut and lyned with aishcoloure Sarceonet.

[10] Item one rounde gowne of aishe Colour Satten cut and laide upon with knottes made of lace of flatt golde and purle with black silke by the edges lyned with yellowe Sarceonet.

[11] Item one rounde gowne of Tawney Satten with a border of leaves cut out laide under with Copwebb Sipers lyned with white Sarceonet.

[12] Item one rounde Gowne of black Taphata cut like leaves lyned with cloth of golde and lyned with Claie Colour Taphata.

[13] Item one Rounde gowne of Orenge Colour Satten corded with silver.

Loc. 'C'. William Jones was entered in 1590 'for makinge of a highe bodied gowne of Orrenge colour Satten corded with Silver the bodies stiffened with Canvas and buckeram, Lyned and bordered with Sarcenenet, with hookes eyes and pockettes of Taffata of our great warderobe'. (Warrant 18 May, 32 Eliz. 1590. PRO, LC5/36, f. 134). He worked on it again later in the year 'alterinnge and newe making the forebodies and Coller of a gowne of Orrendge colour Satten striped with Silver with silver lace about yt and performed with lyk stuff of our great warderobe'. (Warrant 28 Sept., 32 Eliz. 1590. PRO, LC5/36, f. 141).

[14] Item one rounde gowne of blacke tufte Taphata the bodies and sleeves cut upon blacke satten garnished with bugle of sundrye sortes.

Loc. 'C'.

f. 5
Loose Gownes

[1] First one loose gowne of Crymsen satten garded with a passamaine lace of venice golde and silver compas Fashion faced with spotted Coney lyned with Sarceonet.

[2] Item one loose gowne of plaine black vellatt embroidered allover with braunches of Cypers trees lyned with black Taphata.

This may have been a gift, and apparently started out as a French gown, as in 1562 Walter Fyshe had the work of 'alteringe of a Frenche gowne of Blacke Velvet drawne out with sipres trees and making of a newe staie of Fustian of oure great warderobe'. (Warrant 20 Oct., 4 Eliz. 1562. PRO, LC5/33, ff. 3, 4). The following year he worked on it again 'alteringe of a gowne of Black velvet with sipres trees and makinge it longer with velvet And Taffata of oure greate warderobe'. (Warrant 2 Nov., 5 Eliz. 1563. PRO, LC5/33, f. 63). David Smith, the Queen's embroiderer, worked on the gown in the same year 'lengthenynge out of ye forquarters of a gowne of Black velvet and at the skirtes of the forpartes the gowne being w[r]ought allover with Braunches of Black Sipres for silke and workemanshipp therof v s. Item for ij yardes of Blacke Sipres spente upon the same gowne vj s viij d'. (Warrant 4 May, 5 Eliz. 1563. PRO, LC5/33, f. 55). It is first described as a loose gown ten years later when Walter Fyshe was entered for 'lyninge of a lose Gowne with a Traine of blak vellat with sipers trees lyned with blak taphata of our greate guarderobe' (Warrant 1 April, 15 Eliz. 1573. BL, Egerton 2806, ff. 51ᵛ, 52). The train seems to have been removed four years later when Fyshe worked on it again 'alteringe of a gowne of blak vellat embrodered with sipers trees'. (Warrant 12 April, 19 Eliz. 1577. BL, Egerton 2806, f. 111ᵛ).

[3] Item one loose gowne of black wrought vellatt with a Jagg aboute it of plaine black vellatt furred with powdered Armyons.

Walter Fyshe is entered in a warrant of 1570 'for making of a night Gowne of blak wrought vellat with a Jagge about it of playne blak vellat the coller lyned with canvas the wynges lyned with buckeram with bagges and a steye of white taphata the steye lined with fustian all of our greate guarderobe'. (Warrant 12 April, 12 Eliz. 1570. BL, Egerton 2806, f. 22ᵛ). The 'bagges' were probably pocket bags. Fyshe worked on it again when the cold weather was over 'taking oute the furre of the said night Gowne and lyning the same with white sarceonett and fustian' for summer wear (ibid.). Later in the year the furs were put back for the winter, and he was engaged in 'altering and enlargyng of A night gowne of black wrought vellatt being furred with powdered Armyons of our great guarderobe'. (Warrant 14 Oct., 12 Eliz. 1570. BL, Egerton 2806, f. 25ᵛ).

[4]   Item one loose gowne of black Satten with twoe small billement laces of black Silke.

[5]   Item one loose gowne of black vellatt plaine edged with black Satten faced with unshorne vellatt.

[6]   Item one loose gowne of black Taphata cut allover laide with three riche laces of venice golde and Silver like Cheynes, the Jaggs bounde aboute with like lace faced with black Taphata cut lyned with white Sarceonet without sleeves.

[7]   Item one loose gowne of black tuft Taphata the grounde Murrey with three plaine laces of venice golde and flat Silver like waves and owes lined with Murrey Sarceonett.

[8]   Item one loose gowne of Tawney or Murrey Satten embroidered with a border of venice golde and silke of sondrie Colours lyned with chaungeable white and black Sarceonet pinked, faced with aishe coloure Satten.

f. 5ᵛ

[9]   Item one loose gowne of peach colour vellat laide with one brode and twoe narrowe laces of venice golde and silver faced with white Satten cut and razed.

Walter Fyshe is entered in a warrant of 1577 'for making of a night Gowne of peache colour vellat layed with one brode and two narrowe lases of venice golde & silver being taken from another gowne savinge thre yerdes of brode and x yerdes of narrowe lase to perfourme it, fased with white satten the grounde blak cutt and ravelid: the same fase taken oute and the gowne alterid and newe fased with white satten cutt and rased the lase on the oute side of the forequarters taken of and sett upon the fase, the rest of the forequarters lyned and the gowne borderid with chaungeable sarceonett, with pockettes and a steye of like sarceonett lyned with fustian the vellat to make the gowne of our store of the chardge of George Brideman keper of our Palloice at Westminster threst of our great guarderobe'. (Warrant 12 April, 19 Eliz. 1577. BL, Egerton 2806, f. 110).

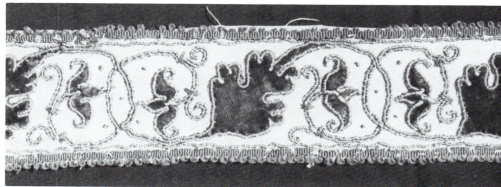

444   *Richly embroidered smock beneath the partlet, embroidered guards on a French gown, and collar of state with hanging jewel, worn by Queen Elizabeth, detail from Figure 12, c. 1570–72. National Trust, Anglesey Abbey*

445   *Ivory satin narrow guard, with applied decoration of leaves in red velvet and gold thread, with red braid on the edges, late sixteenth century. Victoria and Albert Museum, London (546–1892)*

[10]   Item one loose gowne of blewe Satten with Rowes of golde with twoe small passamaine laces of venice golde faced with powdered Armyons. (the furr to bee reserved).

Loc. 'C'.

[11]   Item one loose gowne of white Satten striped with Silver, welted with three weltes of black vellatt whipped over with a small twiste of venice golde.

[12]   Item one loose gowne of Tawnye satten pincked striped downe right allover with lace of venice golde and Crimsen silke furred with Minckes faced and edged with luzarne powtes (the furr to be reserved).

[13]   Item one loose gowne of black Satten striped with golde bound about with a billament lace of Carnacion silke and silver faced with striped lawne and lyned with Carnacion Sarceonet.

This was a New Year's gift: 'By the Barronesse Pagett Cary a lose gowne of blacke Satten stryped with golde bounde aboute with A Byllymente Lace of carnacion silke and silver faced with stryped Lawne & lyned with Carnatyon Taffata. Delivered to the foresaid Ra hope'. ((New Year's Gift Roll, 26 Eliz. 1584. BL, Egerton 3052, printed in *Costume* 9, 1975, p. 28).

[14]   Item one loose gowne of peach Colour Satten prented and razed like half Moones edged with a small plate lace of venice golde and silver furred with Mynnever, and faced with orenge colour plushe.

This was a New Year's gift: 'By the Barrones Paggett Cary A Nyght goune of pechcolored Satten prynted and Rased lyke haulfe monnes edged with A smaull plate Lasse of venis golde and Sylver Furred with myniver and Fased with Orringcolored sylke Fryng. Delivered the forsaid Raulfe hope'. (New Year's Gift Roll, 27 Eliz. 1585. Folger, Z.d.16). Fringe would appear to be an alternative name for silk with a long pile.

[15]   Item one loose gowne of black tufte Taphata with a lace buttons and

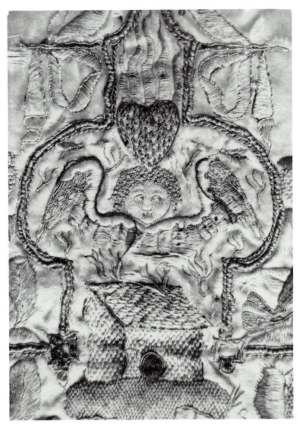

446, 447 *Winged cherub's head below a flaming heart pierced by two arrows, and winged cupid shooting with bow and arrow, two details from a polychrome embroidered white satin panel, probably from a skirt, c. 1600. Victoria and Albert Museum, London (T.138–1981)*

loopes of venice golde and black Silke downe before.

[16] Item one loose gowne of aishe colour silke Burrell with three billament laces of black silk florished with venice golde and Silver.

[17] Item one loose gowne of black wrought vellatt with a brode plate lace of golde and black silke with a face of unshorne vellatt.

[18] Item one loose gowne of tawny Damashe with a lace, buttons and loopes of golde and silver lyned throught with unshorne vellatt.

This gown would seem to have been in the Wardrobe by 1579, although there is not enough detail to identify it with certainty. William Whittell was entered in 1579 'for alteringe of thre lose gownes one tawnye Damaske'. (Warrant 12 March, 21 Eliz. 1579, BL, Egerton 2806, f. 138ᵛ).

f. 6

[19] Item one loose gowne of black stitched cloth striped with golde bounde about with a passamaine lace of venice golde and silver lyned with white sarceonet.

[20] Item one loose gowne of black tuft Taphata {bounde aboute} with passa-

maine lace buttons and loop{es} of venice silver faced and edged with Sables.

This was a New Year's gift: 'By Mrs Skydmour A goune of blacke Tufte Taffataye edged Round Aboute with A lace buttens and Louppes of venis golde and blacke Sylke. Delivered to Rauf Hope'. (New Year's Gift Roll, 27 Eliz. 1585. Folger, Z.d.16).

[21] {Item one} loose gowne of heare colour vellatt laide about with a lase of golde and silver faced and edged rounde about with carnacion plusshe.

This was a New Year's gift: 'By Mr Bruncker one nightgowne of hayre collour vellat laced aboute with a passamayn lace of venice golde and silver faced and edged round aboute with Carnation plusshe. Delivered to the said Sir Tho: Gorges'. (New Year's Gift Roll, 30 Eliz. 1588. BL, Add.8159).

[22] Item one loose gowne of willowe colour vellatt laide rounde aboute and garnished with buttons and loopes of plate lace of venice silver edged and faced with Carnacion plusshe.

[23] Item one loose gowne of white Taphata bounde aboute with a small passamaine lace of venice Silver.

[24] Item one loose gowne of heare colour Taphata the sleeves and border

about embrodered with owes, and drawne oute with lawne.

[25] Item one loose gowne of black Taphata pinked with twoe small plate laces of venice golde and ⟨silver⟩ drawne oute betwene with lawne.

A fine line is drawn through 'silver' to delete it.

[26] Item one night gowne of aishe colour wrought vellatt the grounde silver faced with powdred armyons and furred with pure throughoute.

This was a joint New Year's gift: 'By the Lady Scudamore parte of an Ashe colored wrought vellet gowne the grounde silver faced and edged with powdered Armens furred throughe with pure. Delivered to the Robes'. 'By Sir John Scudamore parte of an ashe colored wrought velvet gowne the grounde silver faced & edged with powdered Armens and furred throughe with pure. Delivered to the Robes'. (New Year's Gift Roll, 41 Eliz. 1599. Folger, Z.d.17).

[27] Item one loose gowne of flame colour tufte Taphata the grounde sylver laide aboute with a faire plate la{c}e of sylver faced with white plushe.

Loc. 'C'. This may have been a New Year's gift. In 1594 William Jones was entered 'for alteringe of a gowne of flame colour tuft taffata the ground silver perfourmed with like stuffe and Sarcenett of our great Warderobe'. (Warrant 27 Sept., 36 Eliz. 1594. PRO, LC5/37, f. 7).

f. 6ᵛ
Kirtells

[1] First one rounde kirtell the outeside b{eing o}f black vellatt, and thinside being russet unsho{rn}e vellat.

[2] Item one french Traine for a kirtle of cloth of silver garded with Murrey vellatt enbrodered covered with a black ⟨vellatt⟩ Nett.

A faint line is drawn through 'vellatt' to delete it.

[3] Item one French kirtle of cloth of silver, prented rewed with golde with a welte of black vellatt, laide with twoe passamaine laces of venice golde and silver.

[4] Item one rounde kirtle of cloth of silver braunched with Flowers of silke of divers colours like peacockes tailes with a border of peach colour satten cut and laide with iiijᵒʳ iijᵒʳ passamaine lace{s} of venice silver and green silke.

[5] Item one rounde kirtle of white golde chamblet with twoe small laces of black silke and golde.

[6] Item one rounde kirtle of green vellat with a garde of twoe wreathes of Carnacion Satten and fower brode Crowne laces of venice golde silver and silke.

[7] Item one rounde kirtle and Dublet of russet satten cut and raised laide with three Compas laces of venice golde silver and Carnacion silke lyned with Carnacion Taphata.

These items were part of a New Year's gift: 'By the Countes of Warwike a foreparte of a kirtell . . . And a rounde kirtell and a Doublet of Russet Satten cut and laide with a Compas lace of venice golde silver and carnation silke lined with Carnation Taphata with xviij buttons of golde. Delivered to the said Rauf hoope'. (New Year's Gift Roll, 7 Eliz. 1565. BL, Add.4827). The forepart is listed in the Stowe inventory, f. 53ᵛ/118.

[8] Item one kirtle of tawnye Satten cut and pinked allover [[laced]] with venice golde allover.

This was made in 1576 by Walter Fyshe: 'a rounde frenche kyrtle of tawnye satten cutt and pinked allover lased with venice golde lyned with white sarceonett of our great guarderobe'. (Warrant 26 Sept., 18 Eliz. 1576. BL, Egerton 2806, f. 101ᵛ).

[9] Item one rounde gathered kirtle of black Satten cut and pinked with three brode weltes of black vellatt drawne oute

with black Cipers lyned with black sarceonet.

[10] Item one rounde kirtle of clothe of golde the grounde orenge colour silke with braunches, with a lace of venice silver and Tawney Silke.

f. 7

[11] Item one rounde kirtle of cloth of silver braunched with golde, with twoe laces of venice golde, and tawny silke.

[12] Item one rounde kirtle of white and yellowe Satten paned Chequerwise laide overthwarte with a plate lace of venice silver and black silke.

This seems to have been a New Year's gift: 'By the Barronesse Cobham a Rounde Kirtle of yellowe and white Satten payned, Cut, layde with A lase of Tawnye silke and silver & lyned with Tawny serceonett. Delivered to the foresaid Rauf Hope'. (New Year's Gift Roll, 23 Eliz. 1581. Eton Coll. BLA 18 192). The 'lase of Tawnye silke and silver' has been changed for one of silver and black silk.

[13] Item one rounde kirtle of white Satten or Capha wrought with knottes of orenge colour silke, and tufte with a passamaine lace of venice golde and black silke.

This was a New Year's gift: 'By the Lady Marben a Kirtle of white wroughte Satten wroughte with Oring Coloured sylke and wyth a passamayne of Black silke and golde and spangles on eyther side lined with blacke serceonett. Delivered to the Roobes by Charles Smyth'. (New Year's Gift Roll, 23 Eliz. 1581. Eton Coll. BLA 18 192).

[14] Item one rounde kirtle of white Satten cut and striped with golde and silver with twoe passamaine laces of venice golde plate and peache colour silke.

[15] Item one rounde kirtle of clothe of silver with workes of Carnacion silke, with buttons and loopes downe before of venice golde.

This was a New Year's gift: 'By the Countes of Lyncolnne A Round kertle of Cloth of Sylver with workes of Carnation sylke with buttens and Lopes doune before of venis golde. delivered the forsaid Raulfe hope'. (New Year's Gift Roll, 27 Eliz. 1585. Folger, Z.d.16).

[16] Item one rounde kirtle of white Satten prented like Skallop shells, and bagg pipes, edged with three plate laces of venice golde.

This was a New Year's gift: 'By Mrs Carre A Round kertle of white Satten prynted with Skallop Shelles & bag pyppes edged with too plate lases of venis golde. Delivered to Rauf hope'. (New Year's Gift Roll, 27 Eliz. 1585. Folger, Z.d.16).

[17] Item one rounde kirtle of white Satten prented, cut lyned with orenge

colour Sarceonet, bounde with a small lace of venice golde.

[18] Item one kirtle of Carnacion Capha with a garde of blacke Taphata laide with lace buttons, and loopes of Silver.

[19] Item one kirtle of cloth of silver striped with blunckett and Carnacion silke bounde with golde and silver and silke lace.

[20] Item one kirtle of black tufte Taphata with a welte of Russet striped vellat frendged with silke.

[21] Item one rounde kirtle of white Taphata cut allover and set with golde owes.

[22] Item one kirtle and a Dublet of orenge colour taphata covered with white networke striped cut and tacked up bounde with a silver lace.

f. 7ᵛ

[23] Item one kirtle and a Dublett of white Taphata cut allover and rased upon Carnacion Taphata sarceonet with a binding lace of Carnacion silke and silver.

Forepartes

[1] Firste one foreparte of blacke vellat enbrodered with oken leaves of venice golde and silver set with spangles.

[2] Item one foreparte of white Saten enbrodered allover with flowers of Crimsen Taphata emboste with flowers of bugles lyned with Crimsen Sarceonet.

[3] Item one foreparte of a kirtle of white Satten cut and enbrodered allover with wreathes of Crimsen Satten like Rondles enbrodered with bugles lyned with {ble}we silver Sarceonet like lilliepotes.

[4] Item one foreparte of Crimsen vellatt striped with golde {with} a garde of white Satten laide with twoe laces of venice golde and flat silver.

[5] Item one verie lardge foreparte and a Dublet of peache colour golde Chamblet lyned with white sarceonet edged with a passamaine of silver and set with Spangles.

f. 8

[6] Item one foreparte of Murrey cloth of silver striped with golde, laide with bonelace of venice golde and silver.

Walter Fyshe is entered in a warrant of 1576 'for making of a gatherid foreparte with bodies & small skyrtes of murrey cloth of silver striped with golde layed with bone lase of venice golde & silver lyned with grene taphata the stuff for thowteside of our store Receyved of Rauf Hope yeoman of our guarderobe of Robes threst of our greate guarderobe'. (Warrant 26 Sept., 18 Eliz. 1576. BL, Egerton 2806, f. 102). He apparently altered the forepart, shortly after it was made. This entry seems to be for the same garment: 'for alteringe & newe gardinge of a foreparte of murrey cloth of silver striped with golde garded with grene taphata the same garde taken of[f] and with a garde of murrey layed with lase of venice golde & silver of our great guarderobe'. (Warrant 26 Sept., 18 Eliz. 1576. BL, Egerton 2806, f. 102ᵛ). Later Fyshe had the work of 'alteringe and making longer of a foreparte of cloth of silver striped with golde perfourmed with like stuff and the lyninge perfourmed with grene taphata of our great guarderobe'. (Warrant 27 Sept., 19 Eliz. 1577. BL, Egerton 2806, f. 117).

[7]   Item <twoe> one gathered forepartes of prented cloth of silver with a garde enbrodered with venice golde.

[8]   Item one foreparte of Murrey or Tawney vellat wrought with Estridge feathers of venice golde.

This was a New Year's gift: 'By Sir William Drury a foreparte of Murry vellate wrought with Estrices feathers of venice golde. Delivered to Rauf hoope'. (New Year's Gift Roll, 19 Eliz. 1577, PRO, C47 3/39).

[9]   Item one gathered foreparte of blacke vellat edged with a turne frenge lace of black silke.

[10]   Item one foreparte of white Satten cut billetwise and owes, allover verie thicke and lyned with tawney Sarceonet.

This was a New Year's gift: 'By the Lady Drury a fore parte and a peir of Sleves of white Satten set with Spangilles and lyned with tawney Sarceonet. Delivered to Rauf hoope'. (New Year's Gift Roll, 20 Eliz. 1578. Soc. of Antiquaries MS 537, printed in *Progr. Eliz.*, II, p. 73).

[11]   Item one foreparte of aishe colour Satten embrodered with Cloudes and wormes of venice golde and silver lyned with yellowe Sarceonet.

This was a New Year's gift: 'By Sir William Drury a fore parte of Asshecollored Satten enbrawdred with Clowdes and wormes of golde and Silver lyned with yelowe Sarceonet. Delivered to Rauf hoope'. (New Year's Gift Roll, 20 Eliz. 1578. Soc. of Antiquaries MS 537, printed in *Progr. Eliz.*, II, p. 75).

[12]   Item one foreparte of peache colour Satten embrodered with eies with a Cordaunte of golde and silke set with spangles and lyned with strawe colour sarceonet.

This was a New Year's gift: 'By [Mrs] Skydmore a foreparte and a peir of Sleves of peche collored Satten with a cordant of golde and sylke and set with Spangilles lyned with yelow sarcenet with two pasmane laces of golde abowte the border. Delivered to Rauf hoope'.

(New Year's Gift Roll, 20 Eliz. 1578. Soc. of Antiquaries MS 537, printed in *Progr. Eliz.*, II, p. 75).

[13]   Item one foreparte of clothe of silver stained the workes enbrodered allover with venice golde silver and silke like dragons and leaves.

[14]   Item one foreparte of heare colour Satten cut and laide with twoe laces of venice golde and silver lyned with tawney Taphata.

[15]   Item one foreparte and a Dublet of clothe of golde prented garnished with passamaine lace of venice golde and blacke silke.

This was a New Year's gift: 'By Mrs Dale a Dublate and a foreparte of clothe of gold, garnisshed with passamayne of golde. delivered to the forsaid Rauf hope'. (New Year's Gift Roll, 21 Eliz. 1579. Folger, Z.d.15, printed in *Progr. Eliz.*, II, p. 260).

[16]   Item one foreparte of black cloth of silver striped with yellowe silke with a brode garde of white Satten laide with twoe brode passamaines of venice golde and silver.

[17]   Item one foreparte of white Cipers florished with venice golde and spangles lyned with Murrey sarceonet.

f. 8ᵛ

[18]   Item one foreparte of a kirtle with a paier of sleeves of white satten prented and striped downeright with a plate lace of golde, the border garnished with some seede p(ear)le.

[19]   Item one foreparte of yellowe Satten cut billetwise enbrodered allover with owes of silver.

[20]   Item one foreparte and a Dublet of dove colour satten cut and prented laide with buttons and loopes of venice golde and silke.

[21]   Item one foreparte of blacke cloth of silver prented like oken leaves with twoe Crowne laces of golde and spangles.

[22]   Item one foreparte of orenge colour satten cut up in puffes enbrodered with owes lyned with white Taphata.

[23]   Item one foreparte of white satten printed tackt up and bounde with silver lace lyned with peache colour satten.

[24]   Item one gathered foreparte of Russet Satten with a Caule of white networke like hartes.

[25]   Item one foreparte of blacke vellat laide over with a net of blacke silke lace and bugle.

[26]   Item one foreparte of yellowe Satten cut and razed with a worke like a skallop shell laide with three laces of venice golde and silver lyned with sarceonet with a networke to the same florished with golde like waves.

Walter Fyshe is entered in a warrant of 1577 'for making of a foreparte of yellowe satten cut and rased with a worke like a scallop shell layed with thre laces of venice golde and silver lyned with white sarceonett'. (Warrant 27 Sept., 19 Eliz. 1577. BL, Egerton 2806, f. 116ᵛ).

[27]   Item one foreparte of a kirtle of white lawne cutworke embrodered with venice golde unlyned.

[28]   Item one foreparte of white networke florished allover with silver with a small passamaine of silver aboute the skirtes lyned with white sarceonet.

This was a New Year's gift: 'By the Lady Cheke a fore parte of a kyrtill of white networke floresshed with silver with a small pasman lace & lyned with white sarcenet. Delivered to Rauf hoope'. (New Year's Gift Roll, 20 Eliz. 1578. Soc. of Antiquaries MS 537, printed in *Progr. Eliz*, II, p. 72).

[29]   Item one foreparte and a Dublet of strawe colour Satten covered with a networke florished with venice silver blacke silke and a fewe spangles.

f. 9

[30]   Item one foreparte of white Satten laide on with white networke with spangles, bounde about with a small passamaine of venice golde and silver.

[31]   Item one foreparte of white cloth of silver rewed enbrodered with Bees, and a border of honiecombes covered with networke enbrodered with braunches of venice golde silver and silke.

[32]   Item one foreparte of networke florished with venice golde lyned Diamondewise with knottes and Crosses.

[33]   Item one foreparte and a Dublet of lawne Cutworke garnished with verie small buttons of silver guilt unlyned.

[34]   Item one foreparte of networke garnished with silver spangles in wide spaces.

This was a New Year's gift: 'By the Lorde Russell A foreparte of network garneshid with silver spangles. Delivered to the foresaid Rauf hope'. (New Year's Gift Roll, 26 Eliz. 1584. BL, Egerton 3052, printed in *Costume* 9, 1975, p. 28).

[35]   Item one foreparte of Cutworke florished with silver plate Diamondwise.

[36]   Item one foreparte of lawne cut allover florished with silver twist{e} aboute the Cuttes.

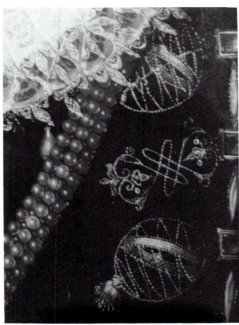

448 'Queen Elizabeth I', panel painting by an unknown artist, c. 1580–85. The Queen wears a 'high-bodied gown', and ruff worked with fleur-de-lis and roses. Present whereabouts unknown

449 Embroidered armillary or celestial spheres and knots, detail from Figure 448. Small tassels hang free from the ends of the spheres

450 Armillary sphere between two trees, detail from a polychrome embroidered white satin panel, probably from a skirt, c. 1600.   (T.138–1981)

[37] Item one foreparte of lawne cut Diamondwise with tuftes of Carnacion silke and spangles of golde cut with lawne betwixt upon a foreparte of orenge colour Satten.

This was a New Year's gift: 'By Mrs Southewell a forparte of a kyrtle of lawne cut dyamondwyse wythe Tuftes of Carnatyon sylke And spangles of golde cut with Lawne betwene. Delivered to the foresaid R hope'. (New Year's Gift Roll, 26 Eliz. 1584. BL, Egerton 3052 printed in *Costume* 9, 1975, p. 30).

[38] Item one foreparte of networke florished with silver and spangles Chevernewise and downeright.

This was a New Year's gift: 'By Mrs Fraunses Howarde the yonger a scarfe of white networke and a foreparte of networke Florysshed with sylver and spangles. The scarf with Mrs Chaworth threst with R hope'. (New Year's Gift Roll, 26 Eliz. 1584. BL, Egerton 3052, printed in *Costume* 9, 1975, p. 30).

[39] Item one foreparte of lawne cut-worke florished with silver and spangles like flower de luces within spaces of black silke and silver owes lyned with Murrey Sarceonet.

This was a New Year's gift: 'By the Ladye Katherin Counstable a foreparte and a paire of Sleeves of lawne cutwourke flourished with silver spangles and Owes. Delivered to the said Sir Thomas Gorges. (New Year's Gift Roll, 30 Eliz. 1588. BL, Add. 8159).

[40] Item one foreparte of black Taphata with a lawne networke florished with blacke silke allover the skirtes.

[41] Item one foreparte of white net-worke florished with flowers of black silke in some places and a lace of venice golde and silver on the skirtes.

f. 9^v

[42] Item one foreparte of lawne Cut-worke with flowers and potts of white and a small lace of white silke.

[43] Item one foreparte and a Dublet of horseflesh colour satten cut laide over-thwarte with waves of twiste of blacke silke and golde.

[44] Item one foreparte of black Taphata covered with networke tuftes with heare colour silke.

'Tuftes' is probably a scribe's error and should be 'tufted'.

[45] Item one foreparte of white Satten gathered enbrodered with three brode gardes beneath of Cipers and Bugle.

[46] Item one foreparte of white Satten enbrodered with Dolphins and Butterflies of black silke.

[47] Item one foreparte of tawnye Satten covered with lawne cutworke flor-ished with golde and silver with twoe bone laces.

[48] Item one foreparte of lawne cut-worke florished with silver and spangles made like puffes or Flowers.

[49] Item one foreparte a paier of sleeves, and a partelett for a gowne of Carnacion Taphata striped with golde covered allover with lawne in rising puffes and owes of silver.

[50] Item one foreparte of Carnacion Satten laide upon with Cutworke florished with owes, and drawne oute with Cop-webb lawne striped with golde plate like puf[f]s.

[51] Item one foreparte of white net-worke florished with venice silver and some Carnacion silke lyned with white Satten.

This was a New Year's gift: 'By the Lady Cheake A foreparte of white nettworke flourished with venis gold silver and Carnation silke layde upon white satten. Delivered to the Roabes'. (New Year's Gift Roll, 31 Eliz. 1589. BL, Lansd. Roll 17, printed in *Progr. Eliz.*, III, p. 8).

[52] Item one foreparte of lawne Cut-worke florished with silver and spangles.

This was a New Year's gift: 'By the Lady Willoughby A foreparte of lawne Cuttwork florished with silver and spangles. Delivered to the Roabes'. (New Year's Gift Roll, 31 Eliz. 1589. BL, Lansd. Roll 17 printed in *Progr. Eliz.*, III, p. 8).

[53] Item one foreparte and a Dublet of white lawne cutworke florished in squares with owes unmade.

Loc. 'C'. This was a joint New Year's gift: 'By the Lady Southwell A dooblet of lawne

454, 455 *Owl, snails and peascods, pansy and a monster, two details from a white linen smock embroidered in crimson silk, c. 1600. Victoria and Albert Museum, London* (T.2–1956)

and in the coller and slevis with buckeram all of our great guarderobe'. (Warrant 9 April, 14 Eliz. 1572. BL, Egerton 2806, f. 41). Later in the year Walter Fyshe had the work of 'making of a payer of newe slevis for a Dou(t)che Cloake of blak vellat with a lase of blak silke & golde of our great guarderobe'. (Warrant 28 Sept., 14 Eliz. 1572. BL, Egerton 2806, f. 46).

[14] Item one rounde cloke of strawe colour clothe laide with three laces of venice golde silver carnacion and greene silke lyned with chaungeable crimsen and blewe Capha striped.

[15] Item one shorte cloake of Abranounsio laide with brode bonelace of venice golde and silver lyned with white satten striped with silver.

Walter Fyshe is entered in a warrant of 1573 'for making of a Cloake of Abramamsio layed with brode bone lase of venice golde and silver lyned with white Satten striped with silver the Stuff to make the Cloake and lyne it of our said store within our said Guarderobe of Robes threst of our great guarderobe'. (Warrant 20 Oct., 15 Eliz. 1573. BL, Egerton 2806, f. 60).

[16] Item one cloake of greene vellat with twoe wreathes of Carnacion satten and a lace on eache side of venice golde and silver lyned with strawe colour Taphata.

f. 13

[17] Item a cloake and a saufegarde of greene Damaske laide rounde aboute and striped downe like waves with a lace of venice silver and Carnacion silke with buttons and loopes of [[like]] silke and silver lyned with Carnacion Taphata.

[18] Item one cloake and a sauefgarde of aishe colour Burrell with twoe laces of venice golde silver and greene silke.

[19] Item one cloake and a saufegarde of blacke vellat bordered aboute and striped downe with twoe passamaine laces of venice golde and aishe colour silke with like buttons and loopes with a cut Jagge bounde with like lace.

[20] Item one cloake of blacke vellat bounde with a passamaine lace buttons and loopes of venice golde.

[21] Item one Cloake and a saufegarde of aishe colour taphata wrought with a border aboute with a Clowde lace of venice silver and Carnacion silke. The saufegarde striped bias, with like lace, the cloake lyned with Carnacion vellat.

Walter Fyshe is entered in a warrant of 1576 'for making of a Cloake and a Saufegarde of ashe colour taphata the Cloake wrought with a border aboute with a cloude lase of venice silver and carnacion silke borderid with ashe colour taphata thinside and the border layed with two lases of venice golde and carnacion silke the coller lyned with canvas the Saufegarde wrought with a border aboute and striped byas allover the quarters with like lase of venice silver & carnacion silke borderid aboute with ashe colour taphata and pockettes of like taphata the taphata to make the same Cloake and Saufegarde of our store threst of our great guarderobe'. (Warrant 26 Sept., 18 Eliz. 1576. BL, Egerton 2806, f. 102ᵛ).

[22] Item one Dutche Cloake of blacke vellat with a lace and frenged with silke.

[23] Item one Cloake of blacke vellat bounde aboute with a bonelace of venice

silver and lyned with prented clothe of silver.

[24] Item one Cloake of blacke clothe of silver striped lyned with white prented satten.

[25] Item one Cloake and a saufegarde of blacke Taphata cut with a billamente lace aboute them and striped allover with lace set with knottes and tuftes, the cloake lyned and the saufegarde bordered with Sarceonet.

William Jones is entered in a warrant of 1584 'for making of a Cloake and a Saufegarde of blak taphata cutt with a billement lase aboute them and striped allover with like lase sett with knottes and tuftes the Cloake lyned and the Saufegarde borderid with sarceonett all of our great guarderobe'. (Warrant 27 Sept., 26 Eliz. 1584. BL, Egerton 2806, f. 200).

f. 13ᵛ

[26] Item one saufegarde of seawater prented satten bounde aboute with a lace of venice golde silver and silke and downe before with like buttons and loopes.

[27] Item one cloake of pale colour vellat with a faire lace buttons and loopes of venice golde and silver lyned with tawnye satten raized.

RMN 'geven to th{e Ladie} Walsingham'.

[28] Item one cloake of blacke taphata with a lace, and caste over with like lace buttons and loopes all of venice golde silver and Carnacion silke lyned with blacke vellat laide aboute with a like lace.

[29] Item one cloake and a saufegarde of Carnacion taphata cut garded aboute

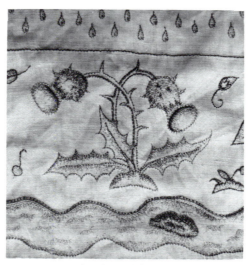

456   Cat embroidered in crimson silk, detail from a white linen smock, c. 1600. Victoria and Albert Museum, London (T.2–1956)

457, 458   Thistle and foxglove, two details from the top of a white linen smock embroidered with polychrome silks, c. 1585–1600. Whitworth Art Gallery, Manchester

with a lace of greene silke and silver lyned with white sarceonet.

[30]   Item one cloake of blacke vellat with twoe bone laces of venice silver lyned with clothe of silver striped with colours.

[31]   Item one Dutche Cloke of rushe coloure vellat with twoe golde laces, the sleeves enbrodered with like lace lined with Taphata pincked.

[32]   Item one Dutche cloake of seawater greene Grograine with three brode gardes of black vellat cut overthwarte and fower small laces of silver lined with blacke Taphata cut.

[33]   Item one cloake of blacke grograine with a passamaine lace of venice golde buttons and loopes lyned with blacke Taphata pincked.

[34]   Item one cloake of Chaungeable heare colour and blacke taphata striped and enbrodered rounde aboute with a purle lace of blewe silke and silver.

f. 14

[35]   Item one cloake and a saufegarde of aishe colour raishe striped downe and rounde aboute with lace of blacke orenge tawny and silver, the Cloake lyned with strawe colour sarceonet.

[36]   Item one shorte cloke of Cloth of silver with flowers of orenge colour silke striped downe and bounde aboute with a lase of venice golde silver and watchet silke lyned with watchet plushe.

[37]   Item one rounde Cloake of aishe colour grograine striped on each side with

buttons and loopes of perle of sondrie bignes, and bugles, lyned with peach colour plushe.

[38]   Item one rounde Cloake of Carnacion silver Capha laide aboute and striped downe with lace of silver and blacke silke lyned with white plushe.

[39]   Item one Juppe and saufegarde of white taphata garded with white Taphata bounde aboute with a white silke lace.

[40]   Item one Juppe and saufegarde of peache colour taphata covered with Copwebb lawne starched the sleeves beinge set with silver owes and spangles bounde aboute with a silver lace.

[41]   Item one rounde cloake of aishe colour cloth of sylver laide aboute and striped downe with twoe laces of venice golde sylver and plate lyned with Carnacion plushe.

f. 14ᵛ

Dublettes

[1]   Item one case for a Dublet of white Cipers garnished with damaske golde and heare colour silke.

[2]   Item one dublet case of lawne cut garnished with golde and spangles.

This was a New Year's gift: 'By Mrs Edmondes a Case for a dublate of lawne Cut garnysshed with gold and spangles. Delivered to the foresaid R. hope'. (New Year's Gift Roll, 26 Eliz. 1584. BL, Egerton 3052, printed in *Costume* 9, 1975, p. 30).

[3]   Item one dublet of lawne allover wroughte with black silke and golde,

bounde aboute with a small passamaine of golde.

This was a New Year's gift: 'By Mrs Dygby a doblett of lawne alover wrought with blacke silke and golde and bownd about withe a smale passamayne of golde. Delivered to R. hope'. (New Year's Gift Roll, 26 Eliz. 1584. BL, Egerton 3052, printed in *Costume* 9, 1975, p. 30).

[4]   Item one Coveringe for a dublet of lawne cutworke.

[5]   Item one Dublet of white Satten prented bounde aboute with a lace buttons and loopes of venice golde lyned with yellowe sarceonet.

[6]   Item one dublet of white Satten embroidered allover with sondrie flowers of venice golde silver and silke in pottes.

[7]   Item one Coveringe for a Dublet of lawne cutworke in spaces.

[8]   Item one Dublet of white satten enbrodered all over with a worke of knottes and flowers with a risinge lace of venice golde and purple silke.

[9]   Item one Dublet of white Satten cut laide overthwarte with twoe laces together of golde and tawny silke.

f. 15

[10]   Item one Dublet of white satten cut enbrodered allover with feathers honiesuckles and other flowers of golde silver and silke of sondrie colours.

[11]   Item one Dublet of tawney satten enbrodered allover with dead trees, and

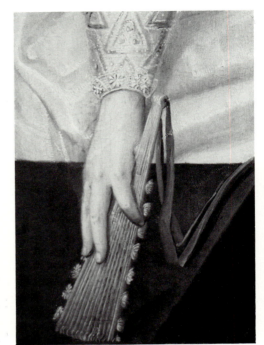

459 'Portrait of an unknown lady in white, called Mary Fitton' by an unknown artist, c. 1595–1600. The Chartered Trustees of the Town of Malden, Moot Hall, Malden

460 Detail from Figure 459 showing the embroidered triangles enriched with silver spangles, 'puffings' of white silk gauze, and wired spangles standing away from the sleevehead

461 Detail from Figure 459 showing a folding fan, similar to those in Figures 424 and 425, decorated with tufts of silk, attached to the girdle with a ribbon

trailes of Eglantine of venice golde and greene silke.

[12]   Item one Dublet of strawe colour taphata slightlie embrodered with roses and honiesuckles of venice silver.

[13]   Item one Dublet of white and orenge colour Capha with tuftes of Carnacion silke and small owes.

[14]   Item one Dublet of lawne embrodered allover with flowers of golde silver and silke of sondrie colours lined with strawe colour Taphata.

This was a New Year's gift: 'By the Countes of Penbroke, a dublet of lawne embrowdred alover with golde, silver & sylke of divers collours, and lyned with yelow taphata. Delivered to Rauf Hoope'. (New Year's Gift Roll, 20 Eliz. 1578. Soc. of Antiquaries MS 537, printed in *Progr. Eliz.*, 11, p. 68).

[15]   Item one Dublet of peache colour satten with a networke florished with golde and spangles.

[16]   Item one dublet of strawe colour taphata covered with aishe colour networke enbrodered allover with sondrie flowers and knottes and wormes of venice golde, silver and spangles.

[17]   Item one Dublet of black satten cut with buttons and loopes like Clowdes with a fewe seede p(ear)le lined with white sarceonet.

This was a New Year's gift: 'By the Lady Drury a dublett of black satten cut with a passamayne lace & buttons of venice gold & the saide buttons & loopes set with seade p(ear)le lyned with white sarceonett. Delivered to Rauf hoope'. (New Year's Gift Roll, 19 Eliz. 1577. PRO, C47/3/39).

[18]   Item one Dublet of russet Satten covered with a lawne cutworke with flowers florished with silver.

[19]   Item one Dublet of Carnacion satten cut slightlie embrodered with a small thred Chevernewise of silver and owes lyned with white sarceonet.

f. 15ᵛ

[20]   Item one Dublet of Tawnye Satten cut and razed laide overthwarte with a small lace of venice silver lyned with white sarceonet.

[21]   Item a Dublet of clothe of silver with a lace of venice golde and Carnacion silke and buttons and loopes set upon Carnacion Taphata with golde and seede p(ear(le.

[22]   Item one Dublet of Carnacion satten cut striped overthwarte with a spangle lace of venice silver.

[23]   Item one Dublet of white satten aboote [sic] bounde aboute with a passamaine lace of venice golde.

[24]   Item one Dublet of blacke satten covered with white lawne networke, and another net upon that of strawe colour and white silke.

[25]   Item one Dublet of Turquey satten cut in risinge panes with a lace of plate silver golde and spangles rounde aboute.

[26]   Item one Dublet of blacke Taphata cut striped downeright with plate lace of silver and golde.

[27]   Item one Dublet of Russet Satten welted Chevernewise, with orenge colour vellat, with a silver lace one eache side.

[28]   Item one Dublet of aishe colour tufte Taphata the grounde silver slightlie embrodered.

[29]   Item a Dublet of Murrey Taphata covered with networke florished with golde and silver.

[30]   Item a Dublet of blacke Satten aboote.

f. 16

[31]   Item one Dublet of Carnacion Satten aboote striped with silver and bounde aboute with a lace of silver.

[32]   Item one Dublet of white Satten cut lyned with Carnacion plushe.

This item might have been either of two doublets listed in the 1588 New Year's Gift

462 *Pendent jewel of a lamb formed from a baroque pearl, hanging from gold chains, second half of the sixteenth century. Museo Lazzaro Galdiano, Madrid*

463 *Carcanet composed of 'cinques' or 'fives' of pearls alternating with cameos in gold settings enamelled with daisies, and a large pointed diamond with pendent pearl at the front, detail from Figure 25, c. 1574–75. Walker Art Gallery, Liverpool*

Roll: 'By the Baronesse Dudley one dublet of white Satten cut lyned with Carnation plushe. Delivered to the said Sir Tho: Gorges' and 'By the Baronesse Paggett Care . . . a Dublett of white satten cut all over in leaves and lyned with Carnation Flusshe. Delivered to the said Sir Tho: Gorges'. (New Year's Gift Roll, 30 Eliz. 1588. BL, Add.8159). The latter gift was accompanied by a petticoat, listed in Stowe f. 61ᵛ/83.

[33] Item one Dublet of Dammaske copper silver turne frenge lace wrought with damaske silver purle edged with a passamaine of venice silver laide upon white sarceonet.

This was a New Year's gift: 'By Sir George Cary A doblett of Copper damaske silver turned freinge lace wrought with purle and edged with a passamayn of silver. Delivered to the Roabes'. (New Year's Gift Roll, 31 Eliz. 1589. BL, Lansd. Roll 17, printed in *Progr. Eliz.*, III, p. 10).

[34] Item one dublet of aishe colour grograine cut like leaves and set with silver owes lyned undernethe with clothe of silver.

[35] Item one Dublet of horsefleshe colour Satten cut allover with leaves and raized up enbrodered allover with silver owes, and bias allover with golde lace.

[36] Item one Covering for a Dublet of lawne striped with silver plate, with puffes like rolles.

Loc. 'C'. This was a New Year's gift: 'By Mrs Townsende a Covering for a dublett of lawne striped with silver plate puffed like Rolles. Delivered to the said Sir Tho: Gorges'. (New Year's Gift Roll, 30 Eliz. 1588. BL, Add.8159).

[37] Item one Dublet of white and Carnacion Satten lyned bias wise with a lace of venice golde.

[38] Item one Coveringe for a Dublet of lawne cutworke with tuftes of Carnacion silke.

This was a New Year's gift: 'By the Ladye Ratcliffe a Covering of a Dublett of lawne Cutwourke with Tuftes of Carnation silke. Delivered to Sir Thomas Gorges'. (New Year's Gift Roll, 30 Eliz. 1588. BL, Add.8159).

f. 16ᵛ

[No entries]

f. 17
Fannes

[1] Firste one Fanne of watchet tawny and strawe colour feathers with a handle of silver white.

[2] Item one Fanne of feathers with a handle of silver white graven with Sir Walter Rawleis armes.

[3] Item one Fanne of Carnacion curled silke garnished with Flowers of seede p(ear)le with Flowers and spiders of ragge[d] pearle.

[4] Item one Fanne of Carnacion white and aishe colour feathers, with a handle of Silver parcell guilte.

f. 17ᵛ
Taken as Fees

[1] Firste one olde robe of purple vellat of the order of the Garter, with laces of purple silke and golde lyned with white Taphata.

[2] Item one saufegarde of blacke vellat laide with brode lace of venice silver.

[3] Item one Peticoate of clothe of silver chamblet striped with golde.

f. 18
A note of suche parcelles as are certefied to bee loste and wantinge.

[1] Firste eight and twentie Buttons of golde made rounde for Jerkines, viz xvᵗᵉⁿᵉ enameled white, and xiijᵗᵉⁿᵉ enameled blacke.

[2] Item fyfteene Buttons of golde enameled greene.

[3] Item nyne small pearles taken from Buttons.

[4] Item twoe small Buttons of golde with a pearle in eache wantinge from a kirtle of greene vellat enbrodered.

 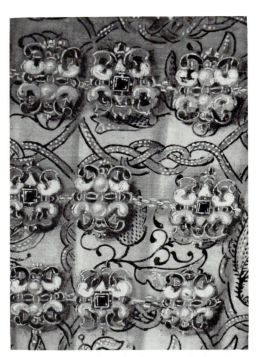

464, 465 *Two details from Figure 391 showing girdle formed of black enamelled gold links, with chains of black enamelled 'pillars', and pearls 'laced on a thread' hanging from the neck. The buttons are enamelled white, red and black, c. 1593–95. Sabin Galleries Ltd, London*

[5]   Item three small aglets of golde wanting from a Mantle of russet stitched clothe.

[6]   Item Fyfteene buttons of golde wanting from a rounde kirtle and dublet of russet Satten etc.

[7]   Item one foreparte of Clothe of silver enbrodered allover with oken leaves of venice golde and peacockes feathers.

[8]   Item one button of golde enameled like a halfe Moone wantinge from a Cloake of purple vellat the ground white Satten.

f. 18ᵛ

[9]   Item xvᵉⁿᵉ paier of Buttons and loopes of pearle wanting from a saufegarde of black vellat.

[10]   Item xvᵗᵉⁿᵉ small buttons of golde wanting from a Cloake of tawney Satten embroidered.

[11]   Item three buttons of golde knotes wantinge from a Dutche cloke of black vellat.

[12]   Item divers greate pearle wantinge from a rounde cloake of blacke vellat enbrodered.

[13]   Item one cloake of blacke knetworke florished with a thred of venice golde lyned with white plushe.

[14]   Item one pece of blacke Networke florished with golde and silver conteyninge xij yardes.

[15]   Item one Fanne of strawe colour and white feathers with a handle of bone slightlie garnished with golde.

f. 19

Jewells loste and wantinge

1   Firste one Button of golde with five pearles in it loste from her Majestes kirtle at a plaie at Richmonde at Xpmas [Christmas] 1595.

2   Item fower paire of small Aglettes of golde loste.

3   Item one Diamonde loste from a Jewell of golde like a double rounde knott at Richmonde xiiijᵗᵒ Januar' 1600.

4   Item three buttons like pressed hartes.

5   Item three buttons of golde with Diamondes of the fourthe sorte and twoe diamondes oute of Collettes of the thirde sorte.

6   Item one Rubie from a button of golde of the firste sorte.

7   Item three buttons of golde with Trueloves of pearl{e} viz' twoe loste xvijᵐᵒ Novembr' 1593 of the thirde sorte and one xxviijᵐᵒ Octobr' 1598 of the seconde sorte.

8   Item one button of golde knotted with three pearles in it loste xvjᵗᵒ Maij 1590.

f. 19ᵛ

9   Item one Diamonde from a button of golde with Cinques of Diamondes loste xxᵐᵒ April' 1590.

10   Item one Diamonde from a Jewell of golde like a harte fullye garnished with diamondes, loste by her Majestie xiiijᵗᵒ Februar' 1596.

11   Item one little pearle from a little flower of gold etc.

12   Item xviijᵗᵉⁿᵉ middle sised pearle from a paire of lawne sleeves.

13   Item twoe little pearles and a pendaunt of a diamonde from a Juell of golde like a halfe Moone loste iijᵗⁱᵒ Februar' 1599.

[14]   Item twelve peeces of golde p(ar)cell of a Cheine and a girdle loste by the Queenes Majestie.

[15]   Item one Opall from a flower of golde etc. loste by her Majestie.

[16]   Item fyve [[small]] buttons of golde enameled with sondrie colours and three perles. loste by her Majestie viz' twoe in anno [[1586,]] one in anno [[1587]] and twoe ijᵈᵒ Maij 1591.

[17]   Item one pendaunt garnished with sparkes of Diamondes and Rubies from a Juell of golde like a pellicane etc.

f. 20

18   Item the Diamondes of one button of golde with ragged staves loste by her Majestie xxiiijᵗⁱᵒ april' 1592.

19   Item three Emerodes from buttons of golde enameled loste by her Majestie.

20   Item one small Rubie from a button of golde enameled with ragged staves etc.

[21]   Item one small Button of golde like roses with small sparkes of Rubies and one sparke of a Diamonde in the middest loste by her Majestie xvjᵗᵒ Marcii 1599.

22   Item one small button of golde with a small diamonde in it.

ff. 21, 22

[These folios were blank and so badly decayed that they were discarded when the MS was repaired].

f. 23

```
              20 li
   (....) first————— 4li 10 s⎤
{I}tem payed—————13li  4 s⎬ 20 li
{I}tem payed————— 2li  6 s⎦
```

Index I
Index of Miscellaneous Subjects including Paintings, Persons, Places, and Events

AS WITH ANY book of this size, a fully comprehensive index is a practical impossibility. For example, page references to donors have been given under 'Gifts of clothes and accessories to Queen Elizabeth', but no attempt has been made to list all those mentioned in the notes given in the Stowe and Folger inventories. All individuals known to be Maids of Honour or Ladies and Gentlewomen of the Privy Chamber and Bedchamber attending on the Queen, at one time or another, are marked thus *; cross references are given for single and married names, where known. It is very easy to confuse ladies with the same surname since Christian names are not always given, as for example with some of the Howards and Staffords; their relationship to each other, if any, is not always clear. Considerable variations in spelling of both Christian names and surnames occur, as for example with Abington and Habington, Bruxsiles and Brussels, Ratcliffe and Radclyffe, Shetz and Skettes, Sidney and Sydney, and it is not always possible to tell if the same person is indicated. Present and former owners and locations of portraits of Queen Elizabeth and other sitters are printed in italics.

Abbreviations

D.	Drawings
E.	Engravings
I.	Illuminations
M.	Miniatures
n.	Note
P.	Paintings
Q.E.	Queen Elizabeth I
T.S.	Tomb sculpture
W.	Woodcuts

Abington [Habington], John, Clerk of the Kitchen of the Household, 101, 102; Dorothy, his wife, 202, 219 (see also under Broadbelt)
Abnett, Ralph, hosier, 12, 206
Accession Day Tilts and celebrations, 6, 57, 91, 94, 112
Act of Apparel, 158
Actors' costumes, 14
Adams, Schoolmaster to the Henchmen, 93, 190
Adderley, Humphrey, Groom of the Robes 168; Yeoman of the Robes, 169
Alcega, Juan de, 124, 139; pattern of farthingale from book by, Fig. 279
Alcherius, Jehan, 77
Alciati, Andreas, 74, 76
Alençon, François, Duke of (later Duke of Anjou), 6, 49, 58, 75, 76
Alington, Richard, T. S. of daughters of, 60, Figs 98, 98a, 213
Alington, Joan, T. S. of, 135, Figs 213, 213a, 213b, 265
Almshouses, founded by David Smith, 190

Alterations, to clothes in paintings and engravings, 19–21, 59, 60, 62, Figs 99, 100, 107
Alterations hand, 180
Altham, Mr, 168
Amman, Jost, engravings by, 131, Figs 208, 258, 261, 263, 273, 276, 304, 315, 331
Amsterdam, Rijksmuseum, P. of Pierre Moucheron and family, Fig. 211
Ampleforth College, P. of Q.E., Fig. 342
Ancaster and Kesteven, Mary Duchess of, Mistress of Robes to Queen Charlotte, 104
Anduxar, Martin de, 125
Anglesey Abbey, National Trust, P. of Q.E., 15, Fig. 12
Anjou, Duke of, see under Henri III, King of France
Anjou marriage negotiations, 122
Anne of Austria, Queen of Spain, P. of, Fig. 194
Anne Boleyn, Queen consort of Henry VIII, 1, 3
Anne of Cleves, Queen consort of Henry VIII, 5, 70
Anne of Denmark, Queen of James I, 64, 70, 72, 87, 89, 104, 175, 210, 216; material suitable for wedding garment of, 97; Q.E.'s clothes altered for, 174; P. of, Fig. 120
Annuities, 101
Anthony, Dericke, engraver at the Mint, 61
Antiquaries, Society of, see under London
Aragon, Katherine of, see under Katherine of Aragon
Arbury Hall, P. of Q.E., 28, 30, 31, Fig. 44
Armada, medal commemorating, Fig. 297
'Armada' portraits of Q.E., 14, 30, 33, 34, 123, 159, Figs 52, 54, 55, Pl. IVA
Armoury at Tower of London, 163
Arnold, John, Yeoman of Revels, 178
Arnold, Lott, pinner, 173
Arrasmakers and tailors, articles controlling, 165
Arthur, Prince of Wales, 123
Artificers, or craftsmen, working for Q.E., 177–234
Ascham, Roger, tutor to Q.E., 4, 134
Ashbourne, Queen Elizabeth's Grammar School, I. of Q.E. on Ashburne Charter, 32, 33, Fig. 48, Pl. IIB
Ashley [Asteley], Katherine, 107
Astle, Thomas, 174, 246, 248, 251
Astraea, Q.E. as, 71
Atherley, see under Adderley
Audley End, Progress to, 217
Audley, Margaret, 56
Ayland, John, cutler, 229
Aylmer, John, Bishop of London, 10, 93

Baby, of pewter, 107, Fig. 163
Bacon, Anthony, 168
Bacon, Sir Francis, 1; letter with gift to Q.E., 98
Bacon, Sir Nicholas, P. of Q.E., 26, Fig. 31
Baker, Sir Richard, 2
Bakewell, All Saints Parish Church, T.S. of Dorothy Vernon, Figs 291, 292

Banyarde, John, tailor, 173
Banghe, John, brusher of Robes, 234
Barcelona, Museum of Catalan Art, P. of Salome wearing farthingale, Fig. 277
Barney, Margaret, hood maker, 203, 204
Baroncelli, Thomasso, 128
Basing Park, Progress at, 12
Bate, John, farthingale maker, 172, 196, 197
Bath, Marquess of, see under Longleat House
Bath, ironwork for moveable, for Q.E., 228
Baynard's Castle, 163, 246
Beale, Robert, 100
Beauchamp, Sir John, 163
Bedford Estates, see under Woburn Abbey
Bedford, Lucy Harington, Countess of, P. of, 64, Fig. 113
Begue, Jehan le, 77
Belon, Pierre, 79
Benabarre, Pedro Garcia de, P. of Salome wearing farthingale by, Fig. 277
Benger, Thomas, Master of Revels, 170, 171; warrant from, Fig. 254
Benlowes, Eleanor, P. of, Fig. 96
Bereleigh, 'Armada' P. of Q.E., 34, Fig. 55
Berkeley Castle, P. of unknown woman by Gheeraerts the Younger, 61, Fig. 103
Berkeley, Lady Elizabeth, 110
Berkeley, Lady Katherine, 110
Berkeley, Sir Thomas, 110
Berlin, Dahlem, Gemaldegalerie Staatliche Museen, P. of Margaret of Parma, by Antonio Mor, Fig. 224
Bermondsey, boat hire to, 179
Berney, Kenelm, 180
Bessborough, Earl of, see under Stansted Park
Bess of Hardwick, see under Shrewsbury, Countess of,
Bettes, John, the Younger, P. of Q.E. by, 26, 29, 30, Figs 40, 45
Bird-cage, curtains for, 231
Blackamoor, 190
Blackfriars, 165
Black Prince's ruby, 43
Blacksmiths, 227–29
Blair Castle, P. of Q.E., 44, Fig. 72
Bland [Blande], Adam, skinner, 53, 58, 59, 106, 107, 167, 171, 173, 177, 192–94
Bland, Peter, skinner, 192–94
Blazonry, 90
Blickling Hall, National Trust, P. of Q.E., 44, Fig. 73
Bodleian Library, see under Oxford
Boissard, Jean Jacques, E. of French women by, 74, 76, 82, Figs 181, 182
Boleyn, Anne, see under Anne Boleyn
Boleyn, Sir Thomas, 113
Bonde, Mrs Karin, 157
Boughton House, P. of Q.E., Fig. 65
P. of Elizabeth Vernon, Countess of Southampton, 110, Figs 138, 164–66, 231

Index II
Clothing, Textiles, Jewels, Motifs, Colours, Techniques, and Articles for the Toilet

THIS INDEX, partly a glossary, has been prepared to enable the reader to trace quickly information on woven and embroidered motifs, designs of jewels, names and symbolism of colours, names of fabrics, technical terms, fashion terminology, and other topics, according to their particular interest.

Modern spellings are used, followed by variations in original spelling, cross-referenced where necessary. Quotations from early dictionaries and other sources come before the modern definition which is only given if there is no full explanation in the text. Page references in the text are followed by selected quotations from the Stowe and Folger inventories and/or their folio references. A selection of Figure references is given at the end of many entries. The size of the book has made it impossible to produce a completely comprehensive index.

Key to abbreviations of sources for quotations given in the text

B   Thomas Blount, *Glossographia*, 1656
BA   John Baret, *An alvearie or quadruple dictionarie*, 1580
C   Randle Cotgrave, *A Dictionarie of the French and English Tongues*, 1611, 1632
HC   Henry Cockeram, *The English Dictionarie, or an interpreter of hard English Words*, 1623
CH   Randle Cotgrave, Robert Sherwood and James Howell, *A French–English and English–French Dictionary with supplements*, 1660
F   Folger inventory. See pp. 335–50 for full transcription
GM   Guy Miege, *A New Dictionary of French and English with Another English and French*, 1679. *A Dictionary of Barbarous French taken from Cotgrave*, 1679
JF   John Florio, *First Fruites*, 1600
M   John Minsheu, *The Guide into Tongues*, 1617
NB   Nathan Bailey, *A Universal Etymological English Dictionary*, 1721
OH   James Orchard Halliwell, *A Dictionary of Archaic and Provincial Words*, 1872
RH   Randle Holme, *The Academy of Armory, or, a Storehouse of Armory and Blazon*, 1688

OED *The Oxford English Dictionary being a corrected re-issue with an introduction, supplement and bibliography of A New English Dictionary on historical principles founded mainly on the materials collected by The Philological Society* edited by James A. H. Murray, Henry Bradley, W. A. Craigie, and C. T. Onions (Oxford, 1933) 12 vols
P   Jehan Palsgrave, *Lesclarcissement de la langue Françoyse*, 1530 (1582)
S   Stowe inventory. See pp. 251–334 for full transcription

The reader will find the following books particularly useful

BOYNTON, LINDSAY (Ed.), *The Hardwicke Hall Inventories of 1601*, The Furniture History Society, 1971. Numerous references to textiles for furnishings.
GERARD, JOHN, *The Herball or Generall Historie of Plantes*, 1597. Photographic reprint, Amsterdam, 1974. Illustrated with woodcuts of flowers used in embroidery.
LEVEY, SANTINA M., *Lace: A History*, 1983. Copiously illustrated with examples of needle and bobbin lace.
LINTHICUM, M. C., *Costume in the Drama of Shakespeare and his Contemporaries*, Oxford, 1936. Numerous references to clothing and textiles from contemporary plays and other documentary sources.
MONTGOMERY, FLORENCE M., *Textiles in America 1650–1870*, 1986. Dictionary of textiles, with illustrations of imported mid-seventeenth-century fabrics which have some bearing on earlier materials.
PUTTNAM, CLARE, *Flowers and Trees in Tudor England*, 1972. Reproductions in colour, from an illuminated manuscript of *c.*1520–30, of flowers used in embroidery.

ABRAHAM, ABRAMAMSIO, ABRANOUNSIO Blount defines Abraham colour as brown, but does not give shade. May also refer to some type of material: p. 121; *shorte cloake of Abranounsio*, F, f.12v/[15]
ACORN, ACKHORNE, AKORNE The fruit or seed of the oak tree, an oval nut growing in a shallow woody cup: used in embroidery,

pp. 30, 31; for gold jewel, p. 32; at ends of partlet laces, p. 150; examples in embroidery, S, f.16/78, f.66/20, f.86v/10. Figs 134, 326, 330
AGATE 'An agath stone . . . so called because it is found in Gange a river in Lycia' (M). A precious stone; a variety of chalcedony, a fine-grained quartz, with the colours arranged in parallel bands: S, f.91/4, f.92/20, f.96v/[25], f.98v/[69]
AGLET, AIGLET, AGLETTE 'An aglet or tag of a point' (M). The metal tag of a lace (formerly called a point) originally used to make it easier to thread through the eyelet holes, but afterwards also as an ornament to the pendent ends, when it might be quite large. Aglets might be of enamelled gold, studded with precious stones, and also of glass or crystal: pp. 41, 144, 222; S, f.7/[4], [5], [6], [7], f.7v/[8], [9], f.95/[3], [7], f.95v/[9], [10], f.101/[17]
AISHCOLOUR, AISHE COLOUR *see under* ASH COLOUR
ALTAR Used in embroidery with butterflies, p. 86; used for jewel, n. to S, f.103/[20]
ALTERATIONS *see also under* TRANSLATING Numerous examples of alterations to Queen Elizabeth's clothes are given in the Stowe and Folger inventories, pp. 255–324 and 335–49: for Anne of Denmark, p. 174; for Queen Elizabeth, pp. 1, 2, 21, 59, 65, 66, 174, 185, 187; to embroidery, pp. 150, 191; to farthingales, pp. 195, 197; from French gown to round gown, p. 184; for gifts, pp. 98, 103, 107; to guards, p. 155; to hose, p. 209; to keep in fashion, p. 184; to linings, p. 184; by Arthur Middleton, p. 180; to jewels, S, f.96/[17]
AMBERGRIS, AMBERGRIZE A wax-like substance of marbled ashy colour, found floating in tropical seas, and as a morbid secretion in the intestines of the sperm whale. It is odiferous and used in perfumery: p. 232, note to S, f.69v/70
ANCHOR Used for jewel design, p. 61. Fig. 102
ANGEL, ANGELL Used for jewel design, S, f.95v/[13]
ANTIQUE 'Antiques or Antique work, is a work for delight sake being a general or irregular composition of all manner of compartments of Men, Beasts, Birds, Flowers, Fruit, and such like, without either rule or reason' (RH, III, 3, p. 145): *embroidered*

and was made of linen, cypress, network and other fine materials; p. 205

BONE LACE   Lace made by twisting bobbins holding gold, silver, silk and linen threads above a pattern marked with pins. The bobbins were originally made of bone, hence bone lace: pp. 23, 49; *a bonelace of venice golde*, S, f.15v/68, f.26v/28; *bonelace of venice silver*, S, f.31/17; *bonelace of venice golde and blacke silke*, S, f.31/18; *bonelace of venice golde and silver*, S, f.32/35; *bonelace of blacke silke*, S, f.32v/40; *bone laces of venice golde and Spangles*, S, f.56/3; *broade bone laces*, S, f.63v/115. Figs 322, 354, 415

BONNET   Worn with caul, p. 112. Fig. 351

BORAGE   *Borago hortensis*, Garden Borage, illustrated in *Gerard*, pp. 652–53. A plant with small, bright blue flowers and stem and leaves covered with prickly hairs: example in embroidery, S, f.52/90

BORDER   'To Border, to brimme, gard or welt' (M). A band, usually embroidered or otherwise decorated, placed round the edges of a garment, and later simply a decorative band: *borders like peramydes*, S, f.32/36; *hanginge sleeves of white satten cut snipte and rufte up with borders betweene*, S, f.52/91

BOOTS   For the fool, p. 213

BOOT HOSE   p. 206

BOUND ABOUT   Braid folded over the edge of a hem on skirts and other garments for decoration and protection, S, f.17/97

BRACES   *see also under* FLAPS *and* SHOULDER PIECES pp. 155, 162 n. 357

BRACELET   With initials ER, p. 70

BRAIDED LACE, BRAID   'Braid-see Curle; Curle -see frize: Frize- frizled, curled, braided or ruffled' (CH). Some arrangement of plaited or interlaced threads making a decorative braid: copper gold lace, also described as braid, p. 106; in chevron design, p. 185; *braided lace*, S, f.33/47; *breade lace*, S, f.34v/69, f.70v/83

BRANCHES   Of a plant or tree, used in embroidery. Term also used for 'branched velvet'. See *Philaster*, v, i, l. 190, where Dion wishes that moths would 'branch their velvets', eating away a pattern in the pile: examples of embroidery designs, S, f.26v/29, f.30v/13; *branches of bugles greate and small*, S, f.19v/26

BRAZIL, BRASELL   Originally the name of the hard brownish-red wood of an East Indian tree, known as sappan, from which dyers obtain a red colour: S, f.76v/11

BREADE LACE   *see under* BRAIDED LACE

BROAD, BRODE   Wide: *brode plate lace of venice golde*, S, f.32/33

BRUSH   Long white, p. 198; rubbing, pp. 181, 234

BUCK, BUCKE   Used in a jewel, S, f.95v/[16]

BUCKET   Gold jewel, p. 75

BUCKLE   On boots, p. 213

BUCKLER   A buckler is a small round shield, so the buttons listed were presumably round and dome-shaped: *buttons called great Bucklers*, S, f.100/[1]; *buttons called small Bucklers*, S, f.100/[2]

BUCKRAM   Apparently a firmly woven material of linen, hemp, or possibly cotton, used for inexpensive garments, linings, and *toiles*. Probably starched or gummed when used for stiffening collars and sleeves: pp. 179, 183, 198; *toiles* of, p. 116; used for stays, p. 188

BUDGE   Lambskin originally coming from North Africa, and later Spain, differentiated

from others by reference to their original association with the Moorish kingdom of Bougie (*Veale*, p. 25): p. 193; used to trim livery gowns, pp. 167, 177

BUGLE, BUGELL   A tube-shaped glass bead, frequently black, used to ornament wearing apparel (OED): p. 184; *bugles like pipes*, S, f.19v/25; *branches of bugles greate and small*, S, f.19v/26; *bugles made like flowers*, S, f.48/31. Fig. 443

BURGONYON GARDES   *see under* GUARD

BURRELL   Material used for gowns, cloaks, and safeguards, exact variety unknown, but perhaps some kind of slubbed wool (from burl — a small knot or lump in wool or cloth, OED) or dressed cloth (from burl — to dress cloth, especially by removing knots and lumps, OED): S, f.88/[1], [2]; F, f.2v/[7], f.13/[18], *aishe colour silke Burrell*, F, f.5v/[16]

BURRIDGE FLOWERS   *see under* BORAGE

BUSK   pp. 12, 110; cases for, p. 231; points for, pp. 110, 111, 147; of whalebone, p. 147, and wire, p. 146; of wood, p. 231

BUSKIN   pp. 215, 216. Fig. 310

BUTTERFLY   In embroidery, pp. 78, 79, 86; for jewel, p. 72; examples in embroidery, S, f.53v/119, f.59v/52, f.70/73, F, f.9v/[46]; *buttons embrodered like Butterflies*, S, f.71v/96; *Brouch . . . with a Butterflie*, S, f.96v/26. Figs 118, 129, 137, 149, 274, 397, 407, 408

BUTTONS   A wide variety are entered in the Stowe and Folger inventories including some set with precious stones: pp. 25, 32, 43, 44, 70; with esses, p. 70; with impresas, p. 94; Scottish. p. 106; buttons and loops, S, f.23/73; lace [braid] buttons and loops, S, f.29/66; *like the birdes of Arabia*, S, f.39v/38; *embrodered like Butterflies*, S, f.71v/96; *with Camewes*, S, f.97v/[49]; *of silver Enbroderers worke*, S, f.28v/58; *enameled like half Moones*, S, f.67/30; *enameled like Paunceis*, S, f.96v/[27]; *like knotts*, S, f.34v/72; *knotted buttons*, S, f.44/117; *knotted with three pearles*, S, f.102/[4]; *of open worke* (possibly filigree), S, f.65v/8; *called Peascoddes*, S, f.102/[5]; *pomaunder buttons like acrones*, S, f.96v/[32]; *like pressed harts*, S, f.96v/[33]; *Suger loafe Buttons*, S, f.95/[5]; *like Tortoises*, S, f.97v/[50], [51], f.102v/[8]; *called Trueloves*, S, f.102v/[3]. Figs 20, 152, 180, 194, 200, 436

BYAS   *see under* BIAS

CAFFA, CAPHA   'Cafas-a kind of course Taffata. Caphetan- a kind of course, or grosse, Taffeta; also a long cassocke of the same' (C, 1611). The silk may have been woven in Caffa or simply taken its name from this town on the coast of the Crimea. Caffa, or Kaffa, was of some importance on the medieval and sixteenth-century trade routes from the East. By the end of the seventeenth century the name of the town was changed to Teodosia, today called Feodosiya: examples in various colours, S, f.24v/95, f.28/52, f.35v/95, f.43/94, 95, f.63v/111, 118, f.74/29

CALICO, CALLACOWE   p. 185

CALLABER   Fur obtained from some species of squirrel from North Italy: pp. 192, 193; S, f.32v/44, f.34v/73, f.68/46, 50

CALTROP   'Caltraps are great prickes of Iron foure square, which are cast in the enemies way when they would breake in on the country side' (M). Metal object with four sharp spikes, which always lies with one point upwards, scattered on the ground to

disable horses. Also name given by sixteenth-century herbalists to Star-thistle (*Centaurea calcitrapa*) from its round head with long sharp spines radiating outwards (OED): example in embroidery, S, f.21/48

CAMBRIC   A kind of fine white linen, orginally made at Cambray in Flanders: S, f.84v/79, 80

CAMEO, CAMEWES   A precious stone, having two layers of different colours in the upper of which a figure is carved in relief, while the lower serves as a ground. Onyx, agate and sardonyx were used. Sometimes described as 'antique head': pp. 3, 31; *buttons with faces of Aggatt or camewes*, S, f.96v/[25]. Fig. 3

CAMERIKE   *see under* CAMBRIC

CAMLET   The name for a ribbed weave, often described as 'repp' today, not a term to describe material from a particular fibre, since silk, camel's hair and wool were all used for camlet in the sixteenth century. In 'gold and silver chamblet' fine metal wire or strip lies on top of the silk ribs in the weft, held with an extra binding warp of silk. The following examples of 'chamblet or tabine' were apparently difficult to tell apart: gold and silver chamblet or tabine, S, f.34v/74, 75, f.76/2

CANDLE   Searing, pp. 181, 183

CANDLESTICK, CANDELLESTICK   Example in embroidery, S, f.62v/99

CANOPY, CANAPIE   'Canapie or canopie, such as hangeth over beds' (M): of tissue with curtains, p. 97; with a handle, possibly a parasol, S, f.94/[5]. Fig. 75

CANVAS   Canvas in English accounts of 1605 was made of hemp. Coarse material made in several qualities, used for household linen, hardwearing shirts and doublets, stage costumes, and interlinings: stiffening for bodies, p. 20; striped gold, for doublet, p. 106; lining for sleeves, p. 183; *strawe colour India Canvas*, S, f.88v/[10]

CAP   pp. 200, 202; case for p. 230

CAP BAND   Band or ribbon put round a cap above the brim: with gold buttons, S, f.98v/[71]; *of Goldesmythes worke*, S, f.95/[4]

CAPE   Ermine-lined, p. 49. Fig. 80

CAPE COLLAR   *see under* COLLAR

CAPHA   *see under* CAFFA

CARNATION, CARNACION   'Carnation colour — incarnat, incarnadine, couleur incarnate. Incarnadin — carnation, of a deep rich or bright carnation. Incarnat — Carnation; and more particularly, light, or pale carnation; flesh coloured or of the colour of our damask Rose' (CH): p. 8; S, f.19v/23, f.20/34, f.20v/43, f.30/3, 5

CARPET   Turkey, p. 98.

CARTRIDGE PLEAT   Modern term for deep even gathering, usually pulled up with three rows of threads, each pleat caught with a single stitch: pp. 20, 185

CARVING TOOLS   To cut gloves, p. 217; to cut shoes, p. 212

CASE   Of cotton, pp. 180, 233; for doublets, pp. 143, 180; of dowlas, p. 233; for petticoats, p. 231; of Milan fustian, p. 233

CASSOCK   p. 142; as gift for William Shenton, p. 105, for blackamoor page, p. 106; in the following example, worn by Edward VI, apparently interchangeable with 'frock', S, f.5v/[5]

CASTELL WALLS   *see under* CASTLE

CASTLE   p. 89; example in embroidery, S, f.82v/47; *wrought in squares like Castell walls*, S, f.64/123. Figs 153a, 155

WITHDRAWN

OVERSIZE DA 356 .A67 1988
Arnold, Janet.
Queen Elizabeth's wardrobe
 unlock'd

DEC 1 1 2007

The College of St. Catherine
ST CATHERINE LIBRARY
WITHDRAWN
2004 Randolph Avenue
St. Paul, MN 55105

KEPT 2010